CLASSICS II
Another Investor's Anthology

CLASSICS II
Another Investor's Anthology

Edited by

Charles D. Ellis
Managing Partner
Greenwich Associates

with

James R. Vertin

AIMR

BUSINESS ONE IRWIN
Homewood, Illinois 60430

This publication is designed to provide accurate and
authoritative information in regard to the subject matter
covered. It is sold with the understanding that neither the
author nor the publisher is engaged in rendering legal, accounting,
or other professional service. If legal advice or other expert
assistance is required, the services of a competent
professional person should be sought.

*From a Declaration of Principles jointly adopted by a Committee
of the American Bar Association and a Committee of Publishers.*

Project editor: Jess Ann Ramirez
Production manager: Diane Palmer
Designer: Jeanne M. Rivera
Compositor: BookMasters, Inc.
Typeface: 11/13 Times Roman
Printer: R. R. Donnelley & Sons Company

Library of Congress Cataloging-in-Publication Data

Classics II : another investor's anthology / edited by Charles D.
  Ellis with James R. Vertin.
        p.   cm.
    ISBN 1-55623-358-2
    1. Investments.   2. Risk management.   3. Stock-exchange.
  I. Ellis, Charles D.   II. Vertin, James R.   III. Title: Classics II.
  HG4522.C57   1991
  332.6'78—dc20   91–2939

Printed in the United States of America
    3 4 5 6 7 8 9 0 DOC 8 7 6 5 4 3 2

For Mina, Barnes, and Mel
with bemused appreciation of our
300 years of cumulative sibling experiences!

As an important part of the celebration of the 30th Anniversary of the CFA program and the founding of the Institute of Chartered Financial Analysts, *Classics I* and *II* are being sent to members of the Association for Investment Management and Research.

What better way to celebrate the 30th Anniversary of the ICFA — with its wonderfully successful commitment to developing a Body of Knowledge — than to share with the membership a collection of several centuries of thoughtful writings on the subject of investing.

Special thanks to AIMR, editors Ellis and Vertin, and Business One Irwin (Richard D. Irwin, Inc.) for their collective efforts in making *Classics I* and *II* available to our membership.

Darwin M. Bayston, CFA
President and CEO
Association for Investment
Management and Research

Preface

The generous reception given to *Classics* when the first volume appeared nearly two years ago has encouraged an even deeper and wider search for unique and important documents in the investment literature. This search has been a happy adventure in discovery, particularly of items not previously known, a delightful introduction to new friends, and a sharing of ideas and memories with old friends.

This new collection goes back farther in time, includes several pieces that are two or more centuries old, and has more documents from the international community. For example, Masanori Owa's special translation of one of Master Honma's prescriptions for successful rice trading takes us back before securities were traded in Japan. (Owa-san graciously translated my *Investment Policy* into Japanese a few years ago; since then, our friendship has blossomed as we visit together in New York and Tokyo.)

Dan Chabris, Arthur Zeikel, Henry Hecht, Peter Darling, and Joe Bower each made important contributions to this collection. Florence Lathrop, librarian for the Kress Collection of rare books at the Baker Library at Harvard Business School, joined in the search with a special combination of interest and expertise, producing a series of significant documents.

The need to hone the collection has been an effective discipline. Less than 1 percent of the material considered made it into this volume. Bold and merciless editing, to be sure that only the best parts of the documents were included, has been matched with a stubborn determination to reject anything that did not absolutely belong. The final arbiter on rejections has been my dear friend, Jim Vertin. Behind his engaging and gentle exterior lies a strict disciplinarian with consistent high standards and the determination to prohibit any "marginal" admittances. His weeding and pruning have been crucial to this collection's value.

A gentle magic comes to the readers and to the collectors of documents written by predecessor colleagues in our profession. We turn a page and engage in communication and thought with people we will never know but with whom we share a deep fascination with investments and markets—people from whom we can learn and to whom, in the learning, we provide a form of immortality. As we join with them in a community of interest that continues on, we pay homage to their wit, their wisdom, and their sharing.

Jim and I gratefully acknowledge the wonderful help we have been given by Katy Sherrerd, Brett Ferguson, Jaynee Dudley, and Charlene Semer.

Charles D. Ellis
Greenwich, Connecticut

Introduction

One of the pleasures of browsing through the contents of *Classics* and *Classics II* is discovering the rich variety of influences—from theology to mathematics—that through the years have shaped the art of investment and continue to do so today. Everyone, it seems, is intrigued by investing, and almost everyone has advice to offer. Shakespeare, for example, captured the full concept of diversification in this speech by Antonio in *The Merchant of Venice:*

> My ventures are not in one bottom trusted,
> Nor to one place; nor is my whole estate
> Upon the fortune of this present year.
> Therefore my merchandise makes me not sad.

More than three centuries later, one of America's best and wisest investment advisors—Will Rogers—summarized in two sentences everything he knew about investing:

> Don't gamble; take all your savings and buy some good stock,
> and hold it till it goes up, then sell it.
> If it don't go up, don't buy it.

All true—and all-encompassing.

Contents

Analysis   337

CLASSICS II
Another Investor's Anthology

HISTORY AND
PERSPECTIVE

The Birth of a Trust Department

Longstreet Hinton

Longstreet Hinton built the Morgan Bank's investment organization into one that set the standards for professionalism, investment results, and fees. It was acknowledged as the best in America when Hinton retired. Because he took the now-remarkable view that corporations are plan sponsors who make contributions but are not clients (because the assets are held in trust for the beneficiaries), Morgan Bank abjured developing "client relationships." After a lengthy, discursive luncheon during which no discussion of the fund or its investments was offered, the "plan sponsor" finally asked: "'Street, how is our pension fund?" He received this complete reply: "Fine." Here, Hinton tells the story of how it all began.

Background

Prior to 1940, J. P. Morgan & Co. was a partnership and under New York law could not act as trustee. Individual partners could act and did, but usually only for family or very close friends. . . .

While the partnership did act as investment advisor for a limited number of accounts, it was not until late 1937 . . . that a department was set up for this specific purpose. No charge, however, was made for

Reprinted from *Some Comments About The Morgan Bank* (1979), pp. 46–54, by permission of J. P. Morgan & Co., Incorporated, New York.

this service; some income was received from handling charges on the execution of purchase and sale orders. . . .

The decision to have a trust department in the incorporated bank created a need for an individual to be the head. Customarily in other banks, the personal trust and corporate trust departments were both under a common head. Mr. Whitney, who had been Chairman of the Trust Committee of Guaranty Trust Company, was determined that the operation should be headed by someone other than a trust lawyer. Mr. Whitney felt that when such a department was headed by a lawyer the primary concern understandably became the legal and administrative aspects of the trust business and, as a result, its investment aspects were seriously handicapped.

The first man approached by the Committee was Bill Gabriel of Wells Fargo; he seemed interested initially but was not willing to leave San Francisco. Dale Sharp was next approached. Guaranty was very reluctant to have him leave; and, as Dale said, "They gave me a big raise."

The reluctance of these two men to leave their jobs was understandable. Considering the circumstances at the time (waiting for people to die), the growth of a new trust department could only be very slow.

Despairing of finding a satisfactory man from outside, the Committee then turned to considering various individuals already in the bank. One night, after dinner at Walter Fletcher's (the partner at Davis Polk who specialized in trust and estate work), when we had rejected various names for one reason or another, Mr. Whitney turned to me and said, " 'Street, I guess you're it."

I had understood that I would be treasurer of the incorporated bank (a job in line with my experience), but in the course of the discussions with Walter Fletcher, I became very interested in the potential of the personal trust business. Although growth would be slow, I felt that the bank's reputation as an investor would in time help establish a profitable business.

Immediately we began planning for the formation of a personal trust and investment department. . . .

Included prominently in the plans was a determination that quality of administrative competence should be first-class and that the operational side of the business should meet the highest standards of performance. . . .

The location of this new department was a problem, because access was necessary for the customers. The solution was to take over the entire third floor—an area smaller than the name might suggest because of the space lost by a center well that provided the only daylight. No windows existed at all on the Wall Street side.

Mr. Morgan's barber shop, with its marbled and mirrored walls, served as a waiting room. The biggest problem was to provide a powder room for the anticipated female customers. This was solved by installing a small one under the staircase to the fourth floor dining room. (The front elevator did not go to the fourth floor.)

The actual setting up of the department—i.e., desks, chairs, tables, and curtains—was superintended by a young employee named Walter H. Page. The same Walter Page felt he should seek guidance from the partners on an issue which perturbed him. The problem involved the choice of a label to be placed on the door of the newly created ladies' room. In spite of much serious consideration, no agreement was ever reached on this delicate matter. To avoid the issue, the door was simply left unmarked, creating from time to time some confusion, embarrassment, and amusement.

The next step was the education of the members of the new department. Weekly lectures (after the close of business) were given by Walter Fletcher. In addition to the members of the department, these lectures were attended by many of the seniors (Messrs. Leffingwell, Whitney, Alexander, Dickey, Davison, Lamont, and others), auguring well for the future. Walter Fletcher could make even trust law interesting. His opening statement was, "It is better to know the judge than know the law." . . .

Building the Business

The Investment Department began with approximately $300 million of advisory business that was already on hand—Carnegie Corporation, St. Paul's School, Exeter, Amherst College, plus a number of individual accounts.

For the trust side, business opened April 1, 1940, with the establishment of four trusts by George Whitney for the benefit of his children. Shortly thereafter, Mrs. John T. Pratt opened trusts for her four children. These together with two trusts established for Archer M. Huntington with shares of Newport News Shipbuilding Company (which he was disposing of), gave us a good start.

Our own Pension Fund was the foundation for that particular area of business.

As previously related, under normal conditions growth of this new department would be very slow. Fortunately our beginning coincided with a decision by the Internal Revenue Service allowing the deduction, for tax purposes, of contributions to a pension trust of payments on account of past service. Previously such payments had been deductible only when paid to an insurance company.

At the same time and for the duration of World War II, emphasis in industry was put on deferred (pension and profit-sharing funds) rather than immediate compensation in order to dampen inflation. Excess profits taxes gave an even greater incentive to corporations to set up such plans (in many cases for the first time) and to make substantial payments on account of past and future service. An example of this was the U.S. Steel Pension Trust set up with us, as well as an additional one with The First National Bank of New York, each with an initial contribution of $6,500,000.

One of our first estates, that of Anna Paton, provided advertisement for us as an executor. Mrs. Paton was the widow of the inventor of the zipper (Talon), and one of her beneficiaries was a prominent clergyman, who other heirs alleged had used undue influence to obtain a legacy. Considerable publicity surrounded the case, including our appearance in court. . . .

To go back to our beginning, we were very fortunate that our start coincided with the boom in trusteed pension plans. Prior to 1940 most plans had been insured, although a few large companies (notably A.T.&T.) had trusteed their plans. Bankers Trust Company had most of this business. The change from the insured type of plan to the trusteed plan was a slow one even though the mathematics strongly favored the latter because the insurance companies were basing their charges on extremely conservative actuarial assumptions. I remember trying (unsuccessfully) to persuade Fred Donner that General Motors should change. At that time, G.M. had a plan for salaried employees with Metropolitan Life Insurance Co. Later, in 1950, the National Labor Relations Board decided that pension plans were a proper subject for collective bargaining. G.M. then decided they wanted some say about the handling of the huge sums to be set aside under plans for wage earners.

We had a similar reaction from many other companies. At the end of 1950, . . . we had become trustees for some 21 plans with a value of $200 million. This compared with a personal trust volume of some $80 million. During this same period investment advisory accounts had doubled to approximately $600 million. . . .

The Trust Committee

In going out for business we made much of J. P. Morgan & Co.'s investment background and of the fact that our Trust Committee, which met weekly, consisted entirely of senior officers long experienced in investment. . . .

Outside directors attended only the special meetings devoted to discussion of general investment problems and review of memoranda prepared by the Research Department on various industries. When other directors had a specific knowledge of an industry, they usually were invited to attend. As time went on the number of outside directors named as members of Trust Committee was increased.

Prior to the weekly meetings, each member of the Committee received a tabulation of the security holdings of the trust and investment accounts under review that week and thus had knowledge of individual accounts. This was in direct contrast to the procedure in other banks where tabulations were available only at the meeting and in such numbers that only a few could be given the attention of the committee. . . .

We also established the practice of reviewing trust accounts twice annually in contrast to the existing practice of annual reviews. Pension trusts and investment accounts were reviewed quarterly.

In the beginning we were able to review each individual account, because we did not have very many. With the development of our IBM system we have been able to continue to do this as we grew. (Remember the man who started lifting an elephant the day it was born and continued to do so daily for the rest of its life?)

This ability to have each account reviewed by senior officials and directors of the bank, long experienced in investment, was without question the most important factor in our becoming (in a relatively short time) one of the outstanding trust and investment departments in the country. . . .

Under ordinary circumstances the Trust Department could not expect to pay for itself for many years; however, the seniors were determined to have a department worthy of the name, J. P. Morgan & Co. This meant building for the future by hiring young people of high quality for the investment, research, and administrative functions at salaries that would attract them.

We were also determined to be selective in the business we accepted and to insist on reasonable compensation. At that time (before pensions) much of the business of trusts and estates came from law firms—usually offered on the condition that you took all or none. Many lawyers resented our insistence on selectivity, and this undoubtedly cost us some business on the short run.

Investment Policy

To return once more to our beginning, investment in 1940 meant investment primarily in bonds, which could be done on the basis of study and of ratings. In the light of investment policy in recent years, with pension funds investing 100 percent in common stocks, it is hard to visualize the atmosphere of the 1940s. The years 1929 to 1932 and the year 1937, when stocks fell almost 50 percent within one year, were periods still vivid in the minds of investors. New York trusts, unless specifically authorized, could invest only in "legals," which at the time consisted of bonds with high ratings. Savings banks and life insurance companies were similarly restricted.

The war years brought price controls and high taxes. As a result, there was little incentive to purchase common stocks and, in fact, many early pension trust agreements limited investments to life insurance legals. This followed naturally from the fact that most pension plans in the past had been insured.

To illustrate, our first investment of the U.S. Steel Pension Fund monies included 150 shares of American Snuff 6% preferred. The balance of some $6,000,000 was invested in bonds including: $300,000 Dow Chemical 1.90% due 9/1/48 and $300,000, L.&N. Equipment 1⅜% due 1944–46, along with other bonds with comparable coupons. The investments of schools, museums, and endowment funds included common stocks but only in relatively small amounts.

The investment atmosphere began to change after the end of World War II. Even then, change came very slowly, even though stocks yielded twice as much as bonds. As time went on, the memories of 1929 to 1932 and the year 1937 faded. Business did not collapse as many had prophesied. Bond yields continued artificially low. Earnings and dividends on stocks were high in relation to price. I remember going with Homer Cochran in the summer of 1949 (the Dow was under 200) to try to persuade C. D. Dickey that we should buy common stocks. He agreed but suggested that we consult R. C. Leffingwell, who was vacationing at Lake George, N.Y. R. C. L. felt that the foreign situation was such that we should not buy common stocks, and he was right in one respect. The Korean War was just around the corner; but, instead of hurting the market, the inflationary boom that came with it sent the market considerably higher.

Although it is hard to believe now, our first purchase of common stock for a pension fund (if we exclude the purchase of bank stocks in 1947) was the purchase in December, 1949 of 1,000 shares of Chesapeake & Ohio common for our own pension fund. The real impetus to the purchase of common stocks for pension trusts came from General Motors, which in establishing trusts in late 1950 with seven banks, of which we were one, suggested in a letter of ground rules that no more than 50 percent be invested in stocks.

Coming as this did with the Korean War boom in the stock market, the maximum soon became the minimum. The Old Colony in Boston, with the Massachusetts "prudent man rule," led the way in the purchase of stocks and for a while was the top bank among G.M.'s "seven dwarfs." We were slow in getting to the 50 percent level. When the reasoning of Devereux Josephs, a director of the bank, member of the Trust Committee, and president of the New York Insurance Company, finally prevailed (that we should pay some attention to the wishes of our clients), our superior choice of stocks put us at the head of the parade. This performance inevitably became known to other companies and resulted in large additional business. . . .

The boom in the stock market that began in 1950 continued, with only a slight interruption in 1953, until 1957. During this period, a considerable change in attitude toward common stocks took place. The New York laws were changed to allow legal trusts to buy common stocks in limited amounts, just as savings banks and insurance companies were permitted to do. The rest is history.

One of our more controversial innovations was our refusal to accept directed brokerage. Up to this time the banks had always accepted such instructions from grantors and beneficiaries. In the days before the growth of the pension trust and the movement into common stocks by endowment funds and other large investors, it was not a matter of serious concern. With the growth of investment in common stocks, however, we felt that we could not accept such instruction. We believed that we could not do a good job as trustee if, in effect, we had to compete with ourselves in using one broker for one trust and a different one for another—in fact, many other brokers. With directed brokerage, there were additional drawbacks: many brokers would know what we were doing; and, in many cases, we were being told to use brokers we felt were incompetent. We lost some business as a result of this policy but were able to convince most of our grantors that it was reasonable. I was convinced (and still am) that this policy was a significant factor in J. P. Morgan's record of performance.

Another reason for our success was the establishment of an outstanding Research Department. This was again in contrast with many other banks, where research often was staffed with excess personnel from other areas.

A competent, outstanding Trading Department was another important factor in our success. J. P. Morgan & Co. had been a member of the New York Stock Exchange until incorporation; for many years it had had active trading departments in bonds and stocks. In contrast to most other banks, these departments were not just passers of orders but were knowledgeable about their markets and their brokers.

The Research Department and the Trading Department were both under the supervision of John Meyer.

For most of our early years we did not advertise, believing that high-grade performance was all that was necessary to get business; also, we were concerned that when you advertise for business you cannot pick and choose.

Harvard College versus Amory

Samuel Putnam

The Prudent Man rule was enunciated by Boston's Judge Samuel Putnam in 1829. Here is his full opinion in this watershed case.

———————— ▬ ————————

John McLean died on October 23d, 1823, and his will and codicil were proved and allowed in the court of probate for the county of Suffolk, on the 3d of November, 1823.

The Will

After an absolute gift to the wife of the testator of a dwellinghouse, certain specified personal property, and $35,000, the will proceeds:—
"I give and bequeath to Jonathan Amory, &c. and Francis Amory &c., jointly, the sum of 50,000 dollars, in trust nevertheless to loan the same upon ample and sufficient security, or to invest the same in safe and productive stock, either in the public funds, bank shares, or other stock, according to their best judgment and discretion, hereby enjoining on them particular care and attention in the choice of funds, and in the punctual collection of the dividends, interest, and profits thereof, and authorizing them to sell out, reinvest, and change the said loans and stock from time to time, as the safety and interest of said trust fund may in their judgment require. And this bequest is upon the further trust, that the said sum of 50,000 dollars so invested, shall constitute a

Reprinted from *The Journal of Portfolio Management* 3 (Fall 1976), pp. 67–71. New York: Institutional Investor, Inc.

separate and distinct fund, the profits and income thereof to be received and collected by the said trustees and paid over to my said wife, Ann McLean, in quarterly or semi-annual payments, as shall be most convenient for said trustees, for and during the term of her natural life. And this bequest of 50,000 dollars is upon the further trust, that the trustees will, after the decease of my said wife, pay over, transfer, and deliver one half, in actual value, of the said entire fund, to the President and Fellows of Harvard College, the income and profits whereof shall be exclusively and forever appropriated to the support of a professor of ancient and modern history, at that college.'' The trustees are directed to pay over the other moiety (after the decease of the wife) to the Trustees of the Massachusetts General Hospital, to be by them held and appropriated to the general charitable objects of that institution.

The testator further says, ''And reposing full and entire confidence in the ability, fidelity, and diligence of the said Jonathan Amory and Francis Amory, and not doubting that they will faithfully and conscientiously discharge and execute the trusts hereby reposed in them, and being desirous of relieving them from the burden of procuring sureties for large sums—I do request and direct that they may not be required to give any other than their own bonds respectively, without sureties, conditioned for the performance and execution of the said trusts; and I do order and direct, that they shall not be held responsible for the acts, doings, and defaults of each other, but shall simply be accountable respectively each for his own acts, doings, and defaults, as such trustees.''

In addition to the foregoing bequests the testator gave pecuniary legacies, amounting to $27,500. . . .

Jonathan Amory and Francis Amory were appointed executors.

The Argument

At a probate court in October, 1828, Francis Amory, the surviving trustee, presented his account as trustee, for allowance, and tendered his resignation of the trust; of which the college and the hospital received due notice. These corporations objected to any settlement of the accounts which should leave upon the fund the loss of capital arising from the investments in trade or manufactories, and at the same time give to the annuitant the whole amount of the dividends thereof. They stated that the shares in insurance stock were then worth about $12,350, the shares in the Boston Manufacturing Company about $8,100, and those in the Merrimack Manufacturing Company about $9,000.

Afterward, on January 12th, 1829, the account was allowed by the judge of probate, and the college and the hospital appealed from his decree, for the following reasons:

1. Because the trustees did not loan the $50,000 upon ample or sufficient security.
2. Because they did not invest that sum in safe and productive stock, either in the public funds, bank shares, or other stock, but on the contrary invested the greater part thereof in trading companies, whereby the principal sum was exposed and still continues to be exposed to great loss.
3. Because in the choice of funds they have solely regarded the interest of the annuitant, for the purpose of giving her large dividends, and have wholly disregarded the interest of the respondents, in exposing the greater part thereof to total loss.
4. Because the trustees, after consulting with the respondents as to the investment of the principal sum, and having obtained their opinion thereon, went contrary to their judgment therein, and invested the same, at their own risk, in such unsafe and improper stock, that a part of the same is now actually lost.
5. Because the trustees, for the sole purpose of giving large dividends to the annuitant, invested the greater part of the principal sum in manufacturing and insurance companies, at a very high rate of advance, and far above what might reasonably be judged to be a fair permanent value.
6. Because they have not only paid out the profits and income of the funds so invested to the annuitant, but have also paid out to her a certain part of the capital thereof, instead of reinvesting the same.
7. Because the judge erred in passing this account, by which the trustees are wholly exonerated from accounting for the deficiency of the principal sum, amounting to $12,000 and upward.
8. Because the entire fund cannot be paid over at the decease of the annuitant, on account of the loss occasioned by the injudicious and improper investment.

9. Because the judge erred in allowing as interest a certain portion of the capital itself.
10. Because the judge erred in not reforming the account by applying the surplus amount received, over and above the common dividends on the stock purchased, and over and above the common rate of interest on the fund, to the making good the loss on the capital.
11. Because the judge passed the account without directing that the trust fund should be made good before the present trustee is discharged and a new one appointed.
12. Because the judge passed the account without directing that the principal sum shall now be invested in the public funds, bank shares, or other stock, or that the same shall be lent upon ample security.

Justice Putnam's Decision: Was the Trust Abused?

The confidence which the testator reposed in his executors, whom he also constituted his trustees, was unbounded. He directed that they, as trustees, should not be required to give any other security than their own bond, without sureties, and that each of them should be accountable "simply for his own acts, doings, and defaults as such trustee."

The general question is, whether the trustees have abused the trust.

The testator made provision for the support of his wife mainly from the proceeds of the trust fund. He speaks of the profits, income, dividends, which were to come from it through their hands. They were to lend the $50,000 upon ample and sufficient security, or invest the same in safe and productive stock, either in the public funds, bank shares, or other stock, according to their best judgment and discretion.

It is very clear that the testator did not intend to limit the income to the simple interest of the fund; for if he had so intended, he would not have spoken of dividends and profits but would have given an annuity of three thousand dollars a year.

It has been argued that the testator gave the sum of fifty thousand dollars as the trust fund, and that the trustees could only have demanded that sum of the executors. But we think that no important inference can be drawn from that fact. It would not follow from thence, that there should have been a sale of the personal property or stocks of the testator and a reinvestment. The trustees and the executors were the same persons, and instead of going through the useless formality of a sale and investment, it was clearly competent for them to select from the ample funds of the estate, those stocks which should form the capital of the trust fund.

And in making that selection, it is very clear to us, that they should have preferred that stock which would probably give her the most profit, and at the same time preserve the value of the capital sum. It would not, for example, have been the exercise of a sound discretion, to have appropriated the trust fund in the stock of an incorporated company which gave great dividends for the time being, but which would, according to the terms of its charter, expire as soon as the death of the wife could be calculated to happen. In such a case nothing would be left of the capital for those in remainder. On the other hand, if the investment of the trust fund were in stock which made large dividends, and which had acquired its value by the prudent management of its proprietors, and might be reasonably calculated upon as a safe and permanent capital, such an investment would seem to be according to the manifest intent of the testator.

It is somewhat remarkable that the testator did not himself appropriate the stock of which the trust fund should consist, but that he should have left the selection to his trustees. But as it would have been necessary to empower them to change, sell out, and reinvest, perhaps it was wise in the testator to leave the whole matter, the selection as well as the management, to them. Be that as it may, he has given them that authority.

But it has happened that the value of the capital stock in which the trust fund was invested, has fallen, and those in remainder call upon the trustees to make up the deficiency.

It was said by Lord *Hardwicke* in *Jackson* v. *Jackson,* 1 Atk. 514. that ''to compel trustees to make up a deficiency not owing to their willful default, is the harshest demand that can be made in a court of equity.'' The statute of *Geo.* 1. for the indemnity of guardians and trustees, provides that if there be a diminution of the principal, without the default of the trustees, they shall not be liable. If that were otherwise, who would undertake such hazardous responsibility?

It is argued for the appellants, that the trustees have not lent the money on good security. The answer is found in the authority which the testator gave to them. They were to lend, or to invest the fund in stocks. They preferred the latter.

Was Their Stock Selection Sound?

But it is argued, that they did not invest in the public funds, bank shares, or other stock, within the true intent and meaning of the authority, but in trading companies, and so exposed the capital to great loss. And we are referred to *Trafford* v. *Boehm,* 3 Atk. 444, to prove the position, that such an investment will not have the support of a court of chancery. The chancellor seems to suppose that *funds or other good securities,* must be such as have the engagement of the government to pay off their capital. Bank stock, as well as South-sea stock, which were in the management of directors, &c. were not considered by that court as good security. But no such rule has ever been recognized here. In point of fact, there has been as great fluctuation in the value of the stock which was secured by the promise and faith of the government, as of the stock of banks. And besides, the testator himself considers that *bank shares* might be a safe object of investment—''safe and productive stock.'' And yet bank shares may be subject to losses which may sweep away their whole value. Lord *Hardwicke* considers that South-sea annuities and bank annuities stand upon different footing, because the directors have nothing to do with the principal, and are only to pay the interest, until the government pay off the capital, and therefore that they only are properly good securities.

This reasoning has very little or no application here; for, in the first place, the stocks depending upon the promise of the government, or, as they are called, the public funds, are exceedingly limited in amount, compared with the amount of trust funds to be invested; and, in the second place, it may well be doubted, more confidence should be reposed in the engagements of the public, than in the promises and conduct of private corporations which are managed by substantial and prudent directors. There is one consideration much in favor of investing in the stock of private corporations. They are amenable to the law. The holder may pursue his legal remedy and compel them or their officers to do justice. But the government can only be supplicated.

It has been argued, that manufacturing and insurance stocks are not safe, because the principal is at hazard. But this objection applies to bank shares, as well as to shares in incorporated manufacturing and insurance companies. To a certain extent, each may be considered as concerned or interested in trade. The bank deals in bills of exchange and notes, and the value of its capital depends upon the solvency of its debtors. It may, for example, very properly discount upon the responsibility of merchants of good credit at the time, but who, before the maturity of their notes, become bankrupts from unavoidable and unforeseen mercantile hazards. In this way a bank becomes indirectly interested in navigation, trade, and merchandise, to an extent very little, if any, short of the trade in which manufacturing companies engage. The capital in both cases may be lost by the conduct of those who direct their affairs, notwithstanding the exercise of reasonable prudence and discretion.

In regard to insurance companies or incorporations, the capital seems, at first view, to be exposed to greater risk, but it is believed that there has not been much, if any, more fluctuation of the capital in those investments, than in incorporated companies for banking or manufacturing purposes. If the insurance be so general as to embrace a fair proportion of all the property risk, it will generally yield a reasonable profit, and preserve the capital entire.

It will not do to reject those stocks as unsafe, which are in the management of directors whose well or ill directed measures may involve a total loss. Do what you will, the capital is at hazard. If the public funds are resorted to, what becomes of the capital when the credit of the government shall be so much impaired as it was at the close of the last war?

Investments on mortgage of real estate are not always safe. Its value fluctuates more, perhaps, than the capital of insurance stock.

Again, the title to real estate, after the most careful investigation, may be involved, and ultimately fail, and so the capital, which was originally supposed to be as firm as the earth itself, will be dissolved.

"All that Can Be Required . . . "

All that can be required of a trustee to invest, is, that he shall conduct himself faithfully and exercise a sound discretion. He is to observe how men of prudence, discretion, and intelligence manage their own affairs, not in regard to speculation, but in regard to the permanent disposition of their funds, considering the probable income, as well as the probable safety of the capital to be invested.

But in the case at bar, the testator referred the management of this trust especially to the judgment and discretion of the trustees whom he appointed; one of whom is the brother, and the other was the cousin of his wife, for whose support this provision was made. These trustees are not to be made chargeable but for gross neglect and willful mismanagement.

The testator expressly authorized the trustees to invest in *"other stock"* than bank shares or the public funds; so they might as well select other stock as that which the testator named.

There can be no doubt but that the shares in manufacturing and insuring incorporations are and were commonly called and known by the name of *stock*. The investment would therefore be clearly within the letter of the authority.

It has been argued, "that the trustees should have invested in safe and productive stock, at their own and *a sound* discretion, without being governed by the known opinion of the testator;" "that *he* was at liberty to speculate, but the trustees were not." If these positions should be granted, the desired inference would not follow. If the testator, for example, had been in the habit of dealing largely in lotteries and games of hazard, it would undoubtedly not have justified the trustees in making such investments, notwithstanding the testator had been the favorite of fortune. But if the testator had invested his funds to remain permanently in any stock, that circumstance might well be taken into consideration by the trustees when called to exercise their own best skill and discretion. They might reasonably and properly inquire and consider what their testator would do in the circumstances in which they were placed. Would he recommend an investment that should give simple interest on a loan, or in stock that would probably give much more, and yet have the principal sum reasonably safe?

The circumstance of the trustees' reposing confidence where the testator had, is one which is always to be considered as tending properly to their discharge. *Thompson* v. *Brown,* 4 Johns. Ch. R. 628. The case of *Rowth* v. *Howell,* 3 Ves. jun. 565, has a strong bearing upon this part of the case. There the testator, having great confidence in his banker, recommended it to his executors not be in a hurry to withdraw the funds from him. But after the death of the testator, the banker misapplied them, and probably stung by remorse on account of his fraud, he committed suicide. It was urged against the executors, that they might have withdrawn the securities from the banker; and they had time enough to do so; but it was considered that the loss arose from the confidence originally reposed in the banker by the testator, and the executors were not subjected to the loss.

In the case at bar, the testator was a man of extraordinary forecast and discretion, in regard to the management of his property. His vast accumulation could not be ascribed to accidental causes, but to calculation and reflection. The fact that he had within three or four years invested nearly half his property in manufacturing stock, was entitled to great consideration and respect, and would, without any change of circumstances, have a strong tendency to justify the selection of the manufacturing stock as part of the trust fund.

We are of the opinion that they had a right to select the stock which they did for that purpose, and that they acted in the premises according to their best skill and discretion. And we have not seen any evidence which would satisfy us, that under all the circumstances of the case, they did not act with sound discretion in making the selection and investment.

The claim now made upon the trustees, to make up the subsequent depreciation, would seem to be justified only on the grounds of gross abuse of their trust, even if it were not barred by the decree in the probate court from which no appeal was made. But upon examining all the documents and evidence, it seems to us that there is no reason whereon to ground that imputation.

Trustees are justly and uniformly considered favorably, and it is of great importance to bereaved families and orphans, that they should not be held to make good, losses in the depreciation of stocks or the failure of the capital itself, which they held in trust, provided they conduct themselves honestly and discreetly and carefully, according to the existing circumstances, in the discharge of their trusts. If this were held otherwise, no prudent man would run the hazard of losses which might happen without any neglect or breach of good faith.

The judgment of this Court is, that the decree of the probate court, from which the appellants appealed, be, and it is hereby affirmed; and that the record be remitted to that court for further proceedings according to law to be there had; and that the appellee recover his costs.

How Fiat Money Inflation Came to France

Andrew Dickson White

Andrew Dickson White, with the help of an endowment from Ezra Cornell, established Cornell University in 1867. In addition to being a scholar, White was a diplomat and served for six years as U.S. ambassador to Germany. This essay was originally presented to a private meeting of senators and representatives in 1876 and subsequently published in 1912. In it, White explains how in 1789, following the French Revolution, well-meaning political leaders launched their nation's economy into a disastrous inflation—for neither the first nor the last time—with all the standard arguments, including the canard about how "this time, things are different." The more things change, . . .

Early in the Year 1789 the French nation found itself in deep financial embarrassment: there was a heavy debt and a serious deficit.

The vast reforms of that period, though a lasting blessing politically, were a temporary evil financially. There was a general want of confidence in business circles; capital had shown its proverbial timidity by retiring out of sight as far as possible; throughout the land was stagnation.

Statesmanlike measures, careful watching, and wise management would, doubtless, have ere long led to a return of confidence, a

Excerpted from *Fiat Money Inflation in France* (Irvington-on-Hudson, New York: The Foundation for Economic Education, Inc., 1959; originally published 1912), pp. 23–36, 42–46.

reappearance of money, and a resumption of business; but these involved patience and self-denial, and, thus far in human history, these are the rarest products of political wisdom. Few nations have ever been able to exercise these virtues; and France was not then one of these few. [1]

There was a general search for some short road to prosperity: ere long the idea was set afloat that the great want of the country was more of the circulating medium; and this was speedily followed by calls for an issue of paper money. The Minister of Finance at this period was Necker. In financial ability he was acknowledged as among the great bankers of Europe, but his was something more than financial ability: he had a deep feeling of patriotism and a high sense of personal honor. The difficulties in his way were great, but he steadily endeavored to keep France faithful to those principles in monetary affairs which the general experience of modern times had found the only path to national safety. As difficulties arose, the National Assembly drew away from him, and soon came among the members renewed suggestions of paper money: orators in public meetings, at the clubs, and in the Assembly, proclaimed it a panacea—a way of "securing resources without paying interest." Journalists caught it up and displayed its beauties, among these men, Marat, who, in his newspaper, "The Friend of the People," also joined the cries against Necker, picturing him—a man of sterling honesty, who gave up health and fortune for the sake of France—as a wretch seeking only to enrich himself from the public purse.

Against this tendency toward the issue of irredeemable paper Necker contended as best he might. He knew well to what it always had led, even when surrounded by the most skillful guarantees. Among those who struggled to support ideas similar to his was Bergasse, a deputy from Lyons, whose pamphlets, then and later, against such issues exerted a wider influence, perhaps, than any others. Parts of them seem fairly inspired. Anyone today reading his prophecies of the evils sure to follow such a currency would certainly ascribe to him a miraculous foresight, were it not so clear that his prophetic power was due simply to a knowledge of natural laws revealed by history.

But this current in favor of paper money became so strong that an effort was made to breast it by a compromise; and during the last months of 1789 and the first months of 1790 came discussions in the National Assembly looking to issues of notes based upon the landed property of the Church, which was to be confiscated for that purpose. But care was to be taken; the issue was to be largely in the shape of notes of 1,000, 300, and 200 livres,[2] too large to be used as ordinary currency, but of convenient size to be used in purchasing the Church lands; besides this, they were to bear interest and this would tempt holders to hoard them. The Assembly thus held back from issuing smaller obligations.

Remembrances of the ruin which had come from the great issues of smaller currency at an earlier day were still vivid. Yet the pressure toward a popular currency for universal use grew stronger and stronger. The finance committee of the Assembly reported that "the people demand a new circulating medium"; that "the circulation of paper money is the best of operations"; that "it is the most free because it reposes on the will of the people"; that "it will bind the interest of the citizens to the public good."

The report appealed to the patriotism of the French people with the following exhortation: "Let us show to Europe that we understand our own resources; let us immediately take the broad road to our liberation instead of dragging ourselves along the tortuous and obscure paths of fragmentary loans." It concluded by recommending an issue of paper money carefully guarded, to the full amount of four hundred million livres, and the argument was pursued until the objection to smaller notes faded from view.

Typical in the debate on the whole subject, in its various phases, were the declarations of M. Matrineau. He was loud and long for paper money, his only fear being that the Committee had not authorized enough of it; he declared that business was stagnant, and that the sole cause was a want of more of the circulating medium; that paper money ought to be made a legal tender; that the Assembly should rise above prejudices which the failures of John Law's paper money had caused, several decades before. Like every supporter of irredeemable paper money then or since, he seemed to think that the laws of Nature had changed since previous disastrous issues. He said: "Paper money under a despotism is dangerous; it favors corruption; but in a nation constitutionally governed, which itself takes care in the emission of its notes, which determines their number and use, that danger no longer exists." He insisted that John Law's notes at first restored prosperity, but that the wretchedness and ruin they caused resulted from their overissue, and that such an overissue is possible only under a despotism.[3]

M. de la Rochefoucauld gave his opinion that "the assignats will draw specie out of the coffers where it is now hoarded."[4]

On the other hand, Cazalès and Maury showed that the result could only be disastrous. Never, perhaps, did a political prophecy meet with more exact fulfillment in every line than the terrible picture drawn in one of Cazalès' speeches in this debate. Still the current ran stronger and stronger; Petion made a brilliant oration in favor of the report, and Necker's influence and experience were gradually worn away.

Mingled with the financial argument was a strong political plea. The National Assembly had determined to confiscate the vast real property of the French Church—the pious accumulations of fifteen hundred years. There were princely estates in the country, bishops' palaces, and conventual buildings in the towns; these formed between one-fourth and one-third of the entire real property of France, and amounted in value to at least two thousand million livres. By a few sweeping strokes all this became the property of the nation. Never, apparently, did a government secure a more solid basis for a great financial future. . . .

There were two special reasons why French statesmen desired speedily to sell these lands. First, a financial reason—to obtain money to relieve the government. Secondly, a political reason—to get this land distributed among the thrifty middle classes, and so commit them to the Revolution and to the government which gave their title.

It was urged, then, that the issue of four hundred millions of paper, (not in the shape of interest-bearing bonds, as had at first been proposed, but in notes small as well as large), would give the treasury something to pay out immediately, and relieve the national necessities; that, having been put into circulation, this paper money would stimulate business; that it would give to all capitalists, large or small, the means for buying from the nation the ecclesiastical real estate; and that from the proceeds of this real estate the nation would pay its debts and also obtain new funds for new necessities. Never was theory more seductive both to financiers and statesmen.

It would be a great mistake to suppose that the statesmen of France, or the French people, were ignorant of the dangers in issuing irredeemable paper money. No matter how skillfully the bright side of such a currency was exhibited, all thoughtful men in France remembered its dark side. They knew too well, from that ruinous experience, seventy years before, in John Law's time, the difficulties and dangers of a currency not well based and controlled. They had then learned how easy it is to issue it; how difficult it is to check its overissue; how seductively it leads to the absorption of the means of the workingmen and men of small fortunes; how heavily it falls on all those living on fixed incomes, salaries, or wages; how securely it creates on the ruins of the prosperity of all men of meager means a class of debauched speculators, the most injurious class that a nation can harbor—more injurious, indeed, than professional criminals whom the law recognizes and can throttle; how it stimulates overproduction at first and leaves every industry flaccid afterward; how it breaks down thrift and develops political and social immorality. All this France had been thoroughly taught by experience. Many then living had felt the result of such an experiment—the issue of paper money under John Law, a man who to this day is acknowledged one of the most ingenious financiers the world has ever known; and there were then sitting in the National Assembly of France many who owed the poverty of their families to those issues of paper. Hardly a man in the country who had not heard those who issued it cursed as the authors of the most frightful catastrophe France had then experienced. . . .

It was no mere attempt at theatrical display, but a natural impulse, which led a thoughtful statesman, during the debate, to hold up a piece of that old paper money and to declare that it was stained with the blood and tears of their fathers.

And it would also be a mistake to suppose that the National Assembly, which discussed this matter, was composed of mere wild revolutionists; no inference could be more wide of the fact. Whatever may have been the character of the men who legislated for France afterward, no thoughtful student of history can deny, despite all the arguments and sneers of reactionary statesmen and historians, that few more keen-sighted legislative bodies have ever met than this first French Constitutional Assembly. In it were such men as Sieyès, Bailly, Necker, Mirabeau, Talleyrand, Du Pont de Nemours, and a multitude of others who, in various sciences and in the political world, had already shown and were destined afterward to show themselves among the strongest and shrewdest men that Europe has yet seen.

But the current toward paper money had become irresistible. It was constantly urged, and with a great show of force, that if any nation could safely issue it, France was now that nation; that she was fully warned by her severe experience under John Law; that she was now a constitutional government, controlled by an enlightened, patriotic people—not, as in the days of the former issues of paper money, an absolute monarchy controlled by politicians and adventurers; that she was able to secure every livre of her paper money by a virtual mortgage on a landed domain vastly greater in value than the entire issue; that, with men like Bailly, Mirabeau, and Necker at her head, she could not commit the financial mistakes and crimes from which France had suffered under John Law, the Regent Duke of Orleans, and Cardinal Dubois.

Oratory prevailed over science and experience. In April 1790, came the final decree to issue four hundred millions of livres in paper money, based upon confiscated property of the Church for its security. The deliberations on this first decree and on the bill carrying it into effect were most interesting; prominent in the debate being Necker, Du Pont de Nemours, Maury, Cazalès, Petion, Bailly, and many others hardly inferior. The discussions were certainly very able; no person can read them at length in the Moniteur, nor even in the summaries of the parliamentary history, without feeling that various modern histories have done wretched injustice to those men who were then endeavoring to stand between France and ruin.

This sum—four hundred millions, so vast in those days—was issued in assignats, which were notes secured by a pledge of productive real estate and bearing interest to the holder at three per cent. No irredeemable currency has ever claimed a more scientific and practical guarantee for its goodness and for its proper action on public finances. On the one hand, it had what the world recognized as a most practical security—a mortgage on productive real estate of vastly greater value than the issue. On the other hand, as the notes bore interest, there seemed cogent reason for their being withdrawn from circulation whenever they became redundant. . . .

As speedily as possible the notes were put into circulation. Unlike those issued in John Law's time, they were engraved in the best style of the art. To stimulate loyalty, the portrait of the King was placed in the center; to arouse public spirit, patriotic legends and emblems surrounded it; to stimulate public cupidity, the amount of interest which the note would yield each day to the holder was printed in the margin; and the whole was duly garnished with stamps and signatures to show that it was carefully registered and controlled. . . .

To crown its work the National Assembly, to explain the advantages of this new currency, issued an address to the French people. In this address it spoke of the nation as "delivered by this grand means from all uncertainty and from all ruinous results of the credit system." It foretold that this issue "would bring back into the public treasury, into commerce, and into all branches of industry strength, abundance, and prosperity."[5]

Some of the arguments in this address are worth recalling, and, among them the following: "Paper money is without inherent value unless it represents some special property. Without representing some special property it is inadmissible in trade to compete with a metallic currency, which has a value real and independent of the public action; therefore it is that the paper money which has only the public authority as its basis has always caused ruin where it has been established; that is the reason why the bank notes of 1720, issued by John Law, after having caused terrible evils, have left only frightful memories. Therefore it is that the National Assembly has not wished to expose you to this danger, but has given this new paper money not only a value derived from the national authority but a value real and immutable, a value which permits it to sustain advantageously a competition with the precious metals themselves."[6]

But the final declaration was, perhaps, the most interesting. It was as follows:

"These assignats, bearing interest as they do, will soon be considered better than the coin now hoarded, and will bring it out again into circulation." The King was also induced to issue a proclamation recommending that his people receive this new money without objection. . . .

The first result of this issue was apparently all that the most sanguine could desire: the treasury was at once greatly relieved; a portion of the public debt was paid; creditors were encouraged; credit revived; ordinary expenses were met, and, a considerable part of this paper money having thus been passed from government into the hands of the people, trade increased and all difficulties seemed to vanish. The anxieties of Necker, the prophecies of Maury and Cazalès seemed proven utterly futile. And, indeed, it is quite possible that, if the national authorities had stopped with this issue, few of the financial evils which afterwards arose would have been severely felt; the four hundred millions of paper money then issued would have simply discharged the function of a similar amount of specie. But soon there came another result: times grew less easy; by the end of September, within five months after the issue of the four hundred millions in assignats, the government had spent them and was again in distress.[7]

The old remedy immediately and naturally recurred to the minds of men. Throughout the country began a cry for another reissue of paper; thoughtful men then began to recall what their fathers had told them about the seductive path of paper-money issues in John Law's time, and to remember the prophecies that they themselves had heard in the debate on the first issue of assignats less than six months before.

At that time the opponents of paper had prophesied that, once on the downward path of inflation, the nation could not be restrained and that more issues would follow. The supporters of the first issue had asserted that this was a calumny, that *the people* were now in control, and that they could and would check these issues whenever they desired.

The condition of opinion in the Assembly was, therefore, chaotic: a few schemers and dreamers were loud and outspoken for paper money; many of the more shallow and easy-going were inclined to yield; the more thoughtful endeavored to breast the current.

Far more important than any other argument against inflation was the speech of Talleyrand. He had been among the boldest and most radical French statesmen. He it was—a former bishop—who, more than any other, had carried the extreme measure of taking into the possession of the nation the great landed estates of the Church, and he had supported the first issue of four hundred millions. But he now adopted a judicial tone—attempted to show to the Assembly the very simple truth that the effect of a second issue of assignats may be different from that of the first; that the first was evidently needed; that the second may be as injurious as the first was useful. He exhibited various weak points in the inflation fallacies and presented forcibly the trite truth that no laws and no decrees can keep large issues of irredeemable paper at par with specie.

In his speech occur these words: "You can, indeed, arrange it so that the people shall be forced to take a thousand livres in paper for a thousand livres in specie; but you can never arrange it so that a man will be obliged to give a thousand livres in specie for a thousand livres in paper—in that fact is embedded the entire question; and on account of that fact the whole system fails."[8]

Greatest force of all, on September 27, 1790, came Mirabeau's final speech. The most sober and conservative of his modern opponents speaks of its eloquence as "prodigious." In this the great orator dwelt first on the political necessity involved, declaring that the most pressing need was to get the government lands into the hands of the people, and so to commit to the nation and against the old privileged classes the class of landholders thus created.

Through the whole course of his arguments there is one leading point enforced with all his eloquence and ingenuity—the excellence of the proposed currency, its stability, and its security. He declares that, being based on the pledge of public lands and convertible into them, the notes are better secured than if redeemable in specie; that the precious metals are only employed in the secondary arts, while the French paper money represents the first and most real of all property, the source of all production, *the land;* that while other nations have been obliged to emit paper money, none have ever been so fortunate as the French nation, for the reason that none had ever before been able to give this landed security; that whoever takes French paper money has practically a mortgage to secure it—and on landed property which can easily be sold to satisfy his claims, while other nations have been able only to give a vague claim on the entire nation. "And," he cries, "I would rather have a mortgage on a garden than on a kingdom!"

Other arguments of his are more demagogical. He declares that the only interests affected will be those of bankers and capitalists, but that manufacturers will see prosperity restored to them. Some of his arguments seem almost puerile, as when he says, "If gold has been hoarded through timidity or malignity, the issue of paper will show that gold is not necessary, and it will then come forth." But, as a whole, the speech was brilliant; it was often interrupted by applause; it settled the question. People did not stop to consider that it was the dashing speech of an orator and not the matured judgment of a financial expert; they did not see that calling Mirabeau or Talleyrand to advise upon a monetary policy, because they had shown boldness in danger and strength in conflict, was like summoning a prize fighter to mend a watch.

In vain did Maury show that, while the first issues of John Law's paper had brought prosperity, those that followed brought misery; in vain did he quote from a book published in John Law's time, showing that Law was at first considered a patriot and friend of humanity; in vain did he hold up to the Assembly one of Law's bills and appeal to

their memories of the wretchedness brought upon France by them; in
vain did Du Pont present a simple and really wise plan of substituting
notes in the payment of the floating debt which should not form a part
of the circulating medium; nothing could resist the eloquence of Mirabeau. Barnave, following, insisted that "Law's paper was based upon
the phantoms of the Mississippi; ours, upon the solid basis of ecclesiastical lands" and he proved that the assignats could not depreciate further. Prudhomme's newspaper poured contempt over gold as security
for the currency, extolled real estate as the only true basis, and was
fervent in praise of the convertibility and self-adjusting features of the
proposed scheme.

In spite of this plausibility and eloquence, a large minority stood firm
to their earlier principles; but on September 29, 1790, by a vote of 508
to 423, the deed was done. . . .

Notes

1. For proof that the financial situation of France at that time was by no means hopeless, see Storch, *Economie Politique,* vol. iv., p. 159.
2. Editor's Note: The livre was the common coin of exchange in France at the beginning
   of the period White describes. The franc became the official monetary unit in 1795,
   with conversion at the rate of 81 livres to 80 francs.
3. See *Moniteur,* sitting of April 10, 1790.
4. *Ibid.,* sitting of April 15, 1790.
5. See *Addresse de l'Assemblée nationale sur les emissions d'assignats monnaies,* p. 5.
6. *Ibid.,* p. 10.
7. Von Sybel, *History of the French Revolution,* vol. i, p. 252; also Levasseur, *Histoires
   des classes ouvrierès et de l'industrie en France de 1789 à 1870,* Paris, 1903, vol. i,
   pp. 137 and following.
8. See speech in *Moniteur;* also in Appendix to Thiers' *History of the French Revolution.*

American Louisiana Stock

Surely the greatest investment ever made was the Louisiana Purchase—over 1 million square miles purchased from France for $11.3 million. It was financed by London's Baring Brothers (with the assistance of Amsterdam's Hope & Co.) with a loan at 3 percent interest. Robert Livingston and James Monroe negotiated the 1804 transaction, with Talleyrand representing Napoleon. For France, by selling an undeveloped property only recently acquired, it was a way to liquidate distant territories exposed to the British navy. For the United States, it was a crucial strategic step forward in the process of becoming a nation. Here is a facsimile of the original loan stock.

London 3 April 1804

AMERICAN LOUISIANA STOCK

is irredeemable for fifteen Years, and then reimbursable in the four following Years, by four equal payments.

This Stock bears Interest, at SIX PER CENT. PER ANNUM, from the first Day of January, 1804; and it is agreed that the Interest shall be payable in LONDON, half-yearly, as it becomes due, and without any protraction of time, namely, on the first Days of July and of January of each Year.

The first Dividend of Three per Cent. will be paid in July next, by SIR FRANCIS BARING AND COMP.Y of London.

The Interest is payable at the Par of Exchange of four Shillings and sixpence Sterling per Dollar, free of Commission and Charges, the risk of Bills being for account of the United States.

The Proprietor of this Stock has the option of exchanging his Certificate for one bearing Interest quarterly, payable in America.

A List of the Proprietors will be sent from Washington every half-year; and those Persons, in whose names the Stock stands on the first of January, are entitled to receive the six months' Dividend, due the first of July following; and in like manner those Persons, in whose names the Stock stands on the first of July, are entitled to receive the six months' Dividend due the first of January following.

Lane, Leadenhall-Street.

Reprinted courtesy of Baring Brothers, London, 1804.

29

A Treatise on Investments

Robert Arthur Ward

Robert Arthur Ward, a British solicitor, wrote A Treatise on Investments: Being a Popular Exposition of the Advantages and Disadvantages of Each Kind of Investment, and of Its Liability to Depreciation and Loss *in 1852. A book for lay persons needing an introductory text, it shines with the clear light of no-nonsense description and forthright opinion. Presented here are brief excerpts from Ward's introductory chapter and from his chapter on investing in mines. He is just as clear, informative, and sound on railways or canals or agricultural properties.*

On Investments Generally

The value of investments depends upon several circumstances: which are, the liability of the investment to depreciation in value, or to entire loss; the annual return, in the shape of rent, interest, dividend, or other produce, which is obtained for the sum invested; the facility with which the investment can be turned into ready money; the ease with which the rent, interest, or other income, can be recovered; and the liability incurred by the person investing, beyond the amount of the sum invested: this latter qualification will not enter into any of the investments mentioned in this work, except partnership, and shares in joint stock companies.

Reprinted from *A Treatise on Investments: Being a Popular Exposition of the Advantages and Disadvantages of Each Kind of Investment, and of Its Liability to Depreciation and Loss* (London: Effingham Wilson, 1852), Chapters 1 and 17, pp. 5, 178–85.

A capitalist seeking a permanent investment for his money, should be guided in his choice, in some measure, by the probable effect of circumstances on the different kinds of property: for example, shortly before the repeal of the corn laws, when their continuance was very doubtful, a person would not have sought for an investment in tithe rent-charges, which were sure to fall in value with the price of corn; and, at the present time, the capitalist will consider how the investment, which he proposes to obtain, will probably be affected by circumstances generally, and, especially, by the importation to a large extent of gold, the probable effect of which is discussed in the next chapter.

The chief object of all investments is, to secure the principal, to obtain as large a rate of interest as possible, and invest upon such a security, that the interest may be readily obtained, when it becomes due, and the principal can be formed into cash with as little delay and expense as possible.

On Mining Speculations

The uncertainty and fluctuating character of mining is such, that no persons should embark in it unless they have a complete knowledge of the subject, or will allow themselves to be guided by those whose experience qualifies them to give a tolerably correct opinion, so that a just and reasonable conclusion may be arrived at.

Mining may be divided into several classes, and in each capacity requires to be treated differently, inasmuch as in the different parts of the United Kingdom the several codes by which it is governed, are entirely dissimilar to each other.

In the north of England and the other districts of the coal formation, the collieries are principally in the possession of a private proprietary, or held by two or three partners in a mercantile firm, who make their own regulations; these mines are seldom or never in the market as joint stock adventures; and, as their accounts are never published, it would be very difficult to obtain any data whereby accurate information could be arrived at.

The iron mines of the Forest of Dean, in Gloucestershire, are worked under special rules, and in most cases are in the hands of galees, who obtain the grant of a gale from the gaveller or his deputy.

The lead mines in Derbyshire have likewise their own regulations, and are held under an officer, the barmaster, who is appointed by the Queen in her right as Duchess of Lancaster. Where speculation is most general, and where the results of investments are best known, is in Cornwall and Devonshire, and those mines which are worked under what is technically styled the "cost book system;" the principal feature of which is that the accounts are made up monthly and discharged by the purser, who enters the monthly cost sheet in a book kept for that purpose, which is denominated the "cost book." A meeting of adventurers is required to take place every two months, when the accounts of the preceding two months, with the balance, and all matters appertaining to the financial affairs of the company, shall be submitted, and minutes of the same entered on the cost book, and signed by the respective adventurers present. At these meetings the adventurers have power to make calls, declare dividends, appoint or remove any agents, and determine the rate of payment for services rendered. Absent adventurers can vote by proxy: the agent of the mine is to prepare a report on the operations of the mine in every case once a fortnight; and such report is to lie open at all times to the inspection of the adventurers on application to the purser or other appointed agent. A copy of the resolutions and abstract of accounts is to be transmitted to every shareholder within seven days after the meeting shall have been held. Any adventurer is at liberty to withdraw from the undertaking on giving notice to the purser of such intention, and paying up his proportion of costs and liabilities; whereupon he is entitled to his like proportion of ores and machinery up to the period of the surrender of his interest in the mine. If any claim remain unpaid for the space of fourteen days after the time fixed for payment of the same, the share in respect whereof it is due, may at any subsequent meeting of the adventurers be declared to be forfeited absolutely, a meeting having been for that purpose previously convened by circular, stating the objects for which it is called. The purser, when required by adventurers holding 50 shares in the undertaking, is to convene a special general meeting for such purpose as may be stated in the requisition, the same being mentioned in the notice calling the meeting, and due notice being given accordingly. This system is said to have originated when tin was the only metal known or worked in the countries of Cornwall and Devon, and was adopted by the tinners, who, unable to keep their own accounts, employed a person for that purpose, and called him the purser. In process of time other parties joined in mining pursuits, who were termed adventurers; and the purser acting as agent for both parties paid the dues to the "lords," dividing the profits among the adventurers. This led to the establishment of the Stannary Court, held every two months for auditing the purser's accounts, and settling any disputes which might arise between any of the parties connected with the mines. This court, however, did not extend beyond tin mines; and, as copper and lead mines were discovered, the authority of the court was extended to those also; and in the year 1834, an Act of Parliament was passed for the purpose of carrying out the rules of the Stannary Court.

Courts of Law and Equity were established under the jurisdiction of a judge, called the Vice Warden, the Prince of Wales being Lord Warden, to whom appeal can be made. The limits of the present work do not allow a more detailed allusion to the system; but it is trusted that the above details, though not copious, will give the reader an insight into the method of keeping mining accounts in Cornwall.

According to the *Mining Journal,* which is considered the authority on all matters connected with the province with which it professes to deal, there are 81 English and 9 foreign mines that have paid dividends; 181 English that have sold ores, but declared no dividends; and 86 English mines which have not sold ores: this is exclusive of private mines.

In order to show the fluctuating nature of mining speculations, a few quotations may be given of the enormous profits, which occasionally arise and tempt persons to embark their capital in the hopes of obtaining an enormous return, which in some few instances is realized. The Devon Great Consols, 1024 shares, 1*l.* paid, dividends declared 262*l.* 10*s.*, present price of shares 300*l.*; from this it will be seen that for a small outlay of 1*l.* in the space of about seven years the sum of 262*l.* 10*s.* has been returned as dividends; East Wheal Rose, 128 shares, 50*l.* paid, dividends declared 2245*l.*, present price per share 330*l.* Phoenix, 200 shares, 30*l.* paid, dividends declared 75*l.*, present price 240*l.* North Roskeur, 140 shares, 10*l.* paid, dividends declared 235*l.* In the same list we have Great Consols, 96 shares, 1000*l.* paid, dividends declared 353*l,* present price of share, 200*l.*; hence it will be seen that should any one have purchased this share at the full price paid up, if he wished to realize at the present time, according to the market value he must sustain a loss of 800*l.* a share. Dolcoath, 180 shares, 252*l.* paid, dividends declared to 1847, 855*l.* 14*s.*, none since, present price 20*l.;* in this instance it will be seen that the adventurers have received nothing for a period of five years. The foreign dividend mines are still worse. The first on the list is the Alten, 5000 shares, 14*l.* 10*s.* paid, dividends declared to 1848, 3*l.*, present price 2*l.;* this mine has been worked by a scrip company since 1833. Imperial Brazilian, 10,000 shares, 24*l.* 10*s.* paid, dividend declared 3*l.* 17*s.* 6*d.* to December, 1844; this is a gold mine, and has been at work since the year 1825, the present price of the shares is 1*l.* 10*s.*, at one period they were worth 150*l.* The only two of the mines on this list which are at premium are the Marmato, 2700 shares, 2⅛*l.* paid, dividends declared, 3*l.* 11*s.* to December 1851, present price 12*l.*; and the St. John del Rey, 11,000 shares, 15*l.* paid, dividends declared to December, 1851, 15*l.* 17*s.* 6*d.*, present price 28*l.* 5*s.* In the second list the mines that have sold ores, the sum paid up and price to be obtained for the share is generally at par; there are, however, some exceptions where they are at premium, the discovery of a course of ore, or the report of agent as to whether they are in soft or hard ground, has a material effect on this class of mines. Shares in those mining companies which have not sold ores, must be considered as purely of a speculative character, and require a great deal of caution to be used with regard to investments in them. Due attention must be given to the character of the promoters, and to the locality in which the property is situated, as well as the reports which have been issued, in order to usher the undertaking into public notice: these may be given by practical men with an honest intention, and yet they will often be found fallacious; since miners, who may have a perfect knowledge of Cornwall, may be very incompetent to judge in Derbyshire and Wales. And the same observation may be applied generally to the opinions of all persons unacquainted with the particular locality to which they belong, and not having perfect knowledge of the strata, dip, and underlay of the lode, as well as of the antecedents of mines, which have been worked in the same formation.

A considerable expense must generally be incurred by the erection of heavy machinery, &c., in order to prove the lodes; and although an investment in this class may turn out profitably, it is not, previous to a sale of ores, readily available for realization. In all cases the investment in home mines is to be recommended in preference to foreign adventures. This is easily accounted for, not because our mines are in every case richer than those in other climates; but the expenses can be calculated and controlled at home better than abroad. In some instances large amounts of money have to be spent for the building of houses, and absolutely colonizing the locality in which the mine may be situated; and though this is taken as stock, and figures yearly on the balance-sheet at the amount which it has cost the shareholders, it is well known if the mine were abandoned and the buildings realized, they would fetch but a very small proportion of their value. In other instances the laws of the country are unfavorable, the expenses of agents are greater, while labor is more expensive; for although the wages are at a lower rate, it is a general and well authorized opinion, that the amount of work performed by the natives is very considerably less than that got through by English workmen. The distance the resident manager is from the board of directors in London, the delay in the transmission of orders, together with the desire single-handed not to assume too much responsibility, all militate against the effectual and economical working of adventures situated in foreign localities.

Where steam is required to be used, it can only be obtained at a much greater cost than in England; while where water is the motive power, the machinery is often not capable of being worked on account of frost in winter or drought in summer. The accounts in the adventurers are in general made up annually or half-yearly, and the present position of the property is in many cases difficult to be obtained. In our home mines the accounts are always submitted every two months, or at least quarterly; the agent is under the control of the committee; the adventurers can at any time ascertain the nature and prospects of the concern in which they have embarked; and should the mine be abandoned, the machinery, stores, &c., will, from the number of adjoining mines, always realize a fair price, while the competition for labour ensures the mines being fairly and cheaply worked. In nearly every instance mines of the baser metals are more profitable than those of gold and silver; and coal mines are more valuable than either.

As none of the California and Australian mining companies have yet actively commenced operations, no results have been derived from them, nor can any safe opinion be formed of their value as investments; hitherto all has been speculation, and the shares have been sought for more with references to the supposed respectability of the promoters, than the intrinsic value of the diggings proposed to be taken. An opinion may however be hazarded, that there will be great difficulty in working the diggings in Australia and California; every one who considers the subject, will see how extremely difficult it will be to restrain the labourers who may be taken to those countries from seeking the precious metal on their own accounts when they get there. In what shape are they to be paid for their labor? Food and all the necessaries of life are already there in abundance; and, if they are paid in gold, they will scarcely feel inclined to receive a less amount from the company than they could procure for themselves; and, unless the company do give a less amount than they receive, they cannot have any surplus to defray even the very considerable expense of organizing and managing the company, much less will they have to divide among shareholders. Machinery may considerably assist the operations of the gold companies; but it will be an expensive undertaking to erect any in California or Australia; and even if erected it does not appear that there is any power strong enough in the gold countries to prevent those who are engaged to work it from doing so on their own account; and the workmen would not be persons likely to be restrained by any moral obligation. In the gold mines of Mexico and Brazil, labourers have worked for others, because the mines were private property, and they had no opportunity of working for themselves; but this is not the case in California and Australia. Few gold mining companies have been successful, even where there has been a monopoly of the precious metal; and I cannot think that those formed for working the recent discoveries will answer the expectations of their shareholders.

. . . Shares in gold mining companies commanded early in the present year a high premium in the market; since then they have declined in value. Not one-half of the projected schemes will be carried out; but when the market is weeded, they may perhaps afford a firmer appearance, and may then be considered as investment, while at present they can only be looked upon as stockjobbing speculations. These companies profess to carry out their projects in a variety of ways: some under the cost book system; others by royal charter; and others under the joint stock companies' act, with a paid up capital; and some, who are connected with France, under the law of commandité.

Investments for the Working Classes

W. R. Greg

W. R. Greg's monograph on *Investments for the Working Classes*
appeared first in the April 1852 issue of the *Edinburgh Review* as a
testament in favor of saving—and in favor of the savings banks and
building societies introduced 40 years before. He also stressed the
importance of sound investment policies and practices by the intermediary institutions. In the quoted passages, Greg makes the
case for encouraging private saving as a means of self-help and as
a public alternative superior to Socialism. A century and a half
later, Socialism is in disarray—but we have not yet mastered the
art of investing for savings and loan and other thrift institutions.
"Society has developed and industry expanded too fast," he says in
1852, "for legislative watchfulness and wisdom to keep pace with
them." How prophetic!

We have often had occasion to remark on the obstacles and perplexities,
the hidden perils, the opposing risks, the surprising and unforeseen dilemmas, which beset the path of active beneficence, especially when
attempted on a great scale. The difficulty of doing good is at least equal
to its luxury. . . .

Sometimes, however, cases will occur to philanthropic effort, in
which the preponderance of good is so evident and so great as to throw

Excerpted from *Investments for the Working Classes* (London: Longman, Brown, Green, and Long-
mans, 1852; originally published in the *Edinburgh Review* 194, April 1852), pp. 1–9, 120–22.

any casual and transient mischief into the shade, and make it of no account. Sometimes, too, a line of action suggests itself, in which, by a moderate amount of care, much benevolent service may be done without the violation of any moral principle or economic rule, and, therefore, without the risk of any counter-balancing harm which we are called upon to foresee. The providing and pointing out of safe and profitable investments for the savings of the frugal and industrious among the humbler classes seems to be one of these. It combines all the requisites and avoids nearly all the prohibitions which mark out the legitimate path of philanthropic aid. It interferes with no individual action: it saps no individual self-reliance. It prolongs childhood by no proffered leading-strings: it [weakens] energy by no hedges or walls of defense, no fetters of well-meant paternal restriction. It encourages virtue and forethought by no artificial incitements, but simply by providing that they shall not be debarred from full fructification, nor defrauded of their natural reward. It does not attempt to foster the infant habit of saving by the unnatural addition of a penny to every penny laid by: it contents itself with endeavouring to secure to the poor and inexperienced that safe investment and that reasonable return for their small economies which is their just and scanty due, and which the better education and wider means of the rich enable them to command.

The custom of hoarding and laying by is no new one in any country; but the form which it has assumed, and the extent to which it has now reached, may well surprise us. Formerly the savings of the poor used to be sewed up in an old stocking, and hid in the thatch or under the hearthstone; and this habit still survives to a great extent in Ireland. But now thousands of societies of every form and constitution receive the savings of hundreds of thousands of depositors, and reckon their accounts by millions. The degree to which this virtue is carried among the working poor, and the class immediately above them, is one of the most hopeful social features of our times; and when we reflect on the severe discouragement, both direct and indirect, which it has met with, both from the system of poor laws, which in times of prolonged pressure placed the frugal and hoarding operatives at so demoralising a disadvantage; and also from the frauds and defalcations of Benefit Societies and Savings' Banks, which have so often deprived them of the small sums scraped together by the industry and self-denial of many years— there is increased reason both for congratulation and astonishment. Of the actual aggregate amount which the savings of the humbler classes have now reached we know something, but are obliged to guess at much more. In 1830, the number of individual depositors in savings' banks was 412,217, and the amount of their deposits 13,507,565*l*. In November, 1849, the depositors were 1,065,031, and their deposits reached 26,671,903*l*. In November, 1850, the depositors were 1,092,581, and their deposits reached 27,198,563*l*. According to Mr. Scratchley there were in 1849, 10,433 *enrolled* Friendly Societies, numbering 1,600,000 members, who subscribe an annual revenue of 2,800,000*l.*, and have accumulated a capital fund of 6,400,000*l*. There are also a vast number of unenrolled Societies. Of the Manchester Unity there are 4000 societies, with 264,000 members, who subscribe 400,000*l*. a-year. In addition there are the unenrolled Foresters, Druids, &c. &c. The total is taken at 33,223 Societies, with 3,052,000 members, who subscribe 4,980,000*l*. a-year, and have a capital fund of 11,360,000*l*. The whole adult male population of the United Kingdom may be taken at about 7,000,000: nearly half of these, therefore, without distinction of rich or poor, are actually members of some of these Societies.

It is difficult to estimate too highly the importance of this tendency to amass, or the duty of removing every obstacle, and affording every facility to its operation. It is matter of deep interest to the state; for the man who has invested a portion of his earnings in securities, to the permanence and safety of which the peace and good order of society are essential, will be a tranquil and conservative citizen. It is matter of deep interest to the moralist; because the soil in which providence and frugality have flourished is a soil favourable to many other virtues. It is matter of deep interest to the social philosopher; for the trenchant line of demarcation between labourers and capitalists—so far more strongly marked in England than elsewhere—is believed by many to be at the root of nearly all, and is allowed by most to be at the root of many, of the most difficult and painful anomalies which meet our view as we look out on the community around us. To have saved money and invested it securely, is to have become a capitalist; is to have stepped out of the category of the *prolétaires* into that of the proprietors; and to have deserted the wide and desolate multitude of those who *have not*, for the more safe and reputable companionship of those who *have*. To have become a capitalist is, for the poor man, to have overleaped a great gulf; to have opened a path for himself into a new world; to have started on a career which may lead him, as it has led so many originally not more favoured by fortune than himself, to comfort, to reputation, to wealth, to power. In proportion to the value and dignity of this step, is it important to make it easy and secure: in that proportion is it the duty of the State to see that there shall be no needless or artificial impediments to the safe keeping and the profitable employment of the first small beginnings of a stream which may swell into such a mighty flood of fertilising waters; and sedulously to take heed that no channel in which it can flow without waste or danger shall be closed to it. It is not for the Legislature to contrive that the guinea of the rich man and the penny of the poor man shall yield an equal revenue: it is for the Legislature diligently to see to it, that by no act, connivance, or negligence of theirs, shall this desirable result be hindered. As it is, many such impediments exist: society has developed and industry expanded too fast for legislative watchfulness and wisdom to keep pace with them. We have been slow to meet new necessities with new provisions; and the consequence is that arrangements and enactments, fitted for other times but unsuitable for these, have a hampering operation which was neither intended nor foreseen; and circumstances and interests have been suffered to grow up, for the free development and adequate security of which no due provision has been made.

The practical discouragements to the virtue of economy which have resulted from the absence of this due provision, can be appreciated only by those who have come into close contact with the operative poor. Every defaulting savings' bank—every absconding treasurer to a sick club or a friendly society—every bankrupt railway—every fraudulent or clumsy building league—every chimerical or mismanaged land association—preaches a sermon on the folly of frugality and providence, not soon forgotten and not easily counteracted. Of late these lessons have multiplied with fearful rapidity. . . .

The principle of association is unquestionably a mighty and prolific one;—if, as Socialists conceive, it does really contain a secret strength by virtue of which society can be purified, its wounds healed, its heart-burnings soothed, and its bitter animosities lulled to rest forever,—why, the fairer field we afford to its development, the sooner and the surer will this vivifying energy be brought to light. If, as older and soberer men—who "stand upon the old way"—incline to fear, these sanguine hopes are in the main delusive, and altogether exaggerated,—why, the more free and unhampered be the opportunities offered for the trial, the more clearly and promptly will the delusion be made manifest. At all events, it is not well to leave to the advocates of Socialism the possibility of ascribing the failure of their schemes, not to the inherent unsoundness of their principles or the native impracticability of their means, but to artificial impediments—to the injustice of the law—to the cnvy or the enmity of the rich and great.

How to Invest and Speculate Safely in Railway Shares

A Successful Operator

Titles nowadays—and reader loyalty—aren't what they used to be. This excerpt comes from a booklet by "A Successful Operator" whose abbreviated title was: *A Short and Sure Guide to Permanent Investments in Railways. A Few Plain Rules.* Published in 1847, it was the ninth edition!

Much has been said and written as to the danger of speculating in Railways.

It may be desirable to ascertain whether, with ordinary precaution, such speculations are attended with greater risk than any other mercantile or monetary transaction.

Operations in Railway Shares are of three kinds; namely,

1. APPLICATIONS FOR ORIGINAL SHARES in Newly Projected Lines.
2. PURCHASES IN THE SCRIP (or Shares) of Lines Projected, or in Course of Construction.
3. PURCHASES IN THE SHARES of Lincs already Established.

Notwithstanding the thousands which have been lost by the follies and deceptions of the last twelve months, investments may be made

Excerpted from *A Short and Sure Guide to Permanent Investments in Railways. A Few Plain Rules. How to Invest and Speculate with Safety and Profit in Railway Shares, with Some Remarks on the Monetary Effect of Deposits and Calls* (London: Effingham Wilson, 1847), pp. 7–11.

with advantage, if made judiciously, even in the first two classes; but it is to the third class, as the safest and most eligible, that the attention of the reader will first be directed. In purchasing into established lines for INVESTMENT, we have merely—as when buying into the Funds—to compare the market price of the stock (or share) with the dividend it has been paying; and this comparison is the more easy, as *Railway dividends* have hitherto been *less liable to diminution* than those of any other description of stock.

It will be remembered that, within no very remote period, the dividend on *Bank of England Stock* has been reduced from TEN to EIGHT, and from EIGHT to SEVEN PER CENT., but upon few, if any, of the Great Lines of Railway have the dividends *ever been reduced, except by spreading them over new creations of capital;* and as the shares into which this new capital has been divided, have usually been distributed amongst the proprietors at par, when they were selling at a considerable premium, the bonus thus given has been more than equivalent to any reduction in the dividend.

The calculation, then, is within the capacity of a school-boy. Taking the value of money at Four per cent., the Shares in a Railway which pays Six per cent. per annum are worth 150*l.* each; or in one which pays Ten per cent. they are worth 250*l.* each. If bought below these prices, the purchaser is receiving, *pro tanto,* a better rate of interest than Four per cent.; and he will expect this better rate, in proportion to any doubt he may have with respect to the dividend being maintained.

Many were long prejudiced against Railways as an investment, because they regarded them rather as an experimental novelty, than as an established system. They must now, however, be considered as forming, for many generations, the only public means of intercommunication. Every previous mode of conveyance is giving place to the Engine and the Train; and the capital which has been embarked in this extensive change, offers a security as ample as the most cautious can require.

In purchasing the shares of an Established Line on SPECULATION, the same rule may be adopted as in buying for investment. If shares already at a premium are expected to rise, they may be purchased with safety, should the dividend yield Three or Four per cent. upon the price of the day, including the premium; as, should the buyer be disappointed in his expectation of an early advance, he is at least receiving a fair rate of interest on the amount he has invested, and may, therefore, wait patiently till the rise takes place. With this view, shares of 100*l.* each, paying Five per cent. dividend, may be worth buying at from 125*l.* up to 165*l.* a share, and others in the same proportion—provided there is a reasonable prospect either of better dividends, or of any other improvement in the value of the property.

For this no general rule can be given. If the party who desires to invest his money has no means of judging for himself, he may have some intelligent friend by whose information he will be guided, or whose connection with a particular line enables him to recommend it with confidence.

The shares of lines which are not paying any dividend at all, or a very trifling one, may be a good investment in the hands of those who are acquainted with the causes of the failure, and who know that this is a probability of their being removed. In this, the most valuable of Railway knowledge, the public generally are slow to participate; and such investments would be dangerous ground for the inexperienced speculator, to whom these brief remarks are addressed.

PURCHASES OF SCRIP (or SHARES) IN PROJECTED OR UNFINISHED LINES can only be made with safety under good information and advice as to their immediate or ultimate prospects; and not even then unless the buyer is prepared to pay the whole of the calls.

Those who look to immediate income should buy into the *established lines*, those who can wait for greater but more remote advantages, should prefer the *lines in progress*.

The next class is one in which it is not likely that there will soon be an opportunity of very extensive transactions.

APPLICATIONS FOR SHARES IN NEWLY PROJECTED LINES have, during the last six months, been to many such a source of loss and misery, that it is scarcely probable such applications would again be numerously made even were the opportunity afforded. It had become evident during the Session of 1845, that Railways were to form one of the important elements of our national greatness; but it happened unfortunately, that the conviction was forced upon the public mind at one of those recurring periods of prosperity when the capital of the country has accumulated beyond the usual means of employing it; and every new project that was brought forward was eagerly embarked in, and supported.

The consequences might very easily have been foreseen. Lines of railway for which there was no necessity but in the imaginary wants of some remote locality, were as favourably received as those which were essential to completing the connecting links of an extensive system. Still the public appetite was unsatisfied; and lines sketched hastily upon the map, without the slightest preference either to engineering difficulties or the prospects of remunerative traffic, were brought forward by adventurers, who saw, in the facility of obtaining deposits, the prospect of a golden harvest which it was impossible to resist the temptation of gathering.

The Shrewdest Leveraged Buyout in History

Leonard Mosley

Of all the leveraged buyouts, the best may well have been the 1902 transaction by which three cousins (and descendants of the founder) with far more bluff than money gained control of $60 million in assets with a cash outlay of 1.5 percent of that amount—and saved the family firm.

On Jan. 27, 1902, Louisa d'Andelot du Pont wrote to her brother Pierre S. du Pont that she had been to visit Cousin Eugene, who was in bed with a heavy cold. Du Pont's senior partner looked so frail and feverish she thought he would not survive the night. He did that, but he died the following day, Jan. 28, age 62.

The death of Eugene du Pont, a grandson of Eleuthère Irénée du Pont, founder of the great gunpowder and explosives combine that bore his name, created a crisis in the affairs of the company. Eugene had served Du Pont[1] for 42 years, and his hand, although shaky, had been the only one on the tiller since the death of General Henry (Boss Henry) du Pont 12 years before. Who would take his place as president?

Shortly after Eugene's burial at Sand Hole Woods, the family burial ground for nearly a century, the five surviving partners were due to hold a meeting to discuss the nomination of a new president, and the future of the company. But Alfred I., Eugene's cousin, did not bother to

Reprinted from *Forbes* (March 17, 1980), pp. 169–83, by permission of the author.

attend. His deafness had grown so serious that he could not always hear what was being said; and in any case, he was alienated from his fellow partners, who strongly disapproved of his notorious affair with Alicia Bradford, an attractive cousin, and his treatment of his wife. He knew they would outvote him on the presidency question and were not likely to listen to his advice. He had a fatalistic feeling that whether he was there or not, they would choose the wrong man.

By length of service, the logical successor to Eugene was his brother Francis Gurney du Pont, and though no one admired his capabilities or believed he had the qualifications for the job, the other four partners were resigned to the prospect of voting him in. But Frank surprised them by saying, the moment the partnership meeting was convened, that he "emphatically refused" to accept the presidency. His family knew what his partners did not: that he was a sick man.

The next logical contender was Colonel Henry Algernon du Pont, son of Boss Henry, but he too demurred. He was now, at 63, doggedly trying to win himself a seat in the Senate or the Congress, and though he was having a frustrating time, he was not ready to give in yet. Moreover, as P. S. du Pont wrote later, he "was inclined to unload business cares and was quite unwilling to take on new responsibilities." And he had had no practical experience. His refusal of the presidency was received with relief.

But who else was there? The other two partners were Charles du Pont and the third brother of Eugene and Frank, Alexis I. du Pont. Charles was already a dying man and did not live out the year. Alexis, who had confined his career at Du Pont to representative and advisory duties, knew nothing about powdermaking and he too was in poor health. (He died within a month of his brother Frank, in 1904.)

That left the fifth partner, Alfred I. du Pont, as the only contender, and since he had not bothered to attend the meeting, they could discuss his qualifications (and his character) freely. Alfred I., a great-grandson of the founder, Eleuthère Irénée, had already proved he knew more about powdermaking than the rest of them put together, but in the eyes of his fellow partners that did not outweigh the disadvantages of his character. Frank Gurney du Pont, as a report later put it, "had formed an exceedingly low estimate of Alfred Irénée's good judgment and business ability, which he did not hesitate to express." The Colonel then cleared his throat and declared that although he was "disposed to be more lenient," he did not think Alfred I. would inspire confidence among other members of the family, let alone in the business community beyond.

The others looked to Alexis, the third senior partner. Alexis would rather not have expressed an opinion but was well aware of what his domineering wife, Elizabeth, would say if he did not block Alfred I.'s progress. Elizabeth Bradford du Pont, a half sister of Judge E. G. Bradford, a pillar of unbending rectitude in Wilmington society, fully shared the judge's disgust over Alfred I.'s scandalous behavior with his outcast daughter, Alicia. Alexis therefore made his opposition loud and clear. In the circumstances, Charles du Pont, Alfred I.'s only friend at the meeting, wisely kept his mouth shut.

But with the last remaining candidate eliminated, what were they to do? Wearily, after hours of fruitless discussion, the four partners reached what seemed to them the only possible solution. They would sell the Du Pont company. They would offer it lock, stock and powder keg to their biggest and most respected rival, the Laflin & Rand Powder Co. For decades the two companies had dominated the explosives business through the Powder Trust, in the formation of which the du Ponts, especially Boss Henry, had played a major role. Laflin & Rand's president, J. Amory Haskell, was an old Du Pont hand who had until recently been head of the Repauno Mineral Co., which Lammot du Pont had started, and they all admired his ability. He would certainly do no harm to Du Pont's reputation or assets.

Then began discussion about who should run the company temporarily while the sale was being arranged. They eventually agreed on the choice of a relative by marriage, Hamilton M. Barksdale (his wife was Charles du Pont's sister). He knew the powder business and had once headed the Repauno Mineral Co. But when Barksdale was approached, he declined. He thought someone with the du Pont name should see the company through to its sale. But by now Alfred I. had dragged himself away from his preoccupation with Alicia and his hearing troubles and had discovered what had been going on in his absence.

On Friday, February 14, 1902, a meeting of the stock holders of the company was called (as a subsequent company report put it) "For the purpose of taking action on the proposed disposal of their property. At this meeting a resolution was offered authorizing a sale to the Laflin & Rand Powder Co. and appointing H. M. Barksdale as agent to negotiate."

Alfred I. made sure he did not miss that meeting. He came straight from the yards, still dressed in his coveralls, hands and face streaked with gunpowder. He took no part in the general discussion until the formal resolution was proposed. Then he rose and put forward an amendment specifying that the company should be sold to the highest bidder. When this was carried, and the meeting seemed to be over, Alfred I. spoke again.

"I will buy the business," he said.

The other partners looked at him in astonishment. The first to speak was Frank Gurney du Pont. It was, he said crisply, simply not possible.

"Why not?" Alfred I. asked.

Despite his outward calmness, he was considerably worked up by the cool way in which the other men around the table were proposing to sell out—just like that—a company that the du Ponts had spent a century to build up to its present eminence, spilling blood and sweat in the process. As he explained to his cousins later, it was an intolerable situation:

> I pointed out [to Frank] that the business was mine by all rights of heritage, it was my birthright. I told him I would pay as much as anybody else, and furthermore, I proposed to have it. I told him I would require a week to perfect the necessary arrangements looking toward the purchase of the business, and asked for that much time.

The partners were struck dumb by this outburst, and no one spoke as Alfred I. shoved back his chair and prepared to leave. Then Colonel Henry rose.

"Gentlemen," he said, "I think I understand Alfred's sentiment in desiring to purchase the business, and I wish to say that it has my hearty approval, and I shall insist he be given the first opportunity to acquire the property."

With that voice in support of Alfred I., even Frank Gurney du Pont could not object. It was agreed that the junior partner be given a chance to produce.

Meanwhile the Colonel had followed Alfred I. out of the room and, grabbing him by the shoulder, said (and the stilted words are his version), "I assume, of course, although you said nothing about it, that Thomas Coleman and Pierre are, or will be, associated with you in the proposed purchase?"

Alfred I.'s reply, as the Colonel later remembered it, was "Yes, although as a matter of fact I have not heard from Pierre as yet."

The Colonel nodded. "With the understanding that Coleman and Pierre are associated with you in the proposition, I assent to it most cordially and will do everything in my power to bring it about."

Pausing only to express his thanks, Alfred I. rushed out and leaped into his automobile. In a noxious cloud of blue smoke and backfires he sped downtown to Delaware Avenue, where Coleman and Elsie du Pont lived. He came right out with the proposition. Would Coleman now join him and help buy out the other partners?

It so happened that Coleman du Pont was going through a sticky financial period in the early part of 1902. He was rumored to have recently lost something like half a million dollars on the stock market, and he might very well have been about to lose more. But when strapped for money, Coleman usually was at his strongest and put his boldest front toward the world. He wore a self-confident mask for Alfred I. now. He too believed that his cousin, though a first class powderman, was a bad organizer and an unstable character. It would never do to have him as president of Du Pont.

So Coleman made two conditions for his own participation. First, he must be given an absolutely free hand in organizing and managing the new company, and that meant he must be given the largest block of stock in the company. Second, their cousin P. S. du Pont must join them in the new venture, since P. S. had long since proved—as guardian of his brothers and sisters and as director of the Johnson Co., a conglomerate of steel and streetcar companies that others in the du Pont family had acquired—that he knew his way around the business world and was, in fact, as good a manager as Coleman himself.

Alfred I. did not hesitate. He put out his hand, and they shook on it.

It was then that Coleman du Pont went to the telephone instrument in the hall and put through a long-distance call to P. S. in Lorain, Ohio, where the Johnson Co. was headquartered. When the connection was made, he told P. S. he had agreed with Alfred I. "to accept the responsibility of the presidency of the reorganization of E. I. du Pont de Nemours & Co.," on the condition that P. S. agreed to oversee the financial part of the business. Would he do it?

P. S. du Pont wrote later:

> This was the most important and far-reaching decision of my life. No position, no salary or interest in the business was offered but the three-minute allowance of a telephone conversation was quite long enough to

receive the account of the proposition placed before me, to make up my mind and give my reply in one word: Yes.

He knew his two cousins were equally enthusiastic about the adventure now facing them:

My commitment to join the enterprise, though made over the telephone only, bound me, by ties much stronger than a written contract, to stand by the old company through thick and thin. Coleman had the same determination and, though only recently a citizen of Delaware and without close family ties, felt a commitment stronger than one to be broken by any unexpected development.

P. S. was convinced that Alfred I. "was equally enthusiastic," but, he added with a hint of superiority that eventually goaded a cousinly quarrel, "as the question of administrative and financial leadership was paramount, perhaps [Alfred I.'s] responsibility seemed the least important of the three."

Now all the three cousins had to do was find the money to make good Alfred I.'s offer. The old regime had put a price of $12 million on the Du Pont assets, and the cousins had a week to find that sum. In available cash and credits they had less than $1 million among them.

It was, of course, the bargain of the century.

The three cousins may not have had the $12 million in ready cash, but there was no doubt, as they quickly discovered, that the Du Pont assets were worth at least double and possibly triple that amount. While P. S. was arranging for a successor in Lorain (he put his brothers William and Irénée in charge for the time being) and getting ready to come East, Alfred I. sneaked into the main office at the powder yards and started hauling out the ledgers in which Du Pont's holdings were listed. As a junior partner, he had never been allowed to peruse them, and from their condition, coated with dust, pages stuck together and yellow with powder, it appeared that none of the senior partners had examined them for some years either. He was astounded at what he found.

Not only did Du Pont own the Brandywine yards (in Delaware) and Carney's Point, but the company also had thriving mills in Pennsylvania, Iowa and Tennessee. It still had the majority block of shares that Lammot du Pont had bought in the California Powder Co. It was the sole owner of the Hazard Powder Co. And it had considerable holdings in several other dynamite companies and explosives concerns. Alfred I., who had been drawing 10% of the profits over the past few years, knew that the enterprise as a whole had never failed to do well, in spite of old-fashioned management and the failure of certain elements in the structure. He now realized he and his cousins had the chance to buy up a gold mine. He computed the assets conservatively at $24 million, and they were almost certainly worth much more. The old partners simply had no idea of what rich resources they possessed, and of what fabulous potentialities they were divesting themselves. But how to pay for it?

The cousins huddled in discussion. Where were they going to find the money? Then Coleman du Pont said:

"We will not need money." And then, as they looked at him in astonishment, he said: "Leave it to me."

Thomas Coleman du Pont was a born promoter, a born seducer. Tall, with a du Pont nose of impressive proportions, a friendly smile, and an air of enormous self-confidence, he had charm that, as one less successful du Pont ruefully said, "could charm birds off trees, blood out of stone, gold bars out of bank vaults, and girls out of their dresses." He exuded capability and trustworthiness.

He went before a meeting of the old partners, and those tired and defeated men were like putty in his hands. He had to tell them, Coleman said, that he and his two cousins did not have the $12 million they were asking for the assets of Du Pont. But did they really want $12 million in cash anyway? Think of what an embarrassment it would be to them. Think of all the trouble they would have reinvesting it in something safe.

He had a much better idea. Instead of $12 million in cash, he would give them a 25% interest in the new company that the three cousins would be forming, and would pay them 4% interest on $12 million over the next 30 years—minus, of course, any interest they received from the profits of the new company.

Alfred I. du Pont was astonished as he listened to Coleman talking. He was well aware that if he had made the proposition, the other partners would angrily have told him he was trying to acquire the company for nothing—which was true—and would undoubtedly have turned him down. But with a surprisingly scant expression of doubt, the proposition advanced by Coleman was accepted. The whole transaction, P. S. wrote later, "was one of mutual faith and intent to win success in the future."

But it was much more than that. It was high-powered salesmanship on the part of Coleman du Pont, and no one else could have got away with it. The three young men had taken over the biggest powdermakers in thc U.S., and probably in the world. And except for $2,100 in incorporation payments, it had not cost them a cent.

P. S. wrote to his brother Irénée to tell him what had been happening, for until now he had kept even members of his family ignorant of these maneuvers:

> This [the purchase] will doubtless come as a great surprise to you. Nevertheless it seems to be a "go." I think there is going to be some tall hustling to get everything reorganized. We have not the slightest idea of what we are buying, but in that we are probably not at a disadvantage as I think the [members of the] old company have a very slim idea of the [value of the] property they possess.

The meeting at which Alfred I. had made his intervention took place on Feb. 14, 1902. Exactly 15 days later P. S. du Pont went down to the Brandywine with the idea of casing himself into the workings of the company while the Old Guard was still *in situ*. But he had a shock waiting for him. As he wrotc later:

> Francis G. du Pont . . . came to the room set aside for me and handed me a number of small papers—morning mail and other matters requiring immediate attention. He shook hands and with hearty good wishes departed, leaving the cntire management of the company to the prospective owners.

The cousins were on their own.

They had certainly taken possession of a viable enterprise. Upon examining the books further, they found they had $1 million in cash in the banks; $3 million in standard securities listed on the New York Stock Exchange; patents, goodwill and other assets worth several million; plants conservatively valued at $10 million; and interests in other companies.

They formally bought the assets of the old company for $2,100, or $700 each, and formed a new company called E. I. du Pont de Nemours and Co. (1902), which, they declared, had a value of $24 million, of which $12 million would be issued in 4% notes and 120,000 shares with a value of $100 each ($12 million in all). All the notes plus 33,600 shares of stock (worth $3.4 million) went to the old partners and stockholders and to the estate of the late Eugene du Pont. The rest of the shares (86,400, worth $8.6 million) the three cousins split among themselves as "promoters' profits."

As the man who had pulled off the deal and who would henceforth head the new company, Coleman reaped 43,200 shares and was named president. P. S. got 21,600 shares and was named treasurer. Alfred I. received 21,600 plus 3,000 shares (this last being his allotment of the purchase price as an old partner), making 24,600 shares in all. He also received $1.2 million in 4% notes as his share of the purchase price. He was named vice president and general manager.

For Alfred I. the position was the fulfillment of a dream. All his life, ever since he had wandered around the Brandywine yards as a boy, he had hoped one day to be master of them. He loved the smell of powder. He enjoyed the comradeship he had with the men and the risks they shared in the mixing sheds and the rolling mills, where a sudden spark could blow them all to blazes.

He was very well aware that the Brandywine mills were by now old-fashioned, their machinery obsolete, their quarters cramped and unnecessarily hazardous, the whole operation far too close to the living quarters where whole colonies of men, women and children—du Ponts among them—were at risk. But he would not have it otherwise. He was a sentimental character who had a quite romantic idea of the working classes, at least so far as the Brandywine labor force was concerned, and it never occurred to him that they might not love the muck and sweat of the yards as much as he did. Had they not broken their backs together to save the nation during the Spanish-American War? He boasted that he considered the powdermen part of his "family." Had anyone asked him why, then, he did not treat them as such, with the kinds of real rewards that "families" get for "belonging," like bonuses and profit-sharing, he would probably have replied that his powdermen were not interested in money, so long as they got enough to live on. All they expected was praise from their boss and recognition of their best endeavors. They were in the yards, he would have added, not to grub for an extra nickel; rather, they were there because they had a pride in their skills, a zest for challenging danger and a respect for the Du Pont tradition. He loved his powdermen as brothers, and he was certain they loved him back. As for the Brandywine yards, he could not imagine life without them, without his faithful labor force working there beside him.

His stupefaction was great, therefore, when Coleman du Pont, having made his first inspection tour of the mills, turned to Alfred I. and said "This place is out of date. Why don't we close it down and raze the whole thing?"

Aghast at the temerity of this outsider, Alfred I. did not stop to argue but raced for the Brandywine offices, where he confronted P. S. with Coleman's outrageous suggestion. He must be mad. Alfred I. had been a fool ever to allow him to become president. If that was how Coleman's mind was working, the new partnership would fail from the start.

P. S. was too keen an expert on cost factors not to know that Coleman was probably quite right. The yards were out of date. But this was not the time to begin a quarrel. He went down to the yards to buttonhole Coleman and tell him to go slowly. So instead of closing the Brandywine, they agreed upon a modernization plan. New machinery was installed. New sheds were built. The water mills were heightened to bring in more power. Roads were regraded and straightened. An internal telephone system was installed. Meters were fitted in all the workers' houses—and those of the du Ponts, too—to encourage people to turn off the lights when not in use, thus reducing the cost of electricity. But at the same time, all the powdermen's houses were fitted at last with baths and toilets.

As general manager, Alfred I. now had control of the du Pont houses on the estate that were still owned by the company, and as it was with his great-grandfather, his grandfather and his uncle before him, it was now in his power to decide who among the du Ponts should live where. Some of the family had, it is true, been allowed over the years to buy their houses. He himself, for instance, had been able to purchase Swamp Hall and some adjoining property, 59 acres of it, for a consideration of ''$5 and more.''

But some of the best and biggest houses remained in the company's hands. Among them was the most palatial house on the estate, Louviers, which had once been the home of Admiral Samuel Francis and Sophie du Pont. But for the past few years the sitting tenant had been Belin du Pont, P. S.' brother. Alfred I. was anxious to get him out. He wanted Louviers for a more active Du Pont employee, one George Maddox, who was just about to marry—though not necessarily live with—Alfred's mistress, Alicia Bradford.

The cousins differed greatly not only in temperament, morals and emotional makeup but also in their ambitions for the Du Pont company. Alfred I. du Pont would not have minded working with black powder on the Brandywine for the rest of his life, so long as the operation turned over a decent profit and left him time for his experiments, his music, his automobiles, his hunting trips and his love affair. Coleman du Pont was interested in the Du Pont company solely as his means of making a fortune large enough to take him away from the Brandywine and provide him with a power base in New York. Du Pont might have made soap, or sausages, as far as he was concerned; all he knew about explosives was that they aggravated the condition of his chronically sore throat.

On the other hand, P. S. du Pont was enlivened, as much as a man of his nature could ever be, by the thought that Cousin Eugene's death had delivered the family business into his hands, and that he was responsible for its destiny. His pioneering forebears had created and fashioned the family business and turned it into a recognized name wherever shots were fired in sport or in anger. He could feel them tugging at him now as he wrestled with ledgers in the office, whispering to him: We have made our family known and we have made it rich. It is now up to you to make it great.

How could that be achieved in any other way than by making Du Pont the biggest explosive company not just in the U.S. but in the world? It must be a company, moreover, that monopolized the explosives business so extensively that in the future no one would be able to make wars or blow up mountains without coming to Du Pont—and paying Du Pont prices. Once upon a time, thanks to the manipulations of old Boss Henry and P. S.' father Lammot du Pont, the company, through Lammot's membership in the Powder Trust, had been able to settle the policies of its rivals and split up the markets among the members of the Trust. But lately, owing to the laxness of the partners of the regime, Du Pont's influence had waned, and the company often had to be content with less than its fair share of the sales and the profits. P. S. hardly found this state of affairs satisfactory. As he told his cousins, what they should aim for now was not their fair share of the market but the lion's share—a monopoly of the orders at the prices Du Pont set.

Going through the company's books, P. S. noticed that Du Pont had some very valuable investments in the shares of rival powder companies, but in only one, the Hazard Powder Co., which Boss Henry had bought up secretly during his reign, did they have a controlling interest. In the eyes of the general public, and of most financial experts too, the three main and competing explosives companies in the U.S. in 1902 were Du Pont, Hazard and Laflin & Rand. No one realized that Hazard was secretly under Du Pont control. And it was this that fired P. S.' imagination and his ambitions. Du Pont already had a minority investment in Laflin & Rand. What if he could turn that into a majority investment—or even take over the whole firm? Then the big three would all be under Du Pont's control, and a monopoly of the explosives industry in America would be in the hands of the three cousins.

The prospect was so tantalizing that P. S. took time off to go to Scranton, Penna., to talk it over with his uncle Henry Belin. Uncle Harry was his mother's brother and the father of Alice du Pont, who had pined over P. S. for years, and she was sorely disappointed when she discovered that it was the professional advice of her father that her young cousin was seeking and not her company. Uncle Harry (like his father before him) had become an expert accountant and was a sought-after adviser of banks and business enterprises, including Du Pont and Laflin & Rand. He had been through the ledgers of both companies and was quite familiar with their contents. He also knew that the three principal directors of Laflin & Rand, like the Old Guard at Du Pont, were "of fairly advanced age, knew the problems before the explosives industry and possibly were disturbed by the changes in the Du Pont management."

As P. S. du Pont described it later, the Laflin & Rand directors were "conservative and willing to drift," whereas they realized that Coleman du Pont had a reputation for being "progressive and aggressive," and they feared a knockdown war with him. If the cousins could come up with a good offer, they would be sorely tempted to sell.

It was at this point that Coleman du Pont was once more wheeled in for a concentrated exercise of his charm and salesmanship. By the time he arrived for the main discussion, the directors of Laflin & Rand had decided that what they wanted for their stockholders was $700 a share. This made P. S. and Alfred I. cringe. But Coleman was not fazed at all. Yes, he said, they would pay $700 a share (provided an examination of Laflin & Rand's books proved them satisfactory). Alfred I. protested that they could not afford such an amount, which came to no less than $6 million. How could a new company, needing all the money it could lay its hands on for raw materials and development, dig up such a sum?

Coleman chuckled, "Don't worry," he said. "We are not going to pay them a nickel."

Once more he persuaded these tough, if tired, businessmen that the last thing they wanted was hard cash. He would pay them in bonds instead. For each $700 share he would give the Laflin & Rand shareholders $400 in 5% bonds of Delaware Security Co. and $300 in 5%

bonds of Delaware Investment Co. Delaware Security Co. and Delaware Investment Co. were two holding companies that he had set up overnight, backed by collateral in Du Pont. To make his proposition seem even more tempting, he offered the Laflin & Rand shareholders a bonus of 20% of the par value of their bonds in the stock of the two companies.

The stockholders, P. S. later reported, "accepted this proposition as being too good to turn down."

As soon as they did so, Coleman sped back to P. S. and told him to get around to Laflin & Rand fast and verify the book value of the company while there was still time to back down. Of that visit, P. S. wrote:

> The *very private ledger* of the company was produced for my inspection. After a couple of hours I retired with a promise to return but instead I went immediately to Wilmington.

For he could hardly believe his eyes. Even more consistently than Du Pont, Laflin & Rand had undervalued its holdings and investments. Shares that Du Pont also possessed, and that the Old Guard had valued at $140, were in the Laflin & Rand books at $31, whereas they were worth at least $200 on the market. Other stocks were estimated according to their 1887 values instead of the much higher ones of 1902. Altogether, the book value of the company was millions of dollars more than the directors seemed to believe.

P. S. went straight to Coleman and urged him to clinch the deal at once:

> [I] advised Coleman to close the transaction at once, lest our inspection might lead the owners to resurvey their property and retire from their commitment. This advice was accepted and the purchase made as of July 1, 1902, though all details of the transfer were not finished until October of that year.

The three cousins and their new Du Pont company were now masters of the U.S. gunpowder industry, the black blasting powder industry and the dynamite industry east of the Mississippi Valley. They were once more kings of the castle so far as the Powder Trust was concerned, for they owned 9 of the 17 companies outright and had large holdings in all but 3 of the 8 remaining companies. Altogether, they now had 54 corporations under their control, and 56% of the national production. Coleman had brought off this financial coup at a cost of a cash outlay of $8,500, divided among the three of them.

Coleman and P. S. began to mold this unwieldy group of companies into a solid corporation. But this necessitated buying out minority stockholders before their companies could be extinguished or incorporated, and in May 1903 Coleman set up the E.I. du Pont de Nemours Powder Co. with an authorized capital of $50 million, of which $30 million was issued in common and preferred stocks. Two thirds of this stock (and the controlling interest) was handed over to E.I. du Pont de Nemours and Co. (1902), which the three cousins had formed after buying out the Old Guard. The other third was to be used, instead of cash, to buy out the minority holdings in the companies they now owned.

John Raskob, who had been brought into the company by P. S., was now working with Coleman du Pont, and these two shrewd operators knew that before the new corporation, the Du Pont de Nemours Powder Co., could begin operations, it must take out licenses to do business in various states of the union. Fees for licenses were calculated on the amount of the capitalization of the company, and the powder company's capitalization had been set at a high figure because the partners needed purchasing power. So yet another company was formed, the E. I. du Pont Co., capitalized at only $10,000. All plants owned by the corporation were transferred to this company. Then the state licenses were applied for through the new company and granted at knockdown rates.

The operation was a brilliant success. The minority stockholders were bought out, and several other companies bought in, including the main California operators. As Marquis James, author of a biography of Alfred I., has written:

> The success of the mopping-up process reduced the authority of the Gunpowder Trade Association [the Powder Trust] to that of a high school debating society. Authority rested with Du Pont. The Association was worse than a hollow shell. It was a source of potential embarrassment, some of its restrictive provisions being clearly in contravention of the Sherman Anti-Trust Law. In 1904 Du Pont pulled out of the Association, abrogating the agreements on prices and trade territories under its aegis. In one instance Du Pont paid $100,000 and in another $140,000 to get rid of such agreements. The Association collapsed.

Du Pont now really controlled the market, and the three cousins set to work driving out every vulnerable competitor. By 1905 they had such a stranglehold on the industry that they manufactured 64.6% of all soda blasting powder sold in the U.S., 80% of all saltpeter blasting powder, 72.5% of all dynamite and 75% of all black sporting powder. They also produced 100% of the smokeless powder manufactured by private firms for military use. (The U.S. government had an ordnance factory making a small amount of smokeless powder.)

Having broken the Powder Trust, Coleman now began to wonder whether he could challenge and beat the international powder manufacturers too. For many years Du Pont had paid dues to an international association that controlled those of the U.S. It not only divided the globe among its members but exchanged patents (as well as markets) in the U.S., Mexico and Central America, while British and German interests controlled the markets in the rest of the world, with the exception of South America, which was, as P. S. described it, a "happy hunting ground for all parties."

> All secret processes were included with the patents [he wrote later]. An annual payment by Du Pont to the Europeans was provided. Undoubtedly, both sides benefited by the acquisition of the patents and secret processes and, equally undoubtedly, the loss of the use of these assets deterred Du Pont from branching out into foreign business, which it had no intention of doing at any rate as it was fully occupied at home. The Europeans were quite willing to surrender their rights for the U.S. though it seemed evident they would have frustrated a Du Pont invasion into any valuable part of their territory.

Should they now go all out for a global market and drive out the British and Germans as they had their home rivals? Coleman was all for it. But P. S., on the urging of John Raskob, was more prudent. He advised his cousin to curb his appetite until Du Pont digested what it had already swallowed.

So, instead, Coleman concentrated on the final stroke of his domestic campaign. He disbanded the $10,000 makeshift company, which had served its purpose now that state licenses had been secured, and transferred all its invaluable assets to Du Pont de Nemours Powder Co., which received as well the assets of all the companies that their other purchases had brought in. When the cousins had first taken over Du Pont, the company controlled 36% of the nation's powder markets. By 1905 Du Pont did 75% of the business. That was an impressive enough figure. But some of the statistics that the financial experts now began to unearth were even more astonishing.

The cousins had taken over Du Pont and Hazard, and then bought out Laflin & Rand, for a cash outlay of $8,500. That was in 1902. By 1905 the value of Du Pont's combined assets was $59,955,000. Commenting on that figure, P. S. noted:

> Of course, since we were du Ponts we were always more likely to under- rather than overvalue our assets, so that sum must be considered a conservative estimate.

Note

1. Since 1961, when company lawyers faced up to over a century of confusion, the company has been Du Pont (upper case ''D''); the family, du Pont (lower case ''d'').

The Great Opportunity

Alfred P. Sloan, Jr.

Alfred Sloan, Jr., describes, in this passage from his book *My Years with General Motors,* the great—but daunting—investment opportunity that GM represented for Du Pont. This was venture capital on a grand scale, made all the more interesting by the omnipresent and extraordinary persona of Mr. William C. Durant.

———— ▪ ————

Two events occurred in 1908 that were to be of lasting significance in the progress of the automobile industry: William C. Durant, working from his base in the Buick Motor Company, formed the General Motors Company—predecessor of the present General Motors Corporation—and Henry Ford announced the Model T. Each of these things represented more than a company and its car. They represented different points of view and different philosophies. History was to assign these philosophies to leading roles in the automobile industry in successive periods. Mr. Ford's was to come first, to last nineteen years—the life of the Model T—and to bring him immortal fame. Mr. Durant's pioneer work has yet to receive the recognition it deserves. His philosophy was an emerging one in the Model T era and was afterward to be realized not by him but by others, including myself.

No two men better understood the opportunity presented by the automobile in its early days than Mr. Durant and Mr. Ford. The automobile was then widely regarded, especially among bankers, as a sport; it was

Reprinted from *My Years with General Motors* (New York: Anchor Books, 1972; originally published 1964), Chapters 1 and 2, pp. 3–44, by permission of Harold Matson Company, Inc. © 1963 by Alfred P. Sloan, Jr.

priced out of the mass market, it was mechanically unreliable, and good roads were scarce. Yet in 1908, when the industry produced only 65,000 "machines" in the United States, Mr. Durant looked forward to a one-million-car year to come—for which he was regarded as a promoter of wildcat ideas—and Mr. Ford had already found in the Model T the means to be the first to make that prediction come true. The industry produced more than a half-million cars in the United States in 1914. In 1916 Mr. Ford alone produced more than a half-million Model T's and at his high point in the early 1920s he produced more than two million in one year. The downfall of that great car in later years, after it had served its historic purpose, is one of the pivotal facts of this story.

Both Mr. Durant and Mr. Ford had unusual vision, courage, daring, imagination, and foresight. Both gambled everything on the future of the automobile at a time when fewer were made in a year than are now made in a couple of days. Both created great and lasting lines of products whose names have been assimilated into the American language. Both created great and lasting institutions. They were of a generation of what I might call personal types of industrialists; that is, they injected their personalities, their "genius," so to speak, as a subjective factor into their operations without the discipline of management by method and objective facts. Their organizational methods, however, were at opposite poles, Mr. Ford being an extreme centralizer, Mr. Durant an extreme decentralizer. And they differed as to products and approach to the market.

Mr. Ford's assembly-line automobile production, high minimum wage, and low-priced car were revolutionary and stand among the greatest contributions to our industrial culture. His basic conception of one car in one utility model at an ever lower price was what the market, especially the farm market, mainly needed at the time. Yet Mr. Durant's feeling for variety in automobiles, however undefined it was then, came closer to the trend of the industry as it evolved in later years. Today each major American producer makes a variety of cars.

Mr. Durant was a great man with a great weakness—he could create but not administer—and he had, first in carriages and then in automobiles, more than a quarter century of the glory of creation before he fell. That he should have conceived a General Motors and been unable himself in the long run to bring it off or to sustain his personal, once dominating position in it is a tragedy of American industrial history.

It may not be generally known that at the turn of the century Mr. Durant—who had started from scratch—was the leading wagon and carriage producer in the United States; that he entered and reorganized the failing Buick Motor Company in 1904 and by 1908 was the leading motorcar producer in the country. He built 8487 Buicks in 1908, as compared with a production in that year of 6181 Fords and 2380 Cadillacs.

Mr. Durant incorporated the General Motors Company on September 16, 1908. Into it he brought first Buick, on October 1, 1908; then Olds, on the following November 12, and then, in 1909, Oakland and Cadillac. The old companies retained their corporate and independent operating identities in the new one, which was a holding company—that is, a central office surrounded by autonomously operating satellites. By various means, mainly exchanges of stock, Mr. Durant between 1908 and 1910 brought into General Motors about twenty-five companies. Eleven were automobile companies; two were electrical-lamp companies, and the remainder were auto-parts and accessory manufacturers. Of the automobile companies, only four, Buick, Olds (now Oldsmobile), Oakland (now Pontiac), and Cadillac, were to have a permanent place—first as companies, later as divisions—in the evolution of the corporation. The other seven early automobile companies were only shadow enterprises; they had principally engineering designs and little plant or production.

Putting together organizations in that period often involved "stock watering" and other manipulations, and this financial alchemy sometimes changed water into gold. I doubt whether that can be said to be the case when the General Motors Company was formed, for Buick was a very profitable enterprise before it became the cornerstone of General Motors. It earned about $400,000 on about $2 million in sales in 1906; about $1.1 million on $4.2 million in sales in 1907, a year of national economic "panic"; and an estimated $1.7 million on $7.5 million in sales in 1908—clearly a nice growth and profitability.

But Mr. Durant was interested in consolidation, through the extension of his product lines and through integration. He was advanced for his time in his general methods of production. Unlike most early motorcar producers, who merely assembled components made by the parts manufacturers, Mr. Durant already had Buick making many of its own parts, and he expected to bring about increasing economies in this direction. A prospectus of his for an unrealized consolidation of Buick with Maxwell-Briscoe Motor Company in 1908 specifies economies expected in purchasing, sales, and integrated production. It notes that one of Buick's plants in Flint "is situated in the midst of a group of 10 independent factories which manufacture bodies, axles, springs, wheels and castings" and reports that options were held on some of them. Mr. Durant thus showed a considerable sophistication in economic matters, very different from the popular image of him as a mere stock-market plunger. I cannot say that he was precise in the application of his economic philosophy; but he emerged prominently from a period that saw the birth and death of a great many automobile companies.

I see three simultaneous patterns in the way Mr. Durant set up General Motors. The first was variety in cars for a variety of tastes and economic labels in the market. That is evident in Buick, Olds, Oakland, Cadillac, and, later, Chevrolet.

The second pattern was diversification, calculated, it seems, to cover the many possibilities in the engineering future of the automobile, in search of a high average result instead of an all-or-none proposition. Among the nonsurvivors in General Motors, there was, for example, the Cartercar, which had a "friction drive" that was then considered a potential rival of the sliding-gear transmission; and also the Elmore Manufacturing Company, an outgrowth of a bicycle-manufacturing enterprise, which had a two-cycle motor that looked as if it might have a chance for a demand of some kind. There were a number of other random gambles which I shall only name: the Marquette Motor Company, the Ewing Automobile Company, the Randolph Motor Car Company, the Welch Motor Car Company, the Rapid Motor Vehicle Company, and the Reliance Motor Truck Company. The last two were combined and named Rapid Truck, which was absorbed by the General Motors Truck Company, organized on July 22, 1911.

The third pattern in Mr. Durant's arrangements was his effort, mentioned in connection with Buick, to increase integration through the manufacture of the parts and accessories that make up the anatomy of the motorcar. Mr. Durant brought into the original company a number of component manufacturers: the Northway Motor and Manufacturing Company, an enterprise producing motors and parts for passenger cars and trucks; and the Champion Ignition Company of Flint, Michigan, a manufacturer of spark plugs, later renamed the AC Spark Plug Company; the Jackson-Church-Wilcox Company, a manufacturer of parts for Buick; the Weston-Mott Company of Utica and later of Flint, a producer of wheels and axles; and others. He also brought in the McLaughlin Motor Car Company, Ltd., of Canada, which had been a fine-carriage maker. This company bought Buick parts and manufactured the McLaughlin-Buick car in Canada. This move brought into association with General Motors the talents of R. Samuel McLaughlin, who was to be largely responsible for the development of General Motors in Canada.

Not all of these additions were companies acquired by Mr. Durant. He created Champion Ignition, for example, by putting up all the money, and gave Albert Champion 25 per cent for his know-how. It remained a partially owned subsidiary until 1929, when General Motors purchased the minority interest from Mr. Champion's widow.

Altogether, from the standpoint of potential integration, Mr. Durant brought into General Motors in the beginning an important group of component enterprises. On the other hand, he also paid more for a property called the Heany Lamp Companies, which became worthless, than he did for Buick and Olds combined. The Heany shares were purchased at a cost of about $7 million, paid for principally in General Motors securities. Heany's main asset consisted of an application for a patent for tungsten lamps, which the Patent Office later threw out.

Mr. Durant's approach, whatever its validity might have been in the long run, was in the short run his undoing. For Buick and Cadillac, especially Buick with its combination of quality and volume, were about all the substance there was to the original General Motors. They accounted for most of its car production, which in 1910 represented about 20 per cent of the automobile output in the United States. The rest of the company's cars were of little consequence. And so, as it turned out, General Motors was soon overextended and in financial difficulties. In September 1910, just two years after he created the General Motors Company, Mr. Durant lost control of it.

An investment banking group, headed by James J. Storrow of Lee Higginson and Company of Boston and Albert Strauss of J. and W. Seligman and Company of New York, came in to refinance General Motors and in this connection took over its operation through a voting trust. A loan was obtained on stiff terms, through a $15-million five-year note issue, from which the proceeds to General Motors were $12,750,000. The note issue carried a "bonus" to the lenders in the form of common stock which would eventually be vastly more valuable than the notes. Mr. Durant, a large shareholder in General Motors, was still a vice president and member of the board of directors, but he was forced to step aside in matters of management.

For five years thereafter, from 1910 to 1915, the banking group ran the General Motors Company efficiently though conservatively. They liquidated the unprofitable units, writing off about $12.5 million—a huge amount at that time—in the value of inventories and other assets. They organized the General Motors Export Company, on June 19, 1911, to sell General Motors products overseas. The automobile industry as a whole expanded rapidly during this period, from about 210,000 units in 1911 to about 1.6 million units in 1916, due mainly to Ford's operations in the low-price field. General Motors increased its sales from about 40,000 units in 1910 to about 100,000 in 1915 but lost in relative position—down from 20 per cent to 10 per cent of the market in units—owing to Ford's rise. General Motors was not then represented in the low-price field. The company, however, was in good shape financially. Its efficiency in operations was due largely to its then president, Charles W. Nash.

Mr. Nash came to General Motors in this way. He had been with Mr. Durant in the Durant-Dort Carriage Company for about twenty years and had stayed on as manager there when Mr. Durant first went into the automobile business. He was as steady and careful as Mr. Durant was brilliant and daring—or reckless, as you may choose to call it. In 1910 Mr. Nash had had little experience in automobiles, but he had demonstrated talent in the art of manufacturing and administration. It was, I understand, at Mr. Durant's suggestion that the banker, Mr. Storrow, engaged Mr. Nash to take over the management of Buick. In any event, Mr. Nash became president of the Buick subsidiary in 1910 and did so well there that he went on to become president of General Motors Company in 1912.[1]

It was no accident that Buick remained the mainstay of General Motors throughout its early years. It had a management of stars. Mr. Storrow, a director of American Locomotive, discovered Walter P. Chrysler in one of that company's shops and recommended him to Mr. Nash. Mr. Nash hired Mr. Chrysler in 1911, I believe, as works manager of Buick. In 1912, when Mr. Nash moved up to be president of General Motors, Mr. Chrysler remained at Buick, where he was later to be president and general manager. Between 1910 and 1915, the period of banking control, Buick together with Cadillac continued to make just about all the profit of the General Motors Company.

General Motors at that time needed the prestige which the banking group gave it. The proceeds of the $15 million five-year note issue enabled the company to liquidate its past-due obligations, but working capital still was needed. This made necessary large borrowings from banks, which at one period rose to about $9 million. By 1915, however, General Motors was in such good financial condition that the directors, at a meeting on September 16 of that year, declared a cash dividend of fifty dollars a share on the common stock, the first cash dividend since the founding of the company seven years earlier. This action involved a distribution of over $8 million divided among the 165,000 shares, and it amazed the financial community, for it was the largest cash dividend per share ever declared on a stock listed on the New York Stock Exchange up to that time. The minutes of the board meeting say that the motion to declare this dividend was made by Mr. Nash and supported by Mr. Durant. However, the period of the voting trust was running out and a momentous conflict between Mr. Durant on the one hand, and the banking group and the Nash management on the other, was brewing as Mr. Durant sought to regain control of the company.

After being forced to step aside from the management of General Motors in 1910, Mr. Durant once again showed his enterprising spirit in the automobile industry. He backed Louis Chevrolet in experiments with a light car. In 1911 Mr. Durant and Mr. Chevrolet together started the Chevrolet Motor Company. Within four years Mr. Durant had built it into a nationwide organization, with several assembly plants and wholesale offices across the country and in Canada. At some time or other in this period he also began increasing the amount of stock of the Chevrolet Company and offering it in exchange for General Motors stock. He hoped thus through Chevrolet to regain a controlling interest in General Motors.

It was about this time that the du Ponts came into the picture and began their significant role in the story of General Motors.

The man chiefly responsible for bringing the du Ponts into General Motors was John J. Raskob, then treasurer of the du Pont Company and personal financial adviser to Pierre S. du Pont, then president of that company. Mr. du Pont, testifying in 1953 in a suit brought by the government attacking the relationship between the du Pont company and General Motors, said that he had bought about 2000 shares of General Motors around 1914 as a personal investment. One day in 1915, he said, Louis G. Kaufman, president of the Chatham and Phenix National

Bank, of which Mr. du Pont was a director, explained to him the situation in General Motors. Mr. Kaufman described the history of the company and the forthcoming expiration of the bankers' voting trust. There was to be a meeting in September 1915 to propose a new directorate for election in November. Mr. du Pont and Mr. Raskob accepted an invitation to attend the meeting. This was the first time that Mr. du Pont remembered meeting Mr. Durant.

Mr. du Pont also said:

> Instead of a harmonious meeting as Kaufman had expected to find, the two factions were at loggerheads; the Boston bankers on one side, Durant on the other. They failed to come to an agreement as to what the new directorate slate would be.
>
> . . . After much conversation, Mr. Kaufman drew me aside. Then we returned to the meeting and it was announced that if I would name three neutral directors for the company, they would make up the slate from that, each faction having seven directors and I would name three.
>
> In the meantime, they had appointed me chairman of the meeting. . . .

The slate was agreed upon and elected by the shareholders at the annual meeting on November 16, 1915. At the organization meeting of the board on the same day, Pierre S. du Pont was elected chairman of the General Motors Company and Mr. Nash was re-elected president. The Boston bankers and Mr. Durant, however, continued to be in deadlock over control of the company, and it was widely rumored then that Mr. Durant held the upper hand. He asserted a claim to control and a proxy contest loomed up, but did not materialize. The bankers chose not to fight and abdicated in 1916. Through his control of Chevrolet, Mr. Durant had control of General Motors.[2]

After Mr. Durant's victory, inducements were offered to Mr. Nash to stay with General Motors. But on April 18, 1916, he resigned from the presidency of the company, and, with the backing of Mr. Storrow of the Boston banking group, started the Nash Motors Company. In July 1916 he bought the Thomas B. Jeffery Company of Kenosha, Wisconsin, a former bicycle manufacturer which was producing an automobile called the Rambler. I bought some of the Nash Motors stock at the time. It was very profitable. When Mr. Nash died some years ago he was reputed to have left an estate of between $40 million and $50 million, an impressive record for a conservative businessman.

On the day Mr. Nash's resignation was formally accepted by the board, June 1, 1916, Mr. Durant took over the presidency of General

Motors and the big show was on again. He soon transformed the General Motors Company—a New Jersey corporation—into the General Motors Corporation—a Delaware corporation—and increased its capitalization from $60 million to $100 million.[3] The car-manufacturing subsidiary companies—Buick, Cadillac, and the others—were made operation divisions, so that the General Motors Corporation became an operating company, as distinguished from the old holding company. In August 1917 the new corporation and its operating divisions were formally joined.

Mr. Durant, it appears, then sought a substantial financial partner and looked to the du Pont group. The question arose in the du Pont Company whether they should come in. Mr. du Pont outlined the events as follows:

> He [Raskob] believed it [General Motors] was a very good investment for du Pont, and gave the reason that the du Pont Company needed an investment of good earning power and good dividend power in order to supplement its current dividend. Du Pont had lost the military business, or we knew it would be lost very shortly, and in the interim between the earnings of the military business and what might come after that, we needed something to support the dividends of the du Pont Company.
>   . . . General Motors was already in full swing. They had established a good line of cars, and they were very popular, and there was every promise that their dividends would continue at the then rate which was good, or maybe would be higher. That was the attractive point to Raskob and it also became my idea that it was a very good investment, and one that could not be duplicated, so far as we knew, anywhere else.

Mr. du Pont stated further:

> The General Motors Corporation and the industry itself had not advanced to a general acceptance. It was regarded as being something very risky, and consequently the stock was selling at about par at that time, which was a very good investment apparently from the actual earnings, but the public hadn't learned to believe that, so that the investment that was possible to make was extremely interesting, and that was the starting of the proposition to the du Pont Company. . . .
>   We had been through a great many financial arrangements in relation to the military business of the du Pont Company, and Durant needed financing or financial management in his corporation. He acknowledged that he wanted that, and he was very glad to take on du Pont interest to run that part of his business. . . .

In a memorandum to the Finance Committee of the du Pont Company dated December 19, 1917, Mr. Raskob, with extraordinary insight into the future of the automobile industry, argued for du Pont Company participation in General Motors. Mr. Raskob wrote:

> The growth of the motor business, particularly the General Motors Company, has been phenomenal as indicated by its net earnings and by the fact that the gross receipts of the General Motors–Chevrolet Motor companies for the coming year will amount to between $350,000,000 and $400,000,000. The General Motors Company occupies a unique position in the automobile industry and in the opinion of the writer with proper management will show results in the future second to none in any American industry. Mr. Durant perhaps realizes this more fully than anyone else and is very desirous of having an organization as perfect as possible to handle this wonderful business. . . . Mr. Durant's association with . . . [the du Pont group] has been such as to result in the expression of the desire on his part to have us more substantially interested with him, thus enabling us to assist him, particularly in an executive and financial way, in the direction of this huge business. The evolution of the discussion of this problem is that an attractive investment is afforded in what I consider the most promising industry in the United States, a country which in my opinion holds greater possibilities for development in the immediate future than any country in the world; that rather than have a coterie of our directors taking advantage of this in a personal way, thus diverting their time and attention (to some degree at least) from our affairs, it would be far preferable for the Company to accept the opportunity afforded, thus giving our directors the interest so desired through their stock ownership in the du Pont Company.[4]

Mr. Raskob summarized his views in favor of the investment in five points, as follows: The first was that with Mr. Durant the du Pont Company would have joint control. The second was that the du Pont people would "assume charge and be responsible for the financial operation of the Company." The third was a forecast of expected return. The fourth was that the purchase would be made on better than an asset basis. The fifth I quote: "Our interest in the General Motors Company will undoubtedly secure for us the entire Fabrikoid, Pyralin, paint and varnish business of those companies, which is a substantial factor."[5]

On December 21, 1917, the du Pont board, on the recommendation of Pierre S. du Pont and Mr. Raskob, authorized the purchase of $25 million worth of the common stock of General Motors and Chevrolet. Whereupon, at the beginning of 1918, the du Pont Company took a position in General Motors amounting to 23.8 per cent of General Motors common stock, which was purchased in the open market and from individuals. The du Pont Company investment in General Motors was increased to $43 million, or 26.4 per cent, at the end of 1918.

The period of co-operation between the du Pont Company and Mr. Durant began when the first investment was made. du Pont representatives took over the responsibility of the General Motors Finance Committee, John J. Raskob becoming its chairman. Mr. Durant was the only member of the Finance Committee not from the du Pont Company. Financial affairs were assigned exclusively to this committee; it also set compensation for top executives. The Executive Committee, on the other hand, took complete charge of all operations, except matters assigned to the Finance Committee. Its chairman was Mr. Durant, and J. A. Haskell, who served as liaison man for du Pont in operations, was a member. Mr. Haskell, like Mr. Durant, sat on both the Executive Committee and the Finance Committee.

By the end of 1919, with the further expansion of General Motors, the du Pont Company increased its investment in the corporation to about $49 million, giving it ownership of 28.7 per cent of the General Motors common. Then, Pierre S. du Pont has said, "they made a declaration that that would be the end of their investment, and they would take no more." But events dictated otherwise.

In the period 1918 through 1920 Mr. Durant took General Motors through a large expansion of operations, in which he was enthusiastically supported by Mr. Raskob and the Finance Committee, which obtained the capital for the expansion.

The acquisition of Chevrolet in 1918 gave the corporation a car that was potentially competitive with Ford in the low-price class, although it could not compete with Ford at that time in quality and was priced above it. Along with Chevrolet came Scripps-Booth, a small car company owned by Chevrolet.

The important association with Fisher Body was begun in 1919 with the acquisition of a 60 per cent interest in that company and a contract for the manufacture of bodies.

The Sheridan car, made by a small outfit, was purchased in 1920, giving the corporation for a time a line of seven cars. The Cadillac, the Buick, the Olds, the Oakland, and the Chevrolet, along with the General Motors Truck, were already established, although the Cadillac and the Buick were still the only worthwhile cars in the line.

Two special projects, one in tractors and the other in refrigeration, were brought into the corporation on the personal initiative of Mr. Durant. On occasion, when out in the field, he would make informal deals to get something started, and this sometimes caused uneasy moments in the general office. But in the end his intuitive and impulsive moves were supported.

So it was that in February 1917 he caused General Motors to buy into a small enterprise called the Samson Sieve Grip Tractor Company of Stockton, California, which had an invention for driving a tractor like a horse—"the Iron Horse" it came to be called. And to this he later added the Janesville Machine Company of Janesville, Wisconsin, and the Doylestown Agricultural Company of Doylestown, Pennsylvania, to form in General Motors the Samson Tractor Division—a very unprofitable venture, as it turned out. In June 1918, on the other hand, Mr. Durant bought a small company in Detroit, called the Guardian Frigerator Company, and made out his own check for it in the amount of $56,366.50, for which he was repaid by General Motors on May 31, 1919. This embryo enterprise took on importance later as the Frigidaire Division.

A number of other enterprises were started or taken into the corporation in the period 1918–20: General Motors of Canada, Ltd.; the General Motors Acceptance Corporation, which was organized to finance the sale of General Motors cars and trucks; a group of Dayton companies in which Charles F. Kettering was interested; a number of manufacturing divisions which were set up to supply axles, gears, crankshafts, and the like for General Motors' automobile divisions, and a group of parts and accessory companies called United Motors, of which I was president.

Thanks mainly to Mr. Durant, General Motors had then the makings of a great enterprise. But it was in good part physically unintegrated and in management uncoordinated; the expenditures for new companies, plants and equipment, and inventories were terrific—some of them not to bring a return for a long time, if ever—and as they went up, the cash went down. General Motors was heading for the crisis from which the modern General Motors Corporation would emerge.

Notes

1. Mr. Nash, although the first president of General Motors to play a large role in that office, was in fact the fifth person to hold the title. Mr. Durant, in founding the company, chose the position of vice president for himself. The first person with the title of president was George E. Daniels; his term lasted less than a month, from September 22 to October 20, 1908. The second was William M. Eaton, who was in

office about two years, from October 20, 1908, to November 23, 1910. James J. Storrow was an interim president for two months, from November 23, 1910, to January 25, 1911. The fourth was Thomas Neal. His term ran from January 25, 1911, to November 19, 1912.

2. The fact that the Chevrolet Motor Company held a controlling interest in General Motors was proved in 1917. Of the 825,589 shares of General Motors Corporation common stock outstanding (after the exchange of five shares of General Motors Corporation common stock for each share of General Motors Company common stock), 450,000 shares were owned by the Chevrolet Motor Company; thus Mr. Durant clinched his earlier claim.

   This odd knot, in which Mr. Durant controlled General Motors, was not undone until some years later. General Motors, in May 1918, bought the operating assets of Chevrolet and paid for them in General Motors common stock. Still later the General Motors stock owned by the Chevrolet Motor Company was distributed to the latter's shareholders upon the dissolution of the Chevrolet Motor Company. The Chevrolet Motor Company became the Chevrolet Division of the General Motors Corporation.

3. The General Motors Corporation was incorporated on October 13, 1916, under the laws of the state of Delaware. The New Jersey company was dissolved and its assets taken over by the corporation as of August 1, 1917, and the latter became the active operating corporation on that date.

4. In quoting, I have followed original materials as closely as possible. This results in some variation in spelling, punctuation, and the like.

5. The entry of the du Pont interests into General Motors became the basis of a suit by the government against du Pont and General Motors—filed in 1949, or more than thirty years after the fact. The basic charge was that the acquisition violated the anti-trust laws and had enabled du Pont to secure for its own benefit the business of General Motors in products produced by du Pont. This charge was denied by General Motors and du Pont. The district court, after hearing testimony over a period of several months of a broad cross-section of the active participants in the matter and the examination of many documents, found there was no evidence to support the contentions of the government and dismissed the case. The Supreme Court on review held that the acquisition by the du Pont interests, some thirty years earlier, was illegal because there was a reasonable probability that the acquisition was likely to result in a restraint of trade. The Supreme Court agreed, however, with the finding of the trial court, stating that "considerations of price, quality and service were not overlooked by either du Pont or General Motors" and that "all concerned in high executive posts in both companies acted honorably and fairly, each in the honest conviction that his actions were in the best interest of his own company and without any design to overreach anyone, including du Pont's competitors." The trial court's judgment of dismissal was reversed and the case remanded for relief. On remand, and after further litigation and appeal, the district court decreed that the du Pont interests divest themselves of their General Motors stock over a period of years. It appears to me, as a layman, that the reasoning of the Supreme Court in the case is almost purely academic and is not supported by the realities of the situation as found by the district court.

Everybody Ought to Be Rich

John J. Raskob

John J. Raskob, senior financial executive at General Motors, proposed to form Equities Security Company to enable the ordinary
workingman "the same chance that the rich banker has of profiting
by the rise in values of the common stocks of America's most successful companies." The idea, described as "the greatest vision of
Wall Street's greatest mind," would enable an investor to put up
$200 in cash, borrow $300 from a finance subsidiary, and buy $500
in stock—repaying the loan at $25 a month. Although most com-
mentators were delighted, Raskob fortunately decided to wait for
somewhat lower prices before launching the venture. Here is his
proposition—from an interview with Samuel Crowther in the *Ladies
Home Journal* dated August 1929.

Being rich is, of course, a comparative status. A man with a million
dollars used to be considered rich, but so many people have at least that
much in these days, or are earning incomes in excess of a normal return
from a million dollars, that a millionaire does not cause any comment.

Fixing a bulk line to define riches is a pointless performance. Let
us rather say that man is rich when he has an income from invested
capital which is sufficient to support him and his family in a decent and
comfortable manner—to give as much support, let us say, as has ever
been given by his earnings. That amount of prosperity ought to be

Reprinted from *Ladies Home Journal* (August 1929), pp. 9, 36. New York: Meredith Corporation.

attainable by anyone. A greater share will come to those who have greater ability. . . .

The common stocks of this country have in the past ten years increased enormously in value because the business of the country has increased. Ten thousand dollars invested ten years ago in the common stock of General Motors would now be worth more than a million and a half dollars. And General Motors is only one of many first-class industrial corporations.

It may be said that this is a phenomenal increase and that conditions are going to be different in the next ten years. That prophecy may be true, but it is not founded on experience. In my opinion the wealth of the country is bound to increase at a very rapid rate. The rapidity of the rate will be determined by the increase in consumption, and under wise investment plans the consumption will steadily increase.

. . . Suppose a man marries at the age of twenty-three and begins a regular savings of fifteen dollars a month—and almost anyone who is employed can do that if he tries. If he invests in good common stocks and allows the dividends and rights to accumulate, he will at the end of twenty years have at least eighty thousand dollars and an income from investments of around four hundred dollars a month. He will be rich. And because anyone can do that I am firm in my belief that anyone not only can be rich but ought to be rich.

The obstacles to being rich are two: The trouble of saving, and the trouble of finding a medium for investment.

If Tom is known to have two hundred dollars in the savings bank then everyone is out to get it for some absolutely necessary purpose. More than likely his wife's sister will eventually find the emergency to draw it forth. But if he does withstand all attacks, what good will the money do him? The interest he receives is so small that he has no incentive to save, and since the whole is under his own jurisdiction he can depend only upon his own will to save. To save in any such fashion requires a stronger will than the normal.

If he thinks of investing in some stock he has nowhere to turn for advice. He is not big enough to get much attention from his banker, and he has not enough money to go to a broker—or at least he thinks that he has not.

Suppose he has a thousand dollars; the bank can only advise him to buy a bond, for the officer will not take the risk of advising a stock and probably has not the experience anyway to give such advice. Tom can get really adequate attention only from some man who has a worthless security to sell, for then all of Tom's money will be profit. . . .

Recently I have been advocating the formation of an equity securities corporation; that is, a corporation that will invest in common stocks only under proper and careful supervision. This company will buy the common stocks of first-class industrial corporations and issue its own stock certificates against them. This stock will be offered from time to time at a price to correspond exactly with the value of the assets of the corporation and all profit will go to the stockholders. The directors will be men of outstanding character, reputation and integrity. At regular intervals—say quarterly—the whole financial record of the corporation will be published together with all of its holdings and the cost thereof. The corporation will be owned by the public and with every transaction public. I am not at all interested in a private investment trust. The company would not be permitted to borrow money or go into any debt.

In addition to this company, there should be organized a discount company on the same lines as the finance companies of the motor concerns to be used to sell stock of the investing corporation on the installment plan. If Tom had two hundred dollars, this discount company would lend him three hundred dollars and thus enable him to buy five hundred dollars of the equity securities investment company stock. . . . That would take his savings out of the free-will class and put them into the compulsory-payment class and his savings would no longer be fair game for relatives, for swindlers or for himself. . . .

It is difficult to see why a bond or mortgage should be considered as a more conservative investment than a good stock, for the only difference in practice is that the bond can never be worth more than its face value or return more than the interest, while a stock can be worth more than was paid for it and can return a limitless profit.

One may lose on either a bond or a stock. If a company fails it will usually be reorganized and in that case the bonds will have to give way to new money and possibly they will be scaled down. The common stockholders may lose all, or again they may get another kind of stock which may or may not eventually have a value. In a failure, neither the bondholders nor the stockholders will find great cause for happiness— but there are very few failures among the larger corporations. . . .

The old view of debt was quite as illogical as the old view of investment. It was beyond the conception of anyone that debt could be constructive. Every old saw about debt—and there must be a thousand of them—is bound up with borrowing instead of earning. We now know that borrowing may be a method of earning and beneficial to everyone concerned. Suppose a man needs a certain amount of money in order to buy a set of tools or anything else which will increase his income. He can take one of two courses. He can save the money and in the course of time buy his tools, or he can, if the proper facilities are provided, borrow the money at a reasonable rate of interest, buy the tools and immediately so increase his income that he can pay off his debt and own the tools within half the time that it would have taken him to save the money and pay cash. That loan enables him at once to create more wealth than before and consequently makes him a more valuable citizen. By increasing his power to produce he also increases his power to consume and therefore he increases the power of others to produce in order to fill his new needs and naturally increases their power to consume, and so on and on. By borrowing the money instead of saving it he increases his ability to save and steps up prosperity at once. . . .

That is exactly what the automobile has done to the prosperity of the country through the plan of installment payments. The installment plan of paying for automobiles, when it was first launched, ran counter to the old notions of debt. It was opposed by bankers, who saw in it only an incentive for extravagance. It was opposed by manufacturers because they thought people would be led to buy automobiles instead of their products.

The results have been exactly opposite to the prediction. The ability to buy automobiles on credit gave an immediate step-up to their purchase. Manufacturing them, servicing them, building roads for them to run on, and caring for the people who used the roads have brought into existence about ten billion dollars of new wealth each year. . . .

The great wealth of this country has been gained by the forces of production and consumption pushing each other for supremacy. The personal fortunes of this country have been made not by saving but by producing. . . .

The way to wealth is to get into the profit end of wealth production in this country.

Artemisa Mines Finance Corp.

C. W. Fisk

"As your eye follows this line of type across this sheet of paper . . .
Destiny stands at your shoulder." "Here is Opportunity. Are you going to be satisfied to glimpse her from the edge of the crowd, or
are you going to step up and take her by the hand?" Thus begins
and ends a classic example of a mining venture come-on that is a
masterpiece of the genre. This tract, by Artemisa's president, C. W.
Fisk, was written to attract the capital needed, he said, to put into
production a mine like no other in the world. And, so long as you
bought a minimum of 200 shares (at $0.25 per share), you could buy
on credit, with one fifth down and the balance due in four equal
monthly installments. In Greek mythology, Artemisa was, among
other things, goddess of the hunt.

———

THE ARTEMISA MINE AT ARIZPE IN THE STATE OF SONORA,
MEXICO, ONLY 117 MILES FROM THE GREAT SMELTERS AT
DOUGLAS, ARIZONA, WILL PRODUCE UPWARDS OF FIFTEEN
THOUSAND DOLLARS A DAY IN NET PROFITS AS SOON AS
PRESENT DEVELOPMENT WORK IS COMPLETED, ACCORDING
TO CAREFUL ENGINEERING ESTIMATES RECENTLY MADE.
HUNDREDS OF THOUSANDS OF TONS OF GOLD, COPPER, SIL-
VER, LEAD AND ZINC ORES ARE ALREADY BLOCKED OUT.
MINING COST IS LESS THAN $1 A TON, WITH VALUES RUN-
NING FROM $45 TO $3,161.90 A TON!

———

Reprinted from a letter written by C. W. Fisk, Denver, 1931 or 1932.

ARTEMISA is in the Heart of the Sonora Metallurgical Belt, One of the Most Richly Mineralized Areas on the Face of the Earth. Two of its Neighbors are the Famous Cananea and Nacozari properties, Which Have Between Them Produced About a Billion Dollars Worth of Freshly Mined Metallic Wealth. Cananea Stock, Representing a Property That Was Not Nearly as Rich as Artemisa at the Same Stage of Development, Arose from 50¢ to $200 per Share!!

Dear Friend:

Once in the life of every man there comes an outstanding opportunity on which, if he grasps it, he may ride on to ease and fortune; but which, if neglected, becomes in later years of adversity and struggle, only a regretful memory.

As your eye follows this line of type across this sheet of paper which has come to you from a man whom you have never seen, Destiny stands at your shoulder. What will you do? Will you stop here and throw the letter into the waste basket, the fire, the stove, or whatever happens to be handy? Or will you continue to read? From a pile of ordinary mail, of ordinary investment offers, will you pick out this opportunity to achieve REAL WEALTH as a skilled miner washes gold from useless gravel?

It is written, "Hope deferred maketh the heart sick." Have you put your hard-won savings into propositions which have promised you immense profits almost overnight, only to find that after waiting weary months and years, honeyed promises had turned into the Dead Sea fruit of loss?

If you have, what of it? We have all made, at one time or another in our lives, investments or speculations which have not turned out as we hoped they would.

Life is a gamble. Love is a gamble. Marriage is a gamble. Politics is a gamble. Business is a gamble.

It used to be said that only one thing is certain—taxes. Nowadays, however, that saying is no longer entirely true, for there is a second thing that is ABSOLUTELY CERTAIN.

And that second thing is the price paid for GOLD. It is $20 per ounce. It is fixed by law. Any of the great Mints maintained by the Government of the United States in various parts of the country, will pay that price for gold. Not only that, they do it gladly. After paying for your gold, they will ask if you haven't more, so that they can pay you for that, too, for no man-eating tiger that roams the jungle ever had an appetite as insatiable as the Government's appetite for gold.

As a consequence, the demand for gold is always greater than the supply—always has been and in all probability always will be. There is never any question about making money from gold. The trouble is in finding the gold. WE HAVE FOUND IT FOR YOU, and along with it Silver, Copper, Lead and Zinc in almost fabulous quantities. And here we come to the point of this letter which I have written you. We need a few thousand dollars to get mining operations under way on a substantial scale and start the gold, silver, copper, lead and zinc that we have found to market.

WE ARE NOW ENGAGED IN RAISING THOSE DOLLARS. WE ARE GOING TO HAVE THEM SOON. WHEN WE DO, AND HAVE OUR IMMENSELY RICH ORE ON ITS WAY IN HUGE DAILY TONNAGES FROM THE MINE TO THE MILL AND SMELTER, THE OFFER IN THIS LETTER WILL NO LONGER BE IN EXISTENCE!

The best way to arrive at accurate knowledge is through comparisons, as everything in the world, as we all know, is comparative. Let us, therefore, compare the ARTEMISA properties with those of the Homestake Mining Company in the Black Hills of South Dakota, which are now considered the greatest gold mining properties in the 48 states of the Federal Union.

Homestake stock was selling at 25¢ per share in 1877. In January, 1878, it started paying cash dividends of 50¢ per share PER MONTH!—200% EVERY THIRTY DAYS! IT HAS PAID THIS EVER SINCE, WITH ONLY THREE BRIEF INTERRUPTIONS. IN ADDITION, IT USUALLY PAYS ABOUT TWO EXTRA DIVIDENDS EVERY YEAR OF $1 EACH—AND LAST MONTH IT RAISED ITS MONTHLY DIVIDEND RATE FROM 50¢ TO 65¢ PER SHARE! THINK OF IT! THIS STOCK, ONCE SELLING AT 25¢ PER SHARE, SELLS NOW AT SOMEWHERE BETWEEN $118 AND $120—AND IS WORTH EVERY DOLLAR OF THE PRICE.

The total original investment that started Homestake, amounted to about $200,000. With that investment, the properties have produced about $378,000,000.00. Each single dollar of Homestake's original capital has produced $1,890.00 in wealth.

BUT MOST INTERESTING OF ALL IS THIS: THE GOLD CON-
TENT OF THE HOMESTAKE ORES HAVE AVERAGED FROM
$3.72½ IN GOLD TO THE TON TO $6.17½ IN GOLD TO THE
TON ——— NEVER HIGHER.

NOW ——— ACTUAL ASSAYS OF VALUES IN THE AR-
TEMISA ORES SHOW THAT LEAD VALUES ALONE ARE FIVE
TIMES THE VALUE OF HOMESTAKE'S GOLD VALUE PER TON,
ZINC VALUES ALONE ARE OVER FOUR TIMES AS MUCH, SIL-
VER SEVEN HUNDRED AND FIFTY TIMES AS MUCH, AND
GOLD TWO HUNDRED AND FORTY-TWO TIMES AS MUCH!!!

AND WHAT IS MORE—YOU CAN GET STOCK IN ARTEMISA
NOW FOR EXACTLY WHAT YOU COULD HAVE BOUGHT
STOCK IN HOMESTAKE IN 1877—25¢ PER SHARE!

Facts are facts, values are values, gold is gold. Gold mined in Mexico is JUST AS VALUABLE AND COSTS LESS TO MINE than gold
mined in the United States. So the profits from Mexican gold are
GREATER than from gold mined in the United States, because mining
costs are lower.

And here are a few more facts:

ARTEMISA MINES are in the State of Sonora, Mexico,—BUT
THEY ARE ONLY 117 MILES SOUTH OF DOUGLAS, ARIZONA.
The Company is incorporated under the laws of the State of Arizona.
Capitalization is $1,000,000. Par value of the stock is 10¢ per share.
Price at present is 25¢ per share. It is all fully participating, fully paid
and non-assessable common stock. Company owns its valuable mining
ground outright, and has a clear title thereto. Legal description of the
property is as follows: "Patent Republica of Mexico." Company has no
debts. Developments now under way and rapidly nearing completion are
being financed through sale of Treasury stock at 25¢ per share. Active
work at present is in an area of 24½ acres, with an additional 140 acres
annexable. The main tunnel is in 512 feet in SOLID ORE AND THERE
IS NO SPECULATION OR GUESSWORK ABOUT ARTEMISA ORE
VALUES, WHICH ASSAY FROM $45 TO $3,161.90 PER TON!

Over $100,000 has already been spent in the development. Present
financing is for the purpose of adding milling and power capacity to
enable the Company to handle 1,000 tons of ore per day.

Careful engineering estimates indicate that ARTEMISA has over
40,000,000 tons of rich ore in the main vein alone—ENOUGH TO
SUPPLY 1,000 TONS A DAY FOR OVER 100 YEARS!

The latest assays from the main vein, <u>which</u> <u>is</u> <u>solid</u> <u>ore</u> <u>over</u> <u>30</u> <u>FEET</u> <u>THICK</u>, are as follows:

Lead, 28% per ton.
Zinc, 29% per ton.
Silver, 7,383.7 ounces per ton ($2,214.90 at present price).
Gold, 47.35 ounces ($947) per ton.

Watch Silver! We believe it will be 60¢ an ounce by the first of the year, and $1.00 an ounce before you celebrate another Fourth of July. The above assay was computed at 30¢ an ounce,—the present price.

If you have the time, get in your car and run down to ARTEMISA. It's only about 100 miles south of the American border, among as industrious and pleasant a people as you would ever want to see, AND LET US SHOW YOU THESE VALUES IN A BIG VEIN OVER 30 FEET WIDE THAT RUNS ALONG FOR HUNDREDS AND HUNDREDS OF FEET, CARRYING MILLIONS UPON MILLIONS OF DOLLARS WORTH OF PRECIOUS AND USEFUL METALS— <u>WEALTH</u> <u>BEYOND</u> <u>YOUR</u> <u>WILDEST</u> <u>DREAMS</u>!!! UNBELIEVABLE 'TIL YOU SEE IT AND TOUCH IT WITH YOUR OWN HANDS!! IN ALL THE WORLD THERE IS NO OTHER MINE LIKE ARTEMISA!

And why should there be? The late Cecil Rhodes, one of the greatest mining men who ever lived, said of Mexico: "I am not blind to the consensus of opinion as expressed by scientists and experts that Mexico will one day furnish the Gold, Silver, Copper and other minerals that will build the empires of tomorrow and make the future cities of this world veritable Jerusalems."

Are you awake to the revenue from the rising tide of the world's wealth from the mines of Mexico? THIS IS YOUR OPPORTUNITY TO AVAIL YOURSELF OF INTERESTS IN THE WEALTH OF ONE OF THE RICHEST MINES IN MEXICO!

No man deserves wealth who does not earn it in one way or another. ARTEMISA prosperity is going to be enjoyed only by those who put their shoulders to the wheel RIGHT NOW, depression or no depression, and HELP.

We want you with us. We want you to help us. If you do, we will do our part to bring you returns on your investment that we believe will seem like a miracle to you, will open your eyes as nothing ever has before to the tremendous golden wealth that is constantly flowing across the border from Mexico.

You can buy ARTEMISA stock either for cash, or on a basis of one-fifth cash, balance in four equal monthly payments of one-fifth each, at 25¢ per share. No cash orders will be accepted for less than 50 shares, and no deferred payment orders for less than 200 shares. The larger your order, the larger is your share in the wealth of ARTEMISA.

In subscribing to stock of this Company, you are not gambling or speculating in an unproven, untried proposition, YOU ARE ASSIST-ING IN THE PURCHASE OF MACHINERY FOR PUTTING ONE OF THE RICHEST GOLD, SILVER, COPPER, LEAD, AND ZINC MINES IN THE ENTIRE WORLD INTO A PRODUCTION OF 1,000 TONS DAILY, FROM WHICH NET PROFITS SHOULD BE TRE-MENDOUS.

If you never put your last dollar into a proposition, DO IT NOW. You aren't betting on a race, an election, or an untried, unproven, uncertain proposition such as an undrilled oil well or an unexplored mine; YOU ARE INVESTING IN PROVEN VALUES WHICH INCLUDE GOLD ORE ASSAYING $947 TO THE TON.

GOLD can make money for you; GOLD can protect your old age and your children from want AS INVESTMENT IN NO OTHER COM-MODITY CAN!

Don't pass up this wonderful opportunity. THE OFFER IS UN-USUAL. ARTEMISA HAS THE LARGEST RICH VEIN OF GOLD, SILVER, COPPER, LEAD AND ZINC KNOWN TO EXIST ANY-WHERE IN THE WORLD.

Get your order at 25¢ per share in the mail TODAY.

Sincerely yours,
ARTEMISA MINES FINANCE CORPORATION
C. W. Fisk, President

P.S. Here is Opportunity. Are you going to be satisfied to glimpse her from the edge of the crowd, or are you going to step up and take her by the hand?

The Big Bull Market and the Crash

Frederick Lewis Allen

Frederick Lewis Allen achieved great success in his popular accounts of many of the key events which marked the 1920s and the 1930s. Here he recalls the chaotic days which preceded and followed Black Tuesday—October 29, 1929.

The Big Bull Market

One day in February, 1928, an investor asked an astute banker about the wisdom of buying common stocks. The banker shook his head. "Stocks look dangerously high to me," he said. "This bull market has been going on for a long time, and although prices have slipped a bit recently, they might easily slip a good deal more. Business is none too good. Of course if you buy the right stock you'll probably be all right in the long run and you may even make a profit. But if I were you I'd wait awhile and see what happens."

By all the canons of conservative finance the banker was right. That enormous confidence in Coolidge Prosperity which had lifted the business man to a new preeminence in American life and had persuaded innumerable men and women to gamble their savings away in Florida real estate had also carried the prices of common stocks far upward since 1924, until they had reached what many hard-headed financiers

Reprinted from *Only Yesterday* (1931), Chapters 12 and 13, 290–336, by permission of HarperCollins Publishers, New York. © 1931 by Frederick Lewis Allen, © 1957 by Harper & Brothers.

considered alarming levels. Throughout 1927 speculation had been increasing. The amount of money loaned to brokers to carry margin accounts for traders had risen during the year from $2,818,561,000 to $3,558,355,000—a huge increase. During the week of December 3, 1927, more shares of stock had changed hands than in any previous week in the whole history of the New York Stock Exchange. One did not have to listen long to an after-dinner conversation, whether in New York or San Francisco or the lowliest village of the plain, to realize that all sorts of people to whom the stock ticker had been a hitherto alien mystery were carrying a hundred shares of Studebaker or Houston Oil, learning the significance of such recondite symbols as GL and X and ITT, and whipping open the early editions of afternoon papers to catch the 1:30 quotations from Wall Street.

The speculative fever had been intensified by the action of the Federal Reserve System in lowering the rediscount rate from 4 per cent to 3½ per cent in August, 1927, and purchasing Government securities in the open market. This action had been taken from the most laudable motives: several of the European nations were having difficulty in stabilizing their currencies, European exchanges were weak, and it seemed to the Reserve authorities that the easing of American money rates might prevent the further accumulation of gold in the United States and thus aid in the recovery of Europe and benefit foreign trade. Furthermore, American business was beginning to lose headway; the lowering of money rates might stimulate it. But the lowering of money rates also stimulated the stock market. The bull party in Wall Street had been still further encouraged by the remarkable solicitude of President Coolidge and Secretary Mellon, who whenever confidence showed signs of waning came out with opportunely reassuring statements which at once sent prices upward again. In January, 1928, the president had actually taken the altogether unprecedented step of publicly stating that he did not consider brokers' loans too high, thus apparently giving White House sponsorship to the very inflation which was worrying the sober mind of the financial community.

While stock prices had been climbing, business activity had been undeniably subsiding. There had been such a marked recession during the latter part of 1927 that by February, 1928, the director of the Charity Organization Society in New York reported that unemployment was more serious than at any time since immediately after the war. During January and February the stock market turned ragged and unsettled, and no wonder—for with prices still near record levels and the future trend of business highly dubious, it was altogether too easy to foresee a time of reckoning ahead.

The tone of the business analysts and forecasters—a fraternity whose numbers had hugely increased in recent years and whose lightest words carried weight—was anything but exuberant. On January 5, 1928, Moody's Investors Service said the stock prices had "over-discounted anticipated progress" and wondered "how much of a readjustment may be required to place the stock market in a sound position." On March 1st this agency was still uneasy: "The public," it declared, "is not likely to change its bearish state of mind until about the time when money becomes so plethoric as to lead the banks to encourage credit expansion." Two days later the Harvard Economic Society drew from its statistical graphs the chilly conclusion that "the developments of February suggest that business is entering upon a period of temporary readjustment"; the best cheer which the Harvard prognosticators could offer was a prophecy that "intermediate declines in the stock market will not develop into such major movements as forecast business depression." The newspaper advertisements of investment services testified to the uncomfortable temper of Wall Street with headlines like "Will You 'Overstay' This Bull Market?" and "Is the Process of Deflation Under Way?" The air was fogged with uncertainty.

Anybody who had chosen this moment to predict that the bull market was on the verge of a wild advance which would make all that had gone before seem trifling would have been quite mad—or else inspired with a genius for mass psychology. The banker who advised caution was quite right about financial conditions, and so were the forecasters. But they had not taken account of the boundless commercial romanticism of the American people, inflamed by year after plentiful year of Coolidge Prosperity. For on March 3, 1928—the very day when the Harvard prophets were talking about intermediate declines and the *Times* was talking about hesitation—the stock market entered upon its sensational phase.

=====

What on earth was happening? Wasn't business bad, and credit inflated, and the stock-price level dangerously high? Was the market going crazy? Suppose all these madmen who insisted on buying stocks at advancing prices tried to sell at the same moment! Canny investors, reading of the wild advance in Radio, felt much as did the forecasters of Moody's Investors Service a few days later: the practical question, they said, was "how long the opportunity to sell at the top will remain."

What was actually happening was that a group of powerful speculators with fortunes made in the automobile business and in the grain markets and in the earlier days of the bull market in stocks—men like W. C. Durant and Arthur Cutten and the Fisher Brothers and John J. Raskob—were buying in unparalleled volume. They thought that business was due to come out of its doldrums. They knew that with Ford production delayed, the General Motors Corporation was likely to have a big year. They knew that the Radio Corporation had been consolidating its position and was now ready to make more money than it had ever made before, and that as scientific discovery followed discovery, the future possibilities of the biggest radio company were exciting. Automobiles and radios—these were the two most characteristic products of the decade of confident mass production, the brightest flowers of Coolidge Prosperity: they held a ready-made appeal to the speculative imagination. The big bull operators knew too, that thousands of speculators had been selling stocks short in the expectation of a collapse in the market, would continue to sell short, and could be forced to repurchase if prices were driven relentlessly up. And finally, they knew their American public. It could not resist the appeal of a surging market. It had an altogether normal desire to get rich quick, and it was ready to believe anything about the golden future of American business. If stocks started upward the public would buy, no matter what the forecasters said, no matter how obscure was the business prospect.

They were right. The public bought.

Monday the 12th of March put the stock market on the front page once more. Radio opened at 120½—and closed at 138½. Other stocks made imposing gains, the volume of trading broke every known record by totaling 3,875,910 shares, the ticker fell six minutes behind the market, and visitors to the gallery of the Stock Exchange reported that red-haired Michael Meehan, the specialist in Radio, was the center of what appeared to be a five-hour scrimmage on the floor. "It looked like a street fight," said one observer.

Tuesday the 13th was enough to give anybody chills and fever. . . . This time the ticker was twelve minutes late.

And so it went on, day after day and week after week. On March 16th the ticker was thirty-three minutes late and one began to hear people saying that some day there might occur a five-million-share day—which seemed almost incredible. . . .

Several times during the spring of 1928 the New York Stock Exchange had to remain closed on Saturday to give brokers' clerks a chance to dig themselves out from under the mass of paper work in which this unprecedented trading involved them. And of course brokers' loans were increasing; the inflation of American credit was becoming steadily intensified.

The Reserve authorities were disturbed. They had raised the rediscount rate in February from 3½ to 4 per cent, hoping that if a lowering of the rate in 1927 had encouraged speculation, a corresponding increase would discourage it—and instead they had witnessed a common-stock mania which ran counter to all logic and all economic theory. They raised the rate again in May to 4½ per cent, but after a brief shudder the market went boiling on. They sold the Government bonds they had accumulated during 1927, and the principal result of their efforts was that the Government-bond market became demoralized. Who would ever have thought the situation would thus get out of hand?

In the latter part of May, 1928, the pace of the bull market slackened. Prices fell off, gained, fell off again. The reckoning, so long expected, appeared at last to be at hand.

It came in June, after several days of declining prices. The Giannini stocks, the speculative favorites of the Pacific coast, suddenly toppled for gigantic losses. On the San Francisco Stock Exchange the shares of the Bank of Italy fell 100 points in a single day (June 11th). . . .

The next day, June 12th, this Western tornado struck Wall Street in full force. As selling orders poured in, the prophecy that the Exchange would some day see a five-million-share day was quickly fulfilled. The ticker slipped almost two hours behind in recording prices on the floor. Radio, which had marched well beyond the 200 mark in May, lost 23½ points. The day's losses for the general run of securities were not, to be sure, very large by subsequent standards; the *New York Times* averages for fifty leading stocks dropped only a little over three points. But after the losses of the preceding days, it seemed to many observers as if the end had come at last, and one of the most conservative New York papers began its front-page account of the break with the unqualified sentence, "Wall Street's bull market collapsed yesterday with a detonation heard round the world."

. . . But had the bull market collapsed? On June 13th it appeared to have regained its balance. On June 14th, the day of Hoover's nomination, it extended its recovery. The promised reckoning had been only partial. Prices still stood well above their February levels. A few thousand traders had been shaken out, a few big fortunes had been lost, a great many pretty paper profits had vanished; but the Big Bull Market was still young.

===

Election Day came and Hoover swept the country. . . . It was a famous victory, and in celebration of it the stock market—which all through the campaign had been pushing to new high ground—went into a new frenzy. Now the bulls had a new slogan. It was "four more years of prosperity."

===

During that "Hoover bull market" of November, 1928, the records made earlier in the year were smashed to flinders. Had brokers once spoken with awe of the possibility of five-million-share days? Five-million-share days were now occurring with monotonous regularity; on November 23rd the volume of trading almost reached seven millions. Had they been amazed at the rising prices of seats on the Stock Exchange? In November a new mark of $580,000 was set. Had they been disturbed that Radio should sell at such an exorbitant price as 150? Late in November it was bringing 400. Ten-point gains and new highs for all time were commonplaces now. Montgomery Ward, which the previous spring had been climbing toward 200, touched 439⅞ on November 30. The copper stocks were skyrocketing; Packard climbed to 145; Wright Aeronautical flew as high as 263. Brokers' loans? Of course they were higher than ever; but this, one was confidently told, was merely a sign of prosperity—a sign that the American people were buying on the part-payment plan a partnership in the future progress of the country. Call money rates? They ranged around 8 and 9 per cent; a little high, perhaps, admitted the bulls, but what was the harm if people chose to pay them? Business was not suffering from high money rates; business was doing better than ever. The new era had arrived and the abolition of poverty was just around the corner.

In December the market broke again, and more sharply than in June. There was one fearful day—Saturday, December 7th—when the weary ticker, dragging far behind the trading on the floor, hammered out the story of a 72-point decline in Radio. Horrified tape-watchers in the brokers' offices saw the stock open at 361, struggle weakly up to 363, and then take the bumps point by point, all the way down to 296—which at that moment seemed like a fire-sale figure. (The earnings of the Radio Corporation during the first nine months of 1928 had been $7.54 per share, which on the time-honored basis of "ten times earnings" would have suggested the appropriateness of price of not much over 100; but the ten-times-earnings basis for prices had long since been discarded. The market, as Max Winkler said, was discounting not only the future, but the hereafter.) Montgomery Ward lost 29 points that same nerve-wracking Saturday morning, and International Harvester slipped from 368½ to 307. But just as in June, the market righted itself at the moment when demoralization seemed to be setting in. A few uneasy weeks of ragged prices went by, and then the advance began once more.

. . . The Reserve banks had already raised the rediscount rate (in July) to 5 per cent, and speculation had been affected only momentarily. Apparently speculators were ready to pay any amount for money if only prices kept on climbing. The Reserve authorities had waited patiently for the speculative fever to cure itself and it had only become more violent. Things had now come to such a pass that if they raised the rate still further, they not only ran the risk of bringing about a terrific smash in the market—and of appearing to do so deliberately and wantonly—but also of seriously handicapping business by forcing it to pay a high rate for funds. Furthermore, they feared the further accumulation of gold in the United States and the effect which this might have upon world trade. And the Treasury had a final special concern about interest rates—it had its own financing to do, and Secretary Mellon was naturally not enthusiastic about forcing the Government to pay a fancy rate for money for its own current use. It almost seemed as if there were no way to deflation except through disaster.

The Reserve Board finally met the dilemma by thinking up a new and ingenious scheme. They tried to prevent the reloaning of Reserve funds to brokers without raising the rediscount rate.

On February 2, 1929, they issued a statement in which they said: "The Federal Reserve Act does not, in the opinion of the Federal Reserve Board contemplate the use of the resources of the Federal Reserve Banks for the creation or extension of speculative credit. A member bank is not within its reasonable claims for rediscount facilities at its Federal Reserve Bank when it borrows for the purpose of making speculative loans. . . . ''

The immediate result of the statement of February 2, 1929 was a brief overnight collapse in stock prices. The subsequent result, as the Reserve Banks proceeded to bring pressure on their member banks to borrow only for what were termed legitimate business purposes, was naturally a further increase in call-money rates. Late in March—after Herbert Hoover had entered the White House and the previous patron saint of prosperity had retired to Northampton to explore the delights of autobiography—the pinch in money came to a sudden and alarming climax. Stock prices had been falling for several days when on March 25th the rate for call money jumped from 12 per cent to 15, and then to 17, and finally to 20 per cent—the highest rate since the dismal days of 1921. Another dizzy drop in prices took place. The turnover in stocks on the Exchange broke the November record, reaching 8,246,740 shares. Once again thousands of requests for more margin found their way into speculators' mail-boxes, and thousands of participators in the future prosperity of the country were sold out with the loss of everything they owned. Once again the Big Bull Market appeared to be on its last legs.

That afternoon several of the New York banks decided to come to the rescue. Whatever they thought of the new policy of the Federal Reserve Board, they saw a possible panic brewing—and anything, they decided, was better than a panic. The next day Charles E. Mitchell, president of the National City Bank, announced that his bank was prepared to lend twenty million dollars on call, of which five million would be available at 15 per cent, five million more at 16 per cent, and so on up to 20 per cent. Mr. Mitchell's action—which was described by Senator Carter Glass as a slap in the face of the Reserve Board—served to peg the call money rate at 15 per cent and the threatened panic was averted.

Whereupon stocks not only ceased their precipitous fall, but cheerfully recovered!

The lesson was plain: the public simply would not be shaken out of the market by anything short of a major disaster.

During the next month or two stocks rose and fell uncertainly, sinking dismally for a time in May, and the level of brokers' loans dipped a little, but no general liquidation took place. Gradually money began to find its way more plentifully into speculative use despite the barriers raised by the Federal Reserve Board. A corporation could easily find plenty of ways to put its surplus cash out on call at 8 or 9 per cent without doing it through a member bank of the Federal Reserve System; corporations were eager to put their funds to such remunerative use, as the increase in loans "for others" showed; and the member banks themselves, realizing this, were showing signs of restiveness. When June came, the advance in prices began once more, almost as if nothing had happened. The Reserve authorities were beaten.

＝＝

By the summer of 1929, prices had soared far above the stormy levels of the preceding winter into the blue and cloudless empyrean. All the old markers by which the price of a promising common stock could be measured had long since been passed; if a stock once valued at 100 went to 300, what on earth was to prevent it from sailing on to 400? And why not ride with it for fifty or a hundred points, with Easy Street at the end of the journey? . . .

Time and again the economists and forecasters had cried wolf, wolf, and the wolf had made only the most fleeting of visits. Time and again the Reserve Board had expressed fear of inflation, and inflation had failed to bring hard times. Business in danger? Why, nonsense! Factories were running at full blast and the statistical indices registered first-class industrial health. Was there a threat of overproduction? Nonsense again! Were not business concerns committed to hand-to-mouth buying, were not commodity prices holding to reasonable levels? Where were the overloaded shelves of goods, the heavy inventories, which business analysts universally accepted as storm signals? And look at the character of the stocks which were now leading the advance! At a moment when many of the high-flyers of earlier months were losing ground, the really sensational advances were being made by the shares of such solid and conservatively managed companies as United States Steel, General

Electric, and American Telephone—which were precisely those which the most cautious investor would select with an eye to the long future. . . .

On every side one heard the new wisdom sagely expressed. "Prosperity due for a decline? Why, man, we've scarcely started!" "Be a bull on America." "Never sell the United States short." "I tell you, some of these prices will look ridiculously low in another year or two." "Just watch that stock—it's going to five hundred." "The possibilities of that company are *unlimited.*" "Never give up your position in a good stock." Everybody heard how many millions a man would have made if he had bought a hundred shares of General Motors stock in 1919 and held on. Everybody was reminded at some time or another that George F. Baker never sold anything. As for the menace of speculation, one was glibly assured that—as Ex-Governor Stokes of New Jersey had proclaimed in an eloquent speech—Columbus, Washington, Franklin, and Edison had all been speculators. "The way to wealth," wrote John J. Raskob in an article in the *Ladies Home Journal* alluringly entitled "Everybody Ought to Be Rich," [see page 75 of this volume] "is to get into the profit end of wealth production in this country," and he pointed out that if one saved but fifteen dollars a month and invested it in good common stocks, allowing the dividends and rights to accumulate, at the end of twenty years one would have at least eighty thousand dollars and an income from investments of at least four hundred dollars a month. It was all so easy. The gateway to fortune stood wide open.

In September the market reached its ultimate glittering peak. . . . Stop for a moment to glance at a few prices recorded on the overworked ticker on September 3, 1929, the day the Dow-Jones averages reached their high point for the year; and compare them with the opening prices of March 3, 1928, when, as you may recall, it had seemed as if the bull market had already climbed to a perilous altitude. Here they are, side by side—first the figures for March, 1928; then the figures for September, 1929; and finally the latter figures translated into 1928 terms—or in other words revised to make allowance for intervening split-ups and issues of rights. (Only thus can you properly judge the extent of the advance during those eighteen confident months.)

	Opening Price, Mar. 3, 1928	High Price, Sept. 3, 1929	Adjusted High Price, Sept. 3, 1929
American Can	77	181⅞	181⅞
American Telephone & Telegraph	179½	304	335⅝
Anaconda Copper	54½	131½	162
General Electric	128¾	396¼	396¼
General Motors	139¾	72¾	181⅞
Montgomery Ward	132¾	137⅞	466½
New York Central	160½	256⅜	256⅜
Radio	94½	101	505
Union Carbide & Carbon	145	137⅞	413⅝
United States Steel	138⅛	261¾	279⅛
Westinghouse E & M	91⅝	289⅞	313
Woolworth	180¾	100⅜	251
Electric Bond & Share	89¾	186¾	203⅝

The Crash

Early in September the stock market broke. It quickly recovered, however; indeed, on September 19th the averages as compiled by the *New York Times* reached an even higher level than that of September 3rd. Once more it slipped, farther and faster, until by October 4th the prices of a good many stocks had coasted to what seemed first-class bargain levels. Steel, for example, after having touched 261¾ a few weeks earlier, had dropped as low as 204; American Can, at the closing on October 4th, was nearly twenty points below its high for the year; General Electric was over fifty points below its high; Radio had gone down from 114¾ to 82½.

A bad break, to be sure, but there had been other bad breaks, and the speculators who escaped unscathed proceeded to take advantage of the lesson they had learned in June and December of 1928 and March and May of 1929; when there was a break it was a good time to buy. In the face of all this tremendous liquidation, brokers' loans as compiled by the Federal Reserve Bank of New York mounted to a new high record on October 2nd, reaching $6,804,000,000—a sure sign that margin buyers were not deserting the market but coming into it in numbers at least undiminished. . . . And sure enough, prices once more began to climb.

Something was wrong, however. The decline began once more. . . . But there was little real alarm until the week of October 21st. The consensus of opinion, in the meantime, was merely that the equinoctial storm of September had not quite blown over. The market was readjusting itself into a "more secure technical position."

=====

The expected recovery in the stock market did not come. It seemed to be beginning on Tuesday, October 22nd, but the gains made during the day were largely lost during the last hour. And on Wednesday, the 23rd, there was a perfect Niagara of liquidation. . . . The next day was Thursday, October 24th.

On that momentous day stocks opened moderately steady in price, but in enormous volume. Kennecott appeared on the tape in a block of 20,000 shares, General Motors in another of the same amount. Almost at once the ticker tape began to lag behind the trading floor. The pressure of selling orders was disconcertingly heavy. Prices were going down. . . . Presently they were going down with some rapidity. . . . Before the first hour of trading was over, it was already apparent that they were going down with an altogether unprecedented and amazing violence. In brokers' offices all over the country, tape-watchers looked at one another in astonishment and perplexity. Where on earth was this torrent of selling orders coming from?

The exact answer to this question will probably never be known. But it seems probable that the principal cause of the break in prices during that first hour on October 24th was not fear. Nor was it short selling. It was forced selling. It was the dumping on the market of hundreds of thousands of shares of stock held in the name of miserable traders whose margins were exhausted or about to be exhausted. The gigantic edifice of prices was honeycombed with speculative credit and was now breaking under its own weight. . . . There seemed to be no support whatever. Down, down, down. The roar of voices which rose from the floor of the Exchange had become a roar of panic.

. . . In the space of two short hours, dozens of stocks lost ground which it had required many months of the bull market to gain. . . .

A few minutes after noon, some of the more alert members of a
crowd which had collected on the street outside the Stock Exchange,
expecting they knew not what, recognized Charles E. Mitchell, erst-
while defender of the bull market, slipping quietly into the offices of
J. P. Morgan & Company on the opposite corner. It was scarcely more
than nine years since the House of Morgan had been pitted with the
shrapnel-fire of the Wall Street explosion; now its occupants faced a
different sort of calamity equally near at hand. Mr. Mitchell was followed shortly by Albert H. Wiggin, head of the Chase National Bank;
William Potter, head of the Guaranty Trust Company; and Seward
Prosser, head of the Bankers Trust Company. They had come to confer
with Thomas W. Lamont of the Morgan firm. In the space of five minutes these five men, with George F. Baker, Jr., of the First National
Bank, agreed in behalf of their respective institutions to put up forty
millions apiece to shore up the stock market. The object of the two-
hundred-and-forty-million-dollar pool thus formed, as explained subsequently by Mr. Lamont, was not to hold prices at any given level, but
simply to make such purchases as were necessary to keep trading on an
orderly basis. Their first action, they decided, would be to try to steady
the prices of the leading securities which served as bellwethers for the
list as a whole. It was a dangerous plan, for with hysteria spreading
there was no telling what sort of debacle might be impending. But this
was no time for any action but the boldest. . . .

As the news that the bankers were meeting circulated on the floor of
the Exchange, prices began to steady. Soon a brisk rally set in. Steel
jumped back to the level at which it had opened that morning. But the
bankers had more to offer the dying bull market than a Morgan partner's best bedside manner.

At about half-past one o'clock Richard Whitney, vice president of the
Exchange, who usually acted as floor broker for the Morgan interests,
went into the "Steel crowd" and put in a bid of 205—the price of the
last previous sale—for 10,000 shares of Steel. He bought only 200
shares and left the remainder of the order with the specialists. Mr. Whitney then went to various other points on the floor, and offered the price
of the last previous sale for 10,000 shares of each of fifteen or twenty
other stocks, reporting what was sold to him at that price and leaving
the remainder of the order with the specialist. In short, within a space
of a few minutes Mr. Whitney offered to purchase something in the

neighborhood of twenty or thirty million dollars' worth of stock. Purchases of this magnitude are not undertaken by Tom, Dick, and Harry; it was clear that Mr. Whitney represented the bankers' pool.

The desperate remedy worked. The semblance of confidence returned. Prices held steady for a while; and though many of them slid off once more in the final hour, the net results for the day might well have been worse. Steel actually closed two points higher than on Wednesday, and the net losses of most of the other leading securities amounted to less than ten points apiece for the whole day's trading.

All the same, it had been a frightful day. At seven o'clock that night the tickers in a thousand brokers' offices were still chattering; not 'til after 7:08 did they finally record the last sale made on the floor at three o'clock. The volume of trading had set a new record—12,894,650 shares. ("The time may come when we shall see a five-million-share day," the wise men of the Street had been saying twenty months before!) Incredible rumors had spread wildly during the early afternoon—that eleven speculators had committed suicide, that the Buffalo and Chicago exchanges had been closed, that troops were guarding the New York Stock Exchange against an angry mob. The country had known the bitter taste of panic. And although the bankers' pool had prevented for the moment an utter collapse, there was no gainsaying the fact that the economic structure had cracked wide open.

Things looked somewhat better on Friday and Saturday. Trading was still on an enormous scale, but prices for the most part held. At the very moment when the bankers' pool was cautiously disposing of as much as possible of the stock which it had accumulated on Thursday and was thus preparing for future emergencies, traders who had sold out higher up were coming back into the market again with new purchases, in the hope that the bottom had been reached. But toward the close of Saturday's session prices began to slip again. And on Monday the rout was under way once more. . . .

The big gong had hardly sounded in the great hall of the Exchange at ten o'clock Tuesday morning before the storm broke in full force. Huge blocks of stock were thrown upon the market for what they would bring. Five thousand shares, ten thousand shares appeared at a time on the laboring ticker at fearful recessions in price. Not only were innumerable small traders being sold out, but big ones too, protagonists of the new economic era who a few weeks before had counted themselves millionaires. Again and again the specialist in a stock would find himself surrounded by brokers fighting to sell—and nobody at all even thinking of buying. To give one single example: during the bull market the common stock of the White Sewing Machine Company had gone as high as 48; on Monday, October 28th, it had closed at 11⅛. On that black Tuesday, somebody—a clever messenger boy for the Exchange, it was rumored—had the bright idea of putting in an order to buy at 1— and in the temporarily complete absence of other bids he actually got his stock for a dollar a share! The scene on the floor was chaotic. Despite the jamming of the communication system, orders to buy and sell—mostly to sell—came in faster than human beings could possibly handle them; it was on that day that an exhausted broker, at the close of the session, found a large waste-basket which he had stuffed with orders to be executed and had carefully set aside for safe-keeping—and then had completely forgotten. Within half an hour of the opening the volume of trading passed three million shares, by twelve o'clock it had passed eight million, by half-past one it had passed twelve million, and when the closing gong brought the day's madness to an end the gigantic record of 16,410,030 shares had been set. Toward the close there was a rally, but by that time the average prices of fifty leading stocks, as compiled by the *New York Times,* had fallen nearly forty points. Meanwhile there was a near-panic in other markets—the foreign stock exchanges, the lesser American exchanges, the grain market. . . .

The next day—Wednesday, October 30th—the outlook suddenly and providentially brightened. The directors of the Steel Corporation had declared an extra dividend; the directors of the American Can Company had not only declared an extra dividend, but had raised the regular dividend. There was another flood of reassuring statements—though by this time a cheerful statement from a financier fell upon somewhat skeptical ears. Julius Klein, Mr. Hoover's Assistant Secretary of Commerce, composed a rhapsody on continued prosperity. John J. Raskob declared that stocks were at bargain prices and that he and his friends were buying. John D. Rockefeller poured Standard Oil upon the waters: "Believing that fundamental conditions of the country are sound and that there is nothing in the business situation to warrant the destruction of values that has taken place on the exchanges during the past week, my son and I have for some days been purchasing sound common stocks.'' Better still, prices rose—steadily and buoyantly. Now at least the time had come when the strain on the Exchange could be relieved without causing undue alarm. At 1:40 o'clock Vice-President Whitney announced from the rostrum that the Exchange would not open until noon the following day and would remain closed all day Friday and Saturday—and to his immense relief the announcement was greeted, not with renewed panic, but with a cheer.

Throughout Thursday's short session the recovery continued. Prices gyrated wildly—for who could arrive at a reasonable idea of what a given stock was worth, now that all settled standards of value had been upset?—but the worst of the storm seemed to have blown over. The financial community breathed more easily; now they could have a chance to set their houses in order. . . .

Catastrophe

John Brooks

John Brooks has written with wit and understanding of both the highs and lows of Wall Street and investing. Here, in a chapter from *Once in Golconda* (aptly subtitled "A True Drama of Wall Street 1920–1938"), he tells of the disgrace of Richard Whitney. Once an Establishment power and the floor broker for J. P. Morgan & Company, Mr. Whitney's financial failures drove him to a criminal misappropriation of the Gratuity (retirement) Fund of the New York Stock Exchange—and disaster.

George Whitney devoted Thanksgiving Day to trying to salvage his brother's shattered affairs, and perhaps, too, his shattered opinion of his brother's character. That morning, at his insistence, Richard Whitney came to his house and laid before him a hastily assembled set of figures purporting to show the condition of Richard Whitney & Company as of that moment. The figures, which Richard Whitney would later admit were false, showed the firm to be in the black to the extent of about one million dollars. The elder brother, however did not question the *bona fides* of the accounting—only Dick's high valuation of the enormous amount of Distilled Liquors stock that by this time had come to constitute most of the assets of Whitney & Company. After marking the stock down to a more realistic valuation, George Whitney concluded that the firm was still in the black by perhaps half a million—provided the stock could somehow be sold. He also concluded that the Distilled Liquors

Reprinted from *Once in Golconda: A True Drama of Wall Street 1920–1938* (New York, Evanston, and London: Harper & Row, 1969), Chapter 11, pp. 249–69, by permission of Harold Ober Associates, Inc. © 1969 by John Brooks.

debacle demonstrated that Dick's business judgment had gone to pieces, and that the best course now would be for Dick to get out of the brokerage business as quickly as possible, before other debacles ensued. Someone ought to be found who would want to take over a firm with such a fine reputation extending over two decades—some wealthy man, say, might want to put his son into it. Shocking as the notion of giving up his very foothold in the world he had lately ruled must have been to Richard Whitney, he responded like a younger brother whose elder brother had just saved him from a desperate jam by lending him a million dollars; he agreed.

The next step was taken even without waiting for the holiday to be over. George Whitney telephoned his brother's old friend Harry Simmons and asked him to come over and join the brothers that afternoon. Simmons, taken aback, pleaded that he was committed to church and then a family dinner. Nevertheless, late that afternoon he came to George Whitney's house to confer with the two brothers, the elder of whom outlined the situation and explained the plan. Nobody quite came out and said so, but it was clear enough why Simmons had been so hurriedly and urgently invited, if not summoned. Obviously the thought was that *he* might be the man to take over Richard Whitney & Company. Simmons was not having any of that. Without even looking at Richard Whitney's sheet of figures, he volunteered the information that he knew nothing about bonds—ostensibly the principal business of Whitney & Company—and therefore wasn't in the market.

A mood of disappointment settled over the conference. The conversation trailed off in discussion of various possible methods of disposing of the business; it was agreed among the three, for one thing, that a sale of the firm would be preferable to outright liquidation because of the value of its celebrated name. It was agreed that in the days following, Richard Whitney would devote himself energetically to the related matters of finding a buyer for his firm and finding a way—*some* way—of converting all that Distilled Liquors stock, delicately referred to by the conferees as the "slow assets," into cash.

No one at any time mentioned the incident of the Gratuity Fund.

The day after Thanksgiving, George Whitney mentioned to his partner Lamont that he had decided Dick was no longer "capable of handling a business properly and adequately," and that accordingly he was "going to get him to wind up his business." "Well," [Thomas] Lamont replied, with Morgan understatement, "I should think that was a good thing.'' That same weekend, both George Whitney and Lamont left New York for their long-planned vacations in the South. As for Simmons—who, it will be remembered, had no firm evidence that Whitney had embezzled from the Gratuity Fund, and who, indeed, stated later that at this time he had not the faintest doubts as to Richard Whitney's integrity—he had several meetings with Whitney during December at the Stock Exchange Luncheon Club, in the course of which he inquired how the plans for liquidation were coming along. Slowly, Whitney replied, mentioning one group or another that he thought might be interested in taking over the Distilled Liquors account or even the whole firm. In fact, the plans were not proceeding at all; nobody wanted the stock or the firm, and Whitney was continuing his frantic efforts to support the market price of Distilled Liquors and for this purpose of course, to borrow more money. Just before Christmas [Paul] Adler let him have another $100,000 which this time was repaid on the button a week later; but the harder-boiled Abraham, asked for the same sum, this time came through with only $15,000—almost an insult, but Whitney nevertheless took it. On January 3, 1938, Whitney had to report to George, back from the South, that his liquidation negotiations had "fallen through."

Meanwhile Richard Whitney's career as the White Knight was in its appropriately quixotic last phase. Privately defeated and dishonored, he played to the hilt the last act of his public role as man of iron principle. [Charles] Gay had decided by Thanksgiving Day that there was nothing for the Stock Exchange to do but give in gracefully to Douglas and the SEC, and reform itself from top to bottom. The alternative, he understood clearly now, was just what Douglas had warned of—a "takeover" by Washington. Early in December, with the reluctant approval of the Stock Exchange governors, Gay put together a new group, composed partly of outsiders to the Stock Exchange and headed by Carle C. Conway, chairman of the board of Continental Can, and notably including the New Dealer A. A. Berle, Jr., to make recommendations as to reorganization of the Stock Exchange. Here was an all-but-formal concession of defeat; everyone understood that the Conway committee would recommend reorganization of the Exchange along the lines proposed by the SEC, and presumed that the Exchange would have to accept the recommendation. Whitney's Law Committee stubbornly objected to both the existence of the Conway committee and its generally liberal makeup, but in vain. Majority sentiment in the Exchange leadership, while probably still privately on Whitney's side, had opted for expediency; Whitney almost alone continued to stand on principle. By the first of January the Conway committee was writing its report; on the twenty-seventh, when the report was published, it was found to recommend everything—the paid president, the technical staff, the nonmember governors, the provisions for increased influence of liberals within the Exchange—that Douglas had wanted in the first place. Gay instantly endorsed the report in full, and Douglas warmly commended it. To emphasize the new mood of peace and harmony between Wall Street and Washington, the newest appointee to a seat on the SEC was Morgan-worshiping North Carolinian John Wesley Hanes, who, interestingly enough, thereby became the first deep-dyed Wall Streeter since Joe Kennedy to join the New Deal in any top-level domestic capacity.

The long war was all but over at last; a stage had been reached when hostages were being exchanged. But Whitney was not done standing on principle. On January 31 the Governing Committee met to consider the Conway report. Overwhelming sentiment was for immediate and unconditional acceptance. Only Whitney and his cohorts, their ranks thinned to a pathetic few, held out, insisting that the report be accepted only in a general way, leaving leeway for rear-guard struggles on each individual provision, along the lines of the famous fight against the Securities Exchange Act. So great was Whitney's eloquence that for a moment it appeared he might still win the day. But Gay, stepping down from the presidential rostrum into the well of the governors' chamber to emphasize the gravity of what he had to say, replied with an impassioned exhortation that the Exchange at last stop maneuvering and temporizing and accept the inevitable with good grace.

Acceptance was unanimous—but for a single vote. It was, as a matter of fact, to be Whitney's last vote as a Stock Exchange governor.

═══

During January George Whitney applied himself one last time to his brother's affairs, this time taking over the thankless task of personally trying to manage a liquidation of Richard Whitney & Company. Had he succeeded, he would later have been in trouble himself, since the firm, as his brother had not told him, was insolvent. But he did not succeed.

His chief thought now was that the rescuer might be his own firm—that Morgan's itself "might conceivably in some way" arrange to take over the Distilled Liquors stock as collateral for a new loan giving Whitney & Company the cash that would make it more appetizing to a prospective buyer. If the matter were viewed as strictly a business proposition, one formidable obstacle to this course of action was that Whitney & Company still owed Morgan's all but $26,000 of the half-million dollars Whitney had borrowed back in the dark ages of 1931. Nevertheless, George Whitney doggedly, and maybe by this time a little sheepishly, asked Francis Bartow, the Morgan partner most versed in common stocks, to look over the Whitney Distilled Liquors portfolio with a view to seeing whether it might somehow meet his firm's standards for collateral on a new loan.

Bartow had his troubles. Digging into the affairs of Distilled Liquors, he found that the company's assets consisted mainly of about 550,000 gallons of Jersey Lightning ("brandy," Bartow called it elegantly) and one million gallons of cider. As he recounted later, he asked himself, "How can any man living determine that such a volume of liquor can be sold within six months or within a year?" Perhaps some man living could have determined it, but Bartow could not, and neither could the two of his other partners whom he consulted. Thus the matter of the new loan remained in abeyance, and the crisis of Whitney & Company dragged on.

But meanwhile something else had happened. Rumors of financial stringency at Whitney & Company had at last reached the place where they could do the most harm—the Stock Exchange—and set in motion an inexorable chain of events. Simmons, right after Thanksgiving, had tortured himself with the notion that it was his duty to repeat the tale of Whitney's slowness in producing the Gratuity Fund assets to the Stock Exchange's Business Conduct Committee, its disciplinary body. On reflection, though, he had decided that since Whitney had come across with the assets and everything was now square, there was no call for such talebearing on his part. And now there re-enters our story a character who has been missing from it for a long time: Sell 'em Ben Smith, the bullnecked, bellowing speculator and pool operator and the public villain in the bear market of 1930 and 1931. In mid-December President Gay invited Smith, now a solid, respected member of the Exchange community, to lunch privately in his office. During the lunch

Gay asked Smith what he thought could be done to create better public feeling toward the Stock Exchange.

The two men later differed on precisely how Smith had replied. Smith said, "I told him I didn't think he would ever be able to do it as long as he had the Old Guard in there. . . . I cited Mr. Whitney, and I told him that the quicker he got rid of him the better off the Exchange would be; that I felt that he was in a large measure responsible for the discredit in which the Exchange stood today. He wanted to know what I had against him, and I . . . said that he was broke and owed money all over the Street and I didn't think it was befitting for him to be one of the leading governors of the Exchange." Gay later corroborated all of this except that he vehemently denied that Smith had said that Whitney was "broke." He further commented that Smith's attitude toward Whitney, as expressed by his manner during the lunch, had been antagonistic, bitter, and angry.

Perhaps so; the self-made Irishman and the haughty Brahmin were set against each other by almost every *casus belli* that the harsh little society of Wall Street and the harsh big society of the United States could offer them. What had come between them since 1931 and 1932, when Whitney's fervent defense of short selling in Washington had been, after all—in general if not in particular—a defense of Smith? We do not know; but it is easy enough to imagine some offhand slight by the Brahmin or some tactless crudity by the Irishman, at one time or another, on the Exchange floor or somewhere else in the little world they both inhabited. At all events, because of Smith's evident hostility toward Whitney, Gay discounted much of what he had heard. In the month following the lunch he made no effort to inquire into the financial affairs of Whitney & Company. But he was, inevitably, put on the alert for such news when it came.

By the kind of irony that life contrives with ease where art wouldn't dare, the rumor that did start action was a wholly false one. One day in mid-January, John B. Shetlar, Stock Exchange specialist in the stock of Greyhound Corporation, noticed what he called "distress selling" in Greyhound. "It came in five-hundred-share lots," Shetlar would recall later, "but was continuous"; moreover, the lots, coming from many different brokers, "were thrown in for sale at the market regardless of price." Somehow or other—without evidence, but relying on the sixth sense about market operations without which no floor specialist could survive—Shetlar came to the conclusion that the distress selling originated with Richard Whitney & Company (in spite of the blind provided by the multiplicity of brokers) and was the tip-off that that firm was in dire trouble. As a matter of fact, later investigation showed that during mid-January not a single share of Greyhound was offered for sale by Whitney & Company on behalf of either itself or its customers.

If he knew that a member firm was in bad trouble, it was Shetlar's clear-cut duty as a member to notify the authorities. Conscientiously acting on his hunch, he went to Duke Wellington, in his capacities as an Exchange governor and close friend of Whitney. He told Wellington of the distress selling and of his belief as to its source, whereupon Wellington nodded and replied, "I'll take care of the matter." Wellington immediately went to the proper Exchange authority—Howland S. Davis, chairman of the Business Conduct Committee—and passed along what he had heard, pleading with Davis that, in any action that Davis might see fit to take, Wellington's name as the informant be kept out in consideration of his personal relations with Whitney. Davis agreed to that. And then a strange thing happened. Wellington had scarcely moved from the spot on the Exchange floor where he had the conversation with Davis when he was given a message that Whitney wanted to see him. Upon his meeting Whitney, the latter asked for a loan of $25,000, unsecured. Wellington, remembering the years he had waited to get back his original loan, had already turned down one request by his old friend for $100,000, the previous November. Now, with Shetlar's report to add to what he knew already, he had no doubt what he had to say. His answer was no.

The chairman of the Committee on Business Conduct went into action. Howland Davis was by background and inheritance a potential Old Guardsman; son of an old-school gentleman broker, he had grown up in a house in Murray Hill across Madison Avenue from J. P. Morgan's and had gone to the Morgan daughters' coming-out parties; as a broker himself, he was often thought to be a "Morgan man" because he had social relations with several of the Morgan partners, but in fact his firm was never a house pet of No. 23 in a business way. Davis had met both George and Dick Whitney in their boyhood and his, and had taken an instant dislike to them—as he put it years later, he found the two boys "perfect snobs" and "pains in the neck." Still, long after that, when Davis had become a Stock Exchange governor and had thus found himself often in Dick Whitney's company, he had modified his opinion as to that brother, and even become cautiously fond of him, though never close. As to Wall Street politics, for all his connections Davis had never been an Old Guardsman, but neither was he a reformer; as an independent he had remained aloof in the 1935 Stock Exchange fight. Now, when he heard Shetlar's report via Wellington, he saw his duty. One of the reforms that the Stock Exchange had lately adopted under SEC pressure was to institute the practice of sending questionnaires about current financial condition at intervals to all member firms. As it happened, the first of the forms under the new procedure were to be mailed out in just a few days, on January 20; in the normal course, Whitney & Company was not scheduled to receive its first form until mid-May, for reply by the end of May. But Davis now directed that Whitney & Company be advanced to the top of the list, and be sent its questionnaire immediately, for reply by February 15. That, he felt, would straighten out the situation; moreover, since the firms themselves in most cases did not know the Exchange's schedule for mailing out the forms, there would be nothing particular in the early arrival of his questionnaire to arouse Whitney's suspicion that *he* was under suspicion.

Thus a false scent had set the dogs on the true trail. Whitney got his questionnaire. On February 15, the due date for its return, he requested a week's extension, which was granted. He filed his return on February 21; a quick check of it was made by the comptroller of the Exchange that same evening. Whitney's return, although necessarily far more detailed than his Thanksgiving Day accounting for his brother, nevertheless similarly contained omissions that had the force of falsifications; even so, the comptroller's preliminary analysis indicated that the firm's capital position fell far short of the requirements of the Business Conduct Committee. So the next step, routine in such cases, was taken: on February 23 a staff accountant of the Exchange was sent to the Whitney offices at 15 Broad Street to make an audit of the books.

Again, the books themselves were falsified—but insufficiently. Realizing this, Whitney on February 24 called on Davis at his apartment uptown to plead for time. He knew, he said, that his capital fell short of requirements, that his assets were injudiciously concentrated in certain specific securities, and so on. But, he explained, he was actively negotiating for a loan of about $700,000 that would enable him to correct all deficiencies; he very much disliked the prospect of having an even partially unfavorable report on his reputable firm go into the Exchange records; and in view of all this, might not the accountant now in his offices be withdrawn, to return in a few weeks when everything would be to rights?

The reply of the man who had once thought Whitney a pain in the neck, and had later grown fond of him, was that it seemed to him advisable that the accountant be permitted to continue his work in the normal way.

By February 28—five days after he had begun his digging in Whitney's office books—the Exchange accountant had extensive but not conclusive evidence of misappropriation of customers' securities. On March 1, Davis told Gay of the findings so far. The following evening, at the Metropolitan Club, Gay, Davis, Simmons, and the Stock Exchange lawyers met with Whitney's personal lawyer, L. Randolph Mason, to hash the whole thing over. Delicately, they warned Mason that there appeared to be serious doubt as to whether his client's books truly reflected his financial situation. They would be in touch. The day after that—Thursday—Whitney made a second unsuccessful attempt to influence Davis to call off his dogs. On Friday the dogs found the corpse. The Exchange comptroller reported to his superiors that he had now established positive proof that Richard Whitney was an embezzler and that his firm was insolvent.

On Saturday morning, March 5, the comptroller confronted Whitney in person with the evidence he had uncovered. Whitney, as the comptroller put it later, gave a "tacit admission" that he had misused customers' securities. This was a feint; Whitney had not given up yet. That afternoon he spent two hours in Gay's office playing his last card. Readily admitting misconduct, he asked for special consideration—specifically, that the Exchange quietly allow him to sell his membership, then drop charges against him. On what grounds? Gay wanted to know—and then Whitney made his play. "After all, I'm Richard Whitney," he said. "I mean the Stock Exchange to millions of people." Therefore what affected him affected the Stock Exchange—and Wall Street. His exposure as a bankrupt was now inevitable, but his exposure as an embezzler—it would make a mockery of the trust on which all stock trading is based; it would be a triumph for the reformulate forces in Washington; it would be a bonanza beyond the wildest dreams of the SEC. . . .

This was a telling point, and Whitney emphasized it; in the course of the two-hour session he brought the same argument up over and over again. "I wouldn't say that Mr. Whitney was pleading," Gay recounted later. "He assumed more of a reasoning attitude, as if he were discussing somebody else than himself." Indeed he was: the White Knight was discussing a thief. It is possible to imagine that Charley Gay was sorely tempted. He had the deep conservatism of the self-made—had grown up admiring the Wall Street Old Guardsmen with their easy languorous charm, and had spent his life working like a peon to try to become one of them; now he was surely no more anxious than Whitney himself that Whitney should bring the Old Guard and its era crashing down with him. If Whitney were allowed to resign quietly with the announcement that he was going to retire from the bond business and take up some other line of work, there was at least a good chance that nothing would ever come to light about his defalcations and that, after a brief flurry of scandal, the whole thing would blow over and things would be back where they had been before. If, on the other hand . . .

But Gay was also a passionately honest and conscientious man. His horrified conscience triumphed over his desire to preserve the world he had accepted and admired so long. Adamantly, over and over again, he told Whitney that the drawing up of charges and specifications against him would proceed, and that they, along with the evidence, would be presented to the Business Conduct Committee on Monday morning as planned.

==

Through the two months preceding that Saturday afternoon, Whitney, fighting for his life and perhaps his way of life, had indulged in one last binge of cash-raising efforts, the details of which add some bizarre footnotes to his story and indeed to the history of borrowing. Turndowns on loan requests were getting to be commonplace now, and he was learning to accept them without batting an eye. "How about George?" people would ask him, bluntly, when he came to them for money. "My brother is out of town, and if he were here I wouldn't be coming to you," he would reply loftily. "Well, I am very sorry . . . " he would hear again and again, and would simply turn his heel and leave. In January the long-suffering, long-awestruck Paul Adler turned him down; unable to face the idol he saw toppling before him, Adler scrawled on a piece of Stock Exchange notepaper: "Dick, I am sorry, but we have decided that we are not willing to make any loans to anyone at this time, and I deeply regret to say so. Sincerely, Paul." In mid-February he walked up to John H. McMannus, a floor specialist far outside his normal social orbit, and asked for $100,000. McMannus, after a stunned pause, offered to make the loan provided Whitney's note be endorsed by George.

Whitney offered instead his wife's endorsement—"She's worth half a million dollars," he confided without shame. McMannus said he never accepted a woman's endorsement on a note. Whitney nodded. "Don't say anything about this," he remarked casually as he turned away. McMannus said later that the episode had been one of the most surprising events of his business life: "I thought he was the essence of everything fine in the world. I was so shocked I couldn't think clearly." If he had thought clearly, McMannus realized only afterward, he would have known that he didn't have the $100,000 to loan anyway.

Late in February Whitney asked Sidney Weinberg, by this time a partner at Goldman, Sachs and well on his way to becoming the "Mr. Wall Street" of the early postwar years, for $50,000. The only trouble, or one trouble, was that Whitney seems to have thought the gentleman's name was Weinstein.

But simultaneous, and more astonishing, were several spectacular successes. In mid-February Whitney asked Alexander B. Gale, an Exchange member, for the usual amount—$100,000. Gale said he could lend only $75,000, and immediately sent along a check for that amount. Whitney, however, brazenly sent back his note for $100,000. Thus made to feel like a piker, Gale sent along the additional $25,000 to round out the note. At about the same time Whitney approached one Walter T. Rosen for the usual amount—as usual, without offering collateral. Rosen handed over the money along with a charming and flattering little speech: "I have always been much impressed by the attitude of the elder Mr. Morgan, who held the view that the personal integrity of the borrower was of far greater value than his collateral." "Mr. Morgan was entirely right," the Morgan broker graciously allowed as he took the check.

Whitney's two last borrowings were memorable for their own reasons. On March 1, four days before his Saturday showdown with Gay, he approached two partners of Brown Brothers, Harriman & Company, Knight Woolley and W. Averell Harriman—the latter not yet launched on his diplomatic career—for the usual amount. Unlike the elder Mr. Morgan, although members of an equally distinguished and aristocratic firm, Woolley and Harriman wanted collateral. Whitney promised to have the collateral delivered within a few days, and got his loan on the spot; somehow the collateral never arrived. That same day Whitney borrowed $25,000 from an old and none too hale friend of his, a man who has spanned our turbulent story—Colonel John W. Prentiss, the tactful mediator in the 1920 dispute between Allan Ryan and the Stock Exchange. Eighteen days later, Colonel Prentiss, unrepaid, would be dead.

And late in January Whitney had made one last, grand embezzlement—his grandest. On the twenty-sixth, without explanation, he ordered the cashier of his firm, Robert J. Rosenthal, to turn over to him a batch of securities belonging to various customers of the firm, among them the estate of his father-in-law, and having a value of about $800,000. Two days later he took these securities to the Public National Bank and, representing them as his own, pledged them as collateral for a loan of no less than $280,000.

Let us sum up in broad strokes, for the astonishing record, Whitney's true financial condition as of the first week of March, 1938. Over the preceding four months he had negotiated, all told, 111 loans aggregating $27,361,500; of this, more than $25 million had been in more or less soundly secured borrowings from commercial banks, constantly turned over as he made new loans to repay those that came due. Apart from this, he owed, entirely unsecured, $2,897,000 to George Whitney, $474,000 to J. P. Morgan & Company, and about an even million dollars to others. He owed borrowed stocks worth about $390,000. Quite apart, then, from the sums he "owed" to the customers from whom he had embezzled, he had managed to accumulate on the strength of nothing, or almost nothing, more than his character and good name net borrowings well in excess of five million dollars.

In those last days he was walking up to men he didn't know on the Exchange floor and asking them in tones casual to the point of indifference to lend him his standard sum—$100,000. He also did one thing suggesting that madness or something like it was overtaking him at last. On Tuesday of the frantic week that ended with his Saturday-afternoon confrontation, he went to Ben Smith. He made no lame effort to ingratiate himself. Rather, he announced brusquely that he "wanted to get this over quickly"—as if, say, his mission were to administer a justified rebuke to an inferior. Then he said that he wanted to borrow $250,000 "on my face." Smith's reply was, in the circumstances, not startling, and can scarcely be described as ruder than the occasion called for. "I remarked he was putting a pretty high value on his face," Smith recounted later. "So he told me that was his story and his back was to the wall and he had to have $250,000. I told him he had a lot of nerve to ask me for $250,000 when he didn't even bid me the time of day. I told him I frankly didn't like him—that I wouldn't loan him a dime.'' Whitney nodded; that was that.

Of course. But why had he done it? What had he expected from Ben Smith but a harsh rebuff? Was this the ritual of capitulation, the beaten wolf intentionally baring his neck to the teeth of his conqueror? It could not have been; as we know, on that Tuesday Whitney was by no means ready to capitulate. The remaining assumption must be that he was as insensitive in the matter of slights received as he had so long been in that of slights delivered; that he regarded this upstart so little as to be immune to his bad opinion, and had made the approach simply because it could cost him nothing; that, as Smith said, he had a lot of nerve, a rather awesome lot, and the nerve at least had not failed.

Francis Bartow, J. P. Morgan's ''Stock Exchange man,'' was the firm's responsible partner in the absence of Lamont, who had followed his trip South with one abroad, and George Whitney, who early in 1938 had returned to the South to resume a long convalescence from his 1937 illness. Let Bartow tell, with a fine dramatic flair, what happened Saturday night after Whitney's last-ditch attempt to persuade Gay to drop charges:

''On the afternoon of March 5, I was playing bridge with some friends at the Links Club in New York and I was called to the telephone by Richard Whitney. He said he wanted to see me as soon as possible. I explained where I was and inquired where he was and he said at his office. I suggested that he stop by and see me where I was. He said he would.

''Some time later he appeared and we sat down together to talk. As we did so, he drew from his pocket a large folded piece of paper which he proceeded to open. He said, 'I am in a jam.' I said, 'Wait a minute, is your idea in talking to me now to borrow money?' He said, 'Yes.' 'Well,' I said, 'in all frankness I will not agree to that.' I think in my mind at the moment I was a little impatient with him because I assumed he must have known that I had talked with Randolph Mason about his affairs and the promised audit report and other information had not been given to me. He said, 'Well, on Monday at ten-thirty my affairs are coming up for examination before the Business Conduct Committee.' I said, 'Now, wait a minute, stop right there. I am not the proper person for you to talk to. My advice is that you go and get Randolph Mason and tell him.'

"He folded his papers up and left me. I resumed my game with my friends. I think as he left me I said to him, 'I expect to be here some time longer, if you should want me.'

"Quite a considerable time later, word was brought to me that Richard Whitney would like to speak with me in the floor below. As soon as I was free I went there. He and Randolph Mason were together. He said, 'Frank, we have been talking this over and I want to know if you have any suggestions to offer.'

"I said, 'I have already told you that I have no suggestions to offer.'

" 'Well,' he said, 'when my affairs come up for review before the Business Conduct Committee on Monday, it is conceivable some embarrassing questions will arise.'

"I said, 'What do you mean, embarrassing?'

" 'Well,' he said, 'for example, the New York Yacht Club have securities with me and I have taken those securities and I have pledged them in loans.'

"I said, 'How much does the New York Yacht Club owe you?'

"He said, 'They don't owe me anything.'

"I said, 'Do you mean that you have taken a client's securities and pledged them in loans and taken the proceeds of that and placed it in your business when they did not owe you anything?'

"He said, 'Yes, I do.'

"I said, 'That is serious.'

"He said, 'It is criminal.'

"I asked, 'Are there any other cases where this had occurred?'

"He said, 'Yes, two; the Sheldon estate of which I am an executor, and Mrs. Baird.'

"I said, 'Dick, now this is such an entirely different nature than the matter that you originally discussed with me that I will not discuss it with you any further. And I want now to go to the telephone and call my counsel.' "

Does it seem rather odd that a man, on hearing a friend and business associate confess that he has been engaged in criminal activities, should react simply by saying that he is going to call his lawyer? It does, but it should not; remember that, in a time when Wall Street was still very much on the public griddle, Whitney was the most publicized man in

Wall Street and Morgan's the most publicized firm, and that private knowledge of a crime on the part of a Morgan partner raised the possibility of the Morgan firm's being considered an accessory. Bartow called the Morgan lawyer—no lesser lawyer than the former Presidential candidate John W. Davis—and made an appointment to see him that evening at his home at Glen Cove, Long Island. Then he went back to Whitney and Mason. The three of them had a hasty supper together at the Links, and just before or during the meal Whitney said to Bartow, "I would like to explain this to you. I have a loan of $280,000 at the Public National Bank. In that loan are all of the securities taken improperly from the accounts in my office—the Yacht Club, Sheldon, and Baird. If I could borrow $280,000 and pay that loan off, it would enable me to restore all of those improperly used securities and when I went before the Business Conduct Committee on Monday morning I could state truthfully that there were no irregularities in my office."

Bartow gave no immediate answer. A prudent man, he was going to wait for advice of counsel. Immediately after dinner he and Mason left Whitney at the Links and took the hour's drive to Glen Cove to see John W. Davis. Davis, after hearing the story, replied without hesitation that no one could or should do anything to help Whitney now—"Anyone who did would run the risk of taking actions that would be misconstrued," as Davis put it euphemistically.

"All right, Mr. Davis," said Bartow. "I accept your advice and counsel on that. I am glad I came to you." One other question: would it be proper to call Gay, and ask him for a one-day or perhaps even two-day delay in the meeting of the Business Conduct Committee that would consider the Whitney case?

Davis gave it as his opinion that there was no reason not to do that.

So back to New York hurried Bartow and Mason, this time for a midnight meeting, arranged on the spur of the moment, with Gay at the Metropolitan Club. They found Gay there with a Stock Exchange lawyer, who, on hearing Bartow's request, replied most emphatically that under no circumstances would there be a single minute's delay in the scheduled Monday-morning meeting. That seemed to be that. Bartow and Mason went back to the Links, where they gave a glum Dick Whitney their grim news.

On Sunday there was more frantic scrambling. Bartow takes up the story again:

"Quite early, I called my partner, Mr. Anderson, and at the same time called my partner, Charles Dickey, in his home in Philadelphia, and in a general way told them of the events of the day before and asked if they would meet me at my house in New York at two-thirty that afternoon, and they agreed. I then called my senior partner, Mr. J. P. Morgan, at his house at Glen Cove, and made an appointment with him for twelve o'clock. I then called Mr. Randolph Mason and told him of a meeting that was to be that afternoon at my house and asked if he would come. I also asked—if it were possible, I would like to have Mr. Rodewald there, as I wished to learn from him firsthand how long, in his opinion, it would take to make an audit.

"Mr. Mason said he would come and, if possible, arrange for Mr. Rodewald to be there, too.

"I then motored to Glen Cove. I went to Mr. Morgan's house where I told him of the events of the night before, and my advice from John W. Davis, and the conclusions that Mr. Davis had reached. Mr. Morgan was naturally shocked beyond measure and gave it as his judgment, which was mine, that there was no course for us to follow except to abide by the advice that we had received from counsel."

(But in view of what he already knew, can J. P. Morgan have really been all that shocked? Or did the old gentleman put on a show for the benefit of the junior partner?)

"I then left and returned to my house in town. Sunday afternoon Mr. Anderson and Mr. Dickey arrived and we sat down and I told them what I had learned in as great detail as I recalled. I then telephoned Mr. Sunderland, who is Mr. John W. Davis' partner, and asked him if he would come to my house. He did. About that time Mr. Mason arrived. Some while after that Mr. Rodewald arrived. I asked Mr. Rodewald how long, in his judgment, he thought it would take for high-class accountants to make a proper audit. He was vague and to me disappointing because he gave the impression it would take a great deal longer than I presumed it would take. . . .

"When Mr. Sunderland arrived, I told him what I had done, and what I planned. I asked him if he thought it was a proper and right thing for me to do and he said, 'Under no circumstances can you or anyone else from J. P. Morgan & Company go into the office of Richard Whitney & Company to find out anything.'

"I then told Mr. Rodewald that the reason for his being called was over with, and we did not need him any more and I presumed he was busy, and he left to go about his business. A little later . . . one by one I expressed my regret at calling [Anderson, Dickey, and Mason] from their homes in the country, and they went back to where they had come from, I presume. . . .

"Late in the afternoon I determined that the time had come when I must call my partner, George Whitney, on the telephone and advise him of everything that I knew. Accordingly I put in a call to get him on the telephone in Florida, which I did. As guardedly as I could, yet as fully as I could, I told him of my knowledge. . . .

"Mr. Whitney said, 'My God!' "

"My God" indeed: there was apparently little else George Whitney could say, and nothing more he could do.

So on Monday the wheels of Stock Exchange justice turned. That morning, right on schedule, the Business Conduct Committee met, heard the evidence, and voted unanimously to present forthwith the charges against Whitney and the two of his partners who held Exchange memberships, Edwin D. Morgan, Jr. and Henry D. Mygatt, to the Governing Committee for action. Early in the afternoon the Governing Committee considered the charges and voted unanimously that they be served on the three member partners, that the accused be notified that they would have the customary ten days to prepare their answers, and that a hearing on the charges be held at the end of the ten-day period, on March 17. The charges were served on Whitney, Morgan, and Mygatt the same day. That evening, by telephone, Gay notified the SEC in Washington of the affair.

Meanwhile, no public announcement had yet been made and there had rather astonishingly been no leaks to the press; and Whitney's remaining allies, most of them now thinking chiefly of the public disaster for Wall Street that his exposure would be, were continuing with sinking hearts their furious efforts to find some way out. Early Monday morning George Whitney called Bartow back from Florida. He was very much disturbed about not being in New York, he said; shouldn't he come at once? Bartow urged him not to, reminding that he was still not entirely recovered from his illness, and pointing out that there was nothing he could do anyway. Later that morning, grasping at straws, Bartow—after again getting clearance from John W. Davis—called on Roland Redmond, the Stock Exchange lawyer who was perhaps Whitney's closest friend. "Is there anything that anybody can humanly do in this thing that you know of?" Bartow asked. Redmond replied,

"Absolutely not. I don't know of a solitary thing." Poor Redmond was obviously in distress; to him, as Exchange lawyer, fell the duty of drawing up the charges against his friend—a duty he had performed at his office the previous afternoon, with tears actually streaming down his face.

"We parted," Bartow recounted later. "In the afternoon of that day, Randolph Mason called me on the phone and said that he would like to see me that evening. He would probably be late, and would I wait at my house until he came, and I said I would. And that evening he did come, and I am not quite clear now why he came, because there did not seem to me any purpose in it, because the only thing he told me now was that he had been engaged all afternoon and evening on papers dealing with the proposed bankruptcy proceedings of Richard Whitney & Company the next day—and after a very brief talk he left." But in retrospect it is clear enough why Mason came to Bartow's house—he wanted to have a wake.

=

John Wesley Hanes, with mixed emotions, became the SEC's liaison man in the Whitney case. Chairman Douglas on Monday night, right after hearing the news from Gay, picked Hanes for the assignment on the spot and called him shortly before midnight, asking him to take it on.

Hanes took the night train to New York, sleeping little and brooding much en route. "My first and principal concern was the extent of public participation in this failure," he said later. "We were unable to find out the extent of the public interest [in Washington]. I came to New York to find out if I could get any more facts than we had in Washington." Some insisted later that he had had another major concern. Far from lusting for the Morgan broker's scalp, Hanes was indubitably as worried as his idolized friends, the men at No. 23 themselves, for the good name of Wall Street at large and J. P. Morgan & Company in particular, and there was talk in Wall Street early that morning—circulated, it is true, by the die-hard remnants of the Whitney Old Guard—that Hanes was coming to New York with the specific mission of recommending on behalf of the SEC that public announcement of the disaster be postponed while efforts were made to negotiate some kind of accommodation. Whatever his intentions may have been—and he later denied that they were these—Hanes found, on his arrival in Wall Street at nine forty-five, only fifteen minutes before Stock Exchange opening time, that events were wholly beyond reversal. The place, he found, was seething with rumors about Whitney that were, if possible, even worse than the facts; from the point of view of Wall Street's public image, no announcement would be the worst possible course. Hanes accordingly recommended to the Stock Exchange authorities that they go ahead with the announcement as planned. In any case, by that time it was already inexorably in the works. Some three-quarters of an hour earlier, at nine o'clock sharp, the Business Conduct Committee had convened with Howland Davis presiding; on the carpet before it were Mason as Whitney's representative and two of Whitney's partners. Davis had opened the meeting by saying, "Gentlemen, I think the thing the committee is most interested in is whether between now and ten o'clock we have to do something with regard to the plans of Richard Whitney & Company to do business today."

Mason had said, "We don't know all the figures. . . . I am obliged to say . . . that the firm is insolvent."

The chairman then asked Kingsley Rodewald, Whitney's partner—a bewildered man who, like all Whitney's partners, had for years been kept entirely in the dark as to Whitney's defalcations and even as to the desperate financial plight of the firm—whether he had anything to say. Rodewald replied that he had not.

"Can your firm meet its obligations?" the chairman had inquired.

"No, sir," Rodewald had replied.

So the failure was formalized, ipse dixit; now the Exchange under its own rules had no choice. At ten-five, just after the start of the day's trading, Gay mounted the rostrum overlooking the floor; the secretary rang the gong that suspends trading; the hum on the floor faded into dead silence; and Gay read an announcement of the suspension of Whitney & Company for insolvency. Immediately thereafter the Exchange released a statement that did not fail to make clear that wrongdoing was involved in the holocaust:

> In the course of an examination of the affairs of Richard Whitney & Company, the Committee on Business Conduct discovered on March 1, 1938, evidence of conduct apparently contrary to just and equitable principles of trade, and on Monday, March 7, 1938, at 1:30 P.M. presented

to a special meeting of the Governing Committee charges and specifications. Hearing on the charges was set for March 17, 1938. This morning the firm of Richard Whitney & Company advised the Exchange that it was unable to meet its obligations and its suspension for insolvency was announced from the rostrum of the Exchange shortly after 10:00 A.M.

With the fall of its champion, the fall of the Old Guard was accomplished.

U.S. Steel Announces Sweeping Modernization Scheme

Benjamin Graham

This bit of 1936 whimsy was Ben Graham's way of calling attention to some of the accounting absurdities that accompanied the depression years, not all of which have subsequently disappeared with the passage of a full half-century.

———— ▪ ————

Myron C. Taylor, Chairman of U.S. Steel Corporation, today announced the long awaited plan for completely modernizing the world's largest industrial enterprise. Contrary to expectations, no changes will be made in the company's manufacturing or selling policies. Instead, the bookkeeping system is to be entirely revamped. By adopting and further improving a number of modern accounting and financial devices the corporation's earning power will be amazingly transformed. Even under the subnormal conditions of 1935, it is estimated that the new bookkeeping methods would have yielded a reported profit of close to $50 per share on the common stock. The scheme of improvement is the result of a comprehensive survey made by Messrs. Price, Bacon, Guthrie & Colpitts; it includes the following six points:

1. Writing down of Plant Account to Minus $1,000,000,000.
2. Par Value of common stock to be reduced to 1 cent.
3. Payment of all wages and salaries in option warrants.
4. Inventories to be carried at $1.

Reprinted from an unpublished paper given to Warren E. Buffett by Benjamin Graham, 1936.

5. Preferred Stock to be replaced by non-interest bearing bonds redeemable at 50% discount.
6. A $1,000,000,000 Contingency Reserve to be established.

The official statement of this extraordinary Modernization Scheme follows in full:

The Board of Directors of U.S. Steel Corporation is pleased to announce that after intensive study of the problems arising from changed conditions in the industry, it has approved a comprehensive plan for remodeling the Corporation's accounting methods. A survey by a Special Committee, aided and abetted by Messrs. Price, Bacon, Guthrie & Colpitts, revealed that our company has lagged somewhat behind other American business enterprises in utilizing certain advanced bookkeeping methods, by means of which the earning power may be phenomenally enhanced without requiring any cash outlay or any changes in operating or sales conditions. It has been decided not only to adopt these newer methods but to develop them to a still higher stage of perfection. The changes adopted by the Board may be summarized under six heads, as follows:

1. Fixed Assets to Be Written Down to *Minus $1,000,000,000*

Many representative companies have relieved their income accounts of all charges for depreciation by writing down their plant account to $1. The Special Committee points out that if their plants are worth only $1, the fixed assets of U.S. Steel Corporation are worth a good deal less than that sum. It is now a well recognized fact that many plants are in reality a liability rather than an asset, entailing not only depreciation charges, but taxes, maintenance, and other expenditures. Accordingly, the Board has decided to extend the write-down policy initiated in the 1935 report, and to mark down the Fixed Assets from $1,338,522,858.96 to a round *Minus $1,000,000,000*.

The advantages of this move should be evident. As the plant wears out, the liability becomes correspondingly reduced. Hence instead of the present depreciation charge of some $47,000,000 yearly there will be an annual *appreciation credit* of 5%, or $50,000,000. This will increase earnings by no less than $97,000,000 per annum.

2. Reduction of Par Value of Common Stock to 1 cent, and

3. Payment of Salaries and Wages in Option Warrants

Many corporations have been able to reduce their overhead expenses substantially by paying a large part of their executive salaries in the form of options to buy stock, which carry no charge against earnings. The full possibilities of this modern device have apparently not been adequately realized. The Board of Directors have adopted the following advanced form of this idea:

The entire personnel of the Corporation is to receive their compensation in the form of rights to buy common stock at $50 per share, at the rate of one purchase right for each $50 of salary and/or wages in their present amounts. The par value of the common stock is to be reduced to 1 cent.

The almost incredible advantages of this new plan are evident from the following:

A. The payroll of the Corporation will be entirely eliminated, a saving of $250,000,000 per annum, based on 1935 operations.

B. At the same time the effective compensation of all our employees will be increased severalfold. Because of the large earnings per share to be shown on our common stock under the new methods, it is certain that the shares will command a price in the market far above the option level of $50 per share, making the readily realizable value of these option warrants greatly in excess of the present cash wages which they will replace.

C. The Corporation will realize an additional large annual profit through the exercise of these warrants. Since the par value of the common stock will be fixed at 1 cent, there will be a gain of $49.99 on each share subscribed for. In the interest of conservative accounting, however, this profit will not be included in the income account, but will be shown separately as a credit to Capital Surplus.

D. The Corporation's cash position will be enormously strengthened. In place of the present annual cash *outgo* of $250,000,000 for wages (1935 basis), there will be an annual cash *inflow* of $250,000,000 through exercise of the subscription warrants for 5,000,000 shares of common stock. The Company's large earnings and strong cash position will permit the payment of a liberal dividend, which in turn will result in the exercise of these option warrants immediately after issuance, which in turn will further improve the cash position, which in turn will permit a higher dividend rate—and so on, indefinitely.

4. Inventories to Be Carried at $1

Serious losses have been taken during the depression due to the necessity of adjusting inventory value to market. Various enterprises—notably in the metal and cotton-textile fields—have successfully dealt with this problem by carrying all or part of their inventories at extremely low unit prices. The U.S. Steel Corporation has decided to adopt a still more progressive policy, and to carry its entire inventory at $1. This will be effected by an appropriate write-down to be charged to the Contingency Reserve hereinafter referred to.

The benefits to be derived from this new method are very great. Not only will it obviate all possibility of inventory depreciation, but it will substantially enhance the annual earnings of the Corporation. The inventory on hand at the beginning of the year, valued at $1, will be sold during the year at an excellent profit. It is estimated that our income will be increased by means of this method to the extent of at least $150,000,000 per annum which by coincidence will about equal the amount of the write-down to be made each year against Contingency Reserve.

A minority report of the Special Committee recommends that Accounts Receivable and Cash be also written-down to $1, in the interest of consistency and to gain additional advantages similar to those just discussed. This proposal has been rejected for the time being because our Auditors still require that any recoveries of receivables and cash so charged off be credited to surplus instead of to the year's income. It is expected, however, that this auditing rule—which is rather reminiscent of the horse-and-buggy days—will soon be changed in line with modern tendencies. Should this occur, the minority report will be given further and favorable consideration.

5. Replacement of Preferred Stock by Non-Interest Bearing Bonds Redeemable at 50% Discount

During the recent depression many companies have been able to offset their operating losses by including in income profits arising from repurchases of their own bonds at a substantial discount from par. Unfortunately the credit of U.S. Steel Corporation has always stood so high that this lucrative source of revenue has not hitherto been available to it. The Modernization Scheme will remedy this condition.

It is proposed that each share of preferred stock be exchanged for $300 face value of non-interest-bearing sinking-fund notes redeemable by lot at 50% of face value in 10 equal annual installments. This will require the issuance of $1,080,000,000 of new notes, of which $108,000,000 will be retired each year at a cost to the Corporation of only $54,000,000, thus creating an annual profit of the same amount.

Like the wage-and/or-salary plan described under 3 above, this arrangement will benefit both the Corporation and its preferred stockholders. The latter are assured payment for their present shares at 150% of par value over an average period of five years. Since short-term securities yield practically no return at present, the non-interest-bearing feature is of no real importance. The Corporation will convert its present annual *charge* of $25,000,000 for preferred dividends into an annual bond-retirement *profit* of $54,000,000—an aggregate yearly gain of $79,000,000.

6. Establishment of a Contingency Reserve of $1,000,000,000

The Directors are confident that the improvements hereinbefore described will assure the Corporation of a satisfactory earning power under all conditions in the future. Under modern accounting methods, however, it is unnecessary to incur the slightest risk of loss through adverse business developments of any sort, since all these may be provided for in advance by means of a Contingency Reserve.

The Special Committee has recommended that the Corporation create such a Contingency Reserve in the fairly substantial amount of $1,000,000,000. As previously set forth, the annual write-down of inventory to $1 will be absorbed by this reserve. To prevent eventual exhaustion of the Contingency Reserve it has been further decided that it be replenished each year by transfer of an appropriate sum from Capital Surplus. Since the latter is expected to increase each year by not less than $250,000,000, through the exercise of the Stock Option Warrants (see 3 above), it will readily make good any drains on the Contingency Reserve.

In setting up this arrangement the Board of Directors must confess regretfully that they have been unable to improve upon the devices already employed by important corporations in transferring large sums between Capital, Capital Surplus, Contingency Reserves and other Balance Sheet Accounts. In fact it must be admitted that our entries will be somewhat too simple, and will lack that element of extreme mystification that characterizes the most advanced procedure in this field. The Board of Directors however, have insisted upon clarity and simplicity in framing their Modernization Plan, even at the sacrifice of possible advantage to the Corporation's earning power.

In order to show the combined effect of the new proposals upon the Corporation's earning power, we submit herewith a condensed Income Account for 1935 on two bases, viz:

	A. As Reported	B. Pro-Forma Giving Effect to Changes Proposed Herewith
Gross Receipts from all Sources (Incl. Inter-Company)	$765,000,000	$765,000,000
Salaries and Wages	251,000,000	—
Other Operating Expenses and Taxes	461,000,000	311,000,000
Depreciation	47,000,000	cr. 50,000,000
Interest	5,000,000	5,000,000
Discount on Bonds Retired	—	cr. 54,000,000
Preferred Dividends	25,000,000	—
Balance for Common	def. 24,000,000	550,000,000
Av. Shares Outstanding	8,703,252	11,203,252
Earned Per Share	def. $2.76	$49.80

In accordance with a somewhat antiquated custom there is appended herewith a condensed pro-forma Balance Sheet of the U.S. Steel Corporation as of December 31, 1935, after giving effect to proposed changes in assets and liability accounts.

Assets

Fixed Assets, net	Minus $1,000,000,000
Cash Assets	142,000,000
Receivables	56,000,000
Inventory	1
Misc. Assets	27,000,000
Total Minus	$774,999,999

Liabilities

	Stated Value
Common Stock (Par 1¢)	
(Par Value $87,032.52)	*Minus $3,500,000,000
Subsidiaries' Bonds & Stocks	113,000,000
New Sinking Fund Notes	1,080,000,000
Current Liabilities	69,000,000
Contingency Reserve	1,000,000,000
Other Reserves	74,000,000
Initial Surplus	389,000,001
Total Minus	$ 774,999,999

*Given a Stated Value differing from Par Value, in accordance with the laws of the State of Virginia where the company will be incorporated.

It is perhaps unnecessary to point out to our stockholders that modern accounting methods have given rise to balance sheets differing somewhat in appearance from those of a less advanced period. In view of the very large earning power that will result from these changes in the Corporation's Balance Sheet, it is not expected that undue attention will be paid to the details of assets and liabilities.

In conclusion the Board desires to point out that the combined procedure, whereby plant will be carried at a minus figure, our wage bill will be eliminated, and inventory will stand on our books at virtually nothing, will give U.S. Steel Corporation an enormous competitive advantage in the industry. We shall be able to sell our products at exceedingly low prices and still show a handsome margin of profit. It is the considered view of the Board of Directors that under the Modernization Scheme we shall be able to undersell all competitors to such a point that the anti-trust laws will constitute the only barrier to 100% domination of the industry.

In making this statement the Board is not unmindful of the possibility that some of our competitors may seek to offset our new advantages by adopting similar accounting improvements. We are confident, however, that U.S. Steel will be able to retain the loyalty of its customers, old and new, through the unique prestige that will accrue to it as the originator and pioneer in these new fields of service to the user of steel. Should necessity arise, moreover, we believe we shall be able to maintain our deserved superiority by introducing still more advanced bookkeeping methods, which are even now under development in our Experimental Accounting Laboratory.

An Informal History
of Interest Rates

Sidney Homer

Did you know that a wife, if pledged for a loan in Babylonia, could be seized by a creditor, or that doors were valuable collateral? Sidney Homer provides summary highlights from his book *A History of Interest Rates* in this easy overview. Those attracted to the full book will be well rewarded.

Babylonia

In ancient Babylonia, credit was widely used and its terms were closely regulated by the government. The famous Code of Hammurabi, circa 1,800 B.C., established legal maxima for interest on all loans: 20 per cent for loans of silver—by weight, there was no coinage—and 33⅓ per cent for loans of grain. Crop failure caused by storm or drought served to cancel interest due on a land loan for that year. A higher-than-legal rate collected by subterfuge served to cancel the debt.

Any property, real or personal, could be pledged—wife, concubine, children, land, houses, utensils, doors. (Wood was very scarce and house doors were valuable.) If the debtor defaulted, the creditor could seize the property hypothecated. If he seized the wife, he must treat her well and return her at the end of three years in as good condition as

Reprinted from *Institutional Investor* (August 1977), pp. 109–25. New York: Institutional Investor, Inc.

when she was received. Women's property rights were protected by the Code; the husband alone could not dispose of joint property without the wife's consent. Property could not be sold outside the family except for debt.

Greece

In Attica at the beginning of the sixth century B.C., there was a credit crisis. Farmers were heavily in debt and often could not keep more than a sixth part of their produce. They threatened rebellion. At this point the poet and wise man, Solon, was called upon to assume supreme legislative power for a limited period and revise the laws. His reforms were radical and for the most part they endured. He scaled down many debts, abolished personal slavery for debt, removed all restrictions on rates of interest or other credit terms, devalued the drachma by one-quarter, reapportioned political power according to property and granted citizenship to skilled immigrants. Later on, democracy was established in Athens and Athens soon outdistanced all Greek cities in trade and finance, as in arts and culture.

The Athenians took every precaution to maintain the integrity of their currency, the silver "owls," while most Greek cities engaged in unscrupulous alloying of their coins. Athenian owls, made of silver from rich Athenian mines, became the most acceptable currency throughout the Mediterranean world for 600 years, long after Athens lost her political power. They became a valuable item of export.

In her golden age, Athens became a leading trade center and Athenians invested extensively at home and abroad. Bottomry loans at 20 to 30 per cent were popular to finance foreign trade; in these the lender took the risk of disaster at sea and he often went along as a passenger. Speculation in commodities was unpopular as was investment in land. There were private bankers who at times underwrote loans to Greek city-states. The credit standing of the bankers was often better than that of the cities. One city pledged her public colonnades, defaulted and lost their use. "Of all kinds of capital," said Demosthenes, "the most productive is Confidence and if you don't know that, you don't know anything." Demosthenes charged his clients interest at 12 per cent per annum if they delayed paying his legal fees. Even Socrates, the philosopher, had a banker friend to whom he entrusted his investment problems.

In the classical period in Attica ownership of real estate was designated by sunken marking stones called *horoi* which marked the boundaries. Many of these horoi have been found and studied. The visible
half was often engraved, giving notice that the property was encum-
bered, some said for how much, to whom and at what rate of interest.
In the fifth century B.C. these rates were usually 8 to 12 per cent but by
the late third century B.C. some loans in Athens were quoted as low as
6 per cent.

Rome

The Romans were a nation of farmers and soldiers. They left manufacture, commerce and banking largely to foreigners, mostly to Greeks.
Cato said, ''How much worse the money lender was considered by our
forefathers than the thief.'' Nevertheless, Cato himself invested in mercantile loans, probably secretly. In the first century B.C. the legal limit
on interest was 12 per cent. Nevertheless the noble senator Marcus
Junius Brutus loaned money to the city of Salamis at 48 per cent interest. Cicero, when he heard of the transaction, was shocked and repri-
manded Brutus.

Julius Caesar was a daring borrower and financed an important part
of his political rise on credit. When he finally ended his wars in complete victory and returned to Rome, he was confronted with three domestic problems: the rapid rise in the cost of living in Italy, the large
number of unemployed citizens in Rome and the deterioration of the
Italian soil due to centuries of overly intensive farming. His assassina-
tion left these problems for Augustus, his successor.

Roman interest rates, which in early centuries of the republic were
limited to 8⅓ per cent and often exceeded these legal limits, came
down in the late first century B.C. at a time of peace and prosperity to 4
per cent on prime credits. Thereafter as the state was weakened by political chaos and inflation they rose to over 12 per cent.

The Middle Ages

After the fall of Rome and especially after the victories of the Arabs in
the south and the Norsemen in the north, trade and finance in Europe

all but vanished. By the eleventh century it began to revive and the revival was centered in the free cities of northern Europe and Italy which had obtained power and autonomy. They built walls. They were dominated and financed by the new merchant class of burghers.

The credit of the best merchants and free towns was generally much better than the credit of princes. Towns could pledge the wealth of their burghers in perpetuity and had to make good to preserve their sovereignty and credit. So did merchants. Princes on the other hand could not bind their subjects or pledge their successors. Their credit depended on youth, good health and military success. Thus it was that princely loans were often made at much higher interest rates than prime commercial loans or loans to free cities. "Lend not to him that is mightier than thou."

For example the emperor Frederick II (1211–1250) usually paid 20 to 30 per cent interest. Frederick the Fair of Austria (1286–1330) borrowed at 80 per cent interest. In 1364 the Countess of Bar pawned her gold coronet for a loan at 50 per cent. Again in 1494 Charles VIII of France paid 42, 56 and 100 per cent for war loans to finance his invasion of Italy.

In contrast, commercial loans on best private credits in the fourteenth century were negotiated at 10 to 15 per cent in the Netherlands and at 5 to 10 per cent in Italy. At the same time the 5 per cent bonds (*prestiti*, see below) of the republic of Venice were selling in the open market to yield from 5¼ to 8 per cent.

There were also reports of odd collateral on loans in the Middle Ages. Baldwin II, king of Jerusalem, on one occasion hypothecated his beard. Later the emperor of Constantinople borrowed in Venice on the security of the Crown of Thorns.

Commercial credit in the Middle Ages was severely hampered by the fact that all usury—any gain from lending—was usually illegal and also forbidden by the church. Merchants, fearful for their souls, gave large sums for the building of cathedrals. The prohibition, however, did not apply to the purchase and sale of incomes such as perpetual annuities; such income was not considered to be interest or usury. These perpetual annuities were the direct ancestors of our long-term bonds; the investor could not demand his principal but the borrower could redeem after a specified date. They became very popular with wealthy burghers wishing to retire and seeking safety and a fair income.

Venice

In the thirteenth century, Venice, an independent and prosperous nation-city governed by and for her seagoing merchants, financed her wars, usually with Genoa, by what we would call capital levies: assessments levied only on the wealth of the wealthy. However the taxpayer received a credit in a permanent fund that paid him 5 per cent interest on face value of his tax payment until such a time as the state decided to pay him off. In the meantime, however, the taxpayer owner could sell his claim to interest at the market price. Thus were created the famous Venetian *prestiti* which were publicly traded for over 200 years and became a prime and much sought investment. They were exempt from new assessments. All state revenues over expenses had to be applied to their redemption. Earlier loans had to be redeemed first. Considerable amounts were redeemed from time to time but new assessments usually exceeded redemptions.

In 1285 the prestiti were quoted on the rialto at a price of 75 to yield $6\frac{5}{8}$ per cent current income. By 1299, during a disastrous war, they declined to a price of 50 ($8\frac{3}{8}$ per cent). Later a sinking fund was provided. Their long record of regular payment of interest in spite of war and disaster created great confidence. In the fourteenth century the prestiti fluctuated between a high price of 102 and a low of 19 closing the century at 63. In the fifteenth century they fluctuated between 74 and 23.

The prestiti were much sought after throughout Europe. Foreign princes and capitalists bought them as a secure investment. The right to own them was a privilege that a foreigner could obtain only by act of the Council of Venice. They were widely used to endow charities and to secure dowers. They were quoted daily on the rialto and their prices accurately mirrored the fortunes of the state.

The Venetian prestiti were the first actively traded security in our history of credit. Their quotations have come down to us over a long period of centuries. They were in essence the same type of obligation as the perpetual annuities, pledging interest but not promising redemption at any date but subject to call. The Italian free cities in the Middle Ages were responsible for many such ingenious financial innovations.

The Genoese

In the sixteenth century the Genoese contributed another financial innovation. The famous Bank of St. George issued on behalf of the republic a series of perpetual securities called *luoghi*. Their income was secured by specific taxes and dividend payments varied according to the size of the tax take. A free market existed for the luoghi. They were not forced levies as were the Venetian prestiti but were popular and freely subscribed. They were in effect equity securities with highly variable dividends—stocks, not bonds, with dividends based on the state's success in collecting taxes. The luoghi were actively traded for at least a century and publicly quoted and became a favorite medium of speculation and of investment. At one time their price rose to over five times par and their current yield declined to 1.1 per cent; obviously extra dividends were expected.

At this time the practice of *moltiplechi* was devised. Gifts of luoghi were made to charities and to heirs with the legatee required to hold and invest the dividends until the principal reached a specified high figure. The bank was also required to keep its reserves in luoghi.

There was a further interesting novelty: The dividends on the luoghi were declared annually but were paid one half in the fourth year after declaration and one half in the fifth year after declaration. Thus, in the meantime the bank had the use of the earnings. Holders of those dividend claims registered them and could discount the script in the market at going rates of discount. These were pure interest rates on prime credit paper. The script was also traded actively and their rates have come down to us. They were usually low, very low for those times. Starting out in 1522 at 3 to 4 per cent, these discount rates rose at times to 9 per cent but were usually around 5 per cent. Late in the sixteenth century they declined to 3 per cent and lower, reaching a low of 1⅛ per cent in 1619, and then they rose back to 5 per cent.

Genoa prospered greatly as banker for the king of Spain. The vast hoards of Spanish gold and silver from the New World often came to Genoa and not to Spain because the king of Spain had pledged future deliveries against loans at Genoa—sometimes five years into the future. When finally the king of Spain defaulted, the Genoese bankers and investors were ruined.

Antwerp

The dynamic sixteenth century was dominated by the newly great monarchies, France and Spain, and their almost incessant wars.

These wars were financed on credit. As a consequence, a highly efficient money market developed, dominated by Italian and German bankers and centered in Antwerp, the great commercial center. There bankers performed "miracles of finance" in support of their royal patrons. They shifted vast sums from country to country as needed by the use of credit bills. The Fuggers of Augsburg obtained and controlled the mining of metals in the Tyrol in exchange for desperately needed loans. The Fugger bills at Antwerp were considered "as safe as gold." They were the bankers for Charles V.

The exchange at Antwerp dominated European transactions in bills of exchange. These were often foreign exchange bills with interest, which was illicit, sometimes concealed in the exchange rate. The exchange also dealt in other credit investments such as demand notes and loans to states and towns. At one time the exchange had 5,000 members and at times 500 ships a day would enter the port. There was, of course, an extensive trade in commodities.

The rates of interest in this international money market swung widely. Stress alternated with ease as funds were shifted via Antwerp to and from all parts of Europe. For example short-term loans to prime governments in 1510 ranged from 7½ to 24 per cent on the exchange. In 1530 the range was 12 to 24 per cent for such credits. The king of France, Francis I, also borrowed heavily. He fostered a competitive money market at Lyons, dominated by Florentine bankers. He attempted to set a 15 per cent legal limit on loans but at times had to pay more. Even the English Crown kept a financial agent at Antwerp, Sir Thomas Gresham, who borrowed at around 13 per cent.

Finance was essential to the great wars of this century as it is today. These wars more than once came to a full stop when both sides ran out of money. The medieval financial machinery was first overstimulated by royal patronage and then destroyed by royal defaults. In 1570 the city of Antwerp, whose excellent credit had been exploited by the Spanish Crown, defaulted on its debts. In 1576 an unpaid Spanish army sacked Antwerp and ruined its commercial prosperity. At about the same time the king of France defaulted. The vast credit boom of the sixteenth century was over.

Dutch Republic

The reformation in the sixteenth century opened the way for modern credit markets by two basic changes: First, credit at interest at moderate rates was permitted. (Luther thought 5 per cent was a top limit; Calvin went up to 6 per cent.) Commercial credit, which had been illicit or illegal, now became open and accepted in the Protestant countries of northern Europe. Second, a high degree of local autonomy was favored by the reformers and the divine right of kings was no longer accepted. This led to governments in Protestant northern Europe which could effectively pledge the resources of their whole people free of fear of royal defaults.

These reforms first bore fruit in the new small Dutch Republic, a union of the northern provinces of the Spanish Netherlands. Her war of liberation from Spain lasted 80 years, 1568 to 1648, and ended in victory for the tiny Dutch Republic over the greatest empire in the world, backed up by all the wealth of the New World. One chief reason for the Dutch victory was no doubt her superior finance.

The Dutch burghers trusted their own government, composed as it was of Dutch burghers. Nobody trusted the king of Spain, who defaulted on his illegal loans four times in a century. The credit instruments of the Dutch provinces were meticulously serviced and could be secured only by the good name of the province. The credits of the king of Spain were secured by gold and silver from the New World on which the king sometimes borrowed five years in advance. The Dutch provinces, at the end of the seventeenth century, were paying 3 to 4 per cent for long-term loans. The king of Spain at one time paid 40 per cent for short-term illicit loans; it turned out that he had pledged the same property several times.

After the fall of Antwerp in 1576, the financial markets shifted to Amsterdam. The Bank of Amsterdam, founded in 1609, achieved a dominating position in the international bullion trade. Its deposits even commanded a small premium over coined money. In the seventeenth century the Dutch Republic developed a worldwide trading empire. It achieved a near monopoly of shipping and commerce. The Dutch were the carriers of the world—the middle men, the brokers of Europe. This was made possible by the development of the new finance. Usury laws were unknown in Holland and interest rates were the lowest in Europe. A frugal, prosperous population saved regularly and invested in the securities of the Dutch provinces. They had confidence in the integrity of their leaders who could pledge the whole future surplus of all the people.

Dutch government financing was almost all at long-term annuities for one or two or three lives, or more often, perpetual annuities where the holder could never claim principal but the borrower could redeem after a certain number of years. These perpetual annuities were the direct ancestors of our long-term bonds. They were very popular. They permitted the Dutch burgher to retire from risky trade after he had "made his pile" and not only enjoy a safe income but also protect his family even to his grandsons and beyond. During the war of liberation very large sums were raised by the sale of these perpetual annuities and the money was used to hire German mercenaries to hold off the unpaid Spanish army. The Dutch themselves could handle their defense on the water and indeed their navy operated at a profit.

A remarkable series of conversions of these annuities (perpetual bonds) occurred during the seventeenth century. At the outset, sinking fund perpetual annuities were sold at $8\frac{1}{3}$ per cent. This was reduced to $7\frac{1}{7}$ per cent and then to $6\frac{1}{6}$ per cent in 1620. In the 1640s all of these annuities were called or, at the option of the holder, converted to 5 per cent annuities. In 1654 all securities were converted to a rate of 4 per cent. There were bondholder riots protesting the reduction of their income but the conversion was a success. Later, during the crises in the war, the prices of the 4 per cent annuities declined to the point where the yield was $7\frac{1}{2}$ per cent but gradually recovered to par and higher. Finally at the end of the century new loans were floated at as low as 3 per cent.

At the same time, the rates on short term loans in Amsterdam came down from $6\frac{1}{6}$ per cent to $3\frac{3}{4}$ and 3 per cent. Finally at the turn of the eighteenth century the rate of interest on the Amsterdam exchange was reported as falling to 2 per cent.

Great Britain: Eighteenth Century

The revolution of 1688 brought parliamentary government to Great Britain and ended the divine right of kings. The Dutch Statholder became William III of Great Britain and almost immediately Dutch finance, as the Torys contemptuously called it, was adopted and improved upon.

Up to the last decade of the seventeenth century, England had no money market, no substantial bank and no organized national debt. The Stuart kings had borrowed haphazardly from goldsmiths on short term, usually at high rates, and occasionally defaulted in the manner of medieval monarchs. Nevertheless, great wealth was accumulating and commerce was expanding. The need for reliable credit at moderate rates was pressing. Everyone in trade envied the Dutch their financial miracles and their low interest rates. The essential ingredients of Dutch finance were confidence in the ability of the government to pledge the wealth of the country as a whole behind a national debt and confidence in the integrity of the government to live up to its contracts.

In 1695 the Bank of England opened for business. It accepted deposits from the government and the public, issued bank notes payable to bearer and honored drafts against deposits. It also discounted inland and foreign trade bills and dealt in bullion and foreign exchange. Soon the bank helped the Treasury develop a new form of short-term obligation called *exchequer bills* with fixed interest and fixed maturity, usually a year. At the same time the private bill market expanded rapidly under the guidance and support of the Bank of England. County banks sent the savings of agricultural communities to London to finance growing manufacturing communities. Short-term British interest rates were stabilized in the eighteenth century at around 4 to 5 per cent.

More important was the development of the new funded debt, the first in English history. Early in the eighteenth century the government began selling long-term annuities in the Dutch manner—for one to three lives or for 99 years or perpetual. These were often accompanied by prizes and lotteries. The funds became very popular; wealthy British capitalists felt they were loaning money to themselves at good rates and could thus provide for retirement and perpetuate the family fortune without taking the risk of trade or the risk of poor crops. Early in the eighteenth century these perpetual annuities yielded as much as 8.7 per cent but they soon came down to 6 per cent, then 5 per cent, then 4 per cent and by 1726 to 3 per cent. Thus the Dutch experience of one century earlier was repeated.

Shortly after 1750 there was another basic innovation. Gradually almost all the outstanding annuities were called in and converted into a single issue of 3 per cent consolidated annuities—the famous British consols. They are still outstanding as 2½s.

The British had made two basic improvements on Dutch finance: They created a uniform security, the consols, which therefore could be freely traded and thus became highly marketable, while each Dutch annuity was unique and not interchangeable with others; the British provided full disclosure of all details of the funded debt, including the size of the debt and tax receipts, while Dutch official financial statistics were secret.

In the eighteenth century the British 3 per cent consols fluctuated widely between a high of 104⅞ per cent [of par] and a low of 57½ per cent to yield 5.22 per cent. Much later, in the 1890s, they were re-funded into the present 2½ per cent consols which recently sold as low as 14 to yield 18 per cent.

During the eighteenth and nineteenth centuries the British issued vast amounts of these perpetual bonds at various rates of interest. In effect, through the perfection of their capital market, the British borrowed and bought themselves an empire.

So successful was the system of finance initiated in seventeenth-century Holland and perfected in eighteenth-century Britain that in the nineteenth and twentieth centuries all advanced industrial nations adopted it with varying success—depending largely on the key element of confidence in government and confidence of the leading members of the financial communities in each other.

In the twentieth century this financial system was maintained with only small changes, but greatly enlarged in size. It survived the two great world wars in nations which maintained economic freedom and confidence in government. However, the recent strain of gigantic peace-time expenditures, spiraling inflation and quantum increases in all forms of debt in many countries, notably Britain, has at times threatened the entire system and has brought back medieval interest rates.

The Bond Business, circa 1910

Sidney Homer

Sidney Homer's magnificent *History of Interest Rates* is a scholarly exposition of several thousand years of lending—and borrowing—experience. His observation that much has happened to the form of bond markets over time, but surprising little to the substance, is well illustrated by this snippet from a 1974 talk at UCLA. It describes the U.S. bond business early in this century.

I will start with a vignette of one phase of the American bond market in 1910 as it was described to me by my first boss. His first job was that of a salesman for a well-known old Wall Street bond firm. His territory was Connecticut. They gave him a bicycle and a list of bonds to sell. The bonds were mostly second grade 5% western public utility bonds and were usually priced at par. Our grandfathers, it seems, liked good round numbers and scorned fractions. Often the bonds cost this firm, the underwriter, something like ten points lower (plus some free stock), and so the young salesman, who operated on a 50–50 commission basis, made $50 for every bond he sold.

In those days one bond a week would keep a man alive, three bonds a week would be prosperity, and ten bonds a week would be affluence. So he went pedaling around the state looking for prosperous storekeepers, tobacco farmers, or druggists who might buy one or two bonds, or country banks who might buy five or more. He did well, and in five years or so he had accumulated enough capital to start his own firm.

Excerpted from *The Journal of Portfolio Management* 1 (Spring 1975), pp. 6–11. New York: Institutional Investor, Inc.

This is a picture of a retail bond market, perhaps not entirely representative, but in the main valid.

These were not high-grade bonds and so had to be retailed in out of the way places to private investors. However, the record of these western utilities was excellent, and twenty years later many of them were called and others eventually became legal. The prime bonds, in the decade ending in 1910, were the rails, like the New York Central 1st 3½s of '97 non-callable. Prime new issues were also underwritten on a negotiated basis, but these were listed on the New York Stock Exchange, grabbed up by sophisticated investors, and if well priced sold at quick premiums. Indeed, between 1880 and 1900, when prime yields moved from 4½% to 3⅛%, fortunes were made by capitalists carrying big blocks of such bonds on credit. They were usually 100-year maturities and non-callable. One popular issue matured in 2361. The basic business was retail—small country investors or big city investors. Underwriting spreads were so large as to make methodical widespread distribution profitable to dealers even if unit transactions were small. This is not true today.

Investing for the Future of IBM

Thomas J. Watson, Sr.

The transformation of Computing-Tabulating-Recording Co. into IBM is certainly one of the greatest continuing investment stories of the western world. Here is an excerpt from a talk by Thomas J. Watson, Sr., on "Investing for the Future of IBM," given in 1932.

———— ▬ ————

We plan to spend a million dollars in research work this year. We have spent over $800,000 each year in research work in the last two years. In an organization such as we have representing 4,000 stockholders, if we can stand before the Board of Directors and ask them to authorize an expenditure of over $800,000 in one year, simply for research and development work, it means we have absolute faith in the future of this business.

Investing in the Future

We do not need to spend a single cent for research on the products we will sell this year. They have been taken care of. But we are going to spend a great deal every year in research for the future.

Twenty years from now you who will still be comparatively young men may look back and realize that the policy of this company in constantly investing in research has been responsible for its growth. For you are going to see this business within a reasonable number of years

Excerpted from *Men-Money-Minutes* (Rye, New York, 1934), p. 570, by permission of International Business Machines Corporation.

just twice as large as you see it today. I am not talking about twenty-five years. I expect to see this business double within five years from the time the United States is willing to acknowledge that we are out of the depression. Just when that will be I do not know. We are willing to acknowledge it now, because we know we can double our business. In my judgment it is going to be a very long time before all the industries in this country will say business is better. Then business will be better and the depression will be over. Within five years from that point, our business will double itself.

Rapid Growth of IBM

I predicted the same thing on two occasions in the past and I was wrong each time because our business more than doubled in both periods. Young men coming into the business and not knowing its possibilities and the opportunities before them, may say, when they hear these statements from me, "that all sounds too good"; but if you will go back over the convention minutes of all the conventions we have held since I have been connected with this company, which has been over eighteen years, you will find that my predictions have been wrong every time because our business has done more than I predicted for it.

The Product Nobody Wanted

Joseph C. Wilson

Joe Wilson transformed The Haloid Co. into Xerox Corp., in part
because he had the capacity and drive to build a great company,
and in part because he led his associates in a deliberate search
for a great company.

In 1946, Xerox was a small firm known as The Haloid Co., located in
Rochester, N.Y. There was little about Haloid to set it apart from hundreds of other small businesses at the end of World War II. It had a
solid reputation in a narrow field, production of photocopy equipment
and machines.

Haloid had increased its production during the war but was beginning
to experience a profit squeeze. While sales rose from $1.4 million in
1936 to just under $7 million in 1946, profits did not keep pace. They
hit a high of $300,000 in 1939, but drifted down to $150,000 in 1946.

Along with me, a few young men in the company saw very clearly
that Haloid would have to change direction.

I am not at all sure that we knew precisely what avenues we wanted
to explore. We thought ideally of finding some entirely new process or
product that would revitalize our 40-year-old company.

The people responsible for the search that ultimately propelled us
to the forefront of the graphic communications industry were not seeking simply a new product. All who were involved 20 years ago when
The Haloid Co. made its big decision—men like Dr. John J. Dessauer,

Reprinted from *Nation's Business* (February 1969), pp. 67–70. Washington: United States Chamber
of Commerce.

John B. Hartnett, the late Harold Kuhns, and the late Homer A. Piper—shared a feeling that we must direct our energies toward a valuable activity—one that was worthwhile for people, not just for making money.

Today this sort of thinking remains an integral part of our business life. We seek not only to be an effective commercial enterprise, but also to establish an institution that is socially responsible and constructive.

Discovery of an Invention

It was during our search for new directions that John Dessauer ran across a potentially interesting invention. John was then and until recently our director of research. He is now vice chairman of our board, and we still seek his wise counsel. He noticed an abstract referring to an article in the July, 1944 issue of *Radio News* describing a new invention, "electrophotography."

The inventor of that process, the late Chester F. Carlson, had struggled for years despite extreme hardships. Finally he produced the first "electrophotographic" image-making plate on Oct. 22, 1938, in Astoria, Queens. Carlson coated a two-inch by three-inch zinc plate with sulfur, then charged the plate electrostatically by rubbing it with a handkerchief, and exposed it for about 10 seconds to a glass slide on which the words "10–22–38 Astoria" were written.

A dusting of lycopodium powder made the latent image visible, and by pressing a piece of wax paper against the powdered image, Carlson completed the first successful demonstration that his process could make a copy. The experiment, although rudimentary, established the feasibility of completely dry copying. It was later renamed xerography, from the Greek words xeros meaning "dry" and graphein, "to write."

Chet Carlson, with all his laboratory work, had also managed to become a patent lawyer by going to school nights. He prepared and filed his own patent application and later, with additional patent applications that were granted, refined the process somewhat. His persistent efforts to kindle a commercial interest in his invention, however, were disheartening. More than 20 major corporations could see nothing in it worth developing.

Finally in 1944, eight years after his discovery, Chet had a chance meeting with Dr. Russell Dayton of Battelle Memorial Institute in Columbus, Ohio, and the Battelle staff subsequently invited Carlson to discuss his process with them. This led to an agreement under which Battelle would develop the process in exchange for 75 per cent of any royalties from commercial sale or licensing.

Happily for Chet, as it turned out, the agreement allowed him to invest his own money in the research. Battelle ran through the initial budget for the project, and Chet was able to raise enough to continue the research, thereby increasing his royalty interest to 40 per cent.

Shortly after John Dessauer read of Chet's invention, he called my attention to the article. The more we thought about the process, the more it appealed to us. So John and I visited Battelle in 1946. We negotiated a limited agreement with the Institute that went into effect Jan. 1, 1947.

The 22 months that followed before we and Battelle unveiled the process on its tenth anniversary—Oct. 22, 1948, at the annual meeting of the Optical Society of America in Detroit—were hectic at best. Battelle conducted further research, and we at Haloid made a concerted, often frantic, effort to prepare for our own development of the process based on that research. We also made an intensive effort to raise additional money—John Dessauer even mortgaged his house.

By 1948 we recognized it would take a considerable amount of money to bring Carlson's process to market. In the six years following our first visit to Columbus, indeed, Haloid was to raise more than $3.5 million for development and exploitation of xerography, a sizable sum for us then.

We also realized our agreement with Battelle was too limiting in light of our projected investment. A young Rochester lawyer I knew, Sol M. Linowitz, agreed to renegotiate the contract for us. He was later to become our general counsel, negotiate our overseas arrangement with the Rank Organisation, and become chairman of the board before leaving to become U.S. Ambassador to the Organization of American States in 1967.

The new agreement gave us an exclusive license on all xerographic developments in return for a substantial royalty arrangement.

An Unusual Pricing Scheme

In 1949 we introduced the first Xerox non-automatic copier—a similar model is still in use for special purposes—and made the critical decision to offer xerographic products for lease, giving the customer decreasing costs per copy as the number of reproductions increased. It was an unusual pricing scheme and demonstrates the beginning of our innovative sales approach.

Between 1949 and 1956, the company's sales tripled. These were years of technical growth, of developing products and market, of single-minded commitment. We had staked so much on the new process that we had to emphasize commercial success. But I am sure none of us who were caught up in the exciting development of xerography ever forgot our desire to render truly valuable service to mankind.

In 1955 we concluded a new agreement with Battelle: the old licenses and royalties were eliminated and actual title to the basic Carlson patents was transferred to Haloid. In return, Battelle received until 1965 modest cash royalties, a portion of royalties we acquired from sublicensing, and additional royalties in stock, depending on our annual revenues from xerography. Since payment in stock satisfied much of Haloid's continuing obligation to the Institute, we could use our cash and borrowing power to develop the process we believed so promising.

The company made its final payment to the Institute in 1965 (except for a modest research commitment of $25,000 a year), and by then, the total Xerox stock paid to Battelle under the agreement had a market value of more than $355 million. We have never regretted these arrangements, nor, I should guess, has Battelle.

By 1955, a number of office copiers based on technologies other than xerography had been introduced. Our respected neighbor, Eastman Kodak Co., and Minnesota Mining and Manufacturing Co., for instance, were marketing copiers.

That year Dr. Dessauer formed a committee, including Chester Carlson, to study the feasibility of building an automatic copier using our technology. The committee concluded that the machine would have to be as large as a four-drawer filing cabinet and would weigh a thousand pounds. Outside consultants hired by us predicted that those specifications—hardly anything to alarm the existing manufacturers of copiers—would sharply limit the market. But our commitment seemed too great to turn back.

The Dessauer report presented two alternatives: go ahead or go broke.

Our own people were enthusiastic. Between 1955 and 1957, when management recommended to shareholders that our name be changed to

Haloid-Xerox, Inc., we had but one goal—accelerated development of this machine. It was not an easy time.

For every technical problem we solved, we encountered another for which we had no answer.

Considering our excitement about the potential of the Xerox 914 during the years preceding the introduction of it, I wonder in retrospect how we managed to keep it a secret as long as we did. From the very beginning, the major goal of our research program was the development of an automatic office copier based on Chester Carlson's process.

For reasons now lost to history, we had assigned it the code designation E 100.

In 1957 we presented our board of directors a "breadboard" version of the E 100.

Nobody Wanted It

They were interested enough to retain a well-known organization to study market feasibility. Another company that we had approached with the product ordered a similar study. And, again, the consulting firms arrived at substantially the same conclusion—the market for a machine like the E 100 was relatively limited. Another Haloid consultant was slightly more optimistic: there was promise for such a large copier within a systems application, but not as an independently functioning unit for general document copying.

It looked as if we were entering the home stretch with a product nobody wanted.

I suppose by every logical rule of management we should have abandoned the whole idea right there.

Fortunately, some unusually perceptive young men on our staff saw a major flaw in the case against the E 100 made by the consultants. The consultants had applied established criteria to evaluate an entirely new product. Our people identified a much larger market for such a machine because they did not follow conventional guidelines.

In today's complex society, of course, you cannot make much progress by following conventional guidelines. No enterprise is unchanging nor are markets. The results of change depend on the purpose and management of it. If change is successful, in retrospect we call it growth.

At the beginning, it wasn't easy to manage the growth of the E 100. We introduced it to the public in 1959 as the Xerox 914 (it could make copies on ordinary paper up to 9″ by 14″). The first production line machine was delivered in March, 1960. The story of what happened to it from then on is, in a way, the opening chapter of a story that I do not expect to see completed in my lifetime.

The copier's immediate success not only refuted most of the market experts, it also astonished the most optimistic of us. The product that nobody wanted, it seems, had become a product that *everybody* wanted.

By the end of 1960, we were producing machines at a rate 50 per cent greater than we had anticipated—and were working against a huge backlog. Orders taken during the first nine months of the 914's commercial life far exceeded our total projections for it. Even more significant (because of our per-copy charge), users of the machines were making more copies than we expected.

A New Name

We recognized almost immediately that more than three quarters of our revenue during the coming decade would come from xerographic products. So we recommended to our shareholders at the 1960 annual meeting that the name of Haloid Xerox undergo one more change—this time to Xerox Corp.

Our annual reports for the first two full years of 914 production tell the story of the machine's success. People began developing whole new office systems around it. Customers discovered uses we hadn't imagined. A Food and Drug Administration office used it to copy labels without taking them off the bottles; police officers recorded the contents of a suspect's pockets with one pass of the machine.

In 1961, our total revenues were 60 per cent greater than the previous year, while net income jumped 109 per cent. The following year, net income rose 151 per cent on a sales gain of 70 per cent.

The success of the 914 provided abundant evidence that our approach to the copying market was a sound one. We hastened the design and production of machines that covered the entire spectrum of copying and medium-range duplicating. By late 1965, we had introduced a "family of products" meeting diverse needs of the copying market. We are still adding to that family and starting on "second generation" machines.

The field of copying continues to grow, but like all markets it will have a saturation point. To avoid stagnation once we reach that point, we carefully selected new ventures related to our basic field—graphic communications, or more broadly, the dissemination of knowledge.

As early as 1956, we recognized that overseas markets could furnish added growth. That year Haloid agreed to form a jointly owned company with The Rank Organisation of London, then best known in the motion picture field. The product of our union, Rank Xerox Limited, now markets xerographic products throughout the Eastern Hemisphere. In recent years it has grown faster than Xerox itself in revenues and earnings.

In 1962 we began—with University Microfilms the first of our acquisitions in this area—to move from our by-then traditional base in copying to the education field. We now have made a full commitment to serve this field by publishing textbooks, by marketing library services, and by developing supplementary teaching materials and, indeed, whole courses for industrial and public classrooms.

Another goal was to participate in the exciting research taking place for the federal government, and that led us to acquire Electro-Optical Systems, Inc., a company chiefly engaged in military research, aerospace and other advanced technology. At Xerox we believe it is essential to *retain* the concept of change to keep the innovative spirit alive in our organization.

I think an essential quality in a manager, even on a relatively low level, is the ability to know when to depart from the normal, when to take risks. On the other hand, the manager who always upsets the applecart can be a disruptive influence. The art, I think, is to provide an atmosphere in which professional managers can retain the sensitivity so essential to the successful operation of a small business—the entrepreneurial spirit, as it were.

The Day They Red-Dogged Motorola

'Adam Smith'

There are two ways to understand institutional block trading: one is to actually do it at Salomon Brothers or Goldman Sachs, and the other is to read this classic by Jerry Goodman writing as 'Adam Smith.'

When John Kenneth Galbraith sits down to write the history of the great Johnson Bear Market, as he is bound to some day, he ought to pay some attention to September 27, 1966. That is going to be one of those days like December 7, 1941, peculiar to a history, the day Wall Street stopped believing in anything, at least for this Bear Market, and you can mark it by minutes on the clock, just the way it happens in the disaster stories when the water goes gurgling into the Titanic. September 27 was the day they red-dogged Motorola.

At the moment it was happening I was having lunch at the Bankers Club, with a friend of mine who runs a hot go-go fund. By this I mean an investment fund that is supposed to go up fast so that the pressure is on to pick the stock that will move. Then they compare your performance with the other "growth" funds month by month and sometimes week by week. Not recommended for widows. Orphans, maybe, young rich orphans with time to grow. It pays to have lunch with such operators on a friendly basis; sometimes you can get a bit of a ride on what

Reprinted from the *World Journal Tribune,* October 30, 1966, pp. 4–6, by permission of Bell & Howell.

they're promoting. Anyway, my friend—I'll call him Charlie—is sitting there stirring his coffee telling me the bearish news from all over, such as that one of the major New York City banks is busted except for its float, i.e. it is kiting money over the weekends and if they ever speed up the United States mail the bank is in trouble. "Kiting over the weekend" means writing checks on Friday on money that doesn't exist and rushing to cover the checks with new funds by Monday morning.

"They're out," Charlie says. "They can't go to the Fed because the Fed would slam the window on their fingers if they look at their loans, so they have been scrambling around Europe sopping up the Euro-dollars."

If you understand what Charlie said, fine, and if you don't, it doesn't have much to do with Motorola except set a nice, dark, ominous atmosphere, John Kenneth Galbraith please note. Money is tight and Wall Street doesn't like the Viet Nam war at all. Then a fellow we both know comes by and says Motorola is getting red-dogged down on the floor of the Exchange. Already there is a little crowd around the Dow Jones broad tape in the ante room, where the carpet is worn.

Meanwhile, a couple of blocks away at 15 William St. the boys are spilling what is left of the tuna fish in order to get to the phones. All this from a speech by Mr. Robert W. Galvin from Franklin Park, Ill. Mr. Galvin is the chairman of the board of Motorola, one of the 1966 flyers, and he is addressing the sage and august New York Society of Security Analysts. Motorola makes color TV sets, and that's growth, and semiconductors, and that's growth, and two-way radios, and that's growth. Growth, growth, growth. Six months ago all this growth is worth $234 a share. On September 27 it's worth $140. A bad gassing, but how much worse can things be? They're going to earn $8 a share. It says so in Standard & Poor's. Business, Mr. Galvin says, is so good it's bad. They have all the orders they can handle—they just have trouble producing the goods—shortages here, labor problems there. They can sell all the color TVs they can make, they just can't make them fast enough. Earnings will be up—but to $5.50, $6 on the outside. Everything else is rosy.

The sage and august analysts look at each other for a moment: $6? $6? What happened to the other $2? Then it is like the end of the White House news conference, except nobody even has said, "Thank you, Mr. President." They are all running for the phones. Except they are security analysts, not newsmen, so they use the Olympic heel-and-toe walk instead of the outright sprint. There is the question-and-answer period, but Mr. Galvin's audience has been depleted.

Back at the Bankers Club, Charlie has melted into a phone booth and is giving orders to his girl. "Sell 10,000 Motorola," he is saying; that's about a million three. I can tell the girl has the portfolio in front of her and is looking for Motorola, and I can even hear (because I am making a special attempt to do so) her saying, "But we don't *own* any Motorola." Charlie is going to short the Motorola, so he hollers a bit. He'll buy it back some other time. Right now the important thing is to sell it, whether or not you own it. This is one of the pressures of a performance fund.

We stand there watching the tape, and there goes MOT, 137, 136, oof, 134. Big blocks are appearing.

"There goes Gerry Tsai's Motorola," says some wise man behind us. That's the *in* thing to say. Gerry Tsai, who is head of the Manhattan Fund, has that $450 million sitting there bubbling away, and he does move in and out fast, but how anybody can tell it's *his* Motorola is beyond me. He might have sold it long before. It's useful, though. You can always sound wise by saying, "Gerry Tsai is buying," or "Gerry Tsai is selling." He has replaced the "They" from the old days, when "They" were about to put a stock up or down. Gerry Tsai better watch out, though, because if you're They, things have to be good. I know a chartist who says the Dow Jones is going to 380. If it does, I would go long apples because there will be plenty of demand from all the street corner salesmen, and they will be looking for a scapegoat. There will be a book sponsored by the John Birch Society called *The Protocols of the Elders of Shanghai,* in which it is proved that Gerry Tsai was really Mao Tse Tung, and there will be a public ceremony in front of the Federal Reserve Bank while Gerry Tsai is exorcised of demons by a god-fearing chaplain just before they drive the water buffalos he is tied to in opposite directions.

Now down on the Floor the pressure is on the specialist. He is standing there on the floor at Post 18, his Hippocratic Oath bidding him make an orderly market in Motorola, and suddenly there he is, like an adolescent fantasy, a quarterback in Yankee Stadium with the crowd roaring. Only it's the wrong dream. The crowd is roaring because all his receivers are covered, his defense has evaporated, and the red-dog is on: two tons of beef descending on him, tackles grunting and linebackers growling *"killll."* Nothing to do but buckle, eat the ball, and hope you're still alive when they stop blowing the whistle. Guys are bearing down on the specialist and he can tell that if he bends over in a reflex from the first chunk of Motorola that hits him in the stomach, they will hit him over the head with the rest. That's not an orderly market. So they blow the whistle. No more trading in Motorola.

Charlie is chagrined. He needed an uptick to get off his short; they've had that rule since the Great Crash. In the good old days without that rule the bears could all get together and short the stock right down to 0 and into negative territory practically.

"Gee, and I was going to go to Europe next week," Charlie says. Now he thinks he better stick around. I ask Charlie for a prognostication. (Remember, this is September 27 and I am writing this the second week of October, so you have a two-week free ride. This is because of what they call "lead time" in this magazine, which is, I gather, that it takes the printers two weeks to put all the pages together.)

Charlie likes to sound like the Oracle of Delphi, not in print, of course, because that can catch up with you, but just to his friends.

"Everything is going to par," Charlie says. Par is 100, or it used to be and everybody still calls it that, and "everything" means the high flyers that the performance boys have to be in or they lose their union cards. Say: Motorola, Xerox, Fairchild Camera, Polaroid—just look at the list of 10 most active stocks and there they are. Well, the flyers have about 40 points to drop before they hit par and naturally Charlie doesn't mean every one, because they aren't all selling at the same price, but that's a steep drop. "After Motorola, nobody will believe anything," Charlie says. "Tomorrow, they will start saying Fairchild has terrible problems, Xerox gives you cancer, handling Polaroid film makes you sterile." So everything is going to par. At that point John Jerk and his brother will figure the way to make money is to go short.

In more polite circles, John Jerk and his brother are called "the little fellows" or "the odd-lotters"; or "the small investors." I wish I knew Mr. Jerk and his brother. They live in some place called the Hinterlands, and everything they do is wrong. They buy when the smart people sell, they sell when the smart people buy, and they panic at exactly the wrong time. There are services that make a very good living just out of charting the activity of Mr. J. and his poor brother. If I knew them I would give them room and board and consult them like they used to ask the original Jeep in the prewar Popeye comic strip, before a Jeep was a car. I would push the pheasant and champagne through the little hatch of his cell and ask Mr. J. what he was going to do that morning, and if he said, "buy," I would know to sell, and so on.

Charlie and I drifted back to his office. "It's a terrible market for everybody but me," Charlie said. "Nobody believes anything. They don't believe Johnson, they don't believe anything in Washington, they believe taxes are going to go up but not enough, they don't believe we'll ever get out of Viet Nam, and after Motorola, nobody will believe any earnings. Let Peat Marwick the CPA's certify them, they still won't believe them."

This is what the French sociologist Emile Durkheim called *anomie*. In market terms it means anxiety builds up as the market drops, and then as you get all the noise about "resistance levels" and so on and the market goes plunging through them, you get *anomie*. Like alienation, only it means "Where's the bottom? Where's the bottom? Where's the bottom?" Nobody knows where the bottom is; nobody can remember where the top was; they're all way out there in the blue, riding on anxiety and a shoeshine. The Dow Jones Average is going to 0. Only Charlie is in good shape; his fund is a hedge fund and he is short.

"At par," Charlie intones, "there will be a rally, while we chase John Jerk and his brother."

The translation of this is that Mr. J., having lost on the stocks he owned, will try to make up his losses by selling short, and then as Charlie buys, the stocks go up, giving Mr. J. a loss on the short sales. Then he panics and he has to buy all the way up with Charlie chasing him.

Times have changed since the Fifties. Way back then, an "institution" was something with a lot of money that lived in Boston or Philadelphia, and it waited until stocks got seasoned, and then it bought and tucked away the stock. They were run by guys who wore sleeve garters and said "my good man." Now you have computers that tell you exactly what each fund is worth every minute, and a bunch of swingers running them. In the old days the brokerage houses had some hot ideas, and some of their customers bought them, and then the good gray funds would pick out the right seasoned stock for the widows and orphans. No more. Now the guys in the brokerage houses are running into the Regency Hotel where Tsai lives before they clear away the breakfast dishes in case Gerry Tsai has made some notes on the tablecloth while he was drinking his grapefruit juice.

That's a good way to lose, too, because with everything swinging so fast some of these funds buy in the morning and they feel it's sacrilegious to hold stocks overnight. Gerry Tsai is out before the tablecloth goes to laundry. It all adds up to the *anomie*.

I sat in Charlie's office while he cancelled his European vacation. At 3:29 the specialist re-opened Motorola, just as the bell rang. That's like a boxer who manages to get on one knee just as the referee says 10. Motorola re-opened and closed at 119, down 19¼ on the day. In the marketplace it was worth $114 million less at 3:30 than it was at 10:00 A.M., and say $684 million less than it had been a few months before. And it was the same company, more or less, and this year is better than last year and next year will be better than this year.

Now you can talk about tight money and Viet Nam and taxes all you want, but something happened on September 27. It started happening before, of course, when the banks started getting all loaned up and then all the whistles and shrieks and bells and yellow smoke signals of the indicators went off late last spring. On September 27, the bell was tolling for belief.

And what now? Well, the odd-lot figures say Mr. J. and his brother are short a lot of stock, and Charlie has the hounds ready. Our trader says the tape has to stand still for 40 days and 40 nights to prepare the way for the next bull market. Charlie is going to Europe in November. We have come to the moment in Peter Pan when the play stops and Mary Martin or whoever comes to the footlights and says, "Do you believe? Do you believe?" The only times I saw Peter Pan, everybody believed.

Some day, maybe not so far away, Charlie will be back from Europe. Mr. J. will be in the Hinterlands, pantsless, and the first daisy will push through the soil and say, "I believe," and the game will be on again.

I'll tell you about that when we get to it.

How the Terrible Two-Tier Market Came to Wall Street

Carol J. Loomis

Carol Loomis has written many perceptive reports on Wall Street
and investing. Here is her much-discussed article on the "two-tier"
market. It appeared in July 1973 in *Fortune*—just as value stocks
began a two-year ascendance over growth stocks.

———————

To many businessmen the stock market this year has seemed inexplicable, about as bizarre, say, as Watergate. The market has ignored the
large, and often sensational, earnings gains being reported by corporations, and has gone relentlessly down. More than that, it has gone down
with a great unevenness, much as a giant popover might lose steam.

On the one hand, the prices and price-earnings ratios of a few dozen
institutional favorites—known around as "the Vestal Virgins"—have
fallen only moderately. In fact, some of these stocks, among them Eli
Lilly (at about forty times estimated 1973 earnings) and Avon (at about
fifty-two times), were recently selling very near their highest p-e ratios
ever. In contrast, the great majority of stocks have sunk to levels that
suggest they have become virtual pariahs. In the early months of this
year, Wall Street was already talking about a "two-tier market" of
remarkable proportions. By May, stocks that had seemed cheap at
March prices had collapsed still further—many to levels of four or five

Excerpted from *Fortune* (July 1973), pp. 82–88, 186–90. New York: The Time Inc. Magazine Company.

times expected 1973 earnings—and the situation was being described as unique in stock-market history.

The description is probably accurate, though a bit difficult to check out. What can be said with certainty is that there has been no comparable situation in recent history. This conclusion emerges from a special statistical study of price-earnings ratios that *Fortune* made for this article. Covering the period since 1948, the year before the great postwar bull market got under way, the study embraced 382 companies, most of them prominent members of the business community. It ascertained their p-e ratios at the end of every year through 1972 (the year-end price was measured against that year's earnings) and also at the end of the first quarter of 1973. Then for each period a "frequency distribution" analysis was done; that is, *Fortune* determined how many of those 382 companies had p-e ratios under 5 at the end of each period, how many had a p-e between 5 and 10, and so on up the scale.

The results show clearly that 1973 has been an extraordinary year in the market, to be ranked with such aberrant years as 1948 and 1961. In 1948 stocks were so out of favor that a company was a real highflyer if its p-e was above 10. The median p-e for those 382 stocks that year was an incredibly low 5.8. In contrast, 1961 was a euphoric time when a p-e ratio below 10 was an oddity; the median was way up at 19.4.

Two Extremes at Once

But those were periods when the whole market was carried to extremes. The market this year has been something else, a case of two extremes at once, and in between them a very deflated median. Specifically, at the end of 1973's first quarter, before the severe declines of April and May, the median p-e for those 382 stocks was 11.5, the lowest level since 1957. And in a pattern not otherwise seen during the twenty-six years under examination, 128 stocks had a p-e above 30. Moreover, because the stocks in that upper tier were so highly valued by the market, they absorbed a far greater proportion of investment dollars than the number of companies represented there would indicate.

No doubt, then, there *is* today a two-tier market of major dimensions. . . . No doubt, also, that this situation is raising some new and very serious economic questions. The basic questions concern the country's capital markets, which have in the past demonstrated an outstanding ability to deliver equity capital to a broad range of companies. The two-tier market suggests, however, that the range is narrowing and the universe in which investors are willing to sink their money is shrinking. If this situation persists, how are the great majority of companies to raise the equity capital they may need? Beyond that, what happens to the new company seeking equity capital for the first time? Optimistic answers to these questions are hard to come by.

Inevitably, these questions also lead to others about the role of the institutions in the stock market. The two-tier market owes its existence to the actions, and the nonactions, of both institutional and individual investors. But market conditions at the moment suggest that control of the situation lies in the hands of the institutions, and that the two-tier market will disappear only if they—and in particular those giants, the bank trust departments—decide to swerve from the investment policies on which they have leaned very heavily in the last few years. The power of the institutions to shape events seems right now more awesome than ever before—and also more subject to attack.

Already, of course, all sorts of companies in the lower tier of the market have expressed outrage at the low valuations placed on their stocks. Their very specific complaints have lately been joined by others focusing on the broader problem. Two notable protests came recently from Reginald H. Jones, chairman of General Electric, and James M. Roche, retired chairman of General Motors. Jones was brought to worry about the ability of "the industrial backbone" of the economy to attract risk capital, and Roche warned that "our system cannot flourish solely on the basis of the health and strength of seventy-five glamour companies."

Even the Chairman of the New York Stock Exchange, James J. Needham, who would not normally think it his business to tout some stocks over others, was pushed to doing just about that. "It is certainly pertinent to inquire," he said deploringly in a speech, "why the large institutions persist in tightening their concentration in a favorite [few] stocks while ignoring hundreds of other choice investment opportunities."

Inflation Is the Thief

That does sound like a pertinent line of inquiry to follow, and its pursuit should probably begin with a look at the bear market in which stocks have been trapped. This market, it would appear, reflects investors' growing recognition . . . that inflation is robbing stocks of their value. For one thing, the "cost-push" inflation of the late 1960's put enormous pressure on corporate profits. Even now, with inflation more of the "demand-pull" variety and corporate profits booming, investors are obviously looking ahead with apprehension, fearing both a return to a cost-push era and a descent into a recession.

Second, inflation had by 1970 raised interest rates to very high levels and had forced investors to begin reconsidering what returns they expect from stocks. Historically, those returns, taken over the long term and on the average, have worked out to about 9.5 percent, including both capital gains and dividends. As long as interest rates were at much lower levels than 9.5 percent, which was the case during most of the postwar period, an expectation of such a return on stocks shaped up as very satisfactory. But with the yields of high-grade utility bonds above 9 percent, as they were for a time in 1970, or between 7.5 percent and 8 percent, as they have been recently, a return of 9.5 percent on stocks scarcely seems adequate compensation for the added risks that stocks involve.

The logical reaction of investors is to mark down the prices of stocks to levels that suggest future returns will comfortably exceed the rates available on bonds (although one investor's conception of what stock premium is "comfortable" may differ from another's). It would appear that investors have recently been in the process of making such a markdown.

——

It is clear that these institutions do not see in the lower tier those same "choice investment opportunities" that Jim Needham does. Yet *Fortune*'s study of price-earnings ratios shows clearly that a whole army of stocks are at levels that in the postwar periods have come to be considered "cheap." Furthermore, if one focuses on *companies* rather than *stocks,* a good case can be made that there are excellent values around.

All sorts of companies, in cyclical industries mainly, that could recently be bought at book value (or lower) have for at least several years averaged a return on book value of, say, 11 percent or better, and have reasonable expectations of maintaining (or improving) that return. An investor who buys into such a company at no more than book can also figure to earn 11 percent (or better) on his investment, both on the money with which he originally buys a piece of the action and also on every dollar of his earnings that the company retains and puts back to work in the company.

══

Yet the interest of these institutions in that 11 percent proposition appears almost nonexistent. Their attention, instead, is on the companies whose returns on capital are considerably higher—say, 14 percent and up—and whose earnings growth is considerably less subject to cyclical bumps and potentially much faster—perhaps 10 percent or more. These are the "good businesses" of the world, and could all stocks be bought at the same multiple of earnings, these are the ones that everyone would want to own. But the prices of these stocks have been affected relatively little by the bear market that has ravaged the rest of the list, and they can be had only at upper-tier prices. The question then becomes: is it rational for the institutions to stay with these expensive stocks when so many others can be bought at greatly reduced prices?

There are arguments on both sides of that question, and they are best looked at in terms of two forces that dominate the market: the corporate pension funds, which own about $110 billion of stocks (out of total assets of about $150 billion) and earlier this year were adding to stockholdings at a $7-billion annual rate; and the bank trust departments, which manage about 80 percent of all corporate pension-fund dollars. The banks also manage an estimated $240 billion for individuals. These assets, however, do not get the flow of "new money" that the pension funds do, nor turn over as rapidly in the market.

There is vigorous competition for the pension funds' business. Insurance companies and investment advisers would like to steal business away from the banks. The banks down the line would like to steal from the Big Two, Morgan Guaranty ($16.6 billion in employee-benefit assets at the end of 1972) and Bankers Trust ($15 billion). And Bankers Trust, of course, is gunning for Morgan. It so happens that Morgan has a history of investing in growth stocks, and it has outperformed most big banks; some of its accounts have had, with their stock portfolios, a compounded return better than 13 percent over the ten years ending with 1972. Because of its performance and its size, Morgan has become the player that everybody in the game watches. Its influence clearly extends beyond the sums it manages.

Morgan operates under certain constraints that set a rather special pattern. In total, the bank manages $27 billion, about $21 billion of it in stocks, and it fervently wishes to keep most of that in a relatively few stocks in which it has maximum confidence. As a result, it needs big companies in which to invest—those whose stocks can absorb, say, $50 million or more without going into orbit. "Big" companies, by Morgan's definition, are those that have at least $500 million in both market value and revenues; companies of that size, of which there are perhaps 300 in the country, qualify for large, direct investments by the pension funds that Morgan manages. Smaller companies usually are reached through pools of money (rather like mutual funds) that Morgan sets up, and in which its pension accounts participate.

Morgan's employee-benefit accounts recently had $13.3 billion in stocks, of which about $9 billion (or 68 percent) was in fifty big companies. That makes an average investment of $180 million per company. The remaining $4.3 billion was invested in more than 550 companies of assorted sizes, for an average around $7.8 million. In that assortment were 182 relatively small companies (generally with under $100 million in market value and revenues) that Morgan believes to be comers and that are held in a $970-million pooled account. There are varying ways to look at all these numbers. Morgan thinks of them as showing that its arms are wide open to smaller companies. Others would no doubt be struck by the degree of concentration in a relatively few stocks.

When Morgan invests in a big stock, it has every intention of staying in that stock, if not forever, at least for a long time. "We are not traders, we are investors," goes the Morgan pitch for new pension-fund business. "We do not buy stocks with the idea of selling them at a specific price objective. We do not buy with the idea of selling high and buying back low." Morgan's belief in these principles is undoubtedly strong, but it should be noted that the bank really has no alternative strategy open to it. You cannot swing $27 billion around from flower to flower. For that matter, you cannot easily swing even a few billion dollars around.

So Morgan and other big banks are constantly looking for what Wall Street has come to call "one-decision stocks"—i.e., stocks that can be bought and put away, with an expectation that they will produce at least some earnings growth in almost any kind of economic situation and will, over the long term, though not necessarily over any given short-term period, outperform the market as a whole.

Warren Buffett, a well-known and very successful private investor whose own preferences run strongly to investing in low-p-e ''value'' situations, thinks that Morgan's strategy is quite rational—for the bank. ''Morgan is sort of like a large conglomerate which must make decisions for the long term as to what kind of business it wants to be in. Would it be right for a conglomerate to sell its most profitable, best business just because it has a chance to pick up a not-so-great business at a cheap price? I doubt it. So I think, with all that money it's got to worry about, Morgan is probably handling things about as well as it can. Which doesn't mean, of course, that what they're doing is necessarily right for *me*.''

It's Rational Because It Worked

Nor does it mean that what may be rational for a giant like Morgan, or even for a few of its biggest competitors, is necessarily rational for all the smaller banks that are today playing follow-the-leader, and that could instead, if they chose to, go hunting for bargains. Nor are the tactics of any big bank necessarily rational for its clients, the pension funds. These investors are not obligated to place their money with giant institutions whose policies are significantly determined by the huge amounts of money they have to manage. They could instead manage their money themselves, or place it with smaller institutions with greater investment flexibility.

The few banks that have tried to steer a different course by moving into what they see as bargains in the lower tier have lately found the going rather tough. One such bank is First National of Chicago. Its portfolio, though studded with such standbys as I.B.M. and Kodak, is committed also to cyclical stocks and is less concentrated in the very largest companies than most other big bank portfolios are. As a result, the returns First National delivered its pension accounts last year, though these ran to around 14 percent, did not compare well with the returns of more than 20 percent realized by some of the New York banks. . . .

While [First National] waits, it can at least keep telling itself that it has bought its low-tier stocks at prices that can be rationalized. That is clearly more than most top-tier buyers can do. Their thoughts about the intrinsic value of growth stocks—which is admittedly one of the murkier subjects around—tend to be underdeveloped. The banks seem to buy instead mainly on the basis of "feel" and historical p-e ranges. We buy I.B.M., they say, when it approaches the lower limits of its range; we avoid it at the upper limits. The banks tend also to retreat into arguments that price doesn't mean that much anyway. What counts, they say, is to pick the right companies, and even then, they add, you can get by with an occasional misjudgment. "This is a batting-average game," says one trust officer. "You're going to lose a stock now and then—say, a Litton. But if your universe is a bunch of other very profitable companies, you can stand it."

That is true, of course, only so long as the universe itself is not marked down sharply. Were such a markdown to occur today, it would probably imply a switch from buying to selling by the banks themselves. It is not easy to see this kind of a move taking place right now, but it is always possible. Some market commentators identify weakness in the growth stocks with the end of a bear market, and expect firmly to see these stocks begin to crack.

Is It Harder to Be Superior?

There can be no doubt, looking at the data that *Fortune* gathered on the largest holdings of the largest trust departments, that cracks in a few big stocks would do broad damage. Fourteen out of the seventeen banks included in the data have I.B.M., the market's biggest stock, as their No. 1 holding (the other three have it in second place) and better than half have 7 percent or more of their common-stock assets in that one company. (One bank, Chemical, has 13 percent.)

The tendency to bunch their investments in the same few big stocks suggests that the banks have created a kind of neutralized environment in which any one bank will find it extremely difficult to achieve a standout performance. These circumstances should logically prove most adverse to the banks that in the past have done better than others.

Morgan, however, disagrees that superior performance has become harder to achieve; one of its executives describes this premise as another example of the "mythologies" that are forever being created by Wall Street. It is Morgan's contention that the banks will continue to disagree about certain important stocks—as, for example, they are now disagreeing about Polaroid. Other banks also react testily to the thought that they have been "neutralized" and predict that the men will keep separating themselves from the boys.

Still, the banks do not feel at ease with the present degree of concentration, since they appreciate all too well the drastic price changes that can take place if a stock goes bad and everybody, as the saying goes, tries to get through the door at once. "Yes," says Quentin Ford, head of trust investments for Bankers Trust, "it does bother me that everybody is doing the same thing." But he finds "solace" in the quality of his research and is none too surprised that research leads other banks to so many of the same stocks.

CONCEPTS AND PHILOSOPHY

A Letter to a Friend

Arthur Ashley Sykes

In 1717, Arthur Ashley Sykes wrote *A Letter to a Friend,* which was printed in London as a pamphlet. In it, Sykes explains the essential role of sustained trustworthiness in establishing credit for an individual or for a public body and warns against taking an expedient course, no matter how temptingly advantageous it may appear for the present. This lesson, never more pertinent than today, has had to be learned over and over again through the years.

Sir,

Your, Project of raising Money for this Years Service, or of paying Debts by *Taxing* or *Lowering the Interest of the Funds,* meets, I think, with too much Approbation amongst some People, who look no farther than *Themselves,* and consider only the *Present* Difficulty, regardless of the Consequences of their Proceedings. The Importance of the Case seems to require that every body should contribute what they can to set this Matter in a true Light, and Examine, without Prejudice, how much the *Interest* of our Country, its *Reputation* and *Honour,* its *future* Good or Evil may be affected by it. This I can assure you, that as I am not concerned in any of the Funds, and *Interest* cannot mislead me in Prejudice to this Project; so the rack-four Shillings in the Pound which I pay to the Land-Tax, is a Motive which would make me *favour* it, if I were not very apprehensive of its fatal Consequences. I cannot but think that *Conscience* is concerned, and *natural Honesty,* and *Publick Justice,* and

Reprinted from *A Letter to a Friend* (London, 1717), pp. 3–8.

the *Credit* of the Nation: Every thing that is *Sacred* and *inviolable* in *Property,* is nearly affected; All *Obligations* will be in a way of being cancell'd, and in a Word, an indelible Character of *Injustice* cast upon us. I may be mistaken perhaps in my Notions, or mis-informed of the nature of your Project; However I will endeavour to state the Case as fairly as I can, and shew the *Unreasonableness* of *Taxing* or *Lowering the Interest of the Funds.* The Case is This.

The Legislative, *i.e.* King, Lords, and Commons in Parliament assembled, has Occasion for, and *borrows* great Sums of Money of the Subject for the Common Service; and *oblige* Themselves to repay the Money borrowed in such a Term of Years, or sooner if they could, and give a *Parliamentary Security* to repay it; and as an *Encouragement* to the Lender, they engage to pay a certain *Specified Interest,* and enact that the Sums so lent should *not* be *liable* to any *Taxation.* Your Project is, to *Lower their Interests,* or which is the same thing, *to Tax these Funds,* in order to raise Money for, or lessen the Debts of the Nation.

Against this Project, however acceptable perhaps it may be to some, give me leave to propose my Objections, which proceed from neither Interest, nor Favour, nor any other View than the Good of my Country, and a sincere Desire that its *Credit* may remain unsullied to the latest Posterity. And

I*st,* To support and maintain a Mans *Private Credit,* 'tis absolutely necessary that the World have a fixt Opinion of the *Honesty* and *Integrity,* as well as Ability of a Person. If there be good Reason to Object against the One or the Other of These, his *Credit* sinks, no one chooses to *deal* with him, nor does any one care to *trust* him. This is so Universal a Rule, such a First Principle, that no Man ever call'd it in Question, or disputed its Truth; Nay, so uncontested in Practice, that neither *Art,* nor Superior Genius, has been ever able long to support *Credit,* when *upright open* Dealing, or *Performance* of Promises, of Covenants or Contracts, has been wanting. Indeed *Credit* is the natural Result of being persuaded of the Obligation of the Law of Nature, *Be Faithful to Contracts;* and therefore when once a Person is supposed to have laid aside that Principle, or by any *avowed* Acts declares that He thinks himself free from that Bond, 'tis impossible in the Nature of Things to place any *Confidence* in Him; every body is forced to be on his Guard; nor can they with *Assurance* transact any Business of Moment with him. *Uprightness* and *Honesty* are the Bands of humane Society, and *Credit* is not to be purchas'd, nor acquir'd, till by a continued Series of *fair* and *open* Actions the World is satisfied of our *Sincerity,* and *Integrity.*

As These then are the Basis of *Credit,* every Attempt to blast it, be it upon just or unjust Grounds, has this fatal Effect, that it raises *Jealousies* and *Surmises* in Peoples Minds, and in consequence lessens their Opinions of a Man; so much at least it lessens their Opinions, as Evil Rumors prevail upon them. Scarce ever was there an Evil Report spread abroad, but it gain'd over some credulous Persons, 'twas industriously propagated by a Mans Enemies, it met with Encouragement amongst some; and so far it *impaired* the *Credit* 'twas designed to lessen. And was it ever found an easy matter to *regain* the Reputation of *Honesty* and *Upright Dealing,* when these have been industriously struck at? Was it ever found, but that the Person (whom I suppose even unjustly treated) *lost* a vast deal of his *Credit,* and continued *injured,* notwithstanding all the Care that could be taken to recover his Good Name?

And indeed a *Readiness* and *Willingness* to perform ones Engagements is such a *Fundamental of Credit,* that all the Affluence of Money, and the most immense Riches are of no Consequence, if there be Ground for the *least* Suspicion of Disingenuity. The *Ability* of a Person without *Natural Justice,* rather makes Men *cautious* than *forward* to deal with him. And the Reason of it is plain, because by his *Power* he is able to keep a Creditor out of his Right longer, and to put him to infinite more Trouble and Inconvenience than otherwise 'twould be possible to do. *Honour* therefore and *Uprightness* must attend upon Riches and Ability, or else the meanest Honest Person shall have, a better *Credit* and a more settled good repute, than the Richest *Crassus* with all his Money.

This *true,* This *only* Foundation of *Credit* takes in all Cases, and all Persons, *Publick* as well as Private; National as well as Personal. Just and Honourable Practices, Fair and Open Dealings, a strict Performance of Contracts, a steddy Observance of Engagements will necessarily *gain Credit* every where; and Common Experience teaches us that a *Breach* in These as necessarily *destroys* it.

The Nature of the Game

Hal Arbit

Hal Arbit was a pioneer in passive investment management and, at Concord Capital, is concentrating on deliberately disruptive—or creative—approaches to investing. Here he observes the difficulties most investors—who fit new data into preexisting patterns—have in breaking out of their organizational routines to become truly creative.

There are characteristics of professional investing that make it challenging but also frustrating. . . .

Mental Data Processing

The first part of this paper will focus on how the professional investor processes data and why he has chosen that approach. The investment professional faces an awesome environment—one in which almost any event that occurs has some investment implication. The thought process that an investment professional uses to function in this kind of environment has implications for how he is organized and also how successful he will be.

Some scholars have suggested that we process information in the following manner.

In order for the mind to operate efficiently, it must be able to assemble data into patterns that are recognizable and reusable. Those patterns

Excerpted from *The Journal of Portfolio Management* 8 (Fall 1981), 5–9. New York, New York: Institutional Investor, Inc.

then become the basis for decisions and behavior. Once we have formed a pattern, the mind automatically attempts to fit any subsequent data that arrive into the existing pattern. If that is not possible, the next step is to try to combine *existing* patterns into a larger pattern that will accommodate the new data. Only as a last resort will the mind try to break down and restructure existing patterns. Indeed, the operant or pre-existing pattern controls our focus of attention, so that, once data become part of an existing pattern, it is difficult to free up or use that data in a different pattern.

Hence, this process becomes critically dependent on the sequence of arrival of new data. Since data at any given moment are processed into the operant existing pattern, data that have already been processed will determine how we view the new data. While this is an effective thought process for most purposes, it is not effective for encouraging creative thought.

One can think of data analysis as processing data through an existing pattern. In contrast, one can think of creativity or innovation as breaking down an existing pattern to free up the data stored in that pattern so as to create a new one. *The nature of professional investing as it has developed accentuates data analysis as opposed to innovation or creativity.*

The Heavy Heritage of Professional Investors

Professional investing is still in a very immature stage. Indeed it has yet to develop its own tools and perspective.

Consider the tools that the investment professional uses. Many of them have come directly from the accounting profession without being adapted to the purposes of a professional investor. This distinction might become clearer if one were to consider the history of the function of accounting. One can argue that the accounting system as we know it had its roots in the attempt by individuals to account for the success and failure of a specific shipping venture. The aim was not "truth," but rather an equitable and justifiable allocation of profits and losses on a specific one-time venture. The focus was on the past. The major difference between the accounting profession and the investment profession is that the investment professional is concerned with the future and the accountant is concerned with the past.

Further, the profession's perspective on investing is still dominated by the perspective of the legal profession: Prudence is essential. And prudence is defined as acting like a typical, knowledgeable investor in the same circumstances. Prudence is using the tried and true. Following precedent—a cornerstone of law—was made the cornerstone of investing. This may be appropriate if one's objective is to accept the risk and returns offered by the market, but not if one expects to achieve a return in excess of the market. One is unlikely to beat the consensus if one is obliged to do things and analyze things the same way as the consensus. This focus on precedent increases the distrust of what is new: If it has not made money, it is not practical. And if it is not practical, you certainly don't want to use it to try to make money.

In addition to these external influences, almost all of a professional investor's training orients him toward analysis and away from creativity. His training in business school is analytical and his training on the job is an analytical apprenticeship. He tends to work in a highly structured environment. It is structured in the sense that his organization has already accepted and established a framework for doing analysis that is not challenged and that forces a certain perspective. His co-workers have similar investment training, philosophies, and points of view. If there is an investment point of view in the organization, the organization will hire people who either already share that point of view or are expected to be trained to accept that viewpoint.

Organizational Drags

Once in an organization, the investment professional is expected to focus on solutions to specific problems but is not expected to examine the nature of the problem itself. Given the way the mind works, however, accepting the definition of the problem greatly influences how one will see potential solutions to the problem.

The environment is also structured in that the specialization of the typical analyst insures that he will be inundated with specifics as to his area of expertise and not be expected or even able to draw connections that transcend his own area of expertise. Indeed, since he knows that the competition is out there waiting to pounce on any new bit of data in order to give themselves an edge, he is so concerned about keeping up with the competition that he cannot step back from the day-to-day pressure and develop some perspective.

His training also makes him feel much more comfortable interacting in an adversary environment. When an idea is presented, the immediate reaction is to evaluate it, to see its flaws so that it can be discarded. To be "acceptable," an idea must be plausible, defensible, and relevant as soon as it is uttered, since no one can afford to "look foolish." While this type of analysis is necessary, it should occur only at the appropriate stage in the idea generation process. If it is used when ideas are initially generated, it inhibits pattern restructuring and innovation. This is particularly important, as the new idea is often being evaluated within the context of the current idea. There is also a tendency to ignore a suggested idea that may not be able to stand alone. These ideas are often prematurely discarded, in that they could have been usable if combined with other ideas (be they past or future ones). This is especially true in investments where relationships tend not only to change but to be quite complex. Finally, this environment increases the chances that the idea that survives is not necessarily the best, but the idea with the strongest supporter.

If the profession produces information processors and analyzers rather than individuals who question the underlying structure, there are implications for market efficiency. Since most investment professionals process data and do that quite well, the winner of the game becomes the one who can integrate the data into the existing structure most quickly, rather than the one who can use the data to restructure the existing pattern. It is possible for the market to be efficient with respect to the former and quite inefficient with respect to the latter.

For example, most investment organizations take the approach of segmenting the world into basically similar pre-defined groups, such as industries or economic sectors. They then analyze or discard information to the extent that it fits into this pre-defined structure. The benefit of this approach is that the organization can process vast amounts of data efficiently. On the other hand, this institutionalization of pre-defined groupings reinforces the individual's tendency to become a tool of the pattern as well as using the pattern as a tool. The danger is that new information, if it does not fit easily into the existing frame of reference, will tend to be ignored or discredited. Tremendous amounts of energy go into protecting status quo rather than incorporating new concepts. How much scientific insight has come from the individual who, instead of fitting data into a pre-existing framework, tried to hypothesize a new framework that would be more conducive to the new information!

Reliance on these pre-defined groupings tends to be based on relationships and variables that have been most stable in the past. The normal assumption therefore tends to be that a factor that was dominant in one period will continue to be important in another. This leads to the unfortunate tendency of money managers and plan sponsors to organize their information flow and diversification process to protect themselves from the most recent traumatic experience. Yet the professional investor might be of more value to his client if he were able to focus on seeing new patterns. While a new pattern may be a relatively rare event, it is the usual consequence of severe trauma; it may also have much greater impact than processing data.

Even a partial shift toward restructuring and creating new patterns and away from reliance on processing data through existing patterns would have a dramatic impact on the typical investment organization. This is so because of the increased demand and need for intellectual and theoretical support. It is much more difficult to conceive of a relationship that can be supported by a theoretical foundation than it is to put incoming data into a neatly accepted slot.

The Enervating Environment

The very nature of professional investing places unusual pressures on the professional investor's ego, sense of security, and comfort with the external world. Most of these stem from the nature of investment risk and the level of competition. . . .

The Frailty of Judgements

Once the manager has formed his portfolio, that portfolio's record will include a large amount of noise as well as any skill. Aside from such problems as accurate measurement of risk or the correct benchmark portfolio to use, this huge amount of variability or noise in returns means that an investor's past performance will be of almost no help in predicting his future performance.

Yet, the typical investor is judged—primarily on past performance. Not only do we judge him on a basis that tells little about his skill, but we expect him to be able to explain to the client in a knowing manner what is essentially noise: What happened to your performance this quarter/this year? Did you have some insight that the market simply hasn't recognized yet? Did you miss some other bit of insight that the market had already impounded in the price? Did some event occur that swamped the importance of your insight?

The final assault on the professional investor's ego is probably the most difficult to accept. It is the notion that, in terms of excess return, being a good professional investor isn't enough. In most other endeavors being good, i.e. a good attorney, provides value-added to the client. Investing is unusual, in that the collective judgement of all the participants (weighted by the amount of money they control) is reflected in the price of the stock and available for free. It is like trying to guess the number of jelly beans in a large jar. The average estimate of all the participants will tend to be more accurate than the guess of any particular contestant. While any individual's estimate will be too high or too low, the estimates will average out to a fairly good approximation of the correct number if there are no systematic biases.

The same concept is at work in the market. If the level of ability of enough market participants is "good," then being one of those good investors at the margin will not earn a client an excess return. Thus, if a professional investor is to earn excess returns for his client, being good is insufficient—he must be exceptional.

Is the Game Worth the Effort?

This paper attempted to examine two characteristics of professional investing: the analytical thought process and the investor's relationship to his environment. I suggested that the profession of investing is oriented towards processing data rather than pattern restructuring. Further, I argued that pattern restructuring by its very nature was meant to be upsetting to the existing status quo. The paper went on to consider the pressures put on the professional investor from the many uncontrollable factors in his environment. These reduce the likelihood that an individual would choose to increase the seeming chaos in his environment by consciously questioning the patterns that he currently employs.

The conclusion of this paper is not that the game isn't worth playing. It only means that the more one understands the nature of the game, the more one is able to make thoughtful decisions about how to play and win. . . .

On Speculating Successfully

Philip L. Carret

Phil Carret is still investing—successfully—an amazing 55 years after he wrote *The Art of Speculation* from which these rules are taken.

———— ■ ————

Twelve Commandments for Speculators

As in any business there are standards of management which cannot be disregarded by the business man, so in speculative investment it is possible to formulate certain rules which must be followed intelligently if success is to be attained. The speculator will never be a success if he attempts to follow any set of rules blindly. There will always be exceptions, he must apply his intelligence keenly in any given situation. . . .

Twelve precepts for the speculative investor may be stated as follows:

1. Never hold fewer than ten different securities covering five different fields of business.
2. At least once in six months reappraise every security held.
3. Keep at least half the total fund in income-producing securities.
4. Consider yield the least important factor in analyzing any stock.
5. Be quick to take losses, reluctant to take profits.
6. Never put more than 25% of a given fund into securities about which detailed information is not readily and regularly available.

Excerpted from *The Art of Speculation* (Burlington, Vermont, 1979; originally published 1930), Chapter 19, pp. 342–64, by permission of Fraser Publishing Company.

7. Avoid "inside information" as you would the plague.
8. Seek facts diligently, advice never.
9. Ignore mechanical formulas for valuing securities.
10. When stocks are high, money rates rising, business prosperous, at least half a given fund should be placed in short-term bonds.
11. Borrow money sparingly and only when stocks are low, money rates low or falling, and business depressed.
12. Set aside a moderate proportion of available funds for the purchase of long-term options on stocks of promising companies whenever available.

Minimizing Chance

The first rule given suggests a minimum standard of diversification. It is just as important in speculation as in investment that a given fund be divided among several baskets. Diversification accomplishes three important results for the speculator. It minimizes the factor of chance, allows for an occasional error of judgment and minimizes the importance of the unknown factor. As in every other field of human activity, chance plays its part in speculation. An earthquake or some other unforeseeable "act of God" may make a mockery of the best-laid plans. No such accident will affect all securities equally, however, and diversification affords the best possible protection against the effect of accidental factors. Errors of judgment are likewise inescapable. Even the most astute speculator is likely to arrive at wrong conclusions from the data in hand 20% to 25% of the time. If he stakes his entire fund on one security about which his conclusions are wrong, he will suffer heavy loss. On the other hand, a 25% margin of error in judgment will not seriously affect the speculator who has scattered his commitments among ten different securities.

The most important factor affecting the value of any single security at any given moment is the unknown factor. Not even the president of a company knows all the facts affecting the intrinsic value of its securities. The speculator must allow a considerable margin for the unknown, even in the case of companies which make frequent reports of their condition and make an honest attempt to keep their stockholders and the public fully informed regarding their affairs. By sufficient diversification these unknown factors affecting individual securities cancel each other. The loss which is due to the unknown factor in one case will be counterbalanced by an unexpectedly large profit in another.

A Psychological Difficulty

It is conventional advice to the investor that he should go over his holdings in search of weak spots at least annually. The speculator will naturally watch his holdings much more closely. The second rule means something more than a mere scanning of his list of commitments and calculation of the paper profit or loss that they show. It means that the speculator should seek so far as possible to reanalyze each commitment from a detached standpoint. Psychologically this is a very difficult thing to do, to consider dispassionately a venture in which he has already risked his funds. Nevertheless, the speculator should make a determined effort to do just this. If he has 100 shares of a given stock, for example, which is selling at 90, he should disregard entirely the price that he paid for it and ask himself this question: "If I had $9000 cash today and wished to purchase some security, would I choose that stock in preference to every one of the thousands of other securities available to me?" If the answer is strongly in the negative, he should sell the stock. It should make not the slightest difference in this connection whether the stock cost 50 or 130. That is a fact which is entirely beside the point, though the average individual will give it considerable weight.

Patience Essential

It is not suggested that the speculator undertake this process of reanalysis much more frequently than once in six months. If he tries to do it oftener, he is likely to fall into the evil and usually fatal habit of frequently switching his commitments. One of the essential qualifications of the successful speculator is patience. It may take years for the market in a given stock to reflect in any large degree the values which are being accumulated behind it. Twenty years of plowing earnings back into property were followed in the case of the Southern Railway by an advance in its common stock from 25 to 120 within two years. Careful analysis may detect values far in excess of market price behind a given stock. The market may not reflect these values until the combination of a bull market and a change in dividend policy supplies the necessary impetus. Even in a bull market a sound stock may lag behind the procession in a discouraging manner for weeks or months. The trader who is always looking for "action" in the market will usually jump from one stock to another during the course of a bull movement only to find at the end that he has made far less money than he would have made by putting his money in ten or a dozen carefully chosen issues at the beginning and holding them.

The Preservation of Investment Value

Edward Sherwood Mead
Julius Grodinsky

Developing a sound and useful frame of reference within which to consider investment in general—and specific investments in particular—has always been a high art. Here is one of the better achievements, taken from Chapter 25 of the authors' 1939 book.

This discussion of investment income has reached certain conclusions:

1. Obsolescence is a universal characteristic of industry. In expanding industries it is latent, overbalanced by the forces of growing demand. In declining industries, obsolescence is an active infection, certain, if not checked by the application of remedies (corrective factors), first to weaken and then destroy its victims.

2. Obsolescence can be recognized by certain symptoms. The most important symptom, ranking with the rise of body temperature in medical diagnosis, is stationary demand. This primary symptom is accompanied by others: (a) rising prices, (b) emphasis on capital expenditures on betterments, as contrasted with additions, (c) the borrowing of money.

3. When these symptoms are recognized, management attempts to restore earnings by the application of correctives, either through cost reduction or by the shift of production to lines of expanding demand.

Reprinted from *Ebb and Flow of Investment Values* (New York: D. Appleton-Century Company, 1939), Chapter 25, pp. 457–67.

4. The successful application of demand correctives depends upon (a) the possession of a non-specialized plant; (b) upon the quality of management that corresponds to the flexibility of plant; (c) upon the possession of large cash resources above the working-capital requirements of the business, which can be applied to develop the new lines, and (d) upon an efficient and well-maintained research department developed in advance of the need.

5. There is no instance on record among the corporations whose securities are listed on the New York Stock Exchange where the application of cost and quality correctives has revised the downward trend of profits. Cost and quality correctives do not operate upon demand, and so are unable to remedy the trouble, which is due to declining demand.

6. Declining industries, therefore, usually continue to decline until they reach the point where they pay nothing to the investor. This characterization applies with peculiar force to public-utility industries whose profits are limited by law, which are forced to inflate their debt during their period of expansion, and which, when the evil days draw nigh, have no adequate cash resources which might be used to apply demand correctives.

7. Investment in any security issued by companies in any industry is permanent. Losses cannot be avoided—by the entire body of investors—by shifting the ownership and the risks of ownership from one to another. Like the river Thames in Blackstone's famous simile, to describe the corporation—the body of investors remains, although the membership of the body is changing every instant.

This is the paradox of investment. Some investors can preserve their capital intact (barring the effect of sweeping commodity price changes, seriously impairing the purchasing power of money) by shifting their holdings, when symptoms of decay are recognized, to holdings in well-managed corporations operating in expanding industries and whose managements, plants, and financial resources make possible the shifting of production to keep pace with the shifting demand. For the mass of investors, however, and especially for the institutional investor, with their immense holdings of securities, such shifting is impossible. These investors make the market. They can sell only to themselves. They are fixed in their positions. ''O wretched man that I am, who shall deliver me from the body of this death.''

This situation is fraught with danger. The financial structure of the United States is built upon the investment structure of its major industries. Many of the bonds and mortgages issued by private corporations and public (governmental) corporations (exclusive of the bonds issued or guaranteed by Federal and State Governments) are exposed to the hazards of obsolescence. . . . Existing industries, infected by incurable obsolescence, cannot, as a practical matter, be reconstructed. A substantial number of industries, still prosperous, are threatened with active obsolescence.

On the other hand stands the imposing group of expanding industries, with simple capital structures, vast cash reserves, progressive managements, advancing profits, and dividends. Only a small part of the securities of the companies in these industries, aside from light and power securities, are found in the portfolios of life-insurance companies or savings and commercial banks. Property-insurance companies have them, and many private foundations draw large revenues from oil, chemical, and tobacco, among others. As sound investments, however, they are not fully accepted. The conservative manager of trust funds, even as the New York banking department forbids him to purchase— but does not order him to sell—three billions of railroad bonds; as he is forced to abandon the channels of investment tried and true, looks back longingly to the days when simple arithmetic, with an occasional use of logarithms, could solve any investment problem. He knows that he must shift his buying to new channels, and yet he does so with hesitation and regret. Meanwhile cash and government bonds pile up, and finance committees are at their wits' end to invest their funds to yield 3 percent.

In suggesting a solution of this problem, we must base that solution upon the main conclusions which have emerged from the facts already presented: that industry is everywhere, and to an increasing extent, subject to change, that obsolescence is its outstanding characteristic. It follows, therefore, that a sound investment policy must recognize the fact of change and the dangers of change. Nothing is permanent. In the process of transforming one mechanism, process, or product into others more appealing to the buyer, or cheaper and more efficient, existing companies, no matter how liquid their resources, no matter how progressive their management, cannot guarantee that twenty years from now they will be as profitable as they are today. Business structures, no matter how firmly founded, contain the germs of obsolescence. Other managements, in charge of other corporations, in the expanding industries of other days, have broken their hearts and gone to their graves, leaving little save memories behind them, as the gulfs of obsolescence closed over them. Investment policy must recognize this fact. . . .

As long as securities, senior or junior, debt or stock, common or preferred, remain outstanding, they are at risk. The risk may be small, but it is always there. These small risks, like clouds no larger than a man's hand, may expand into serious hazards. As the amount of the outstanding issue is reduced, the risk diminishes. Current-assets restrictions, enforced by prohibition of dividends, or even by threat of default, are well enough in their way, as admonitions to management, but they are not often enforced. Nor has the stipulation of a minimum ratio of stock to bonds, a provision that both the Interstate Commerce Commission and some state commissions have endeavored to enforce, availed to protect the bondholders whose bonds were sold in the land of peace, and matured in the swelling of Jordan. When latent obsolescence develops into active obsolescence, bonds and stocks go down and out together.

The sinking fund reduces the income paid to original subscribers, or purchasers of the bonds which carry the sinking fund. It reduces the amount available for dividends. It reduces the amount of bonds that a given amount of earnings will support. A substantial amount of profits, which would otherwise be available for dividends and to support junior bonds, must be used to return this capital to the investor. When large sinking funds shorten the average maturity of bonds, permanent investment is made more difficult. The investor is forced to shift and change his holdings. His money was at risk. Now he has some or all of it back. He has the opportunity to correct his mistakes, to revise his judgment. He is not forced, because he has lost confidence in his investment, to risk a loss of principal by sale. Within a few years, a substantial amount is restored to him. This he can reinvest in other securities more to his liking. The general use of sinking funds, today, is rightly considered to be insurance against the risks of ownership obsolescence. It is the more valuable because it protects not only the prudent and well-informed investor, who, if a small holder, may need no protection, but the mass of the ignorant and uninformed.

But this is not enough. Few bonds, aside from serials, are paid off in twenty years. Fortunate are their holders to receive back half their principal before maturity. One-third is a more reasonable expectation. To the protection against individual ownership depreciation, as well as the depreciation of institutional and estate holdings which are too large to be sold without heavy losses, there should be added two additional measures of protection: (1) the diversification of holdings, and (2) amortization reserves maintained by the investor. . . .

It is not diversification that is at fault. Institutional investors have not failed to diversify. They have diversified too largely in decadent industries. . . .

Diversification is a sound and necessary principle of investment, but, to exert its full effect of stabilizing values, it should be applied to securities of expanding industries. These are the industries that operate within the prevailing trend of demand, the companies that keep abreast of the time, the companies with large cash reserves, progressive managements, flexible plants, and continued expansion into new fields. The superiority of even common stocks of financially expanding companies over the senior bonds of declining companies is manifest. Diversification in the expanding groups will minimize the risks of mistaken selections. Since 1930, the losses in rubber and oil refining would have been offset by the gains of electrical equipment, chemicals, and containers. On balance, the expanding industries, over a period of years, can absorb the inevitable mistakes of selection among them.

. . . Institutional prejudice against common stock as a vehicle for the investment of trust funds is still strong, although not as strong as it was before the collapse of railroad bonds and real-estate mortgages. This prejudice must give way to the facts. Can it be doubted that if the money invested in the three billion dollars of railroad bonds recently thrown out of the New York legal investment list had been placed in common stocks of a group of companies operating in the expanding industries—this investment could have been easily made during the twenties—the present situation of the fund would have been much greater than that received from bond investments? If experience is a safe guide to future policy, the lessons of the recent past should not be ignored. Stocks should partially take the place of bonds in investment portfolios.

Valid objections to stocks, as compared with bonds, have been removed both by the event and by a recognition of the immobility of institutional investment. As we have shown in the preceding chapter, a large number of common stocks have shown larger returns over a period of years than the senior securities of competing industries. Institutions are not traders. They purchase income. Their returns do not, like those of many investment trusts, come from market realizations. Although many changes are always being made as opportunity offers, the bulk of their holdings remain untouched. This permanency of holding is involved in the size of the holdings. Corporate trustees are faced with the same necessity to hold what they buy, because they cannot discriminate between individual trusts. Too long has the reverence for bonds persisted in law and custom. The investor has already paid a heavy price for his secured priorities. "Though He slay me, yet will I trust Him. . . ."

The amortization of ownership, supplementing the retirement policies of companies that have issued senior securities, based upon diversification within expanding industries, irrespective of the type of securities issued, and confined to companies that are able and determined to keep ahead of the trend of demand, is a policy which, if followed, will reduce to the minimum the hazards of investment. No policy, however conservative, can altogether remove these hazards. To the small return, which at any point of time the investor may count upon, may be added the results of sound judgment in the selection of companies, and of good fortune, "luck," which, as La Rochefoucauld puts it, with good temper, rules the world.

Investment Experiences

Henry G. Davis

Henry Davis enjoyed a distinguished career as an investor and investment advisor from the 1920s to the 1970s. To crystalize his own thinking and to elicit the views of others he respected, he wrote occasional long memoranda examining central concepts. Here, in 1970, he discusses experience with market timing—and concludes that issue selection is far more promising for investment success.

Introduction

This will introduce to you an investment approach which does not rely on some individual's ability and prescience successfully to call turns in the stock market. It first found its way on paper back in 1938. . . . We knew that . . . we should put down on paper the lessons learned so they could be re-read periodically and so not be as quickly forgotten as a New Year's resolution. This work dealt particularly with the selection of the securities to put into portfolios but we knew also that credence should be given to timing as these severe periodic interruptions to the upward trend often cost even the best selections from one to five years of their normal and natural growth. Our intended approach to solve the proper time to become cautious relied not on any particular level in stock prices, but upon continuous selling whenever economic activity approached rates of utilization which had only been exceeded for brief periods of the past. . . .

Excerpted from a 1970 memorandum.

As a clue to finding the key we listed all the rich we knew and what method each had used. . . . It was soon obvious that if we eliminated the fortunes which were gained through marriage or inheritance, the others fell into two categories. Nine out of ten were wealthy because they had been long term stockholders in successful enterprises, the remainder because they had ample liquid buying power at the rare but repetitive times when bargains were available. Obviously, these two groups had found correct answers. . . .

In the small group who had concentrated on the "when" we were surprised to find so few individuals who attained wealth because they sold in 1929 or had gone short in bear markets. There were only a few who had been individually lucky enough to make money both ways by alternating between bullish and bearish positions. This is to be expected, for an individual is basically inclined to be either optimistic or pessimistic and only performs well when his character is in tune with the climate. The successful examples, the Rothschilds, Baruchs, etc., were people who had accumulated buying power long before bargains presented themselves. These people had sold when they felt prices were fair without waiting for their holdings to be obviously overvalued. . . .

It impressed us that the unsuccessful proponents of timing had also been very long term in their concept. . . . One canny Scot at the turn of the century discovered a clue to warn him when a cash position was indicated. . . . In those days there was no Federal Reserve Index, no GNP, nor any of the mass of statistics available today, but cannily he found a substitute. His weekly train ride between New York and Newport took him through the then industrial heart of the U.S. When he saw the factories burning their lights at night, he sold stocks, and then patiently waited to rebuy them until the factories were shut down with grass growing in the yards where they stocked their inventories.

As was said earlier, back in 1938 we thought we could borrow these tools. . . . We realized each cyclical peak probably would look so different from the past that it would again fool all but the occasionally lucky. We set up statistics to show us how close to capacity or past peaks the key industries were operating and resolved to be continuing sellers whenever three-quarters of them were operating at rates which had only been exceeded one-tenth of the time in the past.

To recapitulate, we set the course of our investment philosophy within these two guides—both long term in concept. Any conversion of stocks into cash was not to be timed by a committee's enlightened judgment but became a matter of a slow but continuous process whenever activity in most areas of the economy was at levels which had rarely been exceeded in the past. . . .

Second, we determined that any stocks we did buy should be sought as permanent possessions, to be held at least so long as their performance continued satisfactory due to the more favorable factors affecting the areas in which they were operating. Current price, therefore, was only a minor consideration in our decisions. . . . We resolved . . . not [to] sell the best even if we recognized they were "overpriced" until we had eliminated the less shining ones to provide the cash for a cutback.

Relative Potential of the Two Approaches— "What and When"

Selection is a very much more potent tool in producing a good record than is timing. First, it is more possible of accomplishment for it takes just one decision to get aboard, if you stay there once on, whereas timing, to record its potential, requires frequent decisions when to go out and when to go back in. One miss and you have lost your boat. It requires almost impossible odds to have your guess prove right a number of times in succession. Second, you can prove theoretically that staying in the better growth stocks will produce better results than even a perfect timing formula.

For my own enlightenment, I made some computations as to the results which could have been attained in the last fifty years if one sold every stock he owned at each important market peak and reinvested every cent of the proceeds on the day of the subsequent low. The answer is phenomenal. Had he started with owning but one share of each name in the Average, he would own now 573 shares of each. Of course, this is impossible. A more realistic assumption would be that he sold half and kept half. Mathematics play strange tricks, for on this assumption he would have but 28 shares of each today even if he used the same optimum dates for his buying and selling. . . .

To compare his perfect timing record with what you might have gained in a quality growth stock is not realistic over a period as long as 50 years for no company, even an I.B.M., stays in its fast growing stage for that long. A more practical comparison would cover just the postwar era. If before each of the six such declines, an individual originally owning one share of each stock in the Dow Jones Industrials had sold everything the high day before the sell-off and reinvested all these proceeds on the low day following, his account today would have built up 4.7 shares of each of the thirty stocks. If his selling had been limited to one-half his equities at each top, his portfolio today would hold 2.3 shares of each. To accomplish this record his timing guesses would have to have been absolutely correct twelve times in succession—hardly a likelihood.

Now let us compare this to what could have been gained from buying and holding continuously through the 25-year period one of the better growth stocks. The comparison used is identical, starting with a portfolio owning one share of each of the 30 stocks in the Average, being sold in 1946 and the proceeds all reinvested in the one stock. If this stock were sold in 1970 and reinvested in the Average—how many shares of the DJIA would it rebuy?

Minnesota Mining	15.5 shares
Connecticut General Life	20 shares
I.B.M.	32 shares
Tampax	83 shares
Avon Products	157 shares

NOTE: The above five names were selected to avoid an argument that in 1946 the example selected was an obscure stock not likely to have been bought until some years later after most of its gain had been realized. To the contrary four of these stocks enjoyed a fairly constant rate of gain over the whole 25 years. Only in the case of Connecticut General was most of its gain realized in the earlier half of the period but surely in 1946 this was not an obscure unknown stock so it qualifies as a fair comparison.

All growth stocks do not enjoy such a long youth as 25 years, but there are many examples of shorter spans of holding producing as great or even larger appreciation, as:

American Express	10 shares	1955–1970
Burroughs	14 shares	1965–1970
Holiday Inns	50 shares	1948–1969
H.&R. Block	136 shares	1965–1970
University Computing	166 shares	1966–1968
Polaroid	190 shares	1953–1969
Automatic Data Processing	240 shares	1953–1970
Xerox	250 shares	1953–1970
Lum's	900 shares	1964–1969

This brief list out of a hundred possible examples confirms a conclusion that selection is many, many times as potent in shaping investment results as timing even though the timing has been perfect beyond any human being's ability to produce. . . .

This evidence explains why the performance of any portfolio I have ever heard boasted about by the parties responsible, whether it has been operated here, or in Switzerland, Great Britain or Holland, when dissected as to how the results were obtained inevitably pointed to the continuous long holding of one, two or three situations whose price had multiplied many-fold. What had been done in the balance of the portfolio did not matter much so long as these jewels continued to be held. A Xerox, an I.B.M., a Hoffman-La Roche has covered up countless errors the same manager might have made.

It is much more important to hold on to winners than to weed out the losers. . . .

An Investment Philosophy

Over the years countless systems have been designed to make money in the stock market. They inevitably are constructed from historical data and are, of course, designed to have worked profitably if they had been used as a guide through the months or years through which the economy had just passed, but few have fulfilled this promise long in the future. . . .

After the 1929–1932 debacle, the Cowles Institution made an intensive study of the success of the systems which had been in vogue and concluded that the fruits of success in all but one were no better than could have been obtained by the toss of a coin. The one exception was the assumption that what had been happening was more likely to continue than change, a rule which applies to almost everything in life besides the stock market. This, as you recognize, is the basis for the famous "Dow Theory." Unfortunately, that approach involved suffering a substantial depreciation before there has been a definite confirmation that a long-term decline has set in or conversely a substantial loss of incipient gain waiting for the confirmation of a reversal upturn. Consequently, much of its possible benefits are lost while one sat on the sidelines waiting for proof. . . . The Dow Theory has been so widely followed that for short periods it can make its own success for a time whenever adherents act on its signals. Yet even so, there are an increasing number of instances when the declines or advances which it confirms live only for weeks or occasionally for days and, so in the end produced more harm than good.

Since the Twenties more sophisticated indicators of the future have been devised:

1. Colonel Leonard Ayres' breadth theory still has many disciples. It is based on the percentage of daily price moves among listed stocks which move in concord with the Average compared with those going in the opposite direction.

2. The odd lot theory also has many devotees. It is based on the belief that at crucial points the little trader is always wrong, but there have been many times when he can prove that he has been more astute than the professional—as before the recent decline.

3. Barron's Confidence Index, which measures the spread in yields between the highest grade and lower grade bonds. Of course, when it is large there are worries as to the storms ahead for the economy.

4. The very sophisticated Eliott Wave Theory, which carries the Dow principle considerably further, has always been beyond my understanding although I was trained as a mathematician. I know even among those who claim to have fathomed its workings there are long periods of disagreement as to precisely what part of what wave the market is actually on, an argument that is sometimes not settled until further years of history have made the correct answer identifiable.

. . . It has been an axiom on the Street that whenever a large group of investment soothsayers take a vote of where the market is headed and over 75% see the same path, within a very brief period it will confound the many by doing the opposite.

Nevertheless, a few investors do make money in securities, as we can see because the big white houses on the hill are always occupied. When we examine the source of this wealth, we find it has almost never been derived from stock market trading. It took me ten years to realize that the man did not exist who could call the necessary turns in the market and that successful formulae were always long term in concept—either sticking with a successful enterprise through thick or thin or reaping the benefits from having ample liquidity when bargains were available.

Successful investment obviously will not flow easily from either of these sources unless costly errors simultaneously are eliminated so that the inevitable mistakes never aggregate enough to detract from the pull of the gains. A sound philosophy of investing, therefore, cannot stop with the "do's" but also must stress a long list of the "don'ts". . . . We must disabuse ourselves of three of the commonest "don'ts" which much of the public still steadfastly refuses to recognize as such.

1. That there exists anyone or any system having sufficient acumen to gauge the market's future behavior to time one's moves in and out. . . . It is a rare man who is built with the ability to subdue his innate feelings and so permit himself to look first in one direction and then another. . . . I have known many who were adept at anticipating the time when stocks should be sold, which is the easiest lesson to learn if one recognizes and is not stimulated by the degree of speculation in stock trading. But most people are optimistic and are swayed by the crowd when this contagion grips all, as it has again in recent years. Wise selling of stocks does not provide the answer to success because to complete the circle it is necessary to get back in them at lower prices. . . .

If the Cowles Commission was right that the odds of successful timing are about one in two, then the odds of being twice right—that is, rebuying lower down—become four to one against the person who tries to catch the swing. . . .

2. A second source of common error is the buying of stocks for high income. . . . Just present a client with a long list of investment choices and he will invariably pick the one offering the highest present yield. Later, with the benefit of hindsight, one's records can prove easily that the client almost always would have done best by picking the choice offering the lowest yield. . . .

Too often high income is the product of a mature company. . . . So very often this company is approaching old age and declining earnings, so an apparent high yield is not an omen of things to come but a warning that the dividend is soon to be cut—and there goes the high yield.

3. A third common source of failure is to think that anything good ever comes cheap—except through luck or on "basket days." Common sense should tell us that nothing in a free market is ever cheap unless its value is to be affected by factors as yet unknown except possibly to a very few. There are thousands of experts assessing the value of stocks daily—if any security were really cheap today it would not be a week hence. Cheapness almost always indicates inferior quality or defectiveness somewhere. . . .

Human Foibles

George Ross Goobey

George Ross Goobey, a compelling presence and an engaging speaker and storyteller, has been called upon often to share with others the lessons learned as one of Britain's leading investors over the past half-century. Here he counsels against being captives of our own foibles.

———————

There is an old and, I think, misleading adage which runs ''always take a profit and you will never make a loss''. As a long term investor I have found it more profitable to run profits and cut losses. What I am really leading up to saying is that in considering whether one should sell an investment it is much better to ignore the price paid and to endeavour to judge the future of the Company on the facts of the situation in which the original cost of your own particular investment plays no part whatsoever. Unfortunately, however, human nature being what it is this cost factor seems to play the most important part and one is much more ready to sell an investment standing above the price paid for it than vice versa.

I am often asked to advise which security or securities in a portfolio should be sold when it is necessary to raise funds and it is quite apparent that the questioners own ideas are to sell the stock or stocks which are ''standing at a profit'', quite regardless of the particular Company's future investment prospects. I remember saying to one such enquirer on one of these occasions when he was obviously anxious to sell his best

Reprinted from an unpublished paper, 1963, by permission of the author.

stocks because they were standing at a profit over what he had paid for them "I think you would get a better result by using a pin to make your choice", but if he approached his problem from the right angle, namely, the "forward looking" rather than the "backward jobbing" he would find that he had decided to sell in most cases those which were standing at a loss on what he had paid for them. Time after time when I am confronted with a portfolio of investments I find that the majority are quite sound holdings, but at the bottom of the list there are a few worthless shares. On enquiry one usually elicits the explanation that although the holder had been frequently advised that the future of these shares was in danger, he could not bring himself to sell them at a loss on what had been paid for them with the result that eventually they had become entirely worthless.

There is also a type of investor who gets even more keen to buy when the price of a share falls below the price of his original purchase— "averaging" as it is called. It is a sort of human vanity which cannot admit that the original purchase was wrong and that therefore it must be an even better investment to purchase more shares at a cheaper price.

Barnum's Rules for Success in Business

Phinaeus T. Barnum

Phinaeus T. Barnum is best known for producing the world's first three-ring circus. He also wrote four books (including *The Life of P. T. Barnum,* from which these rules are taken), organized a model industrial community in East Bridgeport, Connecticut, and brought New York City its first hippopotamus.

1. *Select the kind of business that suits your natural inclination and temperament.* Some men are naturally mechanics; others have a strong aversion to any thing like machinery, and so on; one man has a natural taste for one occupation, and another for another. "I am glad that we do not all feel and think alike," said Dick Homespun, "for if we did, every body would think my gal, Sukey Snipes, the sweetest creature in all creation, and they would all be trying to court her at once."

I never could succeed as a merchant. I have tried it unsuccessfully several times. I never could be content with a fixed salary, for mine is a purely speculative disposition, while others are just the reverse; and therefore all should be careful to select those occupations that suit them best.

2. *Let your pledged word ever be sacred.* Never promise to do a thing without performing it with the most rigid promptness. Nothing is more valuable to a man in business than the name of always doing as he agrees, and that to the moment. A strict adherence to this rule, gives a man the command of half the spare funds within the range of his ac-

Reprinted from *The Life of P. T. Barnum* (New York: Redfield, 1885), Chapter 14, pp. 394–99.

quaintance, and always encircles him with a host of friends who may be depended upon in almost any conceivable emergency.

3. *Whatever you do, do with all your might.* Work at it if necessary early and late, in season and out of season, not leaving a stone unturned, and never deferring for a single hour that which can be done just as well *now*. The old proverb is full of truth and meaning, "Whatever is worth doing at all, is worth doing well." Many a man acquires a fortune by doing his business *thoroughly* while his neighbor remains poor for life because he only *half* does his business. Ambition, energy, industry, perseverance, are indispensable requisites for success in business.

4. *Sobriety.* Use no description of intoxicating drinks. As no man can succeed in business unless he has a *brain* to enable him to lay his plans, and *reason* to guide him in their execution, so, no matter how bountifully a man may be blessed with intelligence, if his brain is muddled, and his judgment warped by intoxicating drinks, it is impossible for him to carry on business successfully. How many good opportunities have passed never to return, while a man was sipping a "social glass" with his friend! How many foolish bargains have been made under the influence of the *nervine,* which temporarily makes its victim so *rich!* How many important chances have been put off until to-morrow, and thence for ever, because the wine-cup has thrown the system into a state of lassitude, neutralizing the energies so essential to success in business. The use of intoxicating drinks as a beverage is as much an infatuation as is the smoking of opium by the Chinese, and the former is quite as destructive to the success of the business man as the latter.

5. *Let hope predominate, but be not too visionary.* Many persons are always kept poor, because they are too *visionary.* Every project looks to them like certain success, and therefore they keep changing from one business to another, always in hot water, always "under the harrow." The plan of "counting the chickens before they are hatched" is an error of ancient date, but it does not seem to improve by age.

6. *Do not scatter your powers.* Engage in one kind of business only, and stick to it faithfully until you succeed, or until you conclude to abandon it. A constant hammering on one nail, will generally drive it home at last, so that it can be clinched. When a man's undivided attention is centered on one object, his mind will constantly be suggesting improvements of value, which would escape him if his brain were occupied by a dozen different subjects at once. Many a fortune has slipped through men's fingers by engaging in too many occupations at once.

7. *Engage proper employees.*   Never employ a man of bad habits, when one whose habits are good can be found to fill his situation. I have generally been extremely fortunate in having faithful and competent persons to fill the responsible situations in my business, and a man can scarcely be too grateful for such a blessing. When you find a man unfit to fill his station, either from incapacity or peculiarity of character or disposition, dispense with his services and do not drag out a miserable existence in the vain attempt to change his nature. It is utterly impossible to do so. "You cannot make a silk purse," etc. He was created for some other sphere. Let him find and fill it.

8. *Advertise your business. Do not hide your light under a bushel.* Whatever your occupation or calling may be, if it needs support from the public, *advertise* it thoroughly and efficiently, in some shape or other, that will arrest public attention. I freely confess that what success I have had in my life may fairly be attributed more to the public press than to nearly all other causes combined. There may possibly be occupations that do not require advertising, but I cannot well conceive what they are.

Men in business will sometimes tell you that they have tried advertising, and that it did not pay. This is only when advertising is done sparingly and grudgingly. Homoeopathic [sic] doses of advertising will not pay perhaps—it is like half a potion of physic, making the patient sick, but effecting nothing. Administer liberally, and the cure will be sure and permanent.

Some say, "they cannot afford to advertise;" they mistake—they cannot afford *not* to advertise. In this country, where everybody reads the newspapers, the man must have a thick skull who does not see that these are the cheapest and best medium through which he can speak to the public, where he is to find his customers. Put on the *appearance* of business, and generally the *reality* will follow. The farmer plants his seed, and while he is sleeping, his corn and potatoes are growing. So with advertising. While you are sleeping, or eating, or conversing with one set of customers, your advertisement is being read by hundreds and thousands of persons who never saw you, nor heard of your business, and never would, had it not been for your advertisement appearing in the newspapers.

9. *Avoid extravagance; and always live considerably within your income, if you can do so without absolute starvation!*   It needs no prophet to tell us that those who live fully up to their means, without any thought of a reverse in life, can never attain to a pecuniary independence.

Men and women accustomed to gratify every whim and caprice, will find it hard at first to cut down their various unnecessary expenses, and will feel it a great self-denial to live in a smaller house than they have been accustomed to, with less expensive furniture, less company, less costly clothing, a less number of balls, parties, theatre-goings, carriage ridings, pleasure excursions, cigar smokings, liquor-drinkings, etc., etc., etc.; but, after all, if they will try the plan of laying by a "nest-egg," or in other words, a small sum of money, after paying all expenses, they will be surprised at the pleasure to be derived from constantly adding to their little "pile," as well as from all the economical habits which follow in the pursuit of this peculiar pleasure.

The old suit of clothes, and the old bonnet and dress, will answer for another season; the Croton or spring water will taste better than champagne; a brisk walk will prove more exhilarating than a ride in the finest coach; a social family chat, an evening's reading in the family circle, or an hour's play of "hunt the slipper" and "blind man's buff," will be far more pleasant than a fifty or a five hundred dollar party, when the reflection on the *difference in cost* is indulged in by those who begin to know the *pleasures of saving*.

Thousands of men are kept poor, and tens of thousands are made so after they have acquired quite sufficient to support them well through life, in consequence of laying their plans of living on too expensive a platform. Some families in this country expend twenty thousand dollars per annum, and some much more, and would scarcely know how to live on a less sum.

Prosperity is a more severe ordeal than adversity, especially sudden prosperity. "Easy come easy go," is an old and true proverb. *Pride,* when permitted full sway, is the great undying cankerworm which gnaws the very vitals of a man's worldly possessions, let them be small or great, hundreds or millions. Many persons, as they begin to prosper, immediately commence expending for luxuries, until in a short time their expenses swallow up their income, and they become ruined in their ridiculous attempts to keep up appearances, and make a "sensation."

10. *Do not depend upon others.*   Your success must depend upon your own individual exertions. Trust not to the assistance of friends; but learn that every man must be the architect of his own fortune.

With proper attention to the foregoing rules, and such observation as a man of sense will pick up in his own experience, the road to competence will not, I think, usually be found a difficult one.

Mistakes of the First Twenty-Five Years (A Condensed Version)

Warren E. Buffett

Warren Buffett emerges as a frequent contributor to this collection primarily because he has so much of value to say and because he says it so very well. Here, in the 1989 Annual Report, he shares the lessons he has learned during his first quarter century as Berkshire Hathaway's principal, and controlling, shareholder.

———— ▬ ————

To quote Robert Benchley, "Having a dog teaches a boy fidelity, perseverance, and to turn around three times before lying down." Such are the shortcomings of experience. Nevertheless, it's a good idea to review past mistakes before committing new ones. So let's take a quick look at the last 25 years.

• My first mistake, of course, was in buying control of Berkshire. Though I knew its business—textile manufacturing—to be unpromising, I was enticed to buy because the price looked cheap. Stock purchases of that kind had proved reasonably rewarding in my early years, though by the time Berkshire came along in 1965 I was becoming aware that the strategy was not ideal.

Excerpted from the "Chairman's Letter," *Berkshire Hathaway, Inc. 1989 Annual Report,* by permission of the author.

If you buy a stock at a sufficiently low price, there will usually be some hiccup in the fortunes of the business that gives you a chance to unload at a decent profit, even though the long-term performance of the business may be terrible. I call this the "cigar butt" approach to investing. A cigar butt found on the street that has only one puff left in it may not offer much of a smoke, but the "bargain purchase" will make that puff all profit.

Unless you are a liquidator, that kind of approach to buying businesses is foolish. First, the original "bargain" price probably will not turn out to be such a steal after all. In a difficult business, no sooner is one problem solved than another surfaces—never is there just one cockroach in the kitchen. Second, any initial advantage you secure will be quickly eroded by the low return that the business earns. For example, if you buy a business for $8 million that can be sold or liquidated for $10 million and promptly take either course, you can realize a high return. But the investment will disappoint if the business is sold for $10 million in ten years and in the interim has annually earned and distributed only a few percent on cost. Time is the friend of the wonderful business, the enemy of the mediocre.

You might think this principle is obvious, but I had to learn it the hard way—in fact, I had to learn it several times over. Shortly after purchasing Berkshire, I acquired a Baltimore department store, Hochschild, Kohn, buying through a company called Diversified Retailing that later merged with Berkshire. I bought at a substantial discount from book value, the people were first-class, and the deal included some extras—unrecorded real estate values and a significant LIFO inventory cushion. How could I miss? So-o-o—three years later I was lucky to sell the business for about what I had paid. After ending our corporate marriage to Hochschild, Kohn, I had memories like those of the husband in the country song, "My Wife Ran Away With My Best Friend and I Still Miss Him a Lot."

I could give you other personal examples of "bargain-purchase" folly but I'm sure you get the picture: It's far better to buy a wonderful company at a fair price than a fair company at a wonderful price. . . . I was a slow learner. But now, when buying companies or common stocks, we look for first-class businesses accompanied by first-class managements.

• That leads right into a related lesson: Good jockeys will do well on good horses, but not on broken-down nags. Both Berkshire's textile business and Hochschild, Kohn had able and honest people running them. The same managers employed in a business with good economic characteristics would have achieved fine records. But they were never going to make any progress while running in quicksand.

I've said many times that when a management with a reputation for brilliance tackles a business with a reputation for bad economics, it is the reputation of the business that remains intact. I just wish I hadn't been so energetic in creating examples. My behavior has matched that admitted by Mae West: "I was Snow White, but I drifted."

• A further related lesson: Easy does it. After 25 years of buying and supervising a great variety of businesses, . . . I have *not* learned how to solve difficult business problems. What we have learned is to avoid them. To the extent we have been successful, it is because we concentrated on identifying one-foot hurdles that we could step over rather than because we acquired any ability to clear seven-footers.

The finding may seem unfair, but in both business and investments it is usually far more profitable to simply stick with the easy and obvious than it is to resolve the difficult. On occasion, tough problems must be tackled as was the case when we started our Sunday paper in Buffalo. In other instances, a great investment opportunity occurs when a marvelous business encounters a one-time huge, but solvable, problem as was the case many years back at both American Express and GEICO. Overall, however, we've done better by avoiding dragons than by slaying them.

• My most surprising discovery: the overwhelming importance in business of an unseen force that we might call "the institutional imperative." In business school, I was given no hint of the imperative's existence and I did not intuitively understand it when I entered the business world. I thought then that decent, intelligent, and experienced managers would automatically make rational business decisions. But I learned over time that isn't so. Instead, rationality frequently wilts when the institutional imperative comes into play.

For example: (1) As if governed by Newton's First Law of Motion, an institution will resist any change in its current direction; (2) Just as work expands to fill available time, corporate projects or acquisitions will materialize to soak up available funds; (3) Any business craving of the leader, however foolish, will be quickly supported by detailed rate-of-return and strategic studies prepared by his troops;

and (4) The behavior of peer companies, whether they are expanding, acquiring, setting executive compensation or whatever, will be mindlessly imitated.

Institutional dynamics, not venality or stupidity, set businesses on these courses, which are too often misguided. After making some expensive mistakes because I ignored the power of the imperative, I have tried to organize and manage Berkshire in ways that minimize its influence. . . .

• After some other mistakes, I learned to go into business only with people whom I like, trust, and admire. As I noted before, this policy of itself will not ensure success: A second-class textile or department-store company won't prosper simply because its managers are men that you would be pleased to see your daughter marry. However, an owner—or investor—can accomplish wonders if he manages to associate himself with such people in businesses that possess decent economic characteristics. Conversely, we do not wish to join with managers who lack admirable qualities, no matter how attractive the prospects of their business. We've never succeeded in making a good deal with a bad person.

• Some of my worst mistakes were not publicly visible. These were stock and business purchases whose virtues I understood and yet didn't make. It's no sin to miss a great opportunity outside one's area of competence. But I have passed on a couple of really big purchases that were served up to me on a platter and that I was fully capable of understanding. For Berkshire's shareholders, myself included, the cost of this thumb-sucking has been huge.

• Our consistently-conservative financial policies may appear to have been a mistake, but in my view were not. In retrospect, it is clear that significantly higher, though still conventional, leverage ratios at Berkshire would have produced considerably better returns on equity than the 23.8% we have actually averaged. Even in 1965, perhaps we could have judged there to be a 99% probability that higher leverage would lead to nothing but good. Correspondingly, we might have seen only a 1% chance that some shock factor, external or internal, would cause a conventional debt ratio to produce a result falling somewhere between temporary anguish and default.

We wouldn't have liked those 99:1 odds—and never will. A small chance of distress or disgrace cannot, in our view, be offset by a large chance of extra returns. If your actions are sensible, you are certain to get good results; in most such cases, leverage just moves things along faster. . . . I have never been in a big hurry: We enjoy the process far more than the proceeds—though we have learned to live with those also.

======

We hope in another 25 years to report on the mistakes of the first 50. If we are around in 2015 to do that, you can count on this section occupying many more pages than it does here.

The Policies that Guide Us

Charles E. Merrill
E. A. Pierce

Charles Merrill, likely with some assistance from E. A. Pierce and Robert Magowan, committed his firm to an explicit declaration of policies known within the firm as "The Ten Commandments." Here are two versions: The original, detailed 1940 letter from Merrill and Pierce to the partners and managers of Merrill Lynch, E. A. Pierce & Cassatt (in which note the absence of pension funds and mutual funds from its concluding list of investing institutions), and a short listing from the 1949 Annual Report of Merrill Lynch, Pierce, Fenner & Smith.

March 26, 1940

To Partners and Managers:

We are glad to be able, at last, to write you in some detail about this new firm of ours.

We think you will want to know more about what led to the consolidation of the three companies—E. A. Pierce & Co., Cassatt & Co., Incorporated, and Merrill, Lynch & Co., Inc.—and you will want to know where we go from here.

The first part of the story is simple. It deals with problems with which we are unfortunately all too familiar—problems of general busi-

Reprinted from *A Declaration of Policy,* March 26, 1940, pp. 3–14, and from the *Merrill Lynch, Pierce, Fenner & Smith, Inc. 1949 Annual Report,* by permission of Merrill Lynch & Co., Inc.

ness depression from which our industry has not even begun to recover. In the security business, as in others, the collapse shook our houses beneath us.

Security Business Performs an Essential Service

During the past few years we have been trying to readjust ourselves. Some of us have been a little slow in realizing that the readjustment has to be permanent, and a few doubt the possibilities of any successful readjustment. Nevertheless, we are convinced that the buying and selling of stocks, bonds, and other evidences of liens and ownerships, is a fundamental business which performs an essential service.

That there is no lack of opportunity for us is demonstrated by the fact that even last year the volume of stocks and bonds bought and sold was more than thirteen billion dollars. Essentially the job before us involves adapting our operations so that expenses will be in ratio to existing minimum standards of gross income; and then increasing the gross income by adapting our policies to meet the standards and requirements of our customers and public opinion. The sooner we recognize that the temper of living may never again be identical with what it was twelve or fifteen years ago, the sooner we shall gear ourselves for success under present and future conditions.

All Must Join to Reestablish Faith

We've got a job to do—we in the security business—a job of reestablishing faith in the security market as a place for sound investment. This job ought to be done by everybody in the business, and we think in time will be. But we are not going to wait for someone else to start it. We're no smarter, or better, than our competitors, and we have no thought whatever of driving anyone out of business. But we do recognize certain fundamental facts that have to be coped with by our business in its relations with the public, and we're going to make a beginning.

We will be delighted to have the cooperation of anyone and everyone else who sees the road ahead as we think we see it. There will be no secrets in our plans or operations. What is true of our needs, we consider to be equally true of others having a direct or indirect stake in the business—our competitors, banks, insurance companies, etc. So it will be our purpose to cooperate with everyone who wants to bend his energies and direct his thinking toward the big job of saving the security business as a whole, and saving ourselves in the process.

Let's Eliminate Unnecessary Frills

As we see it, our firm has two important things to do:

One is to get our location expenses under control. Let's get rid of any and all frills which do not make a direct contribution to the fundamental requirements of our customers. For instance, 85% of our customers do most of their business with us over the telephone. They do not need or want elaborate offices. They want simplicity, competent man power, and good, impartial service.

Which brings us to our second objective. We have developed what we consider a sound program of policies, to be put into effect when this merger becomes a reality at the end of this week.

Our Success Depends on Service to Public

These policies rest on a conviction—not always uppermost in our minds, we'll grant you—that in order to win success we business men have to put the public's interest first. *The customer may not always be right, but he has rights, and upon our recognition of his rights and our desire to satisfy them, rests our chance to succeed.*

It's not banal poppycock to say today that we've got to succeed through the service we can render the investing public. And it's only looking facts in the face to say that a legitimate, honest service is the only justification for success.

We think the public is still ready and willing to invest in securities, through brokers and the exchanges. We have been having some surveys made which, along with the surveys made by the New York Stock Exchange, have turned up some disturbing—and encouraging—facts.

Disturbing is the large percentage of potential investors and speculators in securities who are suspicious of the motives and operations of the security business and the people engaged therein. You and we know the reasons for this lack of confidence and we know that it won't be eliminated until we convince the public that our house is now in order.

Confidence, in the Main, Is on the Increase

Encouraging is the even larger percentage of people who now generally express confidence in our business, but also have definite ideas about how we should continue to operate it to retain that confidence.

Our plan is based on our appraisal of what our firms ought to do to meet this situation. If we do the best we can, and if we have properly adjudged what the investing public wants, our plan will succeed.

Here are the ideas which we have developed, and have incorporated in a statement of policy which starts out by saying:

> Policies and services of Merrill Lynch, E. A. Pierce & Cassatt were formulated in a spirit of enlightened self-interest. While based on the conviction that they constitute an important advance in both facilities and protection for the investor and speculator, they represent primarily the kind of a brokerage service that we believe will have the greatest chance for enduring success. It is our opinion, as well, that the customer is entitled to this modernized form of brokerage service.

Financial Stability as the Keystone

The first specific matter set forth in this statement has to do with financial stability, the keystone of our entire operation. We consider that since the firm carries free credit balances of customers, acts as custodian of their securities, functions as pledgee and finances margin transactions, it incurs in those financial relationships a responsibility to its clients which involves not only the maintenance of a high degree of financial stability at all times, but the added duty of supplying the trading public a clear picture of the firm's condition.

To meet the first, the firm will at all times maintain a working capital position well in excess of the requirements of the New York Stock Exchange.

The second objective will be attained by the issuance of a complete financial statement, in a form designed for maximum clarity and understanding.

Now in the matter of departmental policy: we operate a brokerage business in securities and commodities, and also underwrite and distribute securities.

But these are *two distinct businesses, with entirely separate functions. No conditions will be permitted which might create conflicts affecting the interests of our several types of customers.*

To Help Our Customers Appraise the Possibility of Bias

In practically all transactions for account of customers the firm will act only as a commission broker. However, in transactions involving securities in which the firm acts as principal dealer, the customer will be notified in advance.

When supplying informative analytical printed reports concerning a security in which the firm is not acting as principal, the firm intends to indicate in such reports the extent of the aggregate direct and indirect ownership of such security as of the date of the report by the firm and its general partners. Such information will be given as follows: if the aggregate value of such holdings is less than $50,000, it will be described as a "small interest"; if between $50,000 and $100,000, it will be described as a "substantial interest"; if over $100,000, it will be described as a "large interest". The purpose of such disclosure is to help the customer estimate the possibility and extent of bias on the part of the firm in its presentation of facts relating to a particular security.

This has been a general objective of brokers during recent years, but we intend to test this specific practical application as a part of our plans for the year 1940.

Pledge Aid for Still Further Protection

You may be interested in knowing how your senior partners feel about the SEC. We'll tell you. We are in full accord with the fundamental purpose of the Securities and Exchange laws—to give the investor adequate information, and to prohibit manipulation and fraud—and we pledge to our customers a complete cooperation with all future efforts designed to strengthen further these fundamental purposes.

No regulations or policies, however, can pretend to guarantee profits nor insure against loss. But we believe our customers can confidently use the Exchanges for investment and speculation with assurance that there are no stacked cards.

Our Research Department Will Stick to Facts—Clearly Presented

Now as to the question of advising the customer on his investments: we don't believe we can run a brokerage firm and be a good investment counsel at the same time. All that we will have to sell is service and facts. Therefore, we are going to do a little research work on our research department. We don't think there has been anything the matter with our research work, but we want to see that it makes the fullest possible use of all available data, puts that data into the clearest possible form, and then lets the facts speak for themselves. In other words, we are going to provide facts, ungarnished with advice. Advice is going to be out—unless it is specifically asked for, and then only with the approval of one of our partners or managers.

Rumors and "Hot Tips" Are Taboo

Let's take a look at our registered representatives, or customers' men. They are going to represent an important phase of our new job, principally because we think we are going to make it possible for them to operate on a different and sounder basis than in the past. One of the troubles in our business has been a potential conflict in interest between the customer and the customer's man, created by compensation practices which we believe were wrong. We're going to minimize, perhaps even eliminate, that potential conflict of interest.

Between ourselves, we think the best name for these men is service representatives, because it best expresses what we would like them to be in our organization. We think that by serving the customer's interest exclusive of all other considerations, the service representatives will really be doing the best job of serving their own interest, as well as that of the firm. To accomplish this purpose, they will assist their customers in getting all desired factual data; they will offer no advice as to the purchase or sale of securities or commodities except under restrictions we mentioned a few paragraphs back; they will circulate no rumors, "confidential suggestions," or "hot tips" designed to influence purchases or sales.

Customers to Say What Service They Want

Our customers themselves will determine the extent to which they want service. They will be asked to fill out a questionnaire stating exactly the type of service they desire. Representatives will then confine their activities strictly within the limits so outlined.

In order to make this policy genuinely workable, we propose to relate the salaries of our representatives primarily to the quality of service rendered to our clients. Their value will be judged largely by the degree of success with which they satisfy customers, and thus attract more customers. This, in our opinion, also represents the only sound way for our representatives to increase their earning power.

This whole policy means that we believe our best chance for increasing our business lies in constructively building the whole business, rather than by permitting conditions which indirectly create pressures to increase the trading of present customers.

In order that partners and managers may contribute as much as possible to the operation of this new impartial service, we plan to release them to a large extent from routine duties, so that their services may be at the disposal of any trader, large or small, who may require their expert knowledge or skilled assistance.

On Panic Days Our Regular Customers Come First

It is when transactions jump from an average day to several million shares a day that your broker's facilities must meet the test of emergency. And it is on these days that the customer requires top service to protect or establish his position.

We therefore offer the following unconditional guarantee of service in emergencies: *no new accounts will be opened in any day when the volume of trading at any time indicates that the facilities of the firm may be over-taxed.*

Although Merrill Lynch, E. A. Pierce & Cassatt has created one of the fastest and most accurate transmission systems for the execution of orders, we recognize that mistakes or delays can still happen. Where errors are due directly to the firm's personnel, or to any other factor under our control, we shall of course make the proper adjustments. In all other cases, effort will be made to expedite settlement through the regular processes established by the New York Stock Exchange. We trust that occasions for such adjustments will be infrequent. The matter is mentioned here only because where man and equipment are involved, there is always a chance of error.

We believe we have a sound program, but it is not enough to develop and execute a sound program. The people must know about it. That's why we are going to so some advertising.

Security Business Important to Our Whole People

In closing, we'd like to express our unshakable confidence in the future of our country, in the basic soundness of our type of economy—capitalism—and in the essential place that the security business has in that economy. We consider that the security business contributes more than most people realize to the development and the welfare of our whole people. It brings together those who need funds for industrial development and those who have funds to invest. It provides money for businesses to build new factories, buy new machines, finance new production, create and maintain employment.

The security business provides money for government to support public institutions and develop civic projects. It puts savings to work, gives literally millions of people a part-interest in business, and thus contributes to our economic progress.

It is estimated that between six and ten million Americans own bonds, between nine and eleven million own stocks. Fifty million of us own life insurance policies, a large portion of whose assets are invested in securities as a protection to the insured. More than thirteen million of us have savings in mutual savings banks, and twenty-six million have deposits in national and state banks and trust companies, where their money is invested in securities to bring them interest. Hundreds of private schools and colleges, hospitals, and other institutions are supported by security endowments and funds invested in securities.

Our Job Is to Make American Economy Work

Without the security market our whole system would collapse, or be radically altered along the lines of some of the European governments. We don't think we are prejudiced in our opinion that the American system of economy is as good as any yet devised by man—and we mean from the standpoint of the people as a whole, not just the privileged few.

It's our job to make that system work, to continue to improve it along lines already established by the government and by our own voluntary efforts. It's our job to see the other fellow's point of view and to reconcile our interests with his. It's our job to move forward with whatever capacities we may have—moral, mental, financial—to the end that our country may progress and that we ourselves may earn the rewards of intelligent effort, honestly applied.

We think that together we can contribute something worthwhile to our personal and the public welfare.

Cordially yours,

Charles A. Merrill
E. A. Pierce

1949 Annual Report

The public was very skeptical of the brokerage business in 1940. Some of the industry's methods were under attack and others were misunderstood. We believed then, and we believe today, that within the limits of human capacity we should conduct our business as our customers want it conducted. To the extent that it is possible we should give the customer what he wants. Certainly we should never force upon a customer something he does not want.

One of our first jobs after the organization of our expanded firm was to publish a statement of policy. These policies were designed to meet the criticisms and fulfill the demands of the investing public. They represented a public guarantee of how we would conduct our business. Since these policies were first announced they have grown to a whole book-full of rules that govern the daily conduct of every partner and every employee of Merrill Lynch. The basic policies in essence are:

1. In every consideration the interest of our customers must come first.
2. We will make no service charges and charge only minimum commissions.
3. All of our account executives will be paid a flat salary.
4. We heartily endorse the laws designed to protect investors.
5. We will provide a research department to help investors get the facts about securities.
6. We will not foist advice upon our customers.
7. We will disclose the interest of our firm in securities mentioned in our printed literature.
8. When we sell a security owned by the firm we will disclose this fact to the customer before the transaction.
9. Our capital will always substantially exceed the requirements of the law.
10. No additional corporate directorships may be accepted by any partner or employee.

The Private Banker's Code

J. P. Morgan, Jr.

J. P. Morgan, Jr., testifying before Congress after the crash, gave a definition to the professionalism of financial service that serves as a steady beacon for us all.

The Private Banker is a member of a profession which has been practiced since the Middle Ages. In the process of time, there has grown up a code of professional ethics and customs, on the observance of which depend his reputation, his fortune, and his usefulness to the community in which he works. . . .

If, in the exercise of his profession, the private banker disregards this code, which could never be expressed in legislation, but has a force far greater than any law, he will sacrifice his credit. This credit is his most valuable possession; it is the result of years of fair and honourable dealing and, while it may be quickly lost, once lost cannot be restored for a long time, if ever. The banker must at all times conduct himself as to justify the confidence of his clients in him and thus preserve it for his successors.

If I may be permitted to speak of the firm of which I have the honour to be the senior partner I should state that at all times the idea of doing only first class business, and that in a first class way, has been before our minds. We have never been satisfied with simply keeping within the law, but have constantly sought so to act that we might fully observe the professional code, and so maintain the credit and reputation which has been handed down to us from our predecessors in the firm.

Excerpted from a 1933 speech, by permission of the author.

To Get Performance You Have to Be Organized for It

Charles D. Ellis, CFA

At a point in the mid-1960s, the historical role and function of the person in the investment organization we now call "Portfolio Manager" began to change, moving away from one of being primarily the implementer of others' decisions to one of being the focus and location of decision making. Early in this evolutionary period, the imperative for facilitative organizational reform was identified and described by Ellis in this prophetic 1968 article. Subsequently, virtually every investment management firm has been redesigned to resemble the structural model advocated here. An accidental irony can be observed: widespread acceptance may have neutralized the advantage of adoption.

Performance-oriented managements have captured virtually all the attention of both individual and institutional investors in recent years, and their investment records have been enviable. Are these records luck? Or speculative good fortune? Or temporary?

Better research and more astute portfolio management are part of the answer, but only part. Like successful companies in other fields, the most rapidly growing and highly regarded investment companies are developing innovative corporate strategies to make the best use of changes in the business environment. Investment managers who seek compara-

Excerpted from *Institutional Investor* (January 1968), 44–47, 68, 70–71. New York, New York: Institutional Investor, Inc.

ble results should understand the key changes in methods, purposes, and organization which produce sustained portfolio performance.

The successful new capital managers have achieved superior operating results because they are better organized for performance than more traditional investors. Their approach is strategic.

Effective corporate strategy anywhere usually involves several phases:

Specify the goal.
Identify the problems and opportunities presented by the environment.
Determine the internal strengths and weaknesses of the enterprise.
Develop policies that minimize problems and exploit opportunities.

The single objective of the new management is to maximize the profitability of capital under management. Capital productivity (not capital preservation) dominates the structure and activities of the entire organization, and the efforts of every individual are aimed at contributing to portfolio profit.

Traditional investment managers often have strikingly different sets of goals: Capital preservation (not profitability) is their economic objective. An image of quality and conservatism is sought and protected. They seek to avoid risk. Naturally, these other goals can and often do conflict with a determined effort to maximize money making. . . .

====

How the "New" Managers Operate

The new managers are convinced that the traditional organizational structure has important weaknesses that can be reduced or eliminated by changes in management organization and method.

Traditional investment management is oriented towards long-term investments; relies on a committee of senior officers to make all investment action decisions at weekly or semi-monthly meetings; depends primarily on a staff of in-house analysts for information and evaluation; and conducts its affairs in private. Since the principal investment objective is capital preservation (rather than capital productivity), caution and conservatism tend to characterize the decision process and the portfolio.

An investment committee, ideally, has two important and useful capabilities. First, serious errors in judgment seldom survive its open review, because a committee composed of men with diverse attitudes and experience can usually raise most potentially significant questions. Second, an effective committee can establish sound basic policy.

But this does not mean that the committee should also make such operating decisions as security selection, action timing, and the degree of emphasis given individual securities.

In portfolio management, time *is* money, and the necessarily slow decision process of a committee can be very expensive to the portfolio. Memoranda prepared for committees take analysts' time away from productive research efforts. Formal procedures delay actions, often until it is too late to act at all because of price changes.

Committee decisions are not easily reversed (although market liquidity allows it) with the result that tentative, experimental purchases or sales are impossible. Profit opportunities provided by market swings must be ignored, and only long-term opportunities can be considered.

Committees Can't Control

Since a committee can only make a few decisions each meeting, they tend to manage portfolios "by exception," selling "bad" stocks and buying "good" ones. The new management wants portfolio management "by control" and recognizes that investment decisions are seldom clearly identified in blacks and whites, but rather appear in varying shades of gray, which warrant almost continuous change in the emphasis placed on various securities.

The committee system makes it very difficult to assign responsibility and measure results. Who can take credit for good decisions, and who can be held accountable for poor decisions?

An individual investment manager working full time on the problems and opportunities facing his portfolio can exercise management "by control." The logic is in the mathematics of time. A committee that meets for three hours 50 times a year cannot make nearly as many astute decisions as an executive working 40 or more hours, 50 weeks a year.

Moreover, if the committee attempts to run the portfolio, it will seldom give adequate time and attention to its major policy responsibilities and will also make inferior operating decisions. So the new management clearly separates policy decisions from operating decisions by assigning operating authority to a single executive or portfolio manager. The capacity to make more decisions allows more aggressive management and allows the portfolio to capture that many more increments of profit. The portfolio manager need not wait for a committee meeting; decisions can be quite informal; he avoids the delays inherent in the preparation of a formal presentation to an investment committee; and he can act decisively.

Why Individuals Outperform Committees

The competent individual has important advantages over a committee in making decisions. Since he devotes all his time and energies to the success of the portfolio, it stands to reason that he'll know more about each constituent security—why it was bought, why it is held, and why it might be sold.

Since portfolio management is more art than science, and since committees are notoriously not artful, the single portfolio executive who is personally skilled in this art will enjoy a significant competitive strength. He can exploit his intuition, inventiveness, and sense of the market because he is judged, not on how well he can explain his programs, but on results in the market place.

Moreover, since the portfolio manager is judged on the profitability of the portfolio as a whole, he is more clearly motivated to take sensible risks where the rewards are commensurate. He can act boldly, innovate, and seize initiatives to increase portfolio profits. By giving the portfolio manager the authority and direct responsibility for operating decisions, the new managements obtain the advantages of an individual in making and executing decisions while preserving the policy-and-review capabilities of a committee.

How "New" Management Gets Information

The new investment-management organizations strive not only to be highly effective at making profitable decisions, but also at acquiring and evaluating the information upon which decisions must be based. The traditional approach to data collection and appraisal relies upon a permanent private staff of analysts who study statistics, visit managements, and write reports recommending purchases and sales to the investment committee. The research process is treated as proprietary and confidential, and is considered the sole responsibility of the in-house staff.

While this internal resource is highly valuable, it can all too often lead to a constriction on the flow of information to the decision-maker. A major opportunity for improved portfolio profits is presented in the best research and security evaluation supplied by brokers. The view that broker research has great value is coupled with a clear awareness for the service buying power of commissions generated by the portfolio. This commission buying power is managed carefully and expended to acquire that brokerage research and judgment ability that will add the most profit to the portfolio.

Another major innovation in capital management is the way in which broker research is integrated into the capital management process. A communications gap exists between the growing store of brokers' research knowledge and the operating needs of the portfolio manager. The portfolio manager who best bridges this communications gap will have an advantage over his competitors.

Bypassing the Staff Analysts

Whereas the traditional management group insists that all broker research go to the staff analysts, the new approach channels an important part of this information and opinion flow directly to the portfolio manager. This practice derives from an appreciation of subtle human differences between analyst and portfolio manager, their positions within the organization, and how they respond to external opinion.

For many good reasons, staff analysts are usually not well suited to appreciating the merits of broker recommendations. A good analyst is necessarily skeptical and tends to discount what others say. Professionally, he distrusts and disparages relying on the work of others. He knows too much about the particular stocks he follows closely to be impressed by a summary description of other securities, and his professional satisfaction often depends more on the breadth and depth of his company and industry knowledge than on the profitability of recommended purchases and sales. His career development typically depends more upon the consistent accuracy of his research reports than upon the frequency and magnitude of his contributions to the portfolio's profitability. Each year he makes far fewer recommendations than a portfolio manager makes decisions and therefore has a smaller set of commitments over which to obtain a satisfactory average of profitability, and he has less opportunity to reverse his decisions, so he must realistically be more confident of each individual security endorsement. For all these reasons, a staff analyst is ill suited by position, responsibility, and interest to effectively exploit broker research.

The Open-Minded Manager

In contrast, the portfolio manager must always rely heavily on the knowledge and appraisals of others whether they be internal staff analysts or external broker analysts. He is just as receptive to one analyst as he is to another if they can equally increase the profits of the portfolio. His principal skill is in seeing the positive potential in a given situation rather than in identifying possible negatives. . . .

Consequently, the contemporary management philosophy offers the portfolio manager wide access to ideas and information, which he may pass on to a staff analyst for review and evaluation if he is interested but not yet convinced, or may act upon immediately if he sees opportunity.

Another approach for in-house analysts is to redefine responsibility so that each analyst sees himself as an assistant portfolio manager and concentrates his efforts on flowing profit-making ideas into the portfolio. In this new role, analysts can see broker research as an opportunity to save time, broaden knowledge, and use the best opinions of others. The assistant portfolio manager-analyst will build upon the work of these external analysts rather than re-creating their original research, with the strong probability that his annual profit contribution to the portfolio will be greater than if time, efforts, and talents were devoted to independent research.

Beyond recasting the communications net to capture more value from external research, the new management considers outside investment capabilities as an opportunity to improve internal portfolio performance by integrating their knowledge and judgments into the portfolio's management. The most helpful brokers are taken in as effective partners in the management of the portfolio. Their opinions are sought on possible changes in investment policy as well as possible changes in holdings. The result of this "open door" policy is to expand greatly the number of competent persons contributing to the profitable management of the portfolio. With a good understanding of how the portfolio is managed, these outside partners can focus their efforts on providing the particular information and suggestions that are most valuable to the particular portfolio at a particular time.

Market Action Is an Indicator, Too

Since market appreciation is the goal of every purchase, correlations between the market and various economic indicators have to be studied. So do the investment actions of other large investors.

Trading is an important profit opportunity, and one member of the management team ought to have complete responsibility for it. The experienced trader, involved continuously with the market, not only knows quoted prices but has useful—often critical—insights into the structures of supply and demand. With this superior market knowledge, the trader is often able to contribute significantly to the profit goal by advising the portfolio manager on timing of actions and on unusual opportunities to buy or sell created by temporary imbalances of supply and demand in the market. New methods have been used to improve the profitability of open market operations, such as large block transactions that allow rapid redeployment of funds in large amounts at specific prices, and sales of blocks to brokers who make position bids by putting their own capital at risk when the market will not immediately absorb a large supply of shares.

Performance Pays the Performers

The management goal of portfolio profitability is supported with pay and other incentives closely related to the ability to contribute to portfolio profitability. The most important job in terms of income, professional responsibility, prestige, and influence is that of portfolio manager. The personal, non-financial incentives are also important in these free-form, multi-profit-center managements in which each person functions as an entrepreneur, and ability to contribute to portfolio profitability is quickly recognized and quickly rewarded. As a result, the new managements have attracted unusually able, hard working, and creative young men, and then stimulated them to achievements at or near their potential. As in most fields of organized endeavor, the essential ingredient for sustained superior results is the ability and effectiveness of the people in management, and the new concept of capital management has emphasized the importance of profit making people.

In summary, having observed and worked with dozens of different investment organizations, I am convinced that the superior record of achievement of a still small but rapidly growing number of capital managements results from their clearer, deeper, and broader understanding of the environment in which they operate and a careful organization of internal strengths to achieve maximum portfolio profits. The flow of new monies to these new managers is impressive evidence that the public recognizes their success. Investment managers that are organized along more traditional lines should seriously consider the nature and importance of the new approach to capital management.

Organizing for Creativity

Arthur Zeikel

Arthur Zeikel has established himself over the years as an authority on organizing groups to make successful investment decisions.
His working hours are spent as president of Merrill Lynch Asset
Management, one of the largest investment management organizations in the world. Here, he focuses on the identification and use of
creativity in the investment process.

———————————————

Can investment management organizations improve their performance?
The answer depends critically, of course, on how investment markets
really work. Do they offer opportunities for superior returns? If so, are
investment firms organized in such a way as to take advantage of those
opportunities? In particular, do they recognize and use constructively
those creative people in the organization who may be the key to superior returns?

How Markets Work

The process of organization must begin with a premise about how markets really work. (I say "premise" because we may never know for sure
what motivates stock prices; we must rely largely on personal convic-
tions.) Because the market is primarily a reflection of investor hope and
anxiety, an understanding of how investors think and act is critical.

Reprinted from the *Financial Analysts Journal* 39 (November/December 1983), pp. 25–29. Charlottesville, Virginia: Association for Investment Management and Research.

First, investors' emotional expectations are shaped largely by their most recent experience. Second, they integrate their perception of trends and patterns of development with insufficient awareness that "unexpected" events are likely to prove disruptive. Third, they tend to overreact.

To put these views in a capital market context, the market is efficient, but the accepted definition of efficiency is inaccurate because it does not describe well how the market's pricing mechanism actually works. That is, the market is efficient, in that current price generally reflects the consensus view of investor expectations for the market as a whole and for most individual issues. But the consensus view is usually incorrect, because it is based on a more or less simple extrapolation of past trends and events and does not effectively incorporate change into expectations.

Furthermore, theory tells us that value-changing events occur randomly and cannot be predicted accurately or consistently. This is not so. There is a flow to the news because there is a rhythm to events that make the news. People generally, and investors particularly, fail to appreciate the workings of countervailing forces; change and momentum are largely misunderstood concepts. Most investors tend to cling to the course to which they are currently committed, especially at turning points.

Stock price movements actually begin to reflect new developments before it is generally recognized that they have taken place. As the circle of recognition widens, a new perception of the future replaces the old, setting the stage for another change. Thus important trend-changing events tend to be underestimated during their early stages of development, and overestimated when they have matured. Put another way, it is the conventional forecast (of the future) that is embedded in today's price, not the future as it will turn out to be.

Let me amplify. First, new information is not simultaneously available to all. Not all who have it recognize it. Not all who recognize it are capable of translating it immediately into an evaluation of market worth. In any market, some competitors recognize and use new information faster than others, hence enjoy a competitive advantage. Professional portfolio managers are paid for that capacity.

Second, stock prices respond to changes in the most recently perceived set of conventional expectations. And investment expectations are a short-time futures concept. That is, the next change governs how investors react, not long-run future expectations. Investor anticipations are formed at the margin. That is why changes in earnings estimates generally follow changes in stock prices. The important question is not whether conditions are good or bad, but whether they are changing for better or worse.

Third, investor psychology is somewhat perverse. Prices usually begin to rise during periods of extreme pessimism. At such times, market evaluations are usually extremely modest, dividend returns are attractive, the ratio of price to book value is favorable, and portfolios are very conservatively positioned. Yet skepticism prevails. The converse also seems to hold: Prices usually begin to decline when optimism is widespread. The correction is frequently perceived as a mere interruption in the general advance. It isn't.

Finally, events tend to coalesce into trends, but the trends are not endless. The greater the belief in the persistence of a trend, the less likely it is to persist. Consequently, decision-makers must learn not to overemphasize discernible trends. The seeming comfort afforded by extrapolating too far is hazardous. Peter Bernstein puts it best:

> Momentum causes things to run further and longer than we anticipate. The very familiarity of a force in motion reduces our ability to see when it is losing its momentum. Indeed, that is why extrapolating the present into the future so frequently turns out to be the genesis of an embarrassing forecast.[1]

Achieving Successful Performance

The market, in other words, does offer opportunities for superior returns to those investors and investment organizations that can recognize important new information and anticipate its effect on market trends. The records of most professional investment management organizations are, nevertheless, not encouraging. Why?

An extensive study by American Telephone & Telegraph suggests that successful investment management activities require, at a minimum, four key elements:[2]

1. a structured decision-making process that can be easily defined,
2. a stated investment philosophy that is applied consistently to identifying an appropriate investment strategy,

3. a clearly stated and acted upon sell discipline, to prevent reinforcement of mistakes and to realize gains from successful investment, and
4. continuity of key personnel.

I would suggest that superior performance also requires that those key personnel of the organization be creative or, at the least, recognize creativity and encourage it.

===

Recognizing and Using Creativity

Creative people are
intellectually curious.
flexible and open to new information.
able to recognize problems and define them clearly and accurately.
able to put information together in many different ways to reach a solution.
responsive to recognition and praise from colleagues.
antiauthoritarian and unorthodox.
mentally restless, intense and highly motivated.
highly intelligent.
goal-oriented.

Some guidance in recognizing the truly creative is offered by Alfred E. Brown, who notes that imaginative, intuitive approaches, rather than routine or analytical ones, are essential to creativity.[3] Creative people are goal-oriented, rather than method-oriented. They are the "problem-solvers," as contrasted with the "phenomenon studiers" who investigate well and use good judgment and analytical reasoning in interpreting data.

Goal-oriented people never limit themselves to thinking in terms of available methods, which often hinder new approaches to problem-solving. Instead, they feel free to challenge conventional ideas and may appear antiauthoritarian and unorthodox. But they are not merely rebellious.

Creative individuals bring to their work an intelligence that allows them to recognize problems and define them clearly and accurately and an open-mindedness that allows them to accept new information and to put data together in many different ways in order to reach an acceptable solution. Being intellectually curious, they continually ask probing questions such as "Why did this occur?" and "What would happen if I did it this way?'' Being flexible, they don't flatly dismiss ideas on the grounds that, ''We tried that before and it didn't work.''

Creative people are also highly motivated, both internally and externally. Mentally restless and intense, they are often obsessed with achieving their objectives and impatient with anything that gets in their way. At the same time, they seek recognition and praise from colleagues both in their own working environment and in their profession.

I would have to agree with one final comment Brown makes about creative people: They develop very early on in life. It is thus probably futile, if not downright counterproductive, to try to turn uncreative people into creative ones. Investment organizations can, however, learn to make better use of the creative people they do have.

Organizing for Creativity

How can managers of investment organizations create an environment that is conducive to the needs of their creative people? They must begin by populating their organization with able people. It is well known, after all, that ''You can't soar with the eagles if you're surrounded by turkeys.'' Senior management, in particular, should encourage their key researchers and decision-makers to be investigative and intellectually curious.

Creativity flourishes best in an atmosphere that enables participants to express themselves without inhibition. A censorious atmosphere will merely increase people's insecurities, anxieties and desire for self-protection and reduce their willingness to accept new ideas. If people are afraid of making mistakes, they will tend to become overly protective of their own judgments—not because those judgments are correct, or even likely to be correct, but because they are theirs. This leads to resistance to new information and new ideas, regardless of their worth.

An environment that encourages people to take chances and risk making mistakes is more likely to evolve in an organization that keeps office politics to a minimum. This does not mean that management should be undemanding. Performance goals should be challenging and clearly articulated. Creative people like being challenged; they also like being recognized and rewarded for meeting challenges successfully.

Finally, to optimize available creativity, investment organizations should keep their decision-making apparatus short, simple and—this is important—small. *Augustine's Laws* tell us:

In virtually any undertaking, it is found that a very small fraction of the participants produces a very large fraction of the accomplishments. It must, in fairness, be pointed out that a very small fraction of the participants also produces a very large fraction of the problem.

Furthermore, one-tenth of the people involved in a given endeavor produce at least one-third of the output, and increasing the number of participants merely serves to reduce the average performance.[4]

In this regard, it is important to realize that creativity and good investment decision-making are not necessarily one and the same. Experience shows that some people cannot consistently make effective and timely decisions; others cannot make good ones at optimum times; still others are just not comfortable making decisions. These people should not be asked to make decisions. Their capabilities and talents can be utilized in related or ancillary roles—fact-finding, for example.

To encourage creativity
   allow participants to express themselves without inhibition.
   keep office politics to a minimum.
   establish demanding and clearly articulated performance goals.
   keep the decision-making apparatus short, simple and small.
   promote an investigatory and intellectually curious attitude.
   populate the organization with able people.
   conduct the research process away from conventional wisdom.

The Research Function

Thomas Kuhn tells us that, "What a man sees depends upon what he looks at and also what his previous visual conceptual experience has taught him."[5] Members of the investment community, despite a diversity of opinions, prejudices and exposure, have undergone roughly similar educational and professional training. In the process, they have absorbed the same body of literature and technique, reflected upon the same history, and are drawn to many of the same lessons of the past. It is thus not surprising perhaps that we tend toward unanimity when it comes to interpreting new information and toward the same average (mediocre) results when it comes to translating those interpretations into investment decisions.

Concentration of research, combined with extensive publicity regarding who is "first team" and who isn't, means that the information base for most major market participants is very similar and, in some cases, exactly the same. The focus is on the same key analysts, the same important firms, the same economic and business conditions and consultants, the same conference attendance, much the same business problems, the same fears and so on.

A creative approach to research—one that strays off the beaten path, away from the conventional wisdom—can contribute immeasurably to successful investment performance. One particularly good example of creative research has been described by Stephen Timbers. The approach assumed that public brokerage house research is the compendium for a given stock and so defines the limitations of the efficiency of the market; thus any information brokerage houses neglect, misinterpret or fail to anticipate produces an opportunity for creative research.[6]

The function of creative research should be to understand, evaluate and, as much as possible, anticipate change—not merely to collect data. Although it cannot be avoided, the unexpected can at least be incorporated into the decision-making process; one cannot usually predict which piece of new information, fresh idea or original thought will prove productive. But one can narrow the range of uncertainty. Sound technique requires skill in excluding the unnecessary and, as quickly as possible, making some guess as to the unknown.

The search is to ascertain those few elements that are critical—in the extreme, to isolate the one factor upon which the decision may turn. One must conquer the urge to learn everything about some new development or unexpected turn of events. One must distinguish between facts needed to form a foundation for new action and those that merely serve to keep one better informed. . . .

Some Final Words

All investment decision-making systems are a compromise. No single perfect organizational structure exists. The greater the number of people involved, especially creative ones, the more complicated and more difficult the compromises that must be made. The goal, however, is not perfection, but rather the proper balance between conflicting pressures and effective interaction between people. The idea is to manage the ego problem, not eliminate it.

Notes

1. Peter L. Bernstein, "Forecasts Will Be Wrong," *The New York Times*, October 21, 1973.

2. American Telephone & Telegraph, *Pensions & Investment Age*, October 13, 1975.
3. Alfred E. Brown, *Chemical and Engineering News*, October 24, 1960, pp. 102–110.
4. Norman R. Augustine, *Augustine's Laws and Major System Development Programs* (New York: American Institute of Aeronautics and Astronautics, Inc., 1982).
5. Thomas S. Kuhn, *The Structure of Scientific Revolutions* (Chicago: University of Chicago Press, 1970).
6. Stephen B. Timbers, "Equity Research After Modern Portfolio Theory," *The Journal of Portfolio Management*, Spring 1979, pp. 52–54.

Stock Market Primer

Claude N. Rosenberg, Jr.

Claude Rosenberg, the quintessential San Franciscan, in addition to developing Rosenberg Capital Management and RREEF, the institutional real estate firm, has served his profession in a variety of formal and informal leadership roles and is one of the industry's favorite people. Among his several books, *Stock Market Primer* has been in print the longest: over 20 years. This is Chapter 37, "Common Stock Commandments."

The preceding pages have given you some basic facts and fundamentals about investments and the stock market. In addition, I have provided rules in each chapter which I believe will guarantee you greater success in your ventures. I won't bore you by repeating all these rules, but I have some further comments which should be equally helpful to you. I call these "common stock commandments" and here they are:

1. *Do not make hasty, emotional decisions about buying and selling stocks.* When you do what your emotions tell you to—on the spur of the moment—you are doing exactly what the "masses" are doing, and this is not generally profitable. It is better to wait until your emotions have returned to normal, so that you can weigh the pros and cons objectively. . . . In line with this thinking, do not be pressured to buy or sell securities by anyone. Hard-selling techniques hint there may be "stale merchandise on the shelf," and that's not what you want. If you're in doubt about buying, my advice is to *do nothing.*

Reprinted from *Stock Market Primer* (New York: Warner Books, Inc., 1981; originally published 1962), Chapter 37, pp. 320–28, by permission of the author.

2. *If you are convinced that a company has dynamic growth prospects, do not sell it just because it looks temporarily too high.*   You may never be able to buy it back lower in price and you stand to miss a potential *big winner*—which is just what you should be looking for. Perhaps the gravest error I've seen made over the years is selling great companies with bright future prospects just because they temporarily looked a few points too high. . . .

3. *Do not fall in love with stocks to the point where you can no longer be objective in your appraisal of them.*   Stocks are different than women. You'd be a fool to think of your wife all day the way she looks the first thing in the morning—maybe best that you think of her as she appears all dressed up. But you do have to scrutinize stocks and think of their worst points; you have to reassess your love constantly and you have to be brutal and unemotional in your appraisal.

4. *Do not concern yourself as much with the market in general as with the outlook for individual stocks.*   Often times you will see a fine stock come down in price to an unquestionable bargain price, only to let your feeling about the general market sway you away from buying it. As they say, it is not a stock market, but instead a market for (individual) stocks. Buy a good value as it appears and do not let the general market sentiment alter your decision.

5. *Forget about stock market "tips."*   Use your good judgment and you won't have to rely on unreliable information. I realize that this point shows no world-shattering brilliance on my part, but so often I've seen this advice ignored. I'll never forget the day I was visited by a certain client of mine at my office. He wanted a recommendation on a good stock and I suggested he buy American Photocopy Equipment, which looked very attractive to me. I related my reasoning to him about the industry, the company, etc., and I showed him all the facts and figures I had on the stock. I spent 10 or 15 minutes on the glowing outlook of this company, and then my client told me he would think about it and let me know. The next morning he called me and placed an order—for an entirely different stock, one of the "Happyjack Uranium" type. He explained he "had heard some very good things" about this stock and he wanted to own it. A year or so later his purchase was about half of his cost and he visited me again. This time he told me the "source" of his information: he had spent an hour at a very fancy cocktail lounge the evening of our original meeting and he had overheard a very confidential conversation about this stock. A fine thing, I thought (and my

client agreed). Here I had spent hours researching American Photocopy and had given him the benefits of these hours—and he turned around and disregarded this in favor of a hot tip he overheard between two unknown people who had consumed an ample supply of martinis. . . .

6. *You get what you pay for in the stock market (like everything else in life).*   Some people consider a $5.00 stock good just because it's low in price. Nothing could be further from the truth. Most often, high-priced stocks provide far better value than low-priced stocks, in that the former generally have more earnings, dividends, etc. behind them than the low-priced issues. Likewise, high-priced stocks go into "better hands" (many are purchased by large institutional investors and others who are long-term holders), while the low-priced issues most often go into the hands of the public and speculators and gamblers, all of whom are less-informed and subject to occasional panic selling. Also remember that high-priced stocks carry one potential which cheap stocks do not—they are all potential split candidates.

7. *Remember that stocks always look worst at the bottom of a bear market (when an air of gloom prevails) and always look best at the top of a bull market (when everybody is optimistic).*   Have strength and buy when things do look bleak and sell when they look too good to be true.

8. *Remember, too, that you'll seldom—if ever—buy stocks right at the bottom or sell them right at the top.*   The stock market generally goes to extremes: when pessimism dominates, stocks go lower than they really should, based on their fundamentals, and when optimism runs rampant, stocks go higher than they really deserve to. Knowing this, don't expect your stocks to go up in price immediately after you buy them or to go down after you sell them, even though you are convinced that your analysis of their value is correct.

9. *Do not buy stocks as you might store merchandise on sale.*   No doubt you've seen people scrapping and clamoring for goods on sale at stores like Macy's, Penney, etc. They fight to buy this merchandise because the goods are reduced in price and because there is limited supply of the merchandise. Too often people buy things they really don't need or really don't like and they find that they really haven't made a "good buy" at all. *But they simply couldn't resist the urge to join others in competing for something of which there was a limited supply.*

There is not a limited supply of actively-traded common stocks, thus I advise you not to rush to buy as though the supply is going to dry up. If you've ever sat in a stock brokerage office and watched the "tape" (which shows the stock transactions as they take place), you'll know what I mean. A certain stock might suddenly get active and start rising in price: one minute you see it at 35, a few seconds later it's 35½, then 36, 36¼, 36½, 37. By the time it has hit 37, it is human nature to feel an almost irresistible urge to buy the stock (regardless of its fundamentals of earnings, dividends, future outlook, etc.)—to get in on the gravy train, to join the rest of the flock who are clamoring to buy the stock as though it is "sale merchandise." Resist this urge—only buy "goods" which you're sure you'll like and which meet your objectives.

10. *There is no reason always to be in the stock market.* After the stock market has had a long and sizable advance, it is prudent to take a few profits. Too often, after selling, the money from the sale "burns a hole in the pocket" of the investor. It's like working in a candy shop: no matter how much will power you have, after a few weeks, the bonbons look awfully good and it's hard to resist other "bonbon" stocks. Go slowly—there are times when cash can be a valuable asset.

11. *Seek professional advice for your investment.* Find a broker who is honest and who you are convinced will have your best interests at heart. Make sure he knows your financial status, your objectives and your temperament. If you don't know the right broker, consult your bank or your friends and then go in and meet the man who is recommended to you. Take the same pains to find the best broker as you would to find the best doctor for yourself. . . .

12. *Take advantage of the research facilities your broker has to offer.* Certainly you'll agree that *Analysis is a better market tool than a Pin.* The top brokerage firms spend hundreds of thousands of dollars every year to find the most attractive investments for their customers. Read the reports which are published—they will give you insight into the investment firm with whom you are dealing. Keep track of their performance over a period of years (performance over a few months may be deceiving, both because the general market may be against them and because you can't expect recommendations to bloom overnight). . . .

13. *Remember that the public is generally wrong.* The masses are not well informed about investments and the stock market. They have not disciplined themselves correctly to make the right choices in the right industries at the right prices. They are moved mainly by their emotions, and history has proved them to be wrong consistently. . . .

A wise investor should be wary of public over-enthusiasm for anything. Don't you be "one of the herd" and be led to slaughter as have so many who have tossed sound thinking to the wind.

14. *Beware of following stock market "fads."*   Along the same line of reasoning discussed in commandments 9 and 13, I want to emphasize separately this idea of following fads in the market. Remember the "sack" dresses that became the fad a decade ago? . . . Seven or eight years ago it was hula-hoops; five years ago it was trampoline centers; last year it was "Batman" and next year it will be something else. As a general rule, if you get in early in a fad you stand to make money. But if you come along after it is in full swing you are asking for trouble.

The same thing goes for the stock market. Just like sack dresses, hula-hoops, trampolines, tulip bulbs, etc., the stock market occasionally develops fads for certain industries. In almost all cases a sudden rush to buy the fad stocks pushes them to price levels which are totally unwarranted. *When you buy at the height of popularity you almost always pay prices which have little relationship to value. . . .*

15. *Do not be concerned with where a stock has already been—be instead concerned with where it is going.*   Many times I've heard people say, "It must be a bargain now—it's down 20 points from its high." Where a stock *has been* is history, it's "spilt milk." Investors may have bid up ABC stock to $100 last year, but the outlook for the company may have changed entirely since then. Or it may have been emotional speculation (fad-buying) which put it up to an unreasonable price. *The important thing is what lies ahead, not what has already transpired,* and previous market prices have no bearing on the future.

16. *Take the time to supervise your stocks periodically.*   Needless to say, conditions are subject to constant change. Don't shut yourself off from the outside world; take an objective look at your holdings periodically, with the thought of weeding out the "weak sisters" and adding stocks which have more potential. Your broker should be willing to make an analysis of your portfolio for you on a regular basis and I encourage you to take advantage of his service.

17. *Concentrate on quality.*   While big profits are often made through buying and selling poor quality common stocks, your success in the stock market is far, far more assured if you emphasize quality in your stock selections. Too many investors shy away from the top-notch companies in search of rags-to-riches performers. This, of course, is fine for a certain portion of your investment dollars, since most people can afford an *occasional* "flyer." But a person who starts out looking for flyers usually ends up, not with just one or two, but with a host of poor quality stocks—most of which turn out unsuccessful. These low-grade issues are certainly no foundation for a good portfolio; instead,

the fine, well-managed companies should form the backbone. And don't for a minute think you can't make money without wild speculation—fabulous fortunes have been made over the years in such high quality, *non*-speculative stocks as Carnation, Coca-Cola, Procter & Gamble, and others. In other words, place your stress on the elite, not on the so-called "cats and dogs" of the marketplace. "Remember," said one wise stock market philosopher, "if you sleep with dogs, you're bound to get fleas."

Reflections on Market Inefficiency

Dean LeBaron, CFA

Original and unconventional ideas have been streaming for a quarter-century from Dean LeBaron, who founded and built Battery-march Financial Management. Here, he is irreverently challenging his academic friends at a 1982 meeting of the Institute of Quantitative Research in Finance.

Physicists and Buddhists tell us, and most rational people know, that absolutes are only an illusion. But our egos are more attracted to Newton, who would tell us that there is such a thing as absolute scientific precision, and that we are approaching it. Such is also the case with investors and "market inefficiencies." We astute, value-oriented investors would like to believe that we can detect and take advantage of departures from some absolute standard of market efficiency. We want progress toward Newtonian rationality to prevail, to our worthy profit and to the loss of the less well informed and less astute. Calvin should be correct; God's reward is on earth as well as in heaven.

Of course, we usually consider the pricing mechanism to be inefficient only with respect to some ego-based reference standard. In other words, that which is efficient is what we believe to be right, whereas that which is inefficient is what we believe to be not right. That said,

Reprinted from the *Financial Analysts Journal* 39 (May/June 1983), pp. 16–17, 23 (adapted from remarks made to the Institute of Quantitative Research in Finance conference in Scottsdale, Arizona, in October 1982). Charlottesville, Virginia: Association for Investment Management and Research.

however, I'll now proceed to outline six market inefficiencies, or characteristics of inefficiencies. Each has features of value that are readily recognizable, but most are unlikely to be exploited. That's what makes any inefficiency and allows it to last even after recognition.

Agents

Why are there such aberrations as closed-end funds persistently selling at a discount and not liquidating? Why are premium prices paid in mergers and acquisitions? Why do new issues yield abnormal returns? How can knowledge of insider transactions, even when publicized, have investment value?

There must be something going on in practice that is not accounted for in theory. To be sure, no one any longer expects the markets to be absolutely perfect, but are they so inefficient that these large aberrations can exist and even persist? Is it a manifestation of the small firm effect? Or some other missing variable in the Capital Asset Pricing Model?

I offer a hypothesis that may be classed as the "theory of agents." It is related to the idea of the agency costs that arise in the separation of the ownership from the management of the firm, but it involves a different intermediary.

Most payoff systems should be designed so that agents are motivated by the same things the ultimate wealth holder would be motivated by. But institutional markets appear to be heavily influenced—even dominated, if we believe the popular literature—by individuals such as pension managers and investment managers who are not proportionately enhanced by the investment gains from individual transactions. Rather, they have a somewhat different set of payoffs. Their clients' perception that they are capable is one element in this set. Because of this, some good investment decisions are known but not done because they are not acceptable to the client. The guiding principle in this environment seems to be that it is better to make a little money conventionally than to run even the smallest risk of losing a lot unconventionally.

The Capital Market Line, as measured in practice, tells us that investors pay more for downside protection than for upside gain. Why? Is it because we all have to face committees, hence do not act as our trustee and fiduciary charge would have us act—i.e., as reasonable businessmen would act for their own account? Are we willing to forgo somebody else's investment gain for our career gain? Many managers end up paying a good deal in terms of forgone opportunity for the privilege of resting comfortably in the lower part of the second quartile and avoiding ever being in the bottom quartile for even a short period.

Of course, the pension officers—our clients—are themselves agents. They often behave in ways that may be uneconomic to beneficiaries. Take for example, the growing use by pension sponsors of multiple managers, with its corollary of having sharply rising costs. There is little evidence that aggregate results improve enough to justify the expense. This phenomenon may be best explained in terms of the sponsor's desire to minimize short-term career risk from volatility by diversifying across many managers.

Early last year, our firm introduced a new strategy called "Corporate Recovery." Our clients had reason to expect that we would be attracted to contrary investment notions, so it was consistent for us to buy beleaguered companies in packages at a time when illiquidity was a front-page peril. Most of our clients acceded to our wish to try the strategy, but only after great soul-searching. We were told that, although the strategy made sense for a businessman on his own account, it was inappropriate for agents.

Obviously, some forms of money-making are considered out-of-bounds for agents, and the losers are the ultimate wealth holders.

Small Stocks

The small stock effect has been analyzed and reported by academics. Investors know now that small capitalization stocks should yield excess return. Maybe this return is related to liquidity, maybe to taxes, or price-earnings ratios. Perhaps, more likely, it relates to the cost of obtaining relevant information.

No matter. What's interesting is that the academic evidence, to my knowledge, did not become known until the late 1970s, well after the greatest bull market in small stocks was mature. I can well remember discussing market imperfections (as we called them then) with clients in the mid-70s, when investing in anything other than the Nifty Fifty was considered imprudent. Academic evidence would have helped more then.

Perhaps investigative attention is influenced by receptiveness. If so, inefficiencies cease to exist just where and when they are well documented to have been present. The studies may be like traces of high energy particles in a cloud chamber: True selection has already passed through.

Cost

Evidence tells us that individually managed assets perform better than institutionally managed assets. In my view, the 1 percent or so of underperformance sustained by institutionally managed money year after year must be traceable to costs. Why does it cost so much to manage money? After all, one might rationally expect that institutional management would benefit from economies of scale not available to individual investors.

Opportunities for cost savings do exist. Transaction costs can be driven down, yet too few managers make the effort to do so. Can it be that the cookie jar is too much a temptation for the economic Invisible Hand?

Of course, clients themselves may be to blame. If they emphasize short-term returns, they are likely to encourage higher turnover rates. If they use multiple managers, they are likely to pay more in management fees, in many cases, without receiving any commensurate increase in return. . . .

It appears to me that academics have applied their skills more to the development of strategies than to day-to-day cost savings. Some of these strategies, such as index funds, have indeed led to cost savings. I think this area would prove fruitful for further research and application.

Investor Group Uniqueness

There appear to be different sets of payoffs for different market participants. I see no reason why tax effects, for example, shouldn't affect pricing. The evidence admittedly seems sketchy, but there is a theory in real estate that states that prices are set by the single most advantaged investor, that no other investor counts. Maybe this is true in public securities markets.

Furthermore, the quest for wealth maximization seems to be influenced more by expected consumption than by new accumulation. Surely payoffs are important to investors not because they result in nominal enhancement on a report, but only insofar as they lead to changed patterns of behavior. Possibly shifts of dominance from one group of investors to another may result in apparent inefficiencies, almost as a particle shifts from one plane to another instantaneously.

Time

Most models assume that time is a constant and that payoffs are the same through time. The assumption of "continuous time" is undoubtedly inapplicable to the real world. Investment horizons differ across investors and differ over time for the same investor. There are days when the market appears to be discounting events five years out. Then there are days when its ability to discount seems three months back.

Our ability to model the time function is still very poor; when it improves, this inefficiency too may disappear.

Forecasting from Price

We know that economic forecasting, although the prologue to any investment firm's presentation to clients, is not the most intelligent way to arrive at an investment strategy. Corporations, on the other hand, compete desperately in getting an edge in economic forecasting and, in fact, need economic forecasts to run their operations. But the market is much better at forecasting the economy than economists.

My suggestion is to read out from prices an economic forecast that might be used for business planning and corporate strategy. Maybe we've been working the problem backward.

Conclusion

These six inefficiencies are grounded in indifference, or in discomfort with some of the methods that could lead to wealth enhancement. They exist because we do not root out their basic causes. These causes are easy enough to identify, if one looks with enough dispassion and rigor. If the academics point to them, the rest of us can respond and . . . walk by.

High Finance or the Point of Vanishing Interest

C. Northcote Parkinson

Parkinson's law—that work expands to fill the time available for its completion—was also the title for a delightful book spoofing government and business. In chapter 3 on high finance, Parkinson examines how spending decisions are made by finance committees. Some fund managers claim to have observed comparable treatment of asset allocation decisions by investment committees.

People who understand high finance are of two kinds: those who have vast fortunes of their own and those who have nothing at all. To the actual millionaire a million dollars is something real and comprehensible. To the applied mathematician and the lecturer in economics (assuming both to be practically starving) a million dollars is at least as real as a thousand, they having never possessed either sum. But the world is full of people who fall between these two categories, knowing nothing of millions but well accustomed to think in thousands, and it is of these that finance committees are most comprised. The result is a phenomenon that has often been observed but never yet investigated. It

Reprinted from *Parkinson's Law and Other Studies in Administration*, Cambridge, Massachusetts. (1957), Chapter 3, pp. 24–32, by permission of Houghton Mifflin Co. Copyright © 1957, 1960, 1962, 1970, 1979 by C. Northcote Parkinson.

might be termed the Law of Triviality. Briefly stated, it means that the time spent on any item of the agenda will be in inverse proportion to the sum involved.

On second thought, the statement that this law has never been investigated is not entirely accurate. Some work has actually been done in this field, but the investigators pursued a line of inquiry that led them nowhere. They assumed that the greatest significance should attach to the order in which items of the agenda are taken. They assumed, further, that most of the available time will be spent on items one to seven and that the later items will be allowed automatically to pass. The result is well known. The derision with which Dr. Guggenheim's lecture was received at the Muttworth Conference may have been thought excessive at the time, but all further discussions on this topic have tended to show that his critics were right. Years had been wasted in a research of which the basic assumptions were wrong. We realize now that position on the agenda is a minor consideration, so far, at least, as this problem is concerned. We consider also that Dr. Guggenheim was lucky to escape as he did, in his underwear. Had he dared to put his lame conclusions before the later conference in September, he would have faced something more than derision. The view would have been taken that he was deliberately wasting time.

If we are to make further progress in this investigation we must ignore all that has so far been done. We must start at the beginning and understand fully the way in which a finance committee actually works. For the sake of the general reader this can be put in dramatic form thus:

Chairman We come now to Item Nine. Our Treasurer, Mr. McPhail, will report.

Mr. McPhail The estimate for the Atomic Reactor is before you, sir, set forth in Appendix H of the subcommittee's report. You will see that the general design and layout has been approved by Professor McFission. The total cost will amount to $10,000,000. The contractors, Messrs. McNab and McHash, consider that the work should be complete by April, 1959. Mr. McFee, the consulting engineer, warns us that we should not count on completion before October, at the earliest. In this view he is supported by Dr. McHeap, the well-known geophysicist, who refers to the probable need for piling at the lower end of the site. The plan of the main building is before you—see Appendix IX—and the blueprint is laid on the table. I shall be glad to give any further information that members of this committee may require.

Chairman   Thank you, Mr. McPhail, for your very lucid explanation of the plan as proposed. I will now invite the members present to give us their views.

It is necessary to pause at this point and consider what views the members are likely to have. Let us suppose that they number eleven, including the Chairman but excluding the Secretary. Of these eleven members, four—including the chairman—do not know what a reactor is. Of the remainder, three do not know what it is for. Of those who know its purpose, only two have the least idea of what it should cost. One of these is Mr. Isaacson, the other is Mr. Brickworth. Either is in a position to say something. We may suppose that Mr. Isaacson is the first to speak.

Mr. Isaacson   Well, Mr. Chairman. I could wish that I felt more confidence in our contractors and consultant. Had we gone to Professor Levi in the first instance, and had the contract been given to Messrs. David and Goliath, I should have been happier about the whole scheme. Mr. Lyon-Daniels would not have wasted our time with wild guesses about the possible delay in completion, and Dr. Moses Bullrush would have told us definitely whether piling would be wanted or not.

Chairman   I am sure we all appreciate Mr. Isaacson's anxiety to complete this work in the best possible way. I feel, however, that it is rather late in the day to call in new technical advisers. I admit that the main contract has still to be signed, but we have already spent very large sums. If we reject the advice for which we have paid, we shall have to pay as much again. (Other members murmur agreement.)

Mr. Isaacson   I should like my observation to be minuted.

Chairman   Certainly. Perhaps Mr. Brickworth also has something to say on this matter?

Now Mr. Brickworth is almost the only man there who knows what he is talking about. There is a great deal he could say. He distrusts that round figure of $10,000,000. Why should it come out to exactly that? Why need they demolish the old building to make room for the new approach? Why is so large a sum set aside for "contingencies"? And who is McHeap, anyway? Is he the man who was sued last year by the Trickle and Driedup Oil Corporation? But Brickworth does not know where to begin. The other members could not read the blueprint if he referred to it. He would have to begin by explaining what a reactor is and no one there would admit that he did not already know. Better to say nothing.

Mr. Brickworth   I have no comment to make.

Chairman   Does any other member wish to speak? Very well. I may take it then that the plans and estimates are approved? Thank you. May I now sign the main contract on your behalf? (Murmur of agreement.) Thank you. We can now move on to Item Ten.

Allowing a few seconds for rustling papers and unrolling diagrams, the time spent on Item Nine will have been just two minutes and a half. The meeting is going well. But some members feel uneasy about Item Nine. They wonder inwardly whether they have really been pulling their weight. It is too late to query that reactor scheme, but they would like to demonstrate, before the meeting ends, that they are alive to all that is going on.

Chairman   Item Ten. Bicycle shed for the use of the clerical staff. An estimate has been received from Messrs. Bodger and Woodworm, who undertake to complete the work for the sum of $2350. Plans and specification are before you, gentlemen.

Mr. Softleigh   Surely, Mr. Chairman, this sum is excessive. I note that the roof is to be of aluminum. Would not asbestos be cheaper?

Mr. Holdfast   I agree with Mr. Softleigh about the cost, but the roof should, in my opinion, be of galvanized iron. I incline to think that the shed could be built for $2000, or even less.

Mr. Daring   I would go further, Mr. Chairman. I question whether this shed is really necessary. We do too much for our staff as it is. They are never satisfied, that is the trouble. They will be wanting garages next.

Mr. Holdfast   No, I can't support Mr. Daring on this occasion. I think that the shed is needed. It is a question of material and cost. . . .

The debate is fairly launched. A sum of $2350 is well within everybody's comprehension. Everyone can visualize a bicycle shed. Discussion goes on, therefore, for forty-five minutes with the possible result of saving some $300. Members at length sit back with a feeling of achievement.

Chairman   Item Eleven. Refreshments supplied at meetings of the Joint Welfare Committee. Monthly, $4.75.

Mr. Softleigh   What type of refreshment is supplied on these occasions?

Chairman   Coffee, I understand.

Mr. Holdfast   And this means an annual charge of—let me see—$57?

Chairman   That is so.

Mr. Daring   Well, really, Mr. Chairman. I question whether this is justified. How long do these meetings last?

Now begins an even more acrimonious debate. There may be members of the committee who might fail to distinguish between asbestos and galvanized iron, but every man there knows about coffee—what it is, how it should be made, where it should be bought—and whether indeed it should be bought at all. This item on the agenda will occupy the members for an hour and a quarter, and they will end by asking the Secretary to procure further information, leaving the matter to be decided at the next meeting.

It would be natural to ask at this point whether a still smaller sum—$20, perhaps, or $10—would occupy the Finance Committee for a proportionately longer time. On this point, it must be admitted, we are still ignorant. Our tentative conclusion must be that there is a point at which the whole tendency is reversed, the committee members concluding the sum is beneath their notice. Research has still to establish the point at which this reversal occurs. The transition from the $50 debate (an hour and a quarter) to the $20 debate (two and a half minutes) is indeed an abrupt one. It would be the more interesting to establish the exact point at which it occurs. More than that, it would be of practical value. Supposing, for example, that the point of vanishing interest is represented by the sum of $35, the Treasurer with an item of $62.80 on the agenda might well decide to present it as two items, one of $30.00 and the other of $32.80, with an evident saving of time and effort.

Conclusions at this juncture can be merely tentative, but there is some reason to suppose that the point of vanishing interest represents the sum the individual committee member is willing to lose on a bet or subscribe to a charity. An inquiry on these lines conducted on race-courses and in Methodist chapels, might go far toward solving the problem. Far greater difficulty may be encountered in attempting to discover the exact point at which the sum involved becomes too large to discuss at all. One thing apparent, however, is that the time spent on $10,000,000 and on $10 may well prove to be the same. The present estimated time of two and a half minutes is by no means exact, but there is clearly a space of time—something between two and four and a half minutes—which suffices equally for the largest and the smallest sums.

Much further investigation remains to be done, but the final results, when published, cannot fail to be of absorbing interest and of immediate value to mankind.

INVESTMENT POLICY

Master Honma's Strategy of Commodities Speculation

Sokyu Honma

Sokyu Honma (1724–1803), a member of a prominent land-owning family in northern Japan, made huge gains in rice trading and speculation. His book, *Master Honma's Strategy of Commodities Speculation,* became a best-selling classic among commodities speculators and investors during his lifetime—and is still in print today—because of its chart analyses and instructive recommendations. Here, in a special translation by M. Owa, are 2 of the almost 100 chapters of the original book.

When volatile movements result in a huge price rise to reach a peak, followed by a precipitous drop, prices will settle into a pattern of movement within a narrow range. In such circumstances, when it is uncertain whether prices will go up again or decline further, people may be tempted to buy if there is some favorable news from the Osaka market. However, rather than a time to buy, this is a time to sell because this stage is a second peak or a transitory phase of either upward or downward movement, and in this case is not the true bottom. One must be careful to identify the real peaks and the real bottoms in the movement of prices. When prices remain at the bottom without rebounding

Translated from *Master Honma's Strategy of Commodities Speculation* by M. Owa.

quickly, and then begin to rise slowly, one may buy little by little because this stage can be identified as not a transitory phase but rather the real bottom which has begun to move up due to its own force.

There are two types of remorse which investors may feel. One is that felt when one misses 20–30% of possible gains by selling and taking profits at a point that turns out to be five or six days before the real peak. This type of remorse is not taken seriously.

The other type is felt when one misses a good time to sell due to greediness by not selling even though there is a potential gain of 70–80% several days before the true peak, and consequently suffers a severe loss. This type of remorse is very painful. One must restrain oneself.

Long-Term Investing

Jack L. Treynor

Jack Treynor, as editor, made the *Financial Analysts Journal* into a lively, challenging, and intellectually leading center of serious thinking about investing. Here, he clarifies the true role of long-term investing and explains why even highly efficient markets are not truly efficient in terms of profound, original insight by the investor who "buys for keeps."

The investor who would attempt to improve his portfolio performance through unconventional, innovative research is currently being challenged on three fronts: (1) The efficient marketers say he will be unable to find any ideas that haven't been properly discounted by the market. (2) Lord Keynes says that even if he finds these ideas his portfolio will be viewed as "eccentric" and "rash" by conventionally-minded clients and professional peers. (3) The investment philistine says that even if he stands by his ideas he won't be rewarded because actual price movements are governed by conventional thinking, which is immune to these ideas.

Successful response to the first challenge lies in distinguishing between two kinds of investment ideas: (a) those whose implications are straightforward and obvious, take relatively little special expertise to evaluate, and consequently travel quickly (e.g., "hot stocks"); and (b) those that require reflection, judgment, special expertise, etc., for their evaluation, and consequently travel slowly. (In practice, of course, ac-

Reprinted from the *Financial Analysts Journal* 32 (May/June 1976), pp. 56–59. Charlottesville, Virginia: Association for Investment Management and Research.

tual investment ideas lie along a continuous spectrum between these two polar extremes, but we can avoid some circumlocution by focusing on the extremes.) Pursuit of the second kind of idea—rather than the obvious, hence quickly discounted, insight relating to "long-term" economic or business developments—is, of course, the only meaningful definition for "long-term investing."

If the market is inefficient, it is not going to be inefficient with respect to the first kind of idea since, by definition, this kind is unlikely to be misevaluated by the great mass of investors. If investors disagree on the value of a security even when they have the same information, their differences in opinion must be due to errors in analysis of the second kind of idea. If these investors err independently, then a kind of law of averages operates on the resulting error in the market consensus. If enough independent opinions bear on the determination of the consensus price, the law of "large numbers" effect will be very powerful, and the error implicit in the consensus will be small compared to errors made on the average by the individual investors contributing to the consensus.

Under what circumstances, then, will investors' errors in appraising information available to all lead to investment opportunities for some? As the key to the averaging process underlying an accurate consensus is the assumption of independence, if all—or even a substantial fraction—of these investors make the same error, the independence assumption is violated and the consensus can diverge significantly from true value. The market then ceases to be efficient in the sense of pricing available information correctly. I see nothing in the arguments of Professor Eugene Fama or the other efficient markets advocates to suggest that large groups of investors may not make the same error in appraising the kind of abstract ideas that take special expertise to understand and evaluate, and that consequently travel relatively slowly.

According to Fama, "disagreement among investors about the implications of given information does not in itself imply market inefficiency unless there are investors who can consistently make better evaluations of available information than are implicit in market prices." Fama's statement can best be revised to read: "Disagreement among investors *due to independent errors in analysis* does not necessarily lead to market inefficiency." If the independence assumption is violated in practice, every violation represents a potential opportunity for fundamental analysis.

The assertion that the great bulk of practicing investors find long-term investing impractical was set forth almost 40 years ago by Lord Keynes:

> Most of these persons are in fact largely concerned not with most superior long term forecasts of the probable yield of an investment over its whole life, but with foreseeing changes in the *conventional basis of evaluation* a short time ahead of the general public. They are concerned not with what an investment is really worth to a man who buys it for keeps, but with what the market will evaluate it at under the influence of mass psychology three months or a year hence.

Obviously, if an investor is concerned with how the "mass psychology" appraisal of an investment will change over the next three months, he is concerned with the propagation of ideas that can be apprehended with very little analysis and that consequently travel fast.

On the other hand, the investment opportunity offered by market inefficiency is most likely to arise with investment ideas that propagate slowly, or hardly at all. Keynes went on to explain why practical investors are not interested in such ideas:

> It is the long term investor, he who most promotes the public interest, who will in practice come in for the most criticism, wherever investment funds are managed by committees or boards or banks. For it is in the essence of his behavior that he should be eccentric, unconventional and rash in the eyes of average opinion. If he is successful, that will only confirm the general belief in his rashness; and if in the short run he is unsuccessful, which is very likely, he will not receive much mercy. Worldly wisdom teaches that it is better for reputation to fail conventionally than to succeed unconventionally.

Thus Keynes not only described accurately the way most professional investors still behave; he also supplied their reasons for so behaving. He was careful never to say, however, that the long-term investor who sticks by his guns will not be rewarded.

But is the price of unconventional thinking as high as Keynes alleges? Modern portfolio theory says that an individual security can be assessed only in the context of the overall portfolio: So long as the overall portfolio has a reasonable level of market sensitivity and is reasonably well diversified, the beneficiary has nothing to fear from unconventional holdings—and still less to fear from conventional holdings bought for unconventional reasons. There is, of course, marketing advantage in holding securities enjoying wide popular esteem but, as investors as a class become more sophisticated, they are less likely to be challenged on specific holdings.

There is, finally, a school of thought that asserts that research directed toward improving our analytical tools is automatically impractical because it does not describe the behavior of a market consensus based on opinions of investors unfamiliar with these tools. This line of argument puts a premium on investment ideas that have broad appeal or are readily persuasive, while rejecting the ideas that capture abstract economic truths in terms too recondite to appeal to the mass of investors.

The investment philistine who asserts that it is impossible to benefit from superior approaches to investment analysis if the market consensus is not based on these approaches misunderstands what appraisal of a security means: An analyst's opinion of the value of a security is an estimate of the price at which, risk-adjusted, the return on the security is competitive with the returns on other securities available in the market. A superior method for identifying undervalued securities is therefore tantamount to a method of identifying securities that at their present prices offer superior long-term returns. The mere inclusion of such securities in a portfolio will guarantee a superior investment performance.

═

To the threefold challenge, a threefold reply is offered: (1) The efficient marketer's assertion that *no* improperly or inadequately discounted ideas exist is both unproved and unlikely. (2) Keynes' suggestion that unconventional investing is impractical is no longer valid in the age of modern portfolio theory. (3) The investment philistine who says good ideas that can't persuade the great mass of investors have no investment value is simply wrong.

The skeptical reader can ask himself the following question: If a portfolio manager . . . [is consistently right when the consensus is wrong, while] maintaining reasonable levels of market sensitivity and diversification, how long would it be before his investment record began to outweigh, in the eyes of his clients, the unconventionality of his portfolio holdings?

The Value of Patience

James H. Gipson

Jim Gipson has developed a successful investment management
firm and written a "plain-talk" book on investing, *Winning the Investment Game.* This excerpt, extolling the value of patience, is
drawn from a chapter called "The Virtues of Investing."

Patience is a virtue with a strange distribution among investors. Young
investors have all the time in the world to enjoy the long-term benefits
of patient investing, but they generally are the least patient. They want
instant gratification and immediate results. They want everything right
now, including instant investment performance. Young investors who
own stocks are likely to check their prices on a daily or hourly basis
even when they are not actively buying or selling.

Old investors do not have much time left and are actuarially unlikely
to enjoy the long-term results of patient investing. Their lives are entering their twilight years, yet they invest as if there will be an infinite
number of tomorrows. Old investors tend to be patient investors despite
the apparent lack of payoff from that patience.

For both young and old, temperament plays a larger role in their
investing than most care to acknowledge. The young in a hurry in their
business and social lives are likely to be in a hurry to see investment
results too. The old who are patient in most other aspects of life are
likely to be patient in investing too.

Reprinted from *Winning the Investment Game* (1984), Chapter 10, pp. 155–57, by permission of
McGraw-Hill Publishing Company, New York.

For the investors of any age who can rise above their own temperaments and choose rational courses of action which are most likely to enrich them, there are compelling arguments for choosing patience.

Patience is necessary simply by nature of the investing game itself. Over short periods of 1 to 2 years, luck is probably more important than skill. Stock prices have a large random element to them, analogous to Brownian motion in physics. That random motion of stock prices is a more important determinant of profits and losses than are skill and strategy in the short run. Only over periods of 3 to 5 years do the random movements of stock prices cancel each other out, leaving the net result of the investor's intelligence and diligence. . . .

Patience focuses an investor's attention on the goal of compounding money over a long period. Compounding can be magic, even when the compounding rate is modest. Investors who compound their money in real terms at 7 percent per year will double it in 10 years; in 40 years they will have 16 times their original amount. If the Indians and their descendants who sold Manhattan for $24 had been successful in compounding their money at 7 percent after taxes for the last 350 years, they would have about $30 billion today.

That $30 billion demonstrates more than the magic of compounding at even moderate rates of return. The complete absence of any pools of private capital remotely approaching $30 billion suggests that long-term compounding is an extraordinarily difficult feat. Even if one or two generations of investors are capable enough to accumulate and compound a respectable pool of assets, one of the heirs is likely to dissipate or lose it all.

The mortal enemy of compounding is the wipeout. A respectable rate of compounding for a lifetime can be lost with a single bad investment decision. The odds are that an investor will make that decision, or one of the investor's heirs will. Reducing the odds of a wipeout and raising the rate of compounding are the twin goals of this book.

Patience has more than the long-term advantage of focusing an investor's attention on the goals of long-term compounding and avoiding a wipeout. Patience also helps control short-term brokerage costs as well. The patient investor is less likely to buy and sell often, thereby reducing the 6 percent that a real estate broker charges or the roughly 3 to 4 percent that a normal stock broker charges for a round trip to sell one stock and buy another (discount brokers charge much less, and a stockholder should use one). A toll charge of 3 to 6 percent may seem small in relation to the total amount of an investor's principal, but it is large in relation to the annual income and profit received. If, for example, an impatient stockholder makes 10 percent per year in profits and turns over his portfolio twice a year at an average cost of 3 percent per turn, then 60 percent of his annual profits go to his broker! At the end of each year investors should add up their brokerage commissions along with their net profits, and then compare the two figures to see whether it is they or their brokers who are making the most money off the investments.

A New Paradigm for Portfolio Risk

Robert H. Jeffrey

"Risk" is not the same thing as "riskiness." And while agents (portfolio managers) can experience riskiness, or price volatility, only owners can experience true investment risk—the risk of being unable to meet cash obligations—as Tad Jeffrey explains.

Thomas Kuhn, in his landmark book, *The Structure of Scientific Revolutions,* describes the fall of a so-called "rational model" as a paradigm shift. "Scientists in any field and in any time," he writes, "possess a set of shared beliefs about the world, and for that time the set constitutes the dominant paradigm. . . . Experiments are carried on strictly within the boundaries of these beliefs and small steps toward progress are made." Citing the example of the Ptolemaic view of the universe with the earth at its center, Kuhn observes, "Elaborate mathematical formulas and models were developed that would accurately predict astronomical events based on the Ptolemaic paradigm" but it was not until Copernicus and Kepler discovered "that the formulae worked *more easily* . . ." when the sun replaced the earth as the center of the universe model that a "paradigm shift" in astronomy began and laid the foundation for even greater steps toward progress.[1]

Reprinted from *The Journal of Portfolio Management* 11 (Fall 1984), pp. 33–40. New York: Institutional Investor, Inc.

The thrust of this paper is to put forth a similar proposition. I shall assert, on a more mundane level, that our portfolio management process should also "work more easily" and *rewardingly* if a paradigm shift were to occur in the "rational model" or "shared belief" that portfolio risk is strictly a function of the volatility of portfolio returns.

The Case in Brief

This paper will suggest that the current paradigm is incomplete. More important, it is often misleading for a vast number of portfolio owners, because it fails to recognize that risk is a function of the characteristics of a portfolio's *liabilities* as well as of its assets and, in particular, of the cash-flow relationship between the two over time. Consequently, I shall offer a modification in the "rational model's" proxy for risk that, by including consideration of liabilities, which tend to be highly parochial, has the salutary effect of involving the portfolio owner more intimately in the risk determination process.

Finally, the paper will demonstrate how the acceptance of this modification in the definition of portfolio risk can naturally lead, in many cases, to the development of an asset mix policy tailored specifically to the particular, and often peculiar, needs of each portfolio owner. Such an asset mix is, after all, what "sophisticated" investors presumably seek but largely fail to achieve. The result is that most institutions have "look-alike" portfolios, even when the institutions themselves are markedly different.

Some of the ideas that I propose here have already been suggested, at least fragmentally, by others. In this Journal alone, Smidt, in discussing investment horizons and performance measurement, asks "How relevant are conventional risk/reward measures?"[2] and Trainer et al. state that the "holding period is the key to risk thresholds."[3] In fact, I have previously suggested that the holding periods or time horizons of a "major segment of institutional investors . . . (are) really infinity, at least as infinity is perceived by mortal beings."[4] Levy succinctly summarizes the concerns of those who are troubled by the current risk paradigm when he says that "time horizon is just as important as (return) variability in setting asset mixes" and suggests that "what is needed is an appropriate definition of risk."[5]

While this Journal would seem to be read mostly by academics and practitioners, it is my hope that the messages of this paper may eventually reach portfolio owners, and specifically, their chief executive officers and governing boards who, in the last analysis, are solely responsible for determining the measure of risk that is appropriate to their respective situations. On a more ambitious level, I suggest that the concepts here are relevant to *all* owners of assets, not just financial assets, and to all types of portfolios, not just those of institutions.

The conclusion that the acceptance of a new risk paradigm may prove rewarding for many portfolio owners stems from a belief that the current misunderstanding of what truly constitutes risk in a given situation often leads to portfolios with less than optimal equity contents and, therefore, lower long-term returns than might otherwise be achieved.[6] Furthermore, the failure to understand explicitly how much volatility risk can actually be tolerated in a given situation all too often encourages owners to dampen volatility by attempts to "time the market," which, as I—among others—have noted elsewhere, typically leads to mediocre long-term performance results.[7]

The utility of developing a concept of risk that is more intuitively understandable to *all* portfolio situations becomes more apparent when we accept the following three premises (of which only the third may be unfamiliar):

1. To the extent that the market *is* mostly efficient, we can expect only modest improvements in portfolio returns from active asset management.
2. To the extent that well diversified portfolio returns *do* vary directly with volatility over long periods of time, returns are indeed a function of risk as risk is presently defined.
3. Prudent portfolio owners, when confronted with *uncertainties* as to what constitutes an appropriate level of risk, will usually err on the side of accepting too little volatility rather than too much.

Given the first two premises, it follows naturally that the most effective way to enhance returns is to determine the extent to which volatility does indeed affect the portfolio owner's true *risk* situation, and to select a portfolio that provides the maximum level of *tolerable* volatility and thus the highest possible return, given the attendant risk. Since uncertainties concerning appropriate levels of risk usually result in overstatements of the impact of volatility, any change in the "rational model" that reduces portfolio owners' uncertainty of what truly constitutes risk in their particular situations should have a positive effect on future returns.

The Problem with Volatility as a Proxy for Risk

The problem with equating portfolio risk solely to the volatility of port-folio returns is simply that the proposition says nothing about what is being risked as a result of the volatility. For purposes of analogy consider the most common example in our daily lives, the weather. The risk implications of weather volatility are usually minimal for the vast majority of the population, who are not farmers or sailors or outdoor sports promoters or backpackers undertaking a winter hike in the mountains. Feeling "rewarded" by not having the daily burden of carrying a raincoat, many commuters are content to bear the nominal risk of occasionally getting slightly damp on their short walk to the office. On the other hand, on a long backpack in the mountains, where one of the "rewards" is clearly carrying as little weight as possible, prudent hikers will nonetheless hedge their risk of serious discomfort or worse by toting several pounds of raingear and perhaps a tent.

Volatility per se, be it related to weather, portfolio returns, or the timing of one's morning newspaper delivery, is simply a benign statistical probability factor that tells nothing about risk until coupled with a consequence. Its measurement is useless until we describe that probability in terms of the "probability of what." If the "what" is of no concern to the given individual or group, then the probability of "what's" occurring is likewise of no concern, and vice versa, and vice all the gradations in between. As the editor of this Journal reminded his clients some years ago, "The determining question in structuring a portfolio is the *consequence* of loss; this is far more important than the *chance* of loss."[8]

What then is the specific *consequence* whose probable occurrence should concern us?

Risk Is the Probability of Not Having Sufficient Cash with which to Buy Something Important

Since an investment *portfolio* is, etymologically, a collection of noncash pieces of paper (see footnote for *portfolio*'s literal meaning),[9] and since nearly everything we buy or every obligation we retire requires outlays of cash, the real risk in holding a portfolio is that it might not provide its owner, either during the interim or at some terminal date or both, with the cash he requires to make essential outlays, including meeting payments when due. (In the case of pension funds, such purchases include deferred payments for services previously rendered.) As Smidt aptly points out, "Investors are ultimately interested in the future stream of *consumption* they will be able to obtain from their portfolios" by converting noncash assets into cash.[10]

Nevertheless, since a portfolio's "cash convertibility" varies so directly with the volatility of its returns that the two terms are typically used interchangeably, one might argue that this emphasis on cash requirements in no way affects the usefulness of volatility as a proxy for risk. To so argue, however, overlooks the critical fact that *different portfolio owners have different needs for cash,* just as the commuter and the backpacker have different needs for protective clothing.

Ability to purchase, which varies directly with portfolio volatility, should not be confused with need to purchase. The latter . . . as Smidt suggests, is the portfolio's raison d'être, and is, or should be, the governing factor in determining the division of the portfolio's asset mix of holdings between those that are readily convertible into predictable amounts of cash and those that are not. By developing a risk paradigm that places the emphasis on "need to purchase" rather than "ability to purchase," each portfolio owner is encouraged to make a conscious decision as to whether or not to carry a raincoat (i.e., low volatile, "nearer to cash" assets). To carry a raincoat because others are carrying raincoats is simply being fashionable, and being fashionable in investment decisions typically leads to mediocre results, or worse.

From this, we can readily see that, strictly speaking, the widely used term "portfolio risk," standing by itself, is meaningless, because "the possibility of loss or injury," which is Webster's definition of risk, has no abstract significance. Like the weather, portfolios feel no pain; it is only *travelers* in the weather and *owners* of portfolios who bear whatever the attendant risk. What then is "owner's risk"?

Owner's risk is measured by the degree of "fit" that appears when a portfolio's minimum projected cash flows from income and principal conversions into cash are superimposed by time period on the owner's maximum future cash requirements for essential payments. Such a juxtapositioning provides a continuous series of pro forma cash flow statements. The periodic differences between the expected future cash conversion values of the assets, including their income flows, and the expected future cash requirements of the liabilities show up on the pro forma statements either as surpluses, connoting negative risk, or as deficits, connoting positive risk. As in all pro forma statements, however, the problem is not in the arithmetic, but rather in the accuracy of the assumptions used in projecting the cash flows.

A great deal of useful research has been done on the predictability, over varying time frames, of the cash conversion values of various arrays of portfolio assets. In this context, "predictability" can be roughly translated as "volatility" and "cash conversion value" as "total return." What is typically left undone, however, is an equally thorough analysis of the liability side of the equation, i.e., of the essentiality, timing, magnitude, and predictability of the portfolio owner's future cash requirements.

Summary: The Need for Cash Drives the Process

In the last analysis, risk is the likelihood of having insufficient cash with which to make essential payments. While the traditional proxy for risk, volatility of returns, does reflect the probable variability of the cash conversion value of a portfolio owner's assets, it says nothing about the cash requirements of his liabilities, or future obligations. Since fund assets exist solely to service these cash obligations, which vary widely from one fund to another in terms of magnitude, timing, essentiality, and predictability, portfolio owners are being seriously misled when they define risk solely in terms of the asset side of the equation.

Specifically, since both history and theory demonstrate that diversified portfolio returns historically and theoretically increase as return volatility increases, owners should be explicitly encouraged to determine *in their own particular situations* the maximum amount of return volatility that can be tolerated, given their own respective future needs for cash. While the theoreticians are presumably correct in directly relating volatility and returns, it is the owner's future *need for cash* that determines how much volatility he can tolerate and, therefore, the level of portfolio return that can theoretically be achieved.

My intention in emphasizing the *need for cash* has been purposely to shift responsibility for the risk-determination process from the asset manager to the portfolio owner. As one author reminds us, "Spending decisions (and thus future needs for cash) are the one input to the portfolio management equation that is totally controllable by the owner."[11] Furthermore, the cumulative effect of the owner's prior spending decisions on future needs for cash can, in most cases, best be fathomed and thus planned for, conceivably modified, and insured against, within the owner's own shop and not by an outside agent.

Finally, by letting the need for cash drive the portfolio management process, the owner can make future spending decisions more wisely. Over time, he can develop and sustain an understandable and defendable asset mix policy that will provide him with an optimum portfolio return given his particular cash requirement situation. In one sentence, the traditional, narrow definition of portfolio risk based solely on volatility encourages owners to apply a universal risk measurement standard, for which they themselves accept little personal responsibility, to what is essentially a highly parochial problem.

Notes

1. T. Kuhn, *The Structure of Scientific Revolutions,* Chicago: University of Chicago Press, 1970, as quoted in T. J. Peters and R. H. Waterman, Jr., *In Search of Excellence,* New York: Harper & Row, 1982, p. 42.
2. S. Smidt, "Investment Horizons and Performance Measurement," *The Journal of Portfolio Management,* Winter 1978, p. 18.
3. F. H. Trainer, Jr.; J. B. Yawitz; and W. J. Marshall, "Holding Period Is the Key to Risk Threshholds," *The Journal of Portfolio Management,* Winter 1979, p. 48.
4. R. H. Jeffrey, "Internal Portfolio Growth: The Better Measure," *The Journal of Portfolio Management,* Summer 1977, p. 10.
5. R. A. Levy, "Stocks, Bonds, Bills, and Inflation over 52 Years," *The Journal of Portfolio Management,* Summer 1978, p. 18.
6. While presumably unnecessary for readers of this Journal, we note here (using Ibbotson and Sinquefield data through 1981) that the annualized total return of the S&P 500 from 1926–1983 was 9.6% versus 3.2% for 90-day Treasury bills.
7. R. H. Jeffrey, "The Folly of Market Timing," *Harvard Business Review,* July–August 1984.
8. P. L. Bernstein, "Management of Individual Portfolios," *The Financial Analyst's Handbook* (S. Levine, ed.), Homewood, Illinois: Dow Jones-Irwin, Inc., 1975, pp. 1373–1388.
9. *Portfolio* derives from the Latin words *portare,* to carry, and *foglio,* leaf or sheet. Since the Romans had a perfectly good word for cash, *moneta,* which they could have used for "cashbox," we can thus infer that *foglio* refers to noncash forms of paper. Etymologically then, a "portfolio," or even a so-called "investment port-

folio," is not and should not be confused with cash, a distinction that most investors fail to make in the "mark-to-market" world in which we live.
10. Smidt, op. cit., p. 21.
11. J. P. Williamson and H. A. D. Sanger, "Educational Endowment Funds," *Investment Manager's Handbook*, Homewood, Illinois: Dow Jones-Irwin, Inc., 1980, p. 839. The actual quotation is, "The spending rate is totally controllable."

Timing Considerations in Investment Policy

Benjamin Graham
David L. Dodd

Ben Graham and Dave Dodd, in this 40-year-old passage from the third edition of their *Security Analysis,* explain why they are skeptics on "timing." "The major consideration," they say, is not when an investor buys or sells, "but at what prices."

Timing Considerations in Investment Policy

The old rule for the ordinary investor was that he should buy sound securities when he had funds available. If he waited for lower prices he would be losing interest on his money; he might "miss his market," even if prices declined; in any case, he was turning himself into a stock trader or speculator. Much of this view retains its validity. However, the time when the investor should clearly *not* buy common stocks is during the upper ranges of a bull market. For most issues this is tantamount to saying that he should not buy them at prices higher than can be justified by conservative analysis—which is something of a truism. But, as we pointed out previously, this warning applies also to the purchase of apparent "bargain issues" when the general price level seems dangerously high.

Excerpted from *Security Analysis: Principles and Techniques,* 3rd edition (1951; originally published 1934), Chapter 5, pp. 47–59, by permission of McGraw-Hill Publishing Company, New York.

There remain two other major questions of investment timing. The first is whether the investor should try to *anticipate* the movements of the market—endeavoring to buy just before an advance begins or in its early stages, and to sell at corresponding times prior to a decline. We state dogmatically at this point that it is impossible for *all* investors to follow timing of this sort, and that there is no reason for any typical investor to believe that he can get more dependable guidance here than the countless *speculators* who are chasing the same will-o'-the-wisp. Furthermore, the major consideration for the investor is not *when* he buys or sells, but at what prices.

This is an aspect of the "timing" philosophy that has been almost completely overlooked. The speculator will always be concerned about timing because he wants to make his profit in a hurry. But waiting for a profit is no drawback to an investor, as compared with having his money uninvested until a propitious buying "signal" is given, unless he thereby succeeds in buying at a sufficiently *lower price* to offset his loss of dividends. This means that *timing,* as such, does not benefit the investor unless it coincides with *pricing*. Specifically, if his aim is to buy and sell repeatedly, then his timing policy must enable him to repurchase his shares at substantially under his previous selling price. We do not believe that the popular approaches to stock-market timing—*e.g.,* the famous Dow theory—will accomplish this for the investor. . . .

A more serious question of timing policy, in our opinion, is presented by the well-defined cyclical movements of the stock market. Should the investor endeavor to confine his buying to the lower reaches of the recurrent bear markets, and correspondingly plan to sell out in the upper ranges of the recurrent bull markets? In such a policy, timing and pricing would clearly coincide—he would be buying at the right time because he would be buying at the right price, and vice versa.

No one can tell in advance how such an investment philosophy will work out in the years to come. Presumably its theoretical justification must be sought in the market's past history. If this is studied with some care, the indications it yields will not be found too encouraging.

. . . For the first half of the past 50-year period [1900–1950] both the amplitude of the price swings and their duration were regular enough to support the idea that the investor could buy his stocks at well-defined cheap levels and sell them out at well-defined dear levels, about once every five years. But since 1925 the market swings have been much less homogeneous in their successive forms, and the time interval between one low (or high) point and the next seems to have widened considerably. In fact since the bull-market peak of 1919 there have been only three subsequent peaks in 30 years—in 1929, 1937, and 1946. Since the bear-market low in 1921 there have been only two well-defined lows—in 1932 and 1942—plus a noncharacteristic market cycle between 1938 and 1942.

The Central Value of the Dow-Jones Industrial Average

We have made some hindsight calculations of results from the use of a "central-value method" of purchasing and selling, as a group, the stocks in the Dow-Jones Industrial Average. This method involves an actual appraisal of the Dow-Jones Unit, together with the decision to buy at a fixed discount below and to sell at a fixed premium above such value. In effect, however, it is not far different from a simple effort to wait for historically indicated low levels to buy and high levels to sell. On paper the results are rather attractive. But we do not believe that they can be projected into the future with any degree of confidence, or that they promise a sufficiently large gain to justify the risks they involve of "missing the market" and of losing investment income for a long period of time. These risks might make the enterprise an essentially speculative one, and apart from the mathematical probabilities of gain or loss, it would not be well suited to the psychology of the typical investor.

Futility of
Stock Market Guessing

David L. Babson

Dave Babson's wonderful reputation for incisive, honest advice was earned from 50 years of blunt truth-telling. This 1951 example shows why his firm's Staff Letter is widely read by competitors, clients, and friends.

In a recent Staff Letter we discussed the futility of trying to forecast the immediate trend of stock prices. It must be apparent to intelligent investors that if anyone possessed the ability to do so consistently and accurately he would become a billionaire so quickly he would not find it necessary to sell his stock market guesses to the general public.

In many of these Letters we have attempted to point out the fundamental difference between basic value and market price. *Values can be analyzed and tested by statistical measurements*. While emotional factors and surprise news developments often temporarily upset the relationship between price and value, eventually the two become correlated.

Consequently, we are strong advocates of basing investment decisions on thorough studies of VALUE rather than wasting time guessing whether PRICES will be higher or lower next week or next month.

If clients had the opportunity to observe the tremendous losses investors have suffered in just the post-war period by either their own guess

Reprinted from the *Weekly Staff Letter* (August 27, 1951), by permission of David L. Babson & Co.

or following someone else's guess on the immediate trend of prices and the market, they would be appalled. Almost every weekly "advisory service" which attempts to "forecast" has advocated selling stocks since 1947 and almost all are bearish today.

The market guesser pays scant attention to the fundamental measurements of value—the relationship of price to current and prospective earnings and dividends. He has no more adequate method of analyzing the future prospects for industrial activity than a guess. The man who is more concerned with price than value places little weight on the differing characteristics of industries and companies.

He assumes everyone interested in securities is a speculator who is concerned only with the immediate fluctuations in price. He does not understand that the real objective of the genuine investor is to conserve his living standards, not just the *number* of dollars he possesses. (If he protects his living standards, the number of dollars he owns will take care of itself.)

The price forecaster does not recognize that the responsible and intelligent man wants to buy an interest in a well-managed, financially-sound business which has above-average prospects of continued growth and expansion, not to gamble on a name which is printed on the quotation page every day. . . .

Likely Gains from
Market Timing

William F. Sharpe

Bill Sharpe, Timken Professor of Finance at Stanford's business school and a principal of William F. Sharpe Associates, is a winner of the Nobel Prize in financial economics who has made many important contributions to the theory and practice of investment management. Here are brief excerpts from his 1975 examination of the level of decision-making superiority necessary to successfully implement a market timing style. Readers will find considerable statistical underpinning in the complete article.

The investment manager who hopes to outperform his competitors usually expects to do so either by the selection of securities within a given class or by the allocation of assets to specific classes of securities. Potentially, one of the most productive forms of the latter strategy is to hold common stocks during bull markets and cash equivalents during bear markets ("market timing").

In a perfectly efficient market, any attempt to obtain performance superior to that of the overall "market portfolio" (taking into account both risk and return) by picking and choosing among securities would fail. Although few investment managers are ready to admit that U.S. security markets are completely efficient, there is a growing awareness that inefficiencies are few: Any divergence between the price of a secu-

Excerpted from the *Financial Analysts Journal* 31 (March/April 1975), pp. 60–69. Charlottesville, Virginia: Association for Investment Management and Research.

rity and the "intrinsic value" that would be assigned to it by well informed and highly skilled analysts is likely to be small, temporary and difficult to identify in advance. Empirical studies of the performance of professionally managed portfolios yield results consistent with this view: Few, if any, provide better-than-average returns relative to risk year in and year out.

Some have argued that abnormal gains from selection of individual stocks or even industry groups are likely to be too small to justify the costs associated with attempts to identify and take advantage of apparent inefficiencies. Instead, it is said, the big gains are to be made by successful market timing. This approach is sufficiently popular to be recognized as one of several major "management styles." When portfolio values shrink in extended bear markets, investors increasingly regard this style as a likely cure for their ills. Thus managers committed to timing strategies with the skill or luck to have moved to cash equivalents in the bear market of 1973–1974 were able to attract money in the latter part of 1974, while their competitors suffered both decreases in the market value of assets and often actual loss of accounts. Market efficiency implies that it should be at least as difficult to predict market turns as to identify specific securities that will perform abnormally well or poorly. Moreover, attempts to take advantage of such predictions entail non-recoverable transaction costs, and expose investment funds to larger losses when errors are made. On the average, stocks outperform short-term money market instruments. Without superior predictive ability, one is likely to forgo return by shifting from stocks to cash equivalents. But this is to state the obvious. How superior must one's predictions be to implement a market timing style effectively?

═══

The conclusion is fairly clear. Attempts to time the market are not likely to produce incremental returns of more than four per cent per year over the long run. Moreover, unless a manager can predict whether the market will be good or bad each year with considerable accuracy (e.g., be right at least seven times out of ten), he should probably avoid attempts to time the market altogether.

This pessimistic view will not appeal to those who feel that they can avoid the next bear market by judicious shifts of funds out of stocks and into short-term low-risk instruments. Some are now doing this, and others are actively considering it. Overall, of course, funds cannot be "shifted" beyond any changes in the market values of relevant securities outstanding. But individual investors can and do make such shifts.

It is said that the military is usually well prepared to fight the previous war. A number of investors now engaging in active market timing appear to be preparing for the previous market. Unfortunately for the military, the next war may differ from the last one. And unfortunately for investors, the next market may also differ from the last one.

Mr. Market, Investment Success and You

Warren E. Buffett

Warren Buffett's affection for Ben Graham, with whom he studied and worked early in his career, is seen again in this passage from the 1987 Annual Report of Berkshire Hathaway.

Whenever Charlie and I buy common stocks for Berkshire's insurance companies (leaving aside arbitrage purchases, discussed later) we approach the transaction as if we were buying into a private business. We look at the economic prospects of the business, the people in charge of running it, and the price we must pay. We do not have in mind any time or price for sale. Indeed, we are willing to hold a stock indefinitely so long as we expect the business to increase in intrinsic value at a satisfactory rate. When investing, we view ourselves as business analysts— not as market analysts, not as macroeconomic analysts, and not even as security analysts.

Our approach makes an active trading market useful, since it periodically presents us with mouth-watering opportunities. But by no means is it essential: a prolonged suspension of trading in the securities we hold would not bother us any more than does the lack of daily quotations on World Book or Fechheimer. Eventually, our economic fate will

Excerpted from the "Chairman's Letter," *Berkshire Hathaway, Inc. 1987 Annual Report,* by permission of the author.

be determined by the economic fate of the business we own, whether our ownership is partial or total.

Ben Graham, my friend and teacher, long ago described the mental attitude toward market fluctuations that I believe to be most conducive to investment success. He said that you should imagine market quotations as coming from a remarkably accommodating fellow named Mr. Market who is your partner in a private business. Without fail, Mr. Market appears daily and names a price at which he will either buy your interest or sell you his.

Even though the business that the two of you own may have economic characteristics that are stable, Mr. Market's quotations will be anything but. For, sad to say, the poor fellow has incurable emotional problems. At times he feels euphoric and can see only the favorable factors affecting the business. When in the mood, he names a very high buy–sell price because he fears that you will snap up his interest and rob him of imminent gains. At other times he is depressed and can see nothing but trouble ahead for both the business and the world. On these occasions he will name a very low price, since he is terrified that you will unload your interest on him.

Mr. Market has another endearing characteristic: He doesn't mind being ignored. If his quotation is uninteresting to you today, he will be back with a new one tomorrow. Transactions are strictly at your option. Under these conditions, the more manic-depressive his behavior, the better for you.

But, like Cinderella at the ball, you must heed one warning or everything will turn into pumpkins and mice: Mr. Market is there to serve you, not to guide you. It is his pocketbook, not his wisdom, that you will find useful. If he shows up some day in a particularly foolish mood, you are free to either ignore him or to take advantage of him, but it will be disastrous if you fall under his influence. Indeed, if you aren't certain that you understand and can value your business far better than Mr. Market, you don't belong in the game. As they say in poker, "If you've been in the game 30 minutes and you don't know who the patsy is, *you're* the patsy."

Ben's Mr. Market allegory may seem out-of-date in today's investment world, in which most professionals and academicians talk of efficient markets, dynamic hedging and betas. Their interest in such matters is understandable, since techniques shrouded in mystery clearly have value to the purveyor of investment advice. After all, what witch doctor has ever achieved fame and fortune by simply advising "Take two aspirins"?

The value of market esoterica to the consumer of investment advice is a different story. In my opinion, investment success will not be produced by arcane formulae, computer programs or signals flashed by the price behavior of stocks and markets. Rather an investor will succeed by coupling good business judgment with an ability to insulate his thoughts and behavior from the super-contagious emotions that swirl about the marketplace. In my own efforts to stay insulated, I have found it highly useful to keep Ben's Mr. Market concept firmly in mind.

Four Cornerstones of a New Investment Policy

James H. Lorie

Jim Lorie, an early instructor in the "random walk" school, was a professor, an economist, and director of the Center for Research in Securities Prices at the University of Chicago. He offers wise advice in this 1971 essay.

The SEC's recent *Institutional Investor Study* "revealed" once again that equities selected by institutions provide about the same total return as equities in general. The SEC indicated in its 1962 study that this was true for mutual funds, and the same point has been abundantly confirmed by others. Results of various portfolios are different; the differences in the short run are reasonably attributed to chance and in the long run to risk.

When the first studies appeared, the findings were startling and widely misinterpreted as indicating that the institutions in question were somehow deficient. By now, it should be recognized that the findings merely indicate that our capital markets are highly efficient, causing prices to reflect very quickly all relevant information. Institutions, through their competent and energetic research, have contributed to this efficiency and should not be criticized for failing to do consistently

Reprinted from *Institutional Investor* (November 1971), pp. 48–50, 85–86. New York: Institutional Investor, Inc.

better than other institutions or other investors managing portfolios of equal riskiness.

An increased understanding that institutions cannot be expected to have superior gifts of prophecy with respect to individual securities has caused many of them to be puzzled about the ways in which they can reasonably expect to achieve superiority. This article offers some solutions to this problem.

Two Truths

One of the most important truths about investing, then, is that stock markets are highly efficient—with the result that investors cannot expect on the average to predict price movements more accurately than others. A second truth is equally important and equally well documented: The market pays a premium to those who bear risk. For example, almost all of the long-run variations observed in rates of return from mutual funds are explained by differences in the riskiness of their portfolios.

Knowledge about risk is valuable. Most things about the market—for instance, changes in earnings or dividends or prospective mergers—if generally known, are not worth knowing since prices of the relevant securities reflect the knowledge. But even commonplace knowledge about risk is valuable, since most investors wish to have their portfolios controlled with respect to risk as well as to return. Further, it is possible to measure risk in a meaningful way and to produce portfolios which in the future will have a specified degree of risk.

These two important truths about investments suggest the following policies for trust departments and investment counseling firms:

1. *Spend less on security analysis, and spend it differently.* As noted previously, commonplace knowledge about a company does not provide the basis for superior investments. And most security analysts are usually capable of knowing only what is generally known. The conventional scrutiny of public information and the conventional quest for private clues produce only conventional wisdom and returns. It is unreasonable to expect that the typical, moderately paid security analyst can achieve superior insights into the complex operations of industries and firms. The first suggestion, therefore, is to abandon conventional security analysis. Its occasional triumphs are offset by its occasional disasters, and on the average nothing valuable is realized.

Some individual institutional investors may forgo security analysis altogether, but almost certainly no institution will. If security analysis must be carried out, it should be done by fewer, more highly paid persons who seek their insights in unconventional ways or can follow companies and industries for which their education and experience give them a reasonable hope of superior understanding.

2. *Provide better investment guidance.* Many trust departments and investment counseling firms make only rudimentary efforts to understand the needs, resources and tastes of their clients whether they be personal clients, corporate managers of pension funds, endowed institutions or others. Almost certainly, the most important determinant of the results of a portfolio is the investment policy selected. It is, therefore, worth trying to do the job well. This means an initial comprehensive analysis of the client's total circumstances and a periodic review to ascertain significant changes.

Typically the only guidance given to portfolio managers is a specific list of prohibitions and a rough indication of a risk category. Often, the portfolio manager is not even aware of the other financial resources available to the client or the current and changing demands upon him. Even with regard to pension funds which are generally large, portfolio managers are guided in part by the work of actuaries and corporate treasurers who do not systematically and comprehensively determine appropriate investment policy. In other words, investment counselors, whether in trust departments or in investment counseling firms, should do more and better investment counseling.

3. *Specify investment policy precisely.* Almost no professional portfolio manager entirely disregards the need to choose an investment policy. Yet, policy prescriptions are typically so crude and imprecise that they fail to give adequate direction to managers or to provide an adequate basis for controlling and evaluating their performance.

Most trust departments and counseling firms rely on "buy" lists, maximum equity ratios, and a diversification requirement to control investment policy for each account. Unfortunately, those standard devices permit wide variation in policies and results for accounts supposedly having the same objectives. Within the limits of a maximum commitment to equities and the necessity for substantial diversification, it is possible to select portfolios from the typical "buy" list which have very different characteristics and produce very different results. This should be totally unacceptable both to institutional investors and their clients. A client who places his funds in the control of an institution deserves to know what investment policy will be, what the reasonable expectations from that policy are, and that the policy will be accurately and efficiently implemented. At the present time, the client is not well treated in those respects.

How does one remedy these shortcomings?

Risk is an elusive and difficult concept, but it is plausible to relate it to the range of feasible outcomes of an investment policy. Investments whose rates of return over a future period are certain can be described as riskless. Those subject to only modest variation are only moderately risky, and those subject to great possible variation are quite risky. These risks can be quantified by measuring actual variability through time in rates of return on the portfolios.

It is possible to measure total variability [over] time, but not to specify in advance the total variability of a portfolio. The impact of one source of variability, however, can be controlled, and this source can be made to account for virtually all the variability that is experienced. The variability in any portfolio can be thought of as arising from changes in the market and from other sources. Further, it is quite simple to select a portfolio virtually all of whose variability is caused by market movements. It is easy to select a portfolio which moves in step with the market, but it is not necessary that the steps taken by the portfolio be of the same size as those taken by the market. By combining the portfolio with appropriate proportions of riskless assets, which are totally insensitive to the market, it is possible to make portfolios which go up and down faster, slower or at the same speed as the market in general. It is also reasonable to say that a measure of the sensitivity of such a portfolio to the market is an appropriate measure of its risk.

Most institutions will not be willing to settle for portfolios whose movements are totally market determined, despite their own disappointing historical experience. The quest for superior performance will undoubtedly continue and may in some instances be successful. This quest means the acceptance of variability in returns for reasons other than market movements. For portfolios subject to such variability, it is necessary in specifying investment policy to do more than specify sensitivity to the market; it is also necessary to specify the proportion of total variability that will be allowed for reasons other than market movements.

Measures of sensitivity to market movement and of the proportion of variability accounted for by the market are the conventional statistics: the regression coefficient (beta) and the coefficient of determination

(r^2), respectively. They are familiar to all statisticians and to all those who have worked with modern portfolio theory. . . . They constitute a feasible and understandable way to specify investment policy (i.e., degrees of risk) for each account, for determining the degree of conformity of each account to that policy and ultimately for evaluating portfolio performance. It is possible to provide portfolio managers with systems for seeing whether the stocks which they have selected or are considering will cause intolerable departures from investment policy.

The two major problems in managing investments are selection and timing. Institutional investors who try to solve the timing problem have in beta an efficient means for doing so. Some institutional officers who foresaw the 1969–1970 decline in the market were shocked to discover that portfolio managers had not reacted appropriately to general admonitions to "build reserves," assume a more "defensive posture," etc. Portfolio managers not sharing the institutional pessimism found ways to conform to the letter of the policy prescription while violating its spirit. They built reserves by reducing the commitment to equities while at the same time shifting to more volatile securities. As a consequence, despite the wisdom of the institutional executives with respect to the timing problem, many portfolios suffered severely as the market declined.

If institutions had adequately discharged their responsibility in reestablishing policy for their portfolio managers, this unhappy result would have been avoided. The timing policy should have been specified in terms of beta. For example, portfolios which in normal times would move up and down as rapidly as the market (i.e., portfolios having a beta of 1.0) would have been required to achieve a beta of, say, 0.25. They would then have fallen only one-fourth as much as the market. Institutions should not permit portfolio managers to adopt widely different policies with respect to timing, and the means for achieving effective control are available.

4. *Control and evaluate portfolio managers.* While a few devout believers in the efficient market would be willing to eliminate all security analysis and select portfolios with computers on the basis of the control mechanisms just described, most financial institutions will continue to analyze securities and have warm, breathing portfolio managers. It thus becomes sensible to control them and evaluate their skills.

The control mechanism is simple to describe and harder to create. A computer periodically—perhaps monthly—indicates whether or not each account is sufficiently in step with the market and has the prescribed degree of sensitivity to its movements. Intolerable departures from prescribed policy are called to the attention of the portfolio manager for correction.

Since the publication of the Bank Administration Institute's study of methods for evaluating pension fund performance, and especially since the recent release of the *Institutional Investor Study,* it is recognized that evaluation of performance must take account of the risk that was assumed. For that purpose, it is necessary to have quantitative measures of riskiness, and the measures specified above can be used. In other words, the rate of return on each account would be evaluated in terms of the constraint imposed upon the manager with respect to risk.

The manager, if believed to have great wisdom and experience, might be allowed to select portfolios which vary substantially for reasons other than market movements. Perhaps other managers would be more narrowly constrained and allowed less discretion in selecting portfolios. Each would be evaluated in terms of the risk actually assumed.

It is, of course, possible to go beyond the mere measurement of performance in order to understand its causes. The most important causes of good or bad performances are the ability to select securities, the magnitude of transaction costs and exposure to taxes. Overall evaluation of performance should be supplemented with efforts at diagnosis focused on those three factors.

A Spur to Service

To sum up, an implication of the efficiency of markets is that the most important nonroutine function of trust departments and investment counselors is choosing an investment policy for each account and specifying that policy so precisely that portfolio managers can be controlled and evaluated. Because of the efficiency of markets, the overwhelmingly most important influence on the returns of portfolios is their riskiness. Investment policy should, therefore, be expressed in terms of risk. Conventional statistics and readily available computer programs facilitate such specification as well as the selection of appropriate portfolios and the evaluation of results.

Institutions which follow these guidelines need not be uneasy if their portfolios do not outperform the market; they will be providing a superior service to their clients.

The Yale Plan

Laurence G. Tighe

The "Yale plan" for investing endowment monies was a $500 million blunder. As post–World War II interest rates were rising—and taking bond prices down—one of history's great bull stock markets took off. Yale's plan, however, drove the endowment fund out of rising stocks and into falling bonds—with disastrous consequences. Here are extracts from the 1940 speech before the Trust Division of the American Bankers Association in which Associate Treasurer Laurence G. Tighe explained how the plan would operate. Yale has still not recovered from it.

One often hears discussions about the relative excellence of various universities; about the size of their libraries; the reputation of their faculties; the prowess or weakness of their athletic teams. But few realize the extent or the scope of these institutions as business organizations. The annual gross income of Yale University is about $9,000,000.

If you will compare this figure with the gross of your own business, you will realize the magnitude of the operation. The collection and expenditure of this sum involve almost every kind of business. An endowment fund of $100,000,000 must be invested and supervised; a plant of $100,000,000 must be maintained and operated; educational facilities with their infinite variations and innumerable ramifications must be provided. Also properties acquired through one means or another must be managed and administered. A farm in North Dakota, a hotel in Du-

Reprinted from *Yale Alumni Magazine* (April 12, 1940), pp. 4–5. New Haven, Connecticut: © Yale Alumni Publications, Inc.

luth, a sporting goods store in Knoxville, a pear orchard in upper New York State, a dry goods store in Bridgeport, and a land development in Greenwich are a few that come to mind.

It is a business, the product of which is education, and in good times or bad, in 1928 or 1932, the demand for this product never slackens. The plant is always operating at capacity. It is difficult and hardly justifiable to attempt to make drastic economies when the factory is producing more goods than ever before, and its personnel working at top speed. A university cannot economize at the expense of the quality of its product. By the very nature of its functions, and with the economic, social, and political developments that are continually taking place, it must always move forward or it inevitably slides back.

The income from investments provides a large percentage of the total needed to operate the institution. The other sources do not fluctuate greatly, so it is upon the stability, the continuity, and even the increase of this investment income that the University must depend for its ability successfully to perform the function for which it was chartered.

Finance Committee

There are many ways of taking advantage of the variations in the price of equities and it is not in any way intended that the method which I shall describe is the only one or the best one. The important thing is to formulate a plan and then adhere to it, no matter what happens. If circumstances change, variations in the plan can be made, but if it is to work effectively, there must be no deviation from the basic principles. The main object should be to set up some plan which works automatically and is not dependent upon the judgment of one individual or a group of individuals. It should take on the nature of a thermostatic control.

Most investment funds are supervised by an investment or a finance committee. The active manager of the fund is pleased to have his responsibility shared by such a committee. He is often, however, harassed by its unwillingness to take action one way or the other and convinced that the doctors, lawyers, and businessmen who so often make up its membership know nothing about investing money. Often, the more intelligent, the more informed, and the more active the members, the more difficult it is to obtain a unanimous decision.

Yale Plan

After considerable research and study the Finance Committee of the Yale Corporation adopted the following plan to handle the equities in the University's Portfolio. It was determined that under present circumstances, fixed-income securities should constitute seventy per cent of the Portfolio and equities thirty per cent thereof. Preferred stocks and bonds in good standing were classified as fixed-income-bearing securities while defaulted bonds, preferred stocks paying no dividends, and common stocks were classified as equities. In figuring these percentages, bonds in good standing were carried at their par value. A bond is a promise to pay and it matters little at what price it sells unless it is in default. All other securities were carried at market values.

It was then determined that if, through market appreciation the percentage of the equities rose to forty, thus making the percentage of income securities sixty, enough equities would be automatically sold and the proceeds invested in income securities so that the resulting ratios would be thirty-five per cent for equities and sixty-five per cent for income securities. When the time to sell arrives, the same proportionate amount of each issue of stock in the Portfolio is disposed of. This necessitates having approximately equal amounts in readily marketable issues, but it is important as it avoids the inevitable and unending arguments among committee members as to the relative merits of duPont and Union Carbide even though the decision to sell something has been reached. If the market continues to advance and the 40–60 ratio is again reached, the process is repeated.

If the market declines so that the ratio of equities is fifteen per cent and of income securities eighty-five per cent, then enough of the latter is sold and equities bought so that the resulting ratio is twenty per cent for equities and eighty per cent for income securities. If the market continues to decline, this operation is again repeated. Between these extremes, any issue can be sold provided the proceeds are invested in the same class of security. Depending on conditions, volatile stocks can be sold and the less spectacular and steadier issue purchased or this process can be reversed.

Before this formula was adopted, and in order to prove whether or not it was effective, a theoretical fund of $1,000,000, invested $300,000 in equities and $700,000 in bonds, was set up as of January 1, 1926. Standard Statistics averages of 90-stocks, which were at 100 at that time, were used as a guide. Various ratios and selling points were tried, but those given above produced by far the best results. The history of this fund is of interest. No action was indicated from January 1, 1926, until April 13, 1928, when the stock averages had risen to 156. Stocks were then sold, and bonds purchased. On January 2, 1929, this process was again repeated. Also on August 22, 1929, with the averages at 244. You will remember that the high was in September of that year with the averages at 253. By September 29, 1931, the averages had dropped to 79. At that point, bonds were sold and stocks purchased. This was repeated on April 4, 1932, with the average at 56 and on May 26, 1932, when they were at 38. The low point was reached in June, 1932, with the averages at 33.

There were two more selling points: November 6, 1935, and July 21, 1936. On or about August 5, 1938, the averages were again at 100 and the fund was valued at $1,246,000 with $874,000 in bonds and $372,000 in stocks. Thus in a cycle where the averages had gone from 100 to 253, down to 33, and back to 100, the fund had increased by about twenty-five per cent, the holdings of bonds had been built up from $700,000 to $874,000 and the holdings of equities were still large enough so that should the market again appreciate, full advantage of the rise would be felt. The effect on the income from the fund was even more satisfactory. This is clear in the case of Eastman Kodak Company stock which would have been sold at an average price of 180, providing at the current dividend of $6 a yield of 3.33 per cent, while it would have been repurchased at an average price of 66, which on the same dividend is a yield of nine per cent.

This formula may sound complicated. But in effect it is very simple and easy to follow and operate. If adopted, it assures a proper relationship between the various classes of securities. It provides for the continual building up of the amount of fixed-income-bearing securities in the Portfolio without lessening the possibilities of appreciation because of the elimination of equity holdings. It does away with the hysteria of optimism or pessimism in determining when to buy or sell and over the period it should materially increase the income. Changing conditions may make it necessary to alter the basic ratio between equities and income securities or make it advisable to buy or sell as result of lesser variations in market prices. These points can easily be adjusted without any change in the basic formula. It may be that this system is not applicable to all accounts. There are in operation others which depend upon the Dow-Jones averages or some similar yardstick. It is important to have a formula that is workable and effective in view of the character of the account under supervision, but the really vital point is to adopt some formula and then stick to it.

The Case for Property Investment by Pension Funds

George Ross Goobey

George Ross Goobey made three extraordinary decisions in his capacity as investment manager of Imperial Tobacco's pension fund. All three were unorthodox, innovative, boldly executed—and correct. First, immediately after World War II, he sold out the fund's bonds (some of which subsequently lost fully two thirds of their value). Second, he went 100 percent into common stocks, catching one of history's great bull markets near its inception. Third, he made a major commitment to real property in the early 1970s— avoiding the drop in stock prices and capturing the gain in property values driven by the major increase in inflation rates that followed. With this troika of striking actions, he made his investment career a triumph. Here, he explores the case for property investment at the 1971 Annual Conference of the National Association of Pension Funds, held in Killarney.

I need hardly remind you that it is only 25 years ago since the British Government issued some £500 million of Treasury 2½% [gilt-edged] Stock at par redeemable in 1975, or after, at the option of the Government, and it would not need a soothsayer to forecast that that option will never be exercised. Even the Fund with which I had become associated shortly after that time, had purchased £½ million of this Stock at

Reprinted from a speech given at the Annual Conference of the National Association of Pension Funds at Killarney, Ireland, 1971.

the issue price and was thereby saddling the Fund with an investment which could at no time earn interest at more than 2½%, in spite of the fact that at that time the Parent Company (Imperial Tobacco) was guaranteeing a minimum rate of interest to the Fund of 5% per annum.

I well remember that one of my early recommendations to the Trustees was that they should cut their losses and sell this investment, the market price of which had already dropped to 83. You can well understand the reluctance of the Trustees to accept voluntarily this capital loss, but I am glad to say they eventually allowed themselves to be persuaded and you will perhaps know that the price today of that Stock is 27¼ because of the radical change in the level of world interest rates which, in a way, is a belated acknowledgment of the fact that we live in a world of inflation.

At that time it was possible to buy the Ordinary shares of our leading industrial companies on a basis of at least 2% higher initial return than gilt-edged. In face of the fact that dividends on Ordinary shares had increased over the years at the rate of 4 to 5% per annum, this bonus of a higher immediate return compared with Stocks which could not increase their rate of interest, was an obvious anomaly. As a result of successfully presenting these facts to my Trustees, they were persuaded to sell all their fixed interest securities and to invest the whole of the funds in equities. Not only were we at that time obtaining a higher immediate return on our equities, but, of course, that income grew each year as dividends increased as we could expect from the evidence that equity dividends had been increased over the years.

Other pension fund investment managers were able to persuade their Trustees and the effect was, of course, that the laws of supply and demand caused equity prices to rise compared with gilt-edged securities, and the 2% yield gap to which I have referred, disappeared. At this stage the financial press were forecasting that this milestone possibly presaged the end of the cult of the equity, as they call it. They were quite wrong, of course, and equity prices quite rightly continued to rise compared with fixed interest and we entered into the era of the reverse yield gap, wherein equity investors were prepared to accept a lower immediate return than fixed interest securities in return for the expectation that the long term income would be greater, by reason of the general overall increase expected in equity dividends. . . .

At successive stages of this evolution the traditionally minded investor called halt; when the *reverse* yield gap got to 2% he thought it was enough. When it got to 4% he was even more apprehensive. But it is quite obvious that this reverse yield gap, certainly to a gross fund such as a pension fund, should be equal to the annual rate at which dividends might be expected to increase in the future and as the evidence of the past is that dividends have increased over the years at the rate of 4–5% per annum, there is a case for stating that the reverse yield gap should be of this order.

However, when the reverse yield gap comes to be of the order of 5–5½%, as it did two years ago, one must reconsider whether one might not be better in the long run to be again in fixed interest securities. You will appreciate that the real crux of our problem is, what is going to be the annual rate of growth of dividends in the future. Will it be more or less than this 4–5% of the past 50 years? The most vital factor in this is, of course, the rate of inflation. If we are visualising inflation in our countries on the South American scale, then fixed interest securities will not be worth considering at any price. I sincerely hope that we will not come to this, and my personal opinion is that we will not.

There are other factors, however, to consider. One simple statistical fact is that in the 4–5% growth of dividends over the past 50 years there has been an upward change in the proportion of profits which companies have declared as dividends and less has been ploughed back to finance future capital developments. There is a school of thought that maintains that new projects should be financed by entirely new capital and not out of retentions of profits on present capital, but obviously 100% distribution is the limit to how far we can go in this direction. The simple point I want to bring out is that even the 4–5% [increases p.a.] of the past includes an element which is of limited recurring effect.

Another factor which we have to take into account in this country is the growing Governmental interference in the affairs of industrial companies. In its attempt to curb the Trade Unions from putting in larger and larger wage claims, we experienced for a year or two recently a limit on the amount by which dividends could be increased of 3½%. One might say that this was merely dividend restraint and not confiscation of profits so that the amount of profits not permitted to be passed on immediately to shareholders was being conserved for their ultimate benefit and might come back to them when the 3½% increase limit was removed, as had happened on a previous occasion. Nevertheless, I fear that our economy requires some sort of incomes and prices policy, whether voluntary or compulsory, and this may have an inhibiting effect on the growth of future dividends. I do not imagine that the rate of annual growth in dividends in the future will be greater than it has in the past, and it therefore behooves us to consider whether the present high returns available on fixed interest securities do not themselves provide a certain protection against inflation. . . .

What worries me today, from attending innumerable Conferences and discussions on pension fund investing, is the way in which quite intelligent pension fund managers and administrators having noted the mouthwatering results achieved by pension funds which had appreciated the investment situation early enough, are at long last convinced that equities are the only investment answer to inflation for pension funds, and they seem anxious to persuade their Trustees today to invest a large proportion of their funds in equities, without realising the implications of the present investment situation.

When the index fell to 305 I heard it said that—"the recent fall in the value of Ordinary shares has called into question their future as a hedge against inflation."

It is not so much the recent fall in the market value of equities, because a lowering of *price* is surely a favourable factor to continuing long term investors so long as the long term outlook has not seriously deteriorated. What has called into question whether equities are the best hedge against inflation, is the fact that there has, over the past year or two, been a dramatic rise in world interest rates, bringing with it a relatively greater fall in the price of fixed interest securities. This, as I indicated earlier, is a belated acknowledgment of the fact that we live in an inflationary world. It is therefore possible that fixed interest securities on present terms might themselves prove a better hedge against inflation for pension funds than equities. . . .

When Dr. Dalton issued his 2½% Treasury Stock at par in an age when the annual rate of inflation was at least 4% per annum, he was in fact offering a negative investment, for the rate of inflation was greater than the rate of interest. Today we can buy "Daltons" on a yield of 9¼%. If the long term rate of inflation is likely to be less than this figure, then it cannot any longer be called a negative investment. In fact, if the politicians can hold the rate of inflation down to a bearable level it might not be an unsuitable investment for pension funds. Many large pension funds invest in British Government securities in the anticipation that by judicious short term anomaly switching operations they can improve the annual yield on their gilt-edged holdings to, say, 10%. Be that as it may, but when a Company of the standing of I.C.I. issues a long term 10¾% Loan Stock below par, then that is good enough for my pension fund money.

My main message to you today, . . . is that even though I suppose our fund has had more advantage than any other pension fund from going 100% into equities at the right time, I do not think that equities will necessarily provide for pension funds the best answer to inflation in the '70's. . . .

I now come to the second part of what is meant by the "Cult of the Equity." I hope that I have indicated to you that I advocated 100% in equities 20 years ago only because I was convinced that they were ridiculously cheap compared with the traditional gilt-edged, and not because I was following a cult or a fad, and I am grateful that I have been proved right.

There is, however, another facet in this expression the "Cult of the Equity" which we might examine in passing. Does it mean that for long term investors in an inflationary age that one is always better to consider the advantages of equities even with their lower immediate return but with sufficient income growth in the future which will compensate, or more than compensate, for the higher continuous income that is available from fixed interest securities at the moment?

Again, to repeat something which I said earlier: if we are contemplating runaway inflation, fixed interest securities may not be worth the paper they are written on, but then neither are equities if the rate of increase in dividends does not keep up with the rate of inflation, especially if one has bought them on a basis which assumes that they will do so.

I grant you that the concept of equities with the income commencing at a lower level and generally rising thereafter, fits in admirably with the long term nature of pension fund liabilities, for, generally speaking, most Funds are still growing rapidly and most income from investment anyhow fails to be re-invested, the present outgoings being covered or nearly covered, by the employers' and employees' contributions. Or, to put it another way, we do not generally need high immediate income to meet pension requirements.

So, having acknowledged that the equity concept at the right price is most suitable for pension funds, I would now like to turn your attention to another type of equity investing which in my opinion fulfills most of the requirements of pension fund investing, namely, the equity of property investment.

Property is a particularly suitable investment for pension funds for the following reasons:

1. It is a very long term investment and in fact if we are dealing with freeholds as we generally are, the investment is undated and therefore fits in very well with the long term liabilities of a pension fund.

2. As I think most of us are convinced that inflation will continue, rents of properties will continue to rise as inflation continues.

3. Even in the unlikely event of no further inflation, this should lead to a real growth in the economy which will permit a marked rise in the overall standards of living and which should also allow margins for increased rents on shop and office premises when present leases fall in.

4. This is not a very important point but I put it in because it is a little ''hobby-horse'' of mine. Because of the expense involved in continually re-valuing properties, one is not embarrassed by the question of market value from time to time. This does not mean that if one had an absurdly over-generous offer for a property which one had purchased as a long term investment one should not consider selling it, provided a suitable replacement can be found and the expenses of finding and securing another good property investment are well covered. The point I am trying to make is that with Stock Exchange securities, with the market value of investments available day by day (or even moment by moment) I am fearful that a lot of investments are sold, which should not be sold, merely because the investment manager is persuaded to take a tempting profit and then he wastes a great deal of his profit by the expense involved in exchanging into another investment of equal value. . . .

Twenty years ago the few pension funds which were investing in property still had to a certain degree, the traditional fixed interest halter round their necks and nothing pleased the Trustees more than to buy a property which was leased to, say, a Government department on a long lease with rent reviews as long as 42 years hence. They were, of course, denying themselves an earlier reversion to the very greatly increased rental values which were taking place, and this quite appreciably altered the value of their investment. This point began to be appreciated and subject to the usual haggle between buyer and seller (which, of course, is a feature of this type of investment more than it is with Stock Exchange securities), property investors managed to obtain concessions on the rent review periods and the accepted normal progressed steadily downwards to 35 years, 28 years, 21 years, 14 years and then 10 years, until the goal is now 7 years, and in the 10 years to come might even get down to 5 or even less.

The pension fund investor (or his agent) has to be very aware in haggling his bargains what the financial effect to him is of a shortening of the term of the reversion to higher rents. It is no use having just a vague idea that a 7-year rent review in an inflationary age is better than a 14-year review, without being able to quantify it. So many years ago I produced some tables which gave me a rough and ready guide to what extra immediate return I required from a 14-year rent review to compensate me for having failed to achieve, say, a 7-year review. Again, as in the case of investing in Ordinary shares, the crux of the whole matter is, what is going to be the rate of rent increases in the future. This, with properties, will vary from place to place; London properties are likely to have a greater growth rate than the Provinces. In this table of mine, therefore, one can exercise one's own judgment as to what the rate of rent increase is likely to be in the particular investment you are considering.

To take an example. Let us assume we are dealing with a property where past experience has shown us that the annual growth rate of rents has been of the order of 5% and we anticipate this will continue. Therefore, if we are looking for, say, an effective long term investment of 11%, we would require an immediate return of some 18% higher if the rent revision clause was 14 years instead of 7. . . .

One great difficulty which I have found in property investing is that not many statistics are available concerning the long term trend in rents over the years. No bright young surveyor for instance, has, as far as I know, yet read a paper to the Chartered Institute of Surveyors on the result of his researches into this subject. . . .

I get the strong impression, however, (and I am sorry it is only an impression for I feel that investment should endeavor to be as much a science rather than just an art) that the rate of growth in rents overall is very much greater than the dividends on industrial Ordinary shares and is likely to continue this way. One of my reasons for saying this is that we have had very much less Government interference in rents in the past than we have had in industrial Ordinary dividends (the recent 3½% per annum maximum increase of dividends is an example) and I suspect this freedom may continue. In fact, the only area in which Governments have taken any interest in rents has been lower level residential property, and for this reason I would exclude residential property from my spread of investments.

We are, in fact, one might say, rather in the same position today as we were 20 years ago with Stock Exchange equities and fixed interest. We are being offered an investment which starts at a higher rate of return and on the face of it the income has more chance of growth. I suppose in passing I might also mention that there is with properties a similar question of equity versus fixed interest (mortgages and the like). Because of the expected growth rate and the smaller differential in the current yield and the fixed mortgage rate, I would certainly recommend the equity of property rather than mortgages which in any case are invariably of medium term and do not therefore fit in with the long term investment picture.

Mr. Chairman, in closing my remarks may I sum up very briefly my main conclusions? . . .

Firstly, that today there is very little to choose as long term investments for pension funds, between Stock Exchange equities and Fixed Interest securities at their current high rates of return, and secondly, that the equity of property, in my opinion, offers a better long term investment than either of them.

Policy in Portfolio Management: Bonds

Charles D. Ellis, CFA

The case for bonds in a truly long-term portfolio is examined—and found wanting—in excerpts from a 1971 Ellis analysis of the long-term safety of income and safety of principal of bonds versus stocks.

———————

The three phases of portfolio management are: *Policy,* which sets the long-term posture of the portfolio towards the capital markets as markets; *Strategy,* which is concerned with the changing economic environment and ways to identify major areas of investment opportunity within the markets; and *Selection,* which deals with buying and selling specific securities at specific times. Portfolio management can and should be conducted on each of these planes simultaneously. . . .

Policy's three market alternatives are cash, bonds, and stocks. In this [discussion], the focus is on bonds, and the basic question is this: Should a truly long-term institutional portfolio have a long-term investment in bonds? This may seem at first to be a curious question whose only answer is "Of course." But can we develop a persuasive, logical argument in favor of sustained, long-term investment in bonds that would explain satisfactorily why the custodians of almost every pension fund, endowment fund, and large personal trust in the nation have

Reprinted from *Institutional Investing* (Homewood, Illinois: Business One Irwin, 1971), Chapter 3, pp. 27–40, by permission of the author.

owned, now hold, and plan to continue investing in long-term corporate and government bonds with a major portion of their funds?

It seems appropriate to question the wisdom of this policy for large, long-term investment portfolios. Proponents of long-term, continuous investment in bonds in large institutional portfolios argue four main propositions:

1. Preservation of principal is assured because at maturity the bond must be repaid in full.
2. The yield on bonds is typically higher than common stock yields and the extra income is often needed now, and income from bonds is assured as to amount and time of payment.
3. If the national economy should suffer a severe and prolonged depression, bonds would once again prove very valuable protection against serious trouble.
4. Trustees of pension funds, trusts, and endowments are bound by the Prudent Man Rule of fiduciary obligations to invest in bonds to have a balanced portfolio.

Let's analyze these propositions carefully, taking them in reverse order, beginning with the fourth. The Prudent Man Rule governing the duty of a trustee in the Commonwealth of Massachusetts, and now recognized quite widely, states: "He is to observe how men of prudence, discretion and intelligence manage their own affairs, not in regard to speculation but in regard to the permanent disposition of their funds, considering the probable income as well as the probable safety of the capital to be invested." In the past, prudent men bought and held bonds in their personal portfolios, but today, sophisticated investors do not buy bonds and hold them for the long term. (Municipal bond holdings of wealthy individuals are a function of the tax incentive without which these investors would not be bond buyers. From time to time, investors will buy long-term bonds in anticipation of capital gains due to a change in interest rates, but this is essentially speculation as they do not intend to hold the bonds for the long term. These two exceptions to the basic statement about owning bonds are just that—exceptions.)

Perhaps the reason bonds are held in most institutional portfolios is just a holdover of a portfolio policy that may have been well enough suited to personal trust and estate problems without being carefully re-evaluated to identify the important differences between the investment problems and responsibilities of estate planners and those of very long-term institutional portfolios. While such an explanation is possible, it would be imprudent to let it go unchallenged. Trust management is historically based on experience in managing the financial affairs of mortal men who unfortunately do not live very long. The investment manager of a personal trust that will not last forever and is subject to an uncertain date of termination may well emphasize conservation of capital for the individual's descendants while planning for an estate settlement and portfolio liquidation.

In contrast, endowments, pension funds, mutual funds, and insurance companies have one unique and distinguishing characteristic: they will continue for very long, virtually indefinite periods. An endowment has an unusually long-term obligation to finance all or at least a considerable portion of the activities of a presumably very long lived organization or institution. A pension fund also has a long-term obligation to provide for the well-being of many workers during their retirement. And even most personal funds will be looked to for such long-term needs as education, retirement, and family security. These cannot be bound by the rules of estate planning because those rules give no explicit attention to the growth of capital and income which any growing institution would naturally seek from its endowment, which any corporation would expect of pension fund investments, and which any individual expects of his capital. . . .

With regard to the third pro-bond argument cited above, the risk of a major economic depression, a powerful case can be built to support the view that, excluding an externally caused calamity such as a major world war, this nation should suffer neither severe nor prolonged economic setbacks such as occurred in the 1930s. . . . This is not intended to suggest that we live in a "new era" from which recession and inflation are banished, but it does seem highly probable that we do not face the prospect of either prolonged or severe economic depression. Consequently, no major portion of long-term portfolios should be aimed at defending against the remote prospect of sustained economic adversity when such a defensive posture means sacrificing the opportunity to invest more positively in the nearly continuous growth of our dynamic economy.

This positive outlook does not deny the remote possibility of unforeseen economic, business, or investment adversities that could reduce current investment income, and a contingency reserve may be desirable. If so, this protection should be provided by a small part of the total assets and held in highly liquid form—from which it could be withdrawn for current spending when and if needed—rather than by allocating 30, 40, or 60 percent of the total fund to bonds for protection against a decline in investment income which may not develop and which is highly uncertain as to timing.

Using a small, "fully spendable" reserve means that the degree of protection or insurance against a drop in income needed by most large and long-term portfolios can be accomplished in most cases with a reserve only 5 to 10 percent of the portfolio. . . . And with that concern satisfied, the rest of the fund is available for profit-maximizing investment. . . .

The remaining pro-bond propositions—assurance of income at a high level and capital preservation—are the key investment considerations and can be tested by comparing a portfolio of long-term bonds with a conservative portfolio of, say, utility common stocks represented by Moody's Utility Average. In questioning the long-term financial validity of bond investments for long-term portfolios, we will use ten-year time periods as the basis for evaluating bonds and the equity alternative. This test period is only for analytical convenience, and the reader should keep in mind that ten years is only a very short-term "proxy" for the truly long-term character of the funds with which we are primarily concerned.

Turning now to the bond advocates' proposition two, and comparing cash income from bond interest to cash income from utility common stock dividends, the record presented in Figure 1 shows that in all but one ten-year period since World War II, total cash income from a portfolio of utility common stocks purchased in the first year and held for ten years, exceeded the income from long-term Aa utility bonds bought in that same first year. On average, over a ten-year span, Moody's utility dividends returned 6.4 percent on cost versus a peak yield of 4.6 percent for the bonds, or an average increase in income earned of 40 percent.

Over longer periods, the advantage of equities increases substantially. On a pure rate of return basis, a dividend yielding 4 percent currently and growing at 6 percent annually earns as much cash income over a 20-year period as a bond yielding 6.5 percent. And over even longer periods, the algebra is inexorable. What bond could compete for very long with an equity portfolio that currently yields 4 percent and is growing at 6 percent? This means the dividend income would double

Figure 1
Ten-Year Cash Income per $1,000 Investment

Period	Interest on Bond Portfolio	Dividends on Utility Portfolio
1945–54	$267	$656
1946–55	258	534
1947–56	267	646
1948–57	292	729
1949–58	276	709
1950–59	268	696
1951–60	295	694
1952–61	305	662
1953–62	332	653
1954–63	300	584
1955–64	313	551
1956–65	343	581
1957–66	403	512
1958–67	392	446
1959–68	456	419
1960–69	453	514

every 12 years producing 8 percent on cost in 12 years, 16 percent on cost in 24 years, 32 percent in 36 years, and, to carry the proposition to century time span, which will really test our capacity to think in truly long terms, the dividend would yield 1,024 percent in the 96th year!

Granted that dividends of conservative common stocks have yielded and are expected to yield more cash income over long periods, are not bond interest receipts more predictable? It is quite clear that the amount of dividends to be received from specific stocks over a period of many years cannot be forecast exactly, but the very probable rate of growth in earnings of a portfolio of seasoned equities can be translated into a highly probable pattern of dividends. And although the pattern of dividend income would be less assured than the pattern of income received on a specific present portfolio of bonds, just the *reverse* would be true for a large, continuing, and therefore always changing, portfolio of bonds. For while we know precisely what interest will be paid on what dates for each individual bond now owned, most issues in any present portfolio will have matured or been called in 20 years and will be replaced with other bonds paying interest rates that are presently unknown. Viewed in this long-term perspective, a bond portfolio's income would be expected to be not *more* but *less* certain than the income from a portfolio of conservative common stocks because we do not know whether bond yields will trend higher or lower, whereas the common stock portfolio's dividend income will almost surely trend higher, and only the rate of increase is uncertain.

The essential conclusion is that while the yield of the present bond portfolio is highly certain, the yield of a future bond portfolio cannot be accurately predicted and is less predictable than the future yield on cost of a conservative common stock portfolio. The evidence substantiates this view. While interest rates have declined nine times on a year-to-year basis during the past two decades, common stock dividends for Moody's Utility Average never once declined in the postwar period. Thus, the utility portfolio provides not only a higher, but also a steadier, more predictable stream of current income than a bond portfolio.

While this discussion of the very long term advantages of common stocks over bonds has been based on a portfolio of electric utility stocks, portfolio managers can and should consider a far broader list of equities. A review of total corporate earnings and dividends indicates quite dramatically that while aggregate dividends rise with increasing earnings, dividends generally do not fall when earnings drop during business recessions. . . . Thus, in the 20 years since World War II, total corporate dividends have declined on a year-to-year basis only once—by a mere 2.3 percent in 1952. Yet, during that same 20-year period dividends rose by nearly 300 percent or at an average annual rate of 7.2 percent compounded. On the record, bonds are clearly inferior as a source of reliable income when compared to equities.

Regarding proposition four, which discusses capital, its preservation and conservation, it is curious that advocates of bond investment appear so convinced that the contractual nature of a bond is always an advantage to the bond buyer. Granted that the contract protects the investor from receiving *less* than stipulated, it also prohibits the investor from receiving any *more*. This situation can be viewed as a source of risk when we consider inflation's erosion of the future purchasing power of both income and capital. In fact, if inflation continues at the long-term historical rate of 2 percent, the assurance that a bond buyer will only recover at maturity the dollars he puts up, is the assurance of an effective *capital loss* in purchasing power terms.

As to the comparison of bonds to the utility stock portfolio, . . . not surprisingly, the utility equity portfolio produces an important capital advantage over the bonds. The magnitude of this advantage is impressive. Using the earlier expectation for utilities of 6 percent growth in earnings, and assuming no change in the price/earnings ratio, the capital invested in utility stocks would increase over a century (if we can contemplate such a long period) to an amount 256 times its present size!

When long-term corporate bonds reached historically high interest rates during 1970, many latent bond buyers argued quite vigorously that if institutional investors could get 8 and 9 percent contractual yields on bonds of satisfactory quality, then surely bonds were attractive. They usually cited the Lorie & Fisher study of long-term returns on common stocks to show that bond buyers could get competitive returns with less risk. The proposition was certainly appealing, but hardly persuasive. To make their case, these bond advocates were comparing *future* returns in bonds with *past* returns in equities. This false logic does not give recognition to the major declines in prices in *both* capital markets and the probability that if the bond market were to recover, so too would the equity market. The only way that bond proponents could legitimately claim that the historical evidence in favor of stocks was not still valid would be to show somehow that the basic and time-tested relationship between the equity and bond markets had been drastically changed. They have not made this case. . . .

The remarkable result of our historical analysis is that a portfolio of conservative equities has been and is very likely to continue to be greatly superior to a bond portfolio on all counts:

1. Capital is safer from inflation in equities than in bonds.
2. Equities produce much higher income.
3. Equity income is more predictable.
4. Equities increase capital substantially.

The evidence is impressively in favor of an investment in conservative equities as the preferred means by which a long-term investment portfolio can achieve its goals. Yet, the question remains: Why do most pension funds, endowment funds, and other large, long-term portfolios continue to commit a large percentage of portfolio capital to long-term investments in bonds? The explanation lies partly in the experience fiduciaries have had with terminal estate planning and partly in the difficulty all investment managers face when asked to deal astutely with long time periods. (For many investors five years into the future is really a working definition of infinity.) For an investment manager faced with a heavy volume of daily business demanding immediate decisions, the really long term is a most awesome challenge to the imagination. Thus, the real problem is perhaps not whether bonds are a better source of income and capital values over the longer term, but rather how can and should the investment manager—and his clients—shift to a strange and unfamiliar time dimension—embracing 10, 20, or even 100 years—in which truly relevant long-term policy can be formulated.

If it were decided to change away from a policy of holding a large permanent portfolio of bonds towards a portfolio of conservative common stocks, how should the change in policy be implemented? At least three choices are available: (1) the change can be made in a single, rapidly executed, "do it now" program at a specific time when conditions are deemed propitious; (2) straight bonds can be replaced by convertible issues which will be subsequently converted into common stocks; or (3) a program of dollar averaging can be used to make the transition from bonds to stocks over a period of years. The choice depends in part on the decision makers' confidence in their ability to time the transition from bonds to equities; in part on their confidence that the policy change is soundly conceived; and in part on their appraisal of the risk that if near-term market developments go against the long-term trend and expectation, a sound long-term policy decision might be interrupted or reversed for essentially short-term reasons. In almost any situation, depending on the politics of policy formulation, a sound means can be chosen to achieve the end result of a policy of holding bonds only as needed for permanent defensive reserves. . . .

Goal-Oriented Bond Portfolio Management

Martin L. Leibowitz

Marty Leibowitz is a pioneer in expanding the frontiers of knowledge and understanding in bond portfolio management. Here, in condensed format, is his introduction of the "Baseline Portfolio" concept, intended to enable clients and managers to set explicit long-term investment policies and to monitor results effectively in the face of growing short-term performance pressures.

Managers of fixed-income portfolios have recently found themselves coming into increasing pressure from various forms of performance monitoring. Primarily, this monitoring has taken the form of total return measurement of portfolio results over relatively short-term measurement periods—*i.e.*, quarters or years. The manager's results are then compared with the returns achieved by general market indices, by short-term investments, or by other portfolios believed to be part of a "peer group." These comparisons increasingly play a major role in the evaluation of the portfolio manager's skills and services.

It is clear that performance monitoring can be helpful in many areas of investment management, especially when the monitoring is based upon objective, concrete measurements. However, the sole reliance upon total return comparisons over short-term periods is subject to a

Reprinted from *The Journal of Portfolio Management* 5 (Summer 1979), pp. 13–18. New York: Institutional Investor, Inc.

number of criticisms. Total return measurements do provide a useful yardstick of the extent to which the portfolio manager took advantage of general market opportunities during the measurement period. But this is only one factor in the complex process of portfolio management. A fundamental problem seems to arise when a *single* yardstick—total return measurement over short-term periods—is taken as *the sole* yardstick for all management activity.

This concentration on the single yardstick of total return can force dangerously simplistic comparisons among portfolios that may actually differ widely in function and purpose. In fact, the same level of achieved return may represent a very satisfactory result for one portfolio while having quite dismal implications for another portfolio with a different set of goals.

Moreover, even within a given portfolio, an over-emphasis on short-term can lead to conflicts with the long-term goals of the fund. For example, it could lead the portfolio manager into concentrating his activity on catching short-term swings in interest rates. In turn, this could lead to a frequent series of major portfolio shifts, thereby introducing considerable timing risk into the overall management process. The resulting volatility risk might be in direct contradiction to the original purpose of placing the funds into a fixed-income portfolio in the first place. This is just one instance of how an exclusive focus on maximization of total return over short periods can violate a fund's policy constraints and cause deviations from the fund's true long-term objectives.

These problems are particularly acute for fixed-income portfolios because of certain distinctive characteristics of the bond market. Much of the institutional investment in bonds is motivated by long-term, risk avoidance purposes. These long-term purposes typically overshadow any specific requirement for total return over short-term periods. Another important characteristic of the bond market is the structural clarity of its asset classes. This clarity enables the return/risk relationships among the different market sectors to be relatively well defined, especially over longer term horizons. The longer-term motivation of investors and the market's structural clarity obviously fit hand-in-glove, allowing for the identification of market sectors that are particularly well suited for serving the specific goals of a given fund.

By taking advantage of these special characteristics of the bond market, we believe that a *practical* technique can be developed for relating performance measurements over short-term periods to the fund's long-term goals.

The Baseline Portfolio

In theory, the portfolio management process can be viewed as consisting of four major steps. . . . The first step is to identify the long-term objectives of the fund. The second step commences with the manager's judgments regarding market prospects. At this point, the manager must make the broad decisions that relate to portfolio strategy, *i.e.*, to determine the portfolio's maturity structure. Once this has been done, the third step consists of deciding upon the detailed portfolio tactics to be employed. These consist of selecting specific sectors to take advantage of perceived market opportunities. The fourth step then consists of a continuing performance monitoring (in the most general sense) to ensure that the portfolio objectives are being fulfilled.

The first step is far more difficult than generally believed. It is no simple matter to identify a full set of portfolio objectives and then to define these objectives in *a useful way*. Such efforts tend to lead to either a frustratingly vague description of the objectives or to lead to an impossibly long collection of goals which mix the minor considerations in with the major ones. . . .

The purpose of the "Baseline Portfolio" is to provide a practical procedure for articulating the fund's long-term objectives in a concrete and useful fashion. The underlying idea is to take advantage of the relatively well-defined sector structure of the bond market. By selecting market sectors to match the fund's objectives and associated risk factors, one should be able to develop a portfolio structure that best suits the fund's long-term goals. This is called the fund's "Baseline Portfolio."

Since the Baseline Portfolio structure should be determined primarily by the long-range considerations, it should be relatively independent of the active manager's day-to-day market judgments. Thus, the Baseline Portfolio could be defined as the most balanced possible fulfillment of all the fund's complex objectives and goals in the absence of an active market-related management activity.

Management Activity Relative to the Baseline Portfolio

From the vantage point of the Baseline Portfolio, one purpose of investment management is to take advantage of market opportunities. Active management can then be viewed as a series of strategic and tactical

judgments that would lead to market-motivated departures from the
Baseline Portfolio in an effort to achieve improved portfolio results. The
resulting portfolio improvements—as well as the incremental risks incurred in achieving them—should theoretically be measured against the
yardstick of the Baseline Portfolio itself.

To see how this measurement can be accomplished, suppose that the
actual portfolio's market value could always be converted into immediate
cash proceeds. (This concept of equating a fund's nominal market value
with a literal cash opportunity value lies at the heart of the conventional
rate-of-return measurement process.) Then, at any moment, the actual
portfolio could be translated into cash and these proceeds used to purchase a Baseline Portfolio. Suppose that this would lead to a purchase
of 100 units of the Baseline Portfolio. If this were done, the manager
would have reverted to the best possible passive portfolio structure. In
other words, he would have converted all his funds into the "currency"
of the fund's long-term objectives, i.e., the Baseline Portfolio itself.

In general, however, the portfolio manager will retain some portfolio
structure other than that of the Baseline. During the course of the subsequent measurement period, this actual portfolio will provide a certain
total return consisting of both income and principal appreciation: perhaps with a certain amount of reinvestment return as well. This total
return may look very acceptable compared to either investment in a
general market index, in short-term investments, or to the relative performance of peer portfolios. At the end of the measurement period,
however, the actual portfolio could again be subjected to the test of a
theoretical repurchase of the Baseline Portfolio. No matter how well the
actual portfolio may have done in terms of the traditional comparisons,
if it converts back into fewer units of the Baseline Portfolio than before,
then the fund has lost ground relative to its long-term objectives.

The gain or loss from this hypothetical repurchase of the Baseline is,
of course, directly related to the incremental return achieved by the actual portfolio relative to the Baseline.

Evaluating Proposed Departures from the Baseline

The Baseline Portfolio can serve both prospective and retrospective
functions. After a given investment period has been completed, the

FIGURE 1
Market-Motivated Departures from the Baseline Portfolio

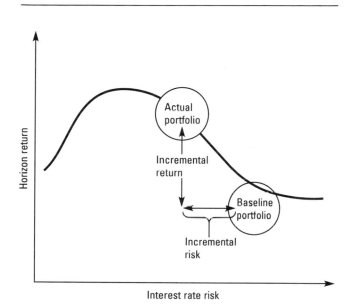

Baseline can help the manager to evaluate, retrospectively, the return achieved in terms of his contribution to the fund's long-term goals. At the beginning of each investment period, however, the Baseline can help the portfolio manager to gauge—in a quantitative, objective fashion— the incremental risk incurred *relative to these same goals.* This *prospective* application of the Baseline Portfolio may be the most important one of all.

Figure 1 illustrates a manager's *prospective* evaluation of the trade-off between expected return (over a short-term horizon) and some measure of "interest rate risk." For example, if the manager was neutral on the market so that the expected case could be represented as "No change in the yield curve," then the expected return would be the Rolling Yield.[1] On the other hand, if the manager's interest rate projections were more optimistic or pessimistic than the neutral case, then these judgments would be reflected in projected returns such as those plotted in Figure 1.

The horizontal axis in Figure 1 represents some measure of "interest rate risk" over the short-term investment period.

As noted earlier, the maturity structure is the most important decision made by an active portfolio manager. By varying the maturity structure, he can control the amount of "interest rate risk" contained in his portfolio. Various proxies for the "interest rate risk" of a portfolio have been proposed—average maturity, historical variability, percentage price volatility, Macaulay's duration, Horizon Volatility, Proportional Volatility.[2] For any of these measures, the Baseline can be viewed as the reference point. To the extent that the active manager departs from this Baseline level of interest rate risk, to that extent, he risks falling below the Baseline's performance.

This holds true for departures in *both directions*. As noted earlier, a defensive departure, while risk-reducing in terms of short-term volatility, runs the risk of an insufficient price appreciation to compensate for the lower income-productivity per dollar of market value under a move to lower yield levels.

Figure 1 illustrates the case of a manager undertaking just such a "defensive departure" from the Baseline's risk level. His motivation is clearly to obtain a sizable improvement in incremental returns. However, he is exposing his portfolio to a considerable shortfall in return relative to the Baseline in the event that interest rates move further downward than the level embedded in his projected return curve.

One should take note of the apparent paradox in the situation portrayed in Figure 1. The greatest risk here is the prospect of a stronger-than-expected *downward* move in interest rates. This action would normally be viewed as an "improving market." Yet, in this case, such a "market improvement" would lead to under-performance relative to the Baseline Portfolio, and hence would constitute the gravest threat to the fund's progress towards its long-term goal.

Figure 1 thus shows how a manager can gauge his incremental interest rate risk relative to the Baseline and, by implication, measure his more generalized risk relative to long-term goals. While there may be some controversy regarding what constitutes a satisfactory measure of interest rate risk, there is not disagreement that a greater level of risk consciousness needs to be introduced into the management process. Once any such volatility measure has been selected, the procedure implied in Figure 1 can be quantified, thereby providing the manager (and the sponsor) with a concrete, numerical indication of the incremental risk associated with a prospective portfolio strategy.

Communication between Sponsor and Manager

The Baseline Portfolio approach can facilitate the communication process between sponsor and manager.

At the outset, the Baseline Portfolio should itself be the result of discussions between the fund's sponsor and the manager. In these initial discussions, the sponsor must try to convey his sense of the fund's purpose, to define his overall objectives and their relative priorities, and to identify and delimit the risk factors that concern him. On the other hand, the manager contributes his knowledge of the behavioral characteristics of the various asset classes, along with his belief as to how they will function in the context of different portfolio structures. (At this point, the manager should try to put aside his perceptions of immediate market value, and concentrate on the general long-term characteristics of the various market sectors.)

In all too many instances, this interchange tends to remain at a rather fuzzy level of generality, with both parties espousing the obviously desirable "Nirvana points," *e.g.*, maximum return with minimum risk, highest yield without sacrifice of quality, minimum volatility with greatest stability of income, etc. If the discussion of goals ends at this point, then neither party has communicated his sense of the appropriate trade-offs. In a rather fundamental sense, no real understanding has been achieved.

A joint determination to specify a Baseline Portfolio can drive these discussions down to the concrete level. It will force the difficult choices to be made—and made *jointly* by both sponsor and manager. The sponsor must articulate the subtle priorities that can organize his many objectives, and he must develop a clear-cut structure by relating these priorities—with the manager's help—to choices between specific market sectors. The manager must rise above his active orientation to define the most balanced, passive portfolio structure matching his client needs. In this fashion, both parties are able to merge and consolidate their different points of view. In essence, by specifying a Baseline Portfolio, they have come to agree on a practical, passive alternative to active management.

As with any real process of communication, these interactions may prove painful and arduous at the outset. Once defined, however, the Baseline can prove a mutual vantage point for interpreting the actual returns achieved over time. The all-too-common confusion between conflicting short-term results and long-term goals will be reduced. Because of the sponsor's role in defining the Baseline, the manager will no longer find himself quite so vulnerable to criticism for the many portfolio effects that are (in reality) mandated by the nature of the fund. In particular, having the Baseline as a "baseline" may considerably reduce artificial pressures on a manager with regard to high volatility, yield give-ups, particularly high or low quality postures, having the portfolio balanced away from the general market structure, or for deviations from the performance returns achieved by general market indices or theoretical peer groups.

Moreover, by concentrating the objective setting in an initial phase shared with the sponsor, the Baseline approach should allow the investment manager to focus more clearly on his day-by-day market activities in the fund's behalf.

Notes

1. See *The Rolling Yield: A New Approach to Yield Curve Analysis* by Martin L. Leibowitz, Salomon Brothers, April 21, 1977.
2. For a more complete discussion, see *The Risk Dimension: A New Approach to Yield Curve Analysis* by Martin L. Leibowitz, Salomon Brothers, October 5, 1977.

How True Are the Tried Principles?

Peter L. Bernstein

President of the company that bears his name and a respected researcher and commentator on economic and investment matters, Peter L. Bernstein is the editor who developed *The Journal of Portfolio Management* into a splendid forum for the exchange of ideas and experience between professional investors and academicians. Here (with apologies for deletion of much documentary data) is one of his typically original, sometimes startling, and always lucid propositions: that bonds should trade places with cash as the "residual stepchild" of asset allocation to reduce portfolio risk and improve returns.

———— ▬ ————

Why is it that the conventional allocation of portfolio assets is between stocks and bonds? Why is cash the portfolio's stepchild, held in lesser amounts and used only as a buying reserve for the two long-term assets? Is there a case for making cash a primary asset in its own right? If so, is it possible that bonds or equities might then become the residual stepchild?

The answers to these questions lead to an unconventional conclusion. Bonds have no legitimate place in a portfolio except under two special and specified conditions. First, unusual short-run opportunities in the bond market do present themselves and should not be ignored. Second,

Reprinted from *Investment Management Review* 3 (March/April 1989), pp. 17–24. New York: DMA Communications, Inc.

bonds may best serve the unique requirements of some portfolios, especially those with high current expenditures relative to the size of their principal.

As a general statement, however, portfolios that hold only stocks and cash can provide higher long-run expected returns, with no increase in risk, as compared with the conventional portfolio that concentrates its assets in stocks and bonds. This means that bonds rather than cash should be the residual stepchild of long-run portfolio asset allocation, except where unique portfolio requirements prevail.

I emphasize that this analysis focuses on what most people today refer to as *strategic* rather than tactical asset allocation. In other words, I consider the range of choice for a portfolio in equilibrium, in its long-run stance, when no unusual opportunities are available in any single sector of the capital markets. This contrasts with tactical asset allocation, which makes temporary shifts away from the strategic allocation in order to take advantage of market disequilibrium.

Diversification and Asset Choices

The overwhelming majority of investors will want to make equities the asset of choice in determining their appropriate strategic asset mix, simply because equities promise the highest rate of return over the long run.

At the same time, most investors find equities too risky to occupy 100% of the portfolio. That is why people diversify: they try to avoid having all their eggs in the equity basket. The essential issue that we confront here is how effectively investors can combine equities with bonds and with cash as diversifying agents.

Let us consider for a moment how diversification actually works. Although diversification helps us avoid the chance that all our assets will go down together, it also means that we will avoid the chance that all assets will go up together. Seen from this standpoint, diversification is a mixed blessing.

In order to keep the mixture of the blessings of diversification as favorable as possible, effective diversification has two necessary conditions:

- The covariance in returns among the assets must be negative; if it is positive, we will still run the risk that all assets will go down together; and

- The expected returns in all the assets should be high; no one wants to hold assets with significant probabilities of loss.

How well do bonds and cash meet these conditions?

Consider covariance first. We know that the correlation between bond and stock returns is variable, but we also know that it is positive most of the time. . . . Stock returns correlate even more weakly with cash, but, such as it is, the correlation between stocks and cash is negative. Bonds and cash also correlate weakly, but the correlation here tends to be positive.

If the correlation between bond and stock returns is positive but stocks have higher expected returns, why does anybody bother to own bonds at all? There are two reasons. First, the long-run expected return on bonds is higher than the expected return on cash. Second, bond returns are usually less volatile than equity returns while providing a higher component of current income.

Nevertheless, bonds have three distinct disadvantages. First, bonds have lower expected returns than stocks most of the time—and this shortfall increases as we lengthen the investment horizon or holding period. Second, bond returns move in the same direction as stock returns too frequently to make bonds a perfect diversifying agent. Finally, bonds are vulnerable to negative returns (prices can fall by more than coupon income); cash suffers from no such vulnerability, in a nominal sense at least. . . .

Monthly and quarterly bond and stock returns are simultaneously positive over 70% of the time. This ratio increases as we lengthen the holding period, as all assets have a higher probability of positive results over the long run.

The meaning is clear: most of the time that bonds are going up, the stock market is also going up. Unless bonds tend to provide higher returns on those occasions, they will be making a reliable contribution to the overall performance of the portfolio only during the relatively infrequent time periods when the bond market is going up and the stock market is going down.

How Can Cash Help?

Although cash tends to have a lower expected return than bonds, we have seen that cash can hold its own against bonds 30% of the time or more when bond returns are positive. Cash will always win out over bonds when bond returns are negative.

The logical step, therefore, is to try a portfolio mix that offsets the lower expected return on cash by increasing the share devoted to equities. As cash has no negative returns, the volatility might not be any higher than it would be in a portfolio that includes bonds.

. . . The results of a portfolio consisting of 60% stocks, 40% bonds, and no cash [are compared] with a portfolio consisting of 75% stocks, no bonds, and 25% cash.

The results are clearly in favor of the bond-free portfolio, which provides higher returns with almost identical levels of risk. The bond-free portfolio outperforms the cash-free portfolio in 88 out of the 138 quarters, or 64% of the time.

Why Bonds at All?

. . . Momentary disequilibrium in the capital markets does provide tactical opportunities for owning bonds. In addition, some portfolios, and especially those whose spending requirements are high relative to capital values, may find that prudence requires investing in the high current income that bonds provide. In addition, active bond management, which involves varying the duration and convexity of fixed-income portfolios, may also have a higher reward/risk profile than a straight cash investment.

None of these considerations dilutes the primary conclusion that long-term bonds are an unsatisfactory asset, with expected returns below stocks and with risk-reducing features below cash. The investor who includes bonds in a portfolio should therefore have clear and positive reasons for doing so; bonds have no place in the portfolio by default.

Telling the "Prospective Returns" Story

Keith P. Ambachtsheer

Canada's Keith Ambachtsheer has developed an international reputation for his insight into investment management. Here he takes us backstage to see how prospective rates of return should be adjusted before using them to determine optimal asset mix.

———— ▬ ————

Getting Asset Mix Religion: A Consequence

Are there still pension fund officers, investment managers, or consultants out there who don't believe that 'asset mix' is the key investment policy decision? If there are, they have not been confessing their heretical views in public lately! It seems we are all asset-allocation-is-the-most-important-decision believers now.

But there is something peculiar in this conversion to devout asset mix disciples of those with key roles in pension fund investing. One can't do much with pension fund asset mix without a view on the return prospects for the investment classes to be mixed. However, we don't yet see the pension investments industry devoting the analytical resources to the return prospects question one would think consistent with its importance to asset allocation.

Reprinted from *The Ambachtsheer Letter* (December 2, 1988), by permission of Keith P. Ambachtsheer & Associates, Inc.

Getting asset mix religion without seriously addressing the prospective asset returns question will miss the mark. Good theology doesn't just ask questions. It demands answers too. With asset mix questions, there can be no answers without views on what kind of returns the capital markets might deliver down the road. . . .

Telling the Story

We do not mean to imply that there are no good prospective capital markets returns stories being told. It is more a sense that many of the ones being told seem incomplete. Most fall into one of two categories:

Category 1: return probability distribution-based stories built on the assumption of efficient markets, on current capital markets prices, and on historical capital market pricing relationships and return realizations;

Category 2: qualitative, often highly individualized stories about economic and capital markets prospects, frequently grounded in a particular ideological and/or theoretical point of view, and focusing on a particular economic or capital markets dimension or theme.

There seems to be a rule operating that you have to tell the capital markets prospects story one way or the other. That is, one must be either a Category 1 objectivist or a Category 2 subjectivist. We intend to challenge that convention. . . . We believe that the best overall story might well be one which blends key elements of objective Category 1 and subjective Category 2 stories together.

Those that Don't Study History . . .

"Those that do not study history are bound to repeat it", said the philosopher Santayana. If this piece of wisdom can be applied to pension fund investing, the implication is that history here will not repeat itself! Few are the pension fund officers, consultants, and investment managers who can not rhyme the key historical long term return numbers off by heart (for the 1926 to 1987 period, from the *SBBI 1988 Yearbook*, Ibbotson Associates, Chicago):

- a 3.0% inflation rate;
- a 0.5% real interest rate on T-Bills;
- a 0.8% maturity premium on long Treasury bonds over T-Bills;

- a 0.6% default premium on long corporates over long Treasury bonds;
- a 5.6% risk premium on stocks over long Treasury bonds and 6.4% over T-Bills;
- a 2.2% smallness premium on small cap stocks over large cap stocks.

But equally few are the pension fund officers, consultants, and investment managers who don't know that these raw historical numbers need adjustments before they can become best estimates of future capital market returns. But what adjustments? That is the heart of the matter . . . and the question we intend to study in some detail.

Converting the Past into the Future

There is no shortage of apparently sensible adjustments one could make to the historical return numbers in order to convert them into best estimate forward-looking expectations. Indeed, our listing of adjustment candidates got so long that we decided to categorize possible adjustments into a four-level hierarchy. This hierarchy recognizes the reality and legitimacy of both objective and subjective elements in telling the best possible capital markets prospects story.

Four Levels of Legitimate Adjustments to Historical Returns

Level #1: Current Yield Curve-Based Adjustments

• these adjustments replace the average historical Treasury bonds/bills yield curve with the actual yield curve today, and use the current inflation rate as the starting inflation rate;

• return prospects are thus generated based on an eventual convergence with the history-derived real rate of return on T-Bills, bond maturity premium structure, and equity risk premiums . . . but these numbers now reflect the possibility of near term divergence from long term historical experience in real bond and bill returns . . . and also the possibility of long term prospective inflation diverging from long term historical inflation experience . . . and hence the possibility of nominal capital markets returns also deviating from long term historical experience;

Level #2: Apparent Biases-in-History Adjustments

• interest rates were pegged at artificially low levels through the 1940's into the early 1950's (for example, T-Bill yields averaged 0.53% over the 1941–1950 period, while the inflation rate averaged 5.91%) . . . while we don't know what yields would have obtained in a free market environment over this period, they would almost certainly have been higher than observed, leading to an upward adjustment of possibly 0.5% to the historical 0.5% real interest rate;

• the pronounced upward trend in inflation and nominal interest rates over the 1926 to 1987 period (eg. long Treasury yields started at 4.5% and ended at 9.1%) produced systematic capital losses to an investment policy of maintaining a long bond portfolio, estimated by Arnott-Sorenson at 0.8% per annum; this annual capital loss is an estimate of the amount by which the historical long bond maturity premium of 0.8% should be adjusted upward if the effect of that trend is to be removed;

• the systematic rise in the per dollar of dividend price of common stocks (ie. the overall dividend yield fell from 5.6% to 3.5% over the 62 year period) produced an annual capital gain estimated by Arnott-Sorenson coincidentally the same as the annual bond capital loss: 0.8%, which then becomes an estimate by how much the equity risk premiums should be adjusted downward if the effect of that trend is to be removed.

Level #3: 'We're Not Just Anywhere in History' Adjustments

• Sharpe points out that the collective risk tolerance of capital markets participants is reasonably related to the value of capital assets per head . . . collective risk tolerance rises as that ratio improves (potentially reducing required maturity, default, and equity risk premiums) and falls as the capital assets/person ratio deteriorates (potentially raising these premiums); if today (a) the ratio is still relatively high and (b) the return covariance structure doesn't embody an abnormally high degree of risk, the implication is that current premium values should be below their historical averages;

• Bernstein points out that capital markets participants are real people with real memories; prolonged bad experiences with a particular asset produces prolonged periods of time where that asset class is 'marked down' by investors; the implication is that the prolonged bout of terrible bond results of the 1970's and early 1980's might still be impacting bond yields even today;

• a third possible adjustment in this category would recognize that the long term historical averages embody a number of reasonably distinct eras with distinctly different capital markets and inflation experience: which one of these eras are the 1990's most likely (and least likely) to resemble? . . . to the degree we assign probabilities to the actual 1990's experience different from the historical frequency of that experience, adjustments to history-neutral return expectations could result.

Level #4: 'The World Is a Different Place' Adjustments

• the 1990's environment in which capital markets must function has dimensions to it where history might be of little use; the current savings/investments–exports/imports disequilibrium of the U.S. economy might top a list of such dimensions, with the apparent recapitalization of Corporate America under way for some time now, and the globalization and integration of capital markets possibly second and third in importance; ignoring these three dimensions in fashioning best-estimate capital markets prospects today seems to us as inappropriate in such an endeavor as ignoring historical capital markets experience itself; serious asset allocators must be prepared to contemplate adjusting history-neutral return expectations for these without-precedent factors, even in the absence of a historical security blanket;

• not only must new capital asset demand-related phenomena be monitored; there is a supply side too; capital assets are supplied as part of the economic growth process; ultimately, their collective return must approximate the rate of economic growth they help generate; different-from-history economic growth prospects demand different-from-history capital market return prospects.

• the absence of comparable historical 1926–1987 numbers for real estate, venture capital, and foreign investments does not justify ignoring these asset classes for pension funds; whatever results are available, together with our understanding of the risk/return characteristics should be used to graft return prospects for these asset classes on to the expectations set for bills, bonds, and stocks.

Building 'Best Estimate' Long Term Return Prospects: A Start

We are clearly not going to get to a set of 'best estimate' return prospects adjusted for Level #1, #2, #3, and #4 considerations in the *LETTER*. But . . . [here is] a look at what long term capital markets prospects look like today, starting with the historical numbers and then adjusting them for Level #1 and #2 considerations:

Building 'Best Estimate' Long Term Return Prospects: A Start [12/88]

In Terms of *'Building Blocks':*	*Pure* *1926–1987* *History*	*With* *Level #1* *Adjustments*	*With* *Level #1 + #2* *Adjustments*
Inflation	3.0%	7.1%	5.9%
Real T-Bill Rate	0.5%	1.0%	1.5%
Bond Maturity Premium	0.8%	0.8%	1.6%
Bond Default Premium	0.6%	0.6%	0.6%
Large Stocks Risk Premium	6.4%	6.4%	5.6%
Small Stocks Risk Premium	8.6%	8.6%	7.8%
In Terms of 'Expected Returns':			
T-Bills	3.5%	8.1%	7.4%
Long T-Bonds	4.3%	9.0%	9.0%
Long Corporate Bonds	4.9%	9.6%	9.6%
Large Stocks	9.9%	14.5%	13.0%
Small Stocks	12.1%	16.7%	15.2%

Historical Performance in Manager Selection

Edgar W. Barksdale
William L. Green

Ed Barksdale and Bill Green are both managing directors of RCB International, one of the leading consultants on the selection of investment managers. Here, they update earlier evidence of manager inconsistency, confront us with a conclusion questioning present-day manager selection practices, and offer an alternative approach.

Historical performance ranking, the primary consideration in most investment manager selection decisions, is a useless, random statistic. In an analysis we've completed using a data base covering 15 years, we asked if past performance was any guide to expected future performance. Our research clearly shows the absence of any predictive value in historical performance rankings of money managers.

Performance statistics, of course, are seductive, because the numbers appear to provide one of the few "concrete" or objective elements of the selection process. But choosing managers is not a numbers game.

Over the years, the industry has learned [that] two dominant factors contribute to a sponsor's successful investment program:

• Suitable investment objectives and policy; and

Reprinted from Pensions & Investments 18 (September 17, 1990), p. 16. Chicago: Crain Communications, Inc.

- Successful selection of the investment managers to implement the policy.

Sponsors have developed broad investment policy guidelines with which they are comfortable. The continuing struggle, however, is in the area of implementation, namely, in the successful evaluation of investment managers. Selections, to a worrisome extent, have resulted in disappointing performance and costly turnover of investment managers.

Countless hours of research and amounts of money have been spent by institutional investors seeking to enhance performance of their investment portfolios. As employee benefit fund assets increase in size, both in absolute terms and in terms relative to the net worth of the sponsoring organizations, the impact of even modest incremental returns easily justifies the use of considerable internal and external resources. All of those efforts notwithstanding, the ongoing turnover of investment management relationships, generally after a substantial period of poor performance, demonstrates the manager selection process is an inexact science and probably close to an art.

Looking back over the period since the enactment of the Employee Retirement Income Security Act of 1974, it's appropriate to examine what we can learn from the industry's practices in managerial selection.

In our analysis, we examined a series of rolling 10-year intervals spanning the period from the end of 1974 through 1989, using a data base of more than 144 equity portfolios, all extending over the full 15-year period, managed by 135 firms. The portfolios' total market value exceeded $22 billion at the end of 1989.

We asked the question of whether knowledge of a manager's ranking during the first half of a decade would be useful in selecting an *above average* manager for the second half of the decade. The accompanying table shows the results of this analysis. To illustrate one of the findings: Of the managers in the top 20% of the sample for the five years from 1980 through 1984, only 45% of them were in the top half during the 1985–89 period.

Scanning the table, no useful predictive pattern emerges. In the best result of the six 10-year periods that were analyzed, only 55% of the managers in the first or second quintile during the initial five-year period were able to finish above average in the succeeding five years.

For eight of 12 observations of managers who performed best by finishing in the first or second quintiles during the six initial five-year periods, less than half were able to do better than average during the

History Is Bunk: Percentage of Managers Performing above Median during Second Half of Decade

Quintile Ranking of Manager during First Half of Decade	1980– 1984	1981– 1985	1982– 1986	1983– 1987	1984– 1988	1985– 1989
1st	31%	52%	48%	45%	48%	45%
2nd	45	55	52	41	41	52
3rd	37	50	57	61	61	43
4th	63	48	45	55	55	48
5th	57	45	48	48	45	57
Decade analyzed	1975– 1984	1976– 1985	1977– 1986	1978– 1987	1979– 1988	1980– 1989

Source: RCB International Inc.

second half of the decade. Revealingly, the subsequent performance of the bottom two quintiles is barely distinguishable from—and certainly no worse than—that of the top two quintiles.

Many institutional investors, oddly, are quick to acknowledge that past performance is not predictive. Yet, after intense "analysis," they tend to be drawn to the managers with the best performance rankings in the past five years. Performance records are more helpful in understanding a manager's investment style, consistency and volatility characteristics than in evaluating ability to produce future superior investment returns.

Qualitative judgments, which we consider much more likely to produce successful long-term choices of managers than *quantitative* judgments, are much more difficult to make. They require far greater depth of knowledge of the manager candidates than is typically practical for, or practiced by, the committee making the selection. Because most committees simply do not spend enough time on the process to be comfortable in making qualitative choices, their decisions are driven by the historical performance numbers.

If the historical performance screen has no discriminating value, to what then should a plan sponsor turn?

We have identified several characteristics—unrelated to investment philosophy, asset class under management or even geographical focus of investing—that are helpful in identifying managers that tend to achieve superior, long-term results.

• Independent thinking. A portfolio manager must, largely through his own evaluation of available information, adopt non-consensus views and build non-consensus portfolios.

• Unencumbered decision-making. If the process to follow through with original ideas is difficult, then only easy and generally less-rewarding decisions will be made. Complex, time-consuming hierarchical information flows within management organizations or large formal committees make decisions more difficult.

• Personal discipline. Successful portfolio managers tend to be highly focused, intense and enthusiastic in their pursuits, whether professional or recreational.

• Flexibility. Portfolio management requires a great commitment to change. All investments must be reviewed continually, reflecting the newest and best available information. The successful manager must always be willing to reverse his earlier decision, regardless of whether it was good or bad, without the slightest hesitation.

• Love of the business. The most successful managers view investing as a personal passion. Although the job pays well, most would do it as an avocation.

The application of these judgmental characteristics requires more time than the typical committee of senior executives spends on the process. It becomes an ad hoc exercise in which a pension officer is forced to quantify and slot a group of managers. It leads to numerically driven selections and avoids difficult qualitative judgments.

A poor performance ranking might indicate more serious problems, but it is important to keep in mind that a poor ranking is a symptom, not the disease. Existing managers, whether performing well or poorly, should be re-evaluated using the same criteria as a new manager. An existing manager who wouldn't be hired today should be terminated.

More successful selections of managers will occur if committees devote the time necessary to fully evaluate managers under consideration, or fully delegate the selection to senior executive staff who have the experience to analyze candidates and who can be held accountable for performance.

Consultants can serve a useful role in rapidly moving their clients up the learning curve. All too often, however, they provide comfort that a sponsor has done a thorough job with relatively little effort.

Pension fund investment, although a good return is its bottom-line objective, is by no means a performance driven selection process.

The Trustees' Meeting—
A City Daydream

J. M. Brew

Anyone who has participated in the discussions of past and prospective investment performance that permeate most meetings of
most investment committees will appreciate the decision dispersal
produced by the study of "hard" data in this delightful piece by
J. M. Brew. It appeared in London's *Journal of the Society of
Investment Analysts* 20 years ago, perhaps inspired by an idea
of Jack Treynor concerning the analysis of U.K. unit trusts. Despite
the passage of time, one suspects that such discussions are still
taking place.

"Well", said the Chairman, "you have all had a few days to consider
the figures of our pension fund's investment performance. Before hand-
ing over to the Secretary who will explain them in detail I must thank
him for his foresight in instituting a scheme which makes performance
so easy to assess. I hear at the club that some other funds have been
having a good deal of trouble in this area. What it comes down to is
that they don't really know whether their pension funds have been invested well or badly. I am confident that in our case the question has
been made unusually straightforward and we shall be able to reach a
decision fairly quickly".

Reprinted from the *Journal of the Society of Investment Analysts* (June 1971), pp. 14–17. Bromley,
Kent: Society of Investment Analysts.

Before seeing the Secretary's comments on the situation the reader should be told the story so far. Some time ago this pension fund decided to divide its equity portfolio into six equal parts and to entrust their management to six organisations which had offered investment management services. The Trustees presciently took the view that ordinary share prices would probably drift down during the period and accordingly made arrangements to put all their new money into property. In order that there should be no ambiguity about the investment performance the powers of management were restricted to investment in shares which were constituents of the F.T.A. All-Share Index with, of course, permission to hold cash and reinvest the dividend income. It was further stipulated that investment should be conducted within the normal bounds of prudence. The Trustees did not know quite what that meant, but it seemed the right sort of thing to say. So the reader will agree that the problem could hardly be simpler. Each management was subject to the same constraints and each portfolio could accurately be compared with the Index. The specific reason for this meeting was the fact that more money was now available for equity investment. Decisions were needed on the allocation of this new money and also, perhaps, on the re-allocation of the management of existing portfolios.

The first figure produced by the Secretary showed the result of quarterly valuations between the starting date, 29 June 1968, and 2 October 1970, all expressed as a percentage of the starting value. The Secretary took the trouble to estimate what the periodic results would have been if the valuations had been exactly in line with the F.T.A. Index and income from the Index constituents had been reinvested as it was received. This is Figure 1.

"Well, Sir, fortunately the figures are sufficiently clear-cut to speak for themselves", the Secretary began, "but perhaps I could be allowed to elaborate very briefly. The first thing to notice is that, even allowing for reinvested income the F.T.A. Index showed a negative rate of return over the period, a rate of minus .131 per cent per quarter to be exact. We should have been much better off to sell out completely and put the proceeds out on loan. So to some extent we can congratulate ourselves on the decision to channel our new money elsewhere during the period. I think most of us believe that the future for equities is now a little more rosy and, with new money to invest, it seems to me that we should take this opportunity of reviewing the performance of our managers. You will see that they all achieved a positive rate of return, and within the

FIGURE 1
Quarterly Valuation Totals Allowing for Reinvested Income

Valuation Date	F.T.A. Index	Fund A	Fund B	Fund C	Fund D	Fund E	Fund F
29. 6.68	100	100	100	100	100	100	100
4.10.68	107.17	135.13	112.10	104.50	115.20	107.30	93.10
3. 1.69	114.89	142.04	127.91	109.73	122.23	115.24	101.12
3. 4.69	108.83	130.86	117.68	105.89	116.61	110.17	97.90
4. 7.69	95.70	111.36	95.32	98.48	89.79	97.17	87.13
3.10.69	94.86	107.79	95.32	97.79	98.14	96.68	87.13
2. 1.70	101.65	113.50	104.85	103.66	107.95	103.84	94.20
3. 4.70	99.49	108.66	102.23	102.11	101.47	101.97	94.20
3. 7.70	88.75	95.62	85.87	95.98	86.25	91.26	88.29
2.10.70	98.83	105.56	103.04	103.66	103.33	102.21	101.65
Effective total quarterly rate of return as calculated by the Secretary	−0.131%	+0.603%	+0.333%	+0.400%	+0.365%	+0.243%	+0.182%
Trend rate of quarterly return as calculated by the Economic Adviser	−1.420%	−2.237%	−1.839%	−0.425%	−1.685%	−1.044%	−0.420%

brief we gave them it was very satisfactory that they all beat the Index by a significant amount. I have designated the managements by letters, and my recommendation is that we should give all the new money to the one at the top of my league table, namely A.''

The Chairman asked for comments and the first one to speak was the Economic Adviser. His economic advice had not been conspicuously successful in the immediate past and he was not in a mood to let anyone get away with praise too easily. ''I should like to know why you have given us all these intermediate valuation results if the end figure is the only one that matters'', he said. ''I thought I ought to keep an eye on what was going on'', replied the Secretary, ''and having arranged for quarterly valuations I thought the Trustees would be interested to see the full result. But you are quite right that my recommendation is based on the last valuation''.

''That is very interesting'', said the Economic Adviser, ''because I have been looking at the intermediate figures and I should like to ask

FIGURE 2
Quarterly Rates of Return Allowing for Both Capital Changes and Income

Quarter	F.T.A. Index	Fund A	Fund B	Fund C	Fund D	Fund E	Fund F
1	+7.17%	+35.13%	+12.1%	+4.50%	+15.20%	+7.30%	−6.90%
2	+7.20%	+5.11%	+14.1%	+5.00%	+6.10%	+7.40%	+8.61%
3	−5.27%	−7.87%	−8.00%	−3.50%	−4.60%	−4.40%	−3.18%
4	−12.07%	−14.90%	−19.00%	−7.00%	−23.00%	−11.80%	−11.00%
5	−0.87%	−3.21%	NIL	−0.70%	+9.30%	−0.50%	NIL
6	+7.15%	+5.30%	+10.00%	+6.00%	+10.00%	+7.40%	+8.12%
7	−2.12%	−4.26%	−2.50%	−1.50%	−6.00%	−1.80%	NIL
8	−11.80%	−12.00%	−16.00%	−6.00%	−15.00%	−10.50%	−6.27%
9	+11.36%	+10.40%	+20.00%	+8.00%	+19.80%	+12.00%	+15.13%
Arithmetic Mean	+0.194%	+1.52%	+1.19%	+0.53%	+1.31%	+0.57%	+0.50%

you if there is any sort of intermediate fluctuation which might have made you change your mind". "I think I see your point", replied the Secretary, "but I am bound to say that it seems to me to be a trifle academic. After all there is no getting away from the fact that A has done a good deal better with our money than any of the others".

But the Economic Adviser was not quite finished. "If you want my specific recommendation it is that we should give the new money to those who are likely to do the best with it in the future rather than give it to those who have done best in the past. Your motive for the study of performance seems to be to reward those who have made the most money for us, on the basis that these will do the best for us in the future. I think we should study your performance tables much more carefully."

Having made this suggestion the Economic Adviser produced Figure 2 which shows the performance of each fund each quarter allowing for both capital and income.

"Is it so obvious now", he said, "that A is such a good manager? He started off like a shot from a gun and was miles ahead of the field at the end of the first quarter. After that he has done noticeably worse than the Index every single time. Contrast this with F who started very badly and has done outstandingly well since. Would you stake any money on A beating F between now and next year, because I certainly wouldn't? My impression is that F is the much better horse but that the finish came a furlong too soon for him. In fact I think we should seriously consider dropping A altogether. He is easily bottom of my league table."

The proposition being put by the Economic Adviser was that F, the management which had put up easily the worst end-to-end performance of all the six, was the one likely to do best in the future. He had some figures to prove it too. He had applied regression methods to the valuation figures (or, to be more accurate, the logarithm of the valuation totals) and derived a trend line for each management which can be used to estimate the rate of total return each is likely to achieve in future. The result is shown in the last line of Figure 1. This new method of assessment turns the ranking order just about completely upside down and shows that only three managements have a trend rate better than the Index. There are other ways of fitting a trend line but the results would not differ substantially. But if the Economic Adviser had been allowed to fit a second degree curve the trend would have been even more strongly in favour of F. His second favourite was C.

At this stage the Finance Director introduced the question of variability and risk which became the subject of a somewhat lengthy argument. It is evident from the tables that some managements produced results which were much more variable than others. But it is not obvious how we should assess variability. Should one consider the periodic valuation totals, or the totals relative to the Index? Perhaps we should consider the variability of the quarterly rates of return, or, probably best of all, the difference between the actual rates of return and those achieved on the Index. The Chairman very much liked E on these grounds, but nobody quite knew how much the better performance should be required or expected before one is justified in pursuing a more risky policy. Still it was evident that E, though he produced rather unexciting results, did so in a way which gave confidence that he would rarely produce a bad performance and would nearly always be above average.

"But there is another, and much better, way of looking at it", said the Finance Director. . . . "The idea is that some managements consistently have portfolios which both go up more and down more than the Index. Others have portfolios which go up less and down less. By examination of Figure 2 you can see roughly what I mean. Fund C moved the same way as the Index each quarter but its movement was always a good deal less pronounced. By contrast, Fund B was more volatile than the Index in both directions. The problem is easily analysed statistically by making a regression of each fund's quarterly rate of total return on the Index return". The results are shown in Figure 3, which shows the equation of the regression line for each management. The variable x represents the performance of the Index expressed as a total return and

FIGURE 3
Regression Equations for Each Management

x = **Quarterly Return on F.T.A. Index**
y = **Quarter Return on the Fund**

		Correlation
Fund A	y = 1.25 + 1.39 x	$r^2 = 0.782$
Fund B	y = 0.88 + 1.61 x	$r^2 = 0.996$
Fund C	y = 0.41 + 0.65 x	$r^2 = 0.994$
Fund D	y = 1.00 + 1.58 x	$r^2 = 0.939$
Fund E	y = 0.38 + 0.99 x	$r^2 = 0.999$
Fund F	y = 0.35 + 0.79 x	$r^2 = 0.789$

the variable y represents the performance of the management under analysis. The gradient of the line for A is 1.39 which means that a 1 per cent increase in the Index tended in the past to be accompanied by a 1.39 per cent increase in the portfolio managed by A. Management C, on the other hand only showed a 0.645 per cent increase in the same circumstances. This line is called the "characteristic line" and there is some evidence that its slope is relatively stable in time.

The Finance Director contended that the choice lay squarely between B and D because these managements had the steepest slopes to their characteristic lines and would therefore perform better in the rising market which the Trustees had agreed was likely to occur. He had a marginal preference for D because though its line was not quite so steep it intersected the vertical axis at a slightly higher point—which is supposed to reflect the amount by which the fund would beat the Index given a nil rate of return on the Index. But the Economic Adviser pointed out that the lines intersected at a point given by an Index return of 4 per cent which was surely less than one could expect in a normal year. The Finance Director then agreed that B was slightly preferable.

The Chairman was a bit dazed by now, but he felt obliged to put in another word for E. "I just don't believe it", he said. "You chaps are being much too clever about it all. Look at E's performance. He beat the Index by a perceptible amount every single time which is more than any of the others did. My second choice would be F who beat it eight times out of nine".

So there we have it. The Secretary chose A. The Economic Adviser chose C and F. The Finance Director chose B and D, and the Chairman chose E and F. About a hundred years ago Mr. Punch summed it up aptly when he said, "You pays your money and you takes your choice".

Postscript

In real life the figures will never be as conveniently clearcut as those in the tables. But the reader will have noticed one respect in which this daydream is realistic. At the time of the meeting there was only one thing on which the trustees were in agreement—that the equity market was likely to rise. At the time of going to press the Index is about 10% lower. But given the fact that they agreed to be bullish it would have been right to prefer B and D whatever Mr. Punch said. If you are going to make quarterly valuations you surely ought to use them.

We can all agree, though, that the matter is not quite so simple as the Secretary supposed.

Seven Rules for Investors

Nigel Lawson

Nigel Lawson wrote this tongue-in-cheek piece long before he became Britain's Chancellor of the Exchequer, but it illustrates the originality and wit that served him well in government. He now serves as vice chairman of BZW.

I am delighted that my colleague "Capitalist" is doing so well with his portfolio of shares. His careful system of selection is plainly a very sound one. But I can't help feeling that—like most accountants—he is obsessed with figures, with the purely statistical facts.

Earnings growth rates and dividend yields are all very well in their way. But the shrewd investor will want to look beyond mere figures, just as the trained psychoanalyst looks beyond the patient's words to discover truths deep in his subconscious.

Happily, I am not alone in this view. So great an authority as the well-known investment trust expert, Mr. George Touche, remarked in the midst of a learned, 25-page address on investment to the Institute of Chartered Accountants at Oxford last summer that "general impressions may be obtained from many sources, apart from the conclusions to be drawn from financial results. The cult of a chairman's personality, combined with constant repetition of his photograph, rarely inspires confidence in the management of a company."

Reprinted from *The Sunday Telegraph* (April 14, 1963), by permission of the Sunday Telegraph, Ltd.

Sole Contribution

So we have investment rule number one:

Avoid companies whose chairman's photograph is published more than four times a year.

Unfortunately this was Mr. Touche's only contribution to the important science of non-statistical investment analysis. But I strongly recommend the following as rule number two:

Avoid companies that publish their balance sheet in front of their profit and loss account in the annual report.

The Companies Act stipulates that both these be published, but it does not lay down the order in which they should appear. So companies invariably put first the document of which they are proudest (or least ashamed).

Obviously a company that is prouder of its assets than its profits is one to be avoided at all costs. This is the very hallmark of an unprogressive company earning an inadequate rate of return (if any) on its capital employed.

How many fortunes might have been saved, for example, had investors noticed that Pressed Steel publishes the parent company's balance sheet in front of the consolidated profit and loss account. You would not catch a growth stock like Elliott-Automation doing that. Again, the Lancashire Cotton Corporation, short of profits but long on assets, publishes its balance sheet first; whereas expansionist I.C.I. . . . but I needn't elaborate. . . .

But perhaps at this stage I ought to warn investors that this particular rule, although in my experience invaluable, is not an infallible guide. Take the two cement companies, for example. Associated Portland Cement puts its profit and loss account first, Rugby Portland Cement its balance sheet. And yet it is Rugby that has by far the better growth record. The explanation of this superficially startling phenomenon brings us to rule number three:

Invest in companies whose chairman is less than 5'8" tall.

What you must look for is the Napoleon of industry, those dynamic individuals who make up for lack of physical stature by making their companies grow instead. Sir Isaac Wolfson and Mr. Charles Clore are obvious examples.

This is also the explanation of the cement conundrum. Rugby's chairman Sir Halford Reddish qualifies with flying colours under the height rule. But A.P.C.'s Mr. John Reiss, although a charming gentleman and fine chairman, is over six feet tall.

The question of average height is also of material importance in determining the geographical spread of your investments. It is no accident that the small Japanese have the fastest rate of growth in the world, the medium size Europeans the next most rapid, and the tall British and Americans the slowest growth rate. . . .

Points System

It is always advisable, therefore, when considering a purchase of any share, to ask your stockbroker to let you know the precise height of the company's chairman. But you should also take a scientific interest in the rest of the board. Which brings us to Rule number four:

Assess the board on the points system as follows—one point for every director, and an extra point for every peer, admiral, general or air marshal. More than 15 points disqualifies, or more than twenty in the case of banks and insurance companies.

Plainly no board meeting will ever reach rapid agreement if there are too many directors; equally, an excessive number of peers and military gentlemen is dangerous because such people were taught by their nannies to believe that trade is no calling for a gentleman.

The shares of Sun Alliance Insurance, for example, are lower today than they were four years ago; whereas those of Legal and General have doubled. The Sun Alliance has 33 members, including eight peers: 41 points, which means instant disqualification. Legal and General's board, however, has only 16 members, including one peer and one admiral. Eighteen points is all right for insurance.

Inner Three

Then again the Rank Organisation board runs to 18 points (which means disqualification for an industrial company) whereas the *Financial*

Times, another leading group in the entertainment field, easily qualifies with nine points in spite of its three peers. But you have to be careful. The Unilever board contains 24 members, which might lead an unsuspecting investor to look elsewhere. But in fact an inner board of only three is what really counts.

This should complete your study of the company's report and accounts, except perhaps for two minor points, rules five and six:

Avoid companies who hold their annual general meetings at awkward times or in unlikely places.

Avoid companies who have just moved into a lush new head office.

The first of these is obvious. A company that announces that the annual meeting will be at 8.30 A.M. at Chipping Sodbury Town Hall is evidently not going out of its way to encourage shareholder participation.

The second derives from one of Prof. Parkinson's laws, viz that new offices are built just as the company reaches its peak, from where it can only decline.

. . . In 1961, when the Bowater Paper Corporation moved into its lavish Knightsbridge skyscraper, profits fell sharply and the company lost its growth stock rating.

But as well as the annual report, it is also well worth paying attention to the announcement of preliminary figures. Here we come to my final, and most important, rule seven:

Longer to Add

Bad figures always take longer to add up than good ones.

From this follows a simple conclusion: you should sell any share in a company whose preliminary profit figures fail to be published within five days of the date on which they were published the previous year. By following this simple rule, you will save far more money than you lose.

Shareholders in both Lombard Banking and Firth Cleveland, for example, could have sold in advance of bad news on three separate occasions, as the following table indicates:

Lombard Banking:—

2/3/1960	Profits up 80 p.c.
9/3/1961	Profits down 25 p.c.
16/3/1962	Profits down 40 p.c.
17/3/1963	Profits unchanged

Firth Cleveland:—

31/5/1961	Profits up by one third
7/6/1962	Profits down by one third

It will be interesting to see what 1963 brings.

Here, then, are my seven rules for investment for Easter. There are, of course, some others. But that's another story.

ANALYSIS

Exposition of a New Theory on the Measurement of Risk[1]

Daniel Bernoulli

Daniel Bernoulli (1700–1782) was a member of a Swiss family of distinguished mathematicians and a professor at the University of Basel. He won the prize of the French Academy no fewer than 10 times. His concept of utility, which forms the basis for all theories of portfolio management, is described in this excerpt from the paper he gave at the Imperial Academy of Sciences in Petersburg in 1738.

§1. Ever since mathematicians first began to study the measurement of risk there has been general agreement on the following proposition: *Expected values are computed by multiplying each possible gain by the number of ways in which it can occur, and then dividing the sum of these products by the total number of possible cases where, in this theory, the consideration of cases which are all of the same probability is insisted upon.* If this rule be accepted, what remains to be done within the framework of this theory amounts to the enumeration of all alternatives, their breakdown into equi-probable cases and, finally, their insertion into corresponding classifications.

§2. Proper examination of the numerous demonstrations of this proposition that have come forth indicates that they all rest upon one hypothesis: *since there is no reason to assume that of two persons*

Reprinted from *Econometrica* 22 (January 1954; originally published 1738, Petersburg), pp. 23–36. Evanston, Illinois: The Econometric Society.

encountering identical risks,[2] *either should expect to have his desires more closely fulfilled, the risks anticipated by each must be deemed equal in value.* No characteristic of the persons themselves ought to be taken into consideration; only those matters should be weighed carefully that pertain to the terms of the risk. The relevant finding might then be made by the highest judges established by public authority. But really there is here no need for judgment but of deliberation, i.e., rules would be set up whereby anyone could estimate his prospects from any risky undertaking in light of one's specific financial circumstances.

§3. To make this clear it is perhaps advisable to consider the following example: Somehow a very poor fellow obtains a lottery ticket that will yield with equal probability either nothing or twenty thousand ducats. Will this man evaluate his chance of winning at ten thousand ducats? Would he not be ill-advised to sell this lottery ticket for nine thousand ducats? To me it seems that the answer is in the negative. On the other hand I am inclined to believe that a rich man would be ill-advised to refuse to buy the lottery ticket for nine thousand ducats. If I am not wrong then it seems clear that all men cannot use the same rule to evaluate the gamble. The rule established in §1 must, therefore, be discarded. But anyone who considers the problem with perspicacity and interest will ascertain that the concept of *value* which we have used in this rule may be defined in a way which renders the entire procedure universally acceptable without reservation. To do this the determination of the *value* of an item must not be based on its *price*, but rather on the *utility* it yields. The price of the item is dependent only on the thing itself and is equal for everyone; the utility, however, is dependent on the particular circumstances of the person making the estimate. Thus there is no doubt that a gain of one thousand ducats is more significant to a pauper than to a rich man though both gain the same amount.

§4. The discussion has now been developed to a point where anyone may proceed with the investigation by the mere paraphrasing of one and the same principle. However, since the hypothesis is entirely new, it may nevertheless require some elucidation. I have, therefore, decided to explain by example what I have explored. Meanwhile, let us use this as a fundamental rule: *If the utility of each possible profit expectation is multiplied by the number of ways in which it can occur, and we then divide the sum of these products by the total number of possible cases, a mean utility*[3] *[moral expectation] will be obtained, and the profit which corresponds to this utility will equal the value of the risk in question.*

§5. Thus it becomes evident that no valid measurement of the value of a risk can be obtained without consideration being given to its *utility,* that is to say, the utility of whatever gain accrues to the individual, or, conversely, how much profit is required to yield a given utility.

Notes

1. Translated from Latin into English by Dr. Louise Sommer, The American University, Washington, D.C., from "Specimen Theoriae Novae de Mensura Sortis," *Commentarii Academiae Scientiarum Imperialis Petropolitanae,* Tomus V.
2. i.e., risky propositions (gambles). [Translator]
3. Free translation of Bernoulli's "emolumentum medium," literally: "mean utility."

The Valuation of Listed Stocks

Arnold Bernhard

Arnold Bernhard built—over more than 50 years—Value Line Inc., an investment service for individual investors that is widely used by professionals; a substantial fortune; and a superior investment record. In this excerpt, he examines the always fascinating and elusive difference between value and price.

At the moment of writing, the Dow Jones Industrial Average stands at 165. Stock prices, as reflected in this Average, are lower in the writer's opinion than values. The reader may agree that stocks are undervalued now, but it is obvious that most investors do not think so, because, if they did, their buying would force prices up to the point where stocks would no longer be undervalued. That raises the question whether it is possible to determine objectively, and in conflict with prevailing opinion, how different the price of a stock ought to be from what it is. More and more one hears the expression: "This or that stock is undervalued and overvalued or fully valued." When an analyst or an investor speaks in such terms, he implies that he has a standard of value in mind, whether he defines that standard or not.

Reprinted from *Readings in Financial Analysis and Investment Management* (Homewood, Illinois: Dow Jones Irwin, Inc., 1963), pp. 235–44, by permission of the Association for Investment Management and Research.

Value Differs from Price

Value often differs from price. Charles H. Dow, whose theory of price trends has had enormous influence in Wall Street, insisted that every student of the market should "first of all know value."

Another famous authority on stock prices, Baron Rothschild, said that the way to succeed in the stock market was to "buy stocks when they are cheap and sell them when they are dear." He too implied a standard of value, though he did not define it. One cannot buy something cheap or sell something dear unless he knows what cheap is and what dear is. Those are relative terms, and they must be related to some kind of a standard.

Value is something that exists in the mind. It is, therefore, as difficult to define as life itself. In all economic history there has never been a definition of pure economic value that has won universal acceptance. All the great economists have attempted to define value—Aristotle, Adam Smith, Ricardo, Bohm-Bawerk, Jevons, Clark, Pareto—but there is no definition of value in the economic sense that has been accorded universal acceptance.

One cannot say that a stock's value is the equivalent of its price. If that were so, it would be a waste of time to discuss value at all. Value would be price and price value, and that is all one would need to know.

The classical definition of the value of a common stock is the one that holds the value of a common stock to be equal to the sum of all the dividends it will pay in the future, discounted to the prevailing interest rate. It is difficult to see how any one could take exception to this theory of value. The only trouble with it is that it is unusable. It is unusable because nobody knows what the sum of all the future dividends will be. If one could determine in advance what the sum of dividends would be over a 20-year span, or whatever life expectancy the company is determined to have, common stocks would not be issued. Capital, instead of being asked to assume a partnership risk, would be granted a contract, specifying the return to be paid on the investment over a period of time and the date when the capital would be returned out of the depreciation reserve. There would be little or no need for common stocks.

The very reason for the existence of common stocks is that nobody knows or is expected to know what the dividends will total in the future. To define the value of a stock, therefore, as the sum of its future dividends, discounted to the interest rate, boils down to this: that the value of a common stock is a mystery.

It is not necessary to give up the search, however, even if no perfectly satisfactory definition of value is available, for it may be found possible to determine value within certain limits.

Up to this point it has been reasoned that value is something different from price and that it cannot be defined. Value is something that exists in the minds of people. But, since the common conception of value is expressed in price at a given moment, we seem to be forced back to the premise that price and value are the same thing, since they are both the expression of value as it exists in the minds of the buyers and sellers who participate in a free market.

The reasoning is not perfectly circular though. There is a break in the circle which offers an opportunity for evolving a practical standard of value. That break lies in this fact: that people—the very same people—do not put the same price tag on a stock at all times. If the market price of General Motors is 30 in March of 1938 and 30 is its value, in the opinion of all buyers and sellers who participate in a free market, and if the price of General Motors should be 50 in October of 1938, also in the opinion of all buyers and sellers, can we find, in this price variation, the clue to those factors that determine value and, through value, price? Admitted that, since value cannot be defined, the verdict of the market as to what value is must be accepted. That does not mean that the verdict of the market must be accepted at every moment. Obviously, the market changes its mind. What causes it to do so?

Classical Definition Impracticable

We reject the theory that the value of a stock is the total of the dividends it will pay during its life, not because this is theoretically incorrect, but because it is impracticable. However, common sense tells us that dividends in some way or other have a bearing on the price at which a stock will sell and, therefore, on its value.

It is known too that dividends can only be paid from profits and that profits are not always the same as dividends. Profits are often reinvested in the business and not paid out in dividends. Although dividends may be said to be a function of profits, they are not the equivalent. Therefore, it may be assumed that profits in their own right have some bearing on what the market will think the price of a stock should be.

Assets also have some weight. Many court tests reveal that book values are given weight in reorganization proceedings in an effort to determine the amount of equity available for apportionment to various claimants.

There is reason also to believe that habit of mind has something to do with price determination. If United States Steel sells for $100 a share during a given year, that figure will influence the thinking of buyers and sellers of United States Steel in the following year, even though other factors significantly related to value have changed.

To repeat the argument to this point: Value and price are not necessarily the same thing. Yet the only determinant of value, which is something that cannot be defined, is price. We find a break in the circle of reasoning in the fact that prices are not the same at all times and that changes in certain variables, such as earnings, dividends, and assets, arc related to the corresponding changes in prices. If it can be found that a certain relationship between prices on the one hand and the variables of earnings and dividends and assets on the other has been maintained for a long period of time, it might then rightly be concluded that at such moments, or even in such years, as the market deviates from this long held relationship, the distortion is a measure of disparity between price and value. It can be said that, at such times when a given level of earnings, assets, and dividends fails to command the price that has been placed on it most of the time in the past, that is a time of overvaluation or undervaluation. And we can logically use this measure, not as a definition of value, but as a description of it, and as a method for determining the direction in which the market price will probably move by way of readjustment. It is the virtue of a normal relationship that it can be expected to prevail most of the time. What we wish to know is what will be the opinion, expressed in price, of all the buyers and sellers participating in a free market, most of the time.

One cannot be perfectly sure that the variables of earnings and dividends and assets and habit of mind will actually determine the opinion of buyers and sellers. But one can make certain assumptions and then test them mathematically, to see whether or not a correlation exists between changes in the variables of earnings, dividends, and assets, and habit of mind on the one hand, and prices on the other, and, if such correlation is found to exist, whether the coefficient is so high as to be beyond the possibility of explanation by pure chance.

If a statistician were to correlate earnings, dividends, assets, and last year's average price of a given stock (last year's average price is the specific way of expressing "habit of mind"), he could do so through a computation known as a multiple variable correlation analysis. The Value Line rating, about which the reader may have heard, is a single line which expresses that correlation. In that line is expressed the price that the market over a 20-year span has placed on earnings, assets, and dividends at the various levels of experience, most of the time.

If through such a correlation over a period of 20 years the market can determine the specific weights to be assigned to each variable, then one could with reason determine what the future value of a stock will be in terms of market price, provided only that the future earnings and dividends and assets of that stock could be forecast with reasonable accuracy. It cannot be said with certainty that the future price will accord with the normal capitalization of earnings and assets as determined by the 20-year experience. But it can be said that the probability that the future price will conform to the long term sense of value is so high as to justify the effort and to provide a basis for a rational investment program.

To summarize: In the absence of a commonly accepted definition of value, we must, to be practical, go on the assumption that value is in the long run the equivalent of price. But we may also proceed on the assumption that price at any given time is not always the same as value, because there is such a thing as a long term price appraisal which may differ from the current price appraisal. We find that the changes in price that occur from year to year can be ascribed in significantly high degree to corresponding changes in such variables as assets, earnings, and dividends, and habit of mind (price lag). We conclude, therefore, that the evolution of a standard of value, based on a correlation between changes in price and changes in factors of value, when found, should enable us to project the probable future of a stock, not with certainty, but with a sufficiently high degree of probability to validate the premise that such a projection is a practical standard by which to identify areas of undervaluation or overvaluation, not only in the stock market as a whole, but in the prices of individual stocks as well.

It is recognized that the practicality of such a rating depends on ability to forecast the future level of earnings and dividends with reasonable accuracy. Although space does not permit a discussion of the methods by which this can be done, there is evidence to prove that it can be and has been done. At the very least, the analysis proves that the normal capitalization of a given level of earnings and assets can be determined in advance and that, because the capitalization is normal, it will probably be realized. The inescapable hazard of projecting future earnings and dividends remains, of course. But the price that the market will probably place on a given level of earnings and dividends need no longer remain in the realm of pure guess.

If this method of evaluation is sound, then it follows that the stocks that are most deeply undervalued according to this standard should give the best account of themselves in the open market during a period of 6 months to 18 months, regardless of the trend of the market as a whole. This, as a matter of fact, is a result that has been proved in experience. That is to say, the stocks most deeply undervalued and therefore most strongly to be recommended have, as a class, outperformed in the market the stocks that, as a class, merit a lower recommendation, and those that merit the second best recommendation have outperformed as a class those that merited the third class recommendation, and so on. In short, it is possible by this method to separate the sheep from the goats in the market, according to value. This is not to say that every stock that merits the strongest recommendation will outperform every stock that deserves the second strongest recommendation, but it is to say that, taken as a group, the most strongly recommended stocks outperform, in a practical market sense, the stocks that are in a less favorable position relative to an objective mathematical standard of value, and this happens consistently, as audited records prove.

The writer is of the opinion that the differences between actual market price and the standard of value expressed in the Value Line rating can be very largely explained in terms of market sentiment. One good measure of market sentiment is the ratio of stock yields to bond yields. If such an average ratio be inserted into the equation as a fifth independent variable, the correlations emerge as almost perfect. (Coefficients of determination as high as 0.96 are not infrequent, and nearly all stock equations have an R^2 of over 0.85.) All this seems to mean, at first blush, is that, if one can predict where the stock market averages and the interest rate will be next year, he can forecast pretty accurately where the price of a particular stock will be too, if he can forecast its earnings and dividends. Actually, though, the exercise is more promising than at first appears, because, for one thing, the stock-bond yield ratio lends itself to forecast better than the stock market averages alone, and, second, even if not forecastable, a stock-bond yield ratio, inserted into a multiple variable correlation analysis, gives a truer weighting to the other variables of earnings, assets, dividends, and price lag. The nonpredictable variable (stock-bond yield ratio) can then be held constant, and a projection of the predictable variables in the equation can be made with greater assurance that they will reveal the true value of the stock, ex sentiment.

Stock Values and Stock Prices

Nicholas Molodovsky

Nicholas Molodovsky, editor of the *Financial Analysts Journal,* brought an old world noblesse and a natural scholarship (with which he also earned a doctorate at the University of Paris) to the study of investments. Here is a representative piece of Nick's work.

———————

A generation or two ago, few investors would have considered putting their money into stocks insufficiently backed by tangible assets. Their net worth was an objective standard of value. Quite independent of the stock's market price, it was a sensible guide for investing. In poor times, the principal was likely to remain safe while providing a reasonably assured and adequate income. And if the stock's earning power increased over the years, both principal and income grew.

Yet, frequently, some of these asset-heavy investment fortresses stood ponderously still at the same levels of earning power and price, while prices and earnings of many equities deeply submerged in asset-accounting water surged irresistibly upward.

Gradually, the effect of earnings on stock prices began to impress investors, and they tried to use them in measuring stock values. One of the early notions was that the fair value of a stock could be ascertained by applying a uniform multiplier to its current earnings.

Excerpted from the *Financial Analysts Journal* 16 (May/June 1960), pp. 9–12, 79–92. Charlottesville, Virginia: Association for Investment Management and Research.

The 'Rule' of Ten-Times Earnings

"Valuation of Common Stocks," in the February 1959 issue of . . . [the *Financial Analysts Journal*], described the circumstances that gave birth to this belief. It mentioned also that, according to an authoritative financial periodical [*The Exchange*], many people still held it. Browsing through earlier issues of the same magazine, we came across some additional comments:

> The table on this page revives a method which enjoyed wide popularity during the securities market upswing of the 1920's and the tortuous downswing of the 1930's for estimating the 'worth' of common stocks. In the buoyant 1920's, when an industrial company's shares were selling at around 10 times earnings, actual or closely estimated, the price was considered by the trading fraternity as reasonable, meaning reasonably low.
>
> Technically, the partisans of such a measure of value spoke of the ratio of price to earnings. [1]

When earnings remain stable, a constant capitalizer makes sense. But the multipliers must reflect changes in earning power.

Price-Earnings Ratios and Stock Market Levels

Another tenacious idea was not helpful to investors: the thesis that when price-earnings ratios are historically high, stocks are overpriced; and that when stocks are cheap, the ratios become invitingly low. To bring the relations between stock prices and price-earnings ratios into sharper focus, let us look at them through the stereoscopic viewer of a scatter diagram.

Figure 1 pictures ratios (horizontal scale) and prices (vertical scale), 1871–1959. To avoid cluttering the chart, we omitted century figures, but there cannot be any confusion. The earliest years plotted are the 1870's, and the most recent years do not extend beyond the 1950's. The years of bull market peaks are marked by triangles, those of bear market troughs by heavy dots. . . .

The absence of correlation between prices and price-earnings ratios is obvious. The points, the triangles, and the heavy dots are scattered throughout the diagram. Evidently, ratios are not always high when prices are forming tops, or low when stocks are scraping bottoms. In the turning areas of stock prices they vary greatly, affording no basis for judgment whether stocks are dear or cheap.

FIGURE 1
Prices and Price-Earnings Ratios: 1871–1959

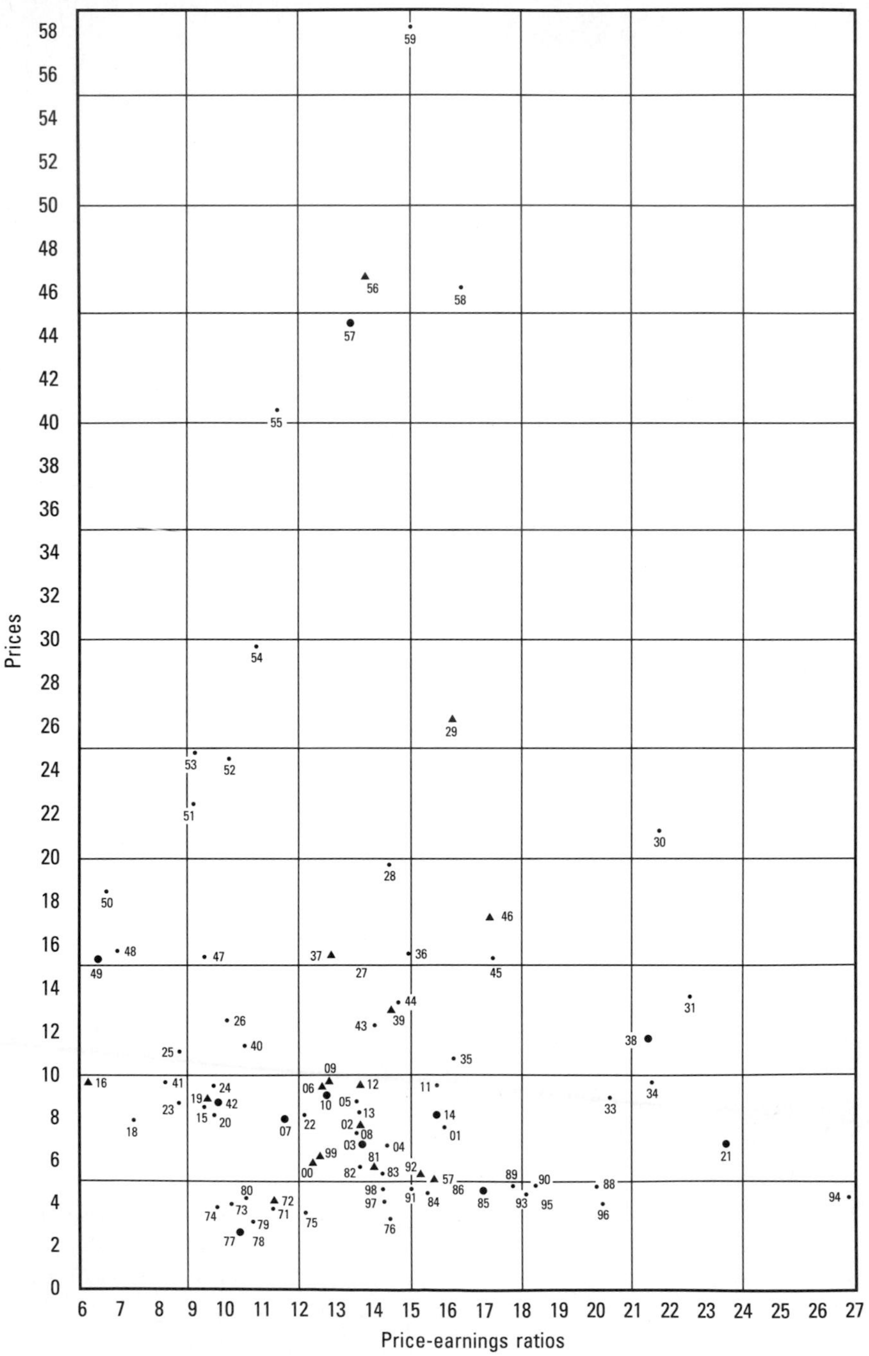

Nor do the ratios rise in bull markets and accompany bear markets in their slides. They do rise in 1926–29, but with similar consistency they decline in 1934–37. At the end of each period, they had reached their respective positions by very different routes and from opposite directions.

The lack of correlation between prices and ratios becomes particularly striking when we observe the tremendous range covered by prices within the same relatively limited zone. Thus, the 13 to 17 times earnings multipliers lie half way on the scale of price-earnings ratios. Within this rather narrow strip, fluctuations in stock prices have been extraordinarily wide, and have encompassed both peaks and troughs of their cyclical movements.

While there is no iron clad pattern in the general structure of the diagram, the price-to-earnings ratios tend to cluster in the middle or "temperate" zone, and the "tropical" zone of the highest ratios is dominated by years of economic and market recessions. The "arctic" region of the lowest ratios has less clearly marked characteristics, but numerous war or rearmament years are in it.

The diagram gives the impression that price-earnings ratios reflect underlying economic conditions and are not associated with any particular level of prices.

On the scale of the ratios, the distance between 1928 and 1929 is small. But between 1929 and 1930, when stock prices declined not quite as much as they had risen in the preceding year, the ratios rose markedly, indicating the passage from economic expansion to contraction. Strange as it may seem, price-earnings ratios are highest during depressions; wars and inflations tend to bring low ratios.

Importance of Adequate Concepts

The story of price-earnings ratios is not unlike that of phlogiston. According to chemistry textbooks, three centuries ago a German scientist "explained" burning by a chemical fluid he dubbed phlogiston, "the thing that makes things burn." Everything flammable, he claimed, contained some phlogiston. When it burned, the phlogiston escaped, causing crackling, sparks, flames and smoke.

While phlogiston presumably accounted for some of the aspects of burning, it led to many difficulties and contradictions until Priestley discovered oxygen. Not only could burning be then understood, but Lavoisier's experiments soon laid the foundations of modern chemistry.

False as were the ideas about what happened in burning, ores were melted into metals and fashioned into tools, ornaments, and weapons for thousands of years before Lavoisier was born. And many years elapsed before his teachings were accepted even by his fellow chemists. Men of affairs—if they heard about him at all—probably considered him a stodgy egghead, an insufferable bore. In their practical work they could get along quite well without dull theorizing. Yet clearer concepts led to technological advances that would have been unimaginable without them.

Our beloved teacher, Frank W. Taussig, once wrote: "Economists are often twitted with being theoretical and out of touch with the facts of industry. Much more unpractical is the attitude of the average business man, who is familiar with but one small corner of the industrial world, contents himself with the most superficial commonplaces, and knows so little of the essential problems of economics that he is hardly aware even of their existence."[2]

Financial Analysts are aware of the importance of basic research for industrial progress. Investors may find a basic valuation approach equally vital.

==

The Factor of Time

The most important dimension of earnings lies along the axis of time. Unless viewed in the perspective of their past and projected future, current earnings have little economic meaning. Time is, in fact, a basic dimension of finance. The concept and practice of the interest rate—the capital's share in the distribution of wealth created by production—express the relation between present and future payments.

To quote F. R. Macaulay: "Investments as a class constitute one family. They each originate in an exchange of present money for an expectation of future money. If it were not for such an expectation they would have no exchange value. And they lose that value as the expectation dies out. The demand that comes from the possibility of buying them and later selling at a profit may exist for a time in a sort of economic vacuum, but it is essentially a derived demand and, in the absence of any (warranted or unwarranted) expectation of future returns, it sooner or later disappears.

"Because the good that the common stock offers to its purchaser is an expectation of future money payments, the relation of its present-money price to its future-money payments is as unmistakably an interest phenomenon as is the relation of the present-money price of a bond to its future-money payments."[3]

At first glance, the value of a common stock may not seem to be related to the future payments to be received from it. Numerous stocks paying small or no dividends often command high prices. However, though the buyer, with an eye to profit alone, may be indifferent to or not even aware of the fact, potential investors' expectations of future payments are the active force supporting the price of his stock.

A comic strip published by a New York evening paper depicted, in the spring of 1946 at the height of the black market, the woeful experience of a lady who committed the blunder of opening a package she had purchased. The food in it was spoiled. Indignantly she rushed back to the store, "My dear lady," exclaimed the clerk, "you opened the package? Good heavens! That's not for eating. It's for BUYING AND SELLING."

So it is too with stocks. Many purchase them for selling, never looking inside. But if the market declines before they succeed in disposing of the package, the value of the contents suddenly acquires a new and decisive meaning.

The only financial return from a common stock comes in the form of a payment, or of a series of payments to the holder. Dividends are the foundation on which common stock values are erected. If expectations of future dividends fail to be realized, the stock becomes worthless. . . .

Notes

1. *The Exchange,* a monthly magazine published by the New York Stock Exchange, December, 1944.

2. F. W. Taussig, *Principles of Economics*, (The Macmillan Company, New York, 3rd ed., 1926), Volume II, p. 45.
3. Frederick R. Macaulay, "Some Theoretical Problems Suggested by the Movements of Interest Rates, Bond Yields and Stock Prices in the U.S. since 1856." (National Bureau of Economic Research, 1938), pp. 129–30.

Common Stocks at the Current Price Level

Dwight C. Rose

In an address to the joint annual meeting of the American Statistical Association and the American Economic Association, Dwight Rose, of Brundage, Story & Rose, always the careful student and quantitative analyst of investments, delivered this sobering "prosecution" of common stocks at their December 1928 prices only months before the crash. And, what a rigorous and relentless prosecutor he was!

———— ▪ ————

December 27, 1928.

Mr. Chairman, and Ladies and Gentlemen:

Those of us who may have become a little timid about the level of the stock market during the last few months have been greatly comforted, I am sure, by the most interesting addresses that Colonel Ayres and Dr. Friday have just given us. I'd even hazard the prediction (loath as I am to predict anything) that several of the gentlemen leaving the hall after Dr. Friday's talk were bound for the telegraph office downstairs to convey their enthusiasm to their brokers in the form of substantial buying

Reprinted from *The Practical Application of Investment Management,* Volume 2 (New York, 1933), Appendix 1, pp. 139–61, by permission of HarperCollins Publishers. © 1933 by Dwight C. Rose. © renewed 1960 by Dwight C. Rose.

orders. But I wonder if the majority of investors in common stocks to-day are in need of more stimulation to their optimistic imaginations. I think I know a few to whom even Dr. Friday might prescribe a sedative, and it probably will not harm any of us to inquire for a few minutes into some of the factors that appear unfavorable to investment in common stocks at the current price level.

===

The common stock during the past three or four years has been most ably defended as a long-term investment medium. And this able defense has been responsible in no small measure for the wide popular support that the leading companies are receiving in the current stock market.

It is only a few years ago that the firm with which I am associated was having real difficulty in persuading most of its clients to reduce their bond holdings in order to introduce a conservative proportion of 40 to 50 per cent in common stocks. Today we are having difficulty in persuading these same clients not to put 150 per cent in common stocks.

The great army of American investors, influenced by the able argument in defense of the common stock, have had a taste of large profits and their appetites have been whetted for more. The courageous ones have realized profits during the last four or five years ranging anywhere from 100 per cent to several thousand per cent. The air is surcharged with optimism. The imagination of American investors has been awakened to tremendous possibilities in the future and there has been developed a sort of hero worship for the common stock. Perhaps a more or less blind confidence in this "hero" has left room for only superficial consideration of some of the more fundamental, though less romantic, factors that will play a large part in determining the rate of return that may be realized over the next few years from a diversified group of high-grade common stocks bought at present levels.

Common stocks perform an important function that is essential to a conservative program for most investors. But perhaps the time is propitious for a temporary application of the brakes. A note of caution does not necessarily imply the advisability of speculating on lower prices to the extent of selling out one's entire commitment in stocks. It may, however, suggest to some the elimination of margin accounts and to others the temporary substitution of bonds in place of some of the stocks held.

In this short discussion I shall, with your permission, assume the role of prosecuting attorney against the common stock bought at the present level of prices. I shall comment on some of the evidence that is available to us and perhaps question some of the character witnesses that have praised the common stock hero and influenced the court of public opinion. On assumption that we have already heard an able defense, I shall point out some of the present weaknesses in the evidence offered before the bar of public opinion.

The evidence upon which the investor must exercise judgment as to the participation he will maintain in high-grade common stocks at the present level of prices may be divided into three broad classifications:

First:—What has the average intelligent investor actually accomplished through common stock investments over the last quarter century?

Second:—What were the fundamental qualities inherent in these common stocks upon which this successful experience was primarily dependent?

Third:—To what extent have important changes in these fundamental qualities altered the character of common stocks as an investment medium?

Let us consider the first one of these three broad classifications of the evidence—What has the average intelligent investor actually accomplished over the last quarter century from a diversified investment in common stocks?

The best evidence of past experience is the actual history of the investments owned by a wide group of intelligent investors. Of course, the difficulty is to get accurate records of representative experience over such a long period of time. There is, however, one group of investors that has been required by law to file an accurate statement of their investment operations every year. I refer to the insurance companies. Of the insurance companies, I have selected the fire companies because they have not been hindered in their investment operations by burdensome legal restrictions; the stockholders have been primarily dependent upon the return from investment operations for their profit; and the directorates have been composed of many of the foremost business and financial men in the country. These fire insurance companies were the nearest thing to investment trusts that we had in operation during that period. What did the twenty-five largest of them accomplish from their stock investments over the last twenty years?

FIGURE 1
Average Accomplishments of 25 Largest Fire Insurance Companies

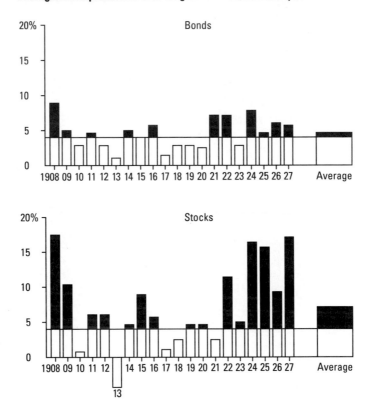

The records kept by these insurance companies permitted us to segregate the return from bonds and stocks only back as far as 1908, and this chart (Figure 1) represents the return from each of these major classes of investment from 1908 up to 1928. The average annual return including both income and changes in market value was for this period 4.81 per cent from bonds and 7.81 per cent from stocks. It is interesting to note from this chart, however, that the large returns from stocks came in the first two years and the last six years. The twelve intervening years showed little if any advantage over bonds. Also the actual average annual return of 7.81 per cent from stocks is substantially lower than that indicated in a number of theoretical studies aimed to portray what the average intelligent investor *should* have been able to accomplish from common stocks during the period.

Misjudgments of the Past

The financier of the early 1900's based his judgment primarily upon the experience of the thirty or forty preceding years which had been attended by an almost constant appreciation in the value of the dollar and a substantial decline in interest rates. The market value of bonds was gradually increasing and the dollars received in interest or at maturity would always buy more in goods and services than the dollars originally invested. A projection of this trend into the future promised large rewards to the investor in long-term bonds, but the twenty years following 1900 exhibited almost a complete reversal in trend. The judgment made by the majority of financiers in the early 1900's with respect to the future trend of bond prices actually proved about 100 per cent wrong.

The judgment of many of our leading financiers at the opening of the year 1929 is based largely upon the experience of the last 7 or 8 years when common stocks have proved a most profitable form of investment. Will the history for the next 7 or 8 years following 1929 turn out to be more favorable to the bond-holder and less favorable to the stockholder or will the experience of the recent past be projected indefinitely into the future?

We are now ready to inquire into the second general classification of the evidence we are examining in this prosecution of our common stock hero. What were the fundamental qualities inherent in common stocks during the last quarter century upon which their favorable experience has been primarily dependent?

The insurance company records that we have just examined show quite conclusively that stocks have proven the more profitable medium of investment during the period studied, but we do not have enough material there to determine *WHY*.

Change in Earnings Basis

. . . To what extent have important changes in the fundamental qualities inherent in common stocks over the past quarter century altered their character as an investment medium?

The outstanding change, to my mind, is the relationship between earnings and selling price. *These Dow-Jones industrial stocks which averaged 11.90 per cent earnings to selling price throughout the last quarter century are now, in a year of unusual prosperity preceded by seven years of expanding credit, selling on an earnings basis of only about 5.40 per cent. During the last period of general prosperity and expanded credit the ratios of earnings to selling price of these stocks were: 1917, 28.5 per cent; 1918, 33.1 per cent; 1919, 22.5 per cent; and 1920, 15.0 per cent. Never before, except in a period of severe depression has the earnings ratio ever approached the present basis of 5.40 per cent.*

The "New Era" Fallacy

Some of our more ardent supporters of the common stock tell us that they do not care at what prices or earnings basis these companies are now selling. They have full confidence that the imagination and inventive genius of the American people must, over a period of years, multiply corporate earnings many times over and consequently push present prices to much higher levels. We have just begun to appreciate the wonders of research, and business men are much more honest in their dealings with the public and their stockholders. Much of the waste incident to the earlier regimes of sharp business practices, lack of knowledge of the economics of production and consumption, and the inflexibility of our crude credit system has now been eliminated. But, do these changed conditions necessarily mean that the *average* corporation is going to show larger earnings on its capital, or a greater increase in earnings than it has in the past?

Is it not more likely that the principal beneficiary from all these influences will be the consumer rather than the producer or the investor? The average efficiency of business has increased. Those that do not keep up with the times must fall by the wayside in competition; those that are ahead of the times will show a correspondingly greater progress; but the *average* company probably will do little better than the average company has done in the past. In the last analysis we have a competition of capital seeking investment in any enterprise offering more than the average return, and more capital will continue to pour into such enterprises until the return of the average concern is on a basis commensurate with that in other fields.

The investor of today is amazed and almost dumbfounded at the new inventions of such fundamental importance that are appearing in rapid succession, one upon the other. It is doubtful, however, if these new inventions and improvements in industry are proportionately any greater than those that took place in the earlier years of this century. Our industrial development has been growing in geometrical ratio as far back as we can measure. The steamboat, railroad train, electric street car, automobile, telephone, the incandescent lamp, motion pictures and hundreds of other major innovations that have taken place in past years were proportionately as great for these years as is the advent of the aeroplane and radio today. We must have more from our industrial research in the next twenty years if our industrial development is to continue to grow in the *same* geometric ratio. But the fact that industry is growing and earnings increasing does not necessarily mean large profits to the common stock investor if all of these favorable factors have been discounted in an inflated market price.

Popularity Promotes Lower Return

One fact that very forcibly strikes the student of actual investment history of the past fifty years is that the majority of investors have usually held the class of security that has shown a relatively poor return. Will the same type of investor that was shrewd enough to hold the highest grade industrial common stocks during the last quarter century continue to maintain his capital in them at present levels if a more attractive opportunity exists elsewhere for its employment?

New capital utilized in the average business today is surely earning above the 5 per cent earnings basis at which the popular industrial common stocks are now being traded. The average chain store, for example, is investing new money to earn 20 per cent or 25 per cent in the chain store field. The purchaser of the common stock in these chain stores is, however, paying a price that shows something between 4 and 5 per cent earnings on his investment. And the average business man, who would not consider investing money in his own business when the opportunity for earnings appeared no greater than 5 per cent, does not hesitate to buy stocks in companies listed on the New York Stock Exchange on this basis.

It is probable that the able defense of the seasoned common stock over the last 4 or 5 years, coincident with a tremendous expansion of our credit structure, has resulted in a concentration of capital in the shares of industry at a faster rate than our business leaders have seen the opportunity for its profitable utilization, and that, therefore, the competitive bidding for seasoned common stocks has inflated their market values to levels from which *there must be a recession*, if and when it becomes apparent that actual earnings will not support these inflated values.

=

Let us now summarize the evidence we have been examining against the common stock:

First, we have found that the actual annual return realized from stocks by a wide group of intelligent investors (the nearest thing we had to investment trusts over the last quarter century) was only 7.81 per cent.

Second, the combined influence of changing commodity prices and changing interest rates may have been responsible for as much as 25 per cent of the upward trend of industrial stock prices during this period. If this influence continues as favorable in the future as it has in the past, the common stockholder may expect to fare as well at its hands over the next twenty years as he has over the last twenty; if this influence should continue on a fairly even keel such as we have observed during the last four or five years, whatever advantage the common stockholder gained from this influence in the past would be eliminated in the future; if, however, the combined influence of changing commodity prices and changing interest rates should be reversed over the next few years, this might operate to the distinct disadvantage of the holder of common stocks. Ever since the World War these two factors have presented a threat to the level of common stock prices, a threat which was only partially removed during the deflation of 1920–21.

Third, as for the most important change that has taken place in the fundamental factors responsible for the favorable experience from common stocks in the past—a reduction in the earnings basis from 12 per cent to 5 per cent—the prosecution suggests two alternatives:

1. Confidence in the long-term results to be accomplished from common stocks, at current prices, may eventually be shaken and some of the risks involved made more apparent, resulting in a drop in stock prices to a substantially lower level—perhaps an earnings basis some-

where near the old ratio of 12 per cent may again come into vogue. If this should eventuate, the purchaser of common stocks at current levels stands to lose anywhere up to 50 per cent of his purchase price.

2. The less probable alternative is that the seasoned common stock may have become permanently entrenched in an accepted investment position (a place heretofore held by the bond alone), where the factor of future growth will always be discounted in an inflated market price. If this should eventuate, and the average annual return on a diversified group of common stocks continues to be only slightly in excess of the earnings basis upon which they are purchased, the investor buying on a 5 per cent earnings basis today should expect an average return of less than half that realized during the last quarter century when the earnings basis was around 12 per cent.

In concluding this case for the prosecution, I would suggest one general question for consideration: If the prospective annual return to an investor in a diversified group of common stocks under the most favorable conditions possible for the next twenty years is not substantially more than the earnings basis upon which purchases are made, how much of a differential are you going to demand between the earnings basis on which you will buy common stocks today and the yield currently available from high-grade bonds? At the present time this differential is less than 1 per cent. Is it enough in this year of unusual prosperity and recognized inflation to compensate for the added risk involved in common stocks at the current price level?

No Crash, but a Bull Market

Arnold Bernhard

In the "lessons for the future" article excerpted here, Arnold Bernhard, the builder of Value Line, forecast a great bull market—a 100
percent rise in the Dow from 850 in 1979 to between 1500 and 2000
three to five years later—based on his historical analysis of dividends and book value as supports for market price.

In this year 1979, the 50th anniversary of the Great Crash of 1929, it
may be appropriate to remark on what seem to be essential differences
between the two periods.

Nineteen hundred twenty-nine was a year when euphoric America
looked forward to a New Era in which poverty would be abolished once
and for all; 1979 is a year when we soberly hope for a lesser increase of
prosperity.

Nineteen hundred twenty-nine ushered in the years of pump-primed
consumption; 1979 is beginning to recognize the need for saving and
capital investing.

Nineteen hundred twenty-nine faced the problem of burdensome surplus; 1979, the problem of scarcity.

In 1929, the business of America, it was proudly asserted, was business; in 1979, the business of America, if it is profitable, is regarded as
an obscenity.

In 1929 our money was tied to an unyielding gold standard; in 1979
it is tied to nothing but the will of the political establishment, which in

Excerpted from *The Journal of Portfolio Management* 6 (Fall 1979), pp. 77–81. New York: Institutional Investor, Inc.

turn is controlled by a thousand pressure groups, each demanding something for nothing, or at least something below cost from housing to food to energy.

In 1929, the Dow Jones Industrial Average was priced at over 20 times earnings; in 1979, at 7 times.

Nineteen hundred twenty-nine, for all its bright hopes was followed by three years of devastating deflation, during which time the Dow stocks lost 90% of their market value; 1979, despite its black forebodings, will be followed, I think, by a 100% rise in the Dow to between 1500 and 2000 in the next three–five years.

This forecast of the Dow in the next three–five years is not an attempt to pinpoint the price in a particular year. Its possible usefulness is in helping to formulate investment strategy. It says in effect that stock prices will probably double some time between now and 1983. Against that prospect, the possibility of moderately lower prices in the more immediate future appears to be a risk worth taking.

Assumptions

Like any forecast over a five-year period, this one rests on certain assumptions. They are as follows:

1. Our country will not become embroiled in a major war.
2. A business recession, if one develops, will last no longer than 12 months.
3. Inflation will persist, but at no higher rate than is reflected in the current 9.25% Aaa bond yield; or, alternatively, inflation may decelerate, lowering the bond yield to 6% by 1983.
4. The American people and their followers, the politicians, will turn away from further socialization toward greater reliance upon the free market.

Although no statistical proof of the validity of these assumptions is attempted, it would probably be in order to explain briefly why they seem more realistic than alternative possibilities.

In this nuclear age, a major war would create a no-win situation for everybody. It could erupt through a series of blunders. If it did, this forecast, like everything else, would be meaningless.

The assumption that any business recession will be short-lived appears more probable than a long depression, because more is known about money and fiscal policy today than in the 1930's, and the political responsibility to prevent depression is a universally accepted imperative.

The expectation that inflation will persist simply recognizes that the market mechanism cannot cope with the unregulated monopoly power of labor unions. They control the major cost of production, and, like any other unregulated monopoly, will press for higher prices regardless of productivity. There will be little political inclination to combat such inflation both because inflation raises the revenues available to politicians for spending and because the unions have great political clout. Hence, for political reasons, money supply will be increased to accommodate the persisting rise in costs forced by wage increases that exceed productivity gains.

Still, a countervailing pressure may well build up to control inflation even if it is not likely to end it. The ordinary citizen is beginning to understand that wage increases beyond increases in productivity only take away from him at the supermarket what he has gained in his paycheck. He sees that inflation so generated promotes him into tax brackets that were originally designed for the rich only. That will make him reactionary enough to demand at least a measure of restraint.

Finally, it is assumed that the electorate will veer away from further socialization and toward greater reliance upon the free market. It has already happened in France, Italy, Britain, and Canada—and perhaps even in China. Bureaucracy and regulation are losing out in public esteem everywhere. They do not produce the goods, and the politicians are getting the message.

—

Is This Good News?

I must admit that I made this same 1500–2000 forecast on December 5, 1974, at the University of California, Los Angeles, Business Forecast Conference. (The Dow price then was below 600.) I expected the 1500–2000 price target to be reached by the end of 1979, but that is obviously out of the question now. My error lay in underestimating the depressing effect inflation would have on the profit margins of corporations, on their payout ratios, and on the multiple the market would place on their dividends.

In this forecast I have tried to address myself more carefully to those factors. I see the profitability of corporations (as related to book value) recovering almost to the historical norm of 5 percentage points over the bond yield, of the payout ratio holding at 45% if the bond yield stays as high as 9.2%, but rising to 55% if the bond yield falls to 6% and, since the dividend growth in either scenario would be greater than the bond yield, I look for the dividend multiple to recover to 22.5 times or higher. That works out to be 1500–2000 on the Dow by 1983.

The picture is not as rosy for stockholders as the numbers suggest. The stockholder doubles his money, but the money is likely to be worth only half as much as today after assuming the rates of inflation. Still, the stockholder does better than the bondholder. The latter's 9.25% yield is reduced by income tax to about 6%. With inflation running at, say, 9%, that leaves him with a negative current return, and there is very little risk that it will be any different.

The stockholder also has a negative annual return—even more negative than the bondholder on a current basis—but the stockholder doubles the number of his dollars, whatever they may be worth. The bondholder winds up with only the same number of depreciated dollars. In the end, the stockholder pays a capital gains tax on his retained earnings. But in the meantime, his retained earnings are tax deferred and compounded.

Proof that Properly Anticipated Prices Fluctuate Randomly

Paul A. Samuelson

Long interested in—and active in—investing, Nobel laureate Paul Samuelson makes the definitive case on the randomness of stock price behavior. This excerpt states the issue and gives the conclusion, neatly deleting the actual proof and its use of equations.

The Enigma Posed

"In competitive markets there is a buyer for every seller. If one could be sure that a price will rise, it would have already risen." Arguments like this are used to deduce that competitive prices must display price changes over time, $X_{t+1} - X_t$, that perform a random walk with no predictable bias.

Is this a correct fact about well-organized wheat or other commodity markets? About stock exchange prices for equity shares? About futures markets for wheat or other commodities, as contrasted to the movement of actual "spot prices" for the concrete commodity?

Or is it merely an interesting (refutable) hypothesis about actual markets that can somehow be put to empirical testing?

Or is it a valid deduction (like the Pythagorean Theorem applicable to Euclidean triangles) whose truth is as immutable as $2 + 2 = 4$? Does its truth follow from the very definition of "free, competitive markets"? (If so, can there fail to exist in New York and London actual

Reprinted from *Industrial Management Review* 6 (Spring 1965), pp. 41–49. Cambridge, Massachusetts: Industrial Management Review Association.

stock and commodity markets with those properties; and must any failures of the "truism" that turn up be attributable to "manipulation,"
"thinness of markets," or other market imperfections?)

The more one thinks about the problem, the more one wonders what
it is that could be established by such abstract argumentation. Is the fact
that American stocks have shown an average annual rise of more than 5
percent over many decades compatible with the alleged "fair game" (or
martingale property) of an unbiased random walk? Is it an exception
that spot wheat prices generally rise (presumably because of storage
costs) from the July harvest time to the following spring and drop during June? Is the fact that the price of next July's future shows much less
strong seasonal patterns a confirmation of the alleged truism? If so,
what about the alleged Keynes-Hicks-Houthakker-Cootner pattern of
"normal backwardation," in which next July's wheat future could be
expected to rise in price a little from July harvest to, say, the following
March (as a result of need of holders of the crop to coax out, at a cost,
risk-disliking speculators with whom to make short-hedging transactions); and what about the Cootner pattern in which, once wheat stocks
become low in March, processors wishing to be sure of having a minimum of wheat to process, seek short-selling speculators with whom to
make long-hedging transactions, even at the cost of having the July
quotation dropping a little in price in months like April and May?

Consideration of such prosaic and mundane facts raises doubt that
there is anything much in celestial *a priori* reasoning from the axiom
that what can be perceived about the future must already be "discounted" in current price quotations. Indeed, suppose that all the participants in actual markets are necessarily boobs when it comes to
foreseeing the unforeseeable future. Why should "after-the-fact" price
changes show *any* systematic pattern, such as non-bias? Are the very
mathematical notions of probability of any relevance to actual market
quotations? If so, how could we decide that this is indeed so?

Whatever the answers to these questions, I think we can suspect that
there is no *a priori* necessity for actual Board of Trade grain prices to
act in accordance with specific probability models. Perhaps it is a lucky
accident, a boon from Mother Nature so to speak, that so many actual
price time series do behave like uncorrelated or quasi-random walks.
Thus, Maurice Kendall[1] almost proves too much when he finds negligible serial correlation in spot grain prices. For reasons that I shall discuss, we would not be too surprised to find this property in futures

price changes. But surely spot prices ought to vary with shifts in such supply and demand factors as weather, crop yields, and crop plantings; or population, income, and taste changes. Who says that the weather must itself display no serial correlation? A dry month does tend to be followed by a dryer-than-average month because of persistence of pressure patterns, etc. Perhaps it is true that prices depend on a summation of so many small and somewhat independent sources of variation that the result is like a random walk. But there is no necessity for this. And the fact, if it is one, is not particularly related to perfect competition or market anticipations. For consider a monopolist who sells (or buys) at fixed price. If the demand (or supply) curve he faces is the resultant of numerous independent, additive sources of variation each of which is limited or small, his resulting quality $\{q_t\}$ may well behave like the normal curve of error.

At this point, the reader may feel inclined to doubt that the arguments of my first paragraph have even a germ of interest for the economist. But I hope to show that such a rejection goes too far.

By positing a rather general stochastic model of price change, I shall deduce a fairly sweeping theorem in which next-period's price differences are shown to be uncorrelated with (if not completely independent of) previous period's price differences. This martingale property of zero expected capital gain will then be replaced by the slightly more general case of a constant mean percentage gain per unit time.

You never get something for nothing. From a nonempirical base of axioms you never get empirical results. Deductive analysis cannot determine whether the empirical properties of the stochastic model I posit come at all close to resembling the empirical determinants of today's real-world markets. That question I shall not here investigate. I shall be content if I can, for once, find definite and unambiguous content to the arguments of the opening paragraph—arguments which have long haunted economists' discussions of competitive markets.

=

Conclusion

. . . One should not read too much into the established theorem. It does not prove that actual competitive markets work well. It does not say that speculation is a good thing or that randomness of price changes would be a good thing. It does not prove that anyone who makes money in speculation is *ipso facto* deserving of the gain or even that he has accomplished something good for society or for anyone but himself. All or none of these may be true, but that would require a different investigation.

I have not here discussed where the basic probability distributions are supposed to come from. In whose minds are they *ex ante?* Is there any *ex post* validation of them? Are they supposed to belong to the market as a whole? And what does that mean? Are they supposed to belong to the "representative individual," and who is he? Are they some defensible or necessitous compromise of divergent expectation patterns? Do price quotations somehow produce a Pareto-optimal configuration of *ex ante* subjective probabilities? This paper has not attempted to pronounce on these interesting questions.

Note

1. Kendall, Maurice G., "The Analysis of Economic Time-Series—Part I: Prices," *Journal of the Royal Statistical Society* 96, Part I (1953), pp. 11–25; also pp. 85–99 in Cootner, Paul H. (editor), *The Random Character of Stock Market Prices.* Cambridge: The M.I.T. Press, 1964.

Higgledy Piggledy Growth

I. M. D. Little

Ian M. D. Little was for many years a most successful investment bursar or portfolio manager at Nuffield College, Oxford. He ran a very "high turnover" portfolio based on frequent calls from his brokers in the city and considered himself an amateur speculator. He is also a first-rate economic observer—with an engaging good sense of humor—as is demonstrated in the conclusions presented here of his extensive analysis of hundreds of British companies in a pioneering 1962 study of whether "past growth behaviour is some sort of guide to future growth."

Conclusions

Mainly for Investors

1. In spite of the heavy ploughing back of profits the growth of adjusted pre-tax earnings per share has lagged behind earned incomes, especially in industries most concerned with exports and investment. That the growth of dividends, except in textiles, has been fast is better known. If the figures had been more up to date, the growth of pre-tax earnings would undoubtedly have been much slower still. Unless there is some fundamental change in the economy making for greater profitability of capital, the prospect for equities is worse than past performance suggests. Equity values cannot continue to ride the surf of reduced taxation and dividend relaxation. This is certainly not, how-

Excerpted from *The Bulletin of the Oxford University Institute of Statistics* 24 (November 1962), pp. 387–412. Oxford, England: Basil Blackwell.

ever, to say that present prices (June 1962) are too high in relation to fixed interest investments.

Since even the smallest investor can avoid the risks attaching to a particular share, or small selection of shares, all that is needed to justify a reverse yield gap is the confident expectation that the sum of the dividend yield and its rate of growth should exceed the redemption yield of fixed interest investments. There is certainly nothing in the past to suggest that equity shares are over-valued, in spite of the relatively sluggish performance of earnings, and the very low apparent rate of return on money ploughed back.

2. It is useless to try to predict future earnings from any single past earnings growth ratio, or from dividend cover, or from asset size. None of these factors should influence the price of a share except insofar as a high dividend cover probably on average results in a higher than average future dividend performance. But a share's price is only loosely tied to its earnings. Mr. Scott has found a correlation between past earnings and the future share price (for up to a year after the last results). . . . This is explicable insofar as future dividends and past earnings growth *are* related: but, probably, the main reason is a naive belief that past growth tends to continue.

Mainly for Economists

1. I wrongly expected that I would be able to find some correlation of future and past growth (in relation to the average for the 'industry'), primarily on the view that some continuity of good and bad management would establish such a correlation. If a good management is one that earns a higher rate of profit on equity capital than the average for the 'industry,' and which maintains this rate on new money for a period of, say, 5–8 years or more, then good and bad management is extremely rare. Statistically speaking, Marks and Spencer does not exist. Evidently, much too high a standard was being expected. Not only may luck play so big a part that steady success or failure is more improbable, but also the forces of competition may operate to prevent above average returns being maintained.

2. It was noted that the variance of the growth distributions had greatly increased since 1955. This can be equated with an increase in uncertainty, which may be associated with a growth in the freedom and competitiveness of markets.

3. The tentative conclusion of the lack of significant correlation between ploughback and growth is disturbing. It shows that among those firms which plough back relatively heavily, about as many decline in relation to the average as grow. It is, of course, possible that the new investments of those which decline are just as profitable as those of the rest, the whole of their relative failure being accounted for by the declining profitability of old assets. Even so, if the heavy 'ploughers-back' contained only their fair share of declining profitability of old assets, one would still expect the group as a whole to grow faster than the average. The lack of correlation could be accounted for by the hypothesis that firms with declining profitability tend to plough back more as a kind of insurance (possibly buying mainly financial assets). But this we know to be in general false, since it is a fact that rapid growth induces a relatively high ploughback. One seems to be left with the conclusion that those which retain a relatively high proportion of profits select relatively unprofitable investments. . . .

Growth Stocks and the Petersburg Paradox

David Durand

The allure of growth stocks is partly in the excitement that is naturally stimulated by highly successful, ever booming businesses—and partly in the potential for very large profits to investors. Ah, but what price should you pay? David Durand linked this fundamental question to the Petersburg Paradox, a problem in valuation presented by Daniel Bernoulli (see p. 338) to the Imperial Academy of Sciences in 1738.

At a time like the present, when investors are avidly seeking opportunities for appreciation, it is appropriate to consider the difficulties of appraising growth stocks. There is little doubt that when other things are equal the forward-looking investor will prefer stocks with growth potential to those without. But other things rarely are equal—particularly in a sophisticated market that is extremely sensitive to growth. When the growth potential of a stock becomes widely recognized, its price is expected to react favorably and to advance far ahead of stocks lacking growth appeal, so that its price-earnings ratio and dividend yield fall out of line according to conventional standards. Then the choice between growth and lack of growth is no longer obvious, and the astute investor must ask whether the market price correctly discounts

Reprinted from *The Journal of Finance* 12 (September 1957), pp. 348–63. New York: The American Finance Association.

the growth potential. Is it possible that the market may, at times, pay too much for growth?

Most problems encountered in appraising growth stocks seem to fall into two categories. First there are the practical difficulties of forecasting sales, earnings, and dividends. Then come the theoretical difficulties of reducing these forecasts to present values. For a long time it seems to have been assumed, altogether too casually, that the present value of a forecasted dividend stream could be represented simply as the sum of all expected future payments discounted at a uniform rate. Doubts, however, are beginning to manifest themselves. As early as 1938, J. B. Williams suggested non-uniform discount rates, varying from payment to payment.[1] More recently, Clendenin and Van Cleave have shown that discounting forecasted dividends at a uniform rate in perpetuity may lead to absurdities or paradoxes, since implied present values of infinity sometimes result. "We have not yet seen any growth stocks marketed at the price of infinity dollars per share," they remark, "but we shall hereafter be watching. Of course, many investors are skeptical and would probably wish to discount the large and remote dividends in this perpetually growing series at a high discount rate, thus reducing our computed value per share to a figure somewhat below the intriguing value of infinity."[2] Clendenin and Van Cleave might have made a good point even better had they noticed a remarkable analogy between the appraisal of growth stocks and the famous Petersburg Paradox, which commanded the attention of most of the important writers on probability during the eighteenth and nineteenth centuries.

The Petersburg Paradox

In 1738 Daniel Bernoulli presented before the Imperial Academy of Sciences in Petersburg a classic paper on probability, in which he discussed the following problem, attributed to his cousin Nicholas: "Peter tosses a coin and continues to do so until it should land 'heads' when it comes to the ground. He agrees to give Paul one ducat if he gets 'heads' on the very first throw, two ducats if he gets it on the second, four if on the third, eight if on the fourth, and so on, so that with each additional throw the number of ducats he must pay is doubled. Suppose we seek to determine the value of Paul's expectation."[3]

FIGURE 1

Sequence of Tosses	Probability	Payment
H.........................	1/2	1
TH........................	1/4	2
TTH.......................	1/8	4
TTTH......................	1/16	8
TTTTH.....................	1/32	16

One may easily obtain a solution according to the principles of mathematical expectation by noting the sequence of payments and probabilities in Figure 1: Paul's expectation is the sum of the products of probability by payment or

$$1/2 + 2/4 + 4/8 + 8/16 + 16/32 + \ldots.$$

If the players agree to terminate the game after n tosses, whether a head shows or not, the series will contain n terms and its sum will be $n/2$; but if they agree to continue without fail until a head shows, as the rules of the game stipulate, then n is infinite and the sum $n/2$ is infinite as well. Thus the principles of mathematical expectation imply that Paul should pay an infinite price to enter this game, but this is a conclusion that virtually no one will accept. A variety of explanations have been given to show that the value of the game to Paul is, in fact, only a finite amount—usually a small finite amount; and all of the explanations are relevant to growth stock appraisal. . . .

Attempts to Resolve the Petersburg Paradox[4]

The many attempts to resolve the paradox, summarized very briefly below, fall mostly into two broad groups: those denying the basic assumptions of the game as unrealistic, and those arguing from additional assumptions that the value of the game to Paul is less than its mathematical expectation.

The basic assumptions of the game are open to all sorts of objections from the practically minded. How, in real life, can the game continue indefinitely? For example, Peter and Paul are mortal; so, after a misspent youth, a dissipated middle age, and a dissolute dotage, one of them will die, and the game will cease—heads or no heads. Or again,

Peter's solvency is open to question, for the stakes advance at an alarming rate. With an initial payment of one dollar, Peter's liability after only 35 tails exceeds the gold reserve in Fort Knox, and after only three more, it exceeds the volume of bank deposits in the United States and approximately equals the national debt. With this progression, the sky is, quite literally, the limit. Even if Peter and Paul agree to cease after 100 tosses, the stakes, though finite, stagger the imagination.

Despite these serious practical objections, a number of writers chose to accept the assumption of an indefinitely prolonged game at face value, and to direct their attention toward ascertaining the value of such a game to Paul. First among these was the Swiss mathematician Gabriel Cramer, who early in the eighteenth century proposed two arbitrary devices for resolving the Petersburg Paradox by assuming that the utility of money is less than proportional to the amount held. First, if the utility of money is proportional to the amount up to $2^{24} = 166,777,216$ ducats and constant for amounts exceeding 2^{24}, so that the utility of the payments ceases to increase after the 24th toss, Paul's so-called moral expectation is about 13 ducats. Second, if the utility of money is assumed equal to the square root of the amount held, Paul's moral expectation is only about 2.9 ducats. Cramer believed that 2.9 was a more reasonable entrance fee than 13.

A little later and apparently independently, Daniel Bernoulli devised a solution only slightly different from Cramer's. Assuming that the marginal utility of money is inversely proportional to the amount held, he derived a formula that evaluates Paul's expectation in terms of his resources at the beginning of the game. From this formula, which does not lend itself to lightning computation, Bernoulli estimated roughly that the expectation is worth about 3 ducats to Paul when his resources are 10 ducats, about 4 ducats when his resources are 100, and about 6 when his resources are 1000. At this rate, Paul must have infinite resources before he can value his expectation at infinity; but then, even his infinite valuation will constitute only an infinitesimally small fraction of his resources.

An interesting variant of Bernoulli's approach was proposed about a century later by W. A. Whitworth[5]—at least, some of us would consider it a variant though its author considered it an entirely different argument. Whitworth was, in fact, seeking a solution to the Petersburg problem that would be free of arbitrary assumptions concerning the utility of money; and he derived a solution by considering the risk of

gamblers' ruin, which is always present when players have limited resources. Thus, for example, if A with one dollar matches pennies indefinitely against B with $10, it is virtually certain that one of them will
eventually be cleaned out; furthermore, A has 10 chances out of 11 of
being the victim. Accordingly, a prudent A might demand some concession in the odds as the price of playing against B. But how much concession? Whitworth attacked this and other problems by assuming a
prudent gambler will risk a constant proportion of his resources, rather
than a constant amount, on each venture; and he devised a system for
evaluating ventures that entail risk of ruin. Applied to the Petersburg
game, this system indicates that Paul's entrance fee should depend
upon his resources. Thus Whitworth's solution is reminiscent of Bernoulli's—particularly when one realizes that Whitworth's basic assumption implies an equivalence between a dime bet for A with $1 and
a dollar bet for B with $10. Bernoulli, of course, would have argued
that the utility of a dime to A was equal to the utility of a dollar to B.
Finally, the notion of a prudent gambler seeking to avoid ruin has
strong utilitarian undertones, for it implies that the marginal utility of
money is high when resources are running out.

But Whitworth's approach—regardless of its utilitarian subtleties—is
interesting because it emphasizes the need for diversification. The evaluation of a hazardous venture—be it dice game, business promotion, or
risky security—depends not only on the inherent odds, but also on the
proportion of the risk-taker's resources that must be committed. And
just as the prudent gambler may demand odds stacked in his favor as
the price for betting more than an infinitesimal proportion of his resources, so may the prudent portfolio manager demand a greater than
normal rate of return (after allowing for the inherent probability of default) as the price of investing more than an infinitesimal proportion of
his assets in a risky issue. . . .

Although the preceding historical account of the Petersburg Paradox
has been of the sketchiest, it should serve to illustrate an important
point. The various proposed solutions, of which there are many, all involve changing the problem in one way or another. Thus some proposals
evaluate the cash value of a finite game, even when the problem specifies an infinite game; others evaluate the utility receipts, instead of the
cash receipts, of an infinite game; and still others forsake evaluation for
gamesmanship and consider what Paul as a prudent man should pay to
enter. But although none of these proposals satisfy the theoretical re-

quirements of the problem, they all help to explain why a real live Paul might be loath to pay highly for his infinite mathematical expectation. As Keynes aptly summed it up, "We are unwilling to be Paul, partly because we do not believe Peter will pay us if we have good fortune in the tossing, partly because we do not know what we should do with so much money . . . if we won it, partly because we do not believe we should ever win it, and partly because we do not think it would be a rational act to risk an infinite sum or even a very large sum for an infinitely larger one, whose attainment is infinitely unlikely."

Implications of Petersburg Solutions for Growth-Stock Appraisal

If instead of tossing coins, Peter organizes a corporation in a growth industry and offers Paul stock, the latter might be deterred from paying the full discounted value by any of the considerations that would deter him from paying the full mathematical expectation to enter the Petersburg game. And again, these considerations fall into two categories: first, those denying the basic assumptions concerning the rate of indefinitely prolonged growth; and, second, those arguing that the value of the stock to Paul is less than its theoretical discounted value.

Underlying J. B. Williams' . . . [way of looking at the problem is] the assumption that Peter, Inc., will pay dividends at an increasing rate g for the rest of time. . . . A slightly different assumption . . . is that Peter will pay steadily increasing dividends until the game terminates with the toss of a head, and that the probability of a head will remain forever constant at $i/(1 + i)$. Under neither assumption is there any provision for the rate of growth ever to cease or even decline. But astronomers now predict the end of the world within a finite number of years—somewhere in the order of 10,000,000,000—and realistic security analysts may question Peter, Inc.'s ability to maintain a steadily increasing dividend rate for anywhere near that long. Williams, in fact, regarded indefinitely increasing dividends as strictly hypothetical, and he worked up formulas for evaluating growth stocks on the assumption that dividends will follow a growth curve (called a logistic by Williams) that increases exponentially for a time and then levels off to an asymptote. This device guarantees that the present value of any dividend stream will be finite, no matter how high the current, and temporary, rate of growth. Clendenin and Van Cleave, though not insisting on a definite ceiling, argued that continued rapid growth is possible only under long-run price inflation.

The assumption of indefinitely increasing dividends is most obviously objectionable when the growth rate equals or exceeds the discount rate ($g \geq i$) and the growth series . . . sums to infinity. . . . If Peter, Inc. is to pay a dividend that increases at a constant rate $g \geq i$ per year, it is absolutely necessary, though not sufficient, that he earn a rate on capital, $r = E/B$, that is greater than the rate of discount—more exactly, $r \geq i/(1 - p)$. But this situation poses an anomaly, at least for the equilibrium theorist, who argues that the marginal rate of return on capital must equal the rate of interest in the long run. How, then, can Peter, Inc. continually pour increasing quantities of capital into his business and continue to earn on these accretions a rate higher than the standard rate of discount? This argument points toward the conclusion that growth stocks characterize business situations in which limited, meaning finite though not necessarily small, amounts of capital can be invested at rates higher than the equilibrium rate. If this is so, then the primary problem of the growth-stock appraiser is to estimate how long the departure from equilibrium will continue, perhaps by some device like Williams' growth curve.

If, for the sake of argument, Paul wishes to assume that dividend growth will continue indefinitely at a constant rate, he can still find reasons for evaluating Peter's stock at somewhat less than its theoretical value just as he found reasons for evaluating his chances in the Petersburg game at less than the mathematical expectation. The decreasing-marginal-utility approach of Cramer and Bernoulli implies that the present utility value of a growing dividend stream is less than the discounted monetary value, because the monetary value of the large dividends expected in the remote future must be substantially scaled down in making a utility appraisal. Or again, Whitworth's diversification approach implies that a prudent Paul with finite resources can invest only a fraction of his portfolio in Peter's stock; otherwise he risks ruinous loss. And either argument is sufficient to deter Paul from offering an infinite price, unless, of course, his resources should be infinite.

The moral of all this is that conventional discount formulas do not provide completely reliable evaluations. Presumably they provide very satisfactory approximations for high-grade, short-term bonds and notes.

But as quality deteriorates or duration lengthens, the approximations become rougher and rougher. With growth stocks, the uncritical use of conventional discount formulas is particularly likely to be hazardous; for, as we have seen, growth stocks represent the ultimate in investments of long duration. Likewise, they seem to represent the ultimate in difficulty of evaluation. The very fact that the Petersburg problem has not yielded a unique and generally acceptable solution to more than 200 years of attack by some of the world's great intellects suggests, indeed, that the growth-stock problem offers no great hope of a satisfactory solution.

Notes

1. John B. Williams, *The Theory of Investment Value* (Cambridge, Mass.: Harvard University Press, 1938), pp. 50–60.
2. John C. Clendenin and Maurice Van Cleave, "Growth and Common Stock Values," *Journal of Finance* 9 (1954), 365–76. Quotation appears on p. 369.
3. Daniel Bernoulli, "Exposition of a New Theory on the Measurement of Risk," *Econometrica* 22 (1954), 23–36, which is a translation by Dr. Louise Sommer of Bernoulli's paper "Specimen Theoriae Novae de Mensura Sortis," *Commentarii Academiae Scientiarium Imperialis Petropolitanae* 5 (1738), 175–92.
4. For a general history of the paradox, see Isaac Todhunter, *A History of the Mathematical Theory of Probability from the Time of Pascal to that of Laplace* (reprint, New York: G. E. Stechert & Co., 1931), pp. 134, 220–222, 259–262, 275, 280, 286–289, 332, 345, 393, 470. For a briefer treatment, see John Maynard Keynes *A Treatise on Probability* (London: Macmillan and Co., 1921), pp. 316ff.
5. W. A. Whitworth, *Choice and Chance* (Cambridge, England: Deighton, Bell & Co., 4th edition, enlarged, 1886), chap. 9.

Picking Growth Stocks for the 1950s

T. Rowe Price

After the Second World War, T. Rowe Price wrote once again in *Barron's* about growth stock investing—an extension, with contemporary modifications, of his prewar articles in the same weekly. (See *Classics*, Volume I.) While his citations of specific companies have been deleted here, removing some of the vitality and charm of the original exposition, this excerpted version serves to concentrate the reader's attention on the underlying principles that he so clearly identified.

February 6, 1950

In the past, a Growth stock was defined as a "share in a business enterprise which has demonstrated long-term growth in earnings and which, after careful research study, gives indications of continuing such growth in the future, reaching new high earnings per share at the peak of each subsequent major business cycle."

No mathematical formula or yardstick alone can be relied upon for identifying Growth stocks. The requirements for an active up-to-date list are a matter of judgment and should be reviewed and revised periodically as factual information and a new appraisal of political and eco-

Reprinted from *Barron's*, February 6, 1950, pp. 13–14, and February 20, 1950, p. 19. © Dow Jones & Company, Inc. All rights reserved worldwide

nomic trends dictate. We can list eight fundamental factors to consider in forming one's judgments:

1. *Management* must be aggressive, efficient, understand social trends and have the good will of its employees. Directors and officers should have a substantial stock ownership in their companies, the value of which and the income from which are not overshadowed by excessive salaries and pensions.

2. *Intelligent research* which develops new products, new markets for existing products, or both, is essential if a company is to forge ahead in a rapidly changing world. It is easier for a company to realize high profits on new products than on old ones which have attracted competition.

3. *Competition* of a cut-throat nature should be guarded against, as it impedes growth.

4. *Finances* must be strong enough to permit companies to weather periods of adverse earnings.

5. *Return on invested capital* must be reasonable—8% or above—and not experiencing a long-term decline of dangerous magnitude. Investors should seek a company that can lower the cost of production and develop an expanding market without materially reducing the return on capital invested in the business.

6. *Profit margins before taxes* must be reasonable, the percentage varying with the industry. A profit margin of 6% is satisfactory for a company which retails consumers' goods such as food, clothing, and low-priced sundries, having a rapid turnover. On the other hand, a 10%–15% profit margin is necessary for the company which sells high-priced products and has a low turnover.

7. *Socialist influences* restrict earnings. Companies whose actions are circumscribed by government regulations of rates, wages, and profits should be avoided. The majority of companies furnishing the necessities of life, such as public transportation, communications, heat and light, and retailing bread, milk, meat, and many other food products fall in this category. When living costs rise and the consumer's pocketbook is pinched, the public is opposed to such corporations earning large profits, and works through governmental bodies to subordinate the profit motive to the public welfare.

8. *Employees* should be well paid, but the total payroll should be relatively low and easily adjusted to changes in business volume.

These are some of the most important factors which should be checked when picking Growth stocks, but it must be remembered that few companies meet all the requirements listed above. Capable management is the most important. If such management takes over the operation of a company which is in an industry with unlimited opportunities for expansion but which has had poorly organized research, weak finances, and low profit margins, it is only a matter of time until these conditions are corrected. . . .

The fundamental factors to consider in picking "Growth" stocks for the 1950's are very similar to those of the past, but some change in emphasis is necessary. World War II has established the United States as the dominant power in international affairs. A continuation of heavy expenditures for armament will be necessary to maintain that position. Large investment of both public and private capital seems probable in foreign countries for economic development. Socialization of basic industries and the development of a welfare state are being accelerated in this country as well as abroad. These changes have had an inflationary influence on our economy, resulting in permanently higher taxes and lower purchasing power of the dollar.

The greater emphasis placed on research during and after the war has advanced our scientific knowledge at such a rapid rate that changes in the fortunes of whole industries as well as individual companies will take place more rapidly than ever before. Atomic energy will undoubtedly have an effect on some basic industries before the end of the next decade. Consequently, many of the Growth stocks selected today will undoubtedly be replaced as new opportunities are afforded the investor.

February 20, 1950

Due to the inflation that has already taken place in our economy, and the probability of further inflation during the next 10 years, a definition of a Growth stock should be revised to read as follows: "A share in a business enterprise which has demonstrated long-term growth of earnings, reaching a new high level per share at the peak of each subsequent major business cycle and which, after careful research, gives indications of continuing growth at a rate faster than the rise in the cost of living.'' Thus, if the cost of living has increased 30% at the peak of the next business cycle, a company's earnings must have increased more than 30%. . . .

The [enterprises] which appear to offer the greatest promise are:

1. *Companies which manufacture labor-saving devices.* This is a broad classification which, in addition to machines which reduce labor costs in factories and offices, includes automatic vending machines for the distribution of low-priced consumers goods such as candy, tobacco products, and soft drinks. It seems reasonable to expect that more and more items of food and clothing will be sold through automatic merchandising machines which will eliminate the high cost of distribution involved in sales personnel.

2. *Companies which prepare materials used in packaging the many items of merchandise dispensed by the automatic machines, as well as the pre-packaged items sold in stores.*

3. *Businesses with new products or processes with promising commercial possibilities.*

4. *Companies which will benefit from the development of atomic energy.*

5. *Companies which,* through engineering and technical know-how, or through direct investment, *will benefit from the development of backward nations.*

6. *New businesses which will develop with the growth of the Air Age.*

7. *Established businesses rejuvenated by the installation of new management.* . . .

It should be remembered that we have not had a serious business depression for twelve years and that the managements of many of the candidates for this list have not been subjected to a testing period of unfavorable business conditions.

When picking a list of Growth stocks for long-term investment, broad diversification of the risk is the first and most important principle to follow. No one can look ahead five or ten years and say what is the most promising industry or the best stock to own. A common stock portfolio should contain at least 20 issues, preferably 25 to 40.

Investing for Growth

Robert R. Barker

Bob Barker has been a marvelously successful long-term investor in growth stocks and a splendidly articulate advocate of the concepts and strict disciplines with which he has invested for more than 40 years. His objective is stated in simple and undiluted terms: maximum long-term capital appreciation. The record has been outstanding. As a footnote, Barker—as chairman of the Ford Foundation Advisory Committee—wrote the report on investing that appears on pages 366–69 in *Classics*, Volume I.

There are many different ways to invest successfully and I do not claim that mine is the best. Furthermore, I realize that what we do is not suited to the temperament of most people. What I do know is that our way is the best for us and also the most fun. Thus, much of what I have to say may be more personal than profound.

Many different strategies can be followed to achieve long-term success in this business. I understand that Warren Buffett, who ran an investment partnership during the nineteen fifties and sixties, compounded his capital by about 25% per annum during that period. This was the same rate over the same period as the firm with which I was associated. So far as I know, neither of us ever owned a stock the other did during those two decades. The two strategies were completely different from each other.

The one absolute truth I have learned about investing—and it is the only one—is that long-range success comes not from any simple rule or

Excerpted from a speech to the Senior Men's Club of New Canaan on September 7, 1979, by permission of the author.

rules that can be followed by everyone but only from the most rigorous pursuit of disciplines designed to neutralize the emotional pressures that inevitably descend from time to time upon anyone who is responsible for investing other people's money.

Those disciplines must be self-evolved because we all have different strengths and weaknesses. The things they have in common are: (1) defining precisely what we are trying to do; (2) clearly understanding the reasons for the strategy; (3) recognizing in advance what problems will sooner or later accompany the strategy—for there will always be such problems; and (4) developing the strength to "stay the course" even during troubled times. Successful investing requires constant inquisitiveness about the new and everlasting, open-minded re-examination of the old. The latter process is more difficult than the former. Not many of us are willing and able to accept the tough disciplines that are involved and not many achieve long-term investment success.

. . . What do I mean by investing for growth? In my firm, we concentrate on finding those few companies that have a clear prospect of very rapid increases in earnings per share over a protracted period ahead. Those are the companies in which our portfolio is entirely invested. We pay no attention to all the other companies there are. Think of the time we save by this concentration! We come to know the companies we care about very well indeed. Furthermore, we also spend almost no time worrying about what the stock market is going to do— an activity that absorbs an astonishingly large amount of the time of most investment managers. . . .

Our objective is simple and undiluted—maximum long-term capital appreciation. We are normally fully invested in common stocks that pay no dividends so we have almost no income. In contrast, our travel and telephone expenses are very heavy and we pay our few people very well when they perform well, which they usually do. Thus, we regularly produce very large operating losses on top of which the partners need to make withdrawals for taxes and living expenses.

The stocks we own are all of companies that are growing very rapidly. Our screen is 40% per annum in earnings per share over the next three to five years. Between one quarter and one third of them are growing at around 100% per annum. Finding and following these companies is the heart of our discipline.

Twenty percent to 25% of the portfolio is in very young companies that have not yet reached the public market. Some call this venture-capital investing, but I dislike that term because the criteria we use are no different from those we apply to publicly traded companies. In fact, every company we buy into we look at as though we were buying the whole company, since we hope to keep the holdings for many years.

What are these criteria? First, the company must have the clear opportunity for very large and very rapid growth in its business. Usually it will be the dominant force in its field, even if it is small and is competing with great companies like IBM, Hewlett-Packard, Texas Instruments, and AT&T. Second, the company must earn a very high rate of return on its invested capital. The best companies will consistently earn 30% to 50% each year on the money they are using—after taxes. Third—and most important—there must be a truly remarkable person or group of people in charge. One hundred percent per annum growth—and even 40% per annum—is *not* an accident. It is the product of soaring imagination, everlasting effort and the constant training and motivating of people. The key qualities are integrity, dedication and intelligence—and in that order. There is only one way to judge those qualities and that is for an experienced portfolio manager to come to know the people first-hand himself and watch them in action over a period of years. . . .

To judge the growth potential, there is no substitute for hard, continuous self-education by the portfolio manager in the industries and technologies where the opportunities are found. This cannot be done well through the eyes of anyone else—even an experienced technology specialist—for the crucial business question is always how the new technology will affect the way people lead their lives. Here the generalist always has the advantage over the specialist.

Studying the past is helpful in selecting growth companies but it can also be dangerously misleading. What really matters is the future. We have to know our industries well enough to know there is potential for very rapid growth. We also have to know the technology well enough to understand whether costs and competitive pressures afford the opportunity for the exceptional profitability that is essential. Finally—and most difficult and important—we must know the management and particularly the man at the top well enough to be sure the integrity, dedication and intelligence . . . are there to realize the potentials.

Perhaps this sounds easy but I can assure you it is not. One comfort for me is that I have come to believe that age provides an advantage in all this. First, it means that we have lived with our industries for a long time and know more about them than most investors. It also means that we have had time to understand some very complex technologies. Even more important, we have come to know the people in the key companies and to understand their strengths and weaknesses. Finally, there has been time to make an enormous number of mistakes of every kind and then to see how they came out. This experience and the ability to look back objectively and learn from it seems to develop an intuitive sense about people and what they say that accelerates our decision-making and increases its soundness in a way that can never be matched by pure logical analysis.

Now, what are the things that are generally emphasized by others that we neglect? First, we pay no attention to dividends, except in very special circumstances. To begin with, we regard any company that pays substantial dividends as unlikely to be attractive. Almost always this means that management cannot find enough attractive investment opportunities to keep and use what it earns. Furthermore, earnings paid out are subject to taxes at both the corporate and the stockholder level. What we look for are companies that have such attractive internal investment opportunities that they are obliged to reinvest all their earnings. In fact, some of the best of them need even more money than they earn and have to sell additional stock now and then. When this happens, however, the return on the new money usually more than offsets the additional shares and eliminates any dilution for existing stockholders. . . .

Sometimes there will be a company like Teledyne that earns a very good return on its existing business but does not have enough continuing rapid-growth opportunities in those fields to use its cash flow. Despite this position, Teledyne never pays a dividend. Instead, it went out and bought other existing companies having greater potentials than its own. Then, when the price of its stock collapsed during the market decline of 1973 and 1974, Teledyne purchased great gobs of its own outstanding shares both in the open market and through tender offers. The number of shares outstanding was reduced from 34 million to under 11 million—before subsequent stock dividends—and earnings per share have risen from just over $1.00 to about $25. More recently, Teledyne has begun to buy stock positions of 20% to 30% in other major companies when they appear to be good long-term investments. Moreover, since the increase in earnings and the decline in the number of shares outstanding have been rapid enough to keep pace with the rise in the price of the stock, the company also continues to buy in its own stock, even though the price has risen from $6 to $150 during the last four and a half years.

A second conventional objective to which we pay little attention is stability—both in terms of the volatility of the business and in terms of the stock market. Most large investment managers feel pressure from the recent ERISA legislation to seek out stocks which are the least likely to go down, even though those stocks may also have very limited upside potential. During inflationary times like these, this seems to us a poor strategy. One of the advantages of being a small firm whose partners understand the strategy we pursue is that we can be less inhibited by the legalities of traditional fiduciary responsibility. Thus, our main attention is focused on the upside potential. We do not neglect volatility, but we know that the lowest-priced growth opportunities are often found in the more volatile industries and we are willing to sacrifice stability for large reward, if the company is sound.

Take the semi-conductor industry as an example. These companies supply parts to other businesses. As with other capital equipment producers, they have greater than average swings in demand over the course of the business cycle. On the other hand, technology is moving so rapidly in this industry that demand is in an almost perpetual long-term boom and costs continue to decline. When we find companies like Mostek, Intel and Advanced Micro Devices that are leading the way in these new developments, we are willing to take major positions in them despite their inherent volatility. Their secular growth is so fast that it softens even the most pronounced cyclical downswings. In addition, the risk-to-reward ratio, which is what we always try to measure, is so much greater on the reward side than on the risk side that the balance seems to us overwhelmingly favorable.

A third widely held objective on which we put little attention is the size of the company. Another advantage of running a small portfolio is that we can build up large enough positions to be significant to us in even the smallest companies. Furthermore, we can accept with equanimity the reduced liquidity that inevitably occurs in less-active over-the-counter stocks during market declines—although I assure you we never enjoy the experience when it comes! Keep in mind, too, that the most rapidly growing companies tend to be the smaller ones. With corporations as with people, rapid growth occurs when they are young. Once a company gains a dominant share of its market, the growth rate is bound to slow down no matter how well run it is. It was failure to recognize this reality on the part of large institutional investors at the end of the nineteen sixties that explains how the great boom in blue-chip growth stocks completely outran itself in 1972. . . .

On the other hand, this rule of size is far from absolute. Two thirds of the companies in our portfolio do less than $100 million worth of business a year and a half of them do less than $30 million. Several of them were doing little or no business when we first invested. However, we also own some large companies like Boeing and Teledyne, Control Data and General Dynamics. We own them because they are growing at 30 percent a year or better during this period of their lives. Their stocks give our portfolio very substantial liquidity in a down market but we buy them only if they "earn their way" in by their performance. We welcome the extra liquidity large companies provide when they meet our standards but we do not seek them out for their own sake.

A fourth generally accepted criterion on which we put much less emphasis than most people is safety. As in the case of the first three criteria, we do not regard safety as an absolute by itself. It has always to be balanced against the potential reward. One of our friends describes our strategy in baseball terms. He said we usually swing for the fences—and I rather like the analogy. The best home-run hitters inevitably also have very high strike-out rates. However, what really matters is the ratio between these two statistics. It seems to us that the search for safety by most portfolio managers—their eagerness to avoid striking out—has led them to settle for rewards that are too small. Consequently, stocks offering a big potential are being largely ignored today. They sell more on the basis of their risks rather than of their much larger rewards. When we come to know these companies well, moreover, we often see that the general perceptions of risk are wrong—even when they are shared by the most reputable people. That is why they sell so far below their true worth measured by any objective risk-to-reward analysis. . . .

What is the rationale for this strategy? Let me try to summarize it for you in three parts. First, the investment community generally has little understanding of the true value of rapid growth and that fact alone keeps growth stocks relatively cheap. . . .

The second part of our rationale lies in understanding what has produced the general unwillingness to accept higher-than-average multiples for growth. That unwillingness stems from the catastrophic price declines that occurred between 1970 and 1974 in all secondary stocks. Looking back on that experience today, most investment managers have concluded that they erred in paying too much for the earnings of younger growth companies—and they want to be certain they never do that again. In contrast, the main lesson of that experience should be that most of us slipped into sloppy analytical disciplines that led us to regard as emerging growth companies hundreds of low-quality, secondary concerns that were never capable of continuing rapid growth and should never have been so classified. It is because of this misunderstanding that the really exciting growth companies of the future are now available at prices that seem to us extraordinarily cheap in relation to their true worth. Furthermore, to the degree that over-exuberance did develop in buying genuine younger growth companies, we now have the reassurance that the experience lies immediately behind us and phenomena of this kind occur no more frequently than once in a generation because the consequences are so searing to those who participated.

The third and last foundation for our approach is the fundamental revolution in using the human brain that is now under way. I call it the computer revolution and I consider it more important in the history of man than the industrial revolution. During the industrial revolution the catapulting growth in our standard of living was caused by using the energy in fossil fuels to leverage the muscles of man and his domestic animals. Notwithstanding all the resulting improvement in productivity, however, very little progress was made in improving human decision-making. Let me give you two sets of figures to show what I mean. . . . At the present time, the average capital investment by American industry for equipment used by blue-collar workers is $24,000 apiece. In contrast, the equipment used by the average white-collar worker costs only $3,000. Gains in productivity have come from leveraging the use of our muscles rather than our brains. . . . Today, over 50 percent of the U.S. work force operates in offices rather than in factories. I quote these figures . . . to show the limits against which our productivity improvement is beginning to press—unless we can find some way to leverage the use of the human mind. This, however, is what the computer revolution has now begun to do. For the first time in history, man is acquiring the ability to multiply the capacity of his brain by using outside capital equipment.

The significance of this revolution is profound. . . . Despite the grievous problems confronting this country in almost every direction, there are also grounds for genuine long-term optimism. The computer revolution is still only beginning to be recognized in the investment community. It provides the cornerstone for our investment strategy.

Let me close with three final thoughts. One is the fact that twenty-five years ago, when we began to develop and follow this growth-stock strategy, there were only fifteen or twenty companies that we could find to follow. Today we track over one hundred really interesting growth companies and there probably are at least as many more that we should follow but do not yet know well enough to be sure. . . .

Second, . . . you might be interested in a simple rule we follow in ferreting out potential new growth stocks. What we are now mostly looking for are substantial, going companies having a major position in some large market that is relatively mature but which also have managements that perceive the opportunity to completely rebuild their product lines by using semi-conductor technology to (1) lower the price of their products, (2) vastly improve the performance of those products, and (3) thus change their demand curves from flat to steeply-rising and their profit margins from routine to glamorous. We have already identified several dozen companies like this and own perhaps eight of them. . . .

Third, and last, I promised to tell you how we can live in peace with a fully invested portfolio when I believe the state of the world is worse than it has been since the nineteen thirties. . . . We have learned to let our own portfolio tell us when to sell or buy. We do not try to anticipate what the market will do because we know that we can't do it and we don't think anyone else can either. When our portfolio has declined 15 percent or 20 percent in value, we will sell 25 percent or 30 percent of it. If it keeps going down still further, we will sell still more until it stops going down. Then, when the portfolio, or what is left of it, turns up, we will start buying back on the same sort of scale upwards.

I know this practice violates all the generally accepted principles of investing because we always sell well after the peak and buy well after the low. However, it has led us to be almost fully invested from early 1976 until the fall of 1978 and then again from January 1979 to the present. To be sure, we were whip-sawed to some degree from last October to this January but the stocks we bought back were better than those we sold, as a general rule, and I am not sure we would have made those changes so fast without this extra discipline. In the end, moreover, whatever the policy cost us, it was not unreasonable as an insurance premium against riding all the way down a major decline in the stock market, fully invested.

. . . Almost everything we do is contrary to the rules accepted by most so-called prudent investment managers. . . . On the other hand, the results have been more than satisfactory to those with whom I have been associated for thirty years and I hope that you may have found some interest in the personal experience of one . . . who has put a large part of his life into this business and enjoys it more all the time.

Are Analysts' Techniques Adequate for Growth Stocks?

Leland E. Dake

The extraordinary difficulties analysts face in trying to determine
what is really going on—and what is likely to be going on in the
future—at a company whose stock is being evaluated are well
illustrated by Leland Dake. He reminds us that there is no substitute for objectivity and persistence in the pursuit of truly insightful
analyses.

———— ▬ ————

The exhilarating phenomena of a "growth" company—rapid growth in
sales, climbing stock price, mergers and diversification—give such a
company a special investment glamour that may obscure basic facts
about the company's operations and create special problems for the Financial Analyst.

Not only are certain facts not readily apparent, but they also tend
to be precisely those fundamental to a decision on the company as an
investment.

It would seem that a great deal of knowledge would be current about
a company that is attracting a great deal of attention—and this is nom-
inally true. However, the very essence of being a "growth" company
tends to make analysis more difficult. In addition, the techniques of
most Financial Analysts seem better fitted to well-established companies

Reprinted from *Readings in Financial Analysis and Investment Management* (Homewood, Illinois:
Dow Jones Irwin, Inc., 1963), pp. 216–22, by permission of the Association for Investment Management and Research.

directed by experienced executives and operating in industries marked by strong competition. The result is that key information about growth companies often will be overlooked in the casual analysis and may even escape the conscientious, dedicated assayer of financial values.

Several months ago I visited a well-known Eastern "growth" company that is very familiar to the financial community. My visit coincided with that of a well-known Analyst from a respected banking house. We visited with the same company executives, witnessed the same things and looked at much of the same data.

My purpose was to orient myself and our organization for a major management survey. The Analyst was reviewing the company's position (its stock was in considerable demand, selling at the time at about 30 times earnings). The two of us were exposed to much the same information because my client reasoned that this was a good way for me to start securing the data needed to develop a survey plan and organize my staff.

We saw the company's plant, its products, its financial records and many of its key people. We listened to the executives answer what I considered to be some particularly intelligent, penetrating questions asked by the Analyst.

We left this company feeling exhilarated. It was exciting to hear great progress detailed and to learn about plans and projects that promised even greater growth. We had seen some marvelous new products and had leafed through some literature which opened up new development vistas for us. Sales were increasing, profits improving; there was an impressive backlog of orders and Uncle Sam had blessed this company with substantial business. In fact, the federal government was the company's biggest customer. We agreed that this truly was a remarkable business organization.

Some months later when a team of my associates was preparing our final report to the management of this company, I happened to meet the Analyst again. He was again reviewing the situation and appeared as enthusiastic as ever. What he had seen and heard the second time gave him no reason to feel otherwise. On the basis solely of the facts at the Analyst's disposal, I would have agreed with him.

But, at our second meeting, I no longer had any illusions about the company's rosy prospects or impregnable position! I now knew the company was now vulnerable in many areas. The differences in our beliefs was the result of the amount of knowledge available to each of us.

The facts available to the Analyst consisted of data and observations given to him by the company's management, his own observations during a plant tour, and a review of management's forecasts. The management was quite sincere and gave him the facts as it saw them—a critical flaw in his analysis.

Management had not concealed its own weaknesses. This omission was not due to dishonesty or subterfuge. Management simply did not and could not reveal weaknesses it wasn't aware of.

By this time, however, I was aware of management weaknesses and the flaws in its plan for the future, because I had the benefits of my survey team's findings.

The differences in viewpoint between my opinion of this company and that of the Analyst can be traced directly to the facts available to us individually and, in turn, to the fact-finding approaches we were able to utilize.

The Analyst, of necessity, had to rely on much information that was subjectively biased and screened through the opinions and judgments of the company's management. On the other hand, my firm was commissioned to audit independently the company's organization, market position and production efficiency; and my staff had given me an objective view of the situation, based on what we had learned for ourselves. While the Analyst was receiving a subjective impression of the company, I had received an objective analysis.

Our analyses were at variance because, in addition to the obvious advantage of having more time to spend on the assignment, and thus an opportunity to explore the company's operations in depth, my associates were analyzing two elements of the company's operations normally out of the reach of the Analyst. They are:

1. Management capabilities of key executives through first-hand observations of their management methods.
2. The company's markets and products as their customers and competitors view them.

Our objective audit reported that this particular company had a well-meaning, aggressive, and enthusiastic management, but one that was also very naive about organizational methods.

We also found that much of the earnings endowed upon this fortunate growth company, by a truly phenomenal growth industry development, were being frittered away. Companies often "plow back" earnings, but this company was simply wasting money in bad organization and inadequate methods. The stockholders, impressed by the prospect of increased future earnings, may never get more than a small fraction of them.

The Growth Stock Mania

William W. Jahnke

When Bill Jahnke questioned the growth stock investing convention in 1972–73, he was in a remarkably small minority. The succeeding dozen years witnessed a profound shift away from growth
stocks into value investing.

Investing in growth stocks has been a rewarding investment strategy in
the recent past and currently enjoys wide popular support as a means of
achieving above average rates of return. However, investments should
never be made on the basis of past record or current popularity. Instead,
the sophisticated investor will evaluate investments in terms of both the
expected rate of return and the attendant risk. Our evaluation of growth
stocks on this basis at current price levels strongly supports the conclusion that a popular list of such issues offers prospects of a below average rate of return.

Common sense and experience tell us that, if we can identify a company whose earnings growth is going to exceed investors' consensus, its
stock is likely to exhibit superior price appreciation. Unfortunately,
consistently identifying growth stocks before the market does is not
easy.

The next best thing to do, at least according to some prestigious investment institutions, is to invest in stocks commonly regarded as
growth stocks. According to the growth stock cult, portfolios should be
invested almost entirely in "core" and "emerging" growth stocks.

Reprinted from the *Financial Analysts Journal* 29 (May/June 1973), pp. 65–68. Charlottesville, Virginia: Association for Investment Management and Research.

Many devotees of growth stocks point to the superior performance records of particular growth stocks to support their investment policy. But does the past record of a list of popular growth stocks mean that they will continue to provide better-than-market returns?

We think not. Common stocks ought to be priced to reflect the consensus of investors' expectations of corporate profits, "discounted" at a rate of return the consensus considers adequate compensation for the risk being borne—the risk being the future possibility that the consensus growth expectations will be revised downward or the consensus discount rate will be revised upward. In more conventional terms, by raising the price earnings ratios for growth stocks, investors are adjusting for higher expected rates of growth in earnings, thereby normalizing expected returns. On the other hand, the expected return for a company whose future earnings growth is very uncertain will be higher, hence the price earnings ratio will be lower, than for a company whose future earnings growth is relatively more certain, given the same growth rate in earnings. The expected return from the riskier stock will be higher, but the expectation will be surrounded by greater uncertainty.

Our analysis of earnings forecasts reveals no systematic upgrading of expected growth rates for popular growth stocks by professional investors and no systematic downgrading for non-growth stocks. If professionals as a group are representative of the larger consensus, then the superior performance of growth stocks must have resulted from changes in the expected rate of return for risk taking. Is this re-evaluation of growth stocks in the marketplace warranted? The question turns on what expected earnings rates and what discount rates are reflected in current price levels of growth stocks relative to non-growth stocks. This study attempts to provide the information necessary to answer the question.

A sample of seasoned quality stocks was drawn from the Wells Fargo Bank Common Stock List (a broadly representative list of securities) using growth classifications provided by a large New York bank. A second sample of non-growth stocks was drawn that excluded any company with a forecasted five-year annual compound earnings growth rate in excess of 13 per cent. The non-growth stocks were chosen to match as closely as possible the risk level of the growth stock sample, using beta as the measure of market relative price volatility. The growth and non-growth samples are reported in Figure 1. The beta of the growth sample is 0.97; the beta of the non-growth sample is 0.98. (A beta of 1.00

FIGURE 1
Company Samples

Growth Stocks	Beta	Non-Growth Stocks	Beta
Lilly Eli Co.	0.68	Northern Ind. Pub. Svc.	0.73
Merck & Co.	0.78	Houston Lighting	0.78
Coca Cola Co.	0.80	Florida Power Corp.	0.80
American Home Products	0.80	General Foods Corp.	0.81
Eastman Kodak	0.83	Morgan, J. P. & Co.	0.86
Warner Lambert	0.84	Commonwealth Edison	0.86
Xerox Corp.	0.84	Mobil Oil Corp.	0.87
Avon Products, Inc.	0.87	Del Monte	0.88
Anheuser-Busch	0.88	Broadway-Hale Stores	0.88
Kresge, S. S.	0.88	Allegheny Power	0.88
Bristol Myers Co.	0.94	Florida Power & Light	0.94
American Hospital Supply	0.95	First National City Bank	0.95
Squibb Corp.	0.97	Shell Oil	0.98
IBM	0.97	Gulf Oil	0.99
Emerson Electric Co.	1.01	Jewel Companies	1.01
Baxter Labs	1.03	Ford Motor	1.02
Pfizer, Inc.	1.03	Goodyear Tire & Rubber	1.04
Sterling Drug, Inc.	1.04	Southern Co.	1.04
Minn. Mining & Mfg.	1.16	Fieldcrest	1.18
Hewlett Packard	1.24	Beneficial Finance	1.23
Polaroid Corp.	1.38	Great Western	1.39
Perkin-Elmer Corp.	1.44	McGraw-Hill	1.44
Average	0.97	Average	0.98

represents the risk of the market.) Hence the expected total return—i.e., the discount rate—ought to be the same for the two samples.

The expected rate of return for each stock was estimated by solving for that discounted rate which equated the present value of our analysts' earnings and payout forecasts with the market price as of February 28, 1973. See the appendix for detail. Figure 2 reports the expected rate of return and the five-year earnings per share growth rate estimates. The average expected annual rate of return, given the forecasts, is 7.7 per cent for growth stocks vs. 10.2 per cent for non-growth stocks. Surprisingly, not one company in the growth stock sample has an expected return above the average for the non-growth stock sample.

To check the reasonableness of the Wells Fargo forecasts a comparison was made with those of [a well-known] New York bank. The average five-year annual compound earnings growth rate forecast for the growth stock sample was 13.3 per cent for Wells Fargo vs. 12.9 per

FIGURE 2
February 28, 1973, Data

Growth Stock Sample

Company	Next 5-Year EPS Growth (%)	Expected Annual Rate of Return (%)
Lilly Eli Co.	13.6	7.7
Merck & Co.	11.6	7.4
Coca Cola Co.	12.0	7.7
Amer. Home Products	10.3	7.2
Eastman Kodak	9.8	6.9
Warner Lambert	10.9	8.0
Xerox Corp.	16.2	8.1
Avon Products, Inc.	16.6	8.0
Anheuser-Busch	13.6	8.5
Kresge, S. S.	15.2	8.1
Bristol Myers Co.	8.2	7.9
Amer. Hosp. Supply	13.7	7.6
Squibb Corp.	10.6	7.6
IBM	12.9	8.0
Emerson Electric Co.	12.4	7.9
Baxter Labs	14.9	7.2
Pfizer, Inc.	9.4	7.9
Sterling Drug, Inc.	10.2	8.2
Minn. Mining & Mfg.	11.3	7.9
Hewlett Packard	14.0	7.2
Polaroid Corp.	32.2	7.2
Perkin-Elmer Corp.	14.9	7.9
Average	13.3	7.7

Non-Growth Stock Sample

Company	Next 5-Year EPS Growth (%)	Expected Annual Rate of Return (%)
Northern Ind. Pub. Svc.	6.6	11.3
Houston Lighting	7.3	9.4
Florida Power Corp.	7.0	10.4
General Foods Corp.	12.4	11.5
Morgan, J. P. & Co.	8.7	9.9
Commonwealth Edison	6.6	11.0
Mobil Oil Corp.	7.2	10.2
Del Monte	8.5	10.8
Broadway-Hale Stores	9.8	8.3
Allegheny Power	3.6	11.1
Florida Power & Light	7.0	10.4
First Natl. City Bank	10.5	9.4
Shell Oil	8.3	9.7
Gulf Oil	10.2	10.6
Jewel Companies	8.7	10.2
Ford Motor	4.2	10.4
Goodyear Tire & Rubber	5.4	10.0
Southern Co.	5.4	10.8
Fieldcrest	9.5	11.7
Beneficial Finance	8.9	10.0
Great Western	4.4	9.1
McGraw-Hill	8.6	10.2
Average	7.7	10.2

cent for the New York bank. If the New York bank's forecasts were used, the expected return from the growth stock sample would be even lower.

For growth stocks to outperform non-growth stocks starting from current price levels, the consensus of investors is required to increase its earnings growth rate projections or decrease the expected rate of return even further. In order for growth stocks to provide the expectations of a 10.2 per cent annual rate of return—that is, the same rate as for non-growth stocks—the forecasted five-year annual compound earnings growth rate for growth stocks would need to be increased to 20 per cent. This rate seems unrealistically high.

In summary, at current price levels growth stocks offer the expectation of a 2½ per cent less return per year than non-growth stocks of similar risk. Indeed, in order to equalize the expected rate of return a price correction for growth stocks relative to non-growth stocks of 50 percentage points would be necessary. A continuation of better-than-market performance by growth stocks requires investors to raise their earnings growth expectations for growth stocks relative to non-growth stocks even further, or to increase the rate spread between what growth and non-growth stocks are expected to return. This is certainly possible, especially in the short run; however, in our opinion, investors in today's growth stocks run a risk beyond the normal one of being disappointed concerning earnings growth expectations. Growth stocks may well be facing a period of below average market performance.

Appendix

The method for determining the discount rate is based on normative capital budgeting theory which is well documented in the literature of finance. The general form of the model used is shown in equation (1). Equation (2), which can be derived from equation (1), is the model used to estimate the expected rate of return, i.e., the discount rate, by setting the present value equal to the current price and solving for r.

$$PV = \sum_{i=1}^{\infty} \frac{D_i}{(1 + r)^i} \tag{1}$$

where:

PV = present value
D_i = expected dividend to be received in the ith year
r = discount rate

$$CP = PV = \sum_{i=1}^{25} \frac{E_i k_i}{(1 + r)^i} + \frac{E_{25} k_{25}(1 + g)}{(r - g)(1 + r)^{25}} \tag{2}$$

where:

CP = current price
PV = present value

E_i = earnings forecast for i^{th} year

k_i = payout ratio for i^{th} year

g = terminal growth rate in earnings

r = discount rate

The forecasted earnings growth rates beyond the fifth year are assumed to decline linearly to 5% at the 25th year and to grow at 5% from that point. The conclusion of this study in our opinion is not easily invalidated by reasonable alternative growth rate assumptions beyond the 5th year. If anything, the assumed sustainability of above average rates of growth beyond the 5th year biases the results in favor of growth stocks.

Investing in Emerging Growth Stocks

Dennis G. Sherva, CFA

Dennis Sherva has managed the research department for Morgan Stanley and is now a partner in that firm's investment management organization, where he concentrates on managing emerging growth stock portfolios.

Introduction

Investing in small, rapidly growing companies can be one of the most rewarding sectors of the stock market for professional money managers as well as individual investors. There are several factors that make emerging growth stocks appealing investments. It is often easier for companies with a small sales base to grow rapidly and earn superior financial returns than it is for large enterprises with a billion or more dollars in revenue. Small or emerging growth companies can focus on specific industry, market, or product niches, allowing the investor an undiluted participation in an attractive business. In addition, with more than 25,000 publicly traded small companies in the United States and frequent new issues being offered, many of the stocks are not widely followed in the investment community and, at times, can be inefficiently priced.

Reprinted from *The Financial Analyst's Handbook* (1988; originally published 1975), Chapter 23, pp. 670–98, by permission of Business One Irwin, Homewood, Illinois.

The attractive characteristics of emerging growth stocks that provide the opportunity to capture superior investment returns are accompanied by business and market risks that are substantially higher than equities in general. It is the management of these risks that determines how much of the potential return in the emerging growth sector will actually be realized. A disciplined approach to stock selection accompanied by an equally rigorous approach to valuation can provide the portfolio manager with the tools that minimize risk while seeking the long-term capital appreciation potential of emerging growth stock investing. Because of the risks inherent in rapidly growing small companies, mistakes cannot be completely avoided and employing appropriate selling disciplines is equally important to having effective buying strategies. Finally, appropriate diversification is necessary in constructing and managing stock portfolios to further control risk.

Criteria for Stock Selection

All companies and industries go through a life cycle with several stages of development. In the idealized evolution of a company, as illustrated in Figure 1, the second, or emerging growth, phase is usually the most

FIGURE 1
Life Cycle of a Company

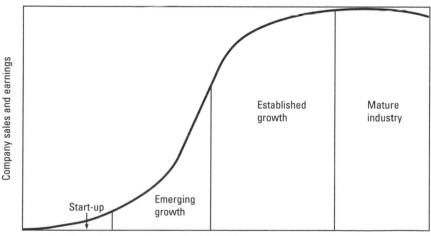

dynamic period in a firm's history and is the time that can yield the greatest returns to investors. The initial stage is the start-up and very early building of a company when products or services are developed, manufacturing and marketing operations put in place, and the business begins to generate revenues. Companies typically lose money until late in the first stage. Venture capital plays an important role in starting and nurturing companies through this early phase. The third, or established growth, phase is associated with companies that continue to grow for many years after they have become large. While the annual growth rate is rarely in excess of 20 percent, companies such as IBM, Merck, Mc-Donald's, and Dun & Bradstreet have maintained a growth pattern for decades and reached billions of dollars in revenues. The fundamental business risks of the established growth companies are typically less than for those enterprises at an earlier and more rapid growth stage. Most companies and industries eventually enter a mature phase characterized by negligible unit growth, increased cyclicality, and where investors seek higher dividend returns. Most automobile, steel, and electric utility companies among others are in this stage.

Identifying the best companies in the second or emerging growth stage of their development is the key to realizing the potentially high-investment returns. Successful emerging growth companies exhibit a set of attributes that are helpful in screening the numerous candidates. By making sure that all portfolio holdings meet the specific criteria, many mistakes can be avoided and the percentage of winners increased. There are eight primary criteria that are particularly important. Additionally, there are a number of secondary characteristics that have been found to be useful and should further improve the selection process.

Primary Criteria

The criteria listed in Figure 2 are straightforward, but need further discussion to narrow the range of interpretation. In the first criterion, earnings per share expansion of at least a 20 percent annual rate is used as the benchmark for growth, but there should also be a reasonably close parallel with sales increases. Profit margin improvement can cause earnings to expand faster than sales for a time, but sales ultimately must keep pace. During the period of high inflation in the late 1970s and early 1980s, the minimum earnings per share growth rate was raised from 15 percent per year to 20 percent. With inflation at lower

FIGURE 2
Emerging Growth Companies—Criteria for Stock Selection

1. Earnings per share growth rate of at least 20 percent per annum over the next five years.
2. High operating or pretax profit margins.
3. High return on shareholders' equity so that as much growth is internally financed as possible.
4. Clean balance sheet with little or no debt.
5. Conservative accounting practices.
6. Leadership position (number one or two) in the industry, product, or market served.
7. Exceptional management to handle sustained, rapid growth.
8. Annual sales of $10 to $100 million.

levels, a 15 percent growth rate hurdle could again be used. The growth rate criterion is based on projected results during the next five years, not on historical data. While past results may be a guide to the future, it is the company's performance in the upcoming quarters and years that is most important. Moreover, a number of small growth companies are recent start-ups with no significant record of sustained performance to serve as a guide. Others are going through the transition from explosive early growth that is clearly unsustainable to a more moderate rate as the sales base increases. A period of five years is chosen because there is a reasonable chance of correctly estimating the size of a market, market share, pricing, the competitive environment, and the numerous other factors that go into making growth rate projections. Rarely is there truly long-term visibility in the sense of forecasting 10 or 15 years into the future. The key is to keep rolling the projections ahead 5 years on an annual basis and challenging the underlying assumptions in the forecast model. The average annual earnings growth rate of the companies in a portfolio of emerging growth stocks will typically be between 20 percent and 30 percent.

One of the best guides to separating the outstanding companies from the mediocre ones is how profitable they are and how sustainable is the profitability. Generally, the higher the profit margin, the stronger the company's competitive position. Pricing flexibility is one of the key factors that enables companies to achieve and maintain high profit margins. The ability of a company to pass on cost increases and be more in control of pricing than competitors is an important attribute of a successful business. The absolute level of profit margins must be analyzed in the context of the company's industry and competition. An 11 percent pretax profit margin would be considered excellent for many retail trade or distribution businesses, but would be unsatisfactory for most high-quality manufacturing or service operations where pretax margins of 20 percent or higher are not unusual. A well-diversified portfolio of emerging growth companies should have an average pretax profit margin near 20 percent. If interest income is a significant contributor to pretax earnings then the operating profit margin will be a better indicator of the profitability of the company's basic business. While numerous companies have had sustained pretax margins of 20 percent to 30 percent or even higher for many years, unusually high margins can be a risk and must be scrutinized carefully to see if they can be maintained. For example, companies with a single ''fad'' product that are the first to enter a market can initially produce high profit margins, but they are not sustainable as competition enters that market or the fad fades.

The third criterion of having a high return on shareholders' equity is a key measure of the health of a business whether the company is small or large. A company with a 20 percent sales and earnings growth rate and no debt on its balance sheet should have at least a 20 percent return on average equity over a complete economic cycle to fund growth internally. With no debt, the return on total capital would also be 20 percent. Companies with a growth rate of 25 percent, 30 percent, or more often cannot generate a high enough return on equity to finance all of the growth internally and must raise capital from external sources such as by selling more common stock. Because of capital-raising efforts or high-internal cash generation, companies can accumulate excess cash which can mask the underlying returns on the operations of the business. By subtracting the excess cash equivalents from shareholders' equity and deducting the related interest income from earnings, one can calculate the return on ''operating'' equity to assess the trends in the basic business. While the level of the return on equity is important, so is the year-to-year trend, which can signal changes in the business. It is not uncommon for a portfolio of emerging growth companies to have a return on shareholders' equity that averages in the 18 percent to 25 percent range.

Because there is so much business and operating risk in rapidly growing small companies, it is prudent to minimize financial risk. Companies should therefore, as a fourth criterion, have little or no short- or long-term debt and where external financing is needed to fund growth, issuance of additional equity is preferred over debt securities. An exception to an unleveraged balance sheet may be the capitalized lease obligations that are frequently part of the liabilities of specialty retailers and restaurant companies. In general, emerging growth companies should be aggressive in their research and development, marketing, and expansion plans but conservative in their financial structure. The debt to total capitalization typically averages less than 12 percent in a portfolio of small-growth companies.

The accounting practices and policies used by emerging growth companies must also be conservative. Since the Financial Accounting Standards Board has clarified practices in several areas in recent years, one area where there is still a lot of management discretion and therefore deserves particularly close examination is revenue recognition policies, which can vary greatly from company to company, even in the same industry. Whether the sale of a computer is booked as revenue at the time of shipment from the factory, when it is installed, or when it is accepted by the customer can greatly affect the quality of reported revenues and earnings. Are long-term service or maintenance contracts booked as revenue when the contract is signed or prorated as the service is performed? The more conservative the accounting, the less chance there is for investors to encounter negative surprises.

If there were one criterion that could be viewed as more sacrosanct than the others, it would be the sixth, which is the requirement for a company to be number one or a close number two in its industry, product, or market niche. One of the most common mistakes investors in emerging growth stocks can make is to identify an attractive area of business, but instead of investing in the leader, buy the shares of the lesser participants in the industry because they may look cheaper than the leader. . . .

Leaders tend to remain leaders in their businesses, which is not surprising, since they produce the largest volume of goods or services, should have the lowest unit costs, and can invest more in research, production, marketing, financial strength, and management controls, in order to stay in front. There is often room for a company in second place to do well, . . . but the error is to go down to the third, fifth, or even lower ranked companies in the industry. The mistake an investor can make is to be drawn by the lower valuation of the lesser companies. If the leading company looks too expensive, the investor should wait for a correction in the market and then buy at a more reasonable price. Buying nonleadership companies when the strong ones are too expensive usually results in a portfolio replete with low-quality companies near the top of a market—a formula for real disaster in emerging growth stocks. . . .

Since companies growing at 20 percent to 50 percent annual rates double in size every two to four years, the seventh criterion takes on immense importance because it takes a talented and dedicated management team to keep the business on track. Judging management capabilities correctly is a difficult, subjective, and imprecise process, but generally the more experience an investor accumulates in meeting and appraising different management teams, the easier it will be to see the differences between weak and strong management groups. With the advent of turnkey computer accounting and material reporting and planning systems, the likelihood of poor financial controls has been reduced in recent years. However, a vitally important function of management that often does not get enough investor scrutiny is marketing and sales. Most publicly traded emerging growth companies have already developed their products, established a manufacturing capability, and have financial controls. At that point, an important part of the future success will be the strength of the marketing and sales organization. In the race for industry leadership, it is often the company with the best marketing, sales, and distribution that will grab and hold the lead.

Another facet of judging the quality of management is to appraise the turnover of key employees. In successful small-growth companies, there is typically little management turnover. This is not surprising since profitable, rapidly growing companies are a good place to work. They are able to pay people competitively, provide significant advancement opportunities, and stock option incentive awards typically reach down several layers into the organization. If a pattern of key people leaving a company begins to develop, the investor must question what could be going wrong. It may be an early tip-off of troubles ahead.

Size per se is not a criterion because it is all of the other characteristics that are most important. However, most small-growth companies typically have sales between $10 million to $100 million at the time the initial investment is made. When a company reaches $400 million or more in revenue, it may still be attractive but is getting beyond the emerging stage of development. What is important is not to set an arbitrary threshold of size before a company will be considered for investment. For example, not buying shares in a company until its sales or market value reaches $100 million only cuts off the investor from some of the early appreciation potential. Similarly, companies with $150 to $250 million in sales are not too big to be included in an emerging growth stock portfolio.

Low P/Es and Value Investing

Paul F. Miller, Jr., CFA

Paul Miller's studies of low P/E stocks at Drexel & Co. in the 1960s provided the foundation rationale upon which "value" investing was subsequently based. An early user of computing power (readers will note in paragraph three of the Introduction the CPU time needed for this study), he is now head of Miller, Anderson & Sherrerd, a major investment management firm.

Introduction

From time to time over the last seven years, Drexel & Co. has conducted basic research studies aimed at investigating the importance of price-earnings ratios as a tool for stock selection and portfolio management.

The best known of these studies were done in 1963 and covered the 30 issues comprising the Dow-Jones Industrial Average for the period 1936 to 1962. These studies together with others covering 62 blue chip issues, published in April and June of 1964, indicated that there has been a strong price performance bias operating in favor of the low price-earnings ranges of the market.

By necessity, the size of our samples in these studies was limited by the tremendous volume of hand calculations. Now with the aid of Standard & Poor's Compustat tapes and a computer, we have been able to significantly expand the study of this area. Of interest is the fact that

Reprinted from *Institutional Service Report,* November 1965, pp. 1–6, Philadelphia: Drexel & Co., by permission of the author.

this study involved approximately 18,000 pieces of data and about 35,000 manipulations and calculations. The total machine time used was about twenty minutes.

Our methodology, and the summary of the results of this new study are described below:

Methodology

Time span.   The study covered time segments from 1948 through 1964.

Sample.   Industrial companies covered in Compustat with sales of over $150 million in a given year. The actual number of companies grew consistently during the period from 110 which had sales over $150 million in 1948 to 334 in 1964. Companies with deficits were eliminated in the years that the deficits occurred. The sample was confined to companies with fiscal year-ends of September 30 to January 31.

Computation of price-earnings ratios.   Price-earnings ratios were computed using year-end prices and calendar year earnings (or fiscal year earnings as long as the fiscal year ended between September 30 and January 31). This procedure assumed that the market had relatively accurate knowledge of calendar year earnings as of each year-end. While this assumption may be open to some question, we feel that the number of companies whose earnings may have differed significantly from the expectations of the market was quite limited. In any event, our subsequent procedure of ranking the stocks into quintiles by price-earnings ratios gives us confidence that the composition of the *quintiles* could not have been altered substantially by earnings surprises.

Ranking of stocks by price-earnings ratios and division of the sample into quintiles.   As of each year-end the companies that qualified on the basis of sales size were ranked by ascending order of price-earnings ratios and then divided into quintiles from the lowest price-earnings ratio quintile to the highest.

Examination of price performance.   The price performances of the qualifying companies were computed for all one-year periods following the year-end price earnings quintile. In a like manner price performances of the quintiles were computed for all three-year periods and all five-year periods in the 1948–1964 time span.

Summary of Results: Performance of Stocks Ranked in Quintiles by P/E at Each Year-End During Subsequent One-Year Periods (1948–1964 incl.)

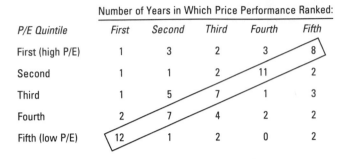

P/E Quintile	Number of Years in Which Price Performance Ranked:				
	First	Second	Third	Fourth	Fifth
First (high P/E)	1	3	2	3	8
Second	1	1	2	11	2
Third	1	5	7	1	3
Fourth	2	7	4	2	2
Fifth (low P/E)	12	1	2	0	2

As can been seen from the above summary, the lowest price-earnings ratio quintile had an average price performance which ranked *first* among all quintiles in 12 out of 17 years, or approximately 71% of the time. The highest price-earnings ratio quintile ranked *last* in one-year price performance in 8 out of 17 years, or 47% of the time.

The channel which has been drawn on the table is the perfect rank correlation channel. That is, if each quintile had had a price performance which correlated in an exact correlative way (inverse to the height of the price-earnings ratio), the numbers appearing in this channel would have been 17. In other words, the fifth quintile would have performed best in the 17 years, the fourth quintile would have performed second best in the 17 years, the third quintile would have performed third best in 17 years, etc. While the correlation is not perfect, note that the largest numbers in every column fall within this correlation channel.

If we examine the average price gain per year for each quintile, we find that here too there is a strong tendency for price performance to vary inversely with the height of the price-earnings ratio. These figures are given below:

Average Price Gain per Year

P/E Quintile

First (High P/E)	7.7%
Second	9.2
Third	12.0
Fourth	12.8
Fifth (Low P/E)	18.4

Interestingly, while each quintile experienced an average loss in 5 out of the 17 years, the average loss *per loss year* did not vary significantly among the various price-earnings quintiles, as seen below.

Average Loss per Loss Year

P/E Quintile	
First (High P/E)	12.1%
Second	10.7
Third	9.4
Fourth	9.5
Fifth (Low P/E)	10.1

Out of curiosity we examined the number of years out of the 17 covered that each quintile outperformed the Dow-Jones Industrial Average.

Number of Years (out of 17) Quintile Outperformed Dow-Jones Industrials

P/E Quintile	
First (High P/E)	5
Second	7
Third	8
Fourth	7
Fifth (Low P/E)	11

As shown, the purely mechanical approach of confining a portfolio to the lowest price-earnings ratio quintiles would have achieved performances better than the Dow-Jones in 11 out of 17 years.

Turning now to the performance over each of 15 three-year periods included in the time span, the same strong bias in favor of low price-earnings ratio quintiles is demonstrated. The low price-earnings quintile was the best performing group in 10 out of 15 periods, whereas the highest price-earnings quintile was the worst performing group in 9 out of 15 periods. Just as the study of one-year periods showed, the perfect inverse correlation channel contained the largest number of periods in each column.

Again the average price gains per [three-year] period correlated perfectly in an inverse manner with the level of the price-earnings ratio.

For five-year periods, the results continued in the same pattern with the low price-earnings quintile ranking first in 10 out of 13 periods, and the high price-earnings quintile ranking last in 8 out of 18 periods. Once

Performance over 15 Three-Year Periods

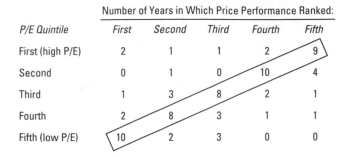

	Number of Years in Which Price Performance Ranked:				
P/E Quintile	First	Second	Third	Fourth	Fifth
First (high P/E)	2	1	1	2	9
Second	0	1	0	10	4
Third	1	3	8	2	1
Fourth	2	8	3	1	1
Fifth (low P/E)	10	2	3	0	0

Average Price Gain per Three-Year Period

P/E Quintile

First (High P/E)	27.6%
Second	29.1
Third	38.1
Fourth	42.2
Fifth (Low P/E)	58.5

again the perfect inverse correlation channel contains the largest number in every column and the average price gain per period again showed the same perfect bias toward the low price-earnings ratio groups.

Average Price Gain per Five-Year Period

P/E Quintile

First (High P/E)	55.7%
Second	59.8
Third	67.7
Fourth	75.2
Fifth (Low P/E)	93.5

Examination of Results

When we first did similar work with the Dow-Jones Industrials, we were criticized for the small sample and the attention we gave to one-year periods. We were also criticized, probably justifiably, for using

June 30 prices and calendar year earnings in the computation of price-earnings ratios. This objection was based on the theory that many of the stocks which were classified as low price-earnings stocks each June 30 based on calendar year earnings were probably stocks which turned out to be low price-earnings stocks as a result of surprisingly good earnings in the last half of the year. (We dealt with this criticism in our April 1963 *Monthly Review.*) We think we have effectively eliminated these objections in this study.

It was thought by some that if we gave consideration to a larger sample and to longer time periods than one year, the earnings growth of the high price-earnings stocks would have had time to work to the price advantage of the high price-earnings issues. Judging from the results of the study of three- and five-year periods, this does not appear to be the case.

We have asked ourselves whether a handful of issues might have accounted for the superior price performance of the lower price-earnings ratio stocks. Consequently, we have examined the distribution of the price performances within the lowest and highest price-earnings ratio quintiles. In doing so we calculated the number of stocks in the lowest and highest quintiles which had a price performance exceeding the average price performance of the quintile.

Summary: Number of Issues in Highest and Lowest Quintiles Whose Performance Exceeded Average Price Performance of Quintile

	Lowest Quintile	Highest Quintile
1 Year	44.5%	48.1%
3 Year	40.4	42.8
5 Year	39.5	41.1

As can be seen, there is some tendency for the lowest quintile to have a slightly more skewed distribution than the highest quintile. We believe, however, that the differences are quite insignificant.

Conclusion

We think that the results of this study support our continuing contention that price-earnings ratios are indeed an important consideration in portfolio management and research direction. However, much further work needs to be done to determine why this bias has been so consistently present in favor of low price-earnings ratio groups. Among the first jobs we have undertaken is a study of the correlation, or lack of it, that exists between price-earnings ratios and subsequent earnings growth. This work is now in process and will be reported on in the near future.

Regressing to the Mean

H. Bradlee Perry, CFA

The Babson Staff Letter is a favorite source of insight and perspective for many investment professionals. Brad Perry's contributions to it are particular favorites, especially for those who can imagine his New Englander's voice pronouncing the words he has written. Here, he is discussing how things seldom stay "changed" for long in investing.

———————

Golfers and baseball players often talk about being "in the groove", having their swing following the particular pattern which has been successful for them. Different businesses also have a "groove", a mode of performance that is typical for them, and individual stocks tend to have a normal valuation "groove".

However, athletes, businesses and stocks deviate from their typical performance from time to time, doing better or worse for a while. Such periods obviously are very significant to sports fans and investors.

Because of aging and other human frailties, golfers and ball players don't always get back into the groove. However, due primarily to competitive forces, businesses and stocks usually do. Statisticians call this "regressing to the mean". Understanding the process and observing it carefully can be very rewarding for investors.

Excerpted from *The Babson Staff Letter,* August 14, 1987, by permission of David L. Babson & Co., Inc.

Industry Patterns

Most types of businesses are influenced by specific factors that give them distinctive characteristics, and all the participants in those particular businesses tend to perform in somewhat similar fashion. When one doesn't, history shows that eventually the "outlier" usually falls back in line with the industry pattern.

Banking is a good example. This is a very homogeneous business. All banks deal primarily with money; it is a commodity because one bank's money is just the same as another's. Through various means they all gather deposits primarily from individuals and businesses and lend those funds to other individuals and businesses.

Some banks are better managed than others so they operate a little more effectively. But in the long run there are rarely major differences in performance in such a homogeneous, competitive industry— especially within geographic areas where economic conditions are similar.

Over the years when a particular bank has been growing faster than its competitors, it has usually been more aggressive in lending. Eventually that leads to greater loan losses and in turn, a reining in of its rapid growth. Occasionally when a bank goes bonkers on profit expansion, it gets into such deep trouble that it has great difficulty regaining its position. Continental Illinois is a recent example and previously First Pennsylvania experienced the same fate (for somewhat different reasons).

However, in most instances overly aggressive banks do regress to the mean. Notable cases are Citizens & Southern many years ago and Chase Manhattan in the late 1970s.

Conversely, banks which go through a period of slower than normal growth and are tagged as "sleepy" usually wake up and get back in the groove. Wells Fargo, First Interstate and State Street Boston are good illustrations.

The same process has occurred in just about every industry: Texaco declining from superiority in the 1970s while Exxon was moving up the scale; Union Carbide losing its position of preeminence in chemicals while Hercules rose from a subpar position to a very good one; Borden and Nabisco waking up in the food business while General Foods was sinking to mediocrity; Pfizer developing much greater strength as Upjohn slipped into the average category; Federated Department Stores

FIGURE 1
Convergence Tendency of Profitability: Five-Year Average Return on Equity

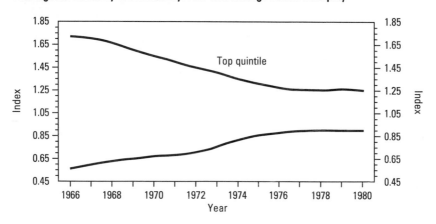

sliding from its very strong position while May Department Stores was advancing from the rear of the pack; etc.

The record is clear that more often than not in a business heavily influenced by a few basic forces, companies rarely perform way above the industry average or way below it indefinitely. There is a constant tendency to regress toward the mean. . . .

This is illustrated in Figure 1 prepared a few years ago by Merrill Lynch. Covering a broad universe of over 1,500 corporations, it shows how those in the top quintile of profitability in 1966 gradually experienced a decline in their return on equity from way above average to moderately above average over the next 14 years—and how those at the bottom of the scale in 1966 improved to just slightly below average. . . .

Stock Market Performance

One lesson we need to remember constantly is that stock prices tend to reflect quite fully the most recent performance of companies. When a business has been going extremely well, almost invariably that fact has *already* been factored into the stock—because everyone has seen the good reports from the company. Similarly, when the recent results of a company have been poor, the stock is usually depressed.

Then when the news on the "good" companies becomes even slightly less favorable—or perhaps merely fails to get more favorable—their shares are likely to underperform the market. On the other hand, even a slight improvement in the news on a "bad" company can spark a major upswing in its stock. . . .

Conclusion

Many years ago we knew a person outside this firm who had developed a very simple—and very effective—method of selecting stocks to buy. He kept careful records of the returns on assets earned by different companies. He would only buy a stock when the firm's profitability was below its historic norm—and he would only sell the stock when profitability had risen above that norm. This gentleman was an extremely successful investor and his commonsense approach (which predates the general understanding of regression to the mean) works just as well today as it ever did.

The reason it does is that most investors take a relatively short-term view and assume that what has happened most recently will continue. They fail to recognize that economic and market forces are always working to press companies (and whole industries) back toward their respective grooves. Furthermore, there is a human element in the equation. As with athletes, it is difficult for managements to play over their heads for long. Nor does any management want to continue performing badly. And if they do for very long, the directors (or an outside buyer) usually step in and replace management.

Appraising where a company is in relation to its normal pattern of performance and how its current status has affected its stock price is a very useful process. Like any other investment technique it doesn't work all the time because exceptions do occur, but clearly this type of analysis can improve one's portfolio batting average.

The Burden of Proof

Simon M. Keane

Shouts of " 'Tis!" " 'Tis not!" " 'Tis!" have all too often characterized discussions of market efficiency. Here, Simon Keane explains the middle ground and how an investor might seek to benefit from being upon it.

———————

It will be shown that the empirical literature falls into two categories, a high proportion of evidence favouring the conclusion that the market is an efficient information processor, and a small proportion that appears to conflict with this conclusion. This raises the issue, therefore, whether the existence of the latter makes it necessary for investors to suspend judgment about the matter. Does the evidence favouring efficiency need to be unequivocal and overwhelming before assent to it as an economic fact is reasonable? Or is it sufficient to be guided simply by the balance of the existing evidence? Does the market have to be perfectly efficient for EMH to be accepted as valid for practical purposes? Upon whom rests the burden of proof?

Exploitable Inefficiency

There can be little doubt that the received wisdom amongst practitioners is that the market's price-setting mechanism is inefficient. In addition, there appears to be a presumption that the onus of proof rests on the

———
Excerpted from *Stock Market Efficiency* (Oxford, England: Philip Allan, 1985), Chapter 3, pp. 23–26, by permission of the author.

proponents of market efficiency to establish their case convincingly before any doubts about the conventional view should be given serious consideration. There are sound reasons, however, for questioning the validity of this presumption, even before any empirical evidence is considered.

First it is essential to recognise that it is not simply a set of beliefs that is at stake but a set of investment strategies. . . . There is a well-defined strategy that follows logically for any investor who believes the market to be efficient, a strategy which involves 'least cost', namely to buy a portfolio as broadly diversified as the market, and to pursue substantially a buy-and-hold policy. In contrast, if the market is assumed to be inefficient, there are incremental costs involved in exploiting the inefficiencies, namely:

1. the costs of searching for mispriced securities,
2. transaction costs in switching securities,
3. the increased risk exposure from inefficient diversification resulting from the pursuit of perceived bargains, and
4. the opportunity costs of holding cash during non-investment periods.

The combined effect of these costs is to place the burden of proof on those who advocate renouncing the market portfolio in pursuit of inefficiency. In addition, it requires proof of more than the mere existence of an inefficiency. To have operational significance, the inefficiency must be *exploitable,* in the sense that an investor should have a reasonable expectation of profiting from it. And to be exploitable, it should satisfy certain criteria, namely it should be:

1. *Authentic*—it should be supportable by properly conducted statistical research, after taking into account all relevant factors such as investors' personal tax effects etc.

2. *Identifiable*- -it is not enough to show that some experts or strategies consistently beat the market if these are not identified. Investors are presented continuously with a bewildering number of advisers and investment rules, and if some of these can achieve genuinely superior performances the investor must have a valid basis for distinguishing them from less successful competitors. Without this basis the inefficiencies that they denote may be of no practical consequence to the investor.

3. *Material*—inefficiencies are not exploitable unless they are sufficient to compensate for the costs and risks of pursuing them.

4. *Persistent*—it is not sufficient that an inefficiency be shown to have existed in the past, if there are no grounds for believing that it will continue to exist in the future. Hence, even when a material inefficiency has been identified and authenticated, one must be reasonably satisfied that the market will not learn from the experience.

It may seem unreasonable, having advanced what for many must appear to be a relatively novel and certainly unorthodox hypothesis about the market's pricing mechanism, to proceed immediately to argue that it falls on those who have long believed the opposing view to demonstrate that this hypothesis is false. But it must be stressed that, although the conventional view has enjoyed a long tradition, it too, no less than the efficient market view, is based on a simple belief or hypothesis, namely that some components of the market portfolio are recognisably not worth holding. The question that presents itself is which hypothesis, in the absence of evidence, is the more reasonable basis upon which to found an investment strategy. Since there are some indisputable benefits in holding the market portfolio, and some equally indisputable costs in attempting to compete with it, it is argued that, despite its long tradition, the conventional view deserves no prior claim upon investors' beliefs. It needs to be demonstrated convincingly that the components of the market portfolio which are not worth holding can clearly be identified as such.

Efficient with Respect to Whom?

Even if an exploitable inefficiency is shown to exist, this is not in itself reason enough for the market to be classified as inefficient in a general sense. It is possible for the market to be inefficient to one investor and efficient to another, depending on whether the individual is in a position, directly or indirectly, to take advantage of the inefficiency. To understand why this is so it is useful to draw a distinction between *'judgmental'* and *'rule-of-thumb'* inefficiencies. The former depend for their recognition on the perceptiveness of the investor. For example, if a specific share price at a particular point in time does not fully reflect all publicly available information, this is a judgmental inefficiency, being directly exploitable only by those who have the necessary insight to perceive its existence. In contrast, if tests show, say, that the market consistently overvalues stocks with high Price-Earnings ratios, this is a rule-of-thumb inefficiency available to any investor, whatever his individual information-processing skills might be. As long as he is aware of the decision rule that all high P/E stocks should be avoided, he does not need to be able personally to see through to the substance of the inefficiency.

Now if the market is found to contain one or more exploitable rule-of-thumb inefficiencies, satisfying the four criteria above, then it can truly be said to be inefficient in a general sense, because it would be irrational for any investor to formulate his investment strategy on the basis that the market is efficient with respect to all securities. But if the market's inefficiencies are judgmental and, therefore, perceptible only to those with special skill or insight, it will remain efficient to the remaining body of investors unless the insights of the experts are transmittible to them. However, the simple act of communicating the information, whether by circular, press comment, or whatever, is itself a piece of data which may be instantaneously captured in the market price, in which case the inefficiency is exploitable by no one other than those who directly perceive it. Under these circumstances, the optimal strategy for the majority of investors may be to behave as if the market is efficient even with the knowledge that for others the market is inefficient. To some extent, therefore, market efficiency is a personal issue, where each individual has to decide whether the market is efficient for him, or whether he has enough evidence to count himself amongst the gifted few.

===

A meaningful verdict on market efficiency can be reached only in terms of how the degree of observed efficiency affects optimal investment behaviour. The market is effectively efficient if it can be shown to serve the interests of investors to behave as if it is efficient. The issue, therefore, is not a simple either/or situation. It is a continuum ranging from perfect efficiency to total inefficiency.

===

The important issue at stake is not whether market efficiency holds in an absolute sense, but whether it holds as a working principle for the great majority of investors. Even if a minority of skilled information-processors are able to earn enough from the market to reward them for their activities, provided their superior insights are not transmittible to the majority, the market can still be classified as near efficient. Hence the burden of proof remains with those who advocate an active strategy to show that the market cannot be classified as efficient.

Bond Quality and
Investor Returns

W. Braddock Hickman

Hickman's extraordinarily careful and detailed pioneering analysis of investor experience in bonds reached two primary conclusions: (1) long-term investors with well-diversified portfolios earn higher net returns from lower quality bond issues and (2) rating agencies are highly successful in rating bond quality *within* an industry, but not *across* industries. A portion of his analysis, used by Michael Milken as the centerpiece of his "junk bonds are good" sales story, is excerpted here.

Investment quality is an elusive concept, as is investor experience. Neither can be defined precisely because of the multiplicity of investor preferences. Since different investors have different objectives, securities suitable for one portfolio may be entirely unsuitable for another. Small investors are unable to diversify against the risk of default and must seek to obtain securities that are individually ''safe'' if they are to avoid ruinous default losses. Large investors may be less directly concerned with the riskiness of individual investments because of the possibility of averaging capital gains and losses, but are frequently restricted by various legal or self-imposed constraints designed to avoid areas of excessively high default risk. Some investors, and they may be large or small, require liquidity in the bond account and therefore seek

Excerpted from *Corporate Bond Quality and Investor Experience* (Princeton, New Jersey: Princeton University Press, 1958), pp. 1–16, by permission of the National Bureau of Economic Research, Inc.

salability and price stability. Others, such as life insurance companies, may have little interest in liquidity per se, if the net flow of funds available for investment is regularly in their favor or if the contracts running against them are typically long term. These are but a few possibilities; the variety of investment objectives is endless. It follows that no single index of investment quality, and no single measure of investment experience, can be equally relevant to all investors.

The field of investigation [in this study] is the universe of straight corporate bonds offered during 1900–1943, including those outstanding on January 1, 1900. Straight corporate bonds are defined as fixed-income, single-maturity bonds offered by domestic business corporations and held by the domestic investing public. The study covers all large straight issues (those with total offerings of $5 million or more) or railroad, public utility, and industrial corporations, and a representative 10 percent sample of small straight issues (under $5 million). Excluded are real estate mortgage bonds (principally issues secured by office buildings and residential property) and bonds of financial corporations. . . .

Aggregate Experience

Before considering the detailed records relating to the default and yield experience of bonds in different quality classes, several points about aggregate behavior are worth noting. Since the basic records cover virtually all large issues offered and outstanding during the period studied, and a large sample of small issues (which were adjusted by weighting to cover all small issues), the aggregates reflect accurately the over-all experience of investors holding corporate bonds.

During the period 1900–1943, $71.5 billion par amount of straight bonds of domestic corporations were offered to and acquired by the investing public. Of that amount 93 percent consisted of regular offerings; the remaining 7 percent, of contract modifications and exchanges growing out of corporate reorganizations. The latter, called irregular offerings in this report, initially sold at extremely high promised yields (12.3 percent on the average), but the yields actually realized from offering to extinguishment were even higher (13.7 percent), so that investors holding them obtained average capital gains of 1.4 percent per annum. The 93 percent of regular offerings breaks down into 12 percent paid in full at maturity, 37 percent called, 18 percent defaulted, and 26 percent outstanding on January 1, 1944, with a perfect contractual record through that date. The zero loss rate on the issues paid in full at maturity has been mentioned (realized yield equaled promised yield). On the defaulted issues the average life-span loss rate was 3.7 percent. But the remarkable fact is that capital losses on defaulted issues were just offset by capital gains on irregular offerings and on regular offerings called or selling in 1944 above amortized book value. The weighted average promised and realized yields on total offerings both worked out at 5.6 percent, so that for the universe of corporate bonds the net loss rate was zero. . . .

Unusual economic developments during the years 1900–1943 also raise questions as to the representativeness of the period studied. Although the loss rate was zero on corporate bonds over the full period, it was definitely not zero for most of the subperiods. Since our records terminate on January 1, 1944, they are heavily weighted by the catastrophic default rates of the Great Depression. For analytical purposes, however, this may be a virtue rather than a weakness since it permits an examination of the behavior of corporate bonds under the most adverse circumstances. . . . Barring another major depression, our estimate of a zero loss rate on corporate bonds held from offering to extinguishment is a conservative one.

Within the full period studied, marked discrepancies occurred in the yields and loss rates on bonds offered and extinguished in different periods. Generally speaking, experience was best with bonds offered and extinguished before, say, 1932, and with bonds offered and extinguished thereafter; it was poorest with bonds offered before 1932 and still outstanding on that date, so that they were exposed to the heavy default risks of the Great Depression. . . .

Behavior of Corporate Bonds in Different Quality Classes

. . . A few summary statistics pertaining to the behavior of straight corporate bonds classified by the more important measures of prospective quality at offering are brought together in Figure 1. The first column contains life-span default rates by composite agency rating at

FIGURE 1
Life-Span Default Rates, Yields, and Loss Rates for Bonds Classified by Industry, Quality, and Other Characteristics at Offering, 1900–1943

	Default Rate	Promised Yield	Realized Yield	Loss Rate
All Industries	17.3%	5.3%	5.4%	−0.1%
Railroads	28.1	5.5	5.2	0.3
Public Utilities	10.6	5.0	5.4	−0.4
Industrials	14.8	5.4	5.8	−0.4
Agency Rating				
I	5.9	4.5	5.1	−0.6
II	6.0	4.6	5.0	−0.4
III	13.4	4.9	5.0	−0.1
IV	19.1	5.4	5.7	−0.3
V–IX	42.4	9.5	8.6	0.9
No rating	28.6	4.8	4.6	0.2
Legal Status				
Legal in Maine	7.1	4.0	4.9	−0.9
Not legal in Maine	19.2	5.5	5.5	0.0
Legal in Massachusetts	7.6	4.0	4.7	−0.7
Not legal in Massachusetts	18.5	5.4	5.5	−0.1
Legal in New York	9.0	4.0	4.5	−0.5
Not legal in New York	18.8	5.5	5.5	0.0
Market Rating				
Under 1/2%	10.5	3.8	3.9	−0.1
1/2–1	13.9	4.5	4.7	−0.2
1–2	20.7	5.4	5.5	−0.1
2% and over	32.4	9.3	9.5	−0.2
Times-Charges-Earned Ratio				
3.0 and over	2.1	4.0	4.9	−0.9
2.0–2.9	4.0	4.3	5.1	−0.8
1.5–1.9	17.9	4.7	5.0	−0.3
1.0–1.4	34.1	6.8	6.4	0.4
Under 1.0	35.0	6.2	6.0	0.2

offering, legal status at offering, and other quality measures. As has been indicated, life-span default rates are retrospective measures of quality: they represent the proportion of the par-amount total of bond offerings in each of the prospective quality classes that went into default at any time between offering and extinguishment.

Even the highest grades of corporate bonds, it is shown, were not entirely free of the risk of default; but virtually all of the prospective measures of quality provided reliable rankings in regard to such risk. In other words, the retrospective quality of bond offerings as measured by default rates declines as we move down the scale of each of the major

FIGURE 1
Continued

	Default Rate	Promised Yield	Realized Yield	Loss Rate
Ratio of Net Income to Gross Income				
25% and over	3.3	4.5	5.0	−0.5
20–24	11.6	4.6	4.6	0.0
15–19	12.7	4.4	4.8	−0.4
10–14	17.6	5.1	5.3	−0.2
Under 10%	27.5	5.0	5.0	0.0
Negative	17.2	8.9	10.7	−1.8
Lien Position				
Secured	18.8	5.3	5.4	−0.1
Unsecured	13.6	5.3	5.3	0.0
Size of Issue				
$50 million and over	16.3	4.9	5.0	−0.1
20–49	16.4	5.2	5.7	−0.5
5–19	19.0	5.7	5.5	0.2
Under $5 million	24.9	6.3	6.1	0.2
Asset Size of Obligor				
$200 million and over	16.4	5.4	5.3	0.1
100–199	17.0	5.0	5.8	−0.8
5–99	18.8	5.6	5.7	−0.1
Under $5 million	23.6	6.6	6.6	0.0

... Data for size of issue and asset size of obligor are based on large issues ($5 million and over) and an adjusted 10 percent sample of small issues; data for other classifications are for large issues only. Default rates exclude irregular offerings (made during corporate reorganizations, etc.)....

prospective measures of quality. The inverse relationship between prospective quality and default rates held almost uniformly throughout the
indicated classes of the figure for agency ratings, legal status, market
ratings, time-charges-earned ratios, ratios of net income to gross income, size of issue, and asset size of obligor. The results thus provide
confirmation of the reasonableness of the quality measures generally
used by investors in selecting corporate bond investments. . . .

One of the most significant points brought out by the figure is the
marked difference among major industry groups in life-span default
rates on their bond offerings. . . . In consequence, the default rates for
bond offerings classified within industry by the various quality measures are usually more closely associated with quality than the figures
for the combined industries indicate. The same is true for outstanding
issues held over assumed chronological investment periods. As a gen-

eral rule, the various rating systems were efficient in ranking issues within industry but were less successful in judging default risks as between major industry groups. . . .

The foregoing may be summarized as follows: (1) Investors, in the aggregate, paid lower prices for, and thus exacted higher promised yields on, the low-grade issues; (2) default rates on the low grades were higher than on the high grades; (3) loss rates, which take into account not only default losses but also capital gains, were higher on low-grade issues; (4) the higher promised returns exacted on the low grades at offering proved to be more than sufficient to offset the higher default losses; (5) in consequence, life-span yields realized on low grades were higher than on high grades. . . .

The major conclusion that investors obtained higher returns on low-grade issues than on high grades should not be accepted without proper qualification. For it cannot be emphasized too strongly that this finding emerges only when broad aggregates of corporate bonds are considered over long investment periods, and given the price and yield relationships that existed during those periods. In effect, the aggregate results reflect the experience of all investors over long periods, rather than that of any particular investor over any given short period. Another qualification is that realized yields and loss rates were not nearly so regularly related to quality as were promised yields and default rates. Because of the disparity in the performance of low-grade bonds, small investors (and many large investors that may have been inhibited from practicing the broadest type of diversification) would frequently have fared best by holding only the highest grade obligations. . . . A third qualification is that realized yields were subject to extreme aberrations over time, since they reflected not only the risks of the business cycle but the state of the capital market as well. The average yields realized over selected periods of offering and extinguishment, or over selected chronological periods during which the issues were outstanding, indicate that the market usually overpriced low-grade issues (and underestimated default risks) at or near peaks of major investment cycles. . . . Low-grade issues of a declining industry rarely worked out as well as high-grade issues.

The finding that realized returns were higher on low-quality corporate bond issues than on high-quality issues has implications for investment theory as well as for practical investment policy. The result appears consistent with either of two views of the factors involved in the formulation of promised yields. One is the neoclassical economists' conception that promised yields contain three roughly additive components: the basic yield on the highest grade of bonds outstanding with similar maturities; a pure risk premium, sufficient, when averaged over a large number of similar obligations, to offset net default losses; and a component for risk bearing. The other view is based largely on institutional considerations.

The concept of a premium for risk bearing, which would explain the higher returns actually obtained on low-grade issues, implies that investors are unable to diversify adequately to average out default losses. This concept would appear to fit best an atomistic market comprised of a large number of small investors. For, if all investors had sufficient funds at their disposal to average out default risk, there would be no need of a component for risk bearing, except possibly for the extra costs incurred in servicing a high risk portfolio. . . . As a general rule, institutional investors are fairly conservative and place a premium on quality, just as do small investors who seek to avoid ruinous default losses through the purchase of high-grade bonds. The result is that promised yields on low grades—averaged over long investment periods—are more than sufficient to offset default losses, so that realized yields on low grades are high. These institutional considerations rest on personal observation rather than on statistical evidence; but either view—the neoclassical or the institutional—is consistent with the record, and indeed both may be partially correct.

Qui Numerare Incipit
Errare Incipit

Oskar Morgenstern

Oskar Morgenstern's thoughtful caution on the imperfections in the statistics used to describe and explain business, the economy, and politics is a summary of his book, *On the Accuracy of Economic Observations.*

Although the natural sciences—sometimes called the "exact" sciences—have been concerned with the accuracy of measurements and observations from their earliest beginnings, they nevertheless suffered a great crisis when it became clear that absolute precision and certainty of important kinds of observations were impossible to achieve in principle. At least all sources of error that occur in the natural sciences also occur in the social sciences: or, in other words, the statistical problems of the social sciences cannot possibly be less serious than those of the natural sciences. But the social sciences pay far less attention to errors than the physical. This is undoubtedly one of the reasons why the social sciences have had a rather uncertain development.

In the physical sciences, when an error is not mentioned explicitly, it is because it can generally be assumed to be well known, or because the values have already entered into physical theories that determine an admissible error level, and their limitations are then those of the respec-

Reprinted from *Fortune* (October 1963), pp. 142–44, 173–80. New York: The Time Inc. Magazine Company.

tive theory. To give an illustration, it may not be necessary to state every time the error in the measurement of the velocity of light because this value is indissolubly tied up with the theory of relativity. But when new measurements are made the error margin must always be stated. Thus exaggeration of the significance of the new results is avoided, and they assume their proper place in physical theory.

It ought to be clear a priori that most economic statistics should not be stated in the manner in which they are so often reported, pretending an accuracy that may be completely out of reach. Changes in consumers' total spending power down to the last billion or less (i.e., variations of less than one-half of 1 percent) are reported and taken seriously. Price indexes for wholesale and retail prices are shown to second decimals, even though there have been so many computing steps that the rounding-off errors alone may preclude such a degree of precision. Unemployment figures of several millions are given down to the last 1,000's (i.e., one-hundredths of 1 percent "accuracy"), when certainly the 100,000's or in some cases perhaps even the millions are in doubt. It will be seen later that national income and consumers' spending power probably cannot be known now in part without an error of plus or minus 10 to plus or minus 15 percent.

Business must be deeply concerned about these matters: its decisions are dependent upon statistical information. For example, wage agreements involving millions of workers are sometimes based on price indexes that record alleged changes of price levels up to one-tenth of 1 percent! Common price and cost-of-living indexes are reported in this form. They are splashed across the front pages of newspapers together with the most important political news of the day. These price changes are then interpreted as a measure of the success or failure of government policy and the existence or absence of inflation. In fact, these minute changes show nothing at all. The public in general and Congress in particular must be made to understand that there cannot be absolute accuracy, that there must be error, and that the important thing to do is to try to uncover, remove, or at least limit the error.

Do Errors Cancel Out?

People gathering statistics all too often face a deliberate attempt to hide information. In other words, economic and social statistics are frequently based on evasive answers and even deliberate lies. Lies arise principally from fear of tax authorities, from dislike of government interference, or from the desire to mislead competitors. Nothing of this sort stands in the path of the physical scientists. Nature may hold back information, is always difficult to understand, but it is believed that she does not lie deliberately. Einstein has aptly expressed this fact by saying: *"Raffiniert ist der Herr Gott, aber boshaft ist er nicht."* ("The Lord God is sophisticated, but not malicious.")

In addition to deliberate lies and evasions there are many other sources of error in the data from which economic observations are made. Anyone familiar with the actual handling of statistical data at the primary level is aware of the great number of possible errors and mistakes and of the frequency with which they occur. The increasing use of machines in handling economic data does not eliminate the main sources of error. These are so deeply rooted that it is impossible, on purely theoretical-probabilistic grounds, to eliminate all of them all of the time. The problem is to appraise them and to reduce them to the minimum.

It is possible that the influence of one error that drives a number in one direction is exactly offset by the influence of another error doing the opposite. In that case, by coincidence, the errors could cancel out— if their "extent" or "strength" balance—and we obtain a "true" figure for our observation. But we have not *made* a true observation. The notion that errors do cancel out is widespread, and when not explicitly stated, it appears as the almost inevitable argument of investigators when they are pressed to say why their statistics should be acceptable. Yet any statement that errors cancel one another has to be proved. The world would, indeed, be even more of a miracle than it is if the influence of one set of errors offset that of another set of errors so conveniently that we need not bother much with the whole matter.

It is also widely believed that more recent statistics are more accurate and trustworthy than earlier ones. This is probably sound, in a vague, general way, but only when sufficiently large intervals of time are taken. There are, however, many instances where statistics produced today are probably no better—and indeed worse—than statistics produced decades ago. It is obviously more difficult, for example, to describe statistically an economy in a state of vigorous development, signified by the introduction of many new products, changes in quality of existing products, and a rapidly advancing technology.

In particular, modern statistics of the value of foreign trade—an enormously important field—are virtually worthless where countries practicing discriminatory exchange rates are concerned; many nations do so right now and did not in earlier years. Domestic statistics do not necessarily improve either. Sometimes governments change rapidly and bring forth the deliberate falsifications associated with Nazi and Communist practices. Or "strategic" considerations play havoc with reliability.

How Old Is the River?

There is a tendency toward specious accuracy, a pretense that things have been counted more precisely than they can be—e.g., the U.S. Army published *enemy* casualties for the Korean war to 1/1,000 of 1 percent, at a time when our own losses were not well known even to the thousands of men! An even better example is given by the official publication of the Austrian Finance Administration, which states that the population of Salzburg Province in 1951 was 327,232 people— *4.719303 percent* of the entire population of Austria. The classical case is, of course, that of the story in which a man, asked about the age of a river, states that it is 3,000,021 years old. Asked how he could give such accurate information, the answer was that twenty-one years ago the river's age was given as three million years. There is a fair amount of this in economic (and other social) statistics.[1] Economic series, reported in billions, are often aggregated with others, reported in millions or thousands, by simple addition. The result is a new series which gives the impression that the aggregate has been measured, counted, or determined to far more digits than is actually the case.

Another kind of specious accuracy is perhaps even more dangerous. It is functional speciousness. Here data are given that, even when they have only a very small margin of error, are nevertheless useless. This is the case, for example, when the exchange rate of a country with exchange control is given at the official rate (quite accurately to any desired number of decimals), although the vast majority of transactions take place at different rates that are not disclosed or cannot be determined.

The success or failure of a government's economic policy is often measured by the number of the nation's involuntary unemployed. "Full employment'' is a national goal in most advanced nations. But as soon as one tries to discover when that desired condition has been reached, considerable difficulties are encountered. They are conceptual as well as statistical.

First, it is known that there is always some ''unemployment'' which may not be truly involuntary, because labor shifts from one place to another, young people enter the labor force, others more or less gradually slip from it because of age, ill health, emigration. These transitions take time for purely technological reasons, such as slow transmission and dissemination of knowledge, time needed to move to other places of employment, etc. This is then the so-called ''frictional'' unemployment, which is at some level unrelated to the state of the economy. There is also possibly a great deal of ''hidden unemployment,'' e.g., when persons becoming unemployed in industry go back to farms for varying periods of time. There is a shift in occupations, for example, when skilled workers are displaced by machines and then have to find employment at lesser skills.

Second, because of the high political significance of unemployment figures, this area is charged with emotions, insinuations, assertions, etc. This applies in particular to times of great stress, of political upheavals and changes in the form of government. Some countries, such as the Soviet Union, flatly assert that they never have unemployment, this allegedly being impossible because of their political system. Others, such as Nazi Germany, ''reduced'' unemployment by drafting men into the army and thereby changed the statistics to their liking.

====

Comparing One Nation with Another

There are two principal questions involved: the first is one referring to the comparability and applicability of concepts, and the second is one referring to the quality of the component data. Conceptually different situations arise for each class or category of countries. For example, home-consumed agricultural produce, which is an enormous part of the total in underdeveloped agricultural countries, is practically irrelevant in the U.S. Clearly, this is much more difficult to measure in the former than in the latter. Yet agricultural statistics in the U.S. are far from satisfactory. How, then, could the agricultural income of, say, Ceylon, the Congo, China, Bolivia, or Tibet be known at least as accurately? How can they be made comparable—e.g., on a per capita basis—when even the number of inhabitants in these countries is in far greater doubt than that in the U.S.?

International comparisons, however, are constantly being made. No doubt some information can be had from existing figures, and whether they are useful depends, as we shall not tire of repeating, on the purposes of the comparisons. To ascertain in a rather general manner the gross differences in the income of different nations, to show that they differ by large factors,[2] and to see whether these differences have changed over the years, etc., is one thing, but to believe that we can state this and much more reliably to two, three, or even four "significant" digits is an entirely different matter.

. . . Figures giving international comparisons of national incomes are among the most uncertain and unreliable statistics with which the public is confronted. The area is full of complicated and unsolved problems, despite great efforts to overcome them. This is a field where politics reigns supreme and where lack of critical economic appraisal is particularly detrimental.

The Accuracy of Growth Rates

In recent years there has been much concern about the rate of economic growth of the U.S. and other countries. In addition to the goals of maintaining a high level of employment and providing for general stability in the price level, a third goal, that of maintaining a satisfactory rate of economic growth, has been added to the responsibilities of fiscal and monetary authorities.

The value of a growth rate depends on the accuracy both of the figure for gross national product and of the prices going into the construction of the deflator indexes. The former are subject to considerable uncertainties; the latter depend on the precision with which actual prices, as distinguished from posted prices, list prices, etc., can be determined and applied to the correct sectors of gross national product.

A reliable growth rate of two significant digits is impossible to establish. Even the first digit is in grave doubt, as will be shown below. Yet the emphasis of the public discussion is on the second digit, usually the first decimal, and it is carried on in all seriousness as if a distinction between, say, 3.2 and 3.3 percent were really possible, and as if the transition, within a short time, from the former to the latter constituted an advance by the country. But a growth rate simply cannot be computed with the stated or demanded degree of refinement and reliability. This applies to the existing national income data of any country in the world.

We know that countries have grown and that, at periods, some have grown faster than others. But such observations and statements can be made with confidence only qualitatively and for longer periods. They are impossible to make for one year (or less), when a nation's growth is as imperceptible as the growth of a person's teeth in a month. . . .

Pick Your Time

The usefulness of growth rates becomes even more dubious when revisions are considered. If the rate of the change from 1947 to 1948 was determined in February, 1949, when the first figures became available, it was 10.8 percent. In July, 1950, using officially corrected figures, it became 12.5 percent; in July, 1956, it fell to 11.8 percent—a full percentage point. All this for the growth from 1947 to 1948! Similar observations apply to the other years for which this computation has been made. There is no consistency in the changes. In stating what the growth rate of the country is, much depends, therefore, on the moment of time when a growth rate is computed. Though not surprising in the light of our previous investigations, this result is nevertheless noteworthy. And all this applies to figures where we have *abstracted* from the fact that they are necessarily afflicted with errors which, when low, must be at least 5 percent.

In addition to all these difficulties, there is the ambiguity in choosing the base year. The need for a base year arises from the desire to compare long periods by means of the compound rate. Such periods will often comprise a whole series of business cycles and therefore several decades. If a year with a high (or low) gross national product is chosen as base year, this will depress (or raise) the growth rate of subsequent years. Since there is no such thing as a "normal" year, the investigator has a great amount of freedom in determining a base year. An unscrupulous or politically oriented writer will choose that base year which produces the sequence of (alleged) growth rates best suited to his aims and programs. An advocate of government spending and inflation will pick a year with a high gross national product as base year in order to show a low rate of growth and thereby strengthen his argument in favor of inflation, government deficits, and the like. An opponent of such policies will choose a relatively poor gross national product as base year, thus obtaining a series of growth rates carrying the comforting message that the development of the country is progressing well. These are, of course, standard tricks, used, undoubtedly, ever since index numbers were invented. . . .

Swimming Pools or Power Plants

There is also a conceptual problem that has to be taken care of even if the statistics are in good shape. Let us say country A expands by adding to its output of automobiles, refrigerators, swimming pools, etc., while country B increases its output of machine tools, power plants, mines, etc. B is laying the foundation for further output increase while A is not. Similar considerations apply when weapons and other tools for war are involved. The ordinary growth rate, computed for the big gross-national-product aggregate, covers up these profoundly different developments and would easily give entirely erroneous and misleading information about the relative development of these countries. Yet this is the figure commonly used to assess past progress and future tendencies. The answer would be to compute instead "power indexes" (of growth), which would have to be based on the information given by special aggregates made up of better related components.

To summarize: precise uses of "growth rates" are entirely inadmissible, whether for comparing different countries or short periods of the same country. Their computation is largely arbitrary. The concept itself is vague and unreliable. . . .

Abandon Old Views

Economics is not nearly so much of a science as the free use of allegedly accurate figures would seem to indicate. On the other hand, there is no reason to conclude that there cannot be or is no theory at all. The belief that we have to get more and more data, make more and more descriptions before we can formulate valid theories is entirely mistaken. A theory means a commitment, and in scientific life that is exactly what is wanted. When new facts come to light and new interpretations are needed, a new situation can arise. This may then call for abandoning the old views and for making a new decision.

There is, however, one definite action that is possible, though it will take time before desirable results will become visible. That is to stop important government agencies, such as the President's Council of Economic Advisers, the various government departments, the Federal Reserve Board, and other agencies, public and private, from presenting to the public economic statistics as if these were free from fault.

Perhaps the greatest step forward that can be taken, even at short notice, is to insist that economic statistics should not be released without an accompanying estimate of their error. Even if only roughly estimated, this would produce a wholesome and perhaps a profound effect. Makers and users of economic statistics both might refrain from making claims and demands that cannot be supported scientifically if the publication of error estimates became a general practice.

Eventually a new generation of economists will have learned to live with data of widely differing quality. In that they will emulate the physicists, who have created a magnificent and terrifying theory though their data range in accuracy from better than 1/100,000,000 percent to only 50 percent—that is, when they can measure at all. In appreciating the true condition of the data, economists cannot fail to develop economic theory in conformity with the high scientific standards set in the physical sciences.

Notes

1. Years ago an example made the rounds: in order to determine the precise height of the Emperor of China, whom none of his subjects has ever seen, it suffices to ask each of 300 million Chinese what he thinks the height is and average their opinions. This will necessarily give a very precise figure.
2. But probably not by as large factors as is suggested by the official statistics. As Kuznets has observed, if the frequently stated low figures were correct the inhabitants of the poorest countries would all have starved a long time ago.

A First Lesson
in Econometrics

John J. Siegfried

Many professional investors skip quickly over those sections of articles on their business that have "too many Greek symbols and formulas." John Siegfried's articles, however, are too good to skim. Pay attention!

Every budding econometrician must learn early that it is never in good taste to express the sum of two quantities in the form:

$$1 + 1 = 2. \tag{1}$$

Any graduate student of economics is aware that

$$1 = \ln e, \tag{2}$$

and further that

$$1 = \sin^2 q + \cos^2 q. \tag{3}$$

In addition, it is obvious to the casual reader that

$$2 = \sum_{n=0}^{\infty} \frac{1}{2^n}. \tag{4}$$

Therefore equation (1) can be rewritten more scientifically as

Reprinted from *The Journal of Political Economy* 78 (November/December 1970), pp. 1378–79. Chicago: University of Chicago Press.

$$\ln e + (\sin^2 q + \cos^2 q) = \sum_{n=0}^{\infty} \frac{1}{2^n} . \tag{5}$$

It is readily confirmed that

$$1 = \cosh p \sqrt{1 - \tanh^2 p} , \tag{6}$$

and since

$$e = \lim_{\delta \to \infty} \left(1 + \frac{1}{\delta}\right)^{\delta} , \tag{7}$$

equation (5) can be further simplified to read:

$$\ln \left[\lim_{\delta \to \infty} \left(1 + \frac{1}{\delta}\right)^{\delta}\right] + (\sin^2 q + \cos^2 q) = \sum_{n=0}^{\infty} \frac{\cosh p \sqrt{1 - \tanh^2 p}}{2^n} . \tag{8}$$

If we note that

$$0! = 1, \tag{9}$$

and recall that the inverse of the transpose is the transpose of the inverse, we can unburden ourselves of the restriction to one-dimensional space by introducing the vector X, where

$$(X')^{-1} - (X^{-1})' = 0 . \tag{10}$$

Combining equation (9) with (10) gives

$$[(X')^{-1} - (X^{-1})']! = 1 , \tag{11}$$

which, when inserted into equation (8) reduces our expression to

$$\left\{\lim_{\delta \to \infty} \left\{[(X')^{-1} - (X^{-1})']! + \frac{1}{\delta}\right\}\right\} + (\sin^2 q + \cos^2 q)$$

$$= \sum_{n=0}^{\infty} \frac{\cosh p \sqrt{1 - \tanh^2 p}}{2^n} . \tag{12}$$

At this point it should be obvious that equation (12) is much clearer and more easily understood than equation (1). Other methods of a similar nature could be used to simplify equation (1), but these will become obvious once the young econometrician grasps the underlying principles.

MARKETS AND
EXCHANGES

Confusion de Confusiones

Joseph de la Vega

Joseph de la Vega's *Confusion de Confusiones,* published in Spanish in Amsterdam just over 300 years ago, is the first book to describe the practices of any stock exchange. Trading was principally in shares of the Dutch East India Company, organized in 1602, and later also in shares of the Dutch West India Company, established in 1621. By 1688, the exchange had puts, calls, inside information, "when issued" trading, pools, and short sales—known as "wind trading."

The text of the book is presented as a dialogue, a popular literary device of that period. These excerpts have been selected from the 1957 version published by Harvard's Kress Library.

Philosopher: And what kind of business is this about which I have often heard people talk but which I neither understand nor have ever made efforts to comprehend? And I have found no book that deals with the subject and makes apprehension easier.

Shareholder: I really must say that you are an ignorant person, friend Greybeard, if you know nothing of this enigmatic business which is at once the fairest and most deceitful in Europe, the noblest and the most infamous in the world, the finest and the most vulgar on earth. It is a quintessence of academic learning and a paragon of fraudulence; it is a touchstone of usefulness and a source of disaster. . . .

Excerpted from *Confusion de Confusiones* (1988; originally published 1688; translated and published 1957 by Kress Library of Business and Economics), pp. 3–14, by permission of Baker Library, Harvard Business School, Boston.

Philosopher: Does my curiosity not deserve a short description from you of this deceit and a succinct explanation of this riddle?

Merchant: That is my wish also, because the importunities of instructions, the shipment of goods, and the circulation of bills of exchange are all so burdensome to me. This load of work leads me to look for another means of acquiring a fortune and, even at the risk of loss, to slough off these many wearisome activities.

Shareholder: The best and most agreeable aspect of the new business is that one can become rich without risk. . . .

I will fulfill your wish to be informed about the origin of this business, and you will see that the stocks do not exist merely for fools but also for intelligent people.

In 1602 a few Dutch merchants founded a company. The wealthiest people [in the country] took an interest in it, and a total capital of sixty-four and a third tons of gold . . . was raised. Several ships were built and in 1604 were sent out to seek adventure Quixote-like in the East Indies. The property of the Company was broken into several parts. . . . There were many, however, who did not subscribe to a whole share, but took only a smaller portion according to their wealth, inclination, or expectation of the future. The ships sailed their courses without encountering windmills or enchanted giants. Their successful voyages, their victorious conquests, and the rich return cargoes meant that Caesar's *Veni, vidi, vici* was surpassed and that a tidy profit was made—which became a stimulus to further undertakings. The first distribution of the profit was postponed till 1612 in order to increase the company's capital. Then the administration distributed 57½ per cent, while in 1613 the dividends amounted to 42½ per cent—so that the shareholders, after having had their capital paid back to them, could enjoy any further return as so much velvet.

Gradually the company developed to such an extent that it surpassed the most brilliant enterprises which have ever been famous in the history of the world. Every year new shipments and new riches arrive, [the proceeds from] which are distributed as profits or are utilized in expenditures in accordance with the stipulations of the administration. (The dividends are sometimes paid in cloves, sometimes in [promissory] notes, at other times in money, just as the directors think fit.) From the founding of the company to the date of this conversation, the dividends have amounted to 1,482½ per cent, while the value of the capital has increased more than five-fold. This treasure is compared to a tree, because it yields fruits [almost] every year, and, although during some years it has only produced blossoms, there have been other years when it has resembled the trees of Uraba[1] which display their fruitfulness two or three times a year, and which competed with the Sibylines[2] whose branches were of gold and whose leaves were of emeralds. Others call the Company the tree of the knowledge of good and evil, such as exists in Paradise, because it is kept informed of everything that happens along all the branches [of its interests]. However, I have come to see that it resembles the tree of life, because innumerable men earn their living in its shadow. And those who are satisfied with the fruits, and do not insist on pulling up the roots . . . , will admit that they do pretty well in such a business.

Philosopher: I think I have fully grasped *usque ad ultimas differentias* the meaning of the Company, its shares, its principles, its reputation, its splendor, its initiation, its progress, its administration, the distribution of profits, and its stability. But what has this to do with that mysterious business you mentioned, with the tricks you pointed out? . . .

Shareholder: [Let me return to my assertions] that this business of mine is a mysterious affair, and that, even as it was the most fair and noble in all of Europe, so it was also the falsest and most infamous business in the world. The truth of this paradox becomes comprehensible, when one appreciates that this business has necessarily been converted into a game, and merchants [concerned with it] have become speculators. Had the conversion of these merchants into speculators been the only change, the harm would have been bearable, but, what is worse, a portion of the stock brokers have become cardsharpers and, though they are familiar with the blossoms, they nevertheless lose the fruits.[3]

For a better understanding of this notable fact, it should be observed that three classes of men are to be distinguished on the stock exchange. The princes of business belong to the first class, the merchants to the second, and the speculators to the last.

Every year the financial lords and the big capitalists enjoy the dividends from the shares that they have inherited or have bought with money of their own. They do not care about movements in the price of the stock. Since their interest lies not in the sale of the stock but in the revenues secured through the dividends, the higher value of the shares forms only an imaginary enjoyment for them, arising from the reflection . . . that they could in truth obtain a high price if they were to sell their shares.

The second class is formed by merchants who buy a share (of 500 pounds) and have it transferred on their name (because they are expecting favorable news from India or of a peace treaty in Europe). They sell these shares when their anticipations come true and when the price rises. Or they buy shares against cash, but try to sell them immediately for delivery at a later date, when the price will be higher (i.e., for which date a higher price is already quoted). They do this from fear of changes in the [political or economic] situation or of the arrival of [unfavorable] information, and are satisfied with [what amounts to] the interest on their [temporarily] invested money. They consider their risk as much as their profit; they prefer to gain little, but to gain that little with [relative] security; to incur no risk other than the solvency of the other party in this forward contract; and to have no worries other than those bound up with unforeseen events.

Gamblers and speculators belong to the third class. They have tried to decide all by themselves about the magnitude of their gains and, in order to do so, . . . they have put up wheels of fortune. Oh, what double-dealers! Oh, what an order of life has been created by those schemers! The labyrinth of Crete was no more complicated than the labyrinth of their plans. . . . The difficulties and the frightful occurrences in the exchange business . . . have taught some precepts. . . . The first principle [in speculation]: *Never give anyone the advice to buy or sell shares,* because, where perspicacity is weakened, the most benevolent piece of advice can turn out badly.

The second principle: *Take every gain without showing remorse about missed profits,* because an eel may escape sooner than you think. It is wise to enjoy that which is possible without hoping for the continuance of a favorable conjuncture and the persistence of good luck.

The third principle: *Profits on the exchange are the treasures of goblins.* At one time they may be carbuncle stones, then coals, then diamonds, then flint-stones, then morning dew, then tears.

The fourth principle: *Whoever wishes to win in this game must have patience and money,* since the values are so little constant and the rumors so little founded on truth. He who knows how to endure blows without being terrified by the misfortune resembles the lion who answers the thunder with a roar, and is unlike the hind who, stunned by the thunder, tries to flee. It is certain that he who does not give up hope will win, and will secure money adequate for the operations that he envisaged at the start. Owing to the vicissitudes, many people make themselves ridiculous because some speculators are guided by dreams, others by prophecies, these by illusions, those by moods, and innumerable men by chimeras. . . .

The expectation of an event creates a much deeper impression upon the exchange than the event itself. When large dividends or rich imports are expected, shares will rise in price; but if the expectation becomes a reality, the shares often fall; for the joy over the favorable development and the jubilation over a lucky chance have abated in the meantime. . . .

Merchant: [As I gather from your description], the terms used on the Exchange are not carefully chosen. I notice that the language there is Arabic grafted upon Greek, and that even the most experienced person needs a new dictionary to understand it. . . .

Shareholder: As to the confusion of tongues on the Exchange, I am not to be blamed for it. The jargon was coined by the necessities of the business. . . .

Notes

1. Uraba is a province in Colombia.
2. The comment on the Sibylines may well have been taken from one of the fabulous books of travels, a type of literature of which many specimens were published in the epoch of the discoveries.
3. Here the author is indulging in a play on words, since in Spanish *flor* means both "flower," and a "trick" of a card-sharp.

A Collection for Improvement of Husbandry and Trade

John Houghton, F.R.S.

In March 1692, John Houghton began a newspaper intended to record industrial progress. After a lead article, the rest of the paper was devoted to commercial intelligence—including the first list of current stock prices. He began with 8 (including East India and Hudson's Bay) and within two years was carrying 64 actively traded securities. In June of 1694, his lead articles offered an explanation of "joint stocks" and, in passing, of what we would now call options.

———— ▬ ————

Joint-Stocks

Friday, June 8, 1694

Having treated in my First Volume of the Nature of Earth, Water, Air, and Fire, which in my Apprehension is the Foundation of most natural Knowledge; and in my Second, the great Sheet of Taxes, Acres, Houses, &c. with the Natural History of Derbyshire. In my Third I treated on the Doctrine of Fermentation, the History of Cider and Clay, so far as room would permit; and in my Fourth Volume I finished my History of Clay, and went through all that was observable of Wheat, in a more compendious and plainer Method than any I have met with. I

Reprinted from *A Collection for Improvement of Husbandry and Trade* 5, Nos. 97, 98, and 99, June 8, 1694, June 15, 1694, and June 22, 1694. London, England.

design to carry on the History of Kine, and all things relating to it; but for a little Diversion from Natural History, and the usefulness of the thing it self, I have thought fit to treat of Joint-Stocks, and of the various dealings therein, commonly called Stock-Jobbing.

And tho' I am not much concern'd in Stocks, and therefore have little occasion to Apologize for Trading therein, yet having undertaken to impart to others some Misteries in Trade, and to rectifie Men's Judgments, whom I find running into Errors and Mistakes, I thought it not amiss to treat upon this Subject; but before I enter upon it, I must desire my Readers to lay aside all Prejudice and Partiality, there being nothing that is so great hinderance to a Man's coming to the true Knowledge of any thing, as false Pre-conceptions and Notions of it. . . . It was the Opinion of that great Man, [des Cartes] that no Person ought to receive or retain any Position for a truth of which they have not a certainty; which certainty only is attainable by an exact Examination and Scrutiny into the reason of such his Opinion, without pre-ingaging his Judgment to one side or other.

And in truth it is for want of this that Men run into so many Errors, for . . . the Foundation being bad, the Super-structure cannot be firm.

If therefore my Reader come pre-possessed against Trading in Stocks, it will be to little purpose for me to go about to assure him of the usefulness or lawfulness of them. Some abuses may probably have been committed by Traders therein; but must we presently thereupon run down all with a full cry that so deal therein? May we not with as much Justice and Reason cry out against all mankind as Devils, because many are guilty of Diabolical Actions? May we not as well prohibit the use of Wine, because we see Men wallowing in the Kennels by drinking too much of it? And the like may be said of all other things which are lawful in themselves; so that it is not the Use but the Abuse of them deserves a Censure. I am the larger in this, because I know many worthy Persons of great Honour and Probity, who deal in Stocks, that do abominate the least unjust Action, and would not for the World have an ill gotten Penny among the rest of their Estates; and it is a great hardship on such Gentlemen to undergo the Censures of Mankind, who inveigh against all Traders and Trading in Stock, tho' at the same time they know little or nothing of it.

I shall therefore in this ensuing Volume give you an Account of the Original, and Necessity of Joint-Stocks, the lawfulness and usefulness of Trading therein, and the Abuses that are so much complained of and charged upon the Traders in them; which I shall do with as much brevity and perspicuity as my Theme will admit, and I shall also make some Remarks of the Advantages that may be expected from some of the most considerable Joint-Stocks, and I doubt not but to give my unbiased Reader full satisfaction; of which he may expect a beginning in my next Friday Paper.

Beginning of Stocks

Friday, June 15, 1694

In my last I promised an History of Stocks, but when these began is not very material to know, tho' I think the East-India Stock, that began in anno 1600 was the first; then followed the Guinny, . . . Hudson's Bay, . . . and by encouragement of an Act of Parliament . . . a great many Stocks have arisen since this War with France; for Trade being obstructed at Sea, few that had Money were willing it should lie idle, and a great many that wanted Employments studied how to dispose of their Money, that they might be able to command it whensoever they had occasion, which they found they could more easily do in Joint-Stock, than in laying out the same in Lands, Houses, or Commodities, these being more easily shifted from Hand to Hand: This put them upon Contrivances, whereby some were encouraged to Buy, others to Sell, and this is it that is called Stock Jobbing.

The plain, honest Proceeding whereof is this, When some one has thought of an Art or Invention, or discovered some Mine, or knows, or thinks of some New (or New manner of) way of Trade, whereby he thinks a considerable gain may be gotten, and yet this cannot well, or not so well as otherwise be carried on by a private Purse, or if it could, the Hazard of it is too great: He then imparts it to some Friend or Friends, who commonly consider or enquire of the Learned, Whether 'twill stand good in Law; and if so, they contrive some Articles for its constitution, whereof to give the first Inventer a Summ of Money for his Invention and charge, or some certain number of the Shares, or both, is certainly, and with good reason one of the principal Articles.

This done, the Parties concerned let it be known, and each brings in his Friend, 'till all the Shares be bought at such a Price as stated, either presently to pay down all the Money, which is generally found to be the best and easiest way, or only some part, which is very often troublesome, one or other being backward of paying his quota, and oblige themselves to pay the rest as the general Court shall call for it.

This general Court consists of every Man who has any Share, and of so many Votes as Men; sometimes of none but those who have such a certain number of Shares; sometimes to have as many Votes as Shares; and sometimes to let none have above Five, Ten, or a certain number of Votes, let their Shares be as many as they will.

This general Court chooses a Committee to manage the whole, except ordering the raising or dividing of Money, or some other great Affairs, for one Year, or what time they think fit; and also a Treasurer and Clerk. This Committee choose a Chair-man for the time they are chose themselves, or else agree to choose a Chair-man every Committee, according as they like the Committee-men that come. Of this Committee they commonly make Five a Quorum, and pay each Committee Man that comes some small Summ of Money for his incouragement. In some great Stocks they have Twenty Shillings apiece each time, in some Ten Shillings, some otherwise; but in a great many of the lesser Stocks, all that come have Half a Crown apiece, or else a certain Summ is allowed if all come, and whoever does not come, his Share is divided among the rest that do.

Places of Meeting

Friday, June 22, 1694

They commonly appoint also some certain place for their meeting; the great Stocks that require Houses, many Offices, and much Warehouse Room at their House: The lesser Stocks usually appoint Coffee Houses, where they may have some refreshment without great charge, which charge is generally paid out of the main Stock; tho' sometimes from the Committee-Money.

This Committee consult the best ways for carrying on the business, examine all Bills that are brought from Workmen, or others that have laid out for their Service, and when adjusted, payment is ordered, and a Warrant to the Treasurer, signed by the Committee for it, is given and all things of moment that are done, are, or ought to be entred in the Minute Book by the Clerk; but ordinarily Ten Pound at a time is paid to the Clerk to discharge the Committee-Money, and other petty Expences.

Very often they subdivide their Committees to Audit the Accounts, to examine, consider, and manage particular parts of their Affairs.

The manner of managing the Trade is this; The Monied Man goes among the Brokers, (which are chiefly upon the Exchange, and at Jonathan's Coffee House, sometime at Garaway's, and at some other Coffee Houses) and asks how Stocks go? and upon Information, bids the Broker buy or sell so many shares of such and such Stocks if he can, at such and such Prices: Then he tries what he can do among those that have stock, or power to tell them; and if he can, makes a Bargain.

Another time he asks what they will have for Refuse of so many Shares: That is, How many Guinea's a Share he shall give for liberty to Accept or Refuse such Shares, at such a price, at any time within Six Months, or other time they shall agree for.

For Instance; When India Shares are at Seventy Five, some will give Three Guinea's a Share, Action, or Hundred Pound, down for Refuse at Seventy Five, any time within Three Months, by which means the Accepter of the Guinea's, if they be not called for in that time, has his Share in his own Hand for his Security; and the Three Guinea's, which is after the rate of Twelve Guinea's profit in a Year for Seventy Five Pound, which he could have sold for at the Bargain making if he had pleased; and in consideration of this profit, he cannot without Hazard part with them the meantime, tho' they should fall lower, unless he will run the hazard of buying again at any rate if they should be demanded; by which many have been caught, and paid dear for, as you shall see afterwards: So that if Three Months they stand at a stay, he gets the Three Guinea's, if they fall so much, he is as he was, losing his Interest, and whatever they fall lower is loss to him.

But if they happen to rise in that time Three Guinea's, and the charge of Brokage, Contract and Expence, then He that paid the Three Guinea's demands the Share, pays the Seventy Five Pounds, and saves himself. If it rises but one or two Guinea's, he secures so much, but whatever it rises to beyond what it cost him, is Gain. So that in short, for a small hazard he can have his chance for a very great Gain, and he will certainly know the utmost his loss can be; and if by their rise he is encouraged to demand, he does not matter the farther advantage the Accepter has, by having his Money sooner than Three Months to go to Market with again; so in plain English, one gives Three Guinea's for all the profits if they should rise, the other for Three Guinea's runs the hazard of all the loss—if they should fall.

Of the Private Cheats Used to Deceive One Another

Daniel Defoe

Daniel Defoe, best known as the author of *Robinson Crusoe* and *Moll Flanders,* was an extraordinarily prolific writer of books, essays, and pamphlets on politics, religion, and finance. He described himself with this couplet:

> No man has tasted differing fortunes more,
> And thirteen times I have been rich and poor!

Perhaps he writes as much from experience as from conviction in this 1719 polemic against London's stock-jobbers.

———

Proving *that* scandalous Trade, as it is now carry'd on, to be Knavish in its Private Practice, and Treason in its Publick:

The General Cry against Stock-Jobbing has been such, and People have been so long, and so justly Complaining of it as a publick Nusance, and which is still worse, have complained so long without a Remedy, that the Jobbers, harden'd in Crime, are at last come to exceed all bounds, and now, if ever, sleeping Justice will awake, and take some Notice of them, and if it should not now, yet the diligent Creatures are so steddy to themselves, that they will some time or other, make it absolutely necessary to the Government to demolish them.

———
Reprinted from *The Anatomy of Exchange-Alley: or, A System of Stock-Jobbing,* First Edition (London: privately printed for E. Smith, 1719), pp. 1–6.

I know they upon all Occasions laugh at the Suggestion, and have the Pride to think it impracticable to restrain them; and one of the top of the Function the other Day, when I casually told him, That if they went on, they wou'd make it absolutely necessary to the Legislature, to suppress them, return'd, That he believ'd it was as absolutely necessary for them to do it now, as ever it could be; But how will they do it? 'Tis impossible, said he, but—if the Government takes Credit, their Funds should come to Market; and while there is a Market we will buy and sell; and there is no effectual way in the World, says he, to suppress us but this, *viz.* That the Government should first pay all the publick Debts, redeem all the Funds, and dissolve all the Charters, viz. *Bank, South-Sea,* and *East-India,* and buy nothing upon Trust, and then, indeed, says he, they need not hang the Stock-Jobbers, for they will be apt to hang themselves.

I must confess, I in part agree that this is an effectual way, but I am far from thinking it the only way to deal with a Confederation of Usurers, who having sold the whole Nation to Usury, keep the Purse-Strings of Poor and Rich in their Hands, which they open and shut as they please.

But before I come to the needful ways for restraining those People, I think 'twill be of some Service to expose their Practices to common view, that the People may see a little what kind of Dealers they are.

And first, they have this peculiar to them, and in which they out do all the particular pieces of publick Knavery that ever I met with in the World, *viz.* That they have nothing to say for it themselves; they have, indeed a particular Stock of hard Ware, as the Braziers call it, in their Faces, to bear them out in it; but if you talk to them of their Occupation, there is not a Man but will own, 'tis a compleat System of Knavery; that 'tis a Trade founded in Fraud, born of Deceit, and nourished by Trick, Cheat, Wheedle, Forgeries, Falshoods, and all sorts of Delusions; Coining false News, this way good, that way bad; whispering imaginary Terrors, Frights, Hopes, Expectations, and they preying upon the Weakness of those, whose Imaginations they have wrought upon, whom they have either elevated or depress'd. If they meet with a Cull, a young Dealer that has Money to lay out, they catch him at the Door, whisper to him, Sir, here is a great piece of News, it is not yet publick, it is worth a Thousand Guineas but to mention it: I am heartily glad I met you, but it must be as secret as the black side of your Soul, for they know nothing of it yet in the Coffee-House, if they should, Stock would rise 10 *per Cent.* in a moment, and I warrant you *South-Sea* will be 130 in a Week's Time, after it is known. Well, says the weak Creature, prethee dear *Tom* what is it? Why really Sir I will *let you into the Secret,* upon your Honour to keep it till you hear it from other Hands; why 'tis this, *The Pretender is certainly taken* and is carried Prisoner to the Castle of *Millan,* there they have him fast; I assure you, the Government had an Express of it from my Lord *St——s* within this Hour. Are you sure of it, says the Fish, who jumps eagerly into the Net? Sure of it! why if you will take your Coach and go up to the Secretaries Office, you may be satisfied of it your self, and be down again in Two Hours, and in the mean time I will be doing something, tho' it is but a little, till you return.

Away goes the Gudgeon with his Head full of Wildfire, and a Squib in his Brain, and coming to the Place, meets a Croney at the Door, who ignorantly confirms the Report, and so sets fire to the Mine; for indeed the Cheat came too far to be baulkt at home: So that without giving himself Time to consider, he hurries back full of the Delusions, dreaming of nothing but of getting a Hundred Thousand Pounds, or purchase Two; and even this Money was to be gotten only upon the Views of his being before-hand with other People.

In this Elevation, he meets his Broker, who throws more Fire-works into the Mine, and blows him up so fierce an Inflamation, that he employs him instantly to take Guineas to accept Stock of any Kind, and almost at any Price, for the News being now publick, the Artists made their Price upon him. In a Word, having accepted them for Fifty Thousand Pounds more than he is able to pay, the Jobber has got an Estate, the Broker 2 or 300 Guineas, and the Esquire remains at Leisure to sell his Coach and Horses, his fine Seat and rich Furniture, to make good the Deficiency of his Bear-Skins, and at last, when all will not go through it, he must give them a Brush for the rest.

Origin of Stock Brokers, Stock Exchanges and Stock Speculation

S. A. Nelson

In a fascinating exercise extending to some 35 chapters, S. A. Nelson explored the entire gamut of speculation-related subjects that might be encountered by a newcomer to the market arena. Aptly entitled "Origin of Stock Brokers, Stock Exchanges and Stock Speculation," here is the first chapter of his 1903 book.

Etymological authorities are not in entire accord respecting the origin of the word "Broker." Jacob's Law Dictionary says: "The etymology of the term Broker has been variously given. By some it has been derived from the Saxon *broc*, misfortune, as denoting a broken trader; the occupation being formerly confined, it is said, to unfortunate persons of that description (Tomlins). According to others it was formed from the French *broieur*, a grinder or breaker into small pieces; a Broker being one who *beats* or draws a bargain into particulars (Termes de la Ley, Cowell). The law Latin from *obrocator*, however, seems to point distinctly to the Saxon *abroecan* (to break), as the true root, which in the old word *abbrochment* (q.v.) or *abroachment*, had the sense of breaking up goods or selling at retail. A Broker, therefore, would seem to have been originally a *retailer*, and hence we find the old word *auctionarius*

Reprinted from *The A B C of Stock Speculation* (New York: S. A. Nelson, 1903), Chapter 1, pp. 11–17.

(q.v.) used in both these senses (Barrill's Law Dict., tit. "Broker"). Wharton gives, as the derivation of the word the French *broceur,* and the Latin *tritor,* a person who breaks into small pieces (Whar. Law Dict., tit. "Broker"). Webster gives as its derivation, the old English *brocour,* Norman French *broggour,* French *brocanteur.* Under the word "broke," to deal in second hand goods, to be a Broker, Webster says it is probably derived from the word *brock.* Worcester derives it from the Anglo-Saxon *brucan,* to discharge an office; *brocian,* to oppress; and the French *broyer,* to grind. See "Broke" and "Broker." The word "Broker" seems first to occur in literature in Pier's Ploughman, "Among burgeises have I be Dwellyng at London. And gart Backbiting be a brocour. To blame men's ware." It clearly means here a *fault finder,* as in Provencal *brac* is refuse. The Broker was originally one who inspected goods and rejected what was below the standard (Wedgwood). Crabb's Dig. of Stat., tit. "Brokers," 261, says, "There were a class of persons known to the Romans who were deemed public officers, and who united the functions of bankers, exchangers, Brokers, commissioners and notaries all in one under the description of *proxe netae.*"

As early as 1285, in England, the term Broker occurs in an Act of Parliament. It enacts that "there shall be no Broker in the city (London), except those who are admitted and sworn before the warden, mayor or aldermen."

John R. Dos Passos, an authority on stock exchange law, says: "The next statute passed in the reign of James the First, more than 300 years later (1604) regulates the calling of Brokers with greater detail than the first act and clearly shows, by the use of the words 'merchandise and wares' that down to this period the Broker in money, stock, and funds had no legal existence. . . . It was not until the latter part of the seventeenth century, when the East India Company came prominently before the public, that trading or speculating in stock became an established business in England; and the term 'Broker,' which had then a well-understood meaning was promptly transferred to those persons who were employed to buy or sell stocks or shares, and who thenceforth became known as 'stock-brokers.' "

In 1697 owing to the "unjust practices and designs" of Brokers and Stock-jobbers in selling tallies, bank stock, bank bills, shares and interest in joint stock, a stringent act was passed permitting only sworn appointees to act as Brokers. In the reigns of William III, Anne and George, statutes were passed regulating the practice and trade of Brokers.

An early legal writer describing Stockbrokers, said: "Stockbrokers are persons who confine their transactions to the buying and selling of property in the public funds and other securities for money, and they are employed by the proprietors or holders of the said securities. Of late years, owing to the prodigious increase of the funded debt of the nation, commonly called the stock, they are become a very numerous and considerable body, and have built by subscription, a room near the Bank, wherein they meet to transact business with their principals, and with each other; and to prepare and settle their proceedings before they go to the transfer-offices at the Bank, the South Sea and India houses, thereby preventing a great deal of confusion at the public offices, where the concourse of people is so great during the hours of transferring stock that if the business was not prepared beforehand it would be impossible to transact it within the given time."

The advantage of having a Broker as an intermediary was recognized by merchants many centuries ago. A sixteenth century writer on the law says: "It is an old proverb, and very true, that between *what you will buy?* and *what you will sell?* there is twenty in the hundred differing in the price, which is the cause that all the nations do more effect to sell their commodities with reputation by means of Brokers than we do; for that which seems to be gotten thereby is more than double lost another way. Besides, that by that course many differences are prevented which arise between man and man in their bargains or verbal contracts; for the testimony of a sworn Broker and his book together is sufficient to end the same."

Dealings in Stock certificates constitute the main business of Stockbrokers, but the origin of stock certificates has not been satisfactorily traced beyond the middle of the seventeenth century. Property in this form was not known to the ancient law. While mercantile or commercial corporations existed among the Romans, history gives us no information regarding their character or methods of conduct.

Ang. & Ames on Corporations (10th ed.) Ch. 18, Sec. 26, says: "A *Collegium Mercatorum* existed at Rome 493 B.C., but the modern bourse from the Latin *bursa,* a purse, originated about the fifteenth century. Bourges and Amsterdam contend for the honor of having erected the first bourse."

"The Roman law," says John R. Dos Passos, "required three persons to organize a corporation; and as each body had at least that number of members, if not more, it would seem but natural that a certificate, or some other substantial muniment of title, should have been issued by the corporation to its respective members, in which the proportion of interest of each in the capital or corporate property of the association appeared. But whether a certificate was, in fact, issued, and, if so, was regarded as property capable of sale or other negotiation, and of vesting in the representatives of the owner, on his decease, or whether the corporations were all of the nature of guilds conferring upon the members more *personal* rights—all of these questions seem now to be incapable of solution; and the Roman law, which sheds such floods of light upon commercial subjects apparently leaves the above matters in total darkness.''

In England, in 1770, Lord Mansfield in a case wherein it was contended that stock certificates were *money* decided against that view, saying: "This is a new species of property *arisen within the compass of a few years.* It is not money.''

The Stock Exchange or Bourse in its present use is a modern creation. Brokers and dealers in stocks and merchandise dealt together in an exchange in Cornhill, London, in 1670, or thereabouts. In 1698, the Stock-brokers of London obtained quarters for their exclusive use.

The first Stock Exchange formed in the United States was that of Philadelphia, where a Board of Stock-brokers formally organized and adopted a constitution in the early part of the eighteenth century.

The New York Stock Exchange, framed on the plan of the one in Philadelphia, was organized in 1817, but curiously enough this institution is in possession of a document bearing date May 17, 1792, signed by a number of Brokers, in which it is stated: "We, the subscribers, Brokers for the purchase and sale of public business, agree to do business at not less than one-fourth of one per cent.''

Medberry, in his "Men and Mysteries of Wall Street,'' describes early stock speculation in this country as follows: . . . "When Washington was President, and Continental money was worth a trifle more as currency than as waste paper, some twenty New York dealers in public stock met together in a Broker's office and signed their names in the bold, strong hand of their generation, to an agreement of the nature of a protective league. The date of this paper is May 17, 1792. The volume of business of all these primitive New York Brokers could not have been much above that of even the poorest first-class Wall Street house in our time (1870). The Revolutionary shinplasters, as the irreverent already styled them, were spread over the land in such plenty that there were $100 to each inhabitant. Something was to be made, therefore, from the fluctuations to which they were liable. Indeed, one of the greatest Broker firms of subsequent years derived its capital from the lucky speculations of its senior member in this currency.

"The war of 1812 gave the first genuine impulse to stock speculation. The Government issued sixteen millions in Treasury notes, and put loans amounting to one hundred and nine millions on the market. . . . Bank stock was also a favorite investment. . . .

"In 1816 one could count up two hundred banks with a capital of $82,000,000. . . . One day in 1817, the New York stock dealers met in the room of an associate and voted to send a 'delegate' over on the stage line to investigate the system adopted in the rival city (Philadelphia). The Philadelphia visit was successful; and the draft of a constitution and by-laws, framed from that of the Philadelphia Board, received the final approbation of a sufficient number of Brokers to enable the New York Stock Exchange to become a definite fact. Three years after, on the 21st of February, 1820, this preliminary code of rules received a thorough revision and the organization was strengthened by the accession of some of the heaviest capitalists in the city. Indeed, with 1820, the real history of the Exchange may properly be said to commence."

In Europe stock speculation historically was marked with white stones by the "Tulip Craze," the South Sea Bubble, the John Law inflation in France, and later by the wild speculation in Kaffirs.

In this country for more than half a century stock speculation had its basis in the securities of the steam railroad. It has ebbed and flowed with the promotion, construction, decline, and reorganization of that industry.

In the last decade speculation has been fostered by the "industrial proposition," which has resulted in offering to the public shares of industrial corporations. Not an industry has been passed by. Like the railroad the industrial corporation is destined to have its periods of promotion, construction, decline and reorganization. It will not be difficult for the reader to determine which period he has under immediate consideration.

Stock Exchange Securities:
An Essay on the General Causes
of Fluctuations in Their Price

Robert Giffen

Robert Giffen's book on the causes of price fluctuations of stock exchange securities was published in London in 1877. Based on a decade of experience as a financial journalist, the book provides opinion on why securities rise and fall in price and offers advice on how investors might best manage their affairs. In this excerpt, he explains why a reserve should be accumulated out of income to offset probable capital losses. The sobriety of Victorian financial mores shines through quite clearly.

It is plain, first of all, that there is always a danger of a partial loss of capital by any investment, apart from any question of its intrinsic unsoundness or the security of the income derived from it. Prices are constantly fluctuating from the state of the money market, the manipulations of the Stock Exchange, and a thousand causes; and although there are natural limits to the fluctuations, and they conform to general laws, which wise people may speculate upon, the great mass who have not the requisite data for speculating may lose by this incessant movement. By buying at a high price and being forced or induced for some

Excerpted from *Stock Exchange Securities: An Essay on the General Causes of Fluctuations in Their Price* (New York: Augustus M. Kelley, Publishers, 1968; originally published 1877), Chapter 12, pp. 148–51.

reason to realise at a low price, their capital may dwindle away. It is no consolation to a particular investor that things right themselves in the aggregate; the difference of nominal capital is always most important, although the real yield of the reduced capital, *i.e.*, the amount of commodities which the income procures, may be as much or greater than it was when unreduced.

An investor, therefore, should in my opinion, no matter how solid the security may be or how trustworthy the income, always set aside a certain proportion of the income as sinking fund to guard against the danger of a loss of capital. There may be cases where it is of no consequence to do this, where capitals are large and are widely distributed among solid investments, so that the investor may trust to the permanent tendencies towards a rise in securities which we have described; but I should doubt whether the majority of investors are in this happy condition. For the sake of income they may consider it desirable to invest in securities not quite of the first class, or they may have only a small sum to invest in a few securities. As occasional realisations are unavoidable in the course of human affairs, there is consequently an unavoidable risk of loss of nominal capital, which must always be material to the mass of investors, and the only way to avoid it is to set aside a portion of the income for the express purpose of meeting this loss. Practically in fact, from an investor's point of view, the apparent yield of an investment should always be looked on as more than the real yield, because a deduction has to be made from it for this important purpose.

Considering how low the yield of good investments is, the advice given may seem hard; but saving money, and what is still more difficult keeping it, are matters lying outside the range of sentiment, and however desirable investors may think it to have an income secure against risk whether of principal or interest, it is impossible to alter the facts for their benefit. Hard as the recommendation is, it is accepted, I believe, and acted upon by soundly conducted banks and other institutions which have reserves invested in the most solid and easily realisable securities, although in fact such institutions are no more likely to be forced to realise, are perhaps less likely to be so forced, than ordinary investors. What they do when they make a purchase of Consols, say, is to write off out of the income for a year or two a certain part of the price. One great joint-stock bank some time ago told its shareholders that its Consols stood in their books at 90, so that realising at any price above 90 would more than replace the capital invested to the bank. It is precisely this course which I recommend all investors to follow. They must not treat all the income they receive as income or profit, to spend or to save, but a portion must be treated as sinking fund to guard against the loss of original capital.

Common-Stock Indexes
1871–1937

Alfred Cowles 3rd and Associates

Alfred Cowles made a pioneering contribution to investors' knowledge--and provided a remarkable opportunity for understanding—when he and his associates on the Cowles Commission undertook the difficult task of creating accurate historical indexes of rates of return from investment in common stocks. These excerpts from the commission's 1938 report give a flavor of its painstaking work—and of the group's conclusions.

Introduction

The Importance of Common Stocks

The movements of common-stock prices, earnings, and yields are of no small importance to the national economy. As a rough approximation it may be stated that, at least in 1929, about 18 per cent of the national income in the United States represented a return on investment.[1] For that year, classifying return on investment into dividends, interest, and net rents and royalties, the National Industrial Conference Board estimates[2] that dividends exceeded by more than 50 per cent the total of interest and net rents and royalties combined. In view of the fact that dividend payments were relatively high in 1929 it would probably be

Excerpted from *Common-Stock Indexes 1871–1937* (Bloomington, Indiana: Principia Press, Inc., 1938), pp. 1–50.

conservative to state that cash dividends from common stocks normally equal about 9 per cent of the national income. . . .

———

The purpose of the Cowles Commission common-stock indexes is to portray the average experience of those investing in this class of security in the United States from 1871 to 1937. The indexes of stock prices are intended to represent, ignoring the elements of brokerage charges and taxes, what would have happened to an investor's funds if he had bought at the beginning of 1871 all stocks quoted on the New York Stock Exchange, allocating his purchases among the individual issues in proportion to their total monetary value, and each month up to 1937 had by the same criterion redistributed his holdings among all quoted stocks. . . . During this 67-year period there were, of course, certain common-stock investors who were considerably more successful than others. However, if all the profits and losses could have been tabulated, the total result would have approximated that shown by the indexes in question, except that deductions would have to be made for brokerage and taxes, important items to the trader but less important to the long-range investor. . . .

The indexes represent separately each of 59 groups, classified according to industry, as well as 10 combinations of these groups. For each of these 69 groups have been computed 7 different series, a total of 483 indexes.

———

Period Covered

On the evidence of an extensive survey[3] it was decided not to extend the Cowles Commission indexes back of 1871 because of the scarcity of data prior to that time. . . .

Further, . . . it will be seen that the value of stocks available for inclusion in the indexes in 1871 equalled only about 2 per cent of the national wealth existing at that time, . . . whereas the stocks included during the 10 years from 1928 to 1937 represented approximately 12 per cent of the national wealth during that period. If the indexes had been extended back to 1861 the stocks available for inclusion in that year would have constituted only about 0.7 of 1 per cent of the national wealth then existing. Prior to 1871 the All Stock index would have been almost completely dominated by one group, the railroads, and would have constituted such a very small fraction of the national wealth that its economic significance would not have been at all comparable with that of later years.

Data Employed

The data employed in the construction of these indexes include, from 1871 to 1917, all industrial and public utility common stocks, and about 93 per cent in market value of the railroad stocks, traded on the New York Stock Exchange. . . .

Subsequent to 1917 (in some cases 1926 or later) are used the stocks included in the Standard Statistics weekly indexes which represent in market value 90 per cent of all common shares listed on the New York Stock Exchange. A survey, covering the years of 1926, 1930, and 1936, showed that approximately 6 per cent of the total market value of stocks so listed afforded incomplete monthly quotations. From this it follows that, from 1918 to 1937, the indexes include about 96 per cent of the market value of stocks listed on the New York Stock Exchange which are sufficiently active for sales to be recorded regularly. Subsequent to 1925, important stocks traded on the New York Curb and a few from other exchanges are included. Sources of data are, in general, the *Commercial and Financial Chronicle, Poor's* and *Moody's Manuals,* and the Standard Statistics Company publications.

In the years 1929–33 the New York Stock Exchange accounted for about 67 per cent of the total volume of stock transactions on the 24 most important exchanges in this country. More than half of the remaining volume was on the New York Curb Exchange.[4] The reason for excluding all Curb quotations from the indexes for the earlier years is indicated by the following statement regularly carried by the *Commercial and Financial Chronicle* at the head of the Curb quotations prior to December 11, 1920:

> It should be understood that no such reliability attaches to transactions on the "Curb" as to those on the regularly organized stock exchanges. . . . It is out of the question for anyone to vouch for the abso-

lute trustworthiness of the record of "Curb" transactions, and we give it for what it may be worth.

Frauds practiced on the New York Curb were so severely criticized in the report of the Hughes Commission in 1909 that organization was begun for the purpose of reform. It was not, however, until 1921, when the activities of the Curb were moved indoors, that it was possible to exercise the necessary control. . . .

On the basis of a rough approximation it was estimated that the stocks included in the Standard Statistics indexes have in recent years been about 73 per cent of the market value of common stocks listed on all of the exchanges in the United States, and about 77 per cent of those which are sufficiently active to be regularly available for inclusion in an index. . . .

The Cowles Commission All Stock index, Series P, indicates that the average rate of increase in market value of common-stock holdings in the United States for the 67 years from 1871 to 1937 has been 1.8 per cent a year. The average annual rate of increase for the Railroad and Utility Stocks has been 0.0 and 0.6 of 1 per cent respectively, whereas for the Industrials it has been 3.0 per cent. . . .

The yield, or ratio of cash dividend payments to stock prices, has averaged 5.0 per cent a year for the All Stock index since 1870. For the Railroads the average yield has been 4.8, for the Industrials 5.3, and for the utilities 5.5 per cent. If we added cash dividend payments to changes in the market values of stocks, determined as described above, the total return has been 4.8 per cent for the Railroads, 6.1 for the Utilities, 8.3 for the Industrials, and 6.8 for the three groups combined. . . . This is to be compared with an average return of about 4.2 per cent obtainable from high-grade bonds and 4.7 per cent from prime commercial paper for this period. . . .

The most profitable group to investors for the entire period from 1871 to 1937 was Miscellaneous Services with a return of 61,898 per cent. This group in the earlier years included principally express companies and more recently has included also finance companies. This apparently fabulous figure represents the gain if an investor had kept his funds continuously from 1871 to 1937 in the stocks included in this index, apportioned according to their monetary importance, and had reinvested in these stocks all cash income which he received. This represents an average return of 10.1 per cent at compound interest for each of the 67 years, which is only 1.9 per cent more than the average annual return of 8.2 per cent[5] on all industrial stocks for this period. The second most profitable group for the 67 years was Telephone and Telegraph with a gain of 23,849 per cent, or slightly over 8.5 per cent per annum. At the opposite extreme is Shipping and Shipbuilding with a shrinkage of 48 per cent, or 0.97 of 1 per cent a year.

Considering the period from 1891 to 1937, it is possible to include 7 additional industries which made their appearance in the quotations subsequent to 1871. One of these new groups, Electrical Equipment, proves to have been the most profitable for this later period, recording a return of 7,406 per cent in 47 years, or 9.6 per cent a year. The second most profitable for this period was Miscellaneous Services with a gain of 6,748 per cent or 9.4 per cent a year, and the least profitable was again Shipping and Shipbuilding with a shrinkage of 33 per cent, or 0.85 of 1 per cent a year.

For the 27 years from 1911 to 1937, there are 17 new industries added which had not appeared as early as 1891. One of these, Chemicals, proved to be the most profitable with a return of 5,010 per cent, or 15.7 per cent a year. The least profitable for this period was Fertilizer with a loss of about 71 per cent, or 4.5 per cent a year. . . .

Looking at the last seven years, 1931 to 1937, the biggest gain was recorded by Miscellaneous Services—the index at this point including finance companies. This group showed a return of 398 per cent, or 25.8 per cent a year. The second most profitable group for the last seven years was Beverages with a gain of 142 per cent, or 13.5 per cent a year, the least profitable being Tobacco Chains with a shrinkage of 83 per cent, or 22.4 per cent a year.

It is evident . . . that conflicting forces have been at work during the last 12 years. Up to that time there was no evidence of a change in yields, earnings-price ratios, or in the trends of stock prices. From 1926 to 1929 there occurred, particularly in industrial and public utility stock prices, a dizzy upsurge which carried them far above the levels usually prevailing in the past with regard to earnings and dividends payments.

This was known as the "New Era" and the rise in prices which occurred was probably to some extent justified on the basis of the history of stocks for the preceding 60 years. During that period there is considerable evidence to support the conclusion that stocks in general sold at about three-quarters of their true value as measured by the return to the investor. However, in the last seven years increased taxation and other governmental controls have constituted factors unfavorable to the outlook for private owners of the means of production. These developments, to some degree at least, form a rational basis for the drastic downward revision in common-stock values which has taken place since 1929.

Notes

1. Maurice Leven, Harold G. Moulton, and Clark Warburton, *America's Capacity to Consume*, Washington, 1934, p. 165.
2. *Conference Board Bulletin*, Vol. 11, No. 5, April 19, 1937.
3. This survey included such sources of information as the *Commercial and Financial Chronicle, Stock Exchange Manual* by Henry Hamon, *Stockholder, Banker's Magazine, Hunt's Merchants Magazine, New York Journal of Commerce, New York Herald, New York Times,* and *New York Tribune.*
4. *The Security Markets*, Twentieth Century Fund, 1935, Appendix IX, p. 748.
5. This figure represents the annual rate of gain as computed between the two points in time, January 1871 and December 1937. For this reason it differs slightly from the annual rate of gain, 8.4 per cent, indicated by a least-squares first-degree parabola fitted to the logarithms of the Series C index of industrial stocks. . . .

Rates of Return on Investments in Common Stocks

Lawrence Fisher
James H. Lorie

When Jim Lorie and Lawrence Fisher produced their 1964 study of rates of return on common stocks from 1926 to 1960, it was a true breakthrough. Those who oversummarized the results as "9 percent" missed two central points: most of the 9 percent came from reinvestment of dividends—not capital gains—and the distribution of returns around the mean was also important. Even so, the study encouraged investors to think more carefully about the truly long term.

This article presents data on rates of return on investments in common stocks. It answers the question of how much gain or loss an individual investor might have realized if he had bought all New York Stock Exchange common stocks—at five different dates and held them for varying lengths of time during the thirty-five years from 1926 through 1960, a total of twenty-two time periods. . . .

Rates of Return on Investments in Common Stocks

It is surprising to realize that there have been no measurements of the rates of return on investments in common stocks that could be consid-

Reprinted from *The Journal of Business* 37 (January 1964), pp. 1–21. Chicago: University of Chicago.

ered accurate and definitive. There have been many efforts, but each has been deficient in at least one crucial respect. Some have lacked comprehensiveness, having dealt only with a selection of individual securities such as those in one of the popular stock market averages. This study embraces all common stock listed on the New York Stock Exchange during the time periods covered—some seventeen hundred of them. Again, earlier studies have dealt only with one or two brief time periods in contrast to the twenty-two time periods within a thirty-five-year span covered here. Finally, all other studies have been deficient because they have ignored taxes and transaction costs. In this study actual New York Stock Exchange round-lot commission rates, as they existed on all purchase, sales and re-investment dates, have been included in the calculations; and all federal taxes, as they applied to income from dividends or capital gains at specific times in selected tax brackets, have been taken into consideration. As can be seen from Figures 1 and 2, taxes and commissions can have large effects on rates of return. This study has shortcomings, but we believe that they are less pronounced than those of previous work.

Rates of Return with Reinvestment of Dividends

Figure 1 shows the results of investing an equal sum of money in each company having one or more issues of common stock listed on the New York Stock Exchange at the beginning of each period *and* of reinvesting dividends as received throughout the periods in the stock of the company making the payment. The results referred to thus include dividends and capital appreciation. Stocks listed at the beginning of any time period receive equal weight. A stock listed after the beginning and before the end of a particular time period is included whenever holders of other stocks receive its shares and also to whatever extent funds for reinvestment became available through the delisting of stocks that still possess value. To be more specific, when a stock is delisted, it is sold over the counter and the proceeds are spread evenly over all stocks listed on that date.

It should be emphasized that Figure 1 represents the rates of return— or rates of capital appreciation—that result from the adoption of only one of a large number of possible investment policies. An illustrative alternative would be the allocation of investment funds in proportion to the value of shares outstanding.

FIGURE 1

Rates of Return on Investment in Common Stocks Listed on the New York Stock Exchange with Reinvestment of Dividends* (Per Cent per Annum Compounded Annually)

Period	Tax Exempt		$10,000 in 1960		$50,000 in 1960	
	Cash-to-Portfolio**	Cash-to-Cash***	Cash-to-Portfolio	Cash-to-Cash	Cash-to-Portfolio	Cash-to-Cash
1/26–12/60	9.0	9.0	8.4	8.2	7.4	6.8
1/26– 9/29	20.4	20.3	20.4	20.3	20.3	19.4
1/26– 6/32	−16.5	−16.8	−16.5	−16.8	−16.5	−13.4
1/26–12/40	2.4	2.3	2.4	2.4	2.2	2.4
1/26–12/50	6.8	6.8	6.3	6.1	5.5	5.1
9/29– 6/32	−48.4	−48.8	−48.4	−48.8	−48.2	−40.6
9/29–12/40	−3.0	−3.1	−3.0	−2.9	−3.0	−2.3
9/29–12/50	4.9	4.8	4.3	4.1	3.5	3.2
9/29–12/60	7.7	7.7	7.0	6.8	5.9	5.4
6/32–12/40	21.3	21.1	21.2	20.8	20.8	19.5
6/32–12/50	18.6	18.6	17.8	17.5	16.5	15.5
6/32–12/60	17.4	17.3	16.5	16.2	15.0	14.1
12/50–12/52	12.5	12.0	11.1	10.0	9.0	7.1
12/50–12/54	17.9	17.6	16.6	15.3	14.4	11.6
12/50–12/56	17.0	16.8	15.8	14.8	13.7	11.4
12/50–12/58	16.5	16.4	15.4	14.6	13.4	11.4
12/50–12/60	14.8	14.7	13.8	13.1	12.0	10.3
12/55–12/56	6.4	5.4	5.7	4.6	4.0	2.8
12/55–12/57	−3.7	−4.2	−4.4	−4.0	−6.0	−4.2
12/55–12/58	13.0	12.6	12.2	11.1	10.5	8.2
12/55–12/59	14.0	13.7	13.3	12.2	11.6	9.2
12/55–12/60	11.2	10.9	10.5	9.6	8.9	7.2

*The data underlying this figure have been exhaustively checked. We are confident that any subsequent refinement or adjustment will do no more than change an occasional figure after the decimal point.

**"Cash-to-Portfolio" means the net rate of return which would have been realized after paying commissions and taxes (if any) on each transaction but continuing to hold the portfolio at the end of each period.

***"Cash-to-Cash" means the net return which would have been realized after paying commissions and taxes (if any) on each transaction including the sale of the portfolio at the end of each period.

Except for the large amount of double-counting involved, this latter policy, in contrast to the one underlying Figures 1 and 2, would indicate the rates of return available to all the investors considered together.[1] That is, new investors as a group might be able to allocate funds among securities in proportion to the value of shares outstanding but could not invest equal amounts in each security without changing many prices by a substantial amount.

The decision to invest equal amounts in each company with common stock listed on the Exchange was based on the desire to calculate rates

FIGURE 2

Rates of Return on Investment in Common Stocks Listed on the New York Stock Exchange without Reinvestment of Dividends* (Per Cent per Annum Compounded Annually)

Period	Tax Exempt		$10,000 in 1960		$50,000 in 1960	
	Cash-to-Portfolio**	Cash-to-Cash***	Cash-to-Portfolio	Cash-to-Cash	Cash-to-Portfolio	Cash-to-Cash
1/26–12/60	6.9	6.9	6.7	6.5	6.2	5.8
1/26– 9/29	19.8	19.7	19.8	19.7	19.8	18.9
1/26– 6/32	−13.2	−13.4	−13.2	−13.4	−13.2	−10.8
1/26–12/40	1.6	1.6	1.6	1.7	1.6	1.8
1/26–12/50	5.1	5.1	4.9	4.7	4.5	4.2
9/29– 6/32	−48.2	−48.6	−48.2	−48.6	−48.1	−40.4
9/29–12/40	−4.9	−5.0	−4.9	−4.7	−4.8	−3.8
9/29–12/50	2.3	2.2	2.0	2.0	1.8	1.7
9/29–12/60	4.9	4.9	4.6	4.4	4.3	3.8
6/32–12/40	24.5	24.4	24.5	24.1	23.8	22.5
6/32–12/50	21.4	21.4	20.8	20.5	19.3	18.5
6/32–12/60	20.5	20.5	19.7	19.5	17.8	17.3
12/50–12/52	12.6	12.1	11.2	10.1	9.1	7.2
12/50–12/54	17.3	17.1	16.1	14.9	14.1	11.5
12/50–12/56	16.6	16.5	15.5	14.6	13.6	11.3
12/50–12/58	16.2	16.1	15.2	14.4	13.3	11.3
12/50–12/60	15.0	14.9	14.0	18.2	12.1	10.4
12/55–12/56	6.5	5.4	5.7	4.6	4.0	2.8
12/55–12/57	−3.3	−3.8	−4.1	−3.7	−5.8	−4.1
12/55–12/58	12.6	12.2	11.9	10.8	10.3	8.1
12/55–12/59	13.7	13.4	13.0	12.0	11.4	9.1
12/55–12/60	11.1	10.9	10.4	9.6	8.9	7.2

*The data underlying this figure have been exhaustively checked. We are confident that any subsequent refinement or adjustment will do no more than change an occasional figure after the decimal point.

**"Cash-to-Portfolio" means the net rate of return which would have been realized after paying commissions and taxes (if any) on each transaction but continuing to hold the portfolio at the end of each period.

***"Cash-to-Cash" means the net return which would have been realized after paying commissions and taxes (if any) on each transaction including the sale of the portfolio at the end of each period.

of return that would on the average be available to the individual investor who selected stocks at random with equal probabilities of selection—that is, exercised no judgment. A policy of allocating funds in proportion to shares outstanding or according to any other criterion implies less neutrality of judgment in making investments.[2]

Since dividends constitute income, the results of reinvesting dividends would obviously vary with the individual investor's tax bracket. For the purposes of this study, three brackets were chosen, although any other set of tax rates could easily be substituted for those used.

The first category, "Tax Exempt," shows the rate of return that might have been realized by a tax-exempt institution.

Results in the $10,000 income class were computed in the following manner:

1. The marginal income tax rate as of 1960 was figured for a married man with standard deductions and an adjusted gross income of $10,000.
2. For each previous year, a tax rate was determined for a man who held the same relative position in the pattern of income distribution existing in those years as the man with $10,000 income in 1960.
3. The appropriate tax rate for such a married man was then applied in all preceding years.

A precisely analogous procedure was used in computing results in the third category, the $50,000 income class.[3]

For each period in each income class, two rates of return are shown. The first, "Cash-to-Portfolio," shows the after-tax rate of interest, compounded annually, which an individual would have had to get on a sum equal to the gross purchase price of the portfolio at the beginning of a period in order to equal the value of the portfolio at the end of the period. The second figure, "Cash-to-Cash," indicates the rate of interest, compounded annually, that would be required on the value of the initial portfolio in order to equal the value of the sum at the terminal date after selling the portfolio and paying the commissions and the capital gains tax applicable.

These rates of return speak for themselves and require little comment. The periods were chosen for obvious reasons. The period from 1925 to 1960 is a long span with booms and depressions—prime examples of each!—and war and peace. The periods beginning in September, 1929, were included to indicate the experience of those who invested at the height of the stock-market boom of the 1920's. The periods beginning in June, 1932, were included to show the results of investing at the nadir of this country's worst depression. The numerous brief, recent periods were included to bring details of postwar experience into sharp focus.

Aside from most periods ending in 1932 or 1940, the rates of return are surprisingly high. For half the twenty-two periods, the rates are above 10 per cent per annum compounded annually; and for two-thirds of the periods, the rates exceed 6 per cent.

Rates of Return without Reinvestment of Dividends

Figure 2 presents the rates of return on common stocks listed on the New York Stock Exchange with no reinvestment of dividends, that is, under the assumption that dividends are spent for consumers goods and services at the time they are received. The method of calculation is analogous to that used to compute the yield-to-maturity of a bond. The cost of the stock at the beginning of a time period is analogous to the purchase price of the bond; dividends are analogous to interest payments; and the value of the stock at the end of the period is analogous to the sum received by the holder of a bond when it matures. The rate of return is the rate of discounting which makes the stream of after-tax cash flows have a present value of zero.

At first, one might expect the rates in Figure 2 to be significantly lower than in Figure 1, whereas in fact the rates are quite similar for most of the periods. This similarity merely reflects the fact that the rate of appreciation in the prices of stocks after the receipt of dividends was on the average about the same as the rate of appreciation before the receipt of dividends. When the latter rate was higher, the rates in Figure 2 are lower than those in Figure 1 and vice versa. The individual who reinvests his dividends is obviously wealthier at an ending date than is the individual who spends them. On the average he also has a great deal more invested in his portfolio. Thus, some rates in Figure 1 are higher than the corresponding rates in Figure 2; some are lower; and several are the same.

Figure 3 shows rate of capital appreciation or gain, ignoring dividends.

Comparison with Other Investment Media

Comparable data for other investment media are not available, but there is some information on realized rates of return on a *before-tax* basis. The most nearly complete data are for savings in commercial banks, mutual savings banks, and savings and loan associations. Savings in these institutions never earned as much as 6 per cent per annum for any of the twenty-two time periods listed in Figure 1 and for most of the period 1926–60 earned less than 4 per cent.[4]

Data on mortgage loans made by commercial banks and life insurance companies on non-farm homes are available for 1920–47 and for

FIGURE 3

Rates of Change in Value of Investment in Common Stocks Listed on the New York Stock Exchange, Ignoring Dividends* (Per Cent per Annum Compounded Annually)

| Period | Tax Exempt | | $10,000 in 1960 | | $50,000 in 1960 | |
	Cash-to-Portfolio**	Cash-to-Cash***	Cash-to-Portfolio	Cash-to-Cash	Cash-to-Portfolio	Cash-to-Cash
1/26–12/60	3.9	3.8	3.9	3.6	4.0	3.3
1/26– 9/29	15.7	15.6	15.7	15.6	15.7	14.8
1/26– 6/32	−21.0	−21.2	−21.0	−21.2	−20.9	−17.8
1/26–12/40	−2.8	−2.9	−2.8	−2.8	−2.7	−2.4
1/26–12/50	1.3	1.3	1.4	1.2	1.5	1.1
9/29– 6/32	−51.5	−51.9	−51.5	−51.9	−51.3	−43.4
9/29–12/40	−8.0	−8.0	−8.0	−7.7	−7.6	−6.4
9/29–12/50	−.5	−.6	−.5	−.6	−.2	−.3
9/29–12/60	2.5	2.4	2.5	2.2	2.7	2.1
6/32–12/40	16.9	16.8	16.9	16.4	16.8	15.1
6/32–12/50	13.1	13.0	13.0	12.5	13.0	11.7
6/32–12/60	11.9	11.9	11.9	11.4	11.8	10.8
12/50–12/52	5.9	5.4	5.9	4.8	5.9	4.0
12/50–12/54	11.4	11.1	11.3	10.1	11.3	8.6
12/50–12/56	10.8	10.7	10.8	9.8	10.8	8.4
12/50–12/58	10.7	10.6	10.7	9.8	10.7	8.5
12/50–12/60	9.6	9.4	9.5	8.7	9.5	7.6
12/55–12/56	1.5	.4	1.4	.4	1.4	.2
12/55–12/57	−8.3	−8.8	−8.3	−7.9	−8.3	−6.6
12/55–12/58	8.0	7.6	8.0	6.9	8.0	5.8
12/55–12/59	9.3	9.0	9.3	8.2	9.3	6.9
12/55–12/60	6.7	6.5	6.7	5.8	6.7	5.0

*The data underlying this table have been exhaustively checked. We are confident that any subsequent refinement or adjustment will do no more than change an occasional figure after the decimal point.

**"Cash-to-Portfolio" means the net rate of return which would have been realized after paying commissions and taxes (if any) on each transaction but continuing to hold the portfolio at the end of each period.

***"Cash-to-Cash" means the net return which would have been realized after paying commissions and taxes (if any) on each transaction including the sale of the portfolio at the end of each period.

some subperiods.[5] When all types of mortgages are considered together, realized yields never exceeded 6 per cent, never fell below 4 per cent, and averaged about 5 per cent.

Realized yields on municipal and U.S. government bonds, as indicated by Standard and Poor indexes, ranged from −7.0 to +7.8 per cent and averaged less than 4 per cent during the twenty-two time periods listed in Figure 2.

Average realized yields on large issues of corporate bonds are available for 1900–58.[6] These yields ranged from −6 per cent to just over

15 per cent during periods from 1920–43. The very high yields were achieved during the recovery from the depression of 1929–32 when prices of industrial bonds, in particular, advanced sharply in price. During most periods, yields varied between 5 and 8 per cent and in recent periods have been lower.

The fact that many persons choose investments with a substantially lower average rate of return than that available on common stocks suggests the essentially conservative nature of those investors and the extent of their concern about the risk of loss inherent in common stocks. And yet their experience with mortgage foreclosures during the 1930's and the substantial rate of default on bonds during the same period shows that even such ''conservative'' investments carry considerable risks.

Conclusions

During the entire thirty-five year period, 1926–60, the rates of return, compounded annually, on common stocks listed on the New York Stock Exchange, with reinvestment of dividends, were 9.0 per cent for tax exempt institutions; 8.2 per cent for persons in the $10,000 income class; and 6.8 per cent for persons in the $50,000 income class. . . . These rates are substantially higher than for alternative investment media for which data are available. It is probably worth noting here that a dollar earning 9.0 per cent per annum, compounded annually, would be worth over $20 in 35 years.

The rates for the postwar periods are substantially higher than for the periods prior to the war except during the period of recovery after 1932. It will perhaps be surprising to many that the rates have consistently been so high. For the postwar period (1950–60), as a whole, rates have exceeded 10 per cent for all tax brackets considered, even after payment of capital gains taxes, and this has been true for most subperiods as well.

Rates of return without reinvestment of dividends varied from period to period above and below rates with reinvestments, but on the whole the rates were similar. This merely reflects the fact that, on the average, rates of appreciation in the prices of stocks after the receipt of dividends were similar to rates before the receipt of dividends.

Notes

1. By "double counting" we mean the ownership by one company of stock in another listed company. For example, Du Pont owns large amounts of stock in General Motors. Allocation of investment funds in proportion to the value of Du Pont and General Motors stock outstanding involves counting some of the General Motors shares twice.
2. We made an estimate of the rates of return available from investing in proportion to the value of shares outstanding by using the Standard and Poor's Index of Common Stocks on the New York Stock Exchange—an index weighted according to the value of shares outstanding—and the Standard and Poor's dividend series. For three of the five starting dates covered in Figure 1, the Standard and Poor's rate of return was generally higher; for two of the starting dates, the yield was lower. No systematic differences were detectable, and on the average the yields based on the two different investment policies were similar.
3. For example, men with incomes of $10,000 or $50,000 in 1960 would have had incomes of $1,780 or $8,950, respectively, in 1933. The ranges of marginal tax rates were from 0 to 25 per cent for dividends for the $10,000 man and from 0 to 62 per cent for the $50,000 man. The capital gains tax rates ranged from 0 to 13 per cent for the $10,000 man and from 5 to 42 per cent for the $50,000 man.
4. Based on (1929–60) figures of U.S. Savings and Loan League *Fact Book*, 1955 and 1962 editions, whose sources are as follows: (1) (savings and loan associations) data of members of Federal Home Loan Bank System, (2) (mutual savings banks) Association of Mutual Savings Banks, (3) (commercial banks) data of Board of Governors of the Federal Reserve System and Federal Deposit Insurance Corporation. The yields for these years were computed by dividing the total cash and credited dividends or interest by the average of deposits at the beginning and end of each year.

   Nineteen twenty-six Figures: (savings and loan associations) R. W. Goldsmith, *A Study of Saving in the United States* (Princeton, N.J.: Princeton University Press, 1955), Vol. I, p. 447; and (savings and commercial banks) J. V. Lintner, *Mutual Savings Banks in the Savings and Mortgage Markets* (Boston, Mass.: Division of Research, Graduate School of Business Administration, Harvard University, 1948), p. 477.
5. J. E. Morton, *Urban Mortgage Lending: Comparative Markets and Experience* (Princeton, N.J.: Princeton University Press, 1956), p.114.
6. W. B. Hickman, *Statistical Measures of Corporate Bond Financing Since 1900* (Princeton, N.J.: Princeton University Press, 1960), pp. 291, 298–301. Hickman's sample included all straight corporate bond issues of $5 million or more.

   See also David Durand, "A Quarterly Series of Corporate Basic Yields, 1952–57, and Some Attendant Reservations," *Journal of Finance,* Vol. XIII, No. 3 (September, 1958).

   Basic yields, together with some discussion of the basic-yield concept, appeared in David Durand, *Basic Yields of Corporate Bonds, 1900–1942* (Technical Paper No. 3 [New York: National Bureau of Economic Research, 1942]). The series was later brought up to date, with additional discussion, in David Durand and Willis J. Winn, *Basic Yields of Bonds, 1925–1947: Their Measurement and Pattern* (Technical Paper No. 6 [New York: National Bureau of Economic Research, 1947]). Later basic-yield figures have appeared in the *Economic Almanac* and the *Statistical Abstract of the United States.*

Stocks, Bonds, Bills, and Inflation: Year-by-Year Historical Returns (1926–1974)

Roger G. Ibbotson
Rex A. Sinquefield

Roger Ibbotson and Rex Sinquefield developed rigorous analyses of historical rates of return in their seminal paper excerpted here. They then went on to show how their analyses of past returns could be used to generate realistic projections of long-term average future return expectations—an important advancement on the road to today's way of thinking about asset allocation decisions.

Introduction

In 1964, Lawrence Fisher and James H. Lorie published in this *Journal* their classic study, "Rates of Return on Investments in Common Stocks."[1] In 1968, they extended their study to include all yearly holding period returns from 1926 to 1965.[2] These two articles prompted a widespread interest in the long-run behavior of stock market returns. Motivated by their example, we present in this paper year-by-year *historical* rates of return for five major classes of assets in the United States. In a companion paper forthcoming in this *Journal*,[3] we show

Excerpted from *Journal of Business* 49 (January 1976), pp. 11–43. Chicago: University of Chicago.

how to use the historical data in simulating *future* return distributions for the same five asset classes.

The five asset classes included in this study are (1) common stocks, (2) long-term U.S. government bonds, (3) long-term corporate bonds, (4) U.S. Treasury bills, and (5) consumer goods (inflation). For each asset we present total rates of return which reflect dividends or interest income as well as capital gains or losses. . . .

Basic Historical Series

We initially construct the five basic return series covering common stocks, long-term government and corporate bonds, Treasury bills, and inflation. Annual returns for each asset are formed by compounding monthly returns. In all cases, returns are formed assuming no taxes or transactions costs.

Common Stocks

Our common stocks total return index is based upon the Standard and Poor's Composite Index.[4] We use this index because it is a readily available, carefully constructed, market value weighted benchmark of common stock performance. By market value weighted, we mean that the weight of each stock in the index equals its price times the number of shares outstanding. Currently the S&P Composite includes 500 of the largest stocks (in terms of stock market value) in the United States; prior to March 1957 it consisted of 90 of the largest stocks. To the extent that the stocks included in the S&P Composite Index represent the market value of stocks in the United States, the weighting scheme allows the returns of the index to correspond to the aggregate stock market returns in the U.S. economy.

Although Standard and Poor's reports its Composite Index exclusive of dividends, it also reports a quarterly dividend series. Except for the most recent years (since 1968) the dividend series is available only in the form of four-quarter moving totals. However, given four separate dividends for any one year, it is possible to unravel the moving totals into separate quarterly dividends for all the years prior to 1968. . . . Monthly dividends are then formed by proportioning the quarterly dividends into the three months of the quarter according to recently observed proportions. . . .

Since there will inevitably be comparisons between our results and those of the Fisher and Lorie studies, . . . some differences in methodology should be noted. Their studies measured annual returns (calculated like ours from monthly returns) of an *equally* weighted portfolio of all New York Stock Exchange (NYSE) common stocks. Thus, their weighting scheme measures the performance of an investor who chose stocks through simple random selection. Ours measures the return to an investor who "bought the market" in the sense that the stocks included in the S&P Composite Index represent most of the value of the U.S. publicly traded stocks.

Another difference between our results and the results of Fisher and Lorie is that they measure returns from a buy and hold strategy, while our portfolio weighting scheme is continuously updated. This allows them to measure the returns on 40 separate portfolios, one starting each year from 1926 to 1965. For example, their 1926–65 period return (compounded annually) is the return on a portfolio equally weighted as of January 1926 and held (not reweighted except by market movements and dividend reinvestment) throughout the entire period. In comparison, our 1926–65 period return (compounded annually) is the return on a portfolio that is market weighted each month throughout the entire period. Our procedure only approximates a buy and hold strategy since our weighting scheme takes into account increases and decreases in the amount of a company's stock outstanding as well as any changes in the stocks included in the S&P Composite Index. An advantage of their buy and hold procedure is that they can present return series for various tax rates with and without commissions. An advantage of our procedure is that our returns can easily be interpreted since they always reflect a market weighted portfolio.

Long-Term U.S. Government Bonds

To measure the total returns of long-term U.S. government bonds, we construct a bond portfolio using the bond data obtained from the U.S. Government Bond File at the Center for Research in Security Prices.[5] Our objective is to maintain a 20-year-term bond portfolio whose returns do not reflect potential tax benefits, impaired negotiability, or special redemption or call privileges. We follow with a brief description of the types of bonds included and excluded from the portfolio. . . .

Prior to March 1941, the income from almost all U.S. government bonds was exempt from "normal" income taxes. However, some of the bonds were subject to the surtax. Since surtax rates were far higher than normal tax rates for large investors, the returns (yields) of the bonds subject to the surtax are not lowered to reflect substantial tax advantages. Therefore, we choose to include in our index only those bonds subject to the surtax during the period 1926–March 1941. Our bond returns are somewhat analogous to our stock returns during most of the period since cash dividends were also exempt from normal income taxes until 1936. The income on all bonds issued subsequent to March 1941 is subject to federal income taxation.

The large size and large number of investors associated with government issues usually ensures high marketability. As direct obligations of the U.S. government, default risk is virtually nonexistent. Consequently, government bonds usually are ideal collateral. However, some 2¼ and 2½ percent bonds issued during the 1940s were restricted until 1953 from bank portfolios, substantially reducing their collateral value. Since returns from bank ineligible bonds are inflated to compensate for their impaired negotiability, these bonds are excluded from the index.

Many government bonds (commonly known as "flower" bonds) have a redemption feature which allows the investor to redeem his bonds at *par* (plus accrued interest) in payment of federal estate taxes. . . . Since part of the return on these bonds is the capital gain from early redemption, the return exclusive of the redemption is lower in general than the return on other bonds not possessing the redemption feature. We therefore seek to avoid using flower bonds in the index. . . . By including only those flower bonds with high yields and prices relative to other existing flower bonds, we effectively restrict the index to bonds whose redemption features are seldom exercised while they are in the index.

Finally, our index must take into account that most long-term government bonds were callable by the U.S. Treasury after a designated first call date. For callable bonds, it is unclear whether the life of the bond should be measured by the first call or the maturity date. We attempt to reduce the problem by avoiding bonds with early first call dates relative to their maturity dates. We then attempt to hold a 20-year life portfolio with the life arbitrarily measured as the simple average of the maturity and first call dates minus the holding period date. . . .

The above-mentioned constraints severely limit the bonds eligible for inclusion in our index. The problem is that the U.S. government bonds available at any one time usually have somewhat homogeneous characteristics. We can either build a multibond index (say by linearly combining bond lives to satisfy our 20-year term objective), or select the one bond which best fits our criteria. We choose to form a one-bond portfolio since there are some periods when only one bond reasonably fits our criteria. However, the lack of diversification in a one-bond portfolio is not a serious defect. Since we assume no default risk, one fairly priced bond adequately reflects the return of other bonds with similar characteristics (maturity date, first call date, coupon, tax, etc.). . . .

Long-Term Corporate Bonds

Since most large corporate bond transactions take place over the counter, the natural source of data is a major dealer. Salomon Brothers has already constructed the High-Grade Long-Term Corporate Bond Index. . . . We use this monthly index from its beginning in 1969 through 1974. For the period 1946–68 we backdate the Salomon Brothers' Index using Salomon Brothers' monthly data and similar methodology. For the period 1926–45 we use the Standard and Poor's monthly High-Grade Corporate Composite Bond Index, . . . assuming a 4 percent coupon and a 20-year maturity.

The purpose of the Salomon Brothers' Index is to approximate the total returns that would be earned by holding the entire high-grade long-term corporate bond market. The relevant market is defined as all industrial and utility issues which were originally publicly offered with a maturity of 1985 or longer, a Moody rating of Aaa or Aa, and an outstanding par amount of at least $25 million.

The Salomon Brothers' Index is constructed by computing a weighted average of the returns from 17 representative bonds. The yields of these bonds are identical with 17 Salomon Brothers' corporate bond monthly yield series listed as industrial or utility by coupon range.[6] Each of the 17 representative bonds is assigned a maturity, a coupon, and a weight by determining the market weighted average maturity and coupon in each coupon range and the weight of each coupon range in the market. Monthly prices and total returns are then computed for each bond given its yield, coupon, and maturity date. The index is formed as a cumulative wealth relative of the weighted average of the 17 bond returns. At the beginning of 1969, the Salomon Brothers' Index had an average maturity of approximately 25 years.

Although the Salomon Brothers' Index is available only from 1969, eight of their 17 corporate bond yield series were initiated prior to 1969 while one series was initiated as early as 1946. We backdate the index by assuming the mean coupon in the coupon range defined for each of the yield series and a 20-year maturity date. Bond prices are then computed, given the yield, coupon, and maturity date. . . .

Since the Salomon Brothers' data starts in 1946, it is necessary to link another index for the period 1926–45. We use the monthly yield series represented in Standard and Poor's High-Grade Composite Bond Index, assuming a 4 percent coupon, a 20-year maturity, and calculate bond prices accordingly. . . .

United States Treasury Bills

For the U.S. Treasury Bill Index, we again use the data in the CRSP U.S. Government Bond File. Our objective is to construct an index that includes the shortest-term bills not less than 1 month in maturity. We also want our index to reflect achievable returns. Therefore, rather than compute yields, we measure 1-month holding period returns for a one-bill portfolio.

Although U.S. Treasury bills were initiated as early as 1929, the U.S. Government Bond File does not include any bills until 1931. Prior to that time, we use short-term coupon bonds. The bills are quoted on a discount basis without coupon, and their returns were exempt from all income taxes until March 1941. Thereafter, their returns were subject to normal income taxes as well as any surtaxes.

Beginning in the early 1940s [and continuing until March, 1951], the yields (returns) on Treasury bills were pegged by the government at low rates. Coupons on new government bond issues were also pegged, but the effect on returns was not as great. . . .

We chose to include in the one-bill portfolio the bill having the shortest term without maturing in less than 1 month, after allowing for delivery dates. . . . This procedure allows us to be continually invested. In the case where the delivery date and the maturity date would be the same, the bond is matured. . . .

Inflation

We utilize the Consumer Price Index (CPI) . . . to measure inflation, which is the rate of change of consumer goods prices. . . .

Although we consider the CPI as the best measure of inflation available at the consumer level, there are numerous problems in applying it as a cost-of-living measure. . . . Its construction is subject to statistical problems related to the sampling and processing of data. It is also subject to conceptual problems. . . . In addition, the index is not continuous since it was substantially revised in the years 1940, 1953, 1964. Numerous minor revisions have also been made from time to time.

. . . The CPI currently includes about 400 items priced in 56 urban regions weighted by their populations. Thus, the CPI reflects a weighted average of many component indices. While most of the components of the CPI are priced monthly, some are priced quarterly, a few are priced semiannually or annually, and some reflect contractual rent agreements rather than current prices.

Historical Highlights

Common Stocks

Some highlights of common stock annual returns are:

1. Over the period of 1926–74, stocks returned 8.5 percent per year compounded annually. Excluding dividends, stocks returned 3.5 percent per year. Over the same period, both risk premia and inflation-adjusted stock returns were 6.1 percent per year.

2. Comparing our stock returns with those measured by Fisher and Lorie over the period 1926–65, we find a return of 10.4 percent from holding a market weighted portfolio with weights updated continually, while they find a return of 9.3 percent from holding a portfolio that is equally weighted as of January 1926. . . .

3. Over the entire period of study, the arithmetic mean of the annual returns was 10.9 percent for stocks and 8.8 percent for risk premia and inflation-adjusted stock returns. Although stocks outperformed the other assets in the study, their returns were also far more volatile. The standard deviation of common stock annual returns was 22.5 percent, while the returns ranged from 54.0 to −43.3 percent.

4. Stock returns were positive almost two-thirds of the years (32 out of 49 years). The longest period over which a year-end investor in our

common stock index would have earned a negative return was the 14-year period 1929–42.

5. The 1974 common stock return was −26.4 percent, the third worst yearly return throughout the period and the worst since 1937. The investor who held our common stock index through year-end 1974 would have lost value if he had purchased the index as of any year-end from 1967 on. On the other hand, the purchaser of the index as of any year-end prior to 1967 would be ahead in (nominal) value as of year-end 1974.

6. Five-year annual calendar holding period returns ranged from a high of 23.9 percent during the period 1950–54 to a low of −12.5 percent during the period 1928–32. The highest 10-year annual return was 20.1 percent earned from 1949 to 1958, while the lowest 10-year annual return was −0.9 percent earned from 1929 to 1938. For 20-year calendar holding periods, the highest annual return was 16.9 percent earned in the period 1942–61, while the lowest annual return was 3.1 percent earned in the period 1929–48.

Long-Term U.S. Government Bonds

Some highlights of long-term U.S. government annual returns are:

1. Long-term U.S. government bonds returned 3.2 percent per year compounded annually over the period 1926–74. The entire period annual returns for both maturity premia and inflation-adjusted long-term government bonds were 1.0 percent.

2. The arithmetic means of the annual nominal returns, maturity premia, and real returns from long-term government bonds are 3.4 percent, 1.1 percent, and 1.3 percent, respectively. These annual return series are far less volatile than the common stock series. However, the maturity premia and the real return series are quite volatile relative to their own historical means.

3. Long-term government bond returns were positive 37 out of the 49 years. Their annual returns ranged from 16.8 percent to −9.2 percent.

4. Five-year annual calendar holding period returns for long-term government bonds ranged from a high of 8.1 percent during the period 1970–74 to a low of −2.1 percent during the period 1965–69. The highest 10-year annual return was 5.7 percent earned during 1932–41, while the lowest 10-year annual return was −0.1 percent earned during

1950–59. For 20-year calendar holding periods, the highest annual return was 4.9 percent earned during the period 1926–45, while the lowest annual return was 0.7 percent earned during the period 1950–69.

Long-Term Corporate Bonds

Some highlights of long-term corporate bond annual returns are:

1. Long-term corporate bonds returned 3.6 percent per year compounded annually over the period 1926–74. Default premia returned 0.3 percent, while the inflation-adjusted corporate bond annual return was 1.4 percent.

2. The arithmetic means of the annual nominal returns, default premia, and real returns resulting from long-term corporate bonds are 3.7 percent, 0.4 percent, and 1.7 percent, respectively. The volatility of long-term corporate bonds is similar to that of long-term government bonds. Again, the default premia and the real return series are quite volatile relative to their historical means.

3. Long-term corporate bonds had positive returns in 39 out of the 49 years. Their returns ranged from 18.4 percent to −8.1 percent.

4. Five-year annual calendar holding period returns for long-term corporate bonds ranged from a high of 10.3 percent during the period 1932–36 to a low of −2.2 percent during the period 1965–69. The highest 10-year annual return was 7.1 percent earned during 1926–35, while the lowest 10-year annual return was 1.0 percent earned during 1947–56. For 20-year calendar holding periods, the highest annual return was 5.5 percent earned during the period 1926–45, while the lowest annual return was 1.3 percent earned during the period 1950–69.

U.S. Treasury Bills and Inflation

Some highlights of U.S. Treasury bill annual returns and annual inflation rates are:

1. During the entire period, U.S. Treasury bills returned 2.2 percent compounded annually, a rate which was approximately equal to the rate of inflation.

2. The entire period inflation-adjusted bill return was 0.1 percent. The inflation-adjusted bill return is a measure of the "real rate of interest."

Notes

1. L. Fisher and J. H. Lorie, "Rates of Return on Investments in Common Stock," *Journal of Business* 37, no. 1 (January 1964): 1–21. [See also page 477 of this volume.]
2. Lawrence Fisher and James H. Lorie, "Rates of Return on Investments in Common Stock: The Year-by-Year Record, 1926–65," *Journal of Business* 41, no. 3 (July 1968): 291–316.
3. Roger G. Ibbotson and Rex A. Sinquefield, "Stocks, Bonds, Bills and Inflation: Simulations of the Future (1976–2000)," *Journal of Business,* [49 (1976): 313–38].
4. See Standard and Poor's *Trade and Security Statistics, Security Price Index Record* (Orange, Conn.: Standard & Poor's Corp., 1974).
5. The U.S. Government Bond File was compiled by Lawrence Fisher and consists of month-end price data on virtually all negotiable direct obligations of the U.S. Treasury for the period 1926–73. We also include 1974 data which is obtained from selected issues of *The Wall Street Journal* (New York: Dow Jones Co.).
6. *An Analytical Record of Yields and Yield Spreads* (New York: Salomon Bros., May 1975).

U.S. Equity Returns from Colonial Times to the Present

Roger G. Ibbotson
Gary P. Brinson, CFA

The power of compound interest—and of long-term investing in equities—is nowhere better demonstrated than in this delightful illustration from *Investment Markets* by Gary Brinson and Roger Ibbotson.

If George Washington had put just $1 from his first Presidential salary check into U.S. equities, his heirs would have been millionaires about five times over by the mid-1980s. U.S. stocks have provided a phenomenal return to investors over the long run. Partly because of this past success, the American equity market is the largest and most closely studied market in the world. Currently, in the mid-1980s, well over 100 million shares are traded each day on the New York Stock Exchange (NYSE), with more than 100 million additional shares traded in the over-the-counter (OTC) market and on other stock exchanges. The value of outstanding equities exceeds $2 trillion.

From price appreciation alone, equities yielded a return, called a *capital appreciation return*, of 2.9 percent, compounded annually,

Reprinted from *Investment Markets—Gaining the Performance Advantage* (1987), Chapter 5, pp. 65, 67, by permission of McGraw-Hill Publishing Company, New York.

Frequency Distribution of U.S. Equity Total Returns, 1790–1985

Summary

Positive Years: 140 or 71%
Negative Years: 56 or 29%
Standard Deviation: 19.6%

−50% to −40%	−40% to −30%	−30% to −20%	−20% to −10%	−10% to 0%	0% to 10%	10% to 20%	20% to 30%	30% to 40%	40% to 50%	50% to 60%	60% to 70%	70% to 80%
					1984							
					1978							
					1970							
					1960							
					1956							
					1953	1972						
					1948	1971						
					1947	1968						
					1939	1965	1983					
					1934	1964	1982					
					1929	1959	1979					
				1981	1923	1952	1976					
				1977	1916	1942	1967					
				1969	1912	1921	1963					
				1966	1911	1909	1961					
				1962	1906	1905	1955					
				1946	1902	1900	1951					
				1941	1896	1899	1950					
				1940	1895	1897	1949					
				1932	1894	1886	1944					
				1914	1892	1878	1943					
				1913	1889	1872	1938					
				1910	1888	1871	1925					
				1890	1882	1868	1924					
				1887	1881	1865	1922					
				1883	1875	1861	1919					
				1877	1874	1855	1918					
				1873	1870	1845	1901					
				1869	1867	1844	1898					
			1973	1859	1866	1840	1891					
			1957	1853	1864	1835	1885					
			1929	1838	1851	1829	1880	1985				
			1920	1837	1849	1824	1860	1980				
			1903	1831	1848	1823	1856	1975				
			1893	1828	1847	1821	1834	1945				
			1884	1825	1846	1820	1830	1936				
			1876	1819	1833	1818	1817	1928				
			1858	1812	1827	1813	1809	1927				
		1974	1842	1811	1826	1806	1800	1915	1958	1954		
		1930	1841	1797	1822	1803	1799	1904	1935	1933		
		1917	1839	1796	1816	1802	1798	1852	1908	1862		
1931	1937	1857	1836	1795	1815	1793	1794	1850	1879	1808		1843
1807	1801	1854	1810	1792	1805	1791	1790	1832	1863	1804		1814

−50% −40% −30% −20% −10% 0% 10% 20% 30% 40% 50% 60% 70% 80%

Ranges of Yearly Returns in Percent

between the 1780s and the 1980s. Without dividends reinvested, a nominal dollar invested in 1789 would have grown to almost $450 in the 1980s. . . .

Total returns, in contrast to capital appreciation returns, include dividend reinvestment as well as price appreciation. Assuming dividends were paid from the 1790s to the 1870s at the same rate as from the 1870s to the 1980s, the compound total return was 8.2 percent per year, resulting in a value [for that nominal dollar] of almost $5 million by year-end 1985.

Nonetheless, this spectacular return came at a substantial risk to investors. Total returns were negative in about 29 percent of the years. These returns have a standard deviation of over 19 percent, another indication of their relatively wide variability. The distribution of annual total returns since 1790 is displayed as a histogram.

Evolution of the U.S. Money Market

Arthur K. Salomon

Arthur Salomon, one of the original Salomon brothers, began a distinguished tradition of research and commentary on the debt markets with a series of articles in *The New York Times.* This is one of them.

To duly appreciate the rapid growth of the United States as a money centre of international importance in 1915, it is necessary to recall events of the latter half of 1914 with which our financial development is so intimately associated.

With these experiences in mind, the financial community began the year 1915. General business being depressed, there was little demand for money with a consequent piling up of bank reserves. Lending institutions were still cautious and sought for the employment of their growing surplus quick negotiable investments, such as call loans, bank acceptances, time loans, and high-grade short-term securities. The course of call and time money against New York Stock Exchange collateral has tended downward, call money having ranged from 2½ per cent to 1½ per cent, and being obtainable at 2 per cent for almost the entire time. Time money for sixty days has ranged from 3½ per cent to as low as 2¼ per cent, for ninety days to four months at 3½ per cent to

Reprinted from *The New York Times,* January 2, 1916, Section 7, Col. 5, p. 3, by permission of The New York Times Company.

2½ per cent, and five and six months from 4 per cent to 2¾ per cent. The low rates quoted are those at which transactions have been negotiated with but slight changes for the last half of the year.

Acceptance Market Broadens

Nineteen-fifteen has witnessed a broadening of the discount market in this country in acceptances. An acceptance in brief is a draft, the payment of which is guaranteed by a second party. This gives a ready marketability depending not only upon the credit of the maker of the draft, but principally upon the credit of the acceptor.

For many years American exporters and importers had financed many of their commitments by drawing drafts on institutions and banking houses abroad which when accepted by them were discounted in European money markets. National banks, trust companies, and private bankers in this country now offered to accept drafts drawn upon them payable at a future date against the export and import of merchandise; trust companies and private bankers to finance domestic transactions based upon commodities. This power vested in our institutions coming at this time was most opportune, as it enabled them to grant credits which furthered our export trade and also assisted in conserving our surplus cotton crop, which was largely financed through the medium of the acceptance. Many hundred millions of acceptances have been discounted in the past year and have been eagerly sought for by all classes of money lenders. The rate of discount for prime acceptances to mature within ninety days ranged from 3¼ to 2 per cent, with 2⅛ to 2¼ per cent the ruling rate the last half of the year.

The degree of importance this country has assumed in the international money markets is more clearly illustrated in the short term note market by the various issues of short term securities of foreign Governments which are now dealt in.

New Foreign Securities

Early in January the Argentine Government sold to an underwriting syndicate of American bankers $15,000,000 of its one, two, and three year 6 per cent notes, which were readily absorbed. This transaction marked the beginning of a public participation in this country in the investment of securities of a South American Republic. This was followed in April by an issue of $50,000,000 one-year 5 per cent notes of the Government of France. Large issues of the Dominion of Canada and its provinces and cities have been placed in this market, maturing in from one to five years. The most important undertaking was the purchase by an American underwriting syndicate of $500,000,000 five-year 5 per cent Anglo-French external loan bonds.

During the past year we have repurchased over $1,000,000,000 of our securities formerly held by European investors. In addition thereto we have loaned European nations, through direct Government loans and credit arrangements, a sum estimated to be over $1,000,000,000.

We begin the new year with the largest gold holdings in our history, a balance of trade in our favor estimated to be $1,000,000,000, and a vast supply of capital in our money market ready to assist in developing our industrial and commercial growth as a nation.

Can the Bond Market Survive?

John F. Lyons

Regression to the mean has, eventually, dominated most market behavior. But in the interim, actual experience can be mightily un-
nerving. John Lyons describes one such example in this excerpt
from a 1969 *Institutional Investor* article.

There was a moment, only a few weeks ago, when everyone who held a
bond had a loss in it. Interest rates were not the highest in history, and
the bond market, if not in a complete rout, was at least in a retreat that
was quite uncomfortable. Institutions, of course, are the chief bond
buyers: they hold 95 per cent of the $370 billion or so outstanding.
Many of them must, by law, hold bonds, but even so, periodic chirps of
optimism have emanated from some of them: *this* is the bottom, *this* is
the bottom, *this* is the bottom.

But now the bear market in bonds is twenty-two years old. It takes a
while for the impulses of pain to travel from the source to the nerve
centers of some of the larger institutions, but it is safe to say, by now,
that the pain impulses have reached all the nerve centers. Institutions
fight to keep from buying bonds: university endowments have upped
their percentage of commons to an average of 60 per cent, and state
pension funds continue to pressure their legislatures for more equities.
And a rather cataclysmic Either/Or is shaping up:

Either a turn in the bear bond market is not far,

Excerpted from *Institutional Investor* (May 1969), pp. 29–36, 100, 105–8. New York: Institutional Investor, Inc.

Or the bond market will not survive as we knew it.

For even institutions can stand only so much pain.

The figures on corporate bond financing right now indicate pretty much what is happening to capital markets—and to the traditional form of straight bond financing. Public corporate straight debt financing declined to $6.8 billion last year from a record of $9.5 billion the year before, registering the first major decline since 1962. A substantial portion of these loans were issued by large, highly rated utility companies; manufacturing companies resorted more and more to convertible bonds, internally generated funds, and Eurodollar bonds for their financing needs. In the first quarter of 1969, new straight debt financing fell to $1.2 billion from $1.5 billion in that quarter a year earlier. On the other hand, new convertible bond financing rose to $2.4 billion from only $0.5 billion a year ago.

What has happened to bonds—and the fortunes of those who believe in them—shows the same pattern. When the prime rate at banks was 3 per cent in 1954, it cost $1,120 to invest in a U.S. government security yielding 2.57 per cent. Today, the safest of all investments can be sold in the marketplace for only about $700, and it is still yielding only about half the return of prime government bonds at the 1954 price. One of the many sweeping effects has been this: The institutions and companies whose investment strategy is built around fixed-income securities have lost an increasing amount of the public investment dollar to investing institutions that stress the equity-type investment vehicle. In the insurance field, for example, Metropolitan Life Insurance Co. had reigned as the asset king of insurance during a good part of the twentieth century by stressing fixed-income investments almost to the exclusion of everything else. But in 1967 Prudential Insurance Co. of America emerged as the asset leader with a growth rate fueled by an aggressive approach toward common stocks.

Holding the Bag

Bonds are carried on the books at cost and the real damage to the institutions has really shown up only lately when medium-grade bond rates went soaring to 8 per cent. This was unmistakable evidence that people who hold bonds have been left holding the bag—and the bag has a gaping hole in it.

Of course, not even the most pessimistic bond-market observer believes for a minute that the credit markets will break down in total disaster. But a look at what happened in Germany in the early 1920's illustrates what happens when inflation gets to real extremes. In early 1922, the German discount rate stood at 5 per cent, slightly lower than the rate in the U.S. today. But by January 1923 that rate had moved to 12 per cent; by April it was 18 per cent. And in August 1923, the German central bank was making loans at rates as high as 90 per cent. It may appear to have been a good time for Germans to short bonds and buy stock, but the cropper was that the cost of living had gone up 600 per cent in five months, and margin loans on the Berlin Stock Exchange drew a rate of 10,500 per cent a year.

The Tulipmania

Charles Mackay

Tulipmania is but one of two *dozen* extraordinary popular delusions recounted in Charles Mackay's 700-page book from 1841. The tales of John Law, the Crusades, and the South Sea Bubble are equally instructive.

——————— ▬ ———————

Quis furor, ô cives!—*Lucan.*

The tulip—so named, it is said, from a Turkish word, signifying a turban—was introduced into western Europe about the middle of the sixteenth century. Conrad Gesner, who claims the merit of having brought it into repute,—little dreaming of the commotion it was shortly afterwards to make in the world,—says that he first saw it in the year 1559, in a garden at Augsburg, belonging to the learned Counsellor Herwart, a man very famous in his day for his collection of rare exotics. The bulbs were sent to this gentleman by a friend at Constantinople, where the flower had long been a favourite. In the course of ten or eleven years after this period, tulips were much sought after by the wealthy, especially in Holland and Germany. Rich people at Amsterdam sent for the bulbs direct to Constantinople, and paid the most extravagant prices for them. The first roots planted in England were brought from Vienna in 1600. Until the year 1634 the tulip annually increased in reputation, until it was deemed a proof of bad taste in any man of fortune to be without a collection of them. Many learned men, including Pompeius

Reprinted from *Extraordinary Popular Delusions and the Madness of Crowds* (New York: Harmony Books, 1980; originally published 1841), pp. 89–97.

de Angelis, and the celebrated Lipsius of Leyden, the author of the treatise "De Constantia," were passionately fond of tulips. The rage for possessing them soon caught the middle classes of society, and merchants and shopkeepers, even of moderate means, began to vie with each other in the rarity of these flowers and the preposterous prices they paid for them. A trader at Harlaem was known to pay one-half his fortune for a single root, not with the design of selling it again at a profit, but to keep in his own conservatory for the admiration of his acquaintance.

One would suppose that there must have been some great virtue in this flower to have made it so valuable in the eyes of so prudent a people as the Dutch; but it has neither the beauty nor the perfume of the rose—hardly the beauty of the "sweet, sweet-pea;" neither is it as enduring as either. Cowley, it is true, is loud in its praise. He says—

> The tulip next appeared, all over gay,
> But wanton, full of pride, and full of play;
> The world can't show a dye but here has place;
> Nay, by new mixtures, she can change her face;
> Purple and gold are both beneath her care,
> The richest needlework she loves to wear;
> Her only study is to please the eye,
> And to outshine the rest in finery.

This, though not very poetical, is the description of a poet. Beckmann, in his *History of Inventions*, paints it with more fidelity, and in prose more pleasing than Cowley's poetry. He says, "There are few plants which acquire, through accident, weakness, or disease, so many variegations as the tulip. When uncultivated, and in its natural state, it is almost of one colour, has large leaves, and an extraordinarily long stem. When it has been weakened by cultivation, it becomes more agreeable in the eyes of the florist. The petals are then paler, smaller, and more diversified in hue; and the leaves acquire a softer green colour. Thus this masterpiece of culture, the more beautiful it turns, grows so much the weaker, so that, with the greatest skill and most careful attention, it can scarcely be transplanted, or even kept alive."

Many persons grow insensibly attached to that which gives them a great deal of trouble, as a mother often loves her sick and ever-ailing child better than her more healthy offspring. Upon the same principle we must account for the unmerited encomia lavished upon these fragile blossoms. In 1634, the rage among the Dutch to possess them was so great that the ordinary industry of the country was neglected, and the population, even to its lowest dregs, embarked in the tulip trade. As the mania increased, prices augmented, until, in the year 1635, many persons were known to invest a fortune of 100,000 florins in the purchase of forty roots. It then became necessary to sell them by their weight in *perits*, a small weight less than a grain. A tulip of the species called *Admiral Liefken*, weighing 400 *perits*, was worth 4400 florins; an *Admiral Van der Eyck*, weighing 446 *perits*, was worth 1260 florins; a *Childer* of 106 *perits* was worth 1615 florins; a *Viceroy* of 400 *perits*, 3000 florins; and, most precious of all, a *Semper Augustus*, weighing 200 *perits*, was thought to be very cheap at 5500 florins. The latter was much sought after, and even an inferior bulb might command a price of 2000 florins. It is related that, at one time, early in 1636, there were only two roots of this description to be had in all Holland, and those not of the best. One was in the possession of a dealer in Amsterdam, and the other in Harlaem. So anxious were the speculators to obtain them, that one person offered the fee-simple of twelve acres of building-ground for the Harlaem tulip. That of Amsterdam was bought for 4600 florins, a new carriage, two grey horses, and a complete set of harness. Munting, an industrious author of that day, who wrote a folio volume of one thousand pages upon the tulipomania, has preserved the following list of the various articles, and their value, which were delivered for one single root of the rare species called the *Viceroy:*

	florins
Two lasts of wheat	448
Four lasts of rye	558
Four fat oxen	480
Eight fat swine	240
Twelve fat sheep	120
Two Hogsheads of wine	70
Four tuns of beer	32
Two tuns of butter	192
One thousand lbs. of cheese	120
A complete bed	100
A suit of clothes	80
A silver drinking-cup	60
	2500

People who had been absent from Holland, and whose chance it was to return when this folly was at its maximum, were sometimes led into awkward dilemmas by their ignorance. There is an amusing instance of the kind related in Blainville's *Travels*. A wealthy merchant, who prided himself not a little in his rare tulips, received upon one occasion a very valuable consignment of merchandise from the Levant. Intelligence of its arrival was brought him by a sailor, who presented himself for that purpose at the counting-house, among bales of goods of every description. The merchant, to reward him for his news, munificently made him a present of a fine red herring for his breakfast. The sailor had, it appears, a great partiality for onions, and seeing a bulb very like an onion lying upon the counter of this liberal trader, and thinking it, no doubt, very much out of its place among silks and velvets, he slily seized an opportunity and slipped it into his pocket, as a relish for his herring. He got clear off with his prize, and proceeded to the quay to eat his breakfast. Hardly was his back turned when the merchant missed his valuable *Semper Augustus*, worth three thousand florins, or about 280*l*. sterling. The whole establishment was instantly in an uproar; search was everywhere made for the precious root, but it was not to be found. Great was the merchant's distress of mind. The search was renewed, but again without success. At last some one thought of the sailor.

The unhappy merchant sprang into the street at the bare suggestion. His alarmed household followed him. The sailor, simple soul! had not thought of concealment. He was found quietly sitting on a coil of ropes, masticating the last morsel of his *"onion."* Little did he dream that he had been eating a breakfast whose cost might have regaled a whole ship's crew for a twelvemonth; or, as the plundered merchant himself expressed it, "might have sumptuously feasted the Prince of Orange and the whole court of the Stadtholder." Anthony caused pearls to be dissolved in wine to drink the health of Cleopatra; Sir Richard Whittington was as foolishly magnificent in an entertainment to King Henry V.; and Sir Thomas Gresham drank a diamond dissolved in wine to the health of Queen Elizabeth, when she opened the Royal Exchange; but the breakfast of this roguish Dutchman was as splendid as either. He had an advantage, too, over his wasteful predecessors: *their* gems did not improve the taste or the wholesomeness of *their* wine, while *his* tulip was quite delicious with his red herring. The most unfortunate part of the business for him was, that he remained in prison for some months on a charge of felony preferred against him by the merchant.

Another story is told of an English traveller, which is scarcely less ludicrous. This gentleman, an amateur botanist, happened to see a tulip-root lying in the conservatory of a wealthy Dutchman. Being ignorant of its quality, he took out his penknife, and peeled off its coats, with the view of making experiments upon it. When it was by this means reduced to half its size, he cut it into two equal sections, making all the time many learned remarks on the singular appearances of the unknown bulb. Suddenly the owner pounced upon him, and, with fury in his eyes, asked him if he knew what he had been doing? "Peeling a most extraordinary onion," replied the philosopher. *"Hundert tausend duyvel!"* said the Dutchman; "it's an *Admiral Van der Eyck.*" "Thank you," replied the traveller, taking out his notebook to make a memorandum of the same; "are these admirals common in your country?" "Death and the Devil!" said the Dutchman, seizing the astonished man of science by the collar; "come before the syndic, and you shall see." In spite of his remonstrances, the traveller was led through the streets followed by a mob of persons. When brought into the presence of the magistrate, he learned, to his consternation, that the root upon which he had been experimentalising was worth four thousand florins; and, notwithstanding all he could urge in extenuation, he was lodged in prison until he found securities for the payment of this sum.

The demand for tulips of a rare species increased so much in the year 1636, that regular marts for their sale were established on the Stock Exchange of Amsterdam, in Rotterdam, Harlaem, Leyden, Alkmar, Hoorn, and other towns. Symptoms of gambling now became, for the first time, apparent. The stock-jobbers, ever on the alert for a new speculation, dealt largely in tulips, making use of all the means they so well knew how to employ to cause fluctuations in prices. At first, as in all these gambling mania, confidence was at its height, and every body gained. The tulip-jobbers speculated in the rise and fall of the tulip stocks, and made large profits by buying when prices fell, and selling out when they rose. Many individuals grew suddenly rich. A golden bait hung temptingly out before the people, and one after the other, they rushed to the tulip-marts, like flies around a honey-pot. Every one imagined that the passion for tulips would last for ever, and that the wealthy from every part of the world would send to Holland, and pay whatever prices were asked for them. The riches of Europe would be concentrated on the shores of the Zuyder Zee, and poverty banished from the favoured clime of Holland. Nobles, citizens, farmers, mechanics, seamen, footmen, maid-servants, even chimney-sweeps and old clotheswomen, dabbled in tulips. People of all grades converted their property into cash, and invested it in flowers. Houses and lands were offered for sale at ruinously low prices, or assigned in payment of bargains made at the tulip-mart. Foreigners became smitten with the same frenzy, and the money poured into Holland from all directions. The prices of the necessaries of life rose again by degrees: houses and lands, horses and carriages, and luxuries of every sort, rose in value with them, and for some months Holland seemed the very antechamber of Plutus. The operations of the trade became so extensive and so intricate, that it was found necessary to draw up a code of laws for the guidance of the dealers. Notaries and clerks were also appointed, who devoted themselves exclusively to the interests of the trade. The designation of public notary was hardly known in some towns, that of tulip-notary usurping its place. In the smaller towns, where there was no exchange, the principal tavern was usually selected as the "show-place," where high and low traded in tulips, and confirmed their bargains over sumptuous entertainments. These dinners were sometimes attended by two or three hundred persons, and large vases of tulips, in full bloom, were placed at regular intervals upon the tables and sideboards for their gratification during the repast.

At last, however, the more prudent began to see that this folly could not last for ever. Rich people no longer bought the flowers to keep them in their gardens, but to sell them again at cent per cent profit. It was seen that somebody must lose fearfully in the end. As this conviction spread, prices fell, and never rose again. Confidence was destroyed, and a universal panic seized upon the dealers. *A* had agreed to purchase ten *Semper Augustines* from *B,* at four thousand florins each, at six weeks after the signing contract. *B* was ready with the flowers at the appointed time; but the price had fallen to three or four hundred florins, and *A* refused either to pay the difference or receive the tulips. Defaulters were announced day after day in all the towns in Holland. Hundreds who, a few months previously, had begun to doubt that there was such a thing as poverty in the land suddenly found themselves the possessors of a few bulbs, which nobody would buy, even though they offered them at one quarter of the sums they had paid for them. The cry of distress resounded everywhere, and each man accused his neighbor. The few who had contrived to enrich themselves hid their wealth from the knowledge of their fellow-citizens, and invested it in the English or other funds. Many who, for a brief season, had emerged from the humbler walks of life, were cast back into their original obscurity. Substantial merchants were reduced almost to beggary, and many a representative of a noble line saw the fortunes of his house ruined beyond redemption.

When the first alarm subsided, the tulip-holders in the several towns held public meetings to devise what measures were best to be taken to restore public credit. It was generally agreed that deputies should be sent from all parts to Amsterdam, to consult with the government upon some remedy for this evil. The government at first refused to interfere, but advised the tulip-holders to agree to some plan among themselves. Several meetings were held for this purpose; but no measure could be devised likely to give satisfaction to the deluded people, or repair even a slight portion of the mischief that had been done. The language of complaint and reproach was in everybody's mouth, and all the meetings were of the most stormy character. At last, however, after much bickering and ill-will, it was agreed, at Amsterdam, by the assembled deputies, that all contracts made in the height of the mania, or prior to the month of November, 1636, should be declared null and void, and that, in those made after that date, purchasers should be freed from their engagements, on paying ten per cent to the vendor. This decision gave no satisfaction. The vendors who had their tulips on hand were, of course, discontented, and those who had pledged themselves to purchase, thought themselves hardly treated. Tulips which had, at one time, been worth six thousand florins, were now to be procured for five hundred; so that the composition of ten per cent was one hundred florins more than the actual value. Actions for breach of contract were threatened in all the courts of the country; but the latter refused to take cognisance of gambling transactions.

The matter was finally referred to the Provincial Council at the Hague, and it was confidently expected that the wisdom of this body would invent some measure by which credit should be restored. Expectation was on the stretch for its decision, but it never came. The members continued to deliberate week after week, and at last, after thinking about it for three months, declared that they could offer no final decision until they had more information. They advised, however, that, in the meantime, every vendor should, in the presence of witnesses, offer the tulips *in natura* to the purchaser for the sums agreed upon. If the latter refused to take them, they might be put up for sale by public auction, and the original contractor held responsible for the difference between the actual and the stipulated price. This was exactly the plan recommended by the deputies, and which was already shown to be of no avail. There was no court in Holland which would enforce payment. The question was raised in Amsterdam, but the judges unanimously refused to interfere, on the ground that debts contracted in gambling were no debts in law.

Thus the matter rested. To find a remedy was beyond the power of the government. Those who were unlucky enough to have had stores of tulips on hand at the time of the sudden reaction were left to bear their ruin as philosophically as they could; those who had made profits were allowed to keep them; but the commerce of the country suffered a severe shock, from which it was many years ere it recovered.

The example of the Dutch was imitated to some extent in England. In the year 1636 tulips were publicly sold in the Exchange of London, and the jobbers exerted themselves to the utmost to raise them to the fictitious value they had acquired in Amsterdam. In Paris also the jobbers strove to create a tulipomania. In both cities they only partially succeeded. However, the force of example brought the flowers into great favour, and amongst a certain class of people tulips have ever since been prized more highly than any other flowers of the field. The Dutch are still notorious for their partiality to them, and continue to pay higher prices for them than any other people. As the rich Englishman boasts of his fine race-horses or his old pictures, so does the wealthy Dutchman vaunt him of his tulips.

In England, in our day, strange as it may appear, a tulip will produce more money than an oak. If one could be found, *rara in terris,* and black as the black swan of Juvenal, its price would equal that of a dozen acres of standing corn. In Scotland, towards the close of the seventeenth century, the highest price for tulips, according to the authority of a writer in the supplement to the third edition of the *Encyclopedia Britannica,* was ten guineas. Their value appears to have diminished from that time till the year 1769, when the two most valuable species in England were the *Don Quevedo* and the *Valentinier,* the former of which was worth two guineas and the latter two guineas and a half. These prices appear to have been the minimum. In the year 1800, a common price was fifteen guineas for a single bulb. In 1835, a bulb of the species called the Miss Fanny Kemble was sold by public auction in London for seventy-five pounds. Still more remarkable was the price of a tulip in the possession of a gardener in the King's Road, Chelsea;—in his catalogues it was labelled at two hundred guineas.

Second Thoughts about the Tulipmania

Peter M. Garber

Peter Garber, professor of economics at Brown University, here provides us in excerpted form with an analysis of the Tulipmania affair
that yields strikingly nonstandard conclusions. Perhaps, after all,
only the uninformed late and greedy entrants to the race got
bagged—and, perhaps, they deserved it. Readers are encouraged
to read Garber's entire article, which examines the famous Mississippi and South Sea episodes as well as John Law's financing
methods. The whole provides trenchant perspectives on "bubbles"
and on the workings of the British Parliament and the French Court
in the early 1700s.

The jargon of economics and finance contains numerous colorful ex-
pressions to denote a market-determined asset price at odds with any
reasonable economic explanation. Such words as "tulip mania," "bubble," "chain letter," "Ponzi scheme," "panic," "crash," and "financial crisis" immediately evoke images of frenzied and probably
irrational speculative activity. Many of these terms have emerged from
specific speculative episodes which have been sufficiently frequent and
important that they underpin a strong current belief among economists
that key capital markets sometimes generate irrational and inefficient
pricing and allocational outcomes.

Excerpted from *Journal of Economic Perspectives* 4 (Spring 1990), pp. 35–54. Nashville, Tennessee:
American Economic Association.

Before economists relegate a speculative event to the inexplicable or bubble category, however, we must exhaust all reasonable economic explanations. While such explanations are often not easily generated due to the inherent complexity of economic phenomena, the business of economists is to find clever fundamental market explanations for events; and our methodology should always require that we search intensively for market fundamental explanations before clutching the "bubble" last resort.

Thus, among the "reasonable" or "market fundamental" explanations, I would include the perception of an increased probability of large returns. The perception might be triggered by genuine economic good news, by a convincing new economic theory about payoffs or by a fraud launched by insiders acting strategically to trick investors. It might also be triggered by uninformed market participants correctly inferring changes in the distribution of dividends by observing price movements generated by the trading of informed insiders. While some of these perceptions might in the end prove erroneous, movements in asset prices based on them are fundamental and not bubble movements.

I aim in these pages to propose a market fundamental explanation for the . . . Dutch tulipmania (1634–37). . . . This [being treated in the modern literature as an outburst of irrationality] may be attributable to the influence of Mackay's (1852) graphic descriptions . . . from our current perspective, though, such "irrational" speculation probably looked a lot like a normal day in a pit of the Board of Trade. . . .

Standard reference sources in economics typically refer to one or more of these events in defining the term "bubble." For example, Palgrave's *Dictionary* (1926, p. 181) defines a bubble as "any unsound commercial undertaking accompanied by a high degree of speculation." It then provides histories of tulipmania, the Mississippi Bubble and the South Sea Bubble as examples. In his article on "bubbles" in *The New Palgrave* (1987), Kindleberger includes the tulipmania as one of the two most famous manias. (His other example is the British railway mania of the 1840s.) Curiously, the entry on "tulipmania" in the *The New Palgrave* does not refer to the 17th century Dutch speculative episode. Instead, Calvo defines "tulipmania" generically, as a situation in which asset prices do not behave in ways explainable by economic fundamentals, and then develops examples of rational bubbles.

In the past few decades, these historical episodes have passed in to the common lore of economics. Samuelson (1957, 1967) refers to the tulipmania and associates it (1967, p. 230) with "the purely financial dream world of indefinite group self-fulfillment," though he is skeptical that such phenomena are important in real markets. Students of Samuelson like Shell and Stiglitz (1967) state, "The instability of the Hahn model is suggestive of the economic forces operating during 'speculative booms' like the Tulip Bulb mania."[1]

The "sunspot" literature has revived references to these famous bubbles. For example Azariadis (1981, p. 380) states that, "The evidence on the influence of subjective factors is ample and dates back several centuries: the Dutch tulip mania, the South Sea bubble in England, the collapse of the Mississippi Company in France are three well-documented cases of speculative price movements which historians consider unwarranted by 'objective' conditions."[2] In a more recent motivational argument for the importance of "sunspots," Azariadis and Guesnerie (1986) state, "And the reading of economic historians may suggest that these factors (sunspots) have some pertinence for the explanation of phenomena like the Dutch tulipmania in the seventeenth century and the Great Depression in our own."

J. van Horne (1985), influenced by mounting evidence of financial market anomalies, accepts the possibility of bubbles and manias and refers to the tulipmania, where a "single bulb sold for many years' salary." With a reference to the tulipmania, Shiller (1986) argues that asset markets are driven by capricious investors acting on the basis of fads and bubbles. In papers related to this literature, Cutler, Poterba, and Summers (1989) refer to the tulipmania, the Mississippi bubble and the South Sea bubble as examples of how trading dynamics may affect asset prices. Finally, in the exchange rate literature, Meese (1986) refers to tulipmania and Krugman (1985) conjures up the images of both the tulipmania and the South Sea Bubble while building a case for a bubble interpretation of the movements of the dollar exchange rate during the 1980s.

The reader can probably provide other cases where these episodes are cited as clear evidence of bubbles in the past. In contrast, I will argue that none of these episodes should actually qualify as bubbles.

The Fundamentals of Tulipmania

Mackay (1852) passed on to economists the standard description of the tulipmania as a speculative bubble.[3] In this description, the Netherlands became a center of cultivation and development of new tulip varieties after the tulip's entry into Europe from Turkey in the mid-1500s. Professional growers and wealthy flower fanciers created a market for rare varieties in which bulbs sold at high prices. For example, a Semper Augustus bulb sold for 2000 guilders in 1625, an amount of gold worth about $16,000 at $400 per ounce. Common bulb varieties, on the other hand, received very low prices.

By 1636, the rapid price rises attracted speculators, and prices of many varieties surged upward from November 1636 through January 1637. In February 1637, prices suddenly collapsed, and bulbs could not be sold at 10 percent of their peak values. By 1739, the prices of all the most prized bulbs of the mania had fallen to no more than 0.1 guilder. This was 1/200 of 1 percent of Semper Augustus's peak price. The story concludes by asserting that the collapse led to economic distress in the Netherlands for years afterwards.

The standard version of the tulipmania neglects discussion about what the market fundamental price of bulbs should have been. Mackay did not report transaction prices for the rare bulbs immediately after the collapse. Instead, he recorded tulip bulb prices from 60 or 200 years after the collapse, interpreting these much lower prices as ones justified by market fundamentals. Yet the dynamics of bulb prices during the tulip episode were typical of any market for rare bulbs, even those existing today. The tulip market involved only bulbs affected by a mosaic virus which had the effect of creating beautiful, feathered patterns in the flowers. Only diseased bulbs were valued by traders and collectors, because a particular pattern could not be reproduced through seed propagation. Only through budding of the mother bulb would a pattern breed true.

A standard pricing pattern arises for new varieties of flowers, even in modern markets. When a particularly prized variety is developed, its original bulb sells for a high price. As the bulbs accumulate, the variety's price falls rapidly; after less than 30 years, bulbs sell at their reproduction cost. This pattern raises two questions. First, why did the price of bulbs increase rapidly? Second, did prices decline faster than should have been expected?

The price increases prior to February 1637 occurred as the status of a variety became clear; and as its renown increased, so would its price. After all, most new varieties were not considered particularly beautiful. This would explain the steady increase in the price of Semper Augustus.

FIGURE 1
Guilder Prices of Tulip Bulbs, 1707, 1722, and 1739

Bulb	1707	1722	1739
1. Premier Noble	409	—	1.0
2. Aigle Noir	110	0.75	0.3
3. Roi de Fleurs	251	10.9	0.1
4. Diamant	71	2.5	2.0

Source: Garber (1989).

FIGURE 2
Post-Collapse Bulb Prices in Guilders

Bulb	Feb. 5, 1637	1642 or 1643
1. English Admiral (bulb)	700.	210.
2. Admirael van Eyck (bulb)	1345.	220.
3. General Rotgans	805.	138.

Source: Garber (1989).

Similarly, a shift in fashion toward the appreciation of tulips in general over a shorter period would generate rising prices for all the rare bulbs.

To form an expectation about a typical rate of price decline of tulip bulbs, I collected data on 18th century bulb price patterns for various highly valued tulip bulbs. The level of 18th century prices was much lower than during the mania. By 1707, an enormous variety of tulip bulbs had been developed; and the tulip itself had been replaced as the most fashionable flower by the hyacinth. Nonetheless, as Figure 1 shows, bulb prices still were falling sharply. The average annual rate of depreciation for these bulbs was 28.5 percent before bulb prices reached floor values.

Figure 2 reports prices of those bulbs for which I have been able to gather price data for years immediately after the mania. February 5, 1637 was the day on which peak prices were attained. For these bulbs from February 1637 to 1642, the average annual rate of price depreciation was 32 percent, not greatly different from the 18th century depreciation rate. If the more rapid annual rate of decline for the tulipmania bulbs was attributed entirely to the crash, and not to factors which materialized in the succeeding five years, the crash can have accounted for no more than a 16 percent price decline: large, but hardly the stuff that legends are made of.

Strangely enough, if one is to speak of tulipmania, it would be more accurate to speak of the rapid price rise and collapse in common bulbs in the last week of January and first week of February 1637. Common bulbs became objects of speculation among the lower classes in a futures market which emerged in November 1636. These markets were located in local taverns, and each sale was associated with a payment of "wine money." In January 1637, prices for some common bulb varieties increased by as much as 25 times. For example, the peak price for a bulb called Switser of .17 guilders/aas was attained on February 5, the apparent peak of the market (1 aas = 1/20 gram). Data from notarized contracts on February 6 and 9 indicate a sudden decline to .11 guilders/aas. This represents a substantial decline from prices in the first five days of February, but it still exceeds the price of .035 guilders/aas attained on January 23. Price increases through mid-January, while rapid, were not as great as in the final two weeks of the speculation; and there is no evidence that they were out of line. Since serious traders ignored this market and participants in this market had almost no wealth, it can have been little more than a mid-winter diversion among tavern regulars mimicking more serious traders.

Finally, there is no evidence of serious economic distress arising from the tulipmania. All histories of the period treat it as a golden age in Dutch development.

Notes

1. Burmeister (1980, pp. 264–286) summarizes the research activity about "the Hahn problem."
2. Actually the company involved was not called the Mississippi Company. Initially it was the *Compagnie d'Occident*; and after a series of corporate takeovers, it became the *Compagnie des Indes*.
3. Mackay plagiarized his description from Beckmann (1846). Beckmann refers to a long sequence of research about the episode, but all sources are ultimately based on a set of three anonymously written pamphlets in dialogue form published in 1637. These pamphlets were among dozens written just after the collapse by anti-speculative partisans launched by the economic oligarchy which wished to assure that speculative capital was channeled through markets which it controlled.

Alice in Taiwanderland

John D. Bolsover

John D. Bolsover, the chief executive officer of Baring Investment in London, spoke to financial analysts in Florida about global investing in February 1990. Having been an early and bold advocate of investing in Japan and Southeast Asia, he took the occasion to share his concerns.

Taiwan has a tiny stockmarket. Many people would believe that we should not be wasting too much time on it, that Taiwan is an irrelevancy. I do not think it is. Taiwan is symptomatic of *the* problem in investing today.

Taiwan is a classic case of entrepreneurship, hard work, saving, and economic success. Yet, I believe that what we are seeing in Taiwan is now going to lead to one of the biggest busts in stockmarket history.

The Taiwan market is up 23 times in US dollars—in the past four years. The market capitalization of Taiwan today is US $296 billion (that is larger than the UK stockmarket in 1985; larger than the whole of EAFE in 1969). In May 1988, there were 14 brokerage companies in Taiwan. They then liberalized, and today there are 250 securities companies registered in Taiwan—with 40 more authorized to open in the next six months. The daily volume in Taiwan is now US $8 billion. That is bigger than the New York Stock Exchange. The total market is being turned over every 10 weeks. The price of participating in Taiwan is 130 times earnings.

Excerpted from a speech at AIMR's Investing Worldwide Conference in Palm Beach, Florida, February 27, 1990, by permission of the author.

Beware of the temptation to say: "This time it is different." Santayana observed: "Those who ignore history are doomed to relive it."

The following is an extract on the Japanese stock market of 1906 from a book that I would recommend to all of you, *The House of Nomura* by Albert Alletzhauser:

> *The great 1906 bull market, one of the greatest in the history of Japan, spread like wild fire. Stocks would suddenly burst into life, setting new highs and doubling or tripling in a matter of weeks. A buying panic would ensue. . . .*

Here is a further extract from Alletzhauser's book. . . .

> *Within days the great bull market of 1906 became the great bear market of 1907—one of the most dramatic declines in the history of the Japanese stockmarket, comparable to the collapse of the St. Petersburg Exchange in 1917 and the Shanghai market in 1949. In the twelve days from the peak on 19th January 1907 to the end of the month, the market shed one-third of its value. By the end of 1907, the selling bloodbath had reduced the market's value by 88%. The final reading on the index at the end of the year was a mere 92 down from 774.*

Of course, I am not telling you that this is something that is going to repeat itself. I am merely telling you about something that has happened in history.

- My concern is that this time is not different.
- My concern is that there is too much greed around.
- My concern is that we ought to start to be happy with making 10–15% per annum rather than wanting to make 25–30%.

No Tears for "The Market"

Mike Royko

Mike Royko is a tough, straight-talking social and political observer whose biography of Chicago's Mayor Richard Daley is a classic of its genre. He is also an economist and a columnist for the *Chicago Tribune,* where this hard-hitting piece on the 1980s divergence between "The Market" and reality appeared.

I can't help it. While it might sound cruel and sadistic, when the stock market takes one of its periodic head-first dives, I enjoy the spectacle.

Not that I really understand it. It baffles me that one day a big corporation can be worth $10 billion. But a day or two later, it is suddenly worth only $8 billion.

It is still making the same products that are selling for the same price in the same quantity. The same people are coming to work and getting the same paychecks. Yet, on paper, the company is worth far less today than it was yesterday.

But what I do understand is that when this happens on a grand scale, to hundreds or thousands of companies, somebody is taking a financial bath, getting clobbered, maybe even losing their shirt, trousers, underwear, driver and limo.

I'd feel bad if I thought that little old widows in three-room flats were being wiped out. Or if those who sweep streets, empty bedpans or put out fires were losing their nest eggs.

Reprinted from *The Chicago Tribune,* October 16, 1989, Sec. 1, Col. 1, p. 3, by permission of Tribune Media Services.

But, from what I read, that isn't the case. The average person is not on the phone telling a broker to buy, sell, go short, go long, go medium, stop, start, hop, skip or whatever all that jargon is.

My guess is that if I called most of the people I know, and asked them if they just took a bath in the market, they'd say: "No, I took a shower in my washroom."

That's because most people have wised up. They'd no more get involved with that strange creature called The Market than they'd buy a gold watch or chain from some seedy guy standing in a doorway.

The Market. All you have to do is look at the headlines or listen to the daily broadcasts and you think you are hearing the latest medical report on someone who ought to be in therapy, on tranquilizers, or strapped down by the attendants. It sounds like a manic-depressive-psycho-head case.

"The Market up on heavy trading this morning, buoyed by reports of . . . The Market closed sharply down on light trading this evening, in the wake of reports. . . . The Market reacted nervously to reports that the President found a pimple on his neck . . . The Market bounced back on reports that the President saw a dermatologist."

What kind of way to do business is that?

No, if we get another Black Monday, Gray Tuesday, or Olive-Drab Wednesday, I won't be shedding tears for those with the vanishing bottom lines. Just as I never offer sympathy for those who try to fill inside straights.

The last time The Market went from manic to depressive, we were told it was caused by computers going berserk or some such thing. If that was the reason, why didn't somebody crawl behind the computer and pull out the plug? That's what I'd do if my TV started spewing smoke.

This time we're told that the sudden drop was caused by the fear that there won't be any more greed-oozing takeovers. If that is so, it's a delight.

That means that the stock prices of companies have been going up and up and up not because anybody thinks that what they make or sell is getting better or more popular. It's because they think that a Wall Street land shark has an eye on a company and is circling. And that the land shark intends to borrow a fortune at high interest rates, break up the company, sell off chunks of it to pay off the big debt, and walk away with a fat profit. In the process, productive careers will be ruined, workers will find their lives turned upside down, companies might no longer exist, but the land sharks and those who finance them will have full bellies.

And that's why—despite the hysteria of Black Monday—the prices of stocks have been creeping upward. It's been a guessing game. Will this or that company be taken over? One little rumor, and the stock becomes manic. No, the rumor goes, now the company is no longer a tasty morsel. So the same stock sinks into a blue funk.

Now on Wall Street, LaSalle Street and all the other places the sharks lurk, they're screaming: "Nobody is going to take over nothing anymore for ever and ever."

And suddenly those who wanted to be in on the kill are in a panic. What? No more feeding frenzies? No more ripping and shredding of slow-swimming companies? Let me out! We keep hearing that the small investor no longer is interested in the stock market. Of course he isn't. Little fish know that it isn't safe to swim with the sharks.

The Emperor's New Clothes

Hans Christian Andersen

The wonder of market crashes is that prices get so amazingly high before they collapse. Here, we receive the wisdom of Hans Christian Andersen in a familiar story about seeing what is truly there— not just seeing what we hope to see. But, must investment professionals depend on others to identify the reality that they are paid to perceive?

Many years ago there lived an emperor, who cared so enormously for beautiful new clothes that he spent all his money upon them, that he might be very fine. He did not care about his soldiers, nor about the theatre, nor about driving in the park except to show his new clothes. He had a coat for every hour of the day; and just as they say of a king, "He is in council," one always said of him, "The emperor is in the wardrobe."

In the great city in which he lived it was always very merry; every day a number of strangers arrived there. One day two cheats came: they gave themselves out as weavers, and declared that they could weave the finest stuff any one could imagine. Not only were their colours and patterns, they said, uncommonly beautiful, but the clothes made of the stuff possessed the wonderful quality that they became invisible to any one who was unfit for the office he held, or was incorrigibly stupid.

"Those would be capital clothes!" thought the emperor. "If I wore those, I should be able to find out what men in my empire are not fit

Reprinted from *The Journal of Portfolio Management* 3 (Winter 1977), pp. 78–79. New York: Institutional Investor, Inc.

for the places they have; I could distinguish the clever from the stupid. Yes, the stuff must be woven for me directly!''

And he gave the two cheats a great deal of cash in hand, that they might begin their work at once.

As for them, they put up two looms, and pretended to be working; but they had nothing at all on their looms. They at once demanded the finest silk and the costliest gold; this they put into their own pockets, and worked at the empty looms till late into the night.

''I should like to know how far they have got on with the stuff,'' thought the emperor. But he felt quite uncomfortable when he thought that those who were not fit for their offices could not see it. He believed, indeed, that he had nothing to fear for himself, but yet he preferred first to send some one else to see how matters stood. All the people in the whole city knew what peculiar power the stuff possessed, and all were anxious to see how bad or how stupid their neighbors were.

''I will send my honest old minister to the weavers,'' thought the emperor. ''He can judge best how the stuff looks, for he has sense, and no one discharges his office better than he.''

Now the good old minister went out into the hall where the two cheats sat working at the empty looms.

''Mercy preserve us!'' thought the old minister, and he opened his eyes wide. ''I cannot see anything at all!'' But he did not say this.

Both the cheats begged him to be kind enough to come nearer, and asked if he did not approve of the colours and the pattern. Then they pointed to the empty loom, and the poor old minister went on opening his eyes; but he could see nothing, for there was nothing to see.

''Mercy!'' thought he, ''can I indeed be so stupid? I never thought that, and not a soul must know it. Am I not fit for my office?—No, it will never do for me to tell that I could not see the stuff.''

''Do you say nothing to it?'' said one of the weavers.

''Oh it is charming—quite enchanting!'' answered the old minister, as he peered through his spectacles. ''What a fine pattern, and what colours! Yes, I shall tell the emperor that I am very much pleased with it.''

''Well, we are glad of that,'' said both the weavers; and then they named the colours, and explained the strange pattern. The old minister listened attentively, that he might be able to repeat it when he went back to the emperor. And he did so.

Now the cheats asked for more money, and more silk and gold, which they declared they wanted for weaving. They put all into their own pockets, and not a thread was put on the loom; but they continued to work at the empty frames as before.

The emperor soon sent again, dispatching another honest statesman, to see how the weaving was going on, and if the stuff would soon be ready. He fared just like the first: he looked and looked, but, as there was nothing to be seen but the empty looms, he could see nothing.

"Is not that a pretty piece of stuff?" asked the two cheats; and they displayed and explained the handsome pattern which was not there at all.

"I am not stupid!" thought the man—"it must be my good office, for which I am not fit. It is funny enough, but I must not let it be noticed." And so he praised the stuff which he did not see, and expressed his pleasure at the beautiful colours and the charming pattern. "Yes, it is enchanting," he said to the emperor.

All the people in the town were talking of the gorgeous stuff. The emperor wished to see it himself while it was still upon the loom. With a whole crowd of chosen men, among whom were also the two honest statesmen who had already been there, he went to the two cunning cheats, who were now weaving with might and main without fibre or thread.

"Is that not splendid?" said the two old statesmen, who had already been there once. "Does not your majesty remark the pattern and the colours?" And then they pointed to the empty loom, for they thought that the others could see the stuff.

"What's this?" thought the emperor. "I can see nothing at all! That is terrible. Am I stupid? Am I not fit to be emperor? That would be the most dreadful thing that could happen to me.—Oh, it is *very* pretty!" he said aloud. "It has our exalted approbation." And he nodded in a contented way, and gazed at the empty loom, for he would not say that he saw nothing. The whole suite whom he had with him looked and looked, and saw nothing, any more than the rest; but, like the emperor, they said, "That *is* pretty!" and counselled him to wear these splendid new clothes for the first time at the great procession that was presently to take place. "It is splendid, tasteful, excellent!" went from mouth to mouth. On all sides there seemed to be general rejoicing, and the emperor gave each of the cheats a cross to hang at his button-hole and the title of Imperial Court Weaver.

The whole night before the morning on which the procession was to take place the cheats were up, and had lighted more than sixteen candles. The people could see that they were hard at work, completing the emperor's new clothes. They pretended to take the stuff down from the loom; they made cuts in the air with great scissors; they sewed with needles without thread; and at last they said, "Now the clothes are ready!"

The emperor came himself with his noblest cavaliers; and the two cheats lifted up one arm as if they were holding something, and said, "See, here are the trousers! here is the coat! here is the cloak!" and so on. "It is as light as a spider's web: one would think one had nothing on; but that is just the beauty of it."

"Yes," said all the cavaliers; but they could not see anything, for nothing was there.

"Does your imperial majesty please to condescend to undress?" said the cheats; "then we will put on you the new clothes here in front of the great mirror."

The emperor took off his clothes, and the cheats pretended to put on him each of the new garments, and they took him round the waist, and seemed to fasten on something; that was the train; and the emperor turned round and round before the mirror.

"Oh, how well they look! how capitally they fit!" said all. "What a pattern! what colours! That *is* a splendid dress!"

"They are standing outside with the canopy which is to be borne above your majesty in the procession!" announced the head master of the ceremonies.

"Well, I am ready," replied the emperor. "Does it not suit me well?" And then he turned again to the mirror, for he wanted it to appear as if he contemplated his adornment with great interest.

The chamberlains, who were to carry the train, stooped down with their hands towards the floor, just as if they were picking up the mantle; then they pretended to be holding something up in the air. They did not dare to let it be noticed that they saw nothing.

So the emperor went in procession under the rich canopy, and every one in the streets said, "How incomparable are the emperor's new clothes! what a train he has to his mantle! how it fits him!" No one would let it be perceived that he could see nothing, for that would have shown that he was not fit for his office, or was very stupid. No clothes of the emperor's had ever had such a success as these.

"But he has nothing on!" a little child cried out at last.

"Just hear what that innocent says!" said the father; and one whispered to another what the child had said. "There is a little child that says he has nothing on."

"But he has nothing on!" said the whole people at length. And the emperor shivered, for it seemed to him that they were right; but he thought within himself, "I must go through with the procession." And so he carried himself still more proudly, and the chamberlains held on tighter than ever, and carried the train which did not exist at all.

OPINION AND COMMENTARY

The Wonders of Lombard Street . . . and a Warning

Walter Bagehot

Walter Bagehot, inventor of the Treasury bill and an editor for many years of *The Economist,* was once described by Gladstone as "the permanent Chancellor of the Exchequer" at least in part because of his continuing and astute commentary on financial matters. "The business of banking ought to be simple," he explained in *Lombard Street* in 1870, "if it is hard it is wrong." In this introductory chapter, Bagehot describes the then-recent phenomenon of the money market and explains how it energized the city and the overall economy of the nation. As was his wont in his essays, he also identified the system's vulnerabilities.

I venture to call this Essay 'Lombard Street,' and not the 'Money Market,' or any such phrase, because I wish to deal, and to show that I mean to deal, with concrete realities. A notion prevails that the Money Market is something so impalpable that it can only be spoken of in very abstract words, and that therefore books on it must always be exceedingly difficult. But I maintain that the Money Market is as concrete and real as anything else; that it can be described in as plain words; that it is the writer's fault if what he says is not clear. . . .

The briefest and truest way of describing Lombard Street is to say that it is by far the greatest combination of economical power and eco-

Reprinted from *Lombard Street: A Description of the Money Market* (1870), Chapter 1, pp. 1–10, by permission of Hyperion Press, Inc., Westport, Connecticut.

nomical delicacy that the world has ever seen. Of the greatness of the power there will be no doubt. Money is economical power. Everyone is aware that England is the greatest moneyed country in the world; everyone admits that it has much more immediately disposable and ready cash than any other country. But very few persons are aware *how much* greater the ready balance—the floating loan-fund which can be lent to anyone or for any purpose—is in England than it is anywhere else in the world. A very few figures will show how large the London loan-fund is, and how much greater it is than any other. The known deposits—the deposits of banks which publish their accounts—are, in

	£
London (31st December, 1872)	120,000,000
Paris (27th February, 1873)	13,000,000
New York (February, 1873)	40,000,000
German Empire (31st January, 1873)	8,000,000

And the unknown deposits—the deposits in banks which do not publish their accounts—are in London much greater than those in any other of these cities. The bankers' deposits of London are many times greater than those of any city—those of Great Britain many times greater than those of any other country.

Of course the deposits of bankers are not a strictly accurate measure of the resources of a Money Market. On the contrary, much more cash exists out of banks in France and Germany, and in all non-banking countries, than could be found in England or Scotland, where banking is developed. But that cash is not, so to speak, 'moneymarket money:' it is not attainable. Nothing but their immense misfortunes, nothing but a vast loan in their own securities, could have extracted the hoards of France from the custody of the French people. The offer of no other securities would have tempted them, for they had confidence in no other securities. For all other purposes the money hoarded was useless and might as well not have been hoarded. But the English money is 'borrowable' money. Our people are bolder in dealing with their money than any continental nation, and even if they were not bolder, the mere fact that their money is deposited in a bank makes it far more obtainable. A million in the hands of a single banker is a great power; he can at once lend it where he will, and borrowers can come to him, because they know or believe that he has it. But the same sum scattered in tens and fifties through a whole nation is no power at all: no one knows where to find it or whom to ask for it. Concentration of money in banks, though not the sole cause, is the principal cause which has made the Money Market of England so exceedingly rich, so much beyond that of other countries.

The effect is seen constantly. We are asked to lend, and do lend, vast sums, which it would be impossible to obtain elsewhere. It is sometimes said that any foreign country can borrow in Lombard Street *at a price:* some countries can borrow much cheaper than others; but all, it is said, can have some money if they choose to pay enough for it. Perhaps this is an exaggeration; but confined, as of course it was meant to be, to civilised Governments, it is not much of an exaggeration. There are very few civilised Governments that could not borrow considerable sums of us if they choose, and most of them seem more and more likely to choose. If any nation wants even to make a railway—especially at all a poor nation—it is sure to come to this country—to the country of banks—for the money. It is true that English bankers are not themselves very great lenders to foreign states. But they are great lenders to those who lend. They advance on foreign stocks, as the phrase is, with 'a margin;' that is, they find eighty per cent of the money, and the nominal lender finds the rest. And it is in this way that vast works are achieved with English aid which but for that aid would never have been planned.

In domestic enterprises it is the same. We have entirely lost the idea that any undertaking likely to pay, and seen to be likely, can perish for want of money; yet no idea was more familiar to our ancestors, or is more common now in most countries. A citizen of London in Queen Elizabeth's time could not have imagined our state of mind. He would have thought that it was of no use inventing railways (if he could have understood what a railway meant), for you would not have been able to collect the capital with which to make them. At this moment, in colonies and all rude countries, there *is* no large sum of transferable money; there is no fund from which you can borrow, and out of which you can make immense works. Taking the world as a whole—either now or in the past—it is certain that in poor states there is no spare money for new and great undertakings, and that in most rich states the money is too scattered, and clings too close to the hands of the owners, to be obtainable in large quantities for new purposes. A place like Lombard Street, where in all but the rarest times money can be always obtained upon good security or upon decent prospects of probable gain, is a luxury which no country has ever enjoyed with even comparable equality before.

But though these occasional loans to new enterprises and foreign States are the most conspicuous instances of the power of Lombard Street, they are not by any means the most remarkable or the most important use of that power. English trade is carried on upon borrowed capital to an extent of which few foreigners have an idea, and none of our ancestors could have conceived. In every district small traders have arisen, who 'discount their bills' largely, and with the capital so borrowed, harass and press upon, if they do not eradicate, the old capitalist. . . . In modern English business, owing to the certainty of obtaining loans on discount of bills or otherwise at a moderate rate of interest, there is a steady bounty on trading with borrowed capital, and a constant discouragement to confine yourself solely or mainly to your own capital.

This increasingly democratic structure of English commerce is very unpopular in many quarters, and its effects are no doubt exceedingly mixed. On the one hand, it prevents the long duration of great families of merchant princes, such as those of Venice and Genoa, who inherited nice cultivation as well as great wealth, and who, to some extent, combined the tastes of an aristocracy with the insight and verve of men of business. These are pushed out, so to say, by the dirty crowd of little men. After a generation or two they retire into idle luxury. Upon their immense capital they can only obtain low profits, and these they do not think enough to compensate them for the rough companions and rude manners they must meet in business. This constant levelling of our commercial houses is, too, unfavourable to commercial morality. Great firms, with a reputation which they have received from the past, and which they wish to transmit to the future, cannot be guilty of small frauds. They live by a *continuity* of trade, which detected fraud would spoil. When we scrutinise the reason of the impaired reputation of English goods, we find it is the fault of new men with little money of their own, created by bank 'discounts.' These men want business at once, and they produce an inferior article to get it. They rely on cheapness, and rely successfully.

But these defects and others in the democratic structure of commerce are compensated by one great excellence. No country of great hereditary trade, no European country at least, was ever so little 'sleepy,' to use the only fit word, as England; no other was ever so prompt at once to seize new advantages. A country dependent mainly on great 'merchant princes' will never be so prompt; their commerce perpetually slips more and more into a commerce of routine. A man of large wealth, however intelligent, always thinks, more or less—'I have a great income, and I want to keep it. If things go on as they are I shall certainly keep it; but if they change I *may* not keep it.' Consequently he considers every change of circumstance a 'bore,' and thinks of such changes as little as he can. But a new man, who has his way to make in the world, knows that such changes are his opportunities; he is always on the look-out for them, and always heeds them when he finds them. The rough and vulgar structure of English commerce is the secret of its life; for it contains 'the propensity to variation,' which, in the social as in the animal kingdom, is the principle of progress.

In this constant and chronic borrowing, Lombard Street is the great go-between. It is a sort of standing broker between quiet saving districts of the country and the active employing districts. . . . Lombard Street is thus a perpetual agent between the two great divisions of England—rapidly-growing districts, where almost any amount of money can be well and easily employed, and the stationary and the declining districts, where there is more money than can be used.

This organisation is so useful because it is so easily adjusted. Political economists say that capital sets towards the most profitable trades, and that it rapidly leaves the less profitable and non-paying trades. But in ordinary countries this is a slow process. . . . English capital runs as surely and instantly where it is most wanted, and where there is most to be made of it, as water runs to find its level.

This efficient and instantly-ready organisation gives us an enormous advantage in competition with less advanced countries—less advanced, that is, in this particular respect of credit. In a new trade English capital is instantly at the disposal of persons capable of understanding the new opportunities and of making good use of them. In countries where there is little money to lend, and where that little is lent tardily and reluctantly, enterprising traders are long kept back, because they cannot at once borrow the capital, without which skill and knowledge are useless. All *sudden* trades come to England. . . .

And not only does this unconscious 'organisation of capital,' to use a contintental phrase, make the English specially quick in comparison with their neighbors on the continent at seizing on novel mercantile opportunities, but it makes them likely also to retain any trade on which they have once regularly fastened. . . .

There are many other points which might be insisted on, but it would be tedious and useless to elaborate the picture. The main conclusion is very plain—that English trade is become essentially a trade on borrowed capital, and that it is only by this refinement of our banking system that we are able to do the sort of trade we do, or to get through the quantity of it.

But in exact proportion to the power of this system is its delicacy—I should hardly say too much if I said its danger. Only our familiarity blinds us to the marvellous nature of the system. There never was so much borrowed money collected in the world as is now collected in London. Of the millions in Lombard street, infinitely the greater proportion is held by bankers or others on short notice or on demand; that is to say, the owners could ask for it all any day they please: in a panic some of them do ask for some of it. If any large fraction of that money really was demanded, our banking system and our industrial system too would be in great danger.

Some of those deposits too are of a peculiar and very distinct nature. Since the Franco-German war, we have become to a much larger extent than before the Bankers of Europe. A very large sum of foreign money is on various accounts and for various purposes held here. And in a time of panic it might be asked for. In 1866 we held only a much smaller sum of foreign money, but that smaller sum was demanded and we had to pay it at great cost and suffering, and it would be far worse if we had to pay the greater sums we now hold, without better resources than we had then.

It may be replied, that though our instant liabilities are great, our present means are large; that though we have much we may be asked to pay at any moment, we have very much always ready to pay it with. But, on the contrary, there is no country at present, and there never was a country before, in which the ratio of the cash reserve to the bank deposits was so small as it is now in England. . . . So far from our being able to rely on the proportional magnitude of our cash in hand, the amount of that cash is so exceedingly small that a bystander almost trembles when he compares its minuteness with the immensity of the credit which rests upon it.

Again, it may be said that we need not be alarmed at the magnitude of our credit system or at its refinement, for that we have learned by experience the way of controlling it, and always manage it with discretion. But we do *not* always manage it with discretion. There is the astounding instance of Overend, Gurney, and Co. to the contrary. Ten years ago that house stood next to the Bank of England in the City of London; it was better known abroad than any similar firm—known, perhaps, better than any purely English firm. The partners had great estates, which had mostly been made in the business. They still derived an immense income from it. Yet in six years they lost all their own wealth, sold the business to the company, and then lost a large part of the company's capital. And these losses were made in a manner so reckless and so foolish, that one would think a child who had lent money to the City of London would have lent it better. After this example, we must not confide too surely in long-established credit, or in firmly-rooted traditions of business. We must examine the system on which these great masses of money are manipulated, and assure ourselves that it is safe and right.

But it is not easy to rouse men of business to the task. They let the tide of business float before them; they make money or strive to do so while it passes, and they are unwilling to think where it is going. Even the great collapse of Overends, though it caused a panic, is beginning to be forgotten. Most men of business think—'Anyhow this system will probably last my time. It has gone on a long time, and is likely to go on still.' But the exact point is, that it has *not* gone on a long time. The collection of the immense sums in one place and in few hands is perfectly new. . . .

I am by no means an alarmist. I believe that our system, though curious and peculiar, may be worked safely; but if we wish so to work it, we must study it. We must not think we have an easy task when we have a difficult task, or that we are living in a natural state when we are really living in an artificial one. Money will not manage itself, and Lombard street has a great deal of money to manage.

Big Business and the Money Power

Henry Ford
in collaboration with
Samuel Crowther

Polemics against "money" and "Wall Street" are familiar and recurring. Here is one from 1926 by Henry Ford, who abhored "debt"
and "financing."

———— ■ ————

Business—that is, the whole material side of life—is threatened by two
classes of people who think they are in opposition, but who actually
have a common cause—the professional financier and the professional
reformer.

Both go about the destruction of business. That is what they have in
common. Their ways are not alike. Their motives are not alike. But,
given a free hand, either can destroy business very quickly.

There is nothing to be said against the financier—the man who really
understands the management of money and its place in life. There is
nothing to be said against the reformer who knows what he is about and
knows the effect of the changes he desires and who is willing to give the
people to be reformed a chance.

But it is very different with the professional financier, who finances
for the sake of financing and what he can get out of it in money, with-

————
Reprinted from *Today and Tomorrow* (1988; originally published 1926), Chapter 3, pp. 26–34, by
permission of Bantam Doubleday Dell Publishing Group, Inc., New York.

out a thought of the welfare of the people. The professional reformer likewise reforms for the sake of reforming and for his own satisfaction, and without a thought of the real welfare of the people.

These two classes are real menaces. The professional financiers wrecked Germany. The professional reformers wrecked Russia. You can take your choice as to who made the better job of it.

＝

Twenty-five years ago, we heard a great deal about big business. There was really no big business twenty-five years ago. What we had was our first mergers of money. Money is not business. Big money cannot make big business.

＝

It becomes plain, therefore, that to confuse business with the money power is to make one thing of two and to unite elements which naturally oppose each other. A business cannot serve both the public and the money power. As a matter of fact, the money power has always lived more by exploiting or wrecking business than by the service of business. There are signs, however, that this may be on the mend.

Money put into business as a lien on its assets is dead money. When industry operates wholly by the permission of ''dead'' money, its main purpose becomes the production of payments for the owners of that money. The service of the public has to be secondary. If quality of goods jeopardizes these payments, then the quality is cut down. If full service cuts into the payments, then service is cut down. This kind of money does not serve business. It seeks to make business serve it.

Money that takes no risks in an industry, but demands its toll whether there be profit or loss, is not live money. It is not whole-heartedly in the business as a part of it; it is a dead weight, and the sooner the business is rid of it, the better. Dead money is not a working partner but an idle charge.

Live money goes into the business to work and to share with the business. It is there to be used. It shares whatever losses there may be. It is asset to the last penny, and never a liability.

Live money in a business is usually accompanied by the active labour of the man or men who put it there. Dead money is a sucker-plant.

The principle of the service of business to the people has gone far in the United States, and it will spread through and remake the world. It was not the war, but the seeming impossibility of restoring conditions as they were before the war, that gave men the first inkling of the lesson they are to learn. They would have accepted the war as an accident or as a mistake had they not been made to see that the war was but the symptom of a deeper malady. The old tricks have failed. The old wisdom has proved foolishness. The old motives are ineffective. If losing a false wisdom and finding a new beginning of learning is progress, then we may say that the world has progressed. Its old principles are disproved by experience. Progress is not marked by a definite boundary across which we step, but by an attitude and an atmosphere. Everything false does not vanish at a given moment, and everything true appear.

Some men know and many others feel that business is something more than money—that money is a commodity and not a power.

Any business is as good as finished when it begins to finance. It is sometimes necessary (although always dangerous) to get money for extensions except out of profits, and there may be emergencies when additional cash is required, but this is very different from financing for the sake of financing—using the business to make money through finance instead of through service.

The danger point of any business is not when it needs money, but when it becomes successful enough to be financed—to be foundation for a great pile of stocks and bonds. The public is gullible and may easily be taken advantage of. For instance, a certain amount of the stock of the Ford Motor Company of Canada is on the market. It could be bought for about $485 a share. Some exploiters bought up a few shares, and against each share issued one hundred of what they called "bankers' shares" at $10 each. That is, they sold for $1,000 what they had bought for $485, and the strange part is that the public fell into the trap and freely paid two dollars for something which they could have bought themselves for a dollar! That shows how easy it is to turn a successful business into a financial tool.

Thus, it is just when an industry becomes most widely useful that its strongest testing comes. The money power will point the way of large stock issues, of profits made out of paper instead of production, of easy gains by mixing water with true worth. This is a temptation to which many concerns succumb under the delusion that it is business. It is not business at all, but only a method of slow suicide. Think, if you can, of a single great industry operating today that was deliberately created and fostered by the money power. Every big business began lowly, grew because it filled a want, and if it attracted the attention of the money power at all, it was only after growth had been attained. A business which can bring itself to the point where it attracts the attention of money should be able to continue on its own feet without being financed.

Another rock on which business breaks is debt. Debt is nowadays an industry. Luring people into debt is an industry. The advantages of debt have become almost a philosophy. Possibly it is true that many people, if not most, would bestir themselves very little were it not for the pressure of debt obligations. If so, they are not free men and will not work from free motives. The debt motive is, basically, a slave motive.

When business goes into debt it owes a divided allegiance. The scavengers of finance, when they wish to put a business out of running or secure it for themselves, always begin with the debt method. Once on that road, the business has two masters to serve, the public and the speculative financier. It will scrimp the one to serve the other, and the public will be hurt, for debt leaves no choice of allegiance.

Business had freed itself from domineering finance by keeping within itself its earnings. Business that exists to feed profits to people who are not engaged, and never will be engaged in it, stands on a false basis. This is being so well understood that it has become a part of the creed of commerce that the service of business is wholly to the public and that the profits of business are due, first, to the business itself as a serviceable instrument of humanity, and then to the people whose labour and contributions of energy make the business a going concern.

But neither business nor finance has power to compel the public to buy here or buy there. The record of financiers in business affairs is full of disaster. If finance had the far-flung power that alarmists say it has, America, like Europe, would be filled with ragged peasants.

But here the service of business always has controlled and always will control. . . .

The true course of business is to follow the fortunes and pursue the service of those who had faith in it from the beginning—the public. If there is any saving in manufacturing cost, let it go to the public. If there is any increase in profits, let it be shared with the public in lowered prices. If there is any improvement in the commodity, let it be made without question, for whatever the capital cost, it was first the public that supplied the capital. That is the true course for good business to steer, and it is good business, for there is no better partnership a business can enter than a partnership of service with the people. It is far safer, far more durable and more profitable than partnership with a money power.

The best defence [sic] any people can have against their control by mere money is a business system that is strong and healthy through rendering wholesome service to the community.

What I Learned from the Depression

Dean Mathey

Dean Mathey was a partner in Dillon Read, headed the Empire Trust Company, and from the 1920s to the 1940s was the remarkably successful chairman of the investment committee at Princeton. In 1966, he privately printed *Fifty Years of Wall Street*, from which these lessons are excerpted.

——— ▬ ———

1. That once in about every 7 to 10 years there is a period of excessive general speculation culminating in a severe panic or depression when the man that is borrowing money is at a great disadvantage and he who has ready cash stands like a tower, four square to the ill winds that blow.

2. Extreme situations do not last, no matter what the apparent justification. No ladder is high enough to reach to Heaven. While we may have "new eras," old laws will still operate.

3. Avoid commitments, particularly of the delayed variety, they are more insidious. These birds may be depended upon to come home to roost when they are least welcome. Also, be definite about commitments made to you by others. When the storm comes, misunderstandings are so easy and so natural. What a joy a good clear record is in such a predicament!

Excerpted from *Fifty Years of Wall Street* (Princeton, New Jersey, 1966), pp. 67–68, by permission of Dean Mathey, Jr., David Mathey, and Macdonald Mathey.

4. Both in 1920 and 1929 the so-called "big fellows" in general said everything was o.k. But if the big fellows in general thought otherwise the stage could not be set for the unexpected. Panics occur because the leaders themselves have lost the way. And panics on Wall Street are notoriously periodic.

5. Never borrow money, without continuously reviewing and questioning your ability to pay it back under the worst conditions. Never borrow short-term money on unmarketable collateral.

6. It's right to be an optimist, but be prepared for the worst.

7. Make a practice of not giving GRATUITOUS ADVICE ABOUT THE PURCHASE OF SECURITIES.

8. People borrow money in good times and pay it back in bad times—just the opposite of what they should do.

9. The public are just as blind to recognizing the bottom of a depression as they are in recognizing the top of the boom. While there is no ladder that reaches to Heaven, the ladder that reaches all the way down to Hell in a country like America is just as fantastic.

Footnote to 1966 Printing

This memorandum was made around 1934 and 1935 after the storm was over. It was a soul-searching review on my part of what my thoughts were on the agonizing experiences I had been through during the depression. It is published just as it was written, without amendments or explanations I might make today.

How Good Is Professional Investment Management?

David L. Babson

Dave Babson's well-earned reputation for straight talk and Yankee integrity is brilliantly illuminated in this excerpted June 4, 1973, speech in Kansas City. The message is timeless.

A big investment feature of the past decade has been the huge increase in institutional investing. As a result, the professional investment management field has mushroomed, too.

Corporations have been placing more and more of their mounting pension fund assets in common stocks, and they've been hiring a host of new managers to supplement or replace their old-time metropolitan trust company advisors.

Scores of colleges and other endowments—spurred on by the famous Ford Foundation Report of the late 1960s—have employed outside investment advisors for the first time in their history. And thousands of wealthy individuals and personal trustees have joined this all-points search for portfolio managers supposed to have the magic touch to leave the market averages far behind.

> Few professional fields have ever grown so much so quickly as investment management in recent years.

Excerpted from *The Commercial and Financial Chronicle,* Thursday, June 28, 1973, pp. 1, 12, 13.

So now an obvious question to ask is: What has this modern professional investment management accomplished for its clients? How good has it really been?

Let's start out by looking at the mutual funds. Their records range all over the lot. A few have had top-notch results over the past five and ten years. But far too many—especially the newer ones—have had a perfectly miserable history.

. . . Over the past five years, the total investment return—income as well as appreciation—has averaged 4.3 per cent annually for all mutual stock funds vs. 7.5 per cent for the S&P 500.

Over the six years ended March 31, only one out of every six mutual funds was able to match the return on the S&P. In fact, one fund out of every ten had a minus return!

And this does not include the results of 1973, which—for many funds—looks like as big a disaster as 1970. Among all 400 U.S. growth funds—as of a week ago—one out of every three was down 25 per cent or more and one out of ten had lost one-third or more since January 1.

Now what about the pension trusts? . . . Over the past ten years, the annual return of these portfolios was 9.3 per cent vs. 9.9 per cent for the S&P—and over the latest five years the pension funds averaged 7.0 per cent vs. 7.5 per cent for the S&P.

American Telephone earlier this year reported that for the previous six years, that part of Telephone's $10 billion pension assets managed by 31 banks had averaged an 8 per cent annual return compared to about 9 per cent for the S&P 500.

These results of professional management may be acceptable in a period that you would not rate as vintage years. But they are a far cry from the rosy promises and expectations of just a few years back. So it may be worthwhile if we try to identify the reasons for the poorer results obtained by many professional money managers than their clients had been expecting. I am going to list five that I think are important:

Reasons for Poor Results

1. *First was the widespread misconception about inflation.* Back in the mid-60's, when the big move to professional management took off, the standard investment view was (a) that inflation would continue

indefinitely, and (b) that stocks—virtually all stocks—were preferable to bonds as inflation hedges.

But inflation doesn't automatically inflate stock prices. This is because it actually hurts the earnings of nearly every company.

When inflation creeps along at 1.2 per cent annually—as it had been doing up to the early 1960's—this fact was concealed by the 5 per cent rate of basic progress which most good companies are able to make.

However, when the annual pace of inflation speeded up to 4 per cent and faster—as it did in the late 1960's—the underlying progress of companies in many industries could no longer outpace inflation and their earnings stopped growing.

As it turned out, only a handful of companies have been able to maintain their rate of earnings expansion under the inflationary surge of recent years. . . .

2. *A second reason why professional management has had underperformance in recent years has been the age-gap in the investment community.* Almost no one came into our field from the early 1930's to the early 50's. As a result, by the late 1960's, only 10 per cent of investment professionals were 45 or older, while at least two-thirds were in their 20's and early 30's.

Now competence and judgment are not the product of age alone. But unless a man is stupid, there has to be a strong correlation between his experience and perspective and his ability to assess the risk factor. Having never seen it happen before, the rookies in our field during the 1960's had no idea that a hot Wall Street favorite like Four Seasons Nursing Homes could—in nine months—plummet from 91 dollars to 91 cents! Or that a sure-fire "now generation" concept like National Student Marketing could turn out to be a confidence game instead of another Xerox!

3. *The third reason why some professional managers have had disappointing results is they try to make investing into a very complicated job* when it is quite a simple and common sense process if you have the discipline to follow a consistent, long-range investment philosophy.

You really don't have to have a degree from the Harvard Business School to know that Eastman Kodak is a unique company or that IBM dominates the computer field or that Merck is one of the truly great research companies we have. Nor do you have to be able to spiel a lot of jargon about "Beta" to know that investors who have bought and held Minnesota Mining and similar leading stocks over the years have had excellent results without taking much risk or even trying very hard.

These new professional managers tend to set their sights too high. They often believe they are smarter than they really are and that they can accomplish things in the future which their own records show they haven't been able to accomplish in the past.

Actually, by setting unrealistic goals, they have been doing the very things that are almost certain to give them poor results—such as churning their portfolios at ridiculously high rates; buying "stories" from Wall Street; paying fantastic prices for unseasoned, speculative, fad stocks; dumping perfectly good companies because of slow earnings for a quarter or two; trying to outguess short-term market swings—*in brief, doing the VERY things that professional investors ought not to be doing.*

Churning is one of the greatest of these faults. . . .

Please note the investment gain for the top ten [mutual funds] averaged plus 71 per cent [for the period measured]—while that for the bottom group averaged minus 38 per cent—quite a swing! . . .

. . . The "churnover ratio" of the ten worst performers averaged 151 per cent during the past three years—five times the 32 per cent average ratio of the top ten funds!

Churning Hurts Performance

The only conclusion I can draw is that the lower the turnover, the better the record—and the higher the turnover, the poorer the results.

Why does the churning hurt investment performance? Primarily because it causes you to put the emphasis on the wrong things. You make poor initial selections; you focus on the temporary short-term factors rather than on the key long-range trends; you try to outsmart the other fellow only to find you are the patsy. In contrast, a buy-to-keep policy forces you to be as sure as possible—before you buy—that you're buying the right stock!

The buy-sell boys who try for a few points here, a few there, always think they can jump out if things go sour. But time after time they get into a disaster and can't get out at all. Even after the blood bath they took in 1970, they've come up with a whole new list of 80–90 per cent losers this year—Mattel, Winnebago, Levitz, etc.

4. *A fourth reason for lacklustre results is that conflicts of interest in the investment community have been multiplying for years.* This trend stems from the fact that everybody in our field has been trying to get into everyone else's specialty.

For example, some brokerage houses and underwriting firms—directly or through new subsidiaries—are managing large amounts of pension assets on a discretionary basis. Huge mutual fund complexes, suffering from redemptions, have moved into the institutional management field.

Insurance companies which have long run their own large portfolios and managed separate equity accounts for pension funds, are now managing and marketing their own mutual funds.

So who can tell whose interests are being represented by whom in these tangles of potential conflict? Damage suits against the trustees and managers of pension funds are appearing more and more frequently. The plaintiffs usually charge conflicts of interest and breach of fiduciary trust—and some of their allegations sound pretty hairy. The investment management field must get rid of these potential conflicts.

5. *A fifth reason for the shortfall of the professionals is a lack of investment knowledge on the part of many of those who make the actual selection of the professional managers of their pension fund or other portfolios.* Because many executives have little background in equity investing, they fall prey to unrealistic promises, hot-shot sales pitches, etc. In other words, there is a lack of investment experience among the personnel of the institutions who hire the professional portfolio managers as well as among the professional managers they hire.

Our firm receives a steady stream of questionnaires from both private and public pension funds seeking replacement or additional managers. Some of the questions asked—such as "what rate of total return do you expect to achieve over the next three years?"—reveal little investment understanding.

Five Crucial Qualifications

And the really crucial questions that ought to be asked often aren't mentioned at all. Having spent all of my adult forty years in the investment profession, I know for sure what five qualifications I would look for if I were selecting an advisory firm for my family, my college or my pension fund. They are:

1. First of all is *independence*. The advisory firm should not be engaged in, affiliated with or controlled by any organization in the brokerage, insurance, underwriting or other financial field. It should not be

owned or organized in any way that could jeopardize its ability to render independent investment advice in the client's best interest.

2. My second qualification would be *philosophy*. It should have a consistent philosophy which does not confuse investing with trading or speculating. And it should have a proven, effective record—in bad as well as in good years—under all types of economic and political conditions, indicating that it has the discipline to follow its philosophy.

3. My third qualification would be *specialization*. The firm should not be a financial department store. Its efforts should be confined to investment analysis and portfolio management rather than spread out over a whole range of other thinly related activities.

4. Fourth is *team work*. A competent and experienced staff which works closely together is more likely, in my judgment, to produce effective results than either the super-star system, on the one hand, or a big, loosely-knit organization whose internal communications are cumbersome and often inconsistent, on the other.

5. The fifth and vital qualification is *responsibility*. This is a tough one to assess. But anyone who manages other people's money must regard it as a serious trust and not as either a "money game" or an exercise in mathematical equations.

How investment management firms stack up on these five counts explains their divergent results in recent years more than anything else. And I see no reason for assuming that the future will be any different.

An Introduction to Warren Buffett from Ben Graham

'Adam Smith'

'Adam Smith' [George J. W. Goodman] provides deft insight into three figures—Ben Graham, Warren Buffett, and himself—in this vignette from his book *Supermoney*.

There is only one Dean of our profession, if security analysis can be said to be a profession. The reason that Benjamin Graham is undisputed Dean is that before him there was no profession and after him they began to call it that. He came to Wall Street in 1914; twenty years later he published the first edition of *Security Analysis*, the first and reigning textbook in the field. Big, black and forbidding, it has gone through four editions. Generations—plural now—of analysts have grown up with Graham and Dodd, as it is called—Dodd being David Dodd, the Columbia professor who was and is coauthor of the book. Graham himself taught at Columbia on and off for eighteen years and also at UCLA. When Graham arrived on the scene, a security analyst was a statistician, an ink-stained wretch wearing a green eyeshade and sitting on a three-legged stool, who gave figures to the partner in

Reprinted from *Supermoney* (New York: Random House, 1972), Chapter 5, pp. 174–78, by permission of the author.

charge of running that day's pool. Now there are examinations and learned analyst societies and the appellation C.F.A., or Chartered Financial Analyst.

That makes Graham Dean, but it would not necessarily make him respected in the downtown canyons, since professors of finance rarely move stocks, and respect is today's buck, after all. But Graham was also an active investor; he put in about twenty-odd years at it, as the head of his own investment company, Graham-Newman, which was considered a very smart outfit one generation ago, and he retired a very comfortable multimillionaire. Graham is now seventy-eight, and travels to his houses in Majorca, in the south of France, and in La Jolla. That makes him respected, in addition to making him Dean.

One day I got a letter from the good Dean, who was at his house in the south of France. It is a nice letter, and so characteristic of the Dean that you might as well read it all; it tells you a lot in a brief moment.

"LA CHAMPOUSSE"
42, AVENUE DE MARSEILLE, 42
AIX-EN-PROVENCE

-Sept. 6, 1968

Mr. "Adam Smith",
c/o Random House,
New York City.

Dear "Adam Smith",

This is an appreciative note about *The Money Game* from the chap you call "the dean of all security analysts". I read your book with a great deal of enjoyment, and with admiration for your many-faceted culture. Also, it gave me a lot of information on what has been happening in Wall Street since I left it some years ago.

I think I understand pretty well everything in the book that's in non-mathematical English. However, your Greek on p. 25 gave me a bit of trouble. The second part is evidently a version of the well-known "Quem deus vult perdere prius dementat." (But your text has φταν instead of όταν.) Does the preceding part mean "When a beam falls every man gathers wood''? (If so, your δουὸς must be changed to οϰός.) And where does the quotation come from?

Thanks in advance for your reply, and sincere congratulations on your book.

Benj. Graham

P.S. Also: shouldn't it be Mme. Récamier instead of de Staël (p. 221) and Hinzelmenschen for—menshen (p. 270). That's for your next printing.

You know something right away. Nobody messes with the Dean as far as the classics are concerned. To many Wall Streeters, Horace is the guy who works in the cage in the back room tallying the margin accounts. Benj. Graham has always been a classicist; the prescript to *Security Analysis* is a marvelously apt quotation from Horace's *Ars Poetica*:

> *Multa renascentur quae iam ce cidera, cadentque*
> *Quae nunc sunt in honore vocabulae . . .*
>
> Many shall be restored that now are fallen, and many
> Shall fall that now are in honor.

It is nice to hear good words from the Dean, even with the ruler-taps on the wrist. We did have to have a special printer for the great quotation, and any good proofreader would have realized that φταν should have been ὅταν. Hinzelmenschen should certainly have a *c;* you can't catch them all. (I did, however, mean Madame de Staël, not Madame Récamier.)

After some further correspondence the good Dean came to town and we had breakfast at the Plaza. Graham is a short, dapper man with a vague resemblance to Edward G. Robinson. He was in town, he said, to see a publisher about the new translation of Aeschylus he had just completed, and then he was going to see some of his grandchildren. When we met, the market was sliding, and the performanceniks were in their final throes. I asked him what he thought of what was going on.

"Oh, I don't keep up any more," he said. "I only own one stock, and the rest is all municipal bonds. But these periods have come before. As it was written once, *hoc etiam transibit,* this too will pass.''

What was the one stock?

"That's just left over, Government Employees Life Insurance; we owned the whole company at one point. I don't even keep up with that. I've reached the stage where I'm just giving things away, not trying to make more."

We talked about events since the last edition of *Security Analysis*. Benj. Graham had an idea he wanted to talk to me about: a new edition of *The Intelligent Investor* was forthcoming, that book being more or less a distillation of the textbook, *Security Analysis*, only for the layman. Graham wanted me to work on it, more or less by long-distance correspondence with him. I could send the relevant chapters to Aix-en-Provence or Majorca or La Jolla, and he would send them back again.

"There are really only two people I would want to work on this," Graham said. "You're one, and the other is Warren Buffett."

"Who's Warren Buffet?" I asked.

That, as it turns out, was a rather extraordinary question at the time. Extraordinary because I knew most of the highly visible professional money managers of the time; they spoke at seminars, delineated their theories, dressed up and trotted out their favorite industries and their favorite stocks. I didn't know Warren Buffett. He was not in the chain letter for Four Seasons or Viatron, or even for Control Data or Polaroid.

That, of course, would have made him atypical but not remarkable. What was remarkable was that Buffett was easily the outstanding money manager of the generation, and what was more remarkable was that he did it with the philosophy of another generation. While the gun slingers of the sixties were promoting each other over drinks at Oscar's then going back to their offices so they could watch the tape, Buffett was compiling the best records in the industry *from Omaha, Nebraska*. No quote machines, no ticker, no Oscar's, no chewed fingernails, no tranquilizers, no Gelusil, no backgammon after the close, no really big spectacular winners, no technological companies, no conglomerates, no "concepts." Just pure Benj. Graham, applied with absolute consistency—quiet, simple stocks, easy to understand, with a lot of time left over for the kids, for handball, for listening to the tall corn grow.

Buffett, it's true, did not manage a public fund, so he was not subject to the pressures of the salesman wanting to sell the fund. While he made his record with the philosophy of another generation, some of his big winners were also well within the growth-stock philosophy. He did not have a committee to deal with, and he did not have a boss. He kept himself out of the public eye, though for most of his career the public eye would not have been on him anyway. If he bought so much of a company that he controlled it, he was willing to step into the business. All of these factors freed him from more typical restraints.

His partnership began in 1956, with $105,000 largely supplied by uncles, aunts and other assorted relatives. It ended in 1969 with $105,000,000, and a compounded growth rate of 31 percent. Ten thousand dollars invested in the partnership in 1957 would have grown to $260,000. Over that time, the partnership *did not have a single losing year,* and it gained in the years of severe market declines, 1962 and 1966 among them.

Ben Graham:
Ideas as Mementos

Charles D. Ellis, CFA

Benjamin Graham's contributions to the professionalization of financial analysis have been recognized for years, but never as adequately or eloquently described as in this article. It outlines
Graham's thinking as revealed through his *FAJ* publications. "To excerpt his thoughts is to explicate his vision, the high personal and
intellectual standards he brought to his work and to the profession,
and the indelible imprint he left on all of us," is the apt way that
Charley Ellis sums up the feelings of all who knew him.

Ben Graham developed the idea of our profession just as surely as Sir
Robert Peel created the idea of an effective policeman, and just as certainly as the London constables are still called Bobbies in respect for
Sir Robert's conceptualization of their mission and qualifications, those
of us who serve in the profession as financial analysts are living out
Ben's idea of what we might be able to do. We are, at least we aspire
to be, adherents to the mission he originated.

My own acquaintance with Ben was all too brief: In his late 70s, he
joined in a series of seminars I was leading for Donaldson, Lufkin &
Jenrette, to which were invited in groups of 20 the leading investment
managers of the day. By common consent, Ben was the best informed,
the most inquisitive, the most delighted with ideas and differences of

Reprinted from the *Financial Analysts Journal* 38 (July/August 1982), pp. 41–48. Charlottesville, Virginia: Association for Investment Management and Research.

view in the group. And, of course, he charmed us all by his grace and wit and appreciation.

Sometimes, the incidental imperfection serves to illuminate the excellence of the man. For me, there is still special pleasure in the impossibility of sorting out one trivial misunderstanding. Ben was very pleased with Jacob Bronowski's television series on *The Ascent of Man,* watched every program, and was reading the book of the program's transcripts. Naturally Ben was delighted with Bronowski's research and ideas: They were the twin dimensions of Ben's work. But Ben was even more enchanted by Bronowski's extraordinary ability, as Ben saw it, to "get every word in every sentence in every performance exactly right— exactly the way it was in the book!" It never occurred to Ben that the book was made *after* the television program, and that it was the book that was accurately repeating Bronowski. Twice I tried to help Ben "get the cart before the horse," to no avail, and then realized he liked it the way he had it, and would rather get on with the serious discussion of ideas.

Here, then, are a few excerpts from a dozen articles Ben wrote for the *Financial Analysts Journal* over 30 years.

The Campaign for Professionalism

Ben was an early advocate of what we now call Chartered Financial Analysts and the extensive examination and education program that is conducted through the CFA Institute. His campaign for this professionalism was evident in a 1945 *FAJ* article where he posed the rhetorical question: Should security analysts have a professional rating? For a mind as quick to isolate the central argument, the analysis was not difficult. First,

> The crux of the question is whether security analysis as a calling has enough of the professional attribute to justify the requirement that its practitioners present to the public evidence of fitness for their work.

Second,

> The right of every individual to practice his chosen trade is subject to the higher right of society to impose standards of fitness where these are advisable.

Third,

> It would seem to follow, almost as an axiom, that security analysts
> would welcome a rating of quasi-professional character, and will work
> hard to develop this rating into a universally accepted warranty of good
> character and sound competence.[1]

The elegance of Ben's thinking was complemented by a plain way
with words—and dress. He wore dark suits of a durable fabric that
would last and last, and he described his work as "stock market operations." In a similar vein, his term for the reorganized professional was
simply Qualified Security Analyst.

In the course of a 1946 article, written as "Cogitator," Ben admonished his colleagues, saying that a professional analyst was "right" in
recommending purchase of a security only when the stock appreciated
in price for the reasons identified by the analyst. You should be right
for the right reason—the one you identified when making your recommendation:

> Recommendations to buy a stock for the main reason that next year's
> earnings are going to be higher . . . are among the most common in
> Wall Street. They have the advantage of being subject to rather simple
> tests. Such a recommendation will be right if both (a) the earnings in-
> crease and (b) the price advances—say, at least 10 per cent—within the
> next 12 months.
>
> The objection to this type of recommendation is a practical one. It is
> naive to believe that in the typical case the market is unaware of the
> prospects for improved earnings next year. If this is so, the favorable
> factor is likely to be discounted, and the batting average of recommenda-
> tions based on this simple approach can scarcely be very impressive.[2]

Evident in this brief excerpt is Ben's respect for the other investors
working in the market. In later years, after many more smart people
had come into the market, he would doubt the ability of any large institutional investor to outperform the market *and* the competition.

Organized Knowledge

Ben enjoyed throughout his life that open-minded thirst for understanding and information that we admire in the term "childlike." At 80, he
was working out a new formulation—and testing it against actual mar-

ket results. In 1946, at the time of the announcement of a new Awards Committee on Corporate Disclosure, Ben addressed the need for organized knowledge in a profession:

> It is amazing to reflect how little systematic knowledge Wall Street has to draw upon as regards the historical behavior of securities with defined characteristics. We do, of course, have charts showing the long-term price movements of stock groups and of individual stocks. But there is no real classification here, except by type of business. (An exception is Barron's index of Low Priced Stocks.) Where is the continuous, ever growing body of knowledge and technique handed down by the analysts of the past to those of the present and the future? When we contrast the annals of medicine with those of finance, the paucity of our recorded and digested experience becomes a reproach.
>
> There are explanations and answers in rebuttal. Security analysis is a fledgling science; give it (and *The Analysts Journal*) time to spread its wings. Contrariwise, many of us believe, perhaps unconsciously rather than consciously, that there is not enough permanence in the behavior of security patterns to justify a laborious accumulation of case histories. If physicians and research men keep on investigating cancer, they will probably end by understanding and controlling it—because the nature of cancer does not change during the years it is being studied. But the factors underlying security values and the price behavior of given types of securities do suffer alteration through the years. By the time we have completed the cumbersome processes of inductive study, by the time our tentative conclusions have been checked and counterchecked through a succession of market cycles, the chances are that new economic factors will have supervened—and thus our hard won technique becomes obsolete before it is ever used.
>
> That is what we may think, but how do we know whether, or to what extent, it is so? We lack the codified experience which will tell us whether codified experience is valuable or valueless. In the years to come we analysts must go to school to the older established disciplines. We must study their ways of amassing and scrutinizing facts and from this study develop methods of research suited to the peculiarities of our own field of work.
>
> To what extent do we address ourselves to the 'classification and methodical exploitation . . . of the salient and recurrent phenomena'? Of this we have as yet only the rudiments. Very little effort has been made to construct systematic inductive studies of our experience with various types of securities, or security situations. The experience we draw upon in forming our judgments is largely a matter of rule-of-thumb, of vague impressions or even prejudices, rather than the resultant of many recorded and carefully studied case histories.[3]

Intrinsic Value

Ben was clearly identified in his investing with "intrinsic value," but not with "growth stocks." The reason for his preference was the confidence he could have in his own work when the analysis focused on present assets and liabilities rather than depending upon estimates of future values. Ben would have, of course, been comfortable with Baron Rothschild's summary of a lifetime's learning: "Buy assets; sell earnings."

Here is Ben's logic from a 1957 article:

> Of the various basic approaches to common-stock valuation, the most widely accepted is that which estimates the average earnings and dividends for a period of years in the future and capitalizes these elements at an appropriate rate. This statement is reasonably definite in form, but its application permits of the widest range of techniques and assumptions, including plain guesswork. The analyst has first a broad choice as to the future period he will consider; then the earnings and dividends for the period must be estimated, and finally a capitalization rate selected in accordance with his judgment or his prejudices. We may observe here that since there is no *a priori* rule governing the number of years to which the valuer should look forward in the future, it is almost inevitable that in bull markets investors and analysts will tend to see far and hopefully ahead, whereas at other times they will not be so disposed to 'heed the rumble of a distant drum.' Hence arises a high degree of built-in instability in the market valuation of growth stocks, so much so that one might assert with some justice that the more dynamic the company the more inherently speculative and fluctuating may be the market history of its shares. (On this point the philosophically inclined are referred to the recent article of David Durand on 'Growth Stocks and the Petersburg Paradox,' in the September 1957 issue of the *Journal of Finance*. His conclusion is 'that the growth-stock problem offers no great hope of a satisfactory solution.')
>
> When it comes to estimating future earnings few analysts are willing to venture forth, Columbus-like, on completely uncharted seas. They prefer to start with known quantities—e.g., current or past earnings—and process these in some fashion to reach an estimate for the future. As a consequence, in security analysis the past is always being thrown out of the window of theory and coming in again through the back door of practice. It would be a sorry joke on our profession if all the elaborate data on past operations, so industriously collected and so minutely analyzed, should prove in the end to be quite unrelated to the real determinants of the value—the earnings and dividends of the future.[4]

The Psychology of the Stock Market

In 1958, Ben was Visiting Professor of Finance at UCLA, and gave a long talk on what he perceived to be speculation in common stock:

> Let me start with a summary of my thesis. In the past the speculative elements of the common stock resided almost exclusively in the company itself; they were due to uncertainties, or fluctuating elements, or downright weaknesses in the industry, or the corporation's individual set-up. These elements of speculation still exist, of course; but it may be said that they have been sensibly diminished by a number of long-term developments to which I shall refer. But in revenge a new and major element of speculation has been introduced into the common-stock arena from outside the companies. It comes from the attitude and viewpoint of the stock-buying public and their advisers—chiefly us security analysts. This attitude may be described in a phrase: primary emphasis upon future expectations.

Ben developed his thesis, to the pleasure of his audience, with a bit of personal history:

> In 1912 I had left college for a term to take charge of a research project for U.S. Express Co. We set out to find the effect on revenues of a proposed revolutionary new system of computing express rates. For this purpose we used the so-called Hollerith machines, leased out by the then Computing-Tabulating-Recording Co. They comprised card-punches, card-sorters, and tabulators—tools almost unknown to businessmen, then, and having their chief application in the Census Bureau. I entered Wall Street in 1914, and the next year the bonds and common stock of C.-T.-R. Co. were listed on the New York Exchange. Well, I had a kind of sentimental interest in that enterprise, and besides I considered myself a sort of technological expert on their products, being one of the few financial people who had seen and used them. So early in 1916 I went to the head of my firm, known as Mr. A. N., and pointed out to him the C.-T.-R. stock was selling in the middle 40s . . . ; that it had earnings of $6.50 in 1915; that its book value—including, to be sure, some non-segregated intangibles—was $130; that it had started a $3 dividend; and that I thought rather highly of the company's products and prospects. Mr. A. N. looked at me pityingly. 'Ben,' said he, 'Do not mention that company to me again. I would not touch it with a ten-foot pole. (His favorite expression.) Its 6% bonds are selling in the low 80s and they are no good. So how can the stock be any good? Everybody knows there is nothing behind it but water.' (Glossary: In those days that was the ultimate of condemnation. It meant that the asset-account on the balance sheet was fictitious. Many industrial companies—notably U.S. Steel—

despite their $100 par, represented nothing but water, concealed in a written-up plant account. Since they had 'nothing' to back them but earning power and future prospects, no self-respecting investor would give them a second thought.)

I returned to my statistician's cubby-hole, a chastened young man. Mr. A. N. was not only experienced and successful, but extremely shrewd as well. So much was I impressed by his sweeping condemnation of Computing-Tabulating-Recording that I never bought a share of it in my life, not even after its name was changed to IBM in 1926. . . .

Always seeking *lessons* to be drawn from experiences, Ben summarized this lesson:

It seems a truism to say that the old-time common-stock investor was not much interested in capital gains. He bought almost entirely for safety and income, and let the speculator concern himself with price appreciation. Today we are likely to say that the more experienced and shrewd the investor, the less attention he pays to dividend returns, and the more heavily his interest centers on long-term appreciation. Yet one might argue, perversely, that precisely because the old-time investor did not concentrate on future capital appreciation he was virtually guaranteeing to himself that he would have it, at least in the field of industrial stocks. And, conversely, today's investor is so concerned with anticipating the future that he is already paying handsomely for it in advance. Thus what he has projected with so much study and care may actually happen and still not bring him any profit. If it should fail to materialize to the degree expected he may in fact be faced with a serious temporary and perhaps even permanent loss.[5]

On Price-Earnings Ratios

Observing how markets change and reverse apparent certainties, Ben gently admonished,

It casts some little doubt in my mind as to the complete dependability of the popular belief among analysts that prominent and promising companies will now always sell at high price-earnings ratios; that this is a fundamental fact of life for investors and they may as well accept and like it. I have no desire at all to be dogmatic on this point. All I can say is that it is not settled in my mind, and each of you must seek to settle it for yourself.

His conclusion draws upon his beloved classics:

When Phaethon insisted on driving the chariot of the Sun, his father, the experienced operator, gave the neophyte some advice which the latter failed to follow—to his cost. Ovid summed up Phoebus Apollo's counsel in three words:

Medius tutissimus ibis

You will go safest in the middle course

I think this principle holds good for investors and their security-analyst advisers.[6]

Beating the Market

In 1963, Ben wrote about the future of financial analysis, in the course of which he mused about technical analysis:

> My views on the validity of stock-market forecasting have been unfavorable for about half a century. This may entitle me to a high mark for consistency, but it hardly qualifies me as an impartial student of the subject. . . . [7]

Judgment and Efficient Markets

Despite his doubts about the ability of large institutions to beat the market regularly, Ben was confident that analysts could be "right" and that markets could be "wrong":

> In its extreme form the hypothesis of the efficient market makes two declarations: (1) The price of nearly every stock at nearly all times reflects whatever is knowable about the company's affairs; hence no consistent profits can be made by seeking out and using additional information, including that held by 'insiders.' (2) Because the market has complete or at least adequate information about each issue, the prices it registers are therefore 'correct,' 'reasonable' or 'appropriate.' This would imply that it is fruitless, or at least insufficiently rewarding, for security analysts to look for discrepancies between price and value.
>
> I have no particular quarrel with declaration one, though assuredly there are times when a researcher may unearth significant information about a stock, not generally known and reflected in the price. But I deny emphatically that because the market has all the information it needs to establish a correct price the prices it actually registers are in fact correct. Take as my example a fine company such as Avon Products. How can it make sense to say that its price of 140 was 'correct' in 1973 and that its

price of 32 was also 'correct' in 1974? Could anything have happened—outside of stock-market psychology—to reduce the value of that enterprise by 77 per cent or nearly six billion dollars? The market may have had all the information it needed about Avon; what it lacked is the right kind of judgment in evaluating its knowledge.

Descartes summed up the matter more than three centuries ago, when he wrote in his 'Discours de la Methode': 'Ce n'est pas assez d'avoir l'esprit bon, mais le principal est de l'appiquer bien.' In English: 'It is not enough to have a good intelligence'—and I add, 'enough information'—'the principal thing is to apply it well.'

I can assure the reader that among the 500-odd NYSE issues selling below the seven times earnings today, there are plenty to be found for which the prices are not 'correct' ones, in any meaningful sense of the term. They are clearly worth more than their current selling prices, and any security analyst worth his salt should be able to make up an attractive portfolio out of this 'universe.'[8]

The pioneer of fundamental research in the 1930s, Ben felt the world of investors had changed—surely more as a result of his work than any ten others—and could say in 1976:

I am no longer an advocate of elaborate techniques of security analysis in order to find superior value opportunities. This was a rewarding activity, say, 40 years ago, when our textbook 'Graham and Dodd' was first published; but the situation has changed a good deal since then. In the old days any well-trained security analyst could do a good professional job of selecting undervalued issues through detailed studies; but in the light of the enormous amount of research now being carried on, I doubt whether in most cases such extensive efforts will generate sufficiently superior selections to justify their cost. To that very limited extent I'm on the side of the 'efficient market' school of thought now generally accepted by the professors.[9]

Later that year, Warren Buffett wrote in his *FAJ* tribute to Ben:

A remarkable aspect of Ben's dominance of his professional field was that he achieved it without that narrowness of mental activity that concentrates all effort on a single end. It was, rather, the incidental by-product of an intellect whose breadth almost exceeded definition. Virtually total recall, unending fascination with new knowledge and an ability to recast it in a form applicable to seemingly unrelated problems made exposure to his thinking in any field a delight. There was an absolutely open-ended, no-scores-kept generosity of ideas, time and spirit. If clarity of thinking was required, there was no better place to go. And if encouragement or counsel was needed, Ben was there.[10]

He still is for those who enjoyed even briefly the pleasure of his company.

Notes

1. "Should Security Analysts Have a Professional Rating?" January 1945.
2. "On Being Right in Security Analysis," First Quarter 1946 (as "Cogitator").
3. "The Hippocratic Method in Security Analysis," Second Quarter 1946 (as "Cogitator").
4. "Two Illustrative Approaches to Formula Valuations of Common Stocks," November 1957.
5. "The New Speculation in Common Stocks," June 1958.
6. Ibid.
7. "The Future of Financial Analysis," May/June 1963.
8. "The Future of Common Stocks," September/October 1974.
9. "A Conversation with Benjamin Graham," September/October 1976.
10. Warren E. Buffett, "Benjamin Graham (1894–1976)," November/December 1976.

The Psychology of
Investment Decision-Making

Peter Carman

Peter Carman serves as chief investment officer at Sanford C. Bernstein Co., whose investment philosophy is based on the expectation that competing investors will have understandable—but profound—distortions in their valuations of securities, creating opportunities for less emotional, more rational investors.

———— ▬ ————

One of the underlying assumptions of the Bernstein investment philosophy is that distortions in value are created by emotions that dominate investor decision-making. . . . These distortions occur regularly and provide opportunities for premium performance for those investors who can capitalize on them. . . . Use of the dividend discount model provides a rational, systematic method that can be used to uncover when these distortions occur and measure how large they are. But why should distortions or inefficiencies exist in the first place? After all, most investors are bright, sophisticated, well educated and well informed. It seems, however, that these irrationalities are a normal part of human behavior.

I came across a survey recently that is particularly appropriate within this context. This survey was taken from a random sample of adult males. The men were asked to rate themselves on a number of param-

Excerpted from a speech at the Sanford C. Bernstein Company's Third Annual Pension Conference, September 9, 1985, by permission of the author.

eters: The first was their ability to get along with others. Every single respondent ranked himself in the top 10% of the population on this score; and a full 25% put themselves in the top 1%. Similarly, 70% rated themselves in the top quintile in leadership ability. And only 2% felt that they were below average leaders. Finally, in an area where self-deception should be difficult for most males, 60% said they were in the top quintile in athletic ability and only 6% said they were below average.

Investment Decision-Making

It also turns out that there are a number of studies in the field of behavioral psychology that strongly suggest that all of us have specific glitches in our thinking patterns that are particularly noticeable in complicated, ambiguous situations, or during periods of stress or uncertainty. Furthermore, these glitches, while not rational, can be measured; they form predictable patterns which tend to confirm, in a systematic fashion, our intuitive beliefs about investor decision-making and pricing in the securities markets. This research leads us to two conclusions.

- First: We don't usually understand the implications of probabilities, and when we do, we don't apply them well in day-to-day situations.
- Second: There are some very strong biases in the way we forecast probabilities in the first place.

The cumulative impact of these two factors results in a number of important and predictable decision-making biases.

- We overvalue certainty.
- We overestimate the value of small chances of large gains or losses.
- We have a disproportionate aversion to losses.

At this point, I would like to introduce some research done primarily by two behavioral psychologists, Daniel Kahneman and Amos Tversky, in the field of prospect theory. Their research tries to measure and explain patterns of decision-making under uncertainty. But first, I would like to provide a little background on the way investment theoreticians have traditionally addressed this issue.

Risk Aversion

I am sure that it doesn't come as a great surprise to any of us that the most easily identifiable bias in decision-making is risk aversion. In order to address this, I would like to explore the idea of utility. Let me ask you a question: Which would you prefer?

 A. An 80% chance of winning $100,000?
    or
 B. An outright gift of $70,000?

The answer that carries the highest expected monetary value is clearly the 80% chance of winning $100,000, which is worth $80,000. Most people, however, opt for the guaranteed $70,000 payment. What happens is that the extra $10,000 that one should statistically earn on that gamble doesn't contribute anywhere near as much to our satisfaction or utility as the earlier increments of $10,000 that make up the guaranteed $70,000. . . .

Utility of Wealth

The utility of wealth is not a linear function of money. Within this frame of reference, a gain of $2,000 contributes less than twice as much to utility or happiness as a gain of $1,000. People tend to feel less and less excited about additional increments of wealth and, as a consequence, are willing to take less and less risk to increase that wealth. The set of relationships postulated by utility theory can be described mathematically and, in its general form, this theory has served an important role in analyzing how investors make decisions.

Useful as this framework has been in modeling human behavior, Kahneman and Tversky's investigations suggest that there are a number of areas where people's decisions are consistently out of line with what would be predicted from utility theory. The psychologists' elaboration of this work is called prospect theory.

They developed prospect theory empirically by asking subjects about their preferences for things. Some of the questions involved preferences related to life, death and health; others involved purely quantitative issues. Many were based on money, sometimes real money. All were gambles of one form or another, thus testing decision-making in an environment of uncertainty. I will now spend the next few minutes talking about some of these choice problems and relating them to investing in general.

General Jones

As a start in exploring this area we can talk about General Jones. Despite his reputation as a crack military strategist, he has found himself in a tough spot. He commands 600 troops and they are cornered. He has two choices. . . . He can choose Strategy A and save 200 of his troops, or the General can adopt Strategy B and risk a one-third chance that all of his troops will be saved and a two-thirds chance that all will die. Which should he choose?

In studies of many groups, some acquainted with the mathematics of probability and some not, the preponderance of people pick A. The expectation for either strategy is identical. But people clearly prefer A. Their motivation? We don't know exactly, but probably it is a distaste for gambling with lives.

Doctor Baker

On the other hand, what about Doctor Baker? He has been called in to treat 600 very sick people. He also has two choices. . . . [Therapy A will cause 400 people to die. With Therapy B, there is a one-third chance everyone will be saved and a two-thirds chance no one will be saved.] What should *he* do? Studies of people faced with these choices show an overwhelming preference for Therapy B. Why? When faced with the possibility of the certain death of 400, why not gamble and try to save them all.

Of course a comparison of the General's and the Doctor's situations indicate that they are in exactly the same position. Strategy A and Therapy A will have the same result—400 people will die. Similarly, the objective result of alternative B in both situations is identical. Yet when the problem is stated in terms of a certain gain (that is, lives saved) versus stating the problem in terms of a certain loss, i.e., lives lost, people react very differently.

When these kinds of choices are framed in terms of financial gain or loss, the results are the same. People normally require very high odds of winning to offset a relatively small probability of loss. In fact, on average, people require a 65% chance of winning $100 to offset a 35% chance of losing $100. . . .

Let's turn to another choice problem. You are now given a choice between:

A. 1% chance of winning $6,000.

or

B. 2% chance of winning $3,000.

Both choices have the same expected value and both are remote chances. In general, people go for A in a ratio of about 7 to 3. Again, the bottom line is that in the case of small chances of very large gains or losses, people seem to turn into risk seekers, despite the fact that this result clearly violates utility theory.

Certainty Effect

The next choice problem is an additional example of this process. Think about the choices offered in the following table:

Choose between:		
A. Amount	**Probability**	**Value**
$2,500	33%	$825
0	67	
B. Amount	**Probability**	**Value**
$2,400	34%	$816
0	66	

In choice A the chance of not winning is miniscule and the expected value of the outcome is a few dollars higher than in choice B. However, studies show choice B to be the overwhelming favorite, 82% to 18%.

This illustrates what is called the certainty effect—that is, the disproportionate interest people have in things that are certain versus things of a moderate probability.

Implications for Money Management

We have gone far enough to draw some important conclusions about prospect theory's implications for money management. The first implication is probably the least provocative: Investors clearly undervalue things they perceive as risky relative to those things they perceive as certain. Characteristics that are frequently associated with overvaluation on this basis include stability of earnings during recessions and consistency of earnings growth at all times.

The second implication is more powerful but doesn't occur with great regularity: Investors can be counted on to overreact to events having small probabilities. This comes in two forms. It causes investors to become risk takers when contemplating large gains and extraordinarily risk averse when contemplating possible large losses. Thus, people can be counted on to overpay for the prospect of a promising new drug in early clinical trials, the potential of a big oil find or a hot rapidly growing technology company. On the flip side, people can also be counted on to overreact to potential calamities and undervalue the affected company, the latest example of which was the Bhopal disaster at Union Carbide.

The third issue is probably most significant for our investment style. It is the disproportionality of people's tolerance for losses as compared to the pleasure of gains. With great frequency, investors find reasons to fear exposure to various sectors of the economy, a particular industry, or individual companies. The prospects for these stocks are then perceived by investors as a pair of choices, one of which implies a loss. The reaction to the potential for loss is to undervalue these stocks relative to others where the probability and magnitude of the potential losses appear small. . . .

Biases in Forecasting

The forecasting process, as you are well aware, is not a simple one. As Mark Twain once said: "The art of prophesy is very difficult, especially with respect to the future." A forecaster is confronted with the problem of collecting massive amounts of information, sorting out the important from the trivial and processing the remaining data in a way that will produce a meaningful approximation of what he is trying to forecast. In addressing this task, we attempt to help ourselves by taking shortcuts that allow us to organize and simplify the process. We do so in a way that seems to be consistent from person to person.

Generally speaking we use the three forecasting tools outlined below:

Forecasting Tool	Technique/Reasoning
Representativeness	What is this similar to?
Availability	How often has this happened?
Anchoring	At what level has the variable been recently?

When using representativeness, we find a model which, in our experience, looks like it has the same characteristics as the thing we are trying to forecast. This helps us decide what the key variables should be. Availability has us look at history, both quantitatively and qualitatively, to try to determine the probable behavior of the key variables that make up the model. And when we employ anchoring we examine the level of each variable today, to establish a base point, and then forecast the future based on steps one and two.

Because of the complexity of the forecasting task, these internalized guidelines are quite useful (one could even say necessary) but they can sometimes lead to severe systematic errors. If we were always totally objective in our thought processes and about ourselves, and if, in addition, we had a good intuitive sense for the laws of statistics, the process outlined above would be fine. Unfortunately, objectivity and appreciation of statistical principles do not often characterize the way we operate. Moreover, the data available to us are usually not complete or are of questionable relevance. Taken together with the way people make judgments, biases are almost assured.

Stereotyping

As the next step in this process, I'll outline some of the more important of these biases as summarized in the following table:

Source	Problem
1. Representativeness	
• Insensitivity to base rate	Stereotyping
• Misconceptions of regression	Importance of recent events overemphasized
• Law of "small" numbers	Overemphasis on small number of events
• Failure of initiative	I can change but no one else can

First let me pose a question. Steven is very shy, withdrawn, invariably helpful, but with little interest in people or in the world of reality. Is Steve a librarian or salesman?

Of course, everyone assumes that Steve is a librarian. Actually, the odds are that Steve is a salesmen because there are 16 times as many salesmen in the workforce as librarians. People are generally aware of this imbalance but disregard it even when the specific information is available. This is stereotyping. . . . In general, stereotyping is extraordinarily compelling and normally overwhelms the discipline required to integrate the laws of statistics into the selection process.

In the stock market, the impact of stereotyping also makes itself felt. For example, when investors were most concerned with problems facing electric utilities with unfinished nuclear facilities, virtually all of those utilities were thrown into the same category. On the other hand there were significant differences among those companies, including relative financial exposure to a plant writeoff, the character of regulation in the state and specific company experience in building nuclear facilities.

Misconception of Regressions

Of greater significance to our business is what is called the effects of misconceptions about regressions. A regression is normally made up of a large number of equally weighted data points that reflect historical relationships. Frequently, forecasters tend to bias historical results by overweighting the most recent data. The effect of this bias is particularly powerful. In our business, for example, investors show a very strong tendency to overreact to either very good or very bad quarterly earnings. They normally act as if such developments are highly unusual, contain new information and frequently decide that something of permanence has occurred. Estimates are changed and elaborate analytical explanations and rationalizations are devised. Instead, the more likely explanation is that such performance is statistically possible, will occur in the future with some frequency, and the next data point will move back toward the average performance of the company or the industry in question.

Law of Small Numbers

Among people's intuitions about statistics is something called "local representativeness." In the case of flipping a coin, people regard getting three heads in a row as much less likely than it really is. As a consequence, they attach much more significance to that event than they should. Because of this intuitive belief, people have far too much confidence in forecasting models inferred from small samples of data that seem to manifest a pattern. The most pernicious of these patterns, from a stock market perspective, is consistency of earnings growth. This kind of bias produces excessive confidence and high stock prices relative to future prospects and is generally associated with stocks that appear overvalued within the framework of a dividend discount model.

Failure of Initiative

Failure of initiative reflects an inclination to believe that existing conditions are unlikely to change and that the world is generally static. To frame this idea in the context of investments: People tend to assume that certain difficult economic or industry-specific problems are intractable and that forecasts should be made accordingly. Actually very few problems are *really* intractable.

One of the most colorful and impressive illustrations of failure of initiative was the Club of Rome report issued by a large distinguished group of international economists and social scientists in the early 1970s, which concluded that we were running out of natural resources. It totally missed the ability of the world economy to conserve and to find new sources of raw materials as prices rose. However, the forecasts that now seem silly in light of the current world-wide commodity glut were then taken very seriously, forming the basis of a significant number of investment strategies.

Availability

Now, let me ask you another question. Do more people die of homicide or of diabetes? The answer is diabetes by a ratio of two-to-one, although people normally vote for homicides. . . .

We just went through an exercise in estimation based on the idea of availability. I'm sure that very few people here carry around death-rate data in their heads, so your judgments on the subject come from impressions that you have gathered from your exposure to the issue. The problem with exposure as a measure of probability is that its frequency may have no relationship to the actual value or mathematical odds of the variable being estimated.

Here's where journalism comes in. News reporting is a business geared towards maximizing market share. As a result, things that attract attention such as death, destruction and financial disaster are reported in great detail and with high frequency.

In addition, all too frequently, the issues that control a forecast have no measurable statistical history. You can look up death rates but you can't look up the probability of an Argentine default or the consequences of that default.

In the absence of concrete data, our judgment tends to be colored by how often we hear and read about a default. Equally important, the more provocative and dramatic the stories are, the more they are remembered and the greater the impact they have on decision-making. It is in this way that availability leads to some of the largest distortions in forecasts and stock prices. It also feels like the hardest bias to fight. After all, we have to read *The Wall Street Journal* every day.

Anchoring

Finally, let me spend a moment on anchoring and the "as if" phenomenon. Anchoring is a term used to describe the inherent conservatism that people seem to have in making single-stage estimates, which is to say that estimates of the future value of a variable will be biased towards its initial value. . . . In a number of tests by several different investigators, this tendency was seen to be quite strong. I think that it is another example of people's intuitions about statistics: We imagine most processes to be less volatile than they really are, and, despite one surprise after another, we never really learn.

"As If" Phenomenon

Lastly, there is the "as if" phenomenon, a concept proposed by psychologists that relates to how people process multistage estimation problems, or in investment terms, scenario forecasts. It appears that once people collect enough information about one stage of a problem to reach a decision with some confidence, they then move on to the next stage "as if" the prior stage is known with certainty. . . . In elaborate scenarios with many stages, the real probability of any given outcome becomes very small. The confidence in the outcome, on the other hand, does not fall nearly as fast as the cumulative probability.

Market Impact

Given the nature of the biases surrounding both the forecasting and decision-making processes, we should expect to find a more or less predictable pattern of distortions in the stock market. Stocks that are cheap, those that have high expected returns, should have the following characteristics:

- Problems will look hopeless if the stock is really cheap because failure of initiative will apply.
- Current financial performance of these companies is likely to be well below what it has been in the past, and their operating situation is likely to leave something to be desired.
- The environment in which these companies operate will appear to have shifted permanently for the worse—the underpriced stocks will feel inherently risky, the possibility of substantial loss will remain high.

Fatal Attractions for Money Managers

Arnold S. Wood

Arnie Wood, president of Martingale Asset Management, a deliberately innovative boutique investment manager, has also been a Batterymarch trustee and head of the Boston Security Analysts Society's outstanding program for continuing professional education. Here, his wry humor is applied to the foibles of institutional money managers.

. . . As a laboratory for the study of human behavior—and, in particular, the triumph of temptation over reason—the field of money management has much to recommend it. We money managers, together with our entourage of economists, analysts and traders, offer a large, robust sample, with observations plentiful enough for all the cross-sectional (snapshot) or longitudinal (historical) analyses you could ask for.

Money managers are, ostensibly, reasonable. We are, by and large, highly educated; many of us hold certificates nearly as demanding to come by as MDs and JDs. One might expect that our investment judgments, given our training and experience, would prove sound and profitable for our clients. But this is, strikingly, not true. (See Figure 1.)

Reprinted from the *Financial Analysts Journal* 45 (May/June 1989), pp. 3–5. Charlottesville, Virginia: Association for Investment Management and Research.

FIGURE 1
Performance of the Experts

Time Period	S&P 500	Annualized SEI Equity Funds	Differences
1962–1974	5.3	4.1	−1.2
1966–1974	2.1	0.4	−1.7
1970–1974	2.2	−0.3	−2.5
1975–1982	14.7	13.4	−1.3
1983	22.3	20.3	−2.0
1984	6.3	−2.0	−8.3
1985	31.7	30.0	−1.7
1986	18.3	16.7	−1.6
1987	5.2	4.0	−1.2

Source: SEI Funds Evaluation.

What makes us so consistently poor at our profession? It seems to me that we are too frequently undone by three very human tendencies.

- Our feelings overcome our reason.
- We take shortcuts that violate logic.
- We don't learn, or want to learn, from experience.

But *why* are we so motivated to behave illogically? Below, I offer a list of 10, not necessarily mutually exclusive, causes of irrational, and occasionally bizarre, behavior.

1. Mindless routine.   Put simply, we are steeped in ritual.

An Indian legend has it that the buffalo return each season in response to the ritual buffalo dance. This is, literally, true. Why? Because the Indians don't stop dancing until the buffalo come back.

As money managers, we place our bets, and when the world comes to us, we feel that it is our persistence that is being rewarded. We accept all evidence that confirms this notion and dismiss any that contradicts it. Psychologists call this "cognitive dissonance."

Die-hard growth-stock apostles of the early '70s are still waiting for the buffalo. Conversely, money managers who never could stomach utilities missed a 12-year spurt in which the S&P 40 provided a 16.9 per cent compound annual return, versus 12.8 per cent for the S&P 500. If you had invested $10 million in utilities in 1976, before the 1979

Three Mile Island disaster, you would be 150 per cent better off than the S&P 500 today—and even better off compared with the median money manager.

One by-product of ritual and routine is comfort, and there's nothing like feelin' good. At the Berkeley Program in Finance in 1987, the word "factors" was used 222 times; I counted. This silly indicator told me that everyone—manager, academic, consultant and client—is hung up on managing and measuring performance by factors. How do you define yourself? By the factor(s) you focus on—defensive . . . , sector rotation, small cap, yield, whatever. Are there any *stock* pickers, people with portfolios that aren't swamped by factor bets, left?

2. The laws of probability.   Consider a pinch hitter with four hits in 10 at-bats during the year. Is he a better hitter than Wade Boggs?

He has, after all, a .400 batting average, and that beats Boggs' .359. But Boggs had 189 hits in 527 at-bats. Probability speaking, there is a 99.9 per cent chance that Boggs is a .300 hitter; there is only an 85 per cent chance that our pinch hitter is.

Now consider an example from money management. Suppose a market timer is correct 55 per cent of the time, and that he makes one decision every two years. How long would you have to wait to determine (with 99 per cent probability) whether he really has any skill? The answer: 167 years!

3. Information overload.   Humans simply cannot process a great deal of data, let alone convert it into action.

Herbert Simon, 1987 Nobel Prize winner, has concluded that humans can digest only five to seven different things at once.[1] A study of horse racing bettors has shown that more information increases bettors' confidence in their bets, but does nothing to increase their accuracy (Figure 2).

Occam's Razor suggests that most complex problems have simple solutions. Why, then, do we make money management so incredibly complex? An MBA with a facility for Lotus Spreadsheet analysis can produce a limitless number of variables that complicate the process of making logical decisions.

4. Psychology of choice.   Decision-framing is an intricate part of how we make choices, how we sort out alternatives. It stands behind one of the central tenets of investing, which is that people, given a 50/50 chance, would rather not lose a dollar than gain a dollar.

FIGURE 2
Changes in Confidence and Accuracy with Increasing Information

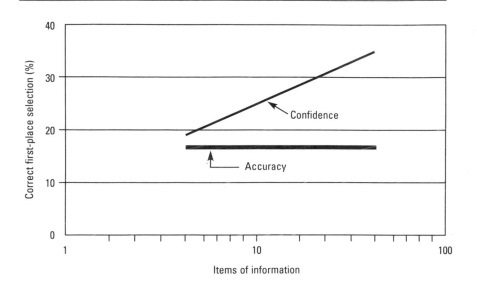

Most choices involving gains are risk-averse, most involving losses are risk-taking. The probabilities assigned to the possible outcomes of a life-and-death decision may be identical, but stating a problem in terms of lives lost versus lives saved evokes very different responses. Investing sometimes equates with loss of life (job), and some irrational decisions result.

Measuring risk is tricky; measuring the perception of risk may be even trickier. Why, for example, do those pension plans with large surpluses tend to elect the more conservative investment policies? Why are people with more money than they ever plan to spend so reluctant to give it away? These choices may appear to be illogical, but we must take into account the entire framework within which the choice is made—and that involves a complex balancing of gain and loss, age and wealth and myriad other factors.

5. Forecasting.   Given our failure to assign accurate statistical probabilities, it is obvious why we are lured into forecasting. But it goes beyond that.

Think of the lottery: Why do people pay to play? Simple: There is a huge payoff if you are right. You are willing to accept essentially a

FIGURE 3
How Good Is that Monkey?

Out of 10 Possible Market Calls

Correct Calls	Number of Monkeys	Total (%)
10	1	0.1
9	10	1.0
8	44	4.4
7	117	11.7
6	205	20.5
5	246	24.6
4	205	20.5
3	117	11.7
2	44	4.4
1	10	1.0
0	1	0.1

negative expected return for the possibility of a huge payoff, plus some fun in playing. Someone calculated that, on average, Massachusetts residents are spending at the rate of $106,000 per person to play the lottery over their collective lifetimes. (Do initial public offerings have a lower probability of payoff than roulette? Probably.)

A little monkey business may help to clarify our fascination with forecasting.[2] Imagine a room full of monkeys, a thousand of them. Each is trying to predict the direction of the market. Figure 3 shows that, at the end of 10 predictions, one monkey has a perfect record of 10 straight calls, while 10 have nine out of 10 and 44 eight out of 10. (By the way, all these outcomes are supported by probability theory.)

What happens next? The 10-for-10 monkey starts its own firm. Large investment counselors hire the nine-for-10 monkeys. Bank trust departments, which can't afford to hire "top talent," lure the 44 who went eight for 10. The unlucky monkeys stay home. This is a pure case of survivorship bias.

Rather than make market predictions, one of the unlucky monkeys figures out a system to predict the market, at least in hindsight. After many iterations, thanks to modern investment technology, the clever monkey figures out what combination of conditions would have led to a 10-for-10 record. With simulated results, this synthetic lucky monkey gets on the same plane with all the lucky monkeys to convince you that market timing is the only game in town.

FIGURE 4
Confidence Judgments

	Low Guess	Best Guess	High Guess
1. UPS delivers twice as many packages as the post office. How many packages did UPS deliver in 1980?			
2. How many credit cards were reported lost or stolen by U.S. consumers on a typical day in 1980?			
3. When you buy a dollar's worth of meat, how much does the rancher get?			
4. How much money was spent on tranquilizers in the U.S. in 1980?			

6. *Overconfidence*. Try answering the questions in Figure 4, giving "high" and "low," as well as "best," estimates for each one.[3]

The narrower the range between your high and low estimates, the more confidence you assign your best answer. Most of us think we know more than we do, or at least pretend a certainty we don't possess.

7. *Follow the leader*. In an uncertain world, we search for sign posts that will allay our fears and doubts.

Suppose you are in a group in a completely dark room, or condition of uncertainty.[4] An intermittent dot of light is flashed on the wall, hitting the same spot each time. Each one in the room is asked how much the light is moving; guesses range from two to eight inches. The whole group is then asked the same question, and the range of answers narrows. Finally, a new person joins the group, declaring that he knows exactly the distance the light travels. The group will cling to this "authority's" estimate, achieving an even narrower consensus. (See Figure 5.)

Why do we all read *The Wall Street Journal?* Perhaps it is to look for leaders in an uncertain world.

8. *Touchy-feely syndrome*. Figure 6 summarizes the results of an experiment in which individuals were either handed a card or selected a card, then asked to "sell" the card.[5]

Those that selected their cards were less likely to sell and received a much higher average price for their cards than those who were handed their cards. Visiting the management of a company can make you feel

FIGURE 5
Convergence of Opinion

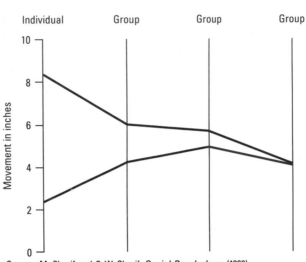

Source: M. Sherif and C. W. Sherif, *Social Psychology* (1969).

FIGURE 6
Illusion of Control

	Those Who Chose Their Own Card	Those Who Were Handed a Card
Initially Said They Would Not Sell	37%	19%
Average Price Offered for Sale	$8.96	$1.96

you know more than you really do. Furthermore, we tend to feel more favorably toward managers we have actually met. (Politicians don't go around shaking hands because they like to meet people.) We tend to overvalue persons and things we have actually "touched."

9. Statistical blockout.   October 19, 1987, when the Dow collapsed over 500 points, has statistically blocked out any logical, sensible response to such events.

FIGURE 7
Friction between Client and Manager

	Corporate Mind	*Investment Mind*
Environment	Controllable	Capricious
Task	Complete	Incomplete
Skill	Measurable	Not Measurable
Pay Check	Medium	High

Fear really damages an otherwise intelligent decision-maker. Our tendency to judge the future on the basis of the more immediate past is one of the most difficult behavioral flaws to overcome.

10. Bad dog.   Your dog chews on the carpet or jumps on a guest. You scold, it, "Bad dog!" The dog looks sheepish.

Managers have their chances, some more than others, to be the Bad Dog. Poor performance, however your master wants to measure it, is ordinarily the reason for the scolding. (Well, that's one reason for paying someone—so you can blame him for not performing. . . .)

The differences between client and manager in environments, tasks, necessary skills and, more often than not, compensation levels make for a tenuous relationship to begin with, one prone to emotional outbursts and apprehensive behavior. (See Figure 7.) When the client sets a benchmark, a performance bogey, and the money manager falls short, more friction is created and the relationship breaks down. Chief Financial Officer to corporate pension officer: "Those guys get too much to underperform. Tell them they're out if we see another quarter like that." The manager's response? Anxiety is an understatement. Is his judgment or skill impaired? I suspect so.

Money managers are human. Their behavioral responses are seldom as rational as might be expected from such an educated sample. Research in behavioral finance is only just getting more formal recognition for its value in identifying and measuring behavior. Clearly, there are managers who have learned from the past, recognize unreasoned behavior and are willing to seize upon the anxieties of others. Perhaps an awareness of the root causes for betraying sound analysis and logic will get us a Good Dog pat more often. Let's hope so.[6]

Notes

1. H. A. Simon, "A Behavioral Model of Rational Choice," *Journal of Economics* (1955), pp. 69, 91–118.
2. I am indebted to William Jacques of Martingale Asset Management for this example.
3. The answers are 1.4 billion packages, 30,000 credit cards, 55¢ and $2.3 billion. The example comes from Professor Fischhoff of Carnegie Mellon University.
4. This experiment is discussed in D. Dreman, *Contrarian Investment Strategy* (New York: Random House, 1979), p. 92.
5. The example comes from E. J. Langer, "The Illusion of Control," in D. Kahneman, P. Slovic and A. Tversky, eds., *Judgment under Uncertainty: Heuristics and Biases* (Cambridge: Cambridge University Press, 1982).
6. Additional examples and insights for this article were provided by Robin Hogarth of the University of Chicago, John Carroll of MIT and Richard Thaler of Cornell.

Three Ways to Succeed as an Investor

Charles D. Ellis, CFA

Charley Ellis has long encouraged investors to commit to determining and staying with a truly long-term investment policy. This excerpt from a 1988 address to the Empire Club in Toronto is yet another such appeal.

There are three ways in which you might try to achieve superior results: one is physically difficult; one is intellectually difficult; and one is emotionally difficult.

Warren Buffett, John Templeton, Dean LeBaron and Warren Goldring and a very few others have staked out the intellectually difficult way of beating the market.

Intellectually difficult investing is pursued by those who have a deep and profound understanding of the true nature of investing, see the future more clearly and take long-term positions that turn out to be remarkably successful. We admire them, but usually only in retrospect. At the time of their doing their best work, we see them as misguided. We do not want to do what they are doing because it looks so unpromising.

Most of the crowd is deeply involved in the physically difficult way of beating the market. See if you don't recognize the physically difficult right away. They come to the office earlier; they stay later. They

Reprinted from a 1988 speech to the Empire Club in Toronto, by permission of the author.

read a larger number of reports more rapidly. They go to more breakfast meetings and more luncheon meetings and more dinner meetings. They are on the telephone, making more calls and receiving more calls than all the rest. They carry huge briefcases home at night, determined to get ahead by reading more reports before the morrow. In every way they possibly can, they put enormous physical energy into trying to beat the market by outworking the competition. What they don't seem to recognize is that so is almost everyone else.

Being incapable of doing the intellectually difficult, and reluctant about the physically difficult, I have set about the emotionally difficult approach to investing. This straightforward, untiring approach is simply to work out the long-term investment policy that's truly right for you and your particular circumstances and is realistic given the history of the capital markets, commit to it and—here is the emotionally difficult part—hold on.

When your friends turn to you and say, "Wow! have I got an opportunity for you! This is a great time to buy!" be absolutely uninterested. And when they turn to you and say, "Oh, Lord, this is it. It's going to be one hell of a crash. Get out now while you can!" you must simply be not interested, absolutely sound asleep. No intellectual effort; no physical effort; but for most, emotionally far too difficult. It suits me just fine. It requires no great genius and no great brawn, but it works.

Comments on the Stock Market

Louis Rukeyser

Louis Rukeyser, through his weekly television program "Wall Street Week," has become the most widely listened-to investment commentator ever. He has also written several books. This passage comes from his *How to Make Money in Wall Street*.

———— ▬ ————

Once you have understood that Sigmund Freud can be as important to the stock market as Adam Smith, you will find it easier to forget the myth that Wall Street—the storied haven of so much of the nation's supposedly "smart money"—is a brilliant forecaster of the nation's economy. It is a myth that ranges from scary newspaper headlines to the government's list of "leading economic indicators," but much of the time you would be just as well off mucking about in soggy tea leaves. It has been calculated, for example, that the stock market predicted eleven of the last four recessions—a performance that may exceed the combined record of the nation's opposition politicians.

Were it not for the market's eventual awakenings to reality, investing would truly seem a hopeless gamble for the ordinary person. But the market's short-term capriciousness can be a source of hypnotic fascination—and a joy when you analyze it correctly. For what the market truly represents is not a crystal ball or anything else of such mystic magnitude; it is an instant photograph of the ephemeral mood of a significant chunk of Americans. Consider the dramatic example of May 1970. President Nixon had ordered a military incursion into Cambodia,

Excerpted from *How to Make Money in Wall Street* (1976; originally published 1974), Chapter 5, pp. 36–42, by permission of Doubleday Book and Music Clubs, Garden City, New York.

the campuses were in an uproar and many prominent Americans who should have known better were vying with one another in prophecies of doom for the republic. Economically, on the other hand, the only sensible forecast was that things were going to get better slowly—which they did. And which siren do you think the so-called smart money heeded? Why, the market staged its very own Cambodia panic—presumably on the theory that if World War III were about to start and we all were going to be hydrogen-bombed into oblivion, the only prudent course was to hold cash instead of IBM.

The Dow Jones Industrial Average, an index of the prices of 30 big old-line stocks that is the market's most familiar indicator, plunged to a sickening low around 630, after nearly touching 1,000 less than eighteen months before. Did Wall Street know something that the rest of the country didn't? All it knew was the hysteria it captured and magnified from its television screens and newspapers. And here is something that to the inexperienced investor is very much worth knowing: The worst pessimistic excesses, the greatest panic selling, took place on the purportedly supersophisticated East and West coasts—the headquarters of most of the lofty financial wise guys and supercilious institutional investors. Investors in the Middle West, in comparison, were heavy net buyers. The real smart money turned out to belong to the Iowa farmer who, perhaps less inclined to stare at his navel and proclaim the demise of America, telephoned his broker to observe calmly that Xerox had gotten down to a level where it looked like a good buy. For lo and behold, the panic passed (as panics do), and less than a year later the same Dow Jones Industrial Average stood fully 50 per cent above its levels of May 1970.

Now, the lesson of this is not that we should all get back to the earth and grow corn, or wave the flag, but that an investor with independence of intellect and spirit is by no means at a disadvantage in a wildly gyrating market. He need not know exactly when his day is coming in order to make the confident assumption that it will. It was John M. Hancock, a partner in Lehman Brothers, who first observed that there are times when the market throws all bad news into the wastebasket, and times when it does the same with all good news. The bulls and bears are often nothing more than the herd on the Street, and the wise individual will remember the maxim of the senior J. P. Morgan, who remarked at a moment of pessimistic frenzy that "it always stops raining."

An Insider's Call for Outside Direction

Elmer W. Johnson

Elmer Johnson, now a senior partner of Kirkland & Ellis, was an executive vice president and director of General Motors. In this brief excerpt, he speaks for many others when he focuses our attention on the need for effective boards of directors in public corporations.

One of history's most remarkable organizational achievements—the large public corporation, governed by an independent board of directors—has served society for most of this century as an unrivaled creator of wealth and employment. Now it is an endangered species, and we must take strong measures to preserve and renew it.

Patient capital is the foundation on which long-lived, wealth-creating institutions rest. But since patient capital is helpless capital unless it has a voice, its prerequisite is a properly functioning board of directors. The people who provide patient capital understand that their managers must enter into long-term, usually implicit compacts with employees, suppliers, and communities, but they also understand that managers can fail and need replacing and that the top personnel needs of even a mature enterprise can change over time. So without boards of directors with the courage and fiduciary conscience to monitor management, there can be no such thing as a public corporation geared to the long-term goals of creating jobs and wealth.

Let's Not Strangle the Golden Goose

Paul C. Cabot

Paul Cabot served as Harvard's treasurer from 1948 to 1965, led the university heavily to common stocks in the early years, and emphasized the importance of spending *less* than total income—so that part could be reinvested to build endowment capital. Here, in an open letter originally published in *The Boston Globe,* Cabot mounts a spirited defense of his policies for Harvard and attacks the growing practice of spending part of an endowment's capital appreciation as well as *all* of income.

Dear President Bok:

I have heard that you and other members of the Harvard Corporation are considering the use of capital for current expenses—specifically, part of capital gains—in addition to your present policy of using *all* of income on the endowment funds of the University. The purpose of this letter is to dissuade you from adopting this dangerous, unfair, unwise and possibly disastrous policy.

Ever since Harvard was founded in 1636, we have had—other than for short periods—higher prices and a declining value for the dollar, i.e., inflation. I would guess that you and the other members of the Corporation would agree with me that this will continue in the future,

Reprinted from *Institutional Investor* (September 1972), pp. 50–51. New York: Institutional Investor, Inc.

regardless of rather futile attempts which, at best, may only slightly slow the present, rather rapid *rate* of inflation.

Unless Harvard and other institutions and individuals recognize this and prepare for it as Harvard has done in the past, the results in the future can indeed be disastrous. If one spends capital, obviously, there will be less in the future to earn money on. It really amounts to robbing the future to take care of the present. Of course, this procedure is tempting to any present incumbent. He'll probably be dead, or out of the picture, long before the inevitable fallacy of such a policy comes home to roost.

Your two predecessors as president of Harvard, with whom I served, always backed me 100 per cent in refusal to spend capital. Indeed, the income we "availed" ourselves of was, in fact, less by a few million every year than the income earned.

Unfortunate Policy?

As of June 30, 1948, the market value of Harvard's General and Special Investments exceeded Yale's by approximately $100 million. At the end of fiscal 1971, the approximate market value of these funds were: Harvard, $1.3 billion and Yale, $547 million. Harvard's investments were three-quarters of a billion larger than Yale's. What caused this? Capital gifts to Harvard were bigger during this period but not enough so to account for this wide difference. Investment policy had most to do with it, but very important was the fact that Harvard saved money *every* year whereas, in many years, Yale dipped into principal. Yale now has a *policy* of doing so regularly. This unfortunate policy is disguised and made unclear by a formula of mathematical hieroglyphics. The simple fact is: It is Yale's policy to spend principal. . . .

To date, Harvard's wise policy of maintaining, indeed augmenting, principal has greatly helped the increase in income and its ability to *more* than meet their percentage of the rising and inflationary costs. Yale's policy has made it impossible for her to do the same.

There are other important reasons not to rob the future to make life easier now. The effect on donors and bequests could be very bad. Most givers of endowment funds assume and expect—and indeed sometimes legally specify—that the principal they give shall be maintained, not dissipated. I realize that all colleges and universities have come on hard

financial times—Harvard maybe less so for past wise preservation and growth of capital. Let's face the facts and not go down the primrose path of capital spending, but *cut expenses.*

There are innumerable areas in this field; I'll only mention a few.

- Fewer students. Every student costs the university money. At least temporarily stop increasing.
- Curtail the further expansion of aids and scholarships out of unrestricted funds. We just haven't got that much money. An undue amount of these can swamp us.
- Reduce the faculty by attrition and see that those that remain on the payroll do in fact *teach* and not spend so much time away from the university and in other peripheral pursuits of less importance than the education of students.
- Stop new building. Most of Harvard's bricks and mortar are a liability and not an asset. They produce no revenue, they have to be maintained, heated, cooled, etc.
- Give up those activities that only involve a very few students but are very expensive to run.

Finally, I beg you and the other members of Harvard's governing boards not to be party to the slow strangulation of Harvard's goose that has laid so many golden eggs over past years.

I hope that this letter will induce alumni and friends of Harvard and Yale to beg the former not to go down this dangerous and probably disastrous road and the latter to return from it.

Sincerely,

Paul C. Cabot
A.B. 1921, M.B.A. 1923, L.L.D. 1966 Harvard;
L.L.D. 1965 Yale;
Treasurer of Harvard 1948–1965

An Open Letter to the Editor of *Business Week*

Leon G. Cooperman, CFA

Lee Cooperman earned an international reputation as investment strategist for Goldman Sachs and as the builder of that firm's research department. Always interested in encouraging constructive critique ("How can we do better?"), he could give as well as take. Here he chastises *Business Week* for not appreciating the extraordinary successes achieved at Teledyne by Henry Singleton, and correctly asserts that Dr. Singleton has been remarkably effective as an investor's investor in guiding Teledyne's strategic development.

I have been a reader of your publication for about 20 years, and only on one previous occasion (cover story, "Death of Equities," August 13, 1979) was I sufficiently aroused to write to the Editor. Now your May 31, 1982 cover story on Teledyne, Inc. and its chairman, Dr. Henry Singleton, is a second such occasion.

I found the article to demonstrate a blatant lack of understanding of the company (bordering on the irresponsible in its thrust) as well as a lack of appreciation of what, in my opinion, is one of the greatest managerial success stories in the annals of modern business history. The reporter simply portrays the company's success to date as the result of an acquisition binge in the 1960s and a stock-buying surge in the 1970s,

Reprinted from an unpublished letter, May 25, 1982, by permission of the author.

the latter being financed by "siphoning-off" the cash flow of its operating businesses to get where it is today. These are gross simplifications of rather elaborate, well-conceived, and, most importantly, well-executed business judgments and strategies for better than 20 years.

Speaking in general terms, Dr. Singleton has followed the principal [sic] of allocating cash to assets (real or financial) that offer, in his view, the highest potential return given the investment risk involved. You criticize this shifting of capital from real to financial assets. An intelligent investor would recognize that, in point of fact, that is precisely the responsibility of management. More importantly, Dr. Singleton has not, as have many other chief executive officers, restricted himself solely to real assets but rather has built a company able to take advantage of returns in both financial markets and the real sector.

More specifically, as a Teledyne observer, I can identify at least five different strategies utilized to foster the company's development over the past 20 years.

Strategy One: Growth through Acquisition

In the period 1960–1969, Dr. Singleton recognized the unusually low cost of equity capital the company enjoyed and relentlessly used the company's common stock as a currency to acquire. In this period of acquisition growth (in excess of 130 acquisitions), the company's sales and net income increased from essentially zero to about $1.3 billion and $58.1 million, respectively.

Strategy Two: Intensively Manage Your Business

In the period 1970–1981, Dr. Singleton *and his management team* demonstrated an ability to manage second to none. *Net income, without* the benefit of *any* acquisitions, rose from $61.9 million in 1970 (a peak year) to $412.3 million in 1981, a compound growth of approximately 19%. (In that period, the S&P 400 earnings grew at a 12% rate off a depressed base.) Net income of the 100%-owned manufacturing businesses rose more than sixfold in that period, to $269.6 million from $46.7 million. . . . The company's ratios of profitability . . . are among the best in American industry—return on equity ranged from

25% to 30% in the past few years, and its return on total capital exceeds 20%, both approaching twice that of American industry. In the last few years, each line of business in the company's manufacturing sector has earned in *excess* of 50% before taxes on identifiable assets, with pretax profit margins in the manufacturing sector in the area of 15%.

Do you possibly believe that this record of growth and profitability could be achieved in a competitive world economy with a tactic of "siphoning-off" the operating earnings to finance the buildup of a stock portfolio? Doubtful. And in fact, . . . the company, while not one of the more aggressive spenders on plant and equipment, has spent well in excess of its cumulative depreciation in the period 1973–1981. More to the point, I would suggest that a conservative approach to capital additions may have been more appropriate given the economic realities of the world economy, which is today awash with excess capacity and is likely to recover in a sluggish fashion.

Strategy Three: Repurchase Your Undervalued Equity

Just as Dr. Singleton recognized he had an unusually attractive stock to trade with in the 1960s, he developed the belief that the company's shares were undervalued in the 1970s. In the period 1971–1980, you correctly point out that the company repurchased approximately 75% of its shares. What you did not point out is that despite the stock's 32% drop from its all-time high reached in mid-1981 to the time of your article, the stock price remains well above the highest price paid by the company (and multiples above the average price paid) in this ten-year period. Contrary to many corporate managements whose stock repurchases have proven ill-timed, Teledyne has been extremely astute from both a stock market standpoint and a return on investment approach. The effect on earnings per share has been dramatic, with earnings-per-share growth about twice that of net income in the 1971–1981 period.

Strategy Four: Stocks Preferable to Bonds for the Taxable Investor

You seem to miss the key aspect of Dr. Singleton's emphasis of common stocks in early 1976. In owning an insurance company, Teledyne, like other insurance companies, has to invest its cash flow and can do so in a number of different financial and nonfinancial assets.

At a time when most insurance companies were still reeling from the devastating effects of the vicious 1973/1974 bear market and were busy buying 9.5%–10% long-term bonds over common stocks, Teledyne determined that stocks were more attractive than bonds—particularly on an after-tax basis given the tax-preferred nature of dividend income from one corporation to another (85% excluded) and the better prospect of capital appreciation and income growth over time. . . . The record thus far suggests that management's judgment was correct. . . . The spread in asset performance is dramatic and quite relevant given the size of the company's asset base.

Lastly, I would point out . . . that the current *market* value of Teledyne's invested assets in stocks and fixed-maturity investments is substantially above its cost basis—a situation very few insurance companies enjoy today because few had his prescience to emphasize stocks over bonds.

Strategy Five: Build Cash for Uncertain Times

At a time when American industry is saddled with the most illiquid financial position and highest debt load in the post–World War II period, Teledyne is in its most liquid financial position ever. I can assure you it is not an accident but rather the result of a correct assessment some 12 months ago of our current economic problems. The company currently has cash and equivalents of nearly $1 billion, no bank debt, and less than $5 million *per year* of maturing long-term debt in the ten-year period, 1984–1993. In addition, at recent levels of profitability, the company (*excluding* noncash equity accounting earnings) generates approximately $400 million per year of cash flow.

In sum, then, you can see the company has utilized not only a multiplicity of strategies (as opposed to just two), but the timing of their adoption has been nothing short of brilliant. While I (and they) will readily concede to having their share of mistakes (International Harvester being the most visible), your article chose to concentrate on what appears to be a half-dozen examples of isolated difficulties without any consideration to the overwhelming successes of the company. Their record of *operating* and *asset management* is second to none. Their strategy in no way has been completely "hooked to cash" as you portray, and I believe your article is a poor excuse for good journalism and borders on a betrayal of the public confidence. While a more effusive person could have "pumped up" your writer, Dr. Singleton marches to his own drummer with a concentration of blood around his brain not his mouth.

The cover picture of the May 31st edition portrays Dr. Singleton as the mythical Greek character, Icarus, who fell to his death when he flew too close to the sun and his wax wings melted. However, I see Dr. Singleton (and his management team) as a group of exceedingly competent industrialists, working for the benefit of the Teledyne shareholder (yes, I am one of them), and my only regret is that I cannot find more Henry Singletons and Teledynes in which to invest.

Leon G. Cooperman, C.F.A., Partner
Chairman, Investment Policy Committee
May 25, 1982

Hiring High, Firing Low

Robert Kirby

Bob Kirby combines good humor and good judgment in the numerous talks and articles through which he has contributed wisdom to his friends in the profession. Here is another example.

In looking at . . . [1987 investment performance]—in particular at the list of 1987's "losers" of pension fund business—it is very disturbing, but not at all surprising, to see among those losers many firms that were among the big winners only a few years ago. It gives one the strong impression that a substantial portion of the pension fund management business has become a slightly modified form of Russian roulette. Apparently, underperforming the market (even modestly) for three or four years is cause for dismissal of a money manager in the eyes of many. If true, then it is not a case of "whether" but "when" the day comes that every manager pulls the trigger and finds a real live bullet in the chamber.

The pension fund management business in its present form is, admittedly, relatively young (it is still shy of its twentieth birthday), but it seems to me high time that those involved in the administration of major pension funds should begin to realize that *markets make money managers*—not vice versa. Any money manager who develops a logical approach based on a modicum of common sense and who applies that approach with a fair degree of consistency (and, sadly, even a few

Reprinted from *Institutional Investor* (May 1988), p. 29. New York: Institutional Investor, Inc.

others who don't) will sooner or later encounter a market that makes him look like a genius for a couple of years. Just as certainly, he will also encounter markets that make him look like an absolute boob.

How can anyone believe that organizations like T. Rowe Price or Pioneering Management or individual investors like Dean LeBaron would suddenly wake up one morning and be dumb? If you believe that this is possible, I daresay that sooner or later Peter Lynch, John Neff and even Warren Buffett will someday wake up dumb. I do not know a great deal about some of the organizations that lost a number of clients, but I daresay they are no smarter or dumber today than they were three or four or five years ago when they were the winners. . . .

Major corporations and their pension fund consultants go through a prolonged and elaborate ritual in the process of selecting money managers. Pretty clearly, however, the single criterion on which at least 80 percent of the selection decision is based is the manager's investment performance during the prior three years. If all you had to do to achieve successful pension fund management was to hire the firm with the best three-year record, wouldn't all the money have long since been in the hands of good managers and wouldn't all bad managers be out of business? Instead, it seems to me that there is more hiring and firing of money managers today than there ever has been. Why?

Moving in Tandem

There is a fairly widespread and possibly growing belief out there in pensionland that size is one of the problems. However, I believe that this would be very difficult to prove scientifically. In 1988 and in years past, some of the . . . winners have been large firms, while many of the losers have had only moderate assets under management. From personal experience, I would not be inclined to blame size itself. I would be more concerned with rate of growth. Everyone hires the same money managers (the ones with the great three-year records) at the same time. An organization grows from ten clients to 25 clients and from $200 million to $1 billion under management in one year. I can testify that it is not easy to build and maintain a stable organization and a consistent decision-making structure under those circumstances.

I am just as confused as everyone else when it comes to determining how to differentiate luck from skill when reviewing the results of a money manager. However, I am quite sure that while an intense focus on the investment results over the past 36 months may not be totally irrelevant, it is damn close.

I have been asked a number of times what I would do if I had responsibility for hiring a money manager. My response has always been the same. I would go through the procedure that a company uses in selecting a law firm, a medical clinic or accountants. Find an organization of quality people with integrity, experience and dedication that is respected by its clients. When you have identified all the money management organizations that meet those specifications, hire the one that has had the *worst* investment performance over the past two to three years. The . . . [recent] list of ''losers'' probably represents a very good place to go looking for a money manager.

Socially Responsible Investing

Burton G. Malkiel

Burt Malkiel, author of *A Random Walk Down Wall Street* and past dean of Yale's School of Management, was chairman of the economics department at Princeton when he gave this talk at the 1971 Endowment Conference in New York City. In it, he deals openly and directly with issues that continue, 20 years later, to be on the agenda of many institutions trying to decide whether moral views can contribute to effective investing.

———————

In recent years, portfolio managers for a wide variety of educational institutions have been faced with a serious challenge to their traditional goals. Formerly, the objective of most portfolio managers was a relatively simple one: the maximization of investment returns from the endowment, subject to some prudent limit on the amount of risk assumed. Similarly, the voting of proxies presented no problem at all for the portfolio manager. The general rule—"support management or sell the shares." Attempting to influence a company through proxy fights or otherwise indicating one's disagreements with management was not even contemplated.

More recently, basic changes occurring both in the political climate of the country and in the investment business have forced many portfolio managers to retreat from such a "business as usual" attitude. I need not recount here the angry demonstrations and even a macing incident that marred annual meetings last year; the picketing, and even bomb-

Reprinted from a speech at the 1971 Endowment Conference, New York, by permission of the author.

ings of some corporate offices and banks; and the proxy fights, such as those at G.M. and Gulf this year, demanding a more socially responsible corporate posture. Nor do I have to review the increasing pressures from students that have been placed on endowment fund managers to consider moral and social criteria as well as economic ones in making investment decisions. The point is that although there are powerful reasons for arguing against institutional investors assuming responsibility for the welfare of society, forces have been gathering which may well necessitate such concerns.

What I propose to do today is to discuss a practical case history of how demands for social involvements were answered in a specific case I know well. A group of students demanded that Princeton University sell its holdings in firms with subsidiaries or affiliates operating in South Africa. This involved stocks valued at $127 million, approximately one-third of the total portfolio. It was argued that these companies were, in effect, supporting a racist government in South Africa and that it was immoral to profit from such securities. Sale of these stocks, it was argued, would make creditable to black people all over the world the university's determination to work toward the abolition of racial discrimination. I was chairman of the committee charged with making recommendations to the university.

I should say at the outset that my committee was unanimous in its unequivocal opposition to the racial policies of the South African government. It is difficult to exaggerate the inhumanity of apartheid. The policy has led to one of the most rigid and tyrannical systems of racial injustice in the world. Moreover, the committee was deeply concerned about the moral issues raised by Princeton's position if, as a by-product of its financial investments, the university was helping to give aid directly to oppressive governments, or was receiving significant profit from the exploitation of black workers.

Despite these concerns, the faculty members of our committee voted unanimously against selling our shares. Several reasons were given, of which the following seem most important to me:

First, it was not at all clear to our committee that selling the particular $127 million of shares chosen by the students would morally cleanse us of association with apartheid. The difficulty is that any company that even trades with countries in southern Africa may be supporting their economies as much as corporations with affiliates or sales subsidiaries there, the ones whose sale was demanded. Indeed, it is not even clear that any portfolio could be found that is not contaminated in some way by relationships with southern Africa.

For example, many U.S. electric utilities, which would appear to be in no way supporting the governments of southern Africa, may buy significant quantities of processed minerals that had been mined in one of the countries of southern Africa. Purely domestic banks and life insurance companies may be even more culpable, since they often hold bonds of the World Bank, which lends money directly to South Africa and thereby actually supports a racist government.

Moreover, one could not even hold a portfolio consisting entirely of cash to escape this contamination. Cash represents the noninterest-bearing debt of the U.S. government, which has given indirect but substantial support to the South African government by buying gold at $35 an ounce. Thus, even if a relatively simple criterion of immorality is chosen (namely, participation in the South African economy) it may be impossible to cleanse the portfolio of all investments that either directly or indirectly may contribute to that immorality.

We also wondered whether, in the final decision about the social responsibility of a company, we should not also consider the good things the company does. For example, Xerox was one of the companies the students insisted we sell. Yet on other grounds we thought that Xerox had been a rather exemplary corporate citizen. Indeed, in a recent article, a Harvard student discussed a group of proposals regarding social investment policy that had been presented to that university's administration. Included was his recommendation "that Harvard invest in companies that have clearly progressive managements, and socially useful products or services. Examples would be Xerox. . . ." Thus a company that has been a leader in providing job training to disadvantaged workers and financial and other aid to ghetto businesses can be considered by some to be a prime example of a socially responsible corporation, while others can consider it to represent an "immoral investment."

The broader issue is, of course, that it is extraordinarily difficult—in a world where our major corporations have a variety of associations and interests—to make any clear moral judgments. We felt that selling the $127 million of securities, as our students demanded, would be settling for an appearance of moral concern while sacrificing its reality.

Our second reason for rejecting the request to sell our shares was based on concerns regarding institutional effectiveness. We doubt that the sale of certain investments was likely to be an effective means for bringing about desirable social goals. We did not believe that sale of our shares would have any influence either on management policies or on the price of the shares. Our blocks of stock would simply be transferred to other buyers.

It would seem that if institutional investors wish to have an influence on corporate policy, a far more effective weapon is the proxy vote and through direct contacts with corporate management. Indeed, pressing one's views through all available channels, consistently and repeatedly, may be more realistic and ultimately perhaps even a more effective solution in the long run. Although the Campaign G.M. experience suggests that the effectiveness of such action is likely to be limited at best in terms of the number of votes obtained, it is already clear that General Motors has been influenced considerably by the pressure that was brought to bear. I will return to this point later.

Our third and final major argument for not selling the shares was based on our estimate of the cost of such action to the university. Based on an analysis of returns over an 18-year period, it turned out that the securities in the portfolio representing companies with some operations in southern Africa had almost a 3% higher average rate of return than the remaining securities in Princeton's portfolio. Moreover, the rates of return for the group with southern African operations tended to be more stable.

These differences in returns cannot be explained as resulting from extra profits that accrue to American companies that exploit black workers. The companies that had provided the largest average annual returns (and thus drove up the average) were leaders in new product development such as International Business Machines, Xerox, Polaroid, and others that were little involved with South Africa and did no manufacturing there.

Of course, past returns cannot be used as a reliable guide to future returns. Nevertheless, innovative and growth-minded companies will generally want to market their products worldwide. Thus, there may well be a systematic relationship between the expected profitability of an investment and the likelihood that the company will operate in all parts of the world, including southern Africa. To the extent that these corporate characteristics can be expected to affect future returns, altering the composition of the portfolio as was requested might well reduce the yield of the endowment.

In addition, the brokerage and other costs of the transactions involved in altering substantially the composition of the portfolio would be very large. In Princeton's case, it was estimated that the costs of the transactions (including brokerage charges and an estimate of the discount necessary to move the large blocks of shares in question) involved in switching all our holdings with affiliates in South Africa would amount to approximately $5 million. (I might say, however, that these estimates were made before the days of negotiated commissions.) The issue is whether a university trustee could adopt such a policy and its cost without violating his trusteeship.

Similarly, a university endowment fund manager cannot deliberately adopt a policy of investing in companies that follow socially desirable policies but which provide below-market rates of return when the university's regular resources are already gravely inadequate to meet its primary educational mission. The use of the university's resources for other social ends will divert them from the purposes for which they have been entrusted to the university, may violate the prudent-man rule of managing its resources, and will prevent the university from taking full advantage of its unique strengths as an educational institution.

For the three major reasons I have outlined, we rejected the proposal that we sell our shares. Nevertheless, the committee was sincere in its desire to do what it could to fight apartheid and racism and to improve the lot of black people in southern Africa. We did, therefore, make several recommendations.

The first set of recommendations, which I will not describe in detail, consisted of a number of suggestions in the field of education and research whereby the university might make positive contributions to aid black people in southern Africa and to influence long-run changes in race relations. The second set of recommendations was that, as members of the stockholding community, we speak out forcefully against corporate practices we consider irresponsible. Let me illustrate by quoting from our report.

> *We are particularly concerned about U.S. corporations and financial institutions that directly aid the South African government. Particularly, we abhor the practices of several U.S. banks in granting South Africa a substantial line of credit, which helped bolster the shaky government after the Sharpsville massacre of 1960. We have reason to believe that the labor practices of many U.S. corporations operating production facilities in South Africa are little different from, and in some cases may even be*

*less progressive than, those of south African-owned corporations. There
exist opportunities, within the laws of South Africa, to improve working
conditions for black workers in at least three areas: job training and
supplementary education, pensions and other employee benefits, and
wage levels. If the U.S. corporation undertakes manufacturing operations
in South Africa, we believe that at the very least it has a humanitarian
responsibility to improve the lot of its black workers. A labor policy of
paying only minimally acceptable wages and benefits by Southern African standards is especially reprehensible, and inconsistent with honor-
able business practices. In addition, we believe that U.S. corporations
operating in South Africa could do much to encourage black African dis-
tributors and suppliers to provide banking and credit facilities to non-
Europeans, and to petition the South African government to liberalize the
'pass laws' and other restrictions bearing on employment.*

The president of Princeton University, Robert F. Goheen, drafted a
letter to the corporations whose shares we held explaining the views of
our committee (and of a wide body of the university community). He
urged particularly that the corporations make greater efforts to improve
the lot of their black workers and made specific proposals in line with
those suggested in our report. It is, of course, impossible to say how
much effect we had, but I am convinced that with continued pressure
from institutional investors, considerable change can be effected.

Let me conclude by indicating the response to pressure of one corporation—Polaroid. That company set up a committee of blacks and
whites from their own company to study whether they should continue
to do business in South Africa. After lengthy deliberations and a trip to
South Africa, during which committee members talked with a large
number of black people, they decided on the following experiment: For
the time being they would continue sales in South Africa to all except
the South African government. Pulling out completely would have an
immediate impact harming black people more than whites. But they
also initiated a number of programs to train and upgrade nonwhites, to
raise their salaries and benefits substantially, and to commit a share of
their profits to encourage black education. Polaroid is under no illusions
that such a policy will quickly hasten the demise of apartheid or satisfy
the company's more radical critics. They do believe, however, that their
programs at least deserve study. Their actions seem to me to be a responsible answer to a highly complex problem.

Whose Firm, Whose Money?

The Economist

The long-term consequences of institutional ownership of corporate equity are increasingly being questioned and explored. Here is a focused review of the issues prepared in 1990 by *The Economist.*

It used to be so simple. Between roughly 1850 and 1880 the capitalist system developed some clear categories of people and the things they did. There were workers, managers, shareholders, creditors, customers, entrepreneurs. Shareholders, creditors and workers provided the vital inputs of capital and labour. Shareholders employed managers to organise these inputs to produce outputs, the goods and services that they sold to their customers. The entrepreneurs buzzed around, full of ideas for new companies or new products. Then as now, it was hard to define an entrepreneur, but you knew one when you saw one.

These clear-cut categories produced clear-cut answers to the age-old question of who gets what? Workers were paid a wage, managers a salary, creditors some interest. Shareholders got the rest, which was sometimes a lot and sometimes nothing, taking it out of the company as dividends or reinvesting it there. Successful entrepreneurs—Carnegie and Rockefeller in America, Krupp in Germany, Pilkington in England, Mitsui in Japan—became immensely rich. Nobody doubted who owned the typical capitalist company. The shareholders did, and they could do pretty much as they liked.

These simple certainties have long since given way to all sorts of complexities. Now workers want a say in management, and a slice of the profits. Managers want to own shares. Many people want their own companies, in which they are manager, shareholder and worker all in one. None of these demands is unnatural; they all reflect a world in which people are richer, better educated, more confident, and praise be for all that. But the demands are running up against other features of mature capitalism, which puts great pressure on the linchpin of the whole system: the way businesses are financed.

The Lure of Tradable Equity

The Carnegie-Rockefeller phase of capitalism did not last for long, and its demise is commonly attributed to politics. More people were getting the vote. Governments could no longer allow a small minority of rich men unfettered power, especially if that power was being used to set up trusts and other quasi-monopolies. So in came antitrust laws, factories acts, laws promoting trade unions, and so on.

All these factors played a part in changing capitalism. But another big agent of change had nothing to do with politics. It owed its development almost entirely to the desire of rich men to make their wealth more marketable, more liquid. It was the publicly quoted company, which issued shares that could then be bought and sold on a stock exchange. Together with the earlier introduction of limited liability, it was what transformed Anglo-Saxon capitalism at the turn of the century into a system that is recognisably the same today.

Stock exchanges had been around a lot longer, of course—in London since 1773, in New York since 1792—but they had dealt mainly in government securities and the shares of railway companies. Then, in the closing decades of the last century, manufacturers and retailers came to market. In America the number of industrial firms with issued shares rose from 30 in 1893 to 170 in 1897; in Britain the rise was from 60 in 1887 to almost 600 in 1907. The habit was convenient, and catching.

Now run ahead to the 1980s. Stockmarkets were springing up in the most improbable places, and the established markets had ballooned. By the end of last year the market capitalisation of the equities traded on the London stock exchange was equivalent to 100% of Britain's GDP. For the world's ten largest markets, their capitalisation was equal to 73% of the combined GDPs of their countries (see Figure 1).

FIGURE 1
Share-Power: Stockmarket Capitalisation as Percent of GDP, End 1989

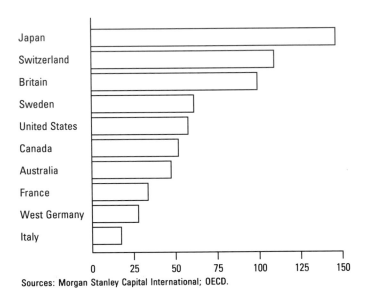

Sources: Morgan Stanley Capital International; OECD.

All that is impressive: anything that grows as fast as stockmarkets have in the past century must have been a success, both for sellers and for buyers. And yet some of the most striking recent changes in Anglo-Saxon stockmarkets tell of failure.

• *Private placements.* A growing number of companies that wish to raise capital do so not through the classic technique of a rights issue to the public, but by placing their extra shares privately with selected investors. In America the amount placed that way in 1988 was worth $200 billion.

• *The decline of the private investor.* The individual who owns shares directly is becoming increasingly rare. American private investors reduced the net value of their equity holdings by around $550 billion between the end of 1983 and the end of 1989, equivalent to 40% of their portfolios in 1983. Over the same period the decline for investing Britons was £17 billion ($26 billion), 32% of their 1983 holdings. Were these trends to continue, the last American to own shares directly would sell his last one in the year 2003.

• *Buy-outs.* Including the purchase of business divisions, the number of buy-outs in America rose from an annual average of 75 in 1979–81 to 190 in 1986–88, and the value of each has soared (see Figure 2). In Britain

FIGURE 2
Urge to Own: Number of Management Buy-Outs

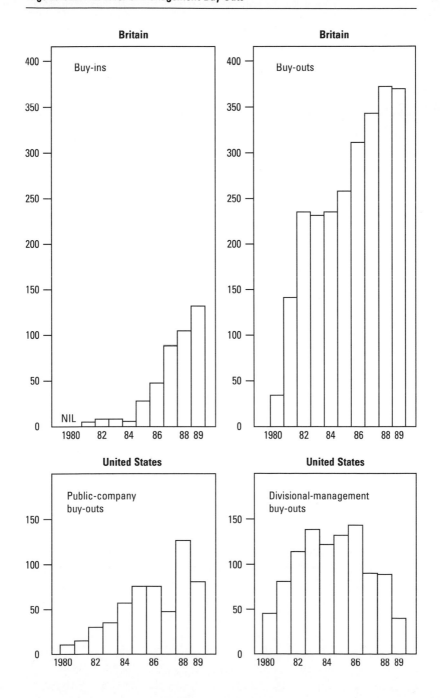

Sources: Centre for Management Buy-Out Research; W. T. Griffen.

last year there were 500 buy-outs, up 10% on 1988; their value, at £7.5 billion ($12.2 billion), was 50% up. Almost all buy-outs involve:

• *Switching from equity to debt.* Buyers round up money from bank loans or by issuing bonds (often to banks), and pay off the equity holders. Some of the new investors get an equity stake; most don't. The growth of America's junk-bond market averaged 26% a year between 1985 and 1989.

These changes . . . serve as a simple but essential warning: in America and Britain during the 1980s, something went wrong with the standard system in which equity is king and the stock exchange its court.

From Proprietors to Punters

At their best, stockmarkets have many merits: convenience, liquidity, unambiguous prices, low dealing costs. Yet there is another side to them. It has little to do with the drawbacks that are usually attributed to stockmarkets—their periodic volatility, their indifference to "real values" (whatever those may be), their gullibility. These alleged defects are, at most, symptoms of a much deeper malaise, which began with the introduction of publicly traded shares and has grown ever since: the change in the meaning of ownership.

To hold equity in a company is to own part of it: that is a legal axiom which has changed hardly at all in more than 100 years. Behind the legal front, however, the functional reality of equity has been transformed. To shareholders in a typical public company in America or Britain—call it Anglo-Saxon Inc.—a share is now little more than a betting slip. It is bought at what a shareholder thinks are good odds, to provide winnings that he hopes will be large. The notion that he owns part of Anglo-Saxon Inc. makes as much sense to him as it would for the average gambler to imagine that he owns part of Lucky Lady, running in the 2.30 tomorrow afternoon. A title deed to a house tells an American or Briton what he knows instinctively: that he owns the place, and must care for it. A share certificate tells him nothing more than that he has the right to a dividend and the chance to make some cash.

This reality has grown partly because of the growth of institutional investors. Millions of people pour money into pension funds, insurance companies and unit trusts (mutual funds). In Britain these bodies

FIGURE 3
Institutional Gush: Flows of Funds into Investment Institutions

Source: UBS Phillips & Drew.

received £26 billion in 1988, more than the entire GNP of New Zealand. In America the inflow was $225 billion, in relative terms slightly more than the British figure. Both have grown massively (see Figure 3). Not all the money goes into equities, of course. The proportion varies from year to year, but roughly half of institutional inflows are put into equities.

The institutions' holdings then grow with staggering speed. Today America's public-pension funds account for one-quarter of all institutional holdings in America—and for 10% of the value of all publicly quoted shares. Their most notable contribution to corporate governance has been to pull many companies out of South Africa. That may or may not be a desirable political goal, but it is low on any list of commercial priorities.

Institutional saving has grown for powerful reasons. Governments encourage it with tax breaks. Savers find it convenient, and they like to think their money is being looked after by expert stewards. The issue, however, is not whether this stewardship system is good or bad, but whether it has anything to do with the ownership of companies. There are three questions worth putting to professional money managers in America and Britain. When they buy a slice of Anglo-Saxon Inc., do they think of themselves as a part-owner? Or are they placing a bet on tomorrow's race? Or, which is increasingly the case, have they bought the shares only because the company is a constituent of a particular stockmarket index which they are tracking?

The answers are usually revealing. Few think of themselves as owners, and they tend to be older than the rest. If the trend continues, every one of the next generation of British and American money managers will be punter-capitalists. Yet they usually gave good, rational reasons for becoming punters. They are there to maximise the returns on the savings entrusted to them.

At this point, one school of critics says

> Ah, but that means only this year's returns, or this quarter's. Are you so short-sighted that you can't see the need to be involved in the long-term health of the companies you invest in?

To most money managers, that question is purely rhetorical. It misses what for them is the vital point: even if an institution wanted to influence the long term, it couldn't. The standard arrangements for exercising influence on Anglo-Saxon Inc.—attending annual meetings, voting on resolutions put before shareholders—are simply too weak and the incentive to use them too small.

The dilemma is obvious. Money managers with holdings in scores of companies cannot really know the details of each of those firms. They cannot use their smallish stakes to exert real influence over the affairs of any of the companies. They cannot easily persuade other institutions to join them so as to enhance their influence, because (a) they are all too busy managing their betting slips and (b) not everybody has the same view on how to improve a company's performance. So the typical money managers prefer to register unease about a company by selling its shares. Selling is quick, cheap and convenient. Above all, it releases money for betting on other shares that look more promising.

These attitudes are shared, in varying degrees, by most individual shareholders in Anglo-Saxon Inc. They too feel uninvolved in its affairs, and powerless to affect its future. It is wrong, therefore, to brand all institutions as bad and all individuals as good. What is wrong with the British and American system is that far too many shareholders, both institutional and individual, do not behave like owners. . . .

When Takeovers Loom

One consequence of punter-capitalism is that the shareholders, detached and uninterested for most of the time, suddenly matter enormously if their company is being bid for. During a takeover they are wooed by both sides, advised by bankers and pundits, promised a glowing future and mighty dividends if only they will/won't accept the bid. For personal shareholders and institutions with small stakes, the betting-slip mentality is never more active than during a takeover battle. This is particularly true of "arbs"—the arbitrageurs who buy shares for just a few days or weeks, hoping to make a quick turn. Perhaps a rival bidder will emerge; even without one, perhaps the bidder will have to raise its offer. The suspense is like waiting for a steward's inquiry: the verdict could go either way, but meanwhile hold on to your slip.

For some institutional shareholders, however, the position is different. Their stakes may be big enough to tip the balance in a takeover battle. They are made more aware of the real issues facing Anglo-Saxon Inc, not least because the bid itself has concentrated their minds. They are told by the bidder of alternative strategies, synergies, new products and much else. In theory, they could behave like the owner of, say, a pedigree puppy, concerned to ensure that it was sold to the person most likely to cherish it and school it on to win at Cruft's. In fact, they don't. In some contested takeovers it is the arbitrageurs who have got enough shares to decide the outcome—and, of all shareholders, they are least likely to behave like a dog-breeder. They probably bought their shares only weeks before. They are not interested in considering rival corporate strategies for the next decade. They want their turn, and quickly.

The position is not much different even for an institution that has held a large stake for a long time. A money manager may have strong reasons for trying to push up the bid price; at a certain stage he has even stronger reasons for accepting. He will be contemplating a sizeable capital gain, which, once it is in the bag, will be good for his reputation and his bonus. And if he holds out to the point where the bid collapses and the price with it, he could be in breach of his fiduciary duty to his clients. He sells, and from his point of view he is right to do so. Only rarely is a bid defeated by arguments over future corporate strategy. Pilkington, a British glassmaker, was one of the exceptions, when shareholders refused to sell to BTR in 1986.

It is time to leave the New York and London stockmarkets, with a quick summary of the main issue so far. It is usually quite rational for most shareholders—whether they be individuals, money managers or arbitrageurs—to take a betting-slip view of their portfolios. None of them has any obvious incentive to behave like the owner of the company, nor any effective way to do so.

All of which begs a big question: who does act as an owner? It is that question which, at root, has prompted the buy-ins, buy-outs and junk bonds of the 1980s, because the Anglo-American stockmarket has created a vacuum at the heart of capitalism. . . .

Contributors

Mr. Barton M. Biggs
Managing Director
Morgan Stanley & Company
1633 Broadway
New York, NY 10019

Mr. David L. Brigham
Managing Director
J. P. Morgan Investment Management,
  Inc.
522 Fifth Avenue
New York, NY 10036

Mr. Arthur Zeikel
President
Merrill Lynch Asset Management
P.O. Box 9011
Princeton, NJ 08543-9011

Mr. Leon G. Cooperman
General Partner
Goldman, Sachs & Co.
85 Broad Street
New York, NY 10004

Mr. Robert S. Salomon
Managing Director and
  Co-Director of Equity Research
Salomon Brothers Inc.
One New York Plaza, 39th Floor
New York, NY 10004

Mr. Walter P. Stern
Vice Chairman and President
Capital Research and
  Management Company
630 Fifth Avenue, 36th Floor
New York, NY 10111

Mr. Dave H. Williams
Chairman
Alliance Capital Management
  Limited Partnership
1345 Avenue of the Americas,
  38th Floor
New York, NY 10105

Professor Andre F. Perold
Harvard University
Graduate School of
  Business Administration
Soldiers Field Road
Boston, MA 02163

Professor John G. MacDonald
Professor of Finance
Stanford University
Graduate School of Business
Stanford, CA 94305

Mr. John J. Cook, Jr.
President
Fidelity Investments Institutional Group
82 Devonshire Street, L11C
Boston, MA 02109

Mr. Lawrence J. Lasser
President and
  Chief Executive Officer
Putnam Management Company
One Post Office Square
Boston, MA 02109

Mr. George J. W. Goodman
Adam Smith's Money World
45 West 45th Street
New York, NY 10036

Mr. Warren E. Buffett
Chairman of the Board
Berkshire Hathaway Inc.
1440 Kiewit Plaza
Omaha, NE 68131

Mr. Claude N. Rosenberg, Jr.
Senior Partner
RCM Capital Management
Four Embarcadero Center, Suite 2900
San Francisco, CA 94111

Sources

David L. Babson & Co.
1 Memorial Drive
Cambridge, MA 02141–1300

Bantam Doubleday Dell Publishing
    Group, Inc.
655 Fifth Ave.
New York, NY 10103

Mr. Robert R. Barker
Barker, Lee & Co.
717 Fifth Ave.
New York, NY 10022

Basil Blackwell
108 Cowley Road
Oxford OX4 1JF England

Bell & Howell
Micro Photo Division
5215 Old Orchard Road
Skokie, IL 60077

Mr. John D. Bolsover
Baring Asset Management Limited
155 Bishopsgate
London EC2M-3XY England

Mr. Warren E. Buffett
Berkshire Hathaway Inc.
1440 Kiewit Plaza
Omaha, NE 68131

Business One Irwin
1820 Ridge Road
Homewood, IL 60430

Mr. Peter Carman
Sanford C. Bernstein Co.
767 Fifth Ave., 22nd Floor
New York, NY 10753–0185

Mr. Leon G. Cooperman
Goldman Sachs Asset Management
32 Old Slip, 34th Floor
New York, NY 10005

Doubleday Book and Music Club
245 Park Ave.
New York, NY 10167

Dow Jones Reprints Service
P.O. Box 300
Princeton, NJ 08543–0300

The Econometric Society
Northwestern University
Department of Economics
2003 Sheridan Road
Evanston, IL 60208

The Economist Newspaper, NA, Inc.
10 Rockefeller Plaza
New York, NY 10020

Mr. Charles D. Ellis, CFA
Greenwich Associates
8 Greenwich Office Park
Greenwich, CT 06830

Financial Analysts Journal
1633 Broadway, Suite 1602
New York, NY 10019

Fortune
Time & Life Building
Rockefeller Center
New York, NY 10020–1393

Fraser Publishing Co.
309 South Willard Street
Burlington, VT 05401

Mr. George H. Ross Goobey
Greystoke
19 Walton Road
Clevedon, Avon BS21 6AE
England

Mr. George J. W. Goodman
141 Fairway Dr.
Princeton, NJ 08540

Harold Matson Company, Inc.
276 Fifth Ave.
New York, NY 10001

Harold Ober Associates, Inc.
425 Madison Ave.
New York, NY 10017

Harper & Row Publishers, Inc.
10 East 53rd Street
New York, NY 10022

Harvard Business Review
Harvard Business School
Boston, MA 02163

Houghton Mifflin Company
2 Park Street
Boston, MA 02108

Hyperion Press, Inc.
47 Riverside Ave.
Westport, CT 06880

IBM Corporation
2000 Purchase Street
Purchase, NY 10577

Industrial Management Review
DMA Communications, Inc.
249 East 55th Street
New York, NY 10022

Institutional Investor, Inc.
488 Madison Ave.
New York, NY 10022

The Investment Analyst
Society of Investment Analysts
211/213 High Street
Bromley, Kent BR1 1NY
England

J. P. Morgan & Co., Incorporated
60 Wall Street, 45th Floor
New York, NY 10260

The Journal of Business
The University of Chicago Press
5801 South Ellis Ave.
Chicago, IL 60637

Journal of Economic Perspectives
American Economic Association
1313 21st Ave. South, Suite 809
Nashville, TN 37212

Journal of Finance
New York University
100 Trinity Place
New York, NY 10006

The Journal of Political Economy
The University of Chicago Press
5801 Ellis Ave.
Chicago, IL 60637

Mr. Simon M. Keane
School of Financial Studies
University of Glasgow
65–71 South Park Ave.
Glasgow G12 8LE Scotland

KPA Advisory Services Inc.
128 Glencairn Avenue
Toronto, Ontario M4R 1M9

Kress Library of Business & Economics
Harvard University
Boston, MA 02163

Ladies Home Journal
Meredith Corporation
100 Park Avenue
New York, NY 10077

Mr. Burton G. Malkiel
Princeton University
Fisher Hall
Princeton, NJ 08544–1021

Mr. David Mathey
c/o Mr. William L. Porter, Jr.
Princeton Bank and Trust Company NA
One Palmer Square, Suite 201
Princeton, NJ 08542

Mr. Dean W. Mathey
c/o Mr. James R. Cogan, Esq.
Walter, Conston, Alexander and Green
90 Park Ave.
New York, NY 10016

Mr. Macdonald Mathey
Thrasher Plat Road
Cornish, NH 03746

McGraw-Hill Book Company
1221 Ave. of the Americas
New York, NY 10020

Merrill Lynch & Co., Inc.
World Financial Center
North Tower, 31st Floor
New York, NY 10281–1331

Mr. Paul F. Miller, Jr.
Miller, Anderson & Sherrerd
One Tower Bridge
West Conshohocken, PA 19428

Mr. Leonard Mosley
c/o Nugent and Associates, Inc.
170 10th Street North
Naples, FL 33940

Nation's Business
1615 H. Street NW
Washington, DC 20062

NBER, Inc.
1050 Massachusetts Ave.
Cambridge, MA 02138

New York Times
Rights and Royalties
229 West 43rd St.
New York, NY 10036

Pensions and Investments
Crain Communications, Inc.
740 Rush St.
Chicago, IL 60611–2590

Mr. Claude N. Rosenberg, Jr.
RCM Capital Management
4 Embarcadero Center, #2900
San Francisco, CA 94111

Mr. Paul A. Samuelson
Massachusetts Institute of Technology
Cambridge, MA 02139

The Sunday Telegraph Ltd.
Ewan MacNaughton Associates
Alexandra Chambers
6 Alexandra Road
Tonbridge, Kent TN9 2AA
England

Tribune Media Services
64 E Concord Street
Orlando, FL 32801

Yale Alumni Magazine
Yale University
New Haven, CT 06520